TAKING THE TOWN

THE THOMAS D. CLARK STUDIES IN EDUCATION, PUBLIC POLICY, AND SOCIAL CHANGE

This series is dedicated to the memory and example of Thomas D. Clark (1903–2004). The breadth and variety of Dr. Clark's contributions to historical understanding in the Commonwealth are unmatched, and he was a tireless advocate for the improvement of public education.

Sponsored by the University of Kentucky's College of Education in cooperation with the University Press of Kentucky, the series puts research on the Commonwealth in the spotlight, research that augments the understanding of national or regional developments or emphasizes the relevance of those same developments to the pace and direction of change here at home. While remaining open to a variety of methodological approaches, the overall aim of the series is to encourage an imaginative engagement with the tasks and opportunities that define the present.

TAKING THE TOWN

Collegiate and Community Culture
in the Bluegrass, 1880–1917

Kolan Thomas Morelock

THE UNIVERSITY PRESS OF KENTUCKY

Copyright © 2008 by The University Press of Kentucky

Scholarly publisher for the Commonwealth,
serving Bellarmine University, Berea College, Centre College of Kentucky,
Eastern Kentucky University, The Filson Historical Society, Georgetown College,
Kentucky Historical Society, Kentucky State University, Morehead State
University, Murray State University, Northern Kentucky University,
Transylvania University, University of Kentucky, University of Louisville,
and Western Kentucky University.

Editorial and Sales Offices: The University Press of Kentucky
663 South Limestone Street, Lexington, Kentucky 40508-4008
www.kentuckypress.com

12 11 10 09 08   5 4 3 2 1

Library of Congress Cataloging-in-Publication Data

Morelock, Kolan Thomas, 1945–
  Taking the town : collegiate and community culture in the Bluegrass,
  1880–1917 / Kolan Thomas Morelock.
      p. cm. — (The Thomas D. Clark studies in education, public policy, and
        social change)
  Includes bibliographical references and index.
  ISBN 978-0-8131-2504-6 (hardcover : alk. paper)
  1. Lexington (Ky.)—Intellectual life—19th century. 2. Lexington
(Ky.)—Intellectual life—20th century. 3. Universities and colleges—Social
aspects—Kentucky—Lexington—History. 4. College students—Kentucky—
Lexington—Societies, etc.—History. 5. Clubs—Kentucky—Lexington—History.
6. Lexington (Ky.)—Social life and customs. 7. Community life—Kentucky—
Lexington—History. 8. Lexington (Ky.)—Social conditions. I. Title.
  F459.L6M67 2008
  306.43'20976947—dc22   2008014637

 Member of the Association of
American University Presses

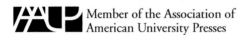

For Betsy

CONTENTS

Foreword   ix

Acknowledgments   xi

PROLOGUE: Panning for Gold   1

CHAPTER ONE: Lexington in the Gilded Age: Public Voices   13

CHAPTER TWO: "Put Me in Class with the Widow Who Gave the Mite": Lexington's Joseph Tanner in the Gilded Age   49

CHAPTER THREE: Campus Prominence: Collegiate Literary Societies in Nineteenth-Century Lexington   71

CHAPTER FOUR: Community Presence: Collegiate Literary Societies in Gilded Age Lexington   109

CHAPTER FIVE: "This City's Never Dull": Public Culture in Progressive Era Lexington   143

CHAPTER SIX: "In Her Most Charming, Characteristic Way": Lexington's Margaret Preston in the Progressive Era   195

CHAPTER SEVEN: The Dramatic Clubs Take the Stage: An Extracurricular Succession in Prewar Lexington   243

EPILOGUE: Postwar Lexington—So Long, Gilded Age   275

Appendixes   285

Notes   303

Bibliography   383

Index   395

FOREWORD

Lexington, Kentucky, was a much smaller place a century ago (the population was only 26,000 in 1900), the proportion of African Americans was larger (39 percent), and the color line ran deep. But more to the point, the landscape of learning was profoundly different from our own, and not just because the revolutionary impact of new information technologies and the modern movement for civil rights were still a long way off. For most people in the 1880s or 1890s—whether they were rich or poor, white or black, male or female—the prolonged school career that would become the norm among generations born after World War II was all but unimaginable. That is not to say that educational opportunity was limited, but only that it was enmeshed in older meanings and different social purposes.

As Thomas Bender, Joseph Kett, Louise Stevenson, and others have suggested, the classroom was but one scene of instruction among many in the nineteenth century, and not the most important scene at that.[1] Of course, the public school movement was already gathering momentum in certain quarters, the same public school movement that would eventually erect a curricular ladder extending from kindergarten to graduate school and help create the entrenched social imperatives that required every child to climb it. But the horizon of educational interest among the middle classes was still broad enough to include the sites and occasions that the nation's cities and towns had to offer. Museums, parks, fairs and expositions, lyceum lectures, libraries, and theaters continued to hold an honored place alongside schools and colleges. And on a more intimate scale, serious reading, journal keeping, correspondence, and conversation were cultivated daily in a spirit that is difficult for us to appreciate today. Whether in the parlor or in literary societies, reading clubs, or church groups, an alert commitment to edification and mutual self-improvement helped set the tone for relationships among family, friends, and associates alike.

Inspired by the work of Bender, Kett, and Stevenson, Kolan Morelock evokes the dynamic, reciprocal relationships that linked campus and community together as the nineteenth century gave way to the twentieth. He describes in detail the last hurrah of a pervasive rhetorical culture, a world in which the competitive performances of student orators mattered most to audiences of townsfolk and fellow students alike. And when the literary societies began to fade into obscurity, as they did by the turn of the century, he shows how student dramatic clubs assumed their place, reflecting the dawning priorities and interests of a new "culture of professionalism." Imaginatively conceived and meticulously researched, *Taking the Town* is local history at its best. By refusing to reduce the history of education to the history of schooling—by refusing to treat the past as a simple prelude to the present—Morelock points the way toward a vast and still largely unexplored region of issues in the experience of the commonwealth of Kentucky and its people. It will be interesting to see who follows him in this effort, and how they will manage to do so.

Richard Angelo
Series Editor

NOTE

1. See Thomas Bender, *New York Intellect: A History of Intellectual Life in New York City, from 1750 to the Beginnings of Our Own Time* (Baltimore: Johns Hopkins University Press, 1987); Joseph Kett, *The Pursuit of Knowledge under Difficulties: From Self-Improvement to Adult Education in America, 1750–1990* (Stanford, Calif.: Stanford University Press, 1994); Louise Stevenson, *The Victorian Home Front: American Thought and Culture, 1860–1880* (Ithaca, N.Y.: Cornell University Press, 2001); Richard Lyman Bushman, *The Refinement of America: Persons, Houses, Cities* (New York: Vintage, 1993); Thomas Augst, *The Clerk's Tale: Young Men and the Moral Life in Nineteenth-Century America* (Chicago: University of Chicago Press, 2003); Elizabeth McHenry, *Forgotten Readers: Recovering the Lost History of African American Literary Societies* (Durham, N.C.: Duke University Press, 2002).

Acknowledgments

Aware of, and grateful for, all the help I have received, I would first like to thank Richard Angelo. Richard, as the chair of my doctoral committee, guided me through the dissertation process several years ago and then more recently encouraged and aided me in reshaping that work into this book. His scholarly example, kind support, patient prodding, and insistence on my best have earned my undying admiration and gratitude. I also owe a debt of gratitude to Stephen Wrinn, director of the University Press of Kentucky. Steve's friendliness and optimism encouraged and motivated me, and his excellent advice was invaluable. My thanks and gratitude also go to Anne Dean Watkins, assistant acquisitions editor of the Press. I greatly appreciate her kindness and helpfulness throughout the publication process. I also want to thank Linda Lotz for copyediting the manuscript so expertly and so beautifully. In addition, I would like to thank James Cibulka, dean of the College of Education at the University of Kentucky, and James W. Tracy, University of Kentucky's vice president for research. Their support of, and funding for, this project made its publication possible. Gratitude and thanks must certainly go to B. J. Gooch, Special Collections librarian at Transylvania University; Frank Stanger and the staff of the Special Collections and Archives at the University of Kentucky; and the staff of the Kentucky Room in the Lexington Public Library. Without their expertise, professionalism, and kind assistance I could not have done the research necessary for the production of this work. Finally, I want to express my heartfelt thanks to my favorite archivist, my wife Betsy. Without her love, encouragement, help, and support this book would never have been written.

PANNING FOR GOLD

> Lexington is a living community bound together by memories, some
> of them bitter, but all remindful of a great history. . . . It is a proud,
> aristocratic city of Southern ancestry, life, and charm.
> —Federal Writers' Project of the Works Progress Administration,
> *Lexington and the Bluegrass Country,* 1938

This is an account of turn-of-the-century southern intellectual life flourishing in a local and regional social environment of considerable turmoil,
violence, and change. More specifically, it is the story of an evolving intersection of community and collegiate life in a small city in the upper South, a
story of extracurricular activities that played a vital role not only in the intellectual lives of the undergraduates but also in the middle- and upper-class
white community as a whole. Why tell this story at all? Why try to unearth
and examine this interplay of town and gown cultural aspirations in Lexington, Kentucky, from the period following Reconstruction to the nation's
entry into the First World War? The answer lies in the importance of region,
locale, and campus-community interaction to the study of American intellectual history. To begin with, academia has sometimes construed southern
intellectual life as an oxymoron—a misguided view that, until recently, has
helped ensure that southern intellectual history would be neglected. Along
with the need to rectify this neglect by further exploration of the historical
life of the mind in the South, there is the need to pay more attention to
specific locales and thus inform a larger context. Or, as one historian put
it, "local history is a prism through which to view the history of the United
States." In addition, American higher education and American society as a
whole achieved modernity in the late nineteenth and early twentieth centuries together, interacting with and affecting each other in the process.
Historian Thomas Bender has argued that, historically, American intellectual life flourished within a "mix of urban cultural institutions. Only later
would one of these institutions, the college converted into the university,

achieve hegemony in intellectual life and transform the urban-based world of learning into university scholarship." Against the backdrop of this historic transformation in American intellectual life and American higher education, a case study of a previously neglected intersection between student and community intellectual life in the Bluegrass city seemed a promising way to contribute to local history as well as to the historiography of American education. This book is the result.[1]

Community Setting and Cultural Change

The social and cultural landscape of Lexington, Kentucky, during the late nineteenth and early twentieth centuries is revisited here through public records, primarily the local press, and through the private and public lives of two Lexingtonians: Joseph Marion Tanner and Margaret Wickliffe Preston. In their own time and in their own way, both Tanner and Preston were civically active and demonstrated a vibrant interest in, and concern for, the life of the mind. From the pages of the local press and from the lives of these two residents, Lexington emerges as a city enveloped by the regional forces characteristic of the New South in the years following Reconstruction and as a late-nineteenth-century Victorian city evolving into an increasingly progressive one before the United States' military entry into the First World War. Enjoying a wealth of popular culture, or what one historian has called "cheap amusement," Lexington was also a community rich in so-called high culture, supporting a vibrant "locality-based" intellectual life outside, though not entirely divorced from, its college campuses. In short, in the decades surrounding the turn of the twentieth century, this small upper South city was awash in a kaleidoscopic array of the mainstream social and intellectual forces prevalent in the region and the nation at the time.[2]

Lexington's turn-of-the-century cultural landscape served as both context and audience for two distinct collegiate student organizations: literary societies and dramatic clubs. These organizations manifested themselves vigorously at two Lexington institutions: Kentucky University, known as Transylvania University before 1865 and after 1908, and State College, known today as the University of Kentucky. These extracurricular groups' higher aspirations included self-improvement and refinement and devotion to the life of the intellect as exercised through the arts of expression, be it behind the lectern or on the stage. Although much of the literature addressing the literary societies has focused on their on-campus, intramural function, in Lexington these societies also clearly participated in and contributed to community intellectual life through public oratorical performances at both on- and off-campus venues—performances designed to inspire and enlighten as well as to entertain. During the Gilded Age the on-campus organizational vitality of Lexington literary societies waxed, as did their notoriety and popularity in the local community. However, this vitality and popularity did not last. As the literary societies waned in the early twentieth century and their off-campus, community role ended in the pre–World War I years, the student dramatic clubs assumed this role. These extracurricular organizations were more in tune with the new century and the public's changing taste in the arts of expression. Moreover, this local succession is suggestive of a major American cultural shift culminating during this period—the shift from a nineteenth-century oratorical culture, wherein the orator's rostrum served as an important locus for both public entertainment and the diffusion of knowledge, to a twentieth-century "culture of professionalism," which increasingly conceded the diffusion of knowledge to professionalized, university-trained experts and public entertainment to the dramatized action of the stage and screen.[3]

THE LITERARY SOCIETIES

The historiography of American higher education since the mid-twentieth century has been characterized as evolving from progressivist formulas and campus memorials to comprehensive overviews and monographs representing analytical works of social or intellectual history. Almost invariably, in these latter works students and student culture appeared as elements of considerable or, in some instances, singular interest. Furthermore, the component of student life generated by the students themselves, the extracurriculum, has occupied much of this continuing interest in the literature. This steadfast attention seems largely attributable to the argument that students, through their extracurricular activities, have contributed much to the collegiate environment, playing a significant role in intellectual and social change on campus. In addition, perhaps an ongoing fascination attaches to the extracurriculum as a *student* creation rather than a product of the adult world—a world typically perceived as always in control and wielding the power. And, in the continuing evolution of the extracurriculum as a power-wielding student force on campus, the literary societies occupy a significant moment. An understanding of the literary societies is essential to an understanding of the historical college student and of the role that student played in the shaping of American academic history.[4]

First established on colonial campuses, literary societies seemingly arose out of youthful students' psychosocial need for fellowship and stimulation in a sometimes austere institutional environment. By most accounts they were an early and significant part of an overall extracurricular movement created as a counterweight by students in revolt against the restrictive climate and formal curriculum of colonial and antebellum colleges. However, it is worth noting that the curriculum (reading, writing, speaking, and debating) taught in these societies has also been characterized as essentially complementary rather than counter to the formal institutional curriculum. The student literary societies spread and rapidly multiplied in the antebellum era and remained vibrant in many places throughout the mid-Victorian period and, in some cases, far beyond. Grounded in the intellectual traditions representing both reason and persuasion, they flowered within a wider oratorical culture of republican ideology and an accompanying rhetoric of public consensus and civic virtue that served this ideology. In this cultural climate, college students were in training, both in the classrooms and in the society halls, for membership in an elite cadre of influential, persuasive leaders of society and, for much of the nineteenth century, for membership in the Victorian middle class. The societies were also training grounds for the competitive and, as the century wore on, increasingly professionalized world of adult work.[5]

The membership of literary societies sometimes included most of the students on campus; these societies were originally inclusive of all economic and social strata represented in the student body and may have remained so even after other extracurricular attractions arose. It has been argued that in many schools well before the Civil War, and certainly after, the students and their extracurricular activities reflected primarily the Anglo-Saxon middle class and its aspirations. This is the cohort that one historian has referred to as the "working elite." Of course, the variations within this pattern were complex and rooted in locale. For example, Kentucky novelist James Lane Allen, a student at Kentucky University in Lexington shortly after the Civil

War, remembered the Bible College students there as being poor relative to the greater affluence of the Arts College students, or at least he styled them so in his novel *The Reign of Law.* At any rate, until the 1880s, with few exceptions, the membership of the societies was exclusively white and male. However, in the relatively more egalitarian and increasingly coeducational atmosphere of the 1870s and 1880s, female and coeducational societies were formed.[6]

While offering their members social fellowship, intellectual stimulation, training in public speaking, and preparation for adult life, the literary societies reputedly made significant contributions to higher education in terms of the evolution of rhetorical practice, the development of academic libraries, and the promotion of academic freedom. Yet, despite the services they offered their members and the contributions they made to their institutions, the literary societies declined and had largely vanished by the turn of the twentieth century or soon thereafter. Their demise is generally attributed to an erosion of student loyalty by competing extracurricular agencies and to an institutional absorption of their educational purposes. In addition, the literature hints at cultural factors beyond the campus. That is, the societies had flowered in an early-nineteenth-century oratorical culture pervaded by republican ideology, and they withered in a late-nineteenth-century culture of professionalism pervaded by liberal-capitalistic ideology. Historian David Potter, writing in the 1940s, broadly encompassed the possibilities in his observation that "chiefly responsible for this decline [of the literary societies] were the changes in national ideals, intellectual interests, and educational purposes."[7]

Lexington's collegiate literary societies were not only a significant on-campus force during their heyday; they also contributed substantially to the cultural life of the surrounding community through public performances or "entertainments" that were often front-page news in the local press throughout much of the Gilded Age and for a few years beyond the turn of the century. These society-sponsored and society-controlled public performances took place both on and off campus. There were two primary modes of on-campus public entertainments: noncompetitive, oratorically centered, recurrent celebrations of special events such as Washington's birthday, and entertainments featuring oratorical competitions. The most notable off-campus entertainments were interinstitutional oratorical competitions featuring society-selected orators representing Kentucky University and State

College as well as other schools throughout the Bluegrass region. The most frequent on-campus site for these public performances was the college chapel, and the primary off-campus venues in Lexington were the opera house and the Chautauqua Assembly auditorium at Woodland Park.

Entertainment considered refined and in good taste, both inside and outside the home, has been referred to as "the central social preoccupation of genteel culture" during the Victorian era, and the Lexington audiences at these literary society–organized entertainments were described by the local press as comprising the area's "best people," the "cultured and refined," or some other phrase denoting gentility. Inside the campus chapels and community auditoriums, these "genteel" audiences saw stages crowded with dignitaries, bedecked with college and society colors, and festooned with elaborate floral decorations. They watched as copious gifts of flowers were bestowed on the orators at the conclusion of their speeches by their admirers and as bejeweled gold medals or cash prizes were awarded to the winners of the competitions. They heard not only eloquent orations but also elegant orchestral music played by professional musicians, as well as the thunderous cheering of the contestants' partisan student supporters. Outside the auditoriums, public performance in the form of mass assembly and parade— complete with ritual yells, flying colors, and heroes (winning orators) hoisted on celebrants' shoulders—was enacted at the railway station, in hotel lobbies, and on the streets of the city on College Day at Chautauqua and before and after the annual intercollegiate oratorical contest at the Lexington Opera House. Having thus commandeered public space for such performances, those outside as well as inside these venues became the students' audience. The local press tended to romanticize its reporting of these events. In the words of one newspaper on such an occasion, "the college boys took the town"; indeed, the exuberant rallies and parades around, in, and through the public buildings and streets of Lexington created exciting, memorable scenes, inspiring the description of students "rollicking through the streets" in celebration of themselves, their literary society competitions, and their public presence. Such public display and ritualistic clamor entertained participants and observers alike, though perhaps more by exciting than by cultivating the senses.[8]

Inside both the campus chapel and the community auditorium, these student performances aspired to provide entertainment, inspiration, and intellectual improvement—indeed, those same products of public speaking that result in what has been called "high amusement." These products, or services, might just as easily be termed amusement, uplift, and education or, as expressed even more simply by the *Lexington Herald* in 1916, "clean amusement and instruction." In these literary society–controlled performances, the student orator, embodying inspirational youth, entertained from the rostrum by rhetorically dispensing eloquence and "culture" for the enjoyment and intellectual improvement of the audience. Such student spectacles, packaged to provide not only amusement but also intellectual enlightenment and aesthetic inspiration, served the quest for self-improvement, for refinement and genteel respectability, and for the intellectual cultural authority that marked the American middle and upper classes in the Gilded Age. Indeed, the audience members attending these celebrations and competitions were, by their presence, engaged in what has been referred to as the "genteel performance."[9]

Lexington collegiate literary societies enjoyed enormous on-campus vitality and off-campus popularity during the Gilded Age and through the first few years of the new century. After this time, however, their off-campus role was negligible, as community interest in them seemingly faded, and their on-campus vitality declined throughout the pre–World War I period. In short, these organizations had become irrelevant, and many were already defunct by the time of the United States' entry into World War I in 1917. Soon after they would vanish so .thoroughly that this author experienced undergraduate life in the 1960s without ever hearing mention of them. As already noted, it has been well argued elsewhere that literary societies everywhere declined in the face of overwhelming on-campus competition for student loyalty from myriad other extracurricular organizations, including social fraternities, which carried little intellectual baggage, and athletics, with neither intellectual nor genteel pretensions. There was, however, an extracurricular "newcomer" in Lexington in the Progressive Era with just such pretensions. As the Lexington literary societies precipitously declined in campus prestige and student interest and loyalty, their former off-campus, public performance role was assumed by another extracurricular agency of "cultured" entertainment—the student dramatic club, which was seemingly in tune with the intellectual interests and entertainment needs of both students and the community in an era that demanded less oratory and more dramatic action.[10]

The Dramatic Clubs

Collegiate dramatic clubs are understood here to have been extracurricular, artistically motivated student organizations engaged in the production of amateur, noncommercial stage plays performed both on and off campus for the benefit of the student body and the playgoing public. Although these student organizations may have received some supportive guidance from faculty members or theatrical professionals from time to time, the clubs were neither under faculty control nor part of the formal institutional curriculum. Although they were not unheard of in pre-Revolutionary colleges, the widespread popularity of student dramatic clubs is generally traced to the 1890s and linked with the revolt against the puritanical mores that had previously been so influential. Timothy Dwight, president of Yale College from 1775 to 1817, certainly exemplified such mores in his rejection of the theater: "To indulge a taste for play going means nothing more nor less than the loss of that most valuable treasure, the immortal soul." Despite Dwight's zealous view, the theater in nineteenth-century America was often associated with genteel culture, and it was widely held that "the purpose of the stage was to entertain, cultivate, refine, and elevate." Also, extracurricular dramatic clubs appear to have both preceded and initially been a part of the so-called Little Theater Movement that originated in Europe in the 1880s and spread to America in the 1910s. In the United States, this movement, which was grounded in the production of amateur, noncommercial stage plays in local venues throughout the country, has been linked, among other things, to the public's thirst for such entertainment due to the professional, commercial theater's withdrawal to New York in the face of withering nationwide competition from the movies in the 1910s. As one early-twentieth-century observer expressed it, amateur theater groups "quickened the intellectual life" of local communities in the wake of the professional theater's retreat. However, the extracurricular nature of college dramatic productions would not endure for long, for the Little Theater Movement of the 1910s has also been linked to the rising popularity of incorporating the study of dramatic arts into the formal curriculum. This co-opting, or absorption, into the formal curriculum was so complete by the late 1920s that Kenneth Macgowan, an observer sympathetic to the curricular approach, could proudly proclaim in 1929: "It is fair to say that today the faculty and the student body of our colleges have united in what is literally a new educational task. . . . It goes beyond undergraduate production of plays. It is the organization of teaching methods in every field of the theater from play writing to direction, from scene design to acting." Nor was Macgowan alone in his pro-curricular sentiments. Many observers of and advocates for the Little Theater Movement and for amateur theater in general, writing from the 1910s through the 1930s, tended to disparage or dismiss the efforts of extracurricular collegiate dramatic clubs; perhaps enamored of what was later referred to as "the culture of professionalism," they applauded a faculty-controlled, curricular system of dramatics production.[11]

In the Progressive Era, student dramatic clubs at Transylvania University and State University (as the University of Kentucky was called between 1908 and 1916) and their performances at the Lexington Opera House and other off-campus venues became very popular in a community saturated with locally produced and performed amateur stage plays. Moreover, these collegiate dramatic clubs largely assumed the public performance role that had formerly been filled by the student literary societies. Indeed, it was these dramatic clubs that "took the town" via their off-campus performances in Lexington during the prewar years. However, although dramatic clubs were among the myriad extracurricular attractions siphoning student interest and loyalty away from literary societies in the early twentieth century, they were not directly responsible for the literary societies' demise. In fact, the literary societies had already abandoned their off-campus public performances and were in steep decline on Lexington campuses before the major collegiate dramatic clubs appeared. Nevertheless, it appears that the dramatic clubs arose, in part, to satisfy the intellectual interests and aesthetic tastes of the new cultural environment. Literary society members themselves were seemingly aware of this changing environment, as they were among the first to experiment with and perform plays on campus.

SILENT VOICES

Many voices are heard in this account of turn-of-the-century Lexington culture and intellectual life, including the (white-controlled) local and campus press, local historians and authors living at the time, the city's college students expressing themselves through their extracurricular literary societies and dramatic clubs, and Lexingtonians Margaret Preston and Joseph Tanner and the people conspicuous in their lives. Other important voices remain silent or largely so, voices that would have the power to enhance, argue strongly against, or even revise the point of view taken here. Among these are voices from the city's black culture, voices of the collegiate administration and professoriat, and voices of college students expressing their curricular choices and career aspirations.

When black life and culture in Lexington during the Gilded Age and Progressive Era are portrayed here, it is through the voices and perspectives of white Lexington. Moreover, although the focus in this account is on the intellectual life of the city's majority population, it was certainly not the only intellectual life in Lexington. Though mentioned only briefly here, the highly successful "Colored Fair," the anti–Separate Coach Law campaign, and amateur dramatic presentations in black churches and schools are a few examples of black cultural and intellectual life in the city. Moreover, there was a vibrant black intelligentsia, as demonstrated by the lives of Professor William Fouse and his wife, Lizzie; again, they are given only passing mention here but are certainly worthy of their own careful and thorough biographies. Although sometimes difficult to recapture (no black newspapers from that time have survived), black voices from this period would enrich, "push against," and doubtless alter the story.

Campus cultures are complex, consisting of student, faculty, and administrative subcultures, each affected by the interplay among the three. In addition, each of these subcultures interacts with, affects, and is affected by the surrounding community and the larger culture. This account offers brief anecdotes hinting at the scope of these complex interactions: faculty members preside at or sit on the stage during literary society oratorical competitions, president James Patterson mentors and is the namesake of a literary society at State College, English professor "Bookie" Taylor speaks before the Woman's Club Department of Literature, the Woman's Club produces a play written by a State University professor to raise money for a local charity effort, and University of Kentucky president Frank McVey reacts to mob violence at the Lexington courthouse by ordering faculty to beseech the students not to participate, to name a few. However, for the most part, the faculty and administration remain silent in this account, and the results and implications of the connections and interactions between institutional culture and the students and the community are largely unexplored. Nevertheless, such relationships could help explain why the students behaved as they did, why the city's collegiate extracurricular world changed, and why the city's intellectual life assumed the shape it did. Like the black perspective on turn-of-the-century life in Lexington, this is a path of inquiry with the potential to enrich, argue with, and reshape the narrative.

Finally, it has already been mentioned that the decline of the student literary societies has been attributed, in part, to the absorption of their educational purposes and activities into the formal curriculum. The same thing happened to the activities of the student dramatic clubs, as once independent student actors fell under the direction of faculty. Along with this institutional curricular change, student curricular choice was changing as well, driven by new cultural and economic priorities. Suggestive of this change, at State College prior to 1900, the majority of graduates were arts students, whereas between 1900 and 1918, the majority were graduates of the engineering school. The voices revealing and shaping these curricular and career changes also remain largely silent in this account. Nevertheless, they too would have influenced the students' extracurricular world and thus the story told here.[12]

The silence of these interesting, informative voices clearly represents challenging opportunities for further research. Historical research is much like panning for gold in an uncharted river: a nugget here, a nugget there, and after considerable time and effort, the prospector joyfully hefts a small bag of glittering gold. Nevertheless, at the inevitable end of his sojourn, he turns away not only with elation but also sadly mindful that other, perhaps richer, treasure lies just out of sight, if not out of reach, beneath the shimmering water.

CHAPTER ONE

LEXINGTON IN THE GILDED AGE

Public Voices

She only requires to be more fully and correctly known to . . . become in
every way the compeer of any inland city.
                                        —*Lexington, the Central City,* 1887

On 2 April 1879 George W. Ranck, educator, newspaper editor, and historian, stood before his audience in Morrison Chapel on the campus of
Kentucky University in Lexington to deliver a historical address during the
centennial celebration of the city's founding. Reconstruction, and the federal military occupation of the South, had ended only two years before.
Lexington and other Kentucky towns and cities had sustained some damage
during the Civil War, but Kentucky had generally been spared the worst of
the physical destruction and desolation visited on the South. Nevertheless,
the war had left the state's economy, infrastructure, political institutions,
and social fabric in "a deplorable condition."[1]

Few remained untouched by the war, and its "bitter legacy" left opinion and loyalty sharply divided and community solidarity badly damaged
throughout the state. Lexington's James Lane Allen dramatically expressed
the situation in Kentucky when he wrote, "not while men are fighting
their wars of conscience do they hate most, but after they have fought; and
Southern and Union now hated to the bottom." The perceived federal excesses during the Reconstruction years only added to the division and rancor. Although legislated racial segregation had not yet become thoroughly
entrenched in the 1870s, white sentiment was reflected in the state legislature's refusal to ratify the Thirteenth, Fourteenth, and Fifteenth Amendments to the U.S. Constitution, abolishing slavery and extending civil rights
and suffrage to blacks—constitutional changes that Lexington attorney and
historian Samuel Wilson still referred to in 1928 as "the three obnoxious

amendments." Race relations between blacks and whites in Lexington, reflecting the situation throughout the emerging New South, were tense and could quickly turn violent. Four of the six known lynchings of black men in Kentucky in 1878, the year before Ranck's centennial oration, had taken place in Fayette County.[2]

Though the bitter divisions of the war were still felt statewide, white sentiment, especially in the Bluegrass region, often favored the South. Moreover, the "Lost Cause" of the Confederacy had become enshrined and memorialized in monuments in Lexington as elsewhere, and ex-Confederates had come to dominate state politics through their control of the Democratic Party. There seems to have been much truth in the assertion by one author that Kentucky "waited until after the war was over to secede from the Union." The political situation in Kentucky paralleled the Democratic "redemption" of one southern state after another in the postwar period. In Kentucky, the Democratic "redeemers" were themselves divided into two factions: the Louisville-based "New Departure" Democrats, who favored accommodation with, and modeling of, the industrialized North, and the more conservative, Bluegrass-centered "Bourbon" Democrats, who sought to maintain their vision of traditional southern ways. Nevertheless, both factions joined in a successful coalition against the Republicans, and "the vanquished ruled the victors" in Kentucky in the years after the war.[3]

Yet no more than a hint of these turbulent social and political conditions found its way into the text of Ranck's centennial address at Morrison Chapel. Rather, employing only acclamatory rhetoric, he insisted that his auditors must congratulate themselves on their "liberal, enterprising and appreciative spirit" and their civilized attention to "sacred duty." Furthermore, he assured them, they had laid aside "political divisions, religious dissensions, and prejudices of nationality and race" to gather as "one harmonious brotherhood . . . to honor the memory of the virtuous and the brave." Invoking "that mysterious hand which marks the eras and the ages on the dial plate of time," Ranck recounted in summary fashion and glowing terms the early history of the founding and settling of Lexington, a city he called "the literary and intellectual centre" of the region. Ranck's address was given during the historical period often referred to as the Gilded Age, a term derived from the title of an 1873 novel by Mark Twain and Charles Dudley Warner. Historian Charles Calhoun succinctly summed up the Gilded Age as the period in which "the central fact of American Life was the evolution of the nation from a largely agricultural, rural, isolated, localized, and traditional society to one that was becoming industrialized, urban, integrated, national, and modern." Perhaps more poetically, Grant C. Knight (biographer of James Lane Allen) characterized this period as a time when the nation was "swelling with national consciousness, girding itself for expansion, confused with a conflict between capital and labor. . . . The whole country was in a ferment." The Gilded Age encompassed, roughly, the years 1870 to 1900. These years were also defined by those values and practices labeled "Victorian" and, in the South, by the social, political, and economic currents of the "New South" era—potent social and cultural forces blending to shape Lexington life at the time.[4]

A VICTORIAN CITY

Values have been well defined as "the broad dominant social attributes, behaviors, and larger goals that are advocated, promoted, and defended by a society," and the term *Victorian* denotes a set of values, ideas, and assumptions widely held by the middle and upper classes during the nineteenth century. Ranck's centennial address, as well as many Lexington press accounts during the period, was laced with elements suggestive of the Victorian mind-set. For instance, examples with regard to women, other cultures, and social welfare concerns can be examined to suggest the Victorian influence in Lexington's public culture in the Gilded Age.[5]

"Feminines"

In rhetoric reflecting the Victorian belief that life is preparation for a higher, often religious purpose and that civilization is "founded on moral law," Ranck reminded his audience that a man's greatness is found not in his wealth, power, or ambitious achievements but rather "in the nobility of his soul." Ranck, however, did not confine this nobility to men alone. He also ascribed high virtue to Kentucky's women and, in doing so, recited a rhetoric of Victorian gender attitudes. For instance, Ranck lauded the pioneer women of the "forest fort" as having "toiled, . . . endured, . . . shuddered at the distant warhoop, . . . cared for the wounded, . . . prayed for the dying and mourned for the dead," and as being "faithful unto death." Though not quite transforming these frontier women into "female allegories"— personifications of civic virtue commonly invoked earlier in the century— Ranck was certainly invoking the Victorian ideal of "True Womanhood," an ideal embodying "piety, purity, obedience, and domesticity."[6]

Similar Victorian sentiments about women also appeared in the Lexington press. Nineteenth-century newspapers both shaped and reflected public perception and opinion, and by midcentury, the prevalent view was that the press acted as "a vast popular educator," informing individual readers as to the general shape and nature of public life and thought. Accounts from local newspapers of any period are "historical exhibits" of publicly expressed attitudes, sentiments, and practices that are suggestive of the social and cultural currents flowing through a community. For instance, a reporter for the *Lexington Daily Press* covering the State College commencement in June 1885 praised a student orator for his "tribute to true womanhood [which] was both beautiful and instructive" and noted that "the ladies covered their champion in flowers." However, praise of an entirely different kind was forthcoming the following day when the *Press* covered the Sayre Female Institute commencement ceremony. The reporter was "grateful" that the female graduates did not speak or read their essays because their ideas would necessarily be "crude" and their opinions "contracted." The account concluded as follows: "Let them write and rewrite, but do not let the public patience be taxed by listening to them. . . . They are visions of beauty when they appear before the public on commencement day, but let them—as they did at the Sayre commencement—appear without the roll of manuscript, aesthetically done up with white or red ribbon."[7]

Unwilling to accord women the public podium or intellectual parity, the Lexington press had no problem relegating women to domesticity—to the private rather than the public realm. Moreover, as was characteristic of Victorian gender stereotyping, the local press seemed quite willing to assign to females more delicate, easily violated sensibilities. Illustrative of both these ideas was "Woman and Home," a regular feature in the *Lexington Morning Transcript* in the 1880s, the title of which assumed that the private world of the home was woman's proper sphere. Centering women within this social and spatial boundary, the column advised and admonished them on everything from housecleaning hints to personal morality.

Such advice followed logically from the widely accepted Victorian idea of "republican motherhood," which held that women properly wielded significant influence on public life through their children, an influence exerted in private life by proper home management and moral role modeling. In the 21 August 1885 issue, "debasement" was associated with both moral and hygienic failure. The reader was advised that "debasement" of either kind was "unnatural" to woman's finer sensibilities, seemingly for both biblical and genetic reasons, and that woman, unlike man, had "a natural desire to fly from base surroundings." Furthermore, the article stated, even a morally debased woman maintained cleanliness "as the governing article of her creed." Such supposedly delicate, fragile female sensibilities were revisited in 1892 in the *Kentucky (Lexington) Leader* when it jocosely ridiculed a local woman and her daughter who had mistaken an innocent noise for a burglar: the headline read, "Victims of Fright: Feminines Are Timid, Especially in the Dark."[8]

"Savages"

George Ranck's remarks about Native Americans in his 1879 centennial address were characteristically Victorian. Referring to American Indians as "raging bands" engaged in "savage butchery" during the colonial and revolutionary periods, Ranck concluded that they had been a "race without a history" conquered by a "race with a history"—indeed, a race "bringing along with the axe and rifle the germ of a civilizing power." Ranck was expressing the Victorians' ideal of civilization as embodied in white, Protestant, Anglo-Saxon culture and their view of those from outside that culture, including Native Americans, as "savage and uncivilized."[9]

If Victorians were critical of, and repulsed by, "exotic," foreign, or "savage" peoples, they were also fascinated by them, and this mixture of attraction and revulsion is clearly evident in the Lexington press of the era. A number of headlines appearing during 1885 are illustrative: an article on Mexico entitled "Creation's Fag End," an account subheaded "Life in the Amphibious and Filthy City of Bangkok: A Queer Land and People," a feature on Syria called "The Children of the Desert: . . . Description of the Manners and Customs of a Romantic Race," a description of the coast of South America entitled "A Picture of Desolation," and a piece headlined

"Groping in the Darkness: The Chinese Still Clinging to Customs of Centuries Ago." The article on the Chinese, in a Victorian articulation of ethnocentrism and racial superiority, quoted an American military officer who found the Chinese "teachable," and it noted that the Chinese of the northern provinces were really quite tall, whereas those from the southern regions were "small inferior physical types. It is from them that the immigrants to this country come."[10]

"Noble Charity"

In January 1885 the *Lexington Daily Press* printed a highly complimentary essay by an unnamed "college maiden" from Hamilton College, a private women's school on North Broadway that was later merged with Kentucky University. The exuberant essayist, praising the benevolence of Lexingtonians, noted that "everyone must know the kindheartedness of the people of Lexington from the numerous asylums they maintain." In his centennial address, George Ranck also alluded to the social consciousness of Lexingtonians when he spoke of "that noble public charity—the Eastern Lunatic Asylum." Founded in 1816 and formally opened in 1824, this asylum was the second hospital for the insane established in the nation. Remarkably, its main building provided space on the top floor for what was called the Lunatic Ball, a prominent community social event that was also an expression of social concern and benevolence. At the turn of the twentieth century, this dance was an annual fund-raising event attended by the elite of Lexington society. There is also evidence that a similar event was held more frequently in the mid-1880s: the *Lexington Daily Press* of 9 December 1885 remarked, "the monthly ball was held at the Asylum last night."[11]

The asylum and its Lunatic Ball were by no means the only expressions of social concern and benevolence in the city. There was the problem of poverty, and Ranck, for one, expressed his interest and concern in 1885 by joining the Lexington Society for Improving the Condition of the Poor. Despite such evidence of organized public empathy, newspaper accounts suggest a rather harsh attitude toward the poor and toward aid for them. In a letter printed in the *Lexington Morning Transcript* in January 1885, the writer expressed disapproval of the city's providing public "relief" for the poor and suggested that "applicants for relief" be made to clean the city streets for what they received in order to "weed out the lazy and unworthy class" and save "good men from pauperization."[12]

This view that many of the poor, especially the homeless, were of the "lazy and unworthy class" was echoed on the pages of the *Lexington Daily Press,* where they were referred to as "tramps" and were styled not as truly impoverished but rather as clever liars and con artists. In a January 1885 *Press* article titled "A Tramp's Philosophy," an "old vagrant" was quoted as cynically advising neophyte beggars to "be truthful and outspoken—that is, tell them you are a Chicago fire sufferer." These "tramps" were portrayed in the *Press* not only as worthless but also as annoyingly numerous. A May 1885 article called "The Tramp Season" described them as an "army on the move" and complained that "among the many nuisances to which Spring is the prelude, tramps deserve the foremost place." The account suggested that they "concocted" a variety of stories to prey on the generosity of the "American housewife." In addition to public "city relief" for the poor, there was the county poorhouse, described by the *Press* in 1885 as simple, clean, neat, and attractive—accommodations, in the *Press*'s view, "in every respect admirably adapted to the pauper class for which they are intended. . . . We are satisfied that it is just the place to send the beggars who infest our city and are a constant annoyance to the public."[13]

Despite such harsh words, the local press exhibited a certain ambivalence toward the poor and their plight. If, on the one hand, the poor were styled as numerous and worthless, an "army" that "infested" the city, they were portrayed, on the other hand, as few in number and worthy of sympathy and benevolence. For instance, the *Lexington Morning Transcript* editorialized in February 1885 that there were few cases of "absolute want at our doors" and little actual destitution in Lexington, which had fared better in this regard "than most cities of her size during the present unusually severe winter." The *Transcript* maintained that this was due to the "thriftiness" of the population and that "deserving people" would have "no trouble in maintaining themselves" at any time in Lexington. Yet only two weeks earlier, the same newspaper had reported a number of people "in extremely destitute circumstances, suffering from hunger and cold . . . whose sore distress is no fault of their own. . . . It is a disgrace upon the city." This sentiment of benevolent concern was echoed in an anonymous letter from "a subscriber" who implored the editor of the *Transcript* to admonish the rich "to give groceries to the starving poor. . . . It is a shame to see so much suffering in this prosperous country."[14]

In addition to the public aid available, Lexington newspaper articles suggest that private benevolence, organized and administered by affluent "ladies," was frequently depended on to cope with social welfare problems in the late nineteenth century. Since colonial times, women had formed benevolent associations to provide "charitable relief," and these groups multiplied after the Civil War as increasing industrialization and urbanization created greater need. Many of these benevolent organizations had begun as women's self-improvement study clubs and then expanded their missions during the Victorian era to render aid to the poor, orphans, "wayward women," and others. A more calloused perspective is that these affluent Victorian women, "under the benign veils" of domesticity and benevolence, "articulated a hierarchical ordering of the social divisions of industrial society" and enacted, in ceremonies and charitable institutions, "gilded class divisions" in the name of charity—enactments whereby the rich paternalistically "cared for" the sick and the poor. At the turn of the twentieth century, novelist and socialist Upton Sinclair styled such benevolence as a combination of curiosity and naïveté: "rich people . . . came . . . to find out about the poor people; but what good they expected it would do them to know, one could not imagine. . . . [They were] standing upon the brink of hell and throwing in snowballs to lower the temperature."[15]

During the winter of 1885 the *Lexington Morning Transcript* reported the organization, for whatever motives, of a "soup house" by three "benevolent ladies" of Lexington to provide soup, bread, and coffee for the "starving poor." According to the account, these women donated their own money to start the enterprise and called on "those young ladies who intend to receive their friends to-day" to solicit funds from their guests for this cause. Another example of an essentially private social welfare effort directed by women in Lexington was the Home of the Friendless, which provided shelter for homeless, destitute women and was, according to the *Lexington Morning Transcript,* "conducted by a lot of ladies . . . trying to do the right thing." In addition to an "allowance" of $50 a month from the city council, the facility relied on private donations secured by these volunteer women "managers." As early as 1877 the Home of the Friendless had sponsored a "sewing school" in the Masonic Hall for "thirty to forty girls . . . of a class whose homes do not afford the advantages offered by the school." These girls were employed in "contract work" as well as in making clothing for themselves, and they were "under the instruction of a number of benevolent young ladies who have given their time . . . to this noble work of instructing the ignorant in useful knowledge."[16]

A BOOMING, FAULTLESS CITY

Above the subtext of Victorian values and attitudes embedded in George Ranck's centennial address, and consonant with his studied disregard of the social and political turbulence in the region and the nation, the major thrust of his speech was an unabashed touting of the city of Lexington and its historic accomplishments and notable attributes. His oration concluded with the bold assertion that the history of Lexington was "substantially the history of Kentucky herself," and that the benefits the city had bestowed on the state had certainly "not been overestimated." Ranck's aggrandizement of Lexington was more than eloquent ceremonial exuberance. He was engaging in what has been called the "civic folk mercantilism" of the era—the view that each city is an economic unit in competition with other cities and that it benefits residents if their city advances and prospers by projecting a positive image and thereby attracting new investment.[17]

To put it another way, Ranck's speech indicates that he was developing into one of the "articulate champions of the New South Creed," those exuberant proponents of southern modernization through business expansion and industrialization. An exemplar of these articulate champions was Henry W. Grady, editor of the *Atlanta Constitution,* whose speech to the New England Club of New York in 1886 exhibited the florid rhetoric of the time: "The new South is enamored of her new work. Her soul is stirred with the breath of a new life. The light of a grander day is falling fair on her face. She is thrilling with the consciousness of growing power and prosperity." Preaching much the same gospel, Ranck would come to fit the description of those "Southern boosters of the early 1880s [who] told everyone who would listen that their region had entered upon the initial stages of a profound and beneficial transformation." Indeed, in 1883 Ranck fully proved himself to be just such a southern booster with the publication of his *Guide to Lexington, Kentucky.*[18]

Although Ranck had previously published, in 1872, a history of early Lexington based primarily on oral history accounts, his *Guide to Lexington, Kentucky,* though containing historical material, was not intended as a historical work. The *Guide* dealt mainly with contemporary conditions in Lexington and was specifically designed to attract commercial and manufacturing concerns, as well as tourism, to the city. The book was the centerpiece of a campaign to promote the city by the newly organized Chamber of Commerce, which had commissioned Ranck to write the work and elected him its president. Apparently, it was well recognized that Ranck was energetic and tireless in his position as the city's chief booster. On 4 January 1885 the *Lexington Daily Press,* reporting on a New Year's Eve party given by Ranck and his wife at "their elegant home on North Broadway" for the members of the Chamber of Commerce, noted, "since Mr. Ranck's election to the Presidency of the Chamber, . . . he has been the soul and body of that work. When an opportunity offered itself to advance the city's interest he has always embraced it." Ranck's popularity and influence were near their zenith at that time, and although it did not bear fruit, in November 1885 the *Lexington Morning Transcript* promoted Ranck for the office of mayor as a man "of character, culture and standing."[19]

Lexington in the early 1880s was portrayed in Ranck's *Guide* as a faultless city with every desirable attribute, a cultural and social mecca on the verge of becoming a manufacturing and commercial mecca as well. Problems were not mentioned. Even the race issue was put aside with a sentimental and paternalistic flourish of the pen: "The negroes of Lexington, light hearted, careless and numerous, and with their peculiar characteristics of speech and manner, are always a novelty to strangers. . . . [Moreover,] the colored agricultural association here is a success and a credit to the race." The *Guide* was crafted to appeal to several groups: for tourists, there was the "pastoral beauty" of a "landscape strikingly English in appearance"; for those who might wish to make Lexington their home, there were many elegant private residences to suit the well-to-do, and the "competent and reliable mechanic" could look forward to a "one story cottage, with yard and reasonable conveniences"; for prospective college students, the *Guide* offered ebullient descriptions of Kentucky University and State College and asserted that "no city in the Union welcomes earnest students more heartily than Lexington"; for commercial interests, Ranck touted the city's already established merchandise market, which annually "disposed of . . . an immense amount of the most elegant and expensive kinds of dry goods, furniture, carpets, jewelry, pianos, clothing, table ware, etc."; for manufacturers, there was abundant water, plentiful, inexpensive coal and lumber, and other inducements "plain and strong" to invite "the capitalist to investment." And for all of the above, there were the advantages of "ten newspapers . . . twenty-two churches, and twenty-three educational institutions," as well as numerous benevolent orders, a flourishing YMCA, an excellent library, and modern conveniences such as telephones, electric lights, free mail delivery, and a street railroad.[20]

The *Guide*'s topics were arranged in a seemingly random manner. For instance, a discussion of the Clay Monument was followed by an appeal for industry to locate in the city, which in turn was followed by descriptions of Fairlawn Farm, the Kentucky Union railway, Centenary Methodist Church, and so forth. Nevertheless, this intermingled cascade of topics was successful in creating the impression that Lexington was an important, bustling place. Arguing that Lexington would become "for the second time the capital of the State," owing to its development as a major railroad center, Ranck asserted, "at no time in fifty years has this city increased so rapidly in population as at present, . . . and the once sleepy city is waking up."[21]

Four years later, in 1887, an even more detailed and elaborate promotional "review" of the city was published by the John Lethem Company of New York. Although no author was listed, *Lexington, the Central City: A Review* credited George Ranck for its historical material. The preface began as follows: "In the firm belief that few places on the American continent deserve so much attention as Lexington, have we published a work wherein we endeavor to give our reader a faithful review of the city as she appears to-day—her attractions as a place of residence, her inducements as a business locality and centre, and her engaging society." Clearly, this publication's promotional motivations render its claims of a "faithful," or objective, presentation of the city suspect; nevertheless, like Ranck's *Guide,* it is useful historical evidence of life in Gilded Age Lexington. Through 136 pages, the *Review* touted Lexington's rich history, fine climate, cultured society, and, most of all, recent growth.[22]

It has been argued that an "urban imperialism" in the early nineteenth century led to fierce competition and bitter rivalry among the cities of Lexington, Louisville, and Cincinnati. The preeminent urban center at the beginning of the century, land-bound Lexington had been eclipsed by its riverbank rivals by the 1830s with the coming of the steamboat. As Allen Share notes, even with the city's rail lines to the Ohio River, it was too late for Lexington to regain its former supremacy. This is not to say that the railroads were insignificant; as the guide to Lexington produced by the Federal Writers' Project in the 1930s pointed out, the railroads "did prevent Lexington from sinking to the level of a crossroads town." The 1887 *Review* indirectly acknowledged Lexington's decline by noting that it was "remarkable that the population in 1850 was less than at the beginning of the century, but it seems to be a fact." The *Review* also conceded that Lexington had experienced little growth between 1870 and 1880 but then pointed out that the city had undergone a rapid population expansion between 1880 and 1886. The *Review* listed the city's 1880 population as 16,656 and the 1886 population as 26,216, with 9,904 of these being "colored." Although the 1880 figure agreed with that reported in the tenth federal census of 1880, the 1886 figure appears to have been inflated, since the 1890 census reported Lexington's population as 21,567—nearly 5,000 less than the *Review*'s numbers four years earlier. Not until the 1900 census did Lexington's population top 26,000.[23]

The *Review* sought to portray Lexington not only as a city experiencing rapid growth but also as a place of prosperity and cultural refinement. Emphasizing both its motto and its aspiration, the *Review* declared, "*commercial prosperity is the first and strongest exponent of social happiness.*" Hoping to characterize life in Lexington as one of "social happiness" grounded in prosperity and refinement, the *Review* focused on Lexingtonians of "opulence and culture" and depicted them as "tall and fine-looking, . . . well educated, . . . genteel and refined. . . . They are rich, and spend money freely . . . [and] boast of their 'fine horses, good whiskey, and pretty women.'" With regard to the city's "pretty women," the *Review* grounded its attitude toward females (just as Ranck had done almost a decade earlier) in the precepts of the Victorian cult of True Womanhood, which has been called the "model of perfect ladyhood." According to the *Review,* Lexington was populated with women who "are justly celebrated in verse and song for their beauty. They are, without exception, well physically developed, while their marked breadth of forehead proclaims them possessed of good common sense and wit in an eminent degree. Their conversational powers are excellent, and as women they are signally suited to fill the highest offices nature has allotted to their sex."[24]

Perhaps nowhere in the *Review* is the commingling of New South and Victorian cultural currents better depicted than on pages twenty-eight and twenty-nine. Page twenty-eight shows a large rendering of the Confederate Monument in Lexington Cemetery. This monument also appeared in Ranck's *Guide,* and he noted that it had been erected in the 1870s by the "Southern ladies" of the city and had been praised as "true art, for it tells its own story—the tragic story of the Lost Cause—without the use of a single word upon its front. It is a poem in stone." Ladies Memorial Associations had sprung up throughout the South after the war, and their monuments and Memorial Day ceremonies quickly grew into a "full-scale civic ritual." These associations helped legitimize southern women's appropriation of public space and helped them place "their own mark on the public calendar." On the facing page of the *Review* is a rendering of the entrance to Woodland Park with the title "Chautauqua Assembly." The *Review* described this event as "the gathering together of teachers, preachers, Sunday School superintendents, students, lecturers, and any interested in the promotion of mental and moral culture and education, or who wish to spend a pleasant and instructive holiday in good society . . . [a place of] cottage tents imparting their homelike air and breathing a welcome to the multitudes—men, women and children there mingling in cheery, orderly intercourse."[25]

Beginning in New York in 1874 and spreading across the nation by the 1880s, the typical independent Chautauqua Assembly—part religious camp meeting, part "college" for self-improvement, and part pure entertainment—was a significant institution of Victorian middle-class intellectual life. Gregory Waller has referred to the Kentucky Chautauqua Assembly as a "model municipality," an archetypal cosmopolitan "city" in a natural setting, without the corruption and "chaotic excess of the metropolis." In similar fashion, Thomas Schlereth has called Chautauqua a "middling landscape of the middle-class," meaning that it was neither howling wilderness nor "over-civilized." Schlereth summarized Chautauqua as "a rural enclave for self-improvement, a sylvan retreat . . . from urban life, and a collective cultural enterprise for moral and intellectual rearmament" and argued that Chautauqua reflected, and had its cultural and spatial origins in, other Victorian "middling" landscapes, including the pleasure park, the college campus, the religious camp meeting, and the communitarian settlement. Commingling Victorian and New South influences, Lexington's first Chautauqua Assembly was capped off, according to the *Lexington Morning Transcript*, with a rousing address to an overflow crowd by Alabama-born Sam Jones, the most widely known and influential evangelist of the New South era.[26]

In tandem with promotional literature such as Ranck's 1883 *Guide* and the 1887 *Review*, Lexington newspapers depicted the city in an idealized fashion. Caught up in the spirit of a "New South creed" that sought to attract and foster commercial and industrial development, the local press frequently printed promotional, laudatory editorials and "booster" advertisements thinly disguised as news. In addition, the newspapers frequently printed letters reputedly from students, tourists, and visitors praising the city and its environs. Indeed, this ardent promotion of the city in the local press would continue beyond the turn of the twentieth century. In this vein of boosterism, a January 1885 editorial in the *Lexington Morning Transcript* boasted that "a Gentleman, . . . just returned after a year's absence, remarked 'I was greatly surprised to see the change in Lexington since I left. Everything is booming and going ahead.'" A useful portrait of the city's physical features and institutions often lay embedded in such hyperbolic rhetoric. A March 1885 *Lexington Daily Press* editorial titled "The Boom" asserted that Lexington had taken "many and decisive strides in the march of progress" since 1880 and went on to list more than forty improvements, including four new factories, 1,500 new homes erected, three new banks established, a new courthouse, and "Woodland Park . . . one of the finest parks in America." The editor was particularly proud of the new "railroad trunk lines," and historian Edward Ayers has noted the extraordinary growth of southern railroads during the New South era and their perceived necessity for local and regional growth and development. Aware of this fact of economic life, as well as Lexington's ongoing struggle to compete despite its recent progress, the editor of the *Transcript* stated flatly on 13 March 1885: "We want another railway. We want it bad. We have got to make an effort to get it." During 1885, the *Daily Press* repeatedly published a Chamber of Commerce advertisement for Lexington, touting its existing railroads and other salient features: "Waterworks, Twenty-three Education Institutions includ-ing Free Schools, Eight Banks, Manufactories, Chamber of Commerce, Eleven Newspapers—Three Daily, Street Railroads, Telephones, Electric Lights, Twenty-two Churches, Fire Alarm, Free Mail Delivery, The Great Feed Depot, the Famous Stock Breeding Center. Healthful, Enterprising, and Wide Awake."[27]

In a similar vein, the same unnamed "college maiden" who praised Lex-ingtonians for their kindheartedness as reflected in their asylums also com-pared the city favorably with its condition five years earlier. She argued that although the Lexington of 1880 might not have been a full-fledged city, the Lexington of 1885 certainly was. She went on to enumerate its positive at-tributes, including streets in "splendid" condition, streetcars, a new public waterworks, a fine hotel, "elegant residences, well-kept churches[,] . . . fine business houses, . . . [and] splendid schools." Then, going beyond praise for the city's physical features and institutions, she characterized the residents' level of "refinement," depicting them not only as benevolent but also as "cultured" and insisting that a new, improved opera house, "a fine, commo-dious building," be erected for the "amusement of a loving public."[28]

HIGH CULTURE

In addition to laudatory student essays, the *Lexington Morning Transcript* published letters from tourists and other outsiders who had stayed in the city, sometimes for extended periods. Like the letter from the "college maid-en," some of these missives contained perceptions of the cultural values and ideals of the city. In one example, reprinted from the *New York Evening Post* by the *Lexington Morning Transcript* in December 1885, an anonymous writer characterized Bluegrass life as follows:

> That one may hear the English language spoken here in purity; that the best magazines are read; that American authors are discussed and intelligently liked or disliked; that young ladies know good music and are as well dressed as those in New York; in short that there is here a class of people who, in all that goes to make up cul-ture—wealth, travel, manners, morals, speech, etc.—are the equals of the best Americans to be found anywhere. . . . [There are] men of

business in [the] town—bank officers, professors, lawyers, etc. And
. . . they are men of ideas [with] private libraries.[29]

By the last decades of the nineteenth century, cultural life had been divided into what is now referred to as *high culture* and *low* or *popular culture.*
These terms denote and define certain activities as well as those who engage
in them, and these distinctions also go by other names. Thus, nineteenth-
century high culture has also been referred to as "genteel culture" or "genteel
high culture," and those who engaged in its recognized activities and lifestyle
as "gentry" or as cultural elites engaged in the "genteel performance." According to Richard Bushman, in the nineteenth century, "culture, in the sense
of beauty, refinement, and taste, was the measure of human development,"
and there was a connection between genteel culture, or "polite" society, and
intellectual life. Moreover, Joseph Kett has argued that a "self-conscious"
intellectual life earnestly pursued by those seeking self-improvement and
refinement was a "leading feature of . . . cultural life" in nineteenth-century
American towns. As Lexington life is characterized in the anonymous letter
quoted above, affluence, refinement, and aesthetic and intellectual pursuits
are interwoven in a description of what Bushman has called the gentility
practiced and assumed by "small-town elites . . . through their implied association with larger circles of refinement in the great world." In a similar
vein, Lawrence Levine has written of the aesthetic and intellectual pretensions of superiority that late-nineteenth-century "highbrow" culture carried
in its quest for cultural authority. Another letter published in the *Lexington
Morning Transcript,* this one from a "Toledo Lady," provides an example of
such highbrow pretensions. Referring to the new courthouse, she wrote: "In
the rotunda is an exquisite piece of statuary, purchased by the ladies of Lexington; the work of Joel Hart, a native of Kentucky, who died in Italy a few
years ago. It is called 'The Triumph of Chastity' and represents the triumph
of womanhood over love."[30]

Then, as now, the question of what constitutes "high" art bred contention. In July 1885, in a front-page article, the *Transcript* lavishly praised
Hart's sculpture, also known as "Woman Triumphant"—a work considered
to be the masterpiece of Lexington's "premier sculptor." The article also
praised the decision to place it in the rotunda of the courthouse. By mid-
August, however, the *Transcript* was forced to defend (in Victorian gendered

metaphors) the statue against public suggestions and complaints that the nude female figure embodied something other than high culture and high art: "True manhood, to which this work of art appeals, will stand before it with reverence as the embodiment of the idea of glorious womanhood. As for the ideas of the vulgar and bestial no one need care or pay the slightest attention to them; nothing good is expected of them." Thus, the letter from the "Toledo Lady" was no doubt welcomed by the paper two months later, as it bolstered the *Transcript*'s position that the statue was high art as well as decorous.[31]

The *Lexington Daily Press* seemed to take the opposite side in the matter. It reprinted a letter to the *St. Louis Globe Democrat* in which the writer argued against nudity-as-art being displayed "for women and children to see." The writer suggested that nudity in art was the product of degenerate European cities and, in the rhetoric of Victorian gendered morality, suggested that an artist's model was a contemptible creature incompatible with "pure" womanhood: "Can a pure thing evolve from an impure source? While such a thing as a pure woman posing naked for a male artist is not an absolute impossibility, yet it is so near so that I do not believe this country contains an American-born woman who would advise her son or brother to marry such a model, or an American-born man who would accept her as a wife, . . . [nor] a good man who would not rather see his mother, wife, or sister dead than to have her follow such an avocation."[32]

In addition to the public display of and argument over art, literary culture found its way into the Lexington press in 1885. Reading was strongly associated in the nineteenth century with self-improvement, refinement, and the development of intellectual culture. Libraries were viewed as key instruments in the diffusion of knowledge, the development of literary culture, and the spread of refinement during the Gilded Age. Moreover, the funding of libraries was one of the important cultural philanthropies of a nineteenth-century elite metropolitan gentry seeking to enhance and maintain its cultural authority. In an article reflecting such intentions, and what has been called the "missionary impulse to diffuse culture" through libraries, the *Lexington Morning Transcript* reported in August 1885 that the private Lexington Library Association was embarked on a campaign to solicit funds for a new library site and building. The proposed new library would provide improved space for "the most valuable collection of books in Kentucky,

. . . reading rooms, an art hall and a lecture hall." The *Transcript* reminded its readers that they should "take enough pride" in this valuable collection of books to help house it in a more suitable facility. The article made much of the fact that one prominent Lexingtonian had already given $5,000.[33]

In addition to an appreciation for art and what has been called "serious reading," Gilded Age Lexingtonians enacting the genteel performance could turn to lectures as a means of seeking refinement and self-improvement. Along with the public square, the white fence, the hotel, and the library, the public lecture was a marker of refinement and gentility in nineteenth-century American towns. In Victorian America the lecture was not only a popular public entertainment but also a cultural pursuit; "by going to a lecture, people announced to others that they aspired to knowledge and self-improvement." One of the "stars" of the lecture circuit, Henry Ward Beecher, spoke at the Lexington Opera House on 1 April 1885. The notice for this event in the *Lexington Morning Transcript* strongly suggested that this was an educational and intellectual event that everyone should attend, but in particular, "every attendant at the schools and colleges should go, as they may never have another opportunity."[34]

In addition to the professional lecture circuit, there were other venues for such intellectual stimulation and entertainment in 1885 Lexington. The student literary societies at both Kentucky University and State College sponsored lectures that were open to the public. These lectures were usually held in the college chapels and were heavily advertised in the local press. On 1 November 1885 the *Lexington Daily Press* printed an announcement of the formation of a "Lecture Association" by members of the literary societies and others at Kentucky University, the purpose of which was not to make money but rather "to secure for the various colleges and the people of the city the best course of lectures we can command." A month later, the *Press* announced the upcoming lecture by "the distinguished orator, Dr. A. A. Willitis." This was to be the first of a planned series of lectures at Morrison Chapel on the Kentucky University campus, tickets for which could be purchased at "J. B. Morton's and Barnes' Drug Store."[35]

Earlier, in February 1885, the Union Literary Society of State College had sponsored a lecture by Belva Anne Lockwood, a famous attorney, women's rights and suffrage leader, and the Equal Rights Party's 1884 presidential nominee. Lockwood's address, "The Woman of Today," was advertised in the *Lexington Daily Press*. Tickets for the event were sold in city businesses and cost thirty-five cents for adults and twenty-five cents for students and children. The *Press* treated the lecture as a major cultural and intellectual event. Praising the "spirit of enterprise and progressiveness" of the literary society members, the editor noted that "the engagement of a lecturer of first-class reputation by a college literary society is something new for Lexington, with all her literary spirit." The *Press* also printed a flattering feature article on Lockwood and encouraged attendance at the lecture, touting the "good walking" provided by a new "substantial elevated plank walkway" extending from town out "along the pike to the gate and up through the campus to the door of the college." The lecture itself was given front-page attention by the *Press,* which noted that the chapel at State College was crowded to capacity by students and "most of the prominent citizens of the city."[36]

POPULAR CULTURE

Just as the city's newspapers yield evidence of pretensions to high culture in Gilded Age Lexington, they also furnish illustrations of lowbrow culture, or the popular entertainment that has been referred to elsewhere as "cheap amusement." To begin with, the Lexington press directly participated in providing popular culture and entertainment to the area's inhabitants. In what might be called a less elitist effort to diffuse literature to the public than that provided by the library, Lexington newspapers provided serialized short stories and novels for their readers' entertainment. By the 1860s, serialized novels had become extremely popular in magazines such as *Harper's Weekly,* and by the last years of the nineteenth century, daily newspapers across the nation had begun using drama to lure readers, both in their news accounts and through serialized fiction. Reflecting this trend locally, the *Lexington Daily Press* in January 1885 ran a serialized story entitled "Mona Scully; or, The Irish Bride of an Englishman," and the *Lexington Morning Transcript* offered "An Actor's Story" beginning on 17 November 1885.[37]

Beyond the serialized popular fiction offered by the press for public amusement, Lexington newspapers advertised, reported on, and reviewed a wide variety of public performances and events. At times, these events blended high and popular culture, often in the same venues; at other times, high and low culture remained separate and in contention with each other.

For instance, "county court days" were extremely popular events for both economic and social reasons, and "of all assemblages treasured by Kentuckians . . . none exceeded the county court days." Yet county court days also led to conflict in Lexington. These monthly events were held on Cheapside, next to the courthouse, from the early nineteenth through the early twentieth centuries. They were a combination of stock trading, merchandise swapping, and socializing "in a chaotic atmosphere of crowded animals and humanity, tobacco chewing, cigar smoking, and whiskey drinking." With Lexington's "growing cosmopolitan and genteel character" came objections to this practice. This clash of values was highlighted in a December 1885 *Lexington Morning Transcript* editorial objecting to the "Cheapside Nuisance" and labeling those who attended either crude mountain "bull whackers" or locals who "would stable 'Woman Triumphant' in a hog-pen." The editorial concluded by noting, "Cheapside is now clean and beautiful, and we trust the City Council will not again see it transformed into a manure pile." Here was disdain for and a challenge to lowbrow culture—which was rendered synonymous with rural culture by the editor. Here too was an expression of Victorian middle-class attitudes regarding the proper uses and segregation of urban space and what has been referred to as a genteel map of the "geography of refinement." By the late nineteenth century, city and country broadly designated separate "cultural regions," a "cultural and social polarity" with fashion and refinement at one end and simplicity and rudeness at the other. "Cheapside Nuisance" was soon answered in a letter signed "Justice" and printed on the front page of the *Transcript.* This angry, anti-elitist letter defended the farmers in populist tones as "that deserving class" and reminded the editor that it was largely the farmers who paid the taxes for the elegant courthouse. The letter writer stated, "while we do not object to the lawyers and criminals having full possession of the inside, we would like to see a deserving people have a little liberty on the outside."[38]

In contrast, the refined and the rustic, the highbrow and the lowbrow, blended without contention at the highly popular fairs held in or near the city during the Gilded Age. Segregated by race, the ninth annual fair of the Kentucky Agricultural and Mechanical (A&M) Association (for whites) opened at the racecourse and fairgrounds on South Broadway on 25 August 1885, while the seventeenth annual "colored fair" was held at a location on the Newtown Pike beginning on 24 September. Judging from the press accounts, these fairs consisted of a kaleidoscopic display of animal husbandry and other agricultural and domestic arts, crafts, and popular amusements, along with more genteel exhibitions as well. At the A&M fair, for instance, there were stock exhibits and contests, trots, "handsomest" baby contests, trained birds, a shooting gallery, and ring-toss games. Along with these agrarian and popular amusements, the press touted the fair's more refined attractions, including an art gallery, a "Floral Hall," and a concert by the "world-renowned Liberati," a cornetist whose playing left the audience with a "wonderfully elevated feeling." There was no hint of animosity between rural "bull whackers" and city elites here.[39]

Along with the mingling of the classes at fairs, there is evidence that the genteel classes, the "best people," mixed with the general public in venues that might seem devoid of highbrow pretensions, such as indoor roller skating rinks. Indoor roller skating became a hugely popular fad in Lexington during the "nickelodeon" era from 1906 to 1912, a period "when readily available cheap amusement exploded," but it was also one of the public entertainments during the Gilded Age. In an era before the title "professor" was reserved for college teachers, the *Lexington Morning Transcript* reported that Professor O. A. Lank, "the champion roller skater," would open a new skating rink on 7 January 1885 at Lell's Hall in Lexington. The account in the *Lexington Daily Press* the following week took pains to make it clear that the genteel enjoyed this popular amusement, thereby making it more respectable: "There was a very large attendance of ladies and gentlemen at the rink last night, and the fun was glorious. There were several elegant ladies present and many of the society young gentlemen of the city. The skating as a rule was good, many practical skaters being on the floor. If you want to have a bushel full of fun go to the rink."[40]

Along with fairs and skating rinks, Gilded Age Lexingtonians both genteel and otherwise were entertained by circuses. In 1885 the Sells Brothers' "Arabian Circus" stopped in Lexington, and the large advertisement in the *Lexington Daily Press* promised the public, in the Victorian rhetoric of cultural and racial superiority, a glimpse of "Dusky Denizens of the Dreadful Desert." A decade later, in 1896, the Adams, Forepaugh, and Sells Circus performed in Lexington to a crowd that included, among others, the "belles and beaus" of polite society.[41]

In 1885 the Lexington Opera House (which would burn the following year and be replaced in 1887 by the facility that still stands today) was a venue that provided, in addition to the intellectually stimulating lectures of Henry Ward Beecher and the like, an eclectic fare reflecting both cheap amusement and pretensions to high culture. Some of the bookings for the opera house advertised in the local press during November 1885 serve to illustrate: on the fourth, the "Mammoth Minstrels" offered "everything New, Fresh, and Novel in Minstrelsy"; on the ninth, "A Parlor Match," a light comedy "So Funny you Can't Describe It," was billed; playing on the fourteenth was a more "serious" piece of theater, "The Banker's Daughter," styled as "The Fashionable Event of the Season," with a "cast especially selected to interpret, in an artistic manner, this, the most beautiful of modern plays"; and on the sixteenth was "Sleeping Beauty," billed as "the Grand Spectacular and Operatic Burlesque," complete with "a carload of new scenery."[42]

Although the opera house offered a mixture of highbrow and lowbrow fare in the same venue, distinctions were sometimes made as to the target audience for a particular performance. As November 1885 ended, the *Lexington Morning Transcript* reprinted on the front page a review of "Baird's Minstrels," which was scheduled to perform at the Lexington Opera House on 3 December. This review, reprinted from the *Newport (R.I.) Times,* chose to accentuate the tension existing between perceptions of high and low culture and argued that a minstrel show could be suitable for a genteel audience: "The difference between the audience present at the opera house last evening to see and hear Baird's minstrels and the audiences which usually attend minstrel shows in this city, was marked, for the seats held many of our best citizens, with their wives and families. Ladies in elegant toilets were the rule, not the exception, and all enjoyed an entertainment pure and pleasing in the highest degree. Baird proves . . . that a . . . minstrel show can be given without resorting to lowness or vulgarity in any form." It has been argued that the late nineteenth century witnessed an increasing impetus to order society through the "sacralization of culture," and it seems clear that this review attempted not only to include at least this exhibition of minstrelsy in the canon of highbrow performance but also to arbitrate the composition and comportment of the audience appropriate for such entertainment. Those responsible for reprinting this review from Rhode Island in the *Transcript* must have assumed that it would resonate with the "best citizens" of Lexington as well.[43]

Along with its fairgrounds and opera house, Lexington's Woodland Park became another significant Gilded Age venue for both activities and entertainments usually associated with popular culture and those identified with the intellectual and aesthetic pursuits of genteel, highbrow life. This fifteen-acre park, developed by the Woodland Park Association from land purchased from the Woodlands estate in 1882, was opened to the public on 9 May 1885. Completely fenced and adjacent to a brick-manufacturing company, the park contained a twin-towered frame auditorium, a baseball field, and four-acre Lake Chenosa; it was accessible from town by a mule-drawn street railway. Two years before the first Chautauqua Assembly would redefine, acquire, and become synonymous with the park, the *Lexington Daily Press* announced its opening with high praise: "It is unnecessary for us to speak of the beauty of these grounds. The present management have expended a large amount of money in improving them, and it is now without doubt the most beautiful park we know of. . . . We know of no more delightful place for recreation or pleasure than our new Woodland Park."[44]

Victorian parks, modeled after Frederick Law Olmsted's New York Central Park, were established for a variety of reasons: as "pleasure gardens" for quiet strolling and contemplation, as healthy outdoor recreational facilities, to promote civic pride, to encourage temperance, and generally to control and civilize urban life. The pleasure garden as anecdote to the metropolitan stress of harried city dwellers "made sense to the middle- and upper-class gentry. . . . To these individuals the pleasure park provided the appropriate environment for promenading and contemplating." These parks have been described as components of a public culture reflecting Victorian middle-class moral values and the attempt to make urban space respectable and safe for middle-class women. Moreover, they have been deemed one of the public spaces on a "map of Gentility"—spaces that carried "immense authority because being there . . . identified a person as genteel." The *Lexington Daily Press* heralded the city's new park in just such rhetoric, styling it as a retreat from city life: "leaving the heat, dust, and smoke of the city, a short drive reaches the entrance to Woodland Park where spring is putting on her most lovely attire, and is rapidly transforming the place into one of unusual beauty and attractiveness." Here was a place where one could spend "an hour wandering over the exquisite grounds, . . . [where] children were overwhelmed with delight . . . and young ladies and gentlemen in rowboats . . .

[made the] beautiful lake [come] alive with fun and beauty." Moreover, "no disreputable persons or persons under the influence of liquor" were allowed on the grounds. The *Lexington Morning Transcript* agreed with the *Press* in all respects, asserting that Woodland Park was "just what our city is so badly in need of—a place of innocent amusement and recreation."[45]

Although newspaper articles described the new park in genteel, highly respectable terms, a quick review of the newspaper advertisements for attractions in the park during the summer of 1885 reveals an eclectic assortment of entertainments, some more genteel than others. For the aesthetically and spiritually inclined, there was a "sacred concert" on 6 September. However, there were also baseball games between a Lexington club and those from other cities scheduled throughout June. In addition, there were circus-like performances, such as the "aquatic feats" of Captain Paul Boyton witnessed by a crowd of more than 2,000 on 23 June, and a 16 July performance by the "Fire King of the World," a daredevil who promised to be "overwhelmed by fierce flames" and survive in them for forty minutes.[46]

In sum, in published letters, editorials, reviews, and advertisements, the Lexington press of the mid-1880s offers evidence of a rich array of attitudes, activities, and entertainments in a variety of venues reflecting both high and popular culture in the city during the Gilded Age. There were, perhaps, some venues that sought and attracted only, or primarily, the more intellectually and aesthetically inclined. More often, however, the venues of public culture such as the fairgrounds, the opera house, and Woodland Park offered both highbrow and popular fare either sequentially or simultaneously, at times distinguishing and separating the classes and at other times mingling them. Moreover, there were also those venues—skating rinks and circuses, to name two—devoid of any highbrow pretensions that nevertheless entertained and amused all classes.

Class was one thing, but race was another. Blacks were excluded from or kept separate within most of the venues of public culture and entertainment in Gilded Age Lexington. Although federal laws and courts thwarted formal moves toward segregation during Reconstruction, the 1883 Supreme Court invalidation of the 1875 Civil Rights Act and the 1896 Supreme Court decision in *Plessey v. Ferguson,* establishing the separate but equal doctrine, opened the gates to a "flood of segregation laws" that hardened racial tension and segregation throughout Kentucky. The last two decades of the nineteenth century "saw the maturing of racial segregation in Kentucky," and in Lexington, the urbanization process that brought large numbers of blacks into the city after the Civil War soon led to informal segregation as well—in housing, in the theater, in the jail, and in the separate fairs previously noted. Even though the laws passed after 1890 ensured statewide racial segregation, "blacks already lived in a segregated world," and libraries were among the many public spaces where blacks were prohibited. Similarly, in an early attempt to open Woodland Park, lessee J. M. Hopson advertised in the *Lexington Daily Transcript* of 1 June 1883 his proposal to establish a "Pleasure Resort" where, for the five-cent price of admission, "All Respectable White People" would be welcome.[47]

Segregation could exclude and divide, but it could also motivate and invigorate, and one important manifestation of black community and intellectual life was the organized black opposition to railway segregation. According to southern historian Edward Ayers, "most of the debates about race relations focused on the railroads of the New South," and laws segregating the railroad coaches by race through the 1880s and 1890s "were the first wave of segregation laws that affected the entire South in anything like a uniform way." Likewise, Kentucky historian George C. Wright has argued that "one of the best-organized, most enduring struggles" by Kentucky blacks centered on railroad discrimination; in particular, members of the Colored Citizens Protective League of Lexington, founded in the late 1880s, lobbied and boycotted to express their resistance to the Separate Coach Law—which was nevertheless passed by the Kentucky legislature in the spring of 1892.[48]

As early as 13 September 1881 the *Lexington Daily Transcript* reported on an "Indignation Meeting" held the previous day by "the colored people of Lexington" at the courthouse. At the meeting there were several well-received orations, a "handsome" collection was taken up, and resolutions were passed denouncing the Cincinnati Southern Railroad for ejecting "a colored woman named Graves" from the train after she attempted to enter the "ladies car." Eleven years later, on 4 April 1892, the Republican *Kentucky Leader* noted with much interest the boycott of white merchants by Lexington blacks in an attempt to forestall the pending Separate Coach Law. It quoted an unnamed black woman as saying, "If we are not good enough to ride together, we are not good enough to trade together." Two days later, the *Leader* editorially opposed both the Separate Coach Law and the black boycott of white merchants. The editor noted approvingly that "determined opposition" to the legislation was coming from the "better element of the colored people." The editor was, in fact, referring to local representatives of the black upper class and emerging middle class, who have been described as having a strong "sense of 'service to the race'" and a strong commitment to the "realization of equal rights for black citizens." Though approving of black opposition to the Separate Coach Law, the editor attributed the ill-advised boycott of local merchants to a "few zealous but hot headed persons" and counseled Lexington blacks to follow the advice of their recognized leaders, "the leading colored people of this section," and thereby avoid "arousing an antagonistic public sentiment." This suggests that although the black community was united as to ends, the means were a matter of contention—or at least the white press thought so. Unfortunately, what the black press had to say has been lost, for no copies of central Kentucky's black newspapers from this era have survived.[49]

The Separate Coach Law was signed in May 1892, and the *Kentucky Leader* reported on 2 October 1892 that black leaders from Lexington, Louisville, and elsewhere were preparing to test its constitutionality in court. These legal maneuvers were ultimately unsuccessful. The Kentucky Supreme Court upheld the law on 7 October 1898, and by the fall of 1903, even the interurban train cars were segregated by law in the Bluegrass. Regardless of the outcome of the railway segregation controversy, even a reading of accounts in the white-controlled press makes it clear that Lexington blacks in the Gilded Age debated the issues of the times in vibrant community organizations and engaged these issues by all means available to them.[50]

A NEW SOUTH CITY

The Race Question

When Henry W. Grady, editor of the *Atlanta Constitution,* rose to the applause of the New England Club of New York in December 1886 and delivered his widely hailed oration titled "The New South," he asked his northern audience rhetorical questions and then offered soothing answers: "But what of the negro? Have we solved the problem he presents or progressed in honor and equity toward solution? Let the record speak to the point. . . . The relations of the Southern people with the negro are close and cordial. . . . Faith has been kept with him, . . . [and] faith will be kept with him in the future if the South holds her reason and integrity." Despite such assuasive rhetoric from the era's southern leaders, manifestations of what was politely referred to as the "race question" in the South—segregation; discrimination; white attitudes of racial superiority that often sanctioned and encouraged the public disparagement and humiliation of blacks; the widespread fear among whites, fostered and fed by press sensationalism, of black crime; and rampant lynching and mob violence—have been widely recognized as hallmarks of New South social arrangements and tensions from Reconstruction through the First World War and beyond.[51]

Accounts in Lexington's white-controlled press during the Gilded Age suggest that these hallmarks of New South culture largely defined the city's race relations. For instance, on 24 March 1877 the *Lexington Daily Press* editorially belittled the rumor of a possible presidential appointment by Rutherford B. Hayes of "Dr. Langston," a Lexington black, and asserted that the man was unpopular even among other blacks, who "charge him with the mortal offense of trying to be a white man." On 26 January 1880, in an obviously partisan letter from "A Democrat and a Taxpayer" printed in the *Lexington Daily Transcript,* the writer railed against any suggestion of social equality for blacks as a "stupid absurdity" and suggested that Democrats, unlike Republicans, had worked "from the rising of the sun to the going down of the same to keep the nigger out." There were those who sought not only to bar blacks from social life and politics but also to remove them from the country. The "back to Africa" movement in the New South era has been described as a "fantasy of black emigration out of the United States" shared by many whites and by some blacks as well. In a 21 October 1883 editorial in the *Lexington Daily Transcript* entitled "What's to Become of the Negro," the editor indulged in this fantasy. Couching his views in a feigned concern for blacks, the editor suggested that "a revolution in sentiment that would move the negro to Africa might be one of the grandest things for him in the world." A decade later, in a commentary published on 3 April 1894, Captain R. H. Fitzhugh suggested that the "negro problem" could perhaps best be settled, in part, by "colonization in Africa." This was a feasible solution, reasoned Fitzhugh, because America had the ships and the means to send "as many as would probably want to go there."[52]

In addition to editorials and commentaries, letters chosen for publication in the white-controlled Lexington press put contemporary racial attitudes on display. For example, in the earlier mentioned letter from the "Toledo Lady," the author not only praised "The Triumph of Chastity" as high art but also expressed her opinion of Lexington's large "colored" population as being "generally well behaved. But [they] have the failing which makes the chicken house and pig sty a scene of nightly terror to their occupants." Quite simply, her assertion was that Lexington's blacks, even the "well behaved," were petty thieves. Other newspaper accounts were equally blatant in displaying racial attitudes and prejudices. On 22 February 1885 the *Lexington Morning Transcript* lauded the police for raiding a "colored" saloon on Vine Street and arresting the "vulgar and obscene" patrons for vagrancy; on the same page, it praised a "popular" white saloon, describing it as "neat and clean as a pin" and crowded with "guests." And in a piece entitled "Captured by the Coons," the 13 August 1885 edition of the *Transcript* complained that the courthouse was not "large enough to accommodate the lazy, idle, dirty negroes who congregate there." Such rhetoric and sentiment were not isolated or infrequent in the Lexington press of 1885, nor were they confined to the *Transcript,* as the following accounts from the *Lexington Daily Press* illustrate: a *Press* article on 21 January assumed that the white students should, and would, walk out of the Board of Home Mission's Williamsburg Academy if blacks were admitted; on 29 March and again on 4 September the paper mimicked black dialect in accounts belittling black courtship and marriage arrangements; on 12 April an article quipped that a black prisoner in Lexington, a "colored rough," would "geologize for the city for a few weary months"; and on 23 June the paper asserted that a deputy marshal in Cynthiana, Kentucky, was "fully justified" in fatally shooting a black prisoner in his jail cell when the man resisted an attempt to chain him to the floor.[53]

It would be a mistake to assume that blacks alone bore the brunt of white racism in the Gilded Age Lexington press. In the rhetoric of Victorian rejection of all cultures not Anglo-Saxon, the press expressed its disdain for Native Americans and Chinese immigrants as well. In a December 1885 account titled "Making 'Good Indians,'" the *Lexington Morning Transcript* signaled its approval of "a war of extermination inaugurated against the murderous Apaches" in New Mexico. And in a *Transcript* article appearing in June of the following year called "Sam, the Injun," Native American intelligence was belittled and it was made clear that "the stolid sort of Indian . . . does as he is told." Moreover, in a September 1885 editorial, the *Transcript* unashamedly advised the Chinese ambassador to "take a hint from the Wyoming massacre of his countrymen [a reference to a recent racial incident] and send them all back home." Nevertheless, despite occasional deprecating remarks about other minorities, the Lexington press in the Gilded Age occupied itself primarily with the various aspects of the "Negro problem," often employing a rhetoric of violence.[54]

Lynching

The New South has been described as a "notoriously violent place," and certainly the history of Kentucky during this era is rife with both interracial and intraracial lawlessness and violence. The Civil War was responsible for spawning "long enduring hatred and violence" in the border states, including Kentucky, and political and economic turmoil in the South of the 1880s and 1890s fueled crime, violence, and racial hatred. Perhaps the most romanticized explanation for this southern propensity to violence appeared in the 1905 novel *The Man of the Hour* by Octave Thanet, who has been described by Ayers as "one of the most insightful observers of the New South." In a chapter entitled "The Southern Way," Thanet styles the violence ingrained in southern life as "the inevitable result when a high-spirited race has its feudal state rent from it by war and is forced into a new order of things for which it is not ready."[55]

When Thanet referred to white southerners as "high-spirited" as an explanation for their tendency toward violence, she may have had in mind the chivalric code of honor endemic in the New South. White southern men frequently aspired to and coveted that principle, which licensed and demanded violence in its defense—violence ranging from fistfights to feuds to, in some circumstances, lynching. Reflected in local newspaper accounts during the period are conflicting views of this chivalric culture that embraced what one historian described as a "quixotic ideal of personal honor." For instance, the *Lexington Daily Press* in August 1885 printed a sermon analyzing and decrying the prevalence of violence and murder in the state. The minister argued that "false sentiments of honor" prevailed within the populace, leading to violent acts committed in revenge for perceived insults—violent acts that were the unworthy "fruits of a barbarous and cruel people." In contrast, the *Lexington Morning Transcript* in January 1888, under the front-page headline "An Affair of Honor," lauded a fistfight between two "highly connected young gentlemen" after an exchange of "high words" and suggested to the public that the fight was a "settlement that commends itself to older heads."[56]

George C. Wright's book *Racial Violence in Kentucky, 1865–1940,* is devoted to chronicling the violence of whites toward blacks after the Civil War. Wright argues that in Kentucky, as throughout the South, white violence toward blacks through lynching, "legal lynching," and mob rule was motivated by the intention to "ensure that Afro-Americans knew 'their place' and remained at the bottom of society." Lynching, it should be understood, includes hanging, shooting, burning, and other means of inflicting violent death extralegally, while "legal lynching" refers to racially motivated, discriminatory execution by legitimate civil authorities. W. Fitzhugh Brundage, in *Lynching in the New South,* agrees that lynching of blacks by whites was a means of "racial repression," but he claims that it was also motivated by the attempt to "enforce social conformity" to perceived community values and standards of conduct. Brundage's work on lynching analyzes the motives and actions of several types of southern lynch mobs: "terrorist" mobs such as the "whitecappers" and "Ku Kluxers," intent on maintaining the social status quo in the South; small, "private" mobs bent on revenge; "posses" determined to provide law enforcement where it was weak or nonexistent; and large, "mass" mobs with a high level of community participation— including many of the "best citizens"—in highly ritualized performances of public torture and murder designed to degrade as well as to punish. Brundage points out that, more than any other type of mob, mass mobs were often congratulated for their actions and applauded in the southern press. Far from feeling guilty, these mobs felt morally justified in their actions. He argues that although all lynchings "were a means to defend the established order against unwelcome change or perceived threats," mass mobs and their ritualized anger "most fully exposed, strengthened, and preserved the social and racial foundations of Southern society."[57]

Lynching was tolerated, and even encouraged, in the New South partly because of a pervasive fear among whites that blacks, freed from the controls of slavery, were becoming habitual criminals and that black crime was spiraling out of control. Ayers also notes that newspapers in the region frequently publicized and exaggerated crimes by blacks and the violent white response. This may have been motivated, in part, by newspapers' increased dependence on drama and sensationalism to increase circulation and revenue in the last decades of the century. African American novelist Charles W. Chesnutt, in *The Marrow of Tradition,* expressed his own perception of the state of affairs in the South in 1901 through the book's black hero: "every . . . crime, committed by a colored man, would be imputed to the race, which was already staggering under a load of obloquy because, in the eyes of a prejudiced and undiscriminating public, it must answer as a whole for the offenses of each separate individual."[58]

Reflecting these trends, the white-controlled Lexington press in the Gilded Age reported on black crime occurring locally and elsewhere in rhetoric that sensationalized the crimes and demonized the criminals. Throughout 1885, for instance, both the *Lexington Daily Press* and the *Lexington Morning Transcript* published accounts of "obstreperous," "lawless," "fiendish" Negroes; "black demons" and "black brutes" who committed "devilish deeds" and "horrible outrages" in crimes ranging from stealing coal to murder and rape. Such rhetoric continued in the Lexington press throughout the last two decades of the century. For example, the *Transcript* of 21 February 1892 reported on the "polluted soul" of a "black demon," and a *Lexington Herald* headline in May 1900 announced that a "black fiend" had committed an "unspeakable crime"—the rape and subsequent murder of a white teenaged girl. Blacks were lynched by whites for any number of offenses ranging from minor infractions to more serious crimes, and rape did not, in fact, incite most lynchings. Nevertheless, rape, the "unspeakable crime," struck at white southerners' personal and community sense of honor; it seized the imagination and ignited the fears of whites more than any other offense and "played a major role in legitimating mob violence."[59]

Brundage has noted that newspaper editors and others "who complained of the 'law's delay' tapped a deep reservoir of disenchantment with the legal system during the late nineteenth and early twentieth centuries." This comment reflects the argument that, in the New South, a weak government and a lack of faith in the criminal justice system often led whites to view extralegal violence as necessary for law enforcement and the maintenance of local community standards of moral conduct, as well as a means of controlling and repressing blacks. Two press accounts from this era illustrate the Lexington newspapers' praise for local, nongovernmental guardianship of community moral standards and outraged citizens' swift administration of what Brundage refers to as "folk justice." Under the headline "Summary Justice," the *Lexington Daily Press* of 19 August 1885 reported, with obvious approbation, an incident in Indiana in which a farmer and his wife discovered three "tramps" burglarizing their house (all the participants were white). The farmer, "a powerful man," subdued and tied up the three burglars with the clothesline supplied by his wife and offered each of them the choice of going to jail or receiving a hundred lashes from him on the spot. The men chose the whipping, and a crowd of neighbors, "all sympathetic to the irate farmer," gathered and watched with approval despite the "piteous cries for mercy" from those being lashed. Almost a decade later, in March 1894, the *Lexington Morning Transcript* commented on the "justified" shotgun killing of a black man on the Leestown Pike by a white farmer who had caught the man stealing chickens: "Notwithstanding the fact that nearly every man in Kentucky will shoot to kill when a chicken thief invades his hen roost, it seems to have no effect upon the Negro chicken thieves in this section. It is almost sure death for a chicken thief to be caught on a man's premises, provided the owner has enough courage to shoot, which is usually the case."[60]

Publicly expressed support not only for extralegal "justice" carried out by individuals but also for violence carried out by "terrorist" mobs is evident in the Gilded Age Lexington press as well. For instance, in March 1885 the *Lexington Morning Transcript* printed a sympathetic "history" of the Ku Klux Klan, maintaining that the organization had begun innocently as a jovial social club for young men seeking "temporary diversion" and that, "by the force of circumstance," they had become "regulators" whose purpose was to "subserve the public welfare, suppress lawlessness and protect property." In September of the same year, the *Transcript* reported approvingly that the Georgia "KuKlux" was determined "to rid the country of bad characters by their own methods" and would continue to "regulate slanderers and other worthless characters."[61]

Accounts of public lynchings of blacks, and occasionally of whites as well, appeared repeatedly in Lexington newspapers during the Gilded Age.

And as has been said of the press in general throughout the New South, the Lexington press appeared to be not only reporting lynchings but also applauding them. The *Lexington Morning Transcript* seemed especially prone to do so, and a few examples from a single year suggest both the rhetoric and the attitude. On 12 September 1885, under the front-page headline "A Good Job," with the subheading "The Negro Rapist . . . Pays the Proper Penalty for His Heinous Crime," the *Transcript* reported the lynching of a black man near Cincinnati by a mass mob that had taken him by force from jail. Later the same month the *Transcript* announced that "A Negro Fiend," a "big, burly . . . black brute," was "Wanted By Judge Lynch" near St. Louis, Missouri, for the "outrage" and "violation" of two white females, noting that the "whole section of the country [had] turned out in pursuit." In October 1885, under the headline "Devilish Incendiarism," the *Transcript* reported that, near Elizabethtown, Kentucky, the hanging of a black man who had attempted to "outrage a popular young lady" had resulted in the "outrageous" burning of her house and barn by blacks bent on revenge. The paper predicted that when the perpetrators of the arson were "fixed to a certainty," there would "certainly be mob work in the neighborhood." A December 1885 article in the *Transcript* reported a case of robbery, arson, and murder by a "black demon" in Laurel, Mississippi, and approvingly concluded that "the villain was captured, and did not live to see the sun go down on his bloody work." Such rhetoric was so common that Chesnutt, satirically expressing his frustration and despair over contemporary race relations, wrote in 1901 that "the Associated Press had flashed the report of another dastardly outrage by a burly black brute—all black brutes it seems are burly."[62]

The approbation, both implicit and explicit, by the Lexington press of lynching and mob violence continued throughout the era. For example, in February 1892 the *Lexington Morning Transcript*'s front-page headline read, "A Rapist Burned at a Stake," with the subheading "A Black Demon's Retribution." It reported that a mob of more than a thousand people in Texarkana, Arkansas, had participated in the public burning at the stake of a black man, and that the torch had been applied to the fuel "by the [white] victim of his own lust." The account concluded by stating that "the good people of Texarkana deplore the necessity of mob law . . . but the opinion is general that [the black man] has been rightly served." Two years later, in 1894, the

Transcript reported in detail a "practical joke" perpetrated on a "gentleman of pronounced color" by two white men, who amused themselves by frightening the black man with a false report of a lynching just outside Lexington on the Newtown Pike. The wording of the account clearly reflected that the *Transcript* reporter was amused as well by this "lynching joke."[63]

Blacks were most often the victims of lynching, but such violence was not directed against them alone. Brundage has explored in detail the lynching of whites in the New South, and he notes that although whites were seldom tortured or mutilated by mobs, and the "gruesome ritual" of burning men alive was reserved for blacks, "the mobs that lynched whites reconfirmed traditional boundaries of conduct." In a matter-of-fact tone, the *Lexington Daily Press* reported in April 1885 that two thieves, one white and one black, had been hanged at the Union City, Tennessee, fairgrounds by a masked mob of 200 men for the "depredations" they had committed. In September 1885 the *Lexington Morning Transcript* made its approval of the lynching of white rapists explicit when it reported on the commission of this crime by two men, one white and one black. The *Transcript*'s headline of the account argued that "The Negro [Was] Lynched . . . The White Man Ought to Be." Of course, as Brundage has pointed out, mob violence and lynching, whether of whites or blacks, was opposed in the New South in the late nineteenth century by a number of adversaries, including powerful, influential whites committed to the New South economic creed. These forces were opposed to such violence because they believed it disrupted the smooth operation of the region's economy and gave the area a negative, unprogressive image. These influential whites, often touting legal segregation as the solution to racial tensions, would help turn the tide against mob violence and lynching in the new century. Nevertheless, Brundage has concluded unequivocally that "lynching came to define Southern distinctiveness every bit as much as the Mason-Dixon line marked the boundary of the region," and true to this southern cultural orientation, the Lexington press in the Gilded Age reflected the New South's preoccupation with, and approval of, lynching.[64]

The Lost Cause

Despite the fact that the New South in the Gilded Age was disturbed by racial turmoil marked by increasing segregation and violence, it looked forward to what it believed would be a bright future of rapid industrialization, a growing commercialism, and an expanding market economy. Simultaneously, the region looked backward to its past and partly defined itself by what has been referred to as the "Cult of the Confederacy." This "cult" began as a strident defense of the Lost Cause of the Confederacy in the 1860s, evolved into a "nostalgic celebration" of Confederate Civil War veterans and the lost southern past in the 1880s, and peaked at the turn of the century in such organizations as the United Confederate Veterans, organized in 1889, and the United Daughters of the Confederacy, organized in 1895. The Bourbon Democrats of the Bluegrass region of Kentucky made a "fetish" of the Lost Cause following the Civil War, and for many Kentuckians, "the 'Lost Cause' appeared as real and dear as a loved one passed on." Clement Eaton, a University of Kentucky historian writing in the late 1960s, suggested that a strong cultural continuity existed between southern pre–Civil War society—the Old South—and the New South; he noted that Old South "civilization" waned slowly and persisted into the twentieth century, and one of the major factors sustaining the survival of Old South culture in the new century was the "rise of the cult of the 'Lost Cause.'"[65]

After the war Confederate monuments were erected throughout the South, first in cemeteries and later in the center of towns. An imposing and highly allegorical Confederate monument was erected in the Lexington Cemetery in the 1870s and was touted in the city's promotional literature of the 1880s. The Lost Cause also assumed a visible presence in print in the Lexington press of the era, and comments published around the time of the death of Ulysses S. Grant in July 1885 are illustrative. This is not to say that ambivalence, confusion, divided loyalties, and new ideas were not present in these accounts as well. The *Lexington Daily Press* remarked on the day following Grant's death on 23 July 1885 that "the great struggle for military supremacy" was forgotten, "those who wore the grey and those who wore the blue" alike were saddened that "a great one" had passed, and it noted that several businesses and private homes in Lexington were draped in black crepe in mourning. A few days later, on 5 August, the *Press* used Grant's death to promote the New South creed of economic growth by emphasizing a national unity, a "community of interest from the lakes to the gulf, and an interstate rivalry in production and manufacture" that would "bind the different sections of our country together with tough cords for the next century." However, less than two weeks later, on 16 August, the same newspaper revealed other sentiments when it published an assertion that Grant himself had been a slaveholder and a Democrat at one time, proving that "he only lacked being a rebel to make him a second Washington."[66]

If Grant's passing elicited a mixed message from the *Lexington Daily Press,* that from the *Lexington Morning Transcript* was less so. The *Transcript* of 30 October 1885 argued that the South was only "by sheer force of numbers whipped," thereby making Grant famous. Earlier, on 9 August, the *Transcript* had grudgingly admitted that there was much to be admired about Grant, but it maintained that Robert E. Lee had been just "as great a soldier as Grant" and at least equal in "personal virtues and the elements of greatness." The editor resented that Lee, unlike Grant, had been "silently buried" with little fanfare because he was the "representative of the Lost Cause." The *Transcript's* sympathies were also clear on 26 September when it proudly reported a Confederate veterans' reunion on page one as "A Large Gathering of the Heros of the Lost Cause." Ayers has argued that the Lost Cause, and the organizations it spawned, provide "ironic evidence" that the South was in step with the nation at large, since the Gilded Age was the "great era of organization" in America. Furthermore, according to Ayers, organizations such as the United Confederate Veterans were made up largely of middle-class, urban businessmen concerned with achieving community and personal prosperity. Therefore, according to Ayers, these men and the monuments to their fallen comrades represented not only the past but also a "thoroughly commercialized present"—indeed, the present George Ranck was celebrating as he touted Lexington in his 1879 centennial address.[67]

Celebratory addresses, promotional literature, and newspaper articles combine to construct a historical exhibit of public "voices" suggesting that Gilded Age Lexington was a place of Victorian values and perspectives, New South attitudes and practices, and a vibrant blend of high and popular culture. This was not a city trapped in the eddies of some provincial backwater; rather, it was one swept along in midchannel by the predominant regional and national currents of the era. Still, public voices generalize—they speak of the "crowd"—and leave open the question of how Gilded Age Lexington could be expressed through a single life.

CHAPTER TWO

"PUT ME IN CLASS WITH THE WIDOW WHO GAVE THE MITE"

Lexington's Joseph Tanner in the Gilded Age

We had many comforts and conveniences that George Washington
and his contemporaries had never dreamed of. . . . [Moreover,] we were
entertained . . . by the oratory of Tom Marshal, Joe Blackburn, and
the two Breckinridges—worthy successors to the eloquent Pat Henry,
Menifee, and Henry Clay.

—Joseph M. Tanner, "Fifty Years' Recollections
of Lexington and Vicinity," circa 1926

In February 1884, thirty-eight-year-old attorney Joseph Tanner, the incumbent Democratic city treasurer for Lexington, Kentucky, entered the race for reelection to that office. He appeared to be an ambitious and rapidly rising politician with many of the right credentials for success: central Kentucky native, white, Protestant (Presbyterian), graduate of Princeton and of Kentucky University College of Law, and a practicing attorney in Lexington since 1873. Tanner occupied a law office in partnership with Stephen G. Sharp at 16 North Upper Street, and he maintained a residence at 48 Drake Street with his wife, Lizzie, and their daughters Bessie, age seven, and Alice, age five. Their first son, Lawrence, the third of the couple's six children, would be born in August.[1]

Tanner first won his seat in city government in 1881, the same year reform-minded Claud M. Johnson won the mayor's race for the second time—to the dismay of Dennis Mulligan, Lexington's political boss since the Civil War. Mulligan had held sway in Lexington political matters since the 1860s, but in the late 1870s and early 1880s, the aging and conservative politician found his power waning and his authority increasingly challenged by a group of young reformers led by Johnson. After the turn of the century, Mulligan's power would pass to William (Billy) Klair, a man Tanner referred to in his memoirs as "my good friend." Meanwhile, Johnson won his fourth term as mayor in 1884, in spite of a determined campaign by Mulligan. Tanner's memoirs, written in the 1920s, do not make it clear, politically speaking, whose "man" (if anyone's) he was in those days, although he practiced law in 1873 with Mulligan's son James and counted the younger Mulligan among his friends. Tanner seemed to admire both Johnson and the elder Mulligan, but he idealized neither. For both men, he stated, "principles were not so much involved . . . and neither side was over squeamish in morals or methods; politics were very practical in those days."[2]

At any rate, Tanner lost his position as city treasurer in 1884, and in fact, he would never be elected to public office again. In retrospect, this political loss seems to have marked the beginning of the decline of his professional life as well, for his career as an attorney essentially ended after the turn of the century. Generally speaking, the power and prestige of the professions rose in the last two decades of the nineteenth century, and the legal profession was steeply stratified by gender, race, social background, and education—all of which should have worked to Tanner's advantage. Nevertheless, there is evidence that he struggled financially as an attorney. After 1884 he turned to the field of real estate to supplement his income, and he finally abandoned the legal profession in favor of the government bureaucracy during the Progressive Era, earning his livelihood as a storekeeper-gauger for the Internal Revenue Service (IRS) beginning in 1905. At the end of his life, Tanner saw himself as less than successful and apologized in his memoirs to his late wife for his undistinguished career and chronic financial problems.[3]

A Man and His Memoirs

Joseph Tanner lived and strived, succeeded and failed, and reached his maturity in Lexington during the last decades of the nineteenth century. His life constitutes, to borrow a phrase, "a single historical exhibit" of Lexington culture in the Gilded Age.[4] Tanner left behind an intriguing memoir, allowing us to partially reconstruct his life and times. Entitled "Fifty Years' Recollections of Lexington and Vicinity, Its People and Institutions," it is a 160-page typewritten manuscript. Although the elderly Tanner lacked the ability to produce a smooth, well-organized text, the document reveals a literate and active mind, churning with a wide variety of interests and a full storehouse of memories.

Including only a short, sketchy autobiographical section, Tanner intended his memoir to be primarily a history, based on his personal recollections, of Lexington and central Kentucky from, roughly, 1870 through 1905. In the text he addresses a wide variety of topics related to the city, its environs, and its culture: architecture, education, economics, the fading of oratorical culture, politics, and theology, to name a few. He describes in some detail the physical space of the city, including city streets and county roads, houses, public buildings, stores and saloons, churches, and college campuses. His work also includes many short biographical sketches of Lexingtonians he had known from the Gilded Age, including businessmen, doctors, ministers, college professors, and, most of all, lawyers, judges, and politicians. The text of Tanner's memoirs, rich in literary allusions, furnishes evidence that he read and cared about literature; he was particularly fond, for instance, of Thomas Gray's "Elegy Written in a Country Churchyard" and John Milton's *Paradise Lost*. His literary interests seem to have been quite eclectic. He also alludes to Greek mythology and to a history of Kentucky then being edited by Lexington attorney and historian Charles Kerr. Suggestive of his love of language and sense of humor, he quotes with obvious amusement an anecdote about a member of the English Parliament who scorned his opponent by asserting that "the gentleman draws upon his imagination for his facts and upon his memory for his wit."[5]

School Days

Joseph Marion Tanner was born 17 May 1846 in Scott County, Kentucky, "nine or ten miles north of Lexington near North Elkhorn Creek and the Fayette line" on Bredalbane farm. Bredalbane was owned by the Reverend Robert J. Breckinridge, a Presbyterian minister, onetime superintendent of public instruction for Kentucky, and, despite being a slave owner, prominent Union advocate during the Civil War. Tanner's father, Oliver Hazard Perry Tanner, worked as slave overseer on Breckinridge's farm. Tanner recalled in his memoirs that he often went horseback riding and swimming in North Elkhorn Creek with Breckinridge's sons, who came out from town to

spend time on the farm in summer. Among them was young W. C. P. Breckinridge, who would later become a Confederate officer, a U.S. congressman,
and, finally, editor of the *Lexington Herald*.[6]

In 1855, a dispute over wages between Tanner's father and Breckinridge
led to a lawsuit. The elder Tanner won a year's wages and moved the family
to Jessamine County. Tanner was fifteen at the start of the Civil War and
wrote in his memoirs, "I was barely old enough to have entered the army
. . . a few joined when younger but I did not." He further lamented, "I
have never ceased to regret that I didn't get in." Tanner knew that at least
part of the reason for his unrealized political ambitions lay in the fact that
he had not fought in the war on the Southern side. From the 1870s on, he
wrote, "it didn't require any great amount of ability to be chosen for public
office if [you] had been a soldier in the Southern army." Tanner understood
the ex-Confederate political domination of Kentucky politics in the Gilded
Age—a domination known as the "Confederate Dynasty."[7]

At the close of the Civil War in 1865, when Tanner was nineteen, his
father was affluent enough to purchase a 110-acre farm in Jessamine County
between the villages of Keene and Troy, adjoining the property of the Eb-
enezer Presbyterian Church, where the Tanners attended services. Tanner
mentioned in his memoirs that he attended, at one time or another, public
schools in Scott, Woodford, and Jessamine counties. However, he did not
confirm the view of later historians who styled the rural schools of the New
South era as woefully inadequate. Rather, he wrote, "the foundations of
education were laid firm and lasting in clear and accurate knowledge of
English, mathematics, and a fair acquaintance with geography and history.
The advanced classes also studied Latin and it seems to me that in these
fundamental branches the training was more thoro than at the present day.
I know that at Pinckard, 4 miles from Keene and 6 from Versailles, the last
school I attended, there were several students able to enter good colleges in
the sophomore class." In this regard, Tanner cannot be considered totally
objective, because he was one of those students who entered the sophomore
class at Kentucky University in 1867.[8]

This was only two years after John Bowman had successfully merged
Kentucky University of Harrodsburg with the all but moribund Transyl-
vania University in Lexington and had opened this new school on the old
Transylvania campus. By 1859, the once proud Transylvania University had

declined from its heyday in the 1820s and was basically operated as a high school by James K. Patterson (who later became the University of Kentucky's first president) until 1865, when Bowman's new school opened with high hopes and expectations. It was a school symbolizing, as James Lane Allen expressed it, the "best passion of the people, measure of the height and breadth of the better times." By the time twenty-one-year-old Joseph Tanner entered the new Kentucky University in 1867, the school boasted a College of Arts, College of the Bible, College of Law, and Commercial College, as well as an Agricultural and Mechanical College located on the combined Ashland and Woodlands farms nearby. Tanner admiringly remembered Bowman more than sixty years later as a man who was "suave, elegant, gracious, and wore becoming whiskers; with these traits and without any appearance of conceit or assumed superiority on account of holding a higher position, and without any air of condescension, he won the confidence and esteem of the young men."[9]

Tanner entered the College of Arts, and an examination of his educational experiences during the next two years reveals a "classical" curriculum. His professors were products and promoters of nineteenth-century oratorical culture, for there was a significant emphasis on Greek, Latin, classical literature, oratory, and rhetoric. The college contained a School of the English Language and Literature directed and taught by Professor Robert Graham, a School of Mathematics under Henry White, a School of Greek Language and Literature under John H. Neville, and a School of Latin Languages and Literature and a School of Philosophy, both under the direction of James K. Patterson. Graham was Tanner's English instructor in the fall of 1867, teaching a course described in the school catalog as the study of "Quackenbos' Rhetoric; Exercises in Composition and Elocution." Tanner did quite well in that class, scoring a 97 on the exam. Tanner also did well in another of Graham's English classes in his junior year, consisting of "Wheately's Rhetoric; Original Essays, Orations, and Forensic Disputations, three times a week." Tanner remembered Professor Graham as being "a native of England and thereby acquainted with its literature, which he was fond of quoting in his sermons and of course in his classes as that was the chief branch taught by him. Quotations from famous authors of both prose and poetry and often from memory was more in vogue then than now, and he recited choice excerpts with fine effect. . . . He was genial with a fine vein of humor, but never permitted it to develop into anything riotous or hilarious in the classroom."[10]

Tanner had Henry White for mathematics during the two years he was at Kentucky University. His courses included geometry, trigonometry, surveying and navigation, calculus, and mechanics, and he consistently scored well on his mathematics exams. Tanner described White as "very accurate and thoro in Mathematics which he had taught for many years, but not I think a man of broad or extensive scholarship[;] he talked but little but exactly to the point and was very fair and open-minded." Unlike the verbally adept Graham, White apparently did not have the gift of public speaking that Tanner so admired throughout his life.[11]

John Henry Neville, who would become professor of Latin and Greek at the Agricultural and Mechanical College in 1880 and vice president of the college in 1899, taught Tanner Greek at Kentucky University. In the spring of 1869, Tanner scored a 93 on the exam for Neville's course. Through their sophomore and junior years, the students were exposed in this class to a wide array of Greek literature in the Greek language, including the orations of Isocrates and the dialogues of Plato, as well as to Professor Neville's lectures on Greek prose composition, dramatic poetry, and Greek theater. Tanner was obviously fascinated by Neville:

> [He was] almost a wizard as instructor in Greek and in manual dexterity in writing the Greek characters. . . . His manner and movements were quick, abrupt, decisive, and he showed little patience with a dullard. Meeting him walking in the middle of the street on account of snow and sleet on the sidewalk, and thinking to anticipate some crisp remark he was likely to make, I called out . . . "tutissimus in media via" to which he instantly responded, correcting my Latin, "mediam viam." On a Sunday in 1868 or 1869 I chanced to meet him on the street and with no preliminaries, without even a good morning he remarked "I am spending my eighth lustrum" from which I inferred he was then 40 years old.

Tanner also took Latin under Patterson as a sophomore in the spring of 1868. He scored an 89 on the exam, having studied, according to the course description, "selections from Tacitus; Terence; [and] Quintilian" that term.

He recalled Patterson as "frail in body, a cripple from boyhood, but in mental and literary attainments and practical achievements he was almost a Hercules. He had a rare combination of book and business sense."[12]

Tanner did not explicitly mention his college extracurricular experiences in his memoirs, but there is evidence that he was a member of the Periclean Society, one of three student literary societies active at Kentucky University at the time. On Wednesday afternoon, 9 June 1869, shortly before the end of the term, the Periclean Society held its "Fourth Annual Exhibition" in Morrison Chapel, and the printed program noted that J. M. Tanner was to take the affirmative in a debate of the question "Was Cromwell a Patriot?" In the fall of 1869 Tanner transferred to Princeton as a senior, where he was a member of the American Whig Society, one of the oldest and most illustrious student literary societies in the nation. Tanner's transfer to Princeton was not unusual, as many young Kentuckians attended college in the Northeast. For instance, Robert Breckinridge had also attended Princeton, as would his grandson, Desha Breckinridge, editor of the *Lexington Herald* in the Progressive Era. Graduating from Princeton with Tanner in 1870 was Lexingtonian John Todd Shelby, W. C. P. Breckinridge's law partner after 1875 and the great-grandson of Isaac Shelby, the first governor of Kentucky. It was no accident that Tanner joined the American Whig Society rather than its competitor at Princeton, the Cliosophic Society. Jacob Beam, the Princeton Whig Society's historian in 1933, noted that as early as 1824 the Transylvania University Whig Society had requested and been granted permission to affiliate with the Princeton Whigs. Beam also wrote that "when Southerners came again after the war they again found their way into Whig. 'Don't go into Whig,' said Clio as reported by the Whig historian of 1868, 'it is nothing but a nest of rebels and copperheads.'"[13]

Three years after graduating from Princeton, Tanner was awarded a master's degree without further academic work, a custom dating back to the eighteenth century and one that has been offered as evidence of the intellectual "poverty" of American higher education in the postbellum years. Nonetheless, Tanner displayed no reluctance, hesitation, or embarrassment about listing the degree in his alumni file in 1906. Tanner moved to Philadelphia in 1870 and worked as "principal male instructor" at the Pennsylvania Institute for Instruction of the Blind until May 1872. From May until October of that year, he was a prefect at Girard College, a school for male orphans also located in Philadelphia. Unfortunately, Tanner's memoirs are silent about the details of his life in Philadelphia, other than to note that he began a course in law at an unnamed school before returning to Lexington to enter the College of Law at Kentucky University in October 1872. The November 1872 edition of the *Collegian,* published by the student literary societies, noted Tanner's return warmly, observing that "his many Periclean [Literary Society] friends will be glad to hear that he is back again." The once distinguished Law Department of Transylvania University had been resurrected in 1865 as the College of Law at Kentucky University. Transylvania, "with one of the finest law libraries in the country," counted among its graduates U.S. Supreme Court Justice John Harlan (class of 1852). Tanner completed his studies in one term and received his law degree on 22 January 1873. Enrollments never flourished, and the law school closed again in 1880.[14]

It is not surprising that young Joseph Tanner would leave a budding career in teaching to pursue another in law. Indeed, his contemporary and the long-time superintendent of Fayette County Schools, M. A. Cassidy, also left schoolteaching to practice both law and journalism before running for the office of superintendent in 1885. Multiple careers were not uncommon for mid- and late-nineteenth-century middle-class Americans, who repeatedly changed their occupations in a quest for success. Moreover, law was commonly perceived as the preeminent profession in 1870, just as Tanner was finding his footing in the world. Even as late as 1896, novelist Harold Frederic's *The Damnation of Theron Ware* reflected both a relaxed attitude toward career mobility and a continued deference toward the legal profession. In the book, an elder in the young, impoverished minister's congregation asks him "whether, looking it all over, he didn't think it would be better for him to study law, with a view to sliding out of the ministry when a good chance offered."[15]

Only a few months before Tanner reentered Kentucky University as a law student, James Lane Allen, a member of the College of Arts class of 1872 and later a celebrated Kentucky novelist and "last champion of the Genteel Tradition," had the honor of delivering the Latin salutatory at the commencement exercises in Morrison Chapel. Allen's speech was highly praised in the *Lexington Daily Press.* Yet the same newspaper account provides local evidence of the swelling national disenchantment with "classical-bound traditions" in higher education in the postbellum era. The less-than-enchanted reporter went on to complain that "it transcends our comprehension [why] . . . colleges will select their brightest young men to pronounce orations which no one can understand."[16]

Like Allen, Tanner would soon be honored with the task of delivering the salutatory, this one in English, at the Law College's commencement in January 1873. The editors of the *Collegian* were not entirely kind in reviewing their fellow student's address, concluding that it was too long and noting, "we thought we saw several points at which he might have closed with good effect, long before the end did come." According to the *Lexington Daily Press,* Tanner's oration, grandly titled "The Advent of Time into Existence, Its Reign on Earth, and Its Blending with Eternity," contained some "appropriate remarks on the choice of a profession . . . and the difficulty which a young man experienced in coming to a decision on the subject. He dwelt on the absurd prejudice which exists against lawyers." This reporter, more generous than the student editors of the *Collegian,* went on to remark that "Mr. Tanner's address on the whole was good, spoken 'trippingly on the tongue,' and his elocution was above the average." Whatever the quality of his address, the *Press*'s summary of the content suggests that the twenty-seven-year-old Tanner was intellectually aware of the "withering attack" endured by the various professions between 1830 and 1880, and emotionally aware of the paralyzing indecision that troubled many young men when faced with a career choice.[17]

Tanner's education coincided with what historian Louise Stevenson has described as a transitional phase in American middle-class culture and higher education: "A college in 1800 prepared graduates to be citizens of the republic; a college in 1900 usually prepared them to enter a profession. Halfway between, the midcentury college prepared students for public life." Her argument suggests that in the early decades of the nineteenth century, educated Americans aspired to the republican values of civic virtue and self-denial for the common good. However, by the beginning of the twentieth century and beyond, there was a profound shift toward the liberal, capitalistic values of materialism, self-assertion, individualism, and specialized professional careerism. During the midcentury transitional years, while individualism was still somewhat limited, the educated were called to serve the public interest through the moral influence of their public rhetoric as well as through their various occupations and activities in public life. Certainly Tanner, in settling on a career in law after a brief flirtation with teaching, along with his inchoate political aspirations, was making an exemplary choice for this transitional era.[18]

CAREER AND FAMILY

Immediately after graduation, Tanner joined the Lexington practice of one of his law professors at Kentucky University, General John B. Huston. Huston, once described in the *Lexington Daily Press* as "an ornament to the bar and beloved by all who know him," was remembered by Tanner as being genial, good humored, and companionable. Tanner also recalled that Huston was "highly moral in principle but rather weak along some lines in practice; he would curse with apparent viciousness when provoked . . . and was quite fond of good liquor." According to Tanner, it was "quite usual" for professional men to be "unable to pay their bills promptly," and Huston, frequently "financially embarrassed," had his own "tactics for meeting the enemy":

> There was a tall young man named Crutchfield who collected for a dry-goods store. . . . He would come in and take his stand near Gen. Huston who was busy reading or writing[,] or pretended to be[,] but fully aware of the young man's presence and mission[.] [Huston] would for a time pay no attention to him until finally becoming a little nervous he would blurt out "What do you want?" Then when the bill was handed to him he would say "this is for things my wife got[.] I don't know a damn thing about it[.] Take it to her." When it was brought back a few days afterwards approved by her he would set another day to pay it.[19]

Despite these fond memories, it was not Huston's character, sense of humor, cleverness, or personality that most impressed Tanner, but rather his oratorical ability. Tanner wrote, "[Huston's] style of oratory was more varied than that of any other member [of the bar] . . . and he was very effective in addressing juries[,] moving them to laughter or tears as the occasion seemed to demand." Although he described W. C. P. Breckinridge as "the most uniformly ready, fluent, and able speaker I have ever known," Tanner felt that

Breckinridge "lacked . . . the humor and pathos of Huston." As these remarks suggest, oratory remained important to Tanner throughout his life. Looking back through the years, he tended to judge teachers, lawyers, judges, politicians, and other professionals he had known by their oratorical skills. On one page of his memoirs entitled "Abandonment of Speech-Making in Schools," he expresses regret that the oratorical emphasis of nineteenth-century education had faded by the 1920s. Tanner's youth had been marked by participation in collegiate literary societies—those nineteenth-century campus incubators of skilled orators—and their effect on him was still evident: "Selections [from literature] memorized in youth supply a stock on which to draw in later life for illustrating and ornamenting mature addresses. . . . Every thought or feeling or sentiment has at some time been crystallized into a form of words . . . these kept ready in the archer's quiver serve as points for his arrows in literary contests."[20]

The years after the mid-nineteenth century have been described as a transitional period during which an oratorical culture of communitarian consensus based on neoclassical rhetoric gave way to another culture that was still quite oratorical in focus but driven by a new rhetoric of individualism and professionalism. By the 1880s, expressive oral performance was giving way to individual, silent reading in the public school classroom; the world of business was "letting high oral expression go the way of William Jennings Bryan"; and nineteenth-century rhetoric was shifting from an oral to a written emphasis. Similarly, rhetoric in the college curriculum moved, over the course of the nineteenth century, from an emphasis on oral practice in the service of public speaking to an emphasis on writing techniques— viewed by some as indicative of a rhetoric in decline. More recently, however, historian Nan Johnson has emphasized development rather than decline, arguing that rhetorical praxis and pedagogy were extended to include both oral and written modes of communication in a "new rhetoric" during the nineteenth century. This view seems more consonant with Tanner's memories of a vibrant oratorical culture in Lexington before the turn of the twentieth century. Evidence suggesting the importance and prevalence of public oratory in Lexington during the Gilded Age is present in an account in the *Lexington Daily Press,* the newspaper that supported Tanner's friend James H. Mulligan for election to the legislature in 1885. The newspaper simply gave notice that over the course of four consecutive evenings at the end of

April, candidate Mulligan would "address the citizens of Lexington" out-doors on a street corner within each of the four wards of the city. There was no indication that this was something out of the ordinary.[21]

Joseph Tanner's career may be seen as threefold, the fate of each entwined with that of the other two: professional, politician, and bureaucratic public servant. He began as a young lawyer with good prospects when he joined the office of Huston and Mulligan at 42½ East Short Street in Lexington in 1873. The young bachelor boarded nearby on East High Street, and he seemed to be making quite a favorable impression in the city. For instance, we find him, as a member of the Fayette Bar Association, eulogizing John C. Breckinridge at an assembly of that organization in May 1875. The funeral of this Lexington native, national political figure, and Confederate hero was a major event in the city, and the Lexington Daily Press gave it front-page coverage. It reported extra trains arriving "laden with passengers," while "carriages crowded the streets and crowds of men thronged every thorough-fare." The twenty-nine-year-old Tanner, sharing the Bar Association's ros-trum with several older, more prominent speakers, "paid a glowing tribute to the memory of the deceased statesman, who was, as the speaker said, the idol of the young men of the country." Tanner remembered the event in his memoirs as his first attempt to give an impromptu speech before the Bar Association when he was "half grown."[22]

On 26 October 1876, a little more than a year after this public speech, Tanner married twenty-year-old Lizzie (Elizabeth) Butler of Jessamine County in the Presbyterian church in Nicholasville, and the marriage was reported in the Kentucky (Lexington) Gazette. Tanner was proud of his wife's background, noting in his memoirs that her father, John Butler, was the uncle of a U.S. senator and that her family boasted of congressmen as well. Tanner cared deeply for his wife, and after her death in 1919, he wrote of his "deep and sincere feeling of indebtedness for a large measure of happi-ness. . . . In her death I have sustained an irreparable loss." As newlyweds with mutually respectable backgrounds and seemingly high expectations, the Tanners settled in Lexington. They did not initially move into a home of their own, however, which might have indicated greater affluence; rather, they boarded at 19 East High Street at least through 1878. By this time, Tanner had left Huston's law office, and the city directory of 1877–1878 lists Tanner as being in partnership with attorney J. L. Jones.[23]

Tanner's early public service included a stint on the local school board and a one-year appointment in 1879 as acting commonwealth attorney in the judicial district that included Fayette County. Then, in 1880, he was elected city treasurer of Lexington. Those four years as city treasurer may have been among the best for Tanner professionally. He, his wife, and their growing family, now lived in their own home, first on Maxwell Street and then at 48 Drake Street. Tanner's law partner during those years was Stephen G. Sharp; they established an office at 42 East Short and then, in 1883, moved to 16 North Upper.[24]

After losing the treasurer's seat in the 1884 election, Tanner continued to practice law but also became involved in real estate, "buying, selling, renting, and examining titles." Newspapers provide evidence of Tanner's real estate dealings. For instance, the *Lexington Morning Transcript* of 13 December 1885 published a list of Lexington businessmen, including the listing "J. M. Tanner, rooms for rent." On 15 December of the same year, the *Transcript* ran an advertisement in the "For Rent" column that read in part: "For Rent—The first floor of house in central part of city, consisting of two rooms, kitchen, front hall, and back porch with all privileges of yard. Suitable for small family; ten dollars per month. Apply to J. N. [*sic*] Tanner." In the same column, G. W. Ranck, Lexington's Gilded Age historian and city booster, was also advertising a house for rent. Ranck was well known to Tanner, who wrote in his memoirs somewhat enviously of Ranck's wealth and property and described him as a man "of small stature, sprightly manner, and pleasing address; . . . he gave his attention mainly to literary work." Money, and the making of it, was undoubtedly a lifelong focus and effort for Tanner. Chiding Ranck for not documenting the cost of things in his historical works, Tanner provided in his memoirs a long list of prices for goods and services during the last years of the nineteenth century, noting that lawyers were paid "$1.50 to 2.50 for drawing deeds and mortgages [and] $5 to $10 for examining titles."[25]

By 1887 the Tanner family had moved again, this time to 219 South Limestone Street. His business, listed in the city directory that year as "lawyer, real estate and loan office," was located at 2½ West Short Street. Tanner would have only one more law partner, listed in the 1888 city directory as W. L. Neal. After that brief partnership, Tanner apparently worked alone until he stopped practicing law in 1905. The year 1888 also saw the birth of the Tanners' fourth child, Louise, to be followed by Mary in 1890 and finally by Thomas in 1892. Between 1888 and 1902 Tanner lived outside the city limits, first "2 miles [out the] Nicholasville Pike" and then, from 1895 on, "4 m[iles out the] Harrodsburg Pike." From 1890 through at least 1896, his office was located at the Northern Bank Building on Short Street. However, by 1902 he had relocated his office to "8 South Mutual Investment Company's Building" and had moved his family back to town, residing at 362 South Mill Street. After 1906 Tanner was listed in the city directories as a "storekeeper-gauger," collecting excise taxes on liquor for the IRS, and was no longer listed as an attorney. The family continued to live at the South Mill address until 1911, when they were boarders at the home of Mrs. E. B. DeLong at 415 South Broadway. By 1912 Tanner again maintained his own residence at 409 East High Street, where he stayed until 1915, when he left Lexington permanently. In 1915 Tanner wrote to Joseph Guernsey, secretary of the Princeton class of 1870, and mentioned his address as being "5 or 6 miles out from Frankfort for the sake of convenience between two of the famous distilleries, Old Crow and E. H. Taylor & Co."[26]

ELUSIVE DREAMS

From the beginning of his law career during Reconstruction until he ceased to practice in 1905, Joseph Tanner changed offices, partners, and residences repeatedly. The reason for this apparent instability is quite suggestive. Although, arguably, the nature of real estate investment and management may have made it financially advantageous for Tanner to frequently change his residence, his business address, and even his business partners, there is reason to believe that Tanner's law and real estate practices were never well established, successful, or consistently lucrative enough to fulfill the early promise and expectations of his youth. First, by the late 1890s, newspaper notices indicated that Tanner was repeatedly delinquent in paying property taxes on both his business property and his residence. Second, if his practice had been satisfyingly successful and lucrative, it seems unlikely that he would have abandoned it at age fifty-nine to work for the IRS at relatively low wages. Indeed, in 1915 IRS employees of the Seventh District met in Frankfort to protest their lack of civil service protection and their low wages, which had not been raised "since some fifty years ago"; Tanner was present at the meeting.[27]

Beyond the evidence provided in the press, the story of Tanner's thwarted expectations is embedded in his own narrative. Although his memoirs never directly or explicitly address the course and fortunes of his career, the rhetoric of several written comments is revealing. For instance, he mentions that when he first entered the law profession in 1873, he "began, *or at least offered,* to practice," suggesting that the business was not as robust or as lucrative as he might have wished. Also, he poignantly apologizes to his deceased wife in his memoirs, saying that "insofar as I have failed to attain high success it has been mainly thru disregard of her concern for our joint welfare, and in not making the best use of the incentive this concern should have inspired." Moreover, in a 1915 letter to Guernsey he notes that "the language of Grey [*sic*] describes pretty accurately the course of my life during recent years—'the short and simple annals of the poor.'" He struck a similar note when he wrote again in 1919. Making a small donation for the upcoming fiftieth reunion in 1920, he remarked to the secretary of his Princeton class, "[I] guess you will have to put me in class with the widow who gave the mite and for like reasons." Taken together, these remarks strongly suggest that Tanner did not regard his career as either highly successful or lucrative. But his memoirs also suggest one reason for this lack of success—a factor directly related to his political ambitions, which were already evident in 1880 when he was elected Lexington city treasurer. When he remarks that not being a Confederate veteran limited his political advancement, Tanner is both expressing his personal regret and citing one reason for his frustrated ambitions. In fact, after he lost his bid for reelection as treasurer in 1884, he never held public office again. His last attempt to be elected to public office took place in 1897, and his defeat not only ended his political hopes but apparently closed the door on his law career as well.[28]

If Tanner's lack of Confederate service was a detriment to his political potential in the 1880s, he may have sensed a new opportunity in the changing political landscape of the mid-1890s. The schism in the Democratic ranks over the silver question and the growing dissatisfaction with the old Bourbon leadership led to the election of the first Republican governor of Kentucky, William O. Bradley, in 1895. Moreover, the presidential campaign in the following year continued to fracture the Democratic Party in Kentucky along Bryan and anti-Bryan lines. William Jennings Bryan, whom biographer Louis Koenig has called "the apostle of the politically deprived," aroused both strong pro- and anti-Populist feelings in the state and "stirred a large crowd to fever pitch at the Fairgrounds" when he visited Lexington in September 1896. The subsequent victory of Republican William McKinley only aggravated the divisions in Kentucky's Democratic ranks. In 1897 a silver Democrat won the state race for clerk of the court of appeals, making it apparent that "a quasi-Populism had captured the Democratic party in the state." Historian Edward Ayers noted the same situation in the entire region, writing, "the ideas and spirit of Populism remained alive in the South long after the death of the party . . . [and] many candidates . . . portrayed themselves as . . . populist in sympathy and intention."[29]

These aggravated divisions in Democratic politics in the last years of the century resulted in a contentious political atmosphere. In the midst of this turmoil, Joseph Tanner announced his intention in the spring of 1897 to enter the primary for the office of Fayette County judge as a silver Democrat, proclaiming, "Except for my repugnance to wearing any man's collar, I would say that I am a Bryan Democrat." The Republican *Lexington Leader,* obviously bemused by Tanner's challenge to the "sound money," gold (National) Democrats, editorialized that Tanner was "the frankest of all the remnants of that host that perished on the 3rd of last November." Tongue in cheek, the editorial concluded by declaring, "the *Leader* takes pleasure in commending him to the Free Silver Bryan Democrats. If Bryanism is not dead, it must respond to such an appeal as Mr. Tanner has issued." Not bemused was the staunchly anti-Bryan, Democratic *Lexington Morning Herald,* now under the leadership of Tanner's childhood swimming companion W. C. P. Breckinridge and Breckinridge's son Desha. The *Herald* launched a vicious, belittling attack on Tanner, referring to him as "our . . . eloquent friend, Jos. M. Tanner, who *thinks* [emphasis added] he is a candidate for County Judge." Accusing Tanner of sowing disharmony among Democrats, the *Herald* continued in sarcastic tones: "As Mr. Tanner is a graduate of Princeton, it is to be presumed that he is acquainted with the meaning of the words he uses, and that his attack upon the sound money Democrats is meant to be offensive; that he uses the words 'fraud' and 'insincerity' intentionally to insult those who were sound money Democrats. Poor Fellow, we pity him. He cannot throw eggs and sling mud enough to make his part in this [race] amount to a walk. If it were otherwise the *Herald* might do something more than give his circular this free advertising."[30]

In fact, the *Lexington Morning Herald* did do "something more" to damage Tanner's candidacy. A week later, on 27 February 1897, the *Herald* published an article suggesting that Tanner was popular only among the more radical, "straight out, original Free Silver Bryan Democrats" and belittling Tanner for complaining that an early primary date and high entry fees were the work of the political bosses of a "ring," which the *Herald* sanctimoniously denied any knowledge of. This was followed on 1 March by a front-page article asserting that "despair" and lack of harmony were leading to "discord in the house of the local free-silverites." Continuing its negative coverage, the *Herald*'s 7 March issue jeered that Tanner was "innocently of the opinion that he is a candidate, and if this gives him pleasure we would not rudely awake him to the realities of the case." Two days later, on 9 March, the *Herald* reported under the headline "Audience Absent" that Tanner's previously announced address to the voters in the county courthouse had been attended by only a few friends, and when Tanner went outside to speak on Cheapside, the "unsympathetic crowd moved off." The article ended by gibing that "Mr. Tanner has been thinking he was a candidate. What does he think now?" On 12 March the *Herald* culminated its attack by reporting that Tanner had quit the race for county judge "and calls on all of his friends to stay out of the primary." The article quoted a nameless member of the party as saying that "if he [Tanner] was so soon done for, what was he begun for? It seems as if he just looked out for a chance to kick and he got it in the neck and now he is sore."[31]

Whether a sore loser or not, this political race was apparently Tanner's last, and the name-calling and public jeering in the press, along with his early withdrawal from the contest, may have humiliated Tanner to the extent that it weakened his professional reputation and his standing in the community. It could not have aided his career. Understandably, perhaps, Tanner does not mention this incident or its impact in his memoirs, other than to make a passing comment that he had once been among the "worshipers of the Bryan idea" but later became disillusioned with the man and his views. It is suggestive, however, that in the years immediately following this political embarrassment, Tanner's taxes were repeatedly in arrears, and less than a decade later, he abandoned the independent practice of law to become a low-level bureaucrat in a federal agency. Of course, the 1890s also witnessed a severe national economic downturn, a complicating factor that might have affected Tanner's personal fortunes. Nevertheless, it is reasonable to assume that Tanner's political misfortunes contributed to his financial woes and to his retreat from professional practice.[32]

Having contended in that broad and crowded space between stellar success and unmitigated failure, Tanner ultimately survived his adversities and managed to earn a living through the Progressive Era until his retirement in 1916 at age seventy. During the 1920s he moved in with a married daughter near Versailles, Kentucky, and died at her home on 19 October 1932 at the age of eighty-six. Obituary articles were published in both the *Lexington Herald* and the *Lexington Leader;* they noted that he had graduated from Transylvania and Princeton and referred to him only as a "retired Lexington Attorney," not mentioning his political life or his years with the IRS. He was buried in the family plot in the Lexington Cemetery, and Mrs. W. S. Hutchinson, the daughter with whom he had lived during his final years, wrote to Princeton University in December 1932 informing the institution of his death.[33]

A Gilded Age Lexingtonian

Joseph Tanner lived through the Progressive Era, World War I, the 1920s, and the beginning of the Great Depression. However, the evidence suggests that he remained a Lexingtonian of the Gilded Age emotionally, intellectually, and culturally, looking back to the decades before the turn of the century as the period most important and vivid to him. Tanner was a resident of Lexington and vicinity from 1873 to 1915, yet his memoirs focus on Lexington and the life he knew there before 1900, thus consciously limiting his recollections to the Gilded Age and his years as a professional attorney. His memoirs clearly suggest that he was emotionally attached to the Lexington of that era. He devotes seven pages to detailed descriptions of Lexington's physical features from 1870 to 1900, including streets, railroads, public buildings, and homes. He praises the city as being superior "in social and home life" to Cincinnati and other larger cities—a place of "commodious and sightly houses, . . . [a city] well-built, well-regulated, and well-governed."[34]

Educated, but neither wealthy nor born of the gentry class, ambitious and seeking to channel that ambition through professional and public service, Tanner was one of the expanding, respectable middle class—the class whose values and attitudes essentially *were* Victorian America. Tanner refers to his wife only briefly in his memoirs, but in phrases that render her in the image of Victorian "True Womanhood." Dedicating his memoirs to her, he writes of her concern for their joint welfare, of the incentive she provided him to attain success, and he attributes their domestic happiness to her. Aside from his wife, women are not mentioned in Tanner's text, and their absence suggests a man whose public life was centered primarily around association with other males.[35]

As an educated man and an attorney, Tanner certainly knew and moved among many of Gilded Age Lexington's notable male professionals, politicians, academics, and intellectuals. In Victorian America, the spoken word was highly valued, and "learning to orate prepared men 'for public usefulness.'" In addition to "public usefulness," oratorical ability was linked in the nineteenth century to social grace, refinement, and nobility of mind; novelist Henry James wrote of one of his characters in *The American* (1877) that "he had no gallantry, in the usual sense of the term; no compliments, no graces, no speeches." Tanner's memoirs recall those Lexington men he knew and admired for their oratorical skills—a preferential social and intellectual value suggesting that he remained situated in the nineteenth-century oratorical culture in which he had grown up and matured.[36]

African Americans are, for the most part, absent from Tanner's own writings, and his views on the "race question" can only be inferred. On the one hand, his Southern sympathies are implied when he refers to the Civil War, expressing his great admiration for Confederate general John Breckinridge as a man who had "cast . . . his fortune with the South." Moreover, we know that Tanner's father was once the overseer on a slave-holding estate. On the other hand, Tanner's memoirs refer to the "evils of slavery," and he clearly admired W. C. P. Breckinridge for his unpopular position "on the admission of Negro testimony" in the courts. Tanner's letter to the Princeton class secretary in 1919 contains his only known direct written comment about an African American. There, he refers to a Lexington attorney in a jocular manner as a "rather light-colored descendent of Ham" and goes on to say that the man had "fair attainments and excellent morals." Tanner was a white man who was educated and came of age in a southern city during Reconstruction and the New South era. Nevertheless, based on the available evidence, he cannot simply be pigeonholed with regard to his views on race. Perhaps the only thing that can safely be said of Tanner is what Ayers has said of southerners of this period in general when it came to race relations: "every human emotion became entangled."[37]

Lexingtonian Joseph Tanner's career is interesting in light of national trends emerging during the Gilded Age and Progressive Era. The Gilded Age was marked by a burgeoning professional class, and Tanner joined this trend by becoming a practicing attorney. Although the status and authority of the legal profession began to decline after the Civil War (first relative to the professoriat and then to medicine), overall, the status, power, and success attached to all the recognized professional vocations were in ascendance throughout the last half of the nineteenth century. Furthermore, in the late nineteenth century, the legal profession was often the mechanism by which ambitious middle-class men climbed the career and social ladder. Middle class, professionally educated, and ambitious—as his repeated forays into the professional polity attest—Tanner was certainly one of those young men. Nevertheless, in some respects, his individual situation ran counter to the broader trend. Tanner was not, ultimately, a successful lawyer-politician, and by 1905, he had ceased to practice law altogether. Progressivism in the early-twentieth-century South was marked by a tendency toward social reform and control through state and (especially during the Wilson era) federal governmental power, regulation, and administration—by means of the effective and efficient use of expertise through bureaucratic organization. This is not to imply that governmental bureaucracy was born after 1900, for it was a feature of the nineteenth century as well. As early as 1854, English novelist Charles Dickens wrote with satirical dread in *Hard Times* of the imminent arrival of "the great public-office Millennium, when Commissioners should reign upon earth." In the United States the federal bureaucracy grew rapidly between the Civil War and World War I. Between 1881 and 1911 the proportion of federal government employees relative to the total population doubled; the same trend toward bureaucratic control was reflected at the state and local levels, creating an administrative state rivaling any of those in Europe in the same era. Tanner, reflecting these trends—or at least participating in and taking advantage of them—turned to the governmental bureaucracy, the IRS, for his livelihood after 1905. All this suggests that Tanner's personal lifetime career path—successful or not—paralleled recognized national trends during the last two decades of the nineteenth century and the first two decades of the twentieth as well.[38]

Finally, although Tanner cannot be fairly characterized as an intellectual in the modern sense of the word—that is, someone who lives by and for ideas—there is ample evidence that he was an educated and literate man who was certainly interested in ideas. Historian Nan Johnson has noted that academic training in the nineteenth century "fostered the view that eloquence in speaking . . . was the mark of the well-educated and thoughtful citizen." Likewise, Tanner's early intellectual training in the classroom and in the student literary societies was heavily oratorical in focus. Oratory and eloquence *mattered* to Tanner and were seen by him as synonymous with education and intelligence. Moreover, he maintained this intellectual stance throughout his life, as evidenced by this passage from his memoirs: "A notion once prevailed that fluency of speech indicated shallowness of brain . . . [as when] a fluent speaker was advised to pluck a feather from the wings of his imagination and place it in the tail of his judgement. Such notions may be true as applied to the fellows spoken of as 'shallow brained' in ordinary conversation, but not I am sure of public speakers; I have never known a fluent speaker who did not have more than average intellectual vigor."[39]

Thus, Joseph Tanner was a lifelong representative and loyal devotee of nineteenth-century oratorical culture. In this respect he was, in large part, a product of those extracurricular, oratorically centered institutions that socialized him in his youth: collegiate literary societies. In Lexington, these student groups were quite conspicuous both on the city's campuses and in the community at large in the decades around the turn of the twentieth century. They both reflected and helped enrich Lexington culture and intellectual life, and more important, they became a mirror of cultural change in the Bluegrass city and beyond.

CHAPTER THREE

CAMPUS PROMINENCE

Collegiate Literary Societies in Nineteenth-Century Lexington

Fast learning the ways of gentlemen, . . . Chad was making himself known. . . . He was elected to the Periclean Society, and astonished his fellow-members with a fiery denunciation of the men who banished Napoleon to St. Helena—so fiery was it, indeed, that his opponents themselves began to wonder how that crime had come to pass.

— John Fox Jr., *The Little Shepherd of Kingdom Come,* 1903

On the morning of Friday, 3 April 1896, attorney Joseph Tanner might well have paused by the window of his office in the Northern Bank Building on Short Street to look down Cheapside, toward Main Street, where a growing crowd of youthful collegiate revelers paraded up and down the city's thoroughfares, shouting college yells as they went. Perhaps Tanner, remembering his own college days, heard them chanting the yell of his alma mater, Kentucky University: "Hoo Gah Hah! Hoo Gah Hah! K.U. K.U.! Rah! Rah! Rah!" The *Lexington Daily Leader* reported that the city was "full of college boys" and of delegations of their well-wishers from throughout central Kentucky, gathered for the ninth annual intercollegiate oratorical contest to be held that evening at the Lexington Opera House on Broadway. In this contest, orators from each of the participating colleges would compete for a golden, bejeweled medal described by the *Daily Leader* as "a specimen of beauty and artistic design." At the conclusion of that evening's oratorical contest, the spectacle spilled back onto the streets and became a boisterous parade as the winner was "taken up and carried in triumph on the shoulders of his companions to the Phoenix Hotel" through a throng of students and townspeople.[1]

Antebellum Literary Societies
at Transylvania University

The victory parade through the streets of Lexington following the 1896 oratorical contest was merely a raucous, late Gilded Age manifestation of one of
the oldest traditions of these student groups. From their antebellum beginnings, student societies enjoyed the merriment, pomp, and status of public
parading, and the notoriety, pride, and rank attached to public procession
offer a point of departure to retrace the evolution of these societies in nineteenth-century Lexington at the city's most notable collegiate institutions.

The early-nineteenth-century parade has been called the "characteristic
genre . . . of civic ceremony," a "cultural performance" that in antebellum
America designated (by the order of march) social class and thereby appor-
tioned honor and status to the participants. On 16 May 1825 members of the
Union Philosophical and Transylvania Whig societies, two of the earliest student literary societies at Transylvania University in Lexington, could be found
walking directly behind university officials and faculty during the "grand procession" in honor of the Marquis de Lafayette's visit to the county named
for him. These student societies also marched in the 15 August 1826 funeral
procession expressing the community's mourning over the loss of Presidents
Thomas Jefferson and John Adams and Kentucky Governor Isaac Shelby.[2]

The minutes of the Union Philosophical Society for 29 July 1829 state
emphatically that it had been established in 1818, five years before the 1823
founding of its campus competitor, the Transylvania Whig Society. The occasion for this assertion of seniority was a heated dispute that had broken
out on 24 July over which society should march first—that is, "have precedence"—in any "public procession," including commencement, in which
they participated. The Whigs had asked the Union Society for equality in
a procession held the previous February and had been rebuffed. Now they
openly challenged the Union's right of precedence, creating "difficulties of an
unpleasant nature" between them. Union Society members strenuously objected and resolved to guard their right of precedence in processions "against
all manner of encroachment"; they also announced that in the future they
would not march in any procession, including commencement, unless their
precedence was maintained. The matter was brought before the Board of
Trustees of Transylvania University, which suggested that, as a compromise,
the students simply march by classes. Both societies refused to abide by the

trustees' decision and continued to negotiate among themselves, suggesting the extent of the on-campus power and prestige of these students and their organizations. The Whig Society continued to protest "most solemnly" against any "idea of the superiority of the U. P. [Union Philosophical] Society." Finally, on 29 July, "from an earnest desire . . . to settle the unhappy difficulties," a compromise was reached: the two societies agreed that the society whose member had taken highest honors at college that year would have precedence in all processions.[3]

The written record of this dispute over public parading suggests that a finely tuned sense of honor, entitlement, and high self-regard was enjoyed by the young gentlemen of these all-male societies. This was perhaps indicative of the fact that their membership comprised the sons of the region's colonial and antebellum elite. The correspondence between the two societies addressing the 1829 dispute, duly recorded in their minutes, reveals that among those members signing the Whig letters was the son of Senator John Breckinridge, W. L. (William Lewis) Breckinridge, who would eventually become president of Centre College in nearby Danville, Kentucky. Among those signing for the Union Society was the later-famous abolitionist C. (Cassius Marcellus) Clay, the son of General Green Clay, a wealthy pioneer landowner and cousin of statesman Henry Clay.[4]

The antebellum Whig and Union societies at Transylvania appear to be directly linked to their antecedents at the College of New Jersey at Princeton, the American Whig and Cliosophic societies—among the oldest student literary societies in America, having been founded in 1769. The connecting factor appears to be Caleb Wallace, who, as a student at Princeton, was one of the founders of the American Whig Society and later, in his maturity, helped found Transylvania University. Wallace, born in 1742, graduated from the College of New Jersey in 1770 at age twenty-eight and counted among his notable classmates both James Madison and Aaron Burr. While at Princeton, Wallace and other students formed the American Whig Society from an earlier student organization known as the Plain Dealing Club. After graduation he moved to Virginia, where he helped establish and organize Hampden-Sydney College in 1775 prior to coming to Kentucky over the Wilderness Road in 1782. In 1783 Wallace began serving in the Kentucky legislature at Richmond and also became the chairman of the original Board of Trustees of Transylvania Seminary. He served on the first supreme court in Kentucky and helped organize the oldest Presbyterian church in the state, Cane Run, near Harrodsburg.[5]

It seems likely that this prominent pioneer Kentuckian carried the seeds of his Princeton literary society experiences and proclivities with him and sowed them in the new school he helped organize and oversee in Lexington. Such conjecture is, in fact, bolstered by several pieces of evidence. The 11 May 1829 minutes of the Transylvania Whig Society clearly state that it considered itself a "branch of the P. W. S. [Princeton Whig Society]" and that the members modeled their organization on the Princeton society's constitution. Confirming this tie is Jacob Beam, the American Whig Society's historian at Princeton in 1933. In his history of the society, Beam notes that as early as 1824, the Transylvania Whig Society requested permission to affiliate itself with the Whigs at Princeton. According to Beam, this overture was accepted by the Princeton Whigs, and the two societies remained formally affiliated until 1837. Beam also mentions that before 1805 there had been an "American Whig Society" at Hampden-Sydney College in Virginia that was formally affiliated with and modeled after the Princeton Whigs. Because Caleb Wallace also helped found Hampden-Sydney, this suggests that his influence may have contributed to the spread of new Whig societies beyond his alma mater—first to Virginia and later to Kentucky. There is also evidence of a tie between the Union Philosophical Society at Transylvania and the Cliosophic Society at Princeton. Beam asserts, but offers no proof, that the Union Society at Transylvania "must" have proposed to establish relations with "Clio" in the 1820s; he goes on to note that a "Union Philosophical Society" of Dickerson College at Carlisle, Pennsylvania, had proposed formal relations with Clio but had been rejected. Interestingly, the society at Carlisle is referred to in the Transylvania Union minutes of 11 May 1829 as the organization's "mother society." At any rate, in one way or another, the early Transylvania literary societies were linked to or modeled on their older counterparts in the Northeast.[6]

From the mid-1820s through most of the 1830s, the Transylvania Whig and Union Philosophical societies were Transylvania's "extracurricular jewels," to borrow a complimentary epithet from higher education historian Frederick Rudolph. But student allegiance and organizational stability would prove transitory, and by the 1840s the Union Society had ceased to function. Meanwhile, on 4 April 1837, at a meeting held at the city library, a new Transylvania student group, the Adelphi Alpha Society, was formally organized and less than a year later (16 February 1838) would be granted a charter from the state legislature. John Hunt Morgan, the future Confederate guerrilla, was a somewhat notorious member of Adelphi in the early 1840s, gaining campus notoriety and a good deal of youthful admiration from some of his peers not for his oratorical ability (for he had little) but rather for his adolescent quest for chivalric honor. Morgan challenged a fellow Adelphi member to what turned out to be a bloodless duel. Morgan was subsequently suspended from the school and never returned, having established "his reputation as a gentleman of valor." Others, however, managed to confine their search for honor and admiration to debate and oratory, and the Adelphi Society flourished in the 1840s and 1850s, establishing at least one "branch," the Adelphi Beta, at Danville, Kentucky, and holding at least three annual "conventions" of the branches between 1838 and 1840. Adelphi developed its own badge to be worn by members, as well as its own diploma to be awarded to members upon their graduation from the college—palpable symbols of both individual achievement and organizational vigor. Also indicative of its vitality is the fact that Adelphi absorbed, through merger, the Transylvania Whig Society in June 1842, receiving its considerable library in the bargain. The June 1915 *Transylvanian* notes that this library contained not only philosophical, theological, and historical works but also "lighter literature" such as *The Last of the Mohicans* and other novels. The 1855 "Library Book" of the Adelphi Society lists 859 volumes, many of them previously belonging to the Whig library, which had been built up since 1829, when the possessions of both the Whig and Union societies were destroyed in a fire. Beginning in July 1843 the secretary began to record the society's name in the minutes as "Adelphoi," without explanation, and this name was used interchangeably with "Adelphi" from then on. The period from 1850 through the Civil War was one of decline for Transylvania and, according to John D. Wright Jr., was "undoubtedly the nadir of the college's . . . history." Interestingly, and perhaps symbolic of this general decline, beginning in the mid-1850s the previously exquisite penmanship and elaborately detailed record keeping of the Adelphi Society's minute book degenerated into intermittent, virtually illegible scribbling, and the organization apparently ceased to function altogether after January 1857.[7]

The antebellum literary societies at Transylvania engaged in a number of activities characteristic of college literary societies. To begin with, they developed their own libraries. As previously noted, a fire on 9 May 1829 destroyed both the Union and Whig libraries, totaling more than 1,500 volumes. The Union Society minutes for 11 May lament the loss of their library and records in the "calamitous fire by which the college edifice was destroyed." Nevertheless, we know that the Whigs, at least, rebuilt their book holdings in the years after the fire. In addition to access to books, these societies offered their members socialization, comradeship, and intellectual stimulation through regular meetings in closed, private sessions held in their "halls" or rooms within the college or, in some cases, in nearby facilities such as the city library. The proceedings of these meetings were customarily recorded in elaborate, handwritten minutes by the society's secretary. Society business was conducted first, after which the members entertained one another with declamations, orations, essay readings, lectures, and debates, all the while gaining practice and experience in the art of public speaking—an art they both sponsored and demonstrated for the public in on- and off-campus performances. The occasions for these public performances included the celebration of George Washington's birthday on 22 February and each society's annual celebration, or "exhibition," of itself.[8]

For instance, on 22 February 1830 the Union Philosophical Society, "for the purpose of celebrating [the] birthday of the Father of our Country," gathered in its college hall and then marched through the streets to a nearby church, where Robert Wickliffe Jr. of Winchester, a graduate of Transylvania and a former Union Society member, delivered the keynote address. Wickliffe, an attorney, was a popular and respected orator who, nine years later in July 1839, would be the featured speaker at the ceremony laying the cornerstone for the new Transylvania Medical Department building to be erected at the corner of Second Street and North Broadway. He surely made an impression on his audience with his 1830 Washington's birthday address, for the Union Society members later published his speech at their own expense. The record is unclear whether society members spoke at this 1830 ceremony, but certainly their public marching and their sponsorship of a well-known orator for the occasion constituted a "performance." Unquestionably, the students themselves were usually the main attraction, delivering all the orations at the Adelphi Alpha Society's annual on-campus celebrations in August 1845 and 1846. Printed programs from these two years reveal that these evening performances in Morrison Chapel were open to the public, began and ended with prayer, and featured several student orations separated by musical interludes. The orations included a wide range of serious topics, from "Characteristics of Statesmen" to "America—her inducements to Intellectual Exertion," and they were delivered by student speakers hailing not only from Kentucky but also from states as distant as Michigan and Alabama.[9]

During the Civil War years, when Transylvania was reduced to little more than a high school run by James K. Patterson and his brothers in the basement of the Second Presbyterian Church and elsewhere, there is no indication that literary societies functioned at the school. However, according to a June 1888 article in the *Kentucky University Tablet*, the college monthly published by the students between 1887 and 1890, there were two literary societies at Bacon College in Harrodsburg: the Newton and the Franklin. These would be replaced by two new societies upon the removal of Bacon College (Kentucky University after 1859) to Transylvania's campus in Lexington in 1865. Moreover, there are surviving minutes of the Franklin Society in the Transylvania University archives. It met during 1864–1865 in its hall in the basement of the Christian Church and inducted George W. Ranck, later Lexington's Gilded Age historian, into regular membership on 29 October 1864. It invited members of the public to its meetings to be entertained by declamations, orations, and debates. Afterward, these visitors were thanked by the society president for coming and were then asked to leave prior to the "business" portion of the meeting.[10]

The surviving accounts strongly suggest that antebellum extracurricular programs at Transylvania consisted largely, if not exclusively, of the literary societies. These societies did not limit themselves to only an intramural, on-campus function; through their public parading and oratorical performances, they participated in, and contributed to, community life beyond the campus. Public parading, though entertaining and symbolic of social status, carried no intellectual pretensions. In contrast, oratorical entertainments, complete with aesthetically pleasing musical interludes, addressed the life of the mind and added to the intellectual life in antebellum Lexington—a community of reputed refinement and gentility and containing, as

John Fox Jr. insisted later, "the proudest families, the stateliest homes, the broadest culture, the most gracious hospitality, the gentlest courtesies, the finest chivalry, that the State has ever known."[11]

Postbellum Literary Societies
at Kentucky University

At the close of the war in 1865, John Bowman moved Kentucky University (formerly Bacon College) from Harrodsburg to the Transylvania campus in Lexington, merging the two nearly moribund schools. Bowman renamed the new institution Kentucky University and had high hopes that it would become, as James Lane Allen later expressed it, "a great institution for the people and by the people in their own land for the training of their sons that they might not be sent away to New England or to Europe." Just as the old Transylvania University had been dissolved, so had its student literary societies, along with all those at the Harrodsburg school, with the exception of the Philothean Society. Organized in 1861, the Philothean, "nursed through the scenes of civil bloodshed," survived the war years and was attached to the Bible College when the new Kentucky University opened in Lexington. The Philothean Society, whose name meant "love of God," had "a ministerial orientation . . . combining 'intellectuality with spirituality.'" Regardless of its orientation, the Philothean was in every way a colligate literary society, complete with its own society "paper," the *Clavis*, which was read aloud at society exhibitions, as was customary. In addition, Lexington college literary societies invariably adopted mottos, and the Philothean was no exception. Its Greek motto, *Agrupneite kai proseuchesthe*, translated as "Watch and pray," reflected its members' religious fervor. The Philothean was joined by the Christomathean Society in the Bible College in 1870, but this short-lived society did not survive the establishment of the College of the Bible as an independent entity in 1878. However, in November 1886, because the Philothean Society "had numerically reached the full extent of its power, . . . the [College of the Bible students] felt the need of an additional society." The students received approval from the faculty to form another literary society and organized the Phileusebian Society, whose name meant "love of piety." This society's paper was called the *Anchor*—an anchor being a symbol representing Christ. Its motto, which was expressed in both Greek and English, was "let us press on to perfection," and its members were characterized as "faithful laborers in the Lord's vineyard." The devout aspirations of both the Philothean and the Phileusebian societies reflected the Christian ideals of the college to which they were attached.[12]

Whereas the number of student societies at the Bible College varied, the Arts College contained at least two complementary and competing societies from the opening of the university in 1865 through the early years of the twentieth century. On 6 October 1865 both the Cecropian and the Periclean literary societies were provisionally organized in Morrison College, the main college building, and were formally established a few weeks later on 17 November. According to a brief history of these societies published in the *Kentucky University Tablet* in 1888, the Cecropian hall occupied the third floor, right-hand wing of Morrison College, while the Pericleans inhabited the third floor, left-hand wing of the building. Former Franklin Society member George W. Ranck, the new Cecropian Society's first president, reportedly wrote much of the constitution. This document began by asserting that the society was formed to "increase our knowledge of literature, to foster the cultivation of oratory, and to strengthen the ties of college friendship." Clearly, Ranck considered these three goals paramount in terms of what such societies should offer college students. Ranck also suggested the society's name and the name of its paper, the *Shield*. According to the *Collegian of Kentucky University*, the college monthly published by the societies in 1872–1873, Cecropia was the original name for Athens, and the founders chose that name (at Ranck's suggestion) because of their admiration for the Greek orators and philosophers of that time and place. The *Collegian* also noted that the Cecropian Society chose as its motto a line from *The Aeneid: Sic itur ad astra* ("Such is the way to immortal fame"). Allusions to ancient Greece also suffused a poem, "The Cecropian Colors," structured around the original society colors, red and white. Written by Ranck, the poem contained five stanzas and ended as follows:

White for the shining palm
That Athens for learning claims
Red for the blood that poured like a flood
From her countless heroes' veins.

And, in further deference to the Hellenic world, the goddess protecting Cecropia, Minerva, became the society's emblematic ideal: "[She was] patron of the liberal arts, standing upon the summit of the Acropolis, and protecting Cecropia or Athens, the home of literature, with her shield, while she direct[ed] the toilers up the rugged path of learning to the stars of immortality." Such allusion to Greek mythology to portray the struggle to attain knowledge and wisdom is reminiscent of the American Whig Society's emblematic selection of "The Choice of Hercules" in the previous century at the College of New Jersey.[13]

The Cecropian Society's twin, the Periclean Society, was named for the famous Athenian statesman and general Pericles. It was reportedly installed in the same room in Morrison College that had been the hall of the Transylvania Whig Society in antebellum days. Like the antebellum societies, the postbellum societies were often officially chartered by the Kentucky legislature, and although the Cecropian Society was chartered by the legislature in February 1866, according to the *Atlantis,* the monthly magazine published by the literary societies at Kentucky University during 1885–1886, the Periclean did not receive its legislative charter until 1886. Regardless, the Periclean Society moved quickly to draft an elaborate constitution whose preamble stated that the society had been formed to promote "the cultivation of our intellectual faculties [as] an object of the highest importance." It also adopted a Latin motto, *Per ardua ad alta* ("Through difficulties to the heights of wisdom"), and established a society paper, the *Owl,* which Kentucky authors James Lane Allen and John Fox Jr. may well have contributed to as members during their student days.[14]

As the result of egalitarian currents surging in the Gilded Age, the male literary societies at Kentucky University would be joined by female counterparts before the century's end. In 1888 Laura Clay, daughter of the famous emancipationist (and onetime Union Philosophical Society member) Cassius Marcellus Clay, helped found the Fayette Equal Rights Association, which was formed in part to open admission to Kentucky University to female students. The association succeeded in its efforts; women were admitted in 1889 to the Arts College, and "thus the oldest university west of the Allegheny Mountains, after 109 years of male isolation, opened its doors to women." When the student editors of the *Kentucky University Tablet* learned in the spring of 1889 that women were coming to Kentucky University, they enthusiastically stated, "We, . . . as the young gentlemen of the institution, promise the best respect and gentlemanly conduct. Our doors are open. We welcome you, come." Soon after their arrival on campus in September 1890, some of the women formed a literary society, the Ossolian Society, which was first mentioned in the university catalog in 1891. The October 1890 issue of the *Focus,* the student magazine published briefly at Kentucky University between June 1890 and June 1891, introduced the new female society to the student body and wished its members "much success in this new enterprise." A month later, in November 1890, the *Focus* printed a long poem written in honor of the Ossolian Society by J. M. Mc'Vey, an admiring Cecropian whose society served as campus mentor to the Ossolians. (The Ossolians, who apparently lacked a room of their own, used the Cecropian hall to meet each Friday afternoon.) The text of his poem makes it clear that the women named their society in honor of Margaret Fuller, the American author and feminist who had helped found the transcendentalist movement in New England in the 1840s and who, while traveling in Italy, had met and married the Marquis Angelo Ossoli.[15]

In some respects, perhaps, the female Ossolians modified the male society traditions by necessity or to express themselves in their own way. For instance, in 1892, they were not yet celebrating Washington's birthday with the male societies on 22 February; they did, however, meet on the twenty-sixth to celebrate both Washington's and Longfellow's birthdays together. Yet any such "departures" were minor, and the Ossolians generally followed the male societies' traditions closely. In keeping with these traditions, the Ossolians adopted a motto, *Pas pour l'ecole mais pour la vie nous apprenons* ("We learn not for school but for life"), and began to conduct public performances. At their second annual open session on 2 June 1892, they entertained students and members of the public in Morrison Chapel with recitations, essays, and the reading of the society paper the *Echo,* with musical interludes provided by Meiler's Orchestra.[16]

It was the Ossolians' namesake and muse Margaret Fuller who had prophesied in the 1840s that the "life of the intellect" would be "carried more and more" in the newspapers, and the Lexington press certainly gave the literary societies' campus performances extensive coverage during the Gilded Age. For example, the annual Washington's birthday celebrations were thoroughly reported in the local press. Not surprisingly, when women began to participate, the press took notice. It was 1894 when, for the first time, a female student orator performed at the 22 February event. The appearance of Julia Mathis, an Ossolian member from Fort Springs, Kentucky, was reported by the *Kentucky (Lexington) Leader* as a "novel feature." The *Leader* described her as a "young lady . . . absolutely fearless upon the platform," who garnered for her successful performance "applause . . . almost deafening." After the following year's event, the *Lexington Press-Transcript* reported that Catherine Darnaby of Lexington, "the fair representative of Ossolia," entertained with "The Woman of the Future and Past" and noted that her performance "went far to remove the little remaining prejudice against woman orators."[17]

Notwithstanding these public successes, the Ossolians struggled to increase their membership. In 1891, in the first issue of the *Transylvanian* to be published since 1837, they expressed the desire to have "all the ladies of the University join us in this good work." Unfortunately, according to the 1897 yearbook, "there had been very little interest" in the Ossolian Society, which had been supported only "by a few girls who hoped to arouse among the students a more laudable college spirit." And so, in 1896, it expired, or rather it evolved into a new society, the Cornelian Society. This female society was named for a second century B.C. Roman noblewoman and, perhaps noting the fate of its predecessor, adopted as its motto *Nulla Vestigia Retrorsum* ("No going backward"). The Cornelians met in the Periclean hall and considered the Pericleans to be their "literary brothers." The Cornelians published a semimonthly paper, the *Jewel;* held bimonthly meetings that gave members the "opportunity for showing our true Kentucky blood and love for speech"; conducted open sessions at which they entertained their "friends" with orations and essays; and participated in the Washington's birthday programs. Their on-campus public entertainments, like those of all the societies, were often covered by the local press. For example, the *Lexington Morning Herald* announced the Cornelian open session during commencement week of 1898, and in 1899 the *Morning Herald* included a photograph of Cornelian member Lulu Cozine (who had declaimed "Fatima") in its coverage of the Washington's birthday celebration.[18]

In January 1900 the *Transylvanian* announced the formation of yet another women's society: "A more beautiful and significant name than Alathea—Truth—could not have been selected to grace a literary society of noble and earnest young women." A second female society was needed, the magazine argued, due to "the increasing attendance of young ladies in Kentucky University." Since the women's societies were not conceived of as competing against the men's, the *Transylvanian* also welcomed the new society for the competition it would offer the female Cornelians, noting that "the prospects are that it will closely rival Cornelia for the literary laurels of the college years." The following month Alatheia (note the new spelling) reported in the *Transylvanian* that it had begun "with flying colors, thanks to our kind friends and earnest, we hope persevering, members." The group reported a membership of sixteen, requested the support of everyone "interested in seeing woman raised to the high intellectual plane for which she is intended," and announced that the society's motto would be *Esse quam videri* ("To be rather than to seem"). By May 1900 the Aletheians (another new spelling; by 1905 it would become "Alethean") were announcing in the *Transylvanian* their first open session planned for June. The session's theme was to be "An Evening with the Representative Literary Women of the Day" and was to consist of readings from the society's paper, the *Truth;* essays of literary criticism; and various authors' works, all interspersed with orchestral music. The *Transylvanian* hoped that "all who can will be present at this the first of Alatheia's public entertainments." The entertainment took place on the evening of 6 June 1900 and was described in detail in the society column of the *Lexington Morning Herald* the following day.[19]

Thus, during the course of the nineteenth century, the campus on North Broadway in Lexington witnessed the disappearance of some of the student societies born there; generally, however, there had been an upsurge in the number of these student groups after the Civil War. In fact, at the turn of the twentieth century, Kentucky University and its "now legally-independent, but functionally-related sister," the College of the Bible, could boast of six active student literary societies: two men's societies, Periclea and Cecropia, and two women's societies, Cornelia and Aletheia, in the Arts College; and two men's societies, Philothea and Phileusebia, in the College of the Bible.[20]

The Kentucky University societies in the Gilded Age continued, and often amplified, the on-campus activities and performances begun by their antebellum forerunners. Like their antebellum predecessors, they maintained libraries within their halls. For instance, by 1898 the Periclean Society librarian's report listed more than 500 volumes in the society's library, categorized as history, biography, philosophy, astronomy, mathematics, rhetoric, and so forth. Most of these books, some in Latin and Greek, were primarily academic in nature, collected to further intellectual pursuits. Such pursuits were collectively carried out in regular, private meetings within society halls, where oratory, debate, and other literary endeavors were practiced. For example, when the Bible College Philotheans met on the afternoon of 10 January 1890, they opened the meeting with a hymn and a prayer. Following this, three members declaimed, and three read their short essays, including one titled "A Visit to the Asylum," referring to the Eastern Lunatic Asylum, located only a short distance down Fourth Street from the campus. Next came a debate on one of the conundrums of the Gilded Age: "Resolved that the Negroes have been Persecuted more than have the Indians by the Whites." Two members took the affirmative and two the negative, with the issue being decided in favor of the affirmative by the judges. The debate was followed by two extemporaneous speeches and, finally, by the business portion of the meeting, which included a report by the society's librarian. The Philotheans then "dismissed with prayer," thereby ending the meeting.[21]

Beyond these private "practice" sessions, the societies displayed their members' oratorical and literary accomplishments in a number of seasonal, recurring on-campus performances, usually held in Morrison Chapel and open to the public. These performances were variously called celebrations, open sessions, exhibitions, exercises, or entertainments. However, one cannot fully appreciate the atmosphere in which these entertainments took place without understanding that they almost invariably included music, often performed by local, commercial orchestral bands. Music was provided to enhance the audience's aesthetic experience. As one State College student editor put it, "music [would] co-operate with literature to render the program attractive and agreeable." In addition to musical preludes and postludes, musical selections filled the interludes between each oratorical effort. The commercial musical groups generally carried the names of their organizers, and those formed by Henry A. Saxton and Herman G. Trost were frequently employed by the societies throughout the Gilded Age. Saxton first organized orchestral bands in 1866, and they soon became a notable feature at Lexington events. Trost had conducted a regimental band in the Union army during the Civil War and was later employed as a music teacher at the new Agricultural and Mechanical (A&M) College at Kentucky University. He went on to become the director of the University of Kentucky band, which performed for him and his wife at their North Broadway home on their fiftieth wedding anniversary celebration in 1916.[22]

Herman Trost was wont to form partnerships. When the cornerstone was laid for the first building on the South Limestone Street campus of the A&M College in October 1880, Wolf and Trost's Band provided music at the ceremony. According to Lexington's city directory of 1883, the musical partnership of Frank Wolf and Herman Trost maintained an office at the corner of Water and Mill streets. That same year, the Cecropian Literary Society at Kentucky University employed the Wolf and Trost Orchestra to play at its 12 January open session in Morrison Chapel. Although there is evidence that Wolf continued to perform with the group, Trost seems to have been the dominant partner; by 1887 the ensemble was simply called Trost's Orchestra when it performed at a Periclean open session. By 1888 Trost had formed a partnership with Henry Saxton, and the Saxton and Trost Orchestra performed at the Cecropian Society's entertainment that February. For the next two years, Saxton's name was absent from the billing when Trost's Orchestra entertained at Cecropian Society open sessions in June 1889 and 1890. Yet in 1890 the city directory contained an advertisement for the Saxton and Trost Military Band and Orchestra, offering "First-Class Music furnished for all occasions." The same directory listed Frank Wolf as a "member of Saxton and Trost's band," suggesting that Wolf continued to play with Trost even after he lost partnership status. In 1892 Saxton's Orchestra (with no mention of Trost) provided music at a public, on-campus oratorical contest among the societies at Kentucky University, and Saxton's Band advertised itself in the biweekly student magazine, the *K.U. Enroll,* in October 1895 as "the only professional Band in the city." Nevertheless, as late as 1914 the two men were advertising themselves together as the Saxton and Trost Band in the city directory. The exact business arrangements and personal relationships between these two men are unclear, but it seems that over the years the partnership between Saxton and Trost was either quite informal, quite fluid, or both. The point is that, flying under whatever colors, professional musical ensembles regularly added to the audience's aesthetic enjoyment at literary society public entertainments throughout the era.[23]

Prominent among these public entertainments held on the Kentucky

University campus during the Gilded Age were the open sessions conducted by the various societies throughout the school year, including the annual open sessions that usually took place during commencement week.
Other public entertainments included the annual Washington's birthday
celebration, in which all the societies participated together; the relatively
rare birthday celebrations of other public figures, such as the celebration of
President James A. Garfield's birthday by the Philotheans in the 1880s; and
the various competitions staged by the Kentucky University societies with
one another, most notably the oratorical contests. Fortunately, the societies
went to some expense to have elaborately decorated programs professionally printed, and the fine examples preserved in the Transylvania Library's
Special Collections offer a glimpse into the nature of these public entertainments intended to intellectually and aesthetically stimulate their audiences.
One program, printed by "Wm. Purnell, Bookseller & Printer, Lexington,
Kentucky," for an open session held in Morrison Chapel by the Cecropian
Society on Friday evening, 12 January 1883, reveals that the entertainment
included a declamation, an oration, a debate whether "the U.S. is Becoming
Morally Better," a reading of the society paper the *Shield,* and interludes of
music by Wolf and Trost's Orchestra. The scheduled dates and content of
these open sessions varied somewhat through the years. In 1888 the Cecropians held their open session on 3 February; the program contained two
orations but no debates, and this time the music was provided by the Saxton and Trost Orchestra. The Cecropians' annual entertainment during the
commencement celebrations of 1885 included music by another local ensemble, George's Orchestra; two orations; the reading of a member's poem;
the presentation of society diplomas; and a valedictory address by member
G. A. Lewellen of Baldwyn, Mississippi, entitled "Southern Statesmanship."
The Periclean Society's annual open session associated with commencement
activities in June 1888 featured music by Saxton and Trost's Orchestra, an
oration, a declamation, a reading of the society's paper the *Owl,* and an
alumnus address by former member and prominent Lexingtonian James
H. Mulligan—judge, legislator, sometime poet, and former law partner of
friend and fellow Periclean alumnus Joseph Tanner. For a final example,
the second annual open session of the women's Ossolian Society in June
1892—consisting of two recitations and the reading of an essay and the
society's paper the *Echo,* with music provided by yet another local orchestra,

Meiler's—suggests that although the content varied somewhat, the Ossolians' intent to display their intellectual proclivities for their public audience in an aesthetically pleasing atmosphere was identical to that of the men's societies.[24]

The printed programs for the annual celebration of Garfield's birthday clearly indicate that the event was solely a Philothean entertainment, complete with orations, declamations, alumni addresses, the reading of the society's paper the *Clavis,* and orchestral music. In contrast, the printed programs describing the annual Washington's birthday celebrations at Kentucky University in the Gilded Age indicate that all the societies active on campus participated in staging this entertainment. These Washington's birthday celebrations were composed almost entirely of orations interspersed with music; Charles L. Loos, Kentucky University president between 1880 and 1897, served as chairman of the student committee overseeing these events and personally presided at them. On 22 February 1889, for instance, Trost's Orchestra provided the music, and one member each from Cecropia, Periclea, Phileusebia, and Philothea delivered an oration suitable for the occasion. By 1897 the women's groups had joined in: Cornelian Nancy Musselman's oration, "The Hero," preceded Periclean Clay Buckner's popular Gilded Age topic, "The Anglo Saxon in Civilization." Frederick Rudolph, among others, has noted that the literary societies were a significant part of an "unseen revolution" to reform the colleges from within and that their activities were at odds with the formal curriculum of college administrations. In contrast, Louise Stevenson has noted that at New York University in the latter part of the nineteenth century, the societies' public speaking curriculum was complementary to the formal curriculum and purposes of the administration. Supporting Stevenson's observations, the Washington's birthday celebrations at Kentucky University stand out as a significant indication that the public speaking curriculum of the societies was consonant with the purposes of the college administration, curricular and otherwise; Loos was apparently quite pleased with the societies and willing to lend his presence and efforts to their entertainments—just as the societies were apparently proud to have him involved.[25]

In addition to the noncompetitive public celebrations, or entertainments, staged by the societies at Kentucky University, there were on-campus competitive contests within and among the societies that were open to the public. Perhaps most notable were the intrainstitutional oratorical contests to select an orator from the men's societies in the Arts College to represent the school at off-campus, interinstitutional contests. These highly competitive contests, which began after the formation of the Inter-Collegiate Oratorical Association of Kentucky in March 1887, were of popular interest beyond the campus, and the Lexington press regularly carried accounts of them. The first "local" (intrainstitutional) contest, held in Morrison Chapel on 6 April 1888, served as a model for the years ahead: the Cecropians and Pericleans each fielded two orators, university president Loos presided, the judges included one professor and four prominent men of the city, and the event was enriched by the music of Saxton and Trost's Band. The victor, who would represent Kentucky University in the intercollegiate contest to be held that April in Richmond, Kentucky, was Periclean Leonard G. Cox of Lexington. Cox's oration, "The Influence of Thought," won the praise of the *Lexington Morning Transcript,* which lauded him for "grace of delivery" and pronounced him a young man whose "promise as an orator is bright."[26]

By the mid-1890s the pattern of on-campus oratorical contests had fully emerged. In March of each year the Pericleans held a "primary" (intrasociety) contest to select their two representatives to the "local," or what was now called the "preliminary" (intersociety), contest held to choose the intercollegiate orator representing Kentucky University. Meanwhile, the Cecropians chose their two representatives to the preliminary by a vote of the members rather than by a contest. Nevertheless, the gladiatorial rhetoric chosen by the *Lexington Press-Transcript* to describe the primary contest held by the Pericleans on the night of 26 March 1895 is suggestive of the highly competitive nature of the selection process, even at the intrasociety level: in air "laden with oratory," the young men were "whetting their swords" so that "the sands of the arena" might "run red with the blood of conflict." By the late 1890s the literary societies from the College of the Bible were also participating in the preliminary oratorical contests at Kentucky University. Philothea, for instance, was represented in 1898, and both Philothea and Phileusebia participated in 1900.[27]

There is one more Kentucky University literary society, to this point unmentioned, whose inception during Reconstruction must be noted. In the spring of 1872, which was, as it happened, the same year Tanner returned to Lexington to seek his law degree, a new literary society, the Union, was organized at Kentucky University's Woodlands campus by the students of the school's Agricultural and Mechanical College. Henry Stites Barker, an early Union member (and the University of Kentucky's second president), recalled that the choice of the name "Union" so soon after the Civil War engendered heated debate among the society's founders. However, it is also likely that the name was chosen, at least in part, in honor and remembrance of the antebellum Union Philosophical Society at Transylvania University. At any rate, in October 1872 the *Collegian of Kentucky University* rather sarcastically vented its doubts about the viability of this fledgling society, expressing feigned surprise and gratification that so many of the "old" members had returned for the fall semester "re-union" meeting in September. The *Collegian* continued to assume a superior tone toward the A&M students for several months thereafter. In November 1872 the student publication mentioned that the A&M students had the opportunity to display their oratorical abilities each morning in chapel, finding it "unnecessary to add" that they had "but little" to display. In like manner, when the *Collegian* "learned" that the Union Society had held an open session on the same night as the Philothean in January 1873, it suggested that the impossibility of being present at both would have to serve as "our excuse for not noticing our Union Society friends further."[28]

By February 1873, however, the editors of the *Collegian* had warmed considerably toward the Union Society, expressing pleasure upon hearing that the legislature had granted the Union a charter and a donation of $100, which would be applied to make "quite a nice addition to the Union Library." That same month the *Collegian* praised as well as criticized the performance of the Union's orator at the Washington's birthday celebration, where, according to the 1894 State College yearbook *Memoria XCIV,* the Union banner, emblazoned with its motto *Jamais Arriere* ("Never Backward"), was first displayed. The *Collegian* also declared the Union Society's second annual exhibition, given 9 May 1873, a success and noted that the society paper, the *Student,* "was well written and read in a lively manner." It would seem that by the end of its second year of existence, the Union Society was accepted by all concerned as a full member of Kentucky University's contingent of literary societies. But the Union's future was linked with that of the Agricultural and Mechanical College, for when that school—made independent from Kentucky University by legislative act in 1878—was moved from the Woodlands campus to its new home on South Limestone Street in February 1882, the Union Society became the first literary society of State College (as the A&M College soon came to be called).[29]

Literary Societies at State College

The Union Literary Society carried its Kentucky University heritage to the new campus. With minor variations in custom, the Union, as well as other societies that subsequently appeared at State College, followed the Kentucky University societies' traditions and patterns of on-campus activities and public entertainments, including regular, private meetings; noncompetitive public celebrations, or entertainments; and, when competitions arose, on-campus, open-to-the-public contests within and among the societies. Notable among Union activities was the annual Washington's birthday celebration, which the Union Society had participated in since 1873. The Union continued to celebrate each 22 February on the new A&M campus with a public entertainment, and by 1885, the year the Washington Monument was dedicated in Washington, D.C., this celebration had become the society's signature event at State College. For a number of years, the Union Society alone provided the Washington's birthday program in the State College chapel, even after other societies had formed on campus. Following the celebratory exercises customarily staged during the morning at Kentucky University's Morrison Chapel, the Union's evening program at State College consisted of orchestral music played in between declamations, orations, guest speakers, and the reading of the society paper the *Student*. One typewritten copy of the *Student* from 1884 remains in the university's archives and offers a rare glimpse of the literary society papers read aloud at public entertainments. This copy is composed primarily of short, serious essays along with humorous quips and jokes related to college life. The Union's 22 February entertainment was open to and attended by the Lexington public and was habitually reported in the local press as a notable cultural event. It was described by the *Lexington Morning Transcript* in 1889 as an "intellectual feast," and other reports noted that overcapacity crowds of "the elite of Lexington," the "cultured and refined," attended these public performances provided each year by what the *Transcript* in 1893 called "this popular and influential society." The Union would retain sole possession of the event until 1895, when other societies at State College began to participate in a joint endeavor, as had always been the custom across town at Kentucky University.[30]

It was inevitable that the Union Society would be joined by others at State College. In 1886, four years after the school moved to South Limestone, the Patterson Society was organized, the result of the rise of contentious "factions" within the Union Society. The first recorded meeting of the Patterson Society occurred on 6 December 1886, and the founding members may have had their dispute with their former Union companions in mind when they adopted the society motto *Post proelia praemia* ("After battles come rewards"). The new society was named, reportedly at the suggestion of Governor James Proctor Knott, in honor of State College president James K. Patterson, who was, no doubt, pleased. Although he was not present at the faculty meeting on 22 December 1886 when a contingent of students petitioned for formal permission to establish a second men's literary society at State College, Patterson allowed the group to meet in his office until it secured its own hall in the main college building in the fall of 1887. From the beginning he was known as a "true friend and benefactor" of the literary society named for him.[31]

The Patterson Society almost immediately came to the attention of the local press. When it held its first annual open session during commencement week in 1887, the *Lexington Morning Transcript* asserted that the *Spectator,* the society paper read by Floyd J. Crum of Louisville, was "very good indeed." Crum, the society's first recording secretary, died on 31 July 1888 at age twenty-one. In his memory, his father, George W. Crum, commissioned and funded a gold medal (crafted by Short Street jeweler Victor Bogaert) to be awarded each year as second prize at the Patterson Society's oratorical contest. Beginning in 1894 this contest was held in connection with Patterson's birthday, which was formally celebrated by the society each March, usually on the twenty-sixth. At the 1894 contest both the Crum Medal and the first-place Patterson Medal, supplied by the president himself, were presented to the winning contestants by Judge James H. Mulligan. Mulligan, scion of a politically powerful Lexington family, was only one of the prominent community figures who took an interest in literary society activities during the Gilded Age, often because they had once been society members themselves. Moreover, Patterson's benevolent support of the society named for him and its annual event honoring him with a display of its public speaking "curriculum" strongly suggests that—as at Kentucky University, where President Loos often presided at society celebrations—the purposes and curriculum of the literary societies and those of the institution were perceived to be in basic harmony by both students and faculty at State College.[32]

The society's annual Patterson's birthday celebration began in 1889 on James K. Patterson's fifty-sixth birthday; it quickly became the group's signature event and received regular coverage by the Lexington press. Until 1894 it was simply a noncompetitive open session consisting of orations, orchestral music, and the reading of the *Spectator*, held in the college chapel in honor of, and usually attended by, Patterson. However, beginning with the sixth celebration in 1894, the program was dominated by an oratorical contest to select the Patterson representative for the intersociety contest, where a winning orator would be chosen to represent State College at the region's popular and increasingly influential intercollegiate oratorical contest.[33]

The all-male Patterson Society, in most respects the competitive "twin" of the older Union, could not, however, claim the honor of being the second literary society on the State College campus. This accomplishment belonged to a group of women. The Normal School had been established within the A&M College by legislative act in 1880, and it admitted the first women to the college during the 1880–1881 school year—a decade before women would be formally admitted to Kentucky University across town. At the same time that Patterson began to preside over faculty meetings at the new college building on South Limestone in 1882, the women of the Normal School were founding the Philosophian Society—predating the Ossolians' first efforts at Kentucky University by eight years.[34]

The seventeen charter members of Philosophia adopted the motto *Nulla Vestigia Retrorsum* ("No going backward"—the same motto chosen by the female Cornelian Society at Kentucky University in 1896). Taking this motto to heart, the society pressed to secure a place for itself on campus. Belle Gunn, the first woman to be granted a degree by State College, served as vice president of Philosophia in 1885 and gave the opening remarks at the society's open session in December 1885. This event, according to the *Lexington Morning Transcript*, was graced by both President Patterson's presence on the rostrum and the "excellent music" furnished by Trost's Orchestra. Although the college yearbook of 1894 maintained that Philosophia had, "with the kind encouragement and approbation of the President and Faculty," prospered since its inception, male privilege may have delimited the boundaries of this support. For instance, according to a story in the *State College Cadet* in March 1893, the Philosophians were displaced from their commodious room in the main college building by the Patterson Society and relegated to a room in the basement "too small for a public entertainment." The women thus had to borrow the room that "once was their own" to hold their open sessions. Without being specific, the *Cadet* suggested in June 1896 that the society had indeed had its "ups and downs" until it reorganized and became independent of the Normal Department in 1892, but from that time forward, it enjoyed a "flourishing condition."[35]

Philosophia's "flourishing condition" entailed a wide range of activities typical of the men's societies, including regular meetings, an annual declamatory contest, an annual banquet, and two semiannual open sessions held during the school year so that "the public [could] obtain some idea of its work and progress." Over the years, Philosophia also frequently participated with (but did not compete against) the men's societies in a variety of programs. For example, at the oratorical contest between the men's societies at State College on the evening of 31 March 1894, Hattie Warner read the Philosophian paper the *Star* to entertain the audience while the judges conferred to choose the winner. Gender roles, though highly bifurcated, were also in transition in Gilded Age Lexington, and the college literary societies were subject to, and doubtless influenced by, these cultural trends. When Colonel W. C. P. Breckinridge gave a speech entitled "Woman's Work: Female Influence and Impress" before the Philosophian Society and its audience at its first public exhibition in June 1882, the *Lexington Daily Transcript* reprinted it in its entirety on the front page. It offers an excellent example of the ambivalence and confusion of a prominent member of the community regarding the role and "place" of college women in the Gilded Age—a "double message" for the Philosophians and their friends. Breckinridge admitted to the assembled that he hardly knew what a proper topic would be at "such an occasion as this, before a young ladies' society in the midst of a boy's college." Nevertheless, he launched into a long oration in which he invoked the Victorian vision of the "true woman": "The greatest work of woman is to bear some man's burdens, that he shall bear his burdens more worthily. She will say: 'Not that I do; but [that] he will be helped to do it. I am the cause that makes his name remembered. I have helped him to make the world happier and nobler and wiser, . . . making his deeds noble and his words wise, . . . and drawing him closer to God.'" Yet before he ended the speech, Breckinridge had anticipated the Progressive Era's "new woman," insisting that the college girl could enter life as "a lecturer, a doctor, an editor, an author, or a woman of business, . . . and should [be given] an honest chance for an honest livelihood, and be paid for it as men are paid."[36]

Just as Breckinridge's speech heralded the changing of gender roles, the Philosophian members' performance of a short play that night, described by the *Lexington Daily Transcript* as a "dialogue, really a little comedy, entitled 'All is Fair in Love,'" served as a harbinger of what would become the society's signature entertainment by the century's end. For instance, in February 1899 the *Lexington Daily Leader* announced that the Philosophians would perform a three-act comedy entitled *Chaperone,* and in December 1900 the *Lexington Leader* praised a Philosophian entertainment consisting of a "play in pantomime," a tableau, and a one-act comedy. These early Philosophian Literary Society theatrical performances were forerunners of the popular public performances of the student dramatic clubs in Lexington during the Progressive Era.[37]

In the meantime, starting in 1890, women at State College also began participating, along with male students, in the coeducational Normal Literary Society. Organized in the Normal Department two years before Philosophia would reorganize and sever its ties with this department, the Normal Society first met in April 1890; it elected Jack Weller as president and Mollie Muncie as vice president, adopted a constitution and bylaws, and chose its motto: "Forward to Excellence." The society minutes of 25 April 1890 indicate that the new society had received a letter from the Union Society congratulating it on the formation of the organization and inviting its members to attend the Union's sessions. The new Normal Society embarked on a full program of literary society activities (including a paper entitled *Roark Enterprise*), gaining the approbation of the *State College Cadet* in 1896 for "some of the best [literary society] work of the college." Though coeducational, the society was divided into male and female "sections" that met both separately and jointly. Normal Society members of both sexes also simultaneously belonged to other literary societies on campus.[38]

The Normal Society reached its zenith in 1895 when the society's representative, Mr. S. B. Ray, won the right to represent State College at Kentucky's eighth annual intercollegiate oratorical contest, held at the Lexington Opera House on 5 April. Though "frequently applauded," Ray's oration, "Will the Republic Endure?" was not the winning address. Nevertheless, the society continued to function until its meeting minutes, and apparently its presence on campus, ended in 1907, only two years after its mentor and "chairman protem," Ruric Roark, was forced to resign as head of the Normal Department after a clash with President Patterson and the Board of Trustees. Roark, apparently quite popular with the students, also inspired or helped organize the Roark Literary Society, which functioned for only a few months prior to his resignation in 1905. Moreover, he may have been a force in establishing another early-twentieth-century coeducational society, the Horace Mann Literary Society, which persisted into the 1920s.[39]

Although the Normal Literary Society was coeducational from its inception, this was not always understood by the local press. In 1896, when a female member of the society entered an oratorical contest for college women in Cynthiana, Kentucky, the *Lexington Press-Transcript* referred to the Normal Society as "one of the two female literary societies" at State College. This was not the case, and in fact, Philosophia would have to wait until 1904 to welcome a "sister" society, the Neville Literary Society, to the campus. The Neville Society adopted the motto *Tout bien ou rien* ("Everything well, or nothing"), along with the trappings of the older societies. This illustrates that although the Neville was formed after the turn of the twentieth century, it was a product, and represented the traditions, of the nineteenth. The Neville was named for John Henry Neville, who in 1904 was the vice president of State College (and, incidentally, had once been Tanner's Greek professor at Kentucky University). Neville took an active interest in the society until his death in 1908. For instance, when the Neville Society met in 1907 for one of its signature events—an annual declamatory contest at which a representative was selected to meet Philosophia's contestant to determine the college's female declamatory championship—the *Lexington Leader* reported that Neville provided a prize of $10 in gold to the winner.[40]

In sum, around the turn of the twentieth century, the State College campus sported two male societies, the Union and the Patterson; two female societies, the Philosophian and the Neville; and the coeducational Normal Literary Society. These complemented the four male (Cecropia, Periclea, Philothea, and Phileusebia) and two female (Cornelia and Aletheia) societies active at the same time across town on the campus of Kentucky University and its associated College of the Bible. Except for the Neville Society, they were all active during the Gilded Age and, taken together, occupied a prominent—and at times, a seemingly preeminent—position in the extracurricular lives of the two schools.

The Student Press

John Wright Jr., in *Transylvania: Tutor to the West*, states that the literary societies at Kentucky University had an outright "monopoly" on much of campus life through the mid-1890s. Likewise, James F. Hopkins, in *The University of Kentucky: Origins and Early Years*, equates the literary societies with oratory and argues that the students' enthusiasm for oratory "reached its peak in the last decade of the nineteenth century." Undergirding these statements is abundant evidence that, throughout the Gilded Age, the Lexington press gave recurrent, conspicuous, often front-page coverage to the literary societies' on-campus performances, especially those that were open to the public and therefore of potential community interest. This press coverage from the surrounding community offers at least indirect evidence of these societies' importance among the students themselves. In addition, the prominent extracurricular position enjoyed by the collegiate literary societies on the campuses of Kentucky University and State College can be inferred from the marked attention they received in the student publications of the period. This assumes, of course, that the students wrote about things they considered worthwhile and important. Although these publications were sometimes produced or significantly controlled by the literary societies themselves, such editorial control can itself be construed as evidence of the societies' prominent and influential role in student life. Furthermore, these student publications chronicled the emergence and growing influence of extracurricular organizations and activities that competed with the literary societies for student loyalty and participation.[41]

Kentucky University

Student publications, themselves a distinct component of student life, began at Kentucky University as a product of the literary societies and existed to serve them. In the early 1870s (between June 1872 and September 1873) a monthly magazine, the *Collegian of Kentucky University,* was published by the school's literary societies as a joint effort. The prospectus of the magazine, published in the September 1872 edition, stated that production of the periodical would "be conducted by Editors, one chosen to represent each of the five Societies of the University." Clearly, this student publication was produced by and for the literary societies, which saw themselves as composing the student body. The *Collegian* invariably contained articles about or of interest to the societies; it mentioned no extracurricular activities other than those of the societies and appears to have unselfconsciously assumed that literary societies *were* the extracurriculum.[42]

As would often be the case with student publications at Kentucky University during the nineteenth century, the *Collegian* was short-lived. In this case, the cause was apparently financial difficulties arising in part from subscribers' failure to pay for their subscriptions. It would be twelve years before another student-produced monthly, the *Atlantis,* made an appearance; it was published by the three literary societies on campus at the time: the Periclean, Cecropian, and Philothean. It, too, was short-lived, publishing only five issues in 1885 before it "died in its infancy," as the 1897 yearbook put it. Based on the surviving issues, the *Atlantis* was largely devoted to the literary and oratorical efforts of the societies' members, although it also contained alumni news, society exhibition announcements, and topical articles of interest or concern, such as one condemning college cliques as evil because they often resulted in "crippling literary societies where they . . . spring up." Like the *Collegian* in the previous decade, the *Atlantis* was produced by, and focused on, the campus literary societies.[43]

Starting publication in February 1887, the monthly *Kentucky University Tablet* represented a departure, in that it was not specifically published by the literary societies, nor were the editors identified in the masthead by their society affiliations. Nevertheless, this magazine focused much of its attention on literary society matters. For example, in March 1887 it published the full text of an oration, "Impending Perils," delivered at a Periclean open session the previous month. The June 1888 issue contained a historical account of the societies, stressing the "manly and praiseworthy rivalry" among them and noting that the "usefulness of society work in an institution of learning cannot be overestimated." A report in the March 1889 issue covered the local oratorical contest (held to select a representative for the annual intercollegiate contest) and observed that Morrison Chapel was filled "with one of the most select audiences to be found in the Bluegrass region."[44]

Although the literary societies' continued extracurricular monopoly is reflected in the pages of the *Kentucky University Tablet,* also reflected is the growing competition for students' attention. For instance, the February 1887 issue extolled the many benefits of college athletics, called for the organization of an "Athletic Association" by the students, and argued that there was "no reason why as strong an institution as Kentucky University should not have a first-class [base]ball club, foot ball team, and gymnasium." Sports, including football and baseball, were played informally among the students of Kentucky University as early as 1880; their formal organization into intercollegiate teams began in earnest in the 1890s. Certainly, this February 1887 article reflects the students' growing interest in athletics and organized sports. The following month, the *Tablet* announced the formation of a Young Men's Christian Association—an extracurricular competitor whose purposes resembled, at least to some extent, the character formation and intellectual improvement aspirations of the literary societies. The YMCA had been founded in England in 1844 by youthful Christian laymen in response to the perceived secular excesses of urban industrial culture, and its stated object from the beginning had been "the improvement of the spiritual and mental condition of young men." Quickly taking root in the United States, the YMCA movement had branched out from its base in the industrial urban setting to the college campus by 1860, and it expanded there through the latter half of the nineteenth century. Moreover, the on-campus associations made energetic appeals for student interest and loyalty, attempting to compete directly with the literary societies by, among other things, "securing 'more beautifully furnished' and strategically located rooms" for members' meetings.[45]

According to the 1897 college yearbook, another student magazine, the *Focus,* was published at Kentucky University simultaneously with the *Tablet* between June 1890 and the fall of 1891. At that time, the two publications merged and reemerged as the *Transylvanian* in October 1891. Like the

Tablet, the *Focus* was heavily devoted to literary society news and features of related interest. For instance, in October 1890 it proudly announced the arrival on campus of the first women's society, the Ossolian, and printed Mc'Vey's poem in honor of the new society the following month. However, also like the *Tablet,* the *Focus* was not produced under the auspices of the societies, and a reading of the three volumes surviving in the Transylvania archives reveals that the magazine, unlike its predecessors, began to compartmentalize the societies within its pages. That is, separate articles or columns, titled with each society's name, dealt with that particular society's news and activities. Among the other regular features was a column titled "Sports"; in October 1890 it was subdivided into "Base Ball," "Tennis," "Football," and so forth, reflecting the students' interest in pursuing these activities. This compartmentalization of each society, along with the existence of columns featuring other extracurricular activities or organizations, is an early indication that the literary societies' monopoly on student life was beginning to wane. This editorial practice would become the norm in the student publications at both Kentucky University and State College in the years ahead.[46]

In October 1891 the student-produced monthly magazine the *Transylvanian* began publication, and it would continue to exist for the remainder of the Gilded Age, throughout the Progressive Era, and beyond. Although, like its recent predecessors, it was not published under the societies' auspices, at least some of the editors were society members. J. M. Mc'Vey, listed in the first issue as an associate editor, was the Cecropian who had penned the poem to the Ossolians the previous year. Beginning with that first issue and continuing through the Gilded Age, the *Transylvanian* tended to cover literary society activities in a section variously titled "Society News" or "The Societies," with each society discussed beneath a subheading consisting of its name. However, the magazine also gave society-related matters extensive coverage outside this section. Typical was the publication of the oration "The Hero of the Future," by Philothean R. H. Crossfield, which ran to six pages in the February 1892 issue. The literary societies and related matters remained a constant and important topic in the *Transylvanian* throughout the remainder of the 1890s, but by 1900 there were definite signs of change. Although the March 1900 issue printed photographs of the orators at the Washington's birthday celebration, as well as the full texts of their orations, other forces were now at work. In the January 1900 *Transylvanian* report on "Cecropia," the student writer acknowledged these forces in a somewhat vexed tone: "The season for that monster detractor of things literary, the foot ball game, has passed, and the colder weather has brought our members indoors and to their Literary Society. As a consequence of all this the members of Cecropia are now more faithful in the performance of their duties." Clearly, this student felt that athletics, especially football, which was poised to enter its "golden era" at the school between 1901 and 1906, had begun to erode literary society productivity and allegiance. In addition, the Greek-letter fraternities were now making their presence felt. For instance, in the February 1900 issue of the *Transylvanian*, the "Societies" section included news about not only the literary societies but also each of the fraternities, suggesting that the former now shared space both in the publication and on the campus with the latter. Fraternities appeared rather late at Kentucky University, officially being allowed on campus beginning in 1896. Nevertheless, the 1900 commencement issue of the *Transylvanian*, published in lieu of a yearbook, featured three: the fraternities Kappa Alpha and Kappa Sigma and the sorority Chi Epsilon Chi.[47]

Other student publications included the *K. U. Enroll*, published biweekly only during the 1895–1896 term, and the *Cloverleaf*, published weekly during the school year from 1895 until near the turn of the century. Although the 1897 Kentucky University yearbook touted both as "newspapers," an examination of the few surviving copies shows that they were actually more like magazines in format. The first student publication on campus that can in all respects be considered a newspaper was the *Crimson Rambler*, which began publication much later, in May 1915. The *K. U. Enroll* and the *Cloverleaf*, in one sense, resembled the *Collegian* and the *Atlantis*, in that they listed editors representing each of the literary societies in the masthead; however, editors representing several other student organizations were listed as well. The *K. U. Enroll* and the *Cloverleaf* were not published totally under the auspices of the literary societies, and although they reported regularly and extensively on each society, they were by no means entirely devoted to literary society news. To illustrate the importance of society matters, as well as distractions from them, a *K. U. Enroll* editorial in September 1895 argued that "the interest taken in the Ossolian society has not been as great as it should have been," and it offered encouragement to the talk of forming a new "young ladies" society—talk that would result in the formation of Cornelia the following year. However, an article on the same page reported that "a meeting of all those who were interested in the formation of a college Glee Club was held in the Cecropian Hall, Monday evening last." Similarly, on the front page of a September 1897 issue of the *Cloverleaf*, the publication gave equal space and attention to the first entertainment of the year by Periclea and to the opening of the school's football season against State College.[48]

The closest thing to a student newspaper at Kentucky University during the Gilded Age might have been the *Daily Transylvanian,* published during the 1890s. However, it was published only during commencement week and was concerned primarily with commencement activities and related topics. A reading of the *Daily Transylvanian* for the second week of June 1893 shows that it was composed largely of reports on literary society entertainments. For instance, the 6 June edition reported that the annual exhibition of the Philothean Society held in Morrison Chapel the evening before had been attended, despite a heavy rain, by a large audience "representing the beauty, intelligence, and aristocracy of Lexington." The piece suggested that "the societies of Kentucky University should certainly appreciate Lexington audiences, for they are loyal enough to come out and hear their entertainments under the most unfavorable circumstances." Two days later, under a picture of *Transylvanian* editor J. M. Mc'Vey—described here as the "Chautauqua [oratorical contest] Representative '92, and Class Poet '93"—the lead story was the annual Cecropian banquet held the night before, where founder George W. Ranck gave a speech. Of course, like the other student publications at Kentucky University in the 1890s, the *Daily Transylvanian* also reflected a variety of student attractions, and the 8 June issue asserted that the school colors, orange and blue, would be upheld the following year by "better ball teams . . . than ever before."[49]

Finally, some student publications at Kentucky University in the late nineteenth century offered a "demographic" glimpse of the on-campus status and influence of the literary societies. An excellent example is the first college yearbook, the *Kentucky University Crimson,* published in 1897. This publication listed all the matriculates of the institution by class and college, as well as their extracurricular affiliations. The yearbook also provided member lists of all the extracurricular organizations. Of the 331 students enrolled in the Arts College, the Bible College, and the Preparatory Academy (there were only 11 in the last), 151, or nearly half, were members of one or more of the five campus literary societies. Of the 35 female matriculates listed, 15, or well over 40 percent, were members of the Cornelian Society. At the same time, there were only 44 student members listed for both the YMCA and YWCA, 21 students in the Kentucky University Athletic Association, and 35 members of the school's three Greek-letter fraternities. The 1897 yearbook also makes clear that most, if not all, of the students belonged to more than one extracurricular organization, and often to several. For instance, senior Betty Berry belonged to the Cornelian Literary Society and the YWCA and was on the staff of the *Cloverleaf*, while senior G. H. Widner belonged to both the Cecropian Literary Society and the Kappa Alpha Fraternity, played football and baseball, was a member of the Kentucky University Athletic Association, and served on the staffs of the yearbook and the *Transylvanian*. Such multiple and combined affiliations were typical, especially among the upperclassmen.[50]

Although not every student on campus was a literary society member, in the late Gilded Age the societies could claim far more members than any other student organization, and their members no doubt wielded influence within the other extracurricular organizations. Moreover, a review of the 1897 *Crimson* suggests that society membership was a mark of high status among the students: in the lists of their extracurricular activities, students' literary society affiliations were listed first. However, unlike in the 1860s and 1870s, when the literary society was virtually the only extracurricular agency at the school, and students were differentiated by *which* society they belonged to, by the century's end, society membership itself served as a proxy for social class on campus. That is, those who were society members could view themselves, and were perhaps viewed by others, as being in a different and higher "class" than nonmembers.[51]

To summarize, in the last three decades of the nineteenth century, the students at Kentucky University wrote in the pages of their publications a narrative of campus life. This narrative suggests that the literary societies stood virtually peerless in the extracurriculum in the 1870s, were preeminent in the 1880s, and were still very prominent in the 1890s amid a widening field of contending attractions.

State College

Across town at State College, there were far fewer student publications than at Kentucky University, but the surviving issues likewise suggest the literary societies' status. The first student publication at State College was the *Bayonet*, a monthly magazine published "for a time" by the Union and Patterson societies. The number of issues produced is unclear, and only the first issue from June 1889 has been preserved in the university's archives. However, this one copy shows that the magazine was professionally printed by a commercial printer, Jas. M. Byrnes, and was very similar in content and format to the *Centre College Magazine* and *Centre College Courant*, well-produced and stylish literary society magazines published during the nineteenth century at the nearby Danville, Kentucky, college. They are so similar, in fact, that it is possible that the editors of the *Bayonet* had these Centre College publications in mind when they stated in the first issue that they were making "a profound bow to the College journals that . . . have already established an enviable reputation."[52]

The *Bayonet* of June 1889 was largely devoted to society news, orations delivered by society members, and other society-related materials. For instance, the magazine reported on the open sessions of both the Union and Patterson societies, noted that a professor at the college had presented the Patterson Society with a bust of Shakespeare, and announced that A. O. Stanley, a former member of the Union Society and State College's representative at the first intercollegiate oratorical contest the year before, would be representing Centre College at the Chautauqua oratorical contest in July 1889. Stanley, who attended State College and subsequently graduated from Centre, would serve six terms in the U.S. House of Representatives in the Progressive Era and would become Kentucky's thirty-eighth governor in 1915. Largely but not exclusively occupied with society matters, the June 1889 *Bayonet* also reported on such things as a meeting to be held in July for the purpose of forming a State College Alumni Association and a report on the baseball team's victories in the four games played. Despite some attention to other matters, the *Bayonet* was clearly by, for, and about the literary societies and, as such, is suggestive of their eminence in campus life in the 1880s.[53]

The *State College Cadet* began as a monthly in 1891 and was published through much of the decade, undergoing some changes in appearance and format in 1896. The title of the publication reflected the fact that the male students at State College were referred to as cadets and were enrolled in a military training program designed to create, among other things, a strict regimen of campus discipline. The *Cadet* was not published by the literary societies, but in the early 1890s the publication listed the names of "correspondents" reporting from each of the societies as well as from other student organizations. Throughout the 1890s the societies appeared prominently and frequently in the pages of the *Cadet*. In the February 1892 issue the editors offered "no apology" for devoting so much of the *Cadet* to literary society matters; they sought a close association with the societies and announced that they were in "full accord" with the societies' genteel aspiration to further "the refinement and culture of the students." The March 1893 *Cadet* also strongly supported the societies' struggle to win faculty approval to participate in the annual intercollegiate oratorical contest. Among many other State College literary society milestones reported by the *Cadet* was the first open session jointly held by the Union and Patterson societies in March 1892 and the first annual declamatory contest held by the Patterson Society in February 1893.[54]

Like the earlier *Bayonet,* the *Cadet* was by no means devoted solely to literary society matters; it also reported on other extracurricular attractions clamoring for student attention as the 1890s unfolded. As it had at Kentucky University, the YMCA made its presence felt at State College in the last years of the century. It was established on the campus in 1889, and by March 1893 the *Cadet* was proudly reporting that 25 percent of the male students belonged to the organization, which had taken part in a YMCA state convention. In June 1896 the *Cadet* announced the organization, in April, of a YWCA chapter on campus that boasted thirty-seven initial members and a typically Victorian ambition "to raise the moral tone [of] and to develop Christian character among the girls." Another article appearing in the same issue clearly reflected this idealized female morality exemplified in the cult of True Womanhood; "our college girls" were touted as "the brightest stars in the constellation of the moral sky[,] the purest gems in the coronet of love."[55]

President Patterson was bitterly opposed to all campus sports, especially football, and sports at State College in the 1890s "struggled to maintain even a tenuous existence." They did, of course, persist to become a significant fact of student life. This persistent presence is well chronicled in the pages of the *Cadet*. For instance, baseball was played at State College as early as 1892, and in April 1893 the *Cadet* reported on the first "base ball" game of the season in the "inter-collegiate series" between Central University of Richmond and State College. According to the article, the game was poorly played despite excellent weather and a large crowd of spectators. By October 1893 the *Cadet* reflected the struggle for student control and regulation of college athletics, arguing for a minimum of "faculty interference." By June 1896 the *Cadet* featured articles on both the track and baseball teams, arguing on 6 June that, with regard to the baseball team, "ours is a bright future." These few examples make it clear that collegiate sports were becoming a significant extracurricular attraction for State College students in the last decade of the century, even as their own publication continued to reflect the prominence of campus literary societies in student life.[56]

One other student publication of the era chronicles the appearance of Greek-letter fraternities on the State College campus and suggests that, in the mid-1890s at any rate, the literary societies remained a potent force on campus despite the rise of competing organizations and attractions. University of Kentucky historian James Hopkins dates the beginning of the institution's annuals, or yearbooks, to the beginning of the twentieth century, but one publication that was clearly a yearbook, *Memoria XCIV*, was published in 1894 by the students, and it substantiates Hopkins's claim that two fraternities appeared there in 1893, Kappa Alpha and Sigma Chi. Hopkins suggests that the fraternities remained relatively weak at State College in the 1890s; they were slow to expand, and it would be seven years before others joined the first two organizations. *Memoria XCIV* provides a demographic glimpse into the relative strength, in terms of membership, of the literary societies and the fraternities in 1894. Although the yearbook provides the membership lists of the two fraternities, of the three societies featured, it provides a complete membership list only for the Philosophian Society. Other sources of such information are scant. For instance, there are no remaining membership lists for the Union Society; membership rolls for the Patterson Society survive in its minute books covering a few years, and assuming a rough parity between the two societies, an extrapolation can be made. Enrollments in the college fell rather sharply for the school year 1893–1894, with a total of only 130 students attending. Of the 34 female students enrolled, *Memoria XCIV* listed 14 as being members of the Philosophian Society. The minutes of the Patterson Society indicated a membership of approximately 33 during that year, and assuming parity for the Union, this suggests that well over half the students on campus belonged to the three societies—indicative of strong campus influence and status. By comparison, *Memoria XCIV* listed a total of 38 undergraduates in the two fraternities—far fewer than the societies could claim that year. Finally, *Memoria XCIV* offers evidence that society members were also members of other extracurricular organizations. For instance, Patterson Society member E. J. Hobdy had not only represented State College in April 1894 at the intercollegiate oratorical contest but also was one of the State College YMCA representatives attending the state convention in Covington, Kentucky. Such multiple memberships suggest that society influence was present within the other extracurricular organizations. Moreover, just as at Kentucky University in the late 1890s, the high status attached to society membership amid a field of multiple extracurricular attractions and affiliations suggests that society membership had become a way for the students at State College to differentiate and rank themselves—in essence, a proxy for social class.[57]

In sum, the pages of the student publications reveal that, from the end of the Civil War to the beginning of the twentieth century at Kentucky University, and throughout the Gilded Age at State College as well, the literary society maintained a constant and prominent position in extracurricular campus life. When, on occasion, a specific society faltered, another usually quickly sprang up to take its place. As the 1890s wore on, the student publications on these Lexington campuses signaled that athletics, Greek-letter fraternities, and other extracurricular attractions were starting to significantly distract students from society work and allegiance. As early as September 1892, an editorial in the *State College Cadet* complained of a lessening of "literary spirit" among the students and questioned whether, among other distractions, a social life luring the students to the "enjoyment of the whirl of the dance" would someday replace the "noble work" of the literary society. The new century would answer this query, but as the old one drew to a close, high status was still attached to literary society membership at both schools, offering student members a way to differentiate themselves from others in a positive way within an environment of multiple extracurricular choices and affiliations. Moreover, literary societies still offered students the pleasure of esprit de corps, an opportunity for intellectual self-improvement outside the classroom, and a campus venue for the "expressive life," most notably manifested in oratorical performances that drew the public onto the campuses. These on-campus public performances—these open sessions, celebrations, and contests—were offered as intellectually and aesthetically pleasing entertainments that contributed to the cultural life of both campus and city. In addition, however, the Lexington collegiate literary societies established, through their chosen member-representatives, an off-campus presence in the city's cultural life. This presence was established by carrying their literary performances out into community venues and into the midst of a local social environment suffused with Victorian attitudes and values, New South boosterism and race relations, and a rich mixture of cultural endeavors and entertainments both high and popular. By turning next to these off-campus, literary society–controlled entertainments, we can venture back along the city's edge to Gilded Age Woodland Park, and back downtown during those days when Joseph Tanner might have watched the shouting college boys marching down Main Street on their way to the opera house.[58]

CHAPTER FOUR

COMMUNITY PRESENCE

Collegiate Literary Societies in Gilded Age Lexington

Along Main street all morning the boys paraded up and down, floating
their college colors in the wind, while many of the pretty young girls . . .
flourished ribbons tied to the handles of their parasols, . . . [and] some
ardent spirits could not content themselves with small bits of ribbons,
but wore streamers yards in length upon their loyal breasts.
—*Kentucky (Lexington) Leader,* 12 July 1896

Let us hurrah for this brief season with the boys and join them as they go
rollicking through the streets . . . for full soon . . . their hallooing will be
hushed.
—*Lexington Morning Herald,* 7 April 1889

On the afternoon of Friday, 5 April 1889, the streets and hotel rotundas of
the city were filled with college students and their friends and well-wishers
who had gathered from throughout central Kentucky for the second annual intercollegiate state oratorical contest to be held that evening at the
Lexington Opera House. Every seat in the house was filled that night, and
hundreds of people reportedly stood in the aisles and lobbies while many
others milled around outside, unable to get in. The audience, consisting
of students, townspeople, and "distinguished box parties" from Richmond
and elsewhere, was described as being "as great in quality as in quantity"; it
was an enthusiastic but orderly audience, which "kept perfect decorum during the orations." On stage were the four student contestants, each selected
by the student literary societies of the four Kentucky schools represented:
Centre College of Danville, Central University of Richmond, and Kentucky University and State College of Lexington. On stage with them were

a number of dignitaries, including several locally prominent ministers along with presidents Charles Loos of Kentucky University and James K. Patterson of State College. Both the *Kentucky (Lexington) Leader* and the *Lexington Morning Transcript* gave this event extensive coverage and described the scene in great detail. The *Transcript,* in its front-page account, stated, "the decorations about the stage were most artistic. An evergreen arch enclosed the four young oratorical gladiators, . . . each submerged in flowers sent by enthusiastic friends, . . . while festoons of evergreens studded with flowers swung gracefully from the ceiling and around the boxes." Orchestral band music preceded and followed each oration, and each orator was attended by an audience that, according to the *Leader,* "kept silent and drank in all his words with a rare appreciation of the speaker's efforts to please them." As each speaker concluded, he was met with thunderous cheering and applause and yet more bouquets of flowers.[1]

The observer from the *Leader* noted that although the State College contestant's oration "bore evidence of the most study," the victory belonged "to the last speaker, Henry Duncan, Jr., of the Periclean Society of Kentucky University," for his oration "The New South," which portrayed the "glorious South as it is today, progressive and untrammeled." Duncan was declared the victor because, "like the true orator that he proved himself to be, he began mildly and gently, and gradually warmed up to the intense beauty of his subject, insinuating himself into the hearts of the audience and judges. He is a fluent speaker, and his gestures . . . were grace itself." His speech also gave voice to the southern leanings and late-century aspirations of a significant portion of his audience and of the Lexington community, for 1889 was the year the United Confederate Veterans was organized—a year during which feelings for the Lost Cause and all things southern ran high throughout the region. And so, when the Periclean orator was announced the winner, "hats whirled in the air, the band played gaily, cheers resounded from pit to dome, . . . the ladies even shed tears from excess of joy, . . . and constituents of Kentucky University and Lexington people in general yelled themselves hoarse, stamped until the air was thick with dust, and clapped their palms red." This remarkable public spectacle would be repeated and embellished over the next decade and would become a regular, almost yearly feature at the opera house through 1903. At the height of the contest's popularity in the 1890s, special chartered trains would carry contestants, guests, and supporters from throughout the region to Lexington, and after the event the winning orator would be hoisted on the shoulders of his fellow literary society members to be carried triumphantly through the streets in an exuberant victory parade.[2]

The *Kentucky Leader* ended its account of the 1889 intercollegiate contest by noting that the Kentucky Chautauqua Assembly, then looking forward to its third annual gathering in Lexington that summer, had invited representatives from several of the region's colleges to compete in an oratorical contest to be held at Woodland Park on 29 June. The assembly was prepared to offer a substantial prize of "$75 to the best orator, and $25 to the second best." Although the intercollegiate contest was only in its second year, both the invitation and the generous enticement to entrants suggest that the managers of the Chautauqua Assembly recognized, and hoped to capitalize on, the public popularity and appeal of intercollegiate oratorical competitions. This recognition opened a second community front in the literary societies' quest to amuse and promote themselves while also providing entertainment for the public—an off-campus campaign that evolved from tentative forays to years of triumph and then to eventual loss and retreat.[3]

1887–1893: MOBILIZING, ADVANCING, AND TAKING THE CITY

Mobilizing in 1887 to organize, exercise, promote, and reward collegiate oratory on a wider scale, students from Kentucky University, State College, Georgetown College, Centre College, and Central University established the Inter-Collegiate State Oratorical Association ("State" was later dropped from the name in common usage). The original purpose of this association was to stage an annual oratorical contest among literary society–selected representatives from each of the participating schools. A printed program of the association's second annual oratorical contest in 1889 indicates that the group was divided into three working committees designed to govern, arrange, and conduct the annual contests: an executive committee made up of two representatives from each of the four schools participating that year, an arrangement committee, and a reception committee. An article in the *Transylvanian* in 1901 clearly indicates that the governance and membership of this association were in the hands of the literary societies of the member schools. In 1901 the presidency of the association was held by a Kentucky University Periclean, and the two executive committee representatives from Kentucky University included one Periclean and one Cecropian. As noted earlier, the collegiate literary societies in Lexington (and presumably elsewhere) developed elaborate intra- and intersociety on-campus contests to select the orator who would compete at the annual intercollegiate contest. However, even though the literary societies controlled the oratorical association, its annual oratorical contest, and the process of selecting each school's representative at that contest, it must be understood that each competitor was then perceived as representing the entire school—as well as his society—at the intercollegiate contest. For this reason, local press reports often identified the contestants and the winners by their institutions rather than their societies. Nevertheless, these intercollegiate oratorical contests were, in essence, performances inspired, organized, controlled, and manned by the student literary societies.[4]

It is uncertain whether the students initially envisioned the intercollegiate oratorical contests as off-campus entertainments, and in fact, the first contest in 1888 was staged on campus in the chapel of Central University in Richmond. In covering the event, the *Lexington Morning Transcript* made no secret of favoring the Lexington schools and suggested that they had not received fair treatment at the hands of the judges. At this first contest, Union Society member and future Kentucky governor A. O. Stanley represented Lexington's State College (he would transfer to Centre College the following year), and Periclean Society member Leonard G. Cox represented Kentucky University. However, Centre College representative Lucien Noel was chosen by the three-judge panel as the winner; in fact, Centre orators would dominate the early years of the contest, winning four of the first six events. Despite the *Transcript*'s disappointment at the outcome, it reported that the event had been well attended and very successful and referred to it as "the great oratorical contest." This first contest in 1888 was the last one to be held on a college campus for the remainder of the century and beyond. As noted earlier, in 1889 it was staged at the Lexington Opera House for the first time, and Periclean Society member Henry T. Duncan Jr. of Kentucky University won for his oration "The New South" by, among other things, "insinuating himself into the hearts of the audience and judges." Upon the judges' decision, Duncan was presented with the first-place gold medal, which the *Transcript* described in detail as a work of fine jewelry. The description is worth repeating as symbolic of the event's claims to quality, dignity, and cultural importance:

> The medal proper is of etruscan and green gold, circular in form, about the size of a silver dollar, hanging from a handsome top bar of etruscan gold. In the center . . . is the monogram I. O. C. A. (Inter-Collegiate Oratorical Contest Association) in relief, enameled in red, blue and black, with book and lamp of knowledge in bas-relief resting on a wreath of green gold at the lower edge of the medal. The top bar is inscribed "1889," and a space is left for the victor's name. The medal is a beauty and well worth a magnificent effort.[5]

Although the second (1889) contest at the Lexington Opera House had been, in the words of the *Lexington Morning Transcript,* "a magnificent success viewed from all sides," the entertainment was still being rotated to the locales of the various member schools, and the third contest in April 1890 was held at the Second Presbyterian Church in Danville. The church was reportedly crowded with spectators, and the two hotels could not accommodate all the visitors. The ladies of the Methodist Episcopal church served dinner to hundreds as a fund-raising scheme. At the appointed hour, a crowd estimated at 1,200 people listened first to an orchestra imported from Louisville and, according to the *Kentucky Leader,* eagerly and impatiently waited for the competition to begin, being "anxious to see what education had done for the quintette of bright young fellows chosen in local contests [at] their respective colleges." The *Leader* account also contains information on two other important aspects of these contests. First, it reported that the length of the orations varied from thirteen to nineteen minutes, with the average being about fifteen minutes. This suggests that these entertainments, including musical interludes, ceremony, and the usual unplanned delays, must have lasted between two and three hours. Second, the *Leader* simply stated that the orations were judged on "thought, expression, and delivery." The *Transcript* confirmed this, describing the winner, again from Centre College, as being "a natural born orator, and [he] has a wonderful voice. His gestures were also perfect . . . [and] his subject . . . gave evidence that he is a hard student and a good thinker." Giving equal weight to content, voice, and gesture suggests that the historical tensions and distinctions between reason and persuasion, between knowledge and eloquence, so often explored by late-twentieth-century historians of rhetoric, were lost on, unknown to, or just ignored by the newspapers' correspondents, the orators, and the local dignitaries who judged their orations. Or perhaps they still viewed oratory as the exercise of Ciceronian, or classical, rhetoric—a rhetoric in which reason and eloquence were not imagined as divorced. Whatever the case, the audience at these intercollegiate contests could expect to be entertained by four or five young men who earnestly aspired to deliver eloquent, thoughtful addresses on subjects of intellectual interest.[6]

In 1891 the intercollegiate contest returned to the Lexington Opera House amid increasing notoriety and excitement. The *Lexington Morning Transcript* reported that trains were bringing delegations into the city from throughout the region and that college boys marched through the streets giving their college yells and stood on every street corner excitedly discussing the upcoming contest. The *Transcript* suggested that "their merriment was infectious, and hundreds of professional men and merchants took a long look backward and wished that they were again college boys." The *Transcript*'s correspondent was present that night to report that every seat and "available foot of space" was taken in the opera house, and 200 people occupied the stage, including "all the college professors and their ladies in town or visiting here[,] the clergy, some city officials and the newspaper people." A "sea" of young men present shouted deafening college yells until it became necessary to quiet them from the stage. Among the judges was General Basil Duke, John Hunt Morgan's second in command during the Civil War and later a Democratic political activist and Civil War historian. In many ways, Duke symbolized the Lost Cause, and "The Lost Cause" was the title of the oration by Centre College's representative, Samuel M. Wilson, who would one day become a noted Lexington jurist, author, and historian. Nevertheless, the day and the winner's medal belonged to eighteen-year-old John M. Stevenson of Georgetown College, "the youngest orator on the platform." Upon the announcement by General Duke, the Georgetown students surged over and through Saxton and Trost's Orchestra to get to the stage to congratulate their hero.[7]

The *Lexington Morning Transcript*'s account of the 1891 contest proclaimed that "an army of bright young men capture[d] the city." However, the incursion was brief, and problems soon arose among the ranks. In 1892 officials at Kentucky University and State College refused to allow their students to enter the oratorical contest, and that year the intercollegiate competition was held at the Scott County courthouse in Georgetown with only Central University, Centre College, and Georgetown College competing—a contest that Centre won. Faculty at Kentucky University and State College objected to these contests on the grounds that the cheering and yelling during and after the events were excessive and rowdy, that the contests interfered with the students' classroom studies, and that they contributed to student drunkenness and gambling. In an April 1892 editorial in the Kentucky University *Transylvanian,* the student editor rejected each of these faculty arguments, countering that exclusion from the contest (as well as from intercollegiate athletics) was damaging college pride and spirit among the students. Things came to a head in February 1893 when the literary societies refused to participate in the annual Washington's birthday celebration at Morrison Chapel. This boycott led to the unprecedented cancellation of the celebration and, ultimately, to the university's acquiescence; Kentucky University was a participant in the intercollegiate contest that April. At State College an article in the *Cadet* in March 1892 seemed to suggest that the students supported the faculty's decision to withdraw the institution from the contest, stating, "we are out of the contest business and very glad of it." However, this viewpoint did not prevail, for a year later, in March 1893, the *Cadet* reported that the Patterson and Union societies had sent a committee to the faculty to request permission to reenter the intercollegiate contest, and in October 1893 the *Cadet* rejoiced that the societies had "obtained from the faculty the revocation of their decision." Regardless of the *Cadet's* assertion, there is evidence in the faculty minutes that they revisited this issue during February 1894 and appointed a committee to study the matter before giving their final approval. At any rate, State College reentered the contest in April 1894.[8]

Beginning in 1893, the Lexington Opera House became the fixed venue for the contest and would remain so for a decade. Indeed, that decade would prove to be the apex for off-campus collegiate oratorical entertainment as a fixture of Lexington cultural life.

Meanwhile, a second venue for off-campus oratorical contests had opened in 1889 at the Chautauqua auditorium in Woodland Park, and student orators from the region's colleges began to compete there each summer during the Kentucky Chautauqua Assembly. By 1900 nearly 200 imitators of the original New York Chautauqua venture had sprung up around the country, and these independent Chautauquas were "primarily for customers in the immediate neighborhoods, and they lasted each summer from a few packed days to a month." Exactly who the Lexington Chautauqua customers were—the audience demographics—has not been preserved in statistical detail, but the local press accounts suggest who the Chautauqua audiences "imagined themselves to be": cultured and intellectual members of the middle and upper-middle classes. The Chautauqua Assembly sessions were always part education, part entertainment. Chautauqua historians Karl Detzer and Harry P. Harrison, writing in the 1950s, recalled that the independent Chautauqua managers "billed the best musicians, orators, and humorists available" and noted that "Chautauqua was show business, genteel, prudent, more respectable than [the circus], but show business just the same." More recently, Frederick Antczak and Edith Siemers argued that even though the increasingly professionalized show-business aspects of the venture largely destroyed the original educational ideals of Chautauqua, prior to its decline it had taken on "a significant mission of democratic education, [and through] . . . its involvement of ordinary people in discussions of . . . matters of real public import . . . it had generated . . . an oratorical culture that was substantively ambitious and publicly influential." Simply put, the Chautauqua movement, though providing popular amusement, also provided a stage for oratory, which in turn contributed significantly to community intellectual life.[9]

Lexington began formal preparations in February 1887 to join those communities touting their own Chautauquas. As reported in the *Lexington Morning Transcript,* the Chamber of Commerce proposed Lexington as the site of "a branch of the Chautauqua University" and encouraged "all the friends of education, Sunday School work, [and] better kinds of popular entertainment" to work to secure the Kentucky Chautauqua Assembly for Lexington. The following month the *Transcript* touted the Chautauqua "idea" as "one of the marked practical products in morals and literature of the present century" and called it an effort "to provide wholesome, moral entertainment and instruction for the masses." One correspondent to the *Transcript,* calling himself "Rusticus," referred to the Chautauqua as "a delight for the refined and intellectual" and argued that the mission of the original Chautauqua in New York, "improvement in Sunday School work," should also be the central idea of the Kentucky Chautauqua, with lectures and music provided as "embellishments." The first Lexington Chautauqua opened on 28 June 1887 and closed eleven days later on 9 July. Managed by the Reverend W. D. McClintock and Claude Buckley, the Chautauqua grounds at Woodland Park that first year boasted one huge meeting tent holding 1,500 people, about 200 small tents for "campers" staying on the grounds, a wooden structure used as the dining hall, and several other small buildings. According to the *Transcript*'s account of opening day, Trost's Band provided music "sweet and melodious as ever," and the assembly opened with prayers, scripture readings, hymns, and introductory remarks. President James K. Patterson of State College delivered the welcoming address in which he argued that the times were progressing not only materialistically but also intellectually and spiritually. After eleven days of orations, stereopticon-enhanced lectures, study classes, a variety of musical programs, balloon ascensions, and fireworks displays, the session closed, as noted approvingly by the *Transcript*, with a verbal "spanking" of the assembled sinners by the famous southern evangelist Sam Jones, whose address drew "an immense . . . multitude" of listeners despite a great deal of rain and mud on closing day. In the years ahead, the park grounds would be modified and improved, the assembly's physical facilities would be enlarged and enhanced, and its program would be embellished, but the basic structure and tone of the annual gathering had been established that first successful summer. The *Transcript* announced on the last day of the session that funds were being gathered to purchase Woodland Park as the permanent site of the Kentucky Chautauqua.[10]

The second Chautauqua Assembly opened in Woodland Park on 26 June 1888 and, according to the *Kentucky Leader,* provided the large crowd with "the intellectual and physical enjoyments of its many pleasures." Beginning at 4:30 that afternoon, Saxton and Trost's Band "discoursed music of bewitching sweetness" from a platform beside a yet-to-be-completed lake. Professor Harry Saxton also played a tuba solo for the throng prior to Reverend McClintock's formal opening of the session. The 1888 program included the annual meeting of the Kentucky College Association, at which several addresses were made; one by the president of Central University,

F. V. Logan, questioned the elective (curricular) system, and one by Professor S. R. Cheek of Centre College considered the "abuses" attending the "secret fraternities." This participation by the region's higher education faculties would be followed the next year by their students' inclusion in the Chautauqua program of events.[11]

The third Chautauqua at Lexington opened on 25 June 1889, and the *Kentucky Leader* declared it "a city of canvass . . . a city born of truth and religion and learning and useful pleasure." The *Leader* seemed to revel in its own rhetoric as it described the efforts of families moving into their tents for the session: "All is bustle on the grounds today. Trunks are coming in, families are taking up their quarters in their snowy houses [white tents]; pretty girls flit hither and thither with their mouths full of tacks; . . . the dictatorial voice of the maiden rings out directing the placing of beds and bureaus and other furniture of a household description and, in short, Chautauqua is begun again." The *Leader* also took pains to tout the educational departments to be conducted—among them the normal, college, Sunday school, and musical departments—and argued that, "while the greatest number of people look at the outside programme only, it is in these departments that the real work for good is being done." Nevertheless, the *Leader* also chronicled many other enticements that were new to the 1889 session, including graveled walks, lemonade stands, lawn tennis and croquet courts, a barbershop, and a college oratorical contest much like the popular intercollegiate event held each spring. Although the Inter-Collegiate Oratorical Association did not stage or totally control the Chautauqua contest, the association did establish and enforce the governing rules for this oratorical entertainment at Woodland Park in the years to come.[12]

The *Leader* reported that on 29 June, the fifth day of the 1889 Chautauqua session, it was obvious that the crowd was going to be enormous because "the city was full of people and the people were all gravitating in one direction, . . . Woodland Park. The occasion was the oratorical contest"— the first collegiate contest to be held at the Chautauqua in Lexington. The *Lexington Morning Transcript* reported that "long before the time for the oratorical contest the immense auditorium [in Woodland Park] began to be crowded with the largest assembly of persons it has ever held . . . [and] boys and young men were even sitting upon the joists that support the roof." According to the *Transcript* account, the audience contained many "girls and young ladies . . . [with] bright eyes and eager faces," and Trost's Band played "some of their sweetest strains" for the occasion. Four schools were represented that day: Central University of Richmond, Centre College, Georgetown College, and Kentucky Wesleyan College of Millersburg. The contestants were viewed as representing their respective schools; however, an article in the *State College Cadet* some years later makes it clear that although the exact details of the process varied over time, the literary societies chose the Chautauqua representatives, usually via on-campus preliminary or local contests held to determine which society orator would have "the honor of representing the college." Neither State College nor Kentucky University was represented at this first contest, and an editorial in the *Kentucky University Tablet* indicates that the school's students, though originally intending to participate, were "reluctant" because they feared that the Chautauqua event might overshadow the springtime contest conducted by the Inter-Collegiate Oratorical Association. In the end, the Kentucky University students decided to stay out of the first Chautauqua oratorical contest. Nevertheless, James Lane Allen, Kentucky University's illustrious Periclean alumnus, was one of the four judges at the event. First place, and the $75 prize, was taken by John Van Lear of Central University for his oration "The Triumph of Truth," while the second-place prize of $25 went to Centre College's A. O. Stanley, the future governor who had represented State College at the intercollegiate contest the year before.[13]

The following year the 1890 Lexington Chautauqua opened on 29 June for another eleven-day session amid claims of increasing financial prosperity for the organization, even though the *Kentucky Leader* noted that "bad weather [thunderstorms] has hitherto interfered with the meetings" in previous years. Having been a popular success, the Chautauqua oratorical contest was scheduled for 7 July, and the *Leader* announced it beforehand as "the feature of the week." On the day of the contest, the *Leader* styled the event as "long looked forward to," reporting, "there is great interest in it and all day long the street cars have been kept busy, . . . people are here from all over the State . . . [and] the auditorium is filled to overflowing to hear the young orators." Although State College would not be represented at the Chautauqua contest until 1894 (nor at the intercollegiate contests in 1892 and 1893), owing to a combination of faculty opposition and lack of student consensus, Kentucky University relented and joined in the Chautauqua entertainment in 1890, but to no avail: first prize was captured by Centre College, and second prize by Georgetown College.[14]

During the early 1890s the Chautauqua at Lexington continued to grow more elaborate and more popular, and its collegiate oratorical contest grew in popularity and notoriety as well. In 1891 an estimated 4,000 people attended the opening night as a "human stream" poured into Woodland Park, and in 1892 the *Kentucky Leader* touted the record number of tents "sold" (rented) in advance. However, this was the New South era, and it was clear that the Chautauqua was for whites only. On 5 July 1891, during the height of the Chautauqua festivities, the *Leader* reported on a Fourth of July march through town to another picnic grounds, where the "colored people ha[d] a merry picnic." The *Leader* took pains to add that "the colored people enjoyed the day thoroughly, and no disturbance of any kind was seen on the grounds." The next day the *Leader* described the "college boys" as the "ruling spirits at Chautauqua" and stated that the grounds had been turned completely over to them as great crowds appeared on that very hot afternoon for the oratorical contest; Central University took first prize, and the Centre College representative won second prize for an oration entitled "Our South." The 1892 session opened "under sunny skies" on 28 June in a purportedly prosperous condition. On 5 July, reflecting the popularity of oratory at the time, the event featured former Tennessee governor Bob Taylor, who, along with his brother, has been described as "probably the most colorful of the political orators of the south." On 8 July the session closed "in a blaze of glory," with special excursion trains bringing in people from the surrounding towns for the collegiate oratorical contest, which was the prominent "drawing card" for closing day; once again, the contest was dominated by the orators from Centre College and Central University.[15]

By 1893 the accommodations at the Chautauqua Assembly were becoming quite elaborate and included a park hotel that could accommodate 25 lodgers and seat 100 patrons in its dining room. In its 27 June coverage of the 1893 session, the *Kentucky Leader* proudly asserted that all of Lexington's churches, benevolent societies, and associations had their own tents, making special mention of the tent of the Confederate Veterans' Association. This seventh assembly seemed to be taking on a more "professional" air as well; the event and the details of its program were publicized weeks ahead of time in large newspaper advertisements that listed Charles Scott—who also managed the Lexington Opera House—as the session's business manager. In addition, a sixteen-piece professional band that specialized in playing at independent Chautauqua assemblies had been imported from Cincinnati. For the first time that year, the day of the collegiate oratorical contest was formally referred to in the press as "college day." The *Leader's* front-page coverage of the contest on 6 July 1893 included brief biographies of each of the contestants and noted that, of the three judges, one had been chosen by the assembly managers, one by the participating orators, and one jointly. At the conclusion of the contest, for the first time at Chautauqua, a representative from a Lexington school was one of the prize winners; Cecropian Society member Phillip W. Breitenbucher of Kentucky University took second place for his oration "Modern Chivalry." State College was still absent but would join the contest with faculty approval the following year. The *Leader* asserted that "college day" was a "magnificent success," noting that the Chautauqua grounds that afternoon were "simply a mass of humanity"; the auditorium was "literally packed . . . with people" for the oratorical contest, and the contest was "the most enthusiastic feature of the [1893] assembly."[16]

By 1894, then, the Inter-Collegiate Oratorical Association, organized and controlled by literary society members, had secured the Lexington Opera House as the "permanent" site for its annual oratorical contest. Moreover, the "college day" oratorical contest at Chautauqua, whose contestants were literary society members chosen by their respective societies to represent their respective schools, had become a popular yearly fixture at Woodland Park. By helping to control and supplying the performers for these two highly popular public entertainments, the men's literary societies of Lexington's Kentucky University and State College had succeeded in establishing a distinct off-campus presence in the community's cultural life. Although these entertainments were highly competitive, exuberant, and sometimes quite rowdy affairs, they clearly carried intellectual pretensions; the orators earnestly, and at times eloquently, addressed their audiences on serious subjects, while the ever-present band music provided an aesthetic counterpoint to the raucous college yells and cheers of the audience. For the remainder of the decade, and perhaps a year or two beyond, the vitality and popularity of these off-campus entertainments would persist.

1894–1900: A Manifest Presence in the City

In 1894 State College reentered the intercollegiate oratorical contest and
sent an orator to the Chautauqua contest for the first time as well. In March
the faculty had given its blessing to the societies' plan to have the orator
who won second place in the campus contest to determine the intercollegiate representative represent the school at Chautauqua. Indeed, from 1894
through 1900, the Lexington schools—State College and Kentucky University—would unfailingly be represented at both events and would often
dominate them. Certainly 1894 was a notable year for Kentucky University students and especially for members of the Cecropian Literary Society,
whose orators won both the intercollegiate and the Chautauqua contests.
The *Kentucky Leader* provided detailed coverage of the primary (intrasociety) and preliminary (intersociety) contests at both Lexington schools,
which resulted in State College Patterson Society orator E. J. Hobdy and
Kentucky University Cecropian Society orator Enoch Grehan representing
their respective schools at the 1894 intercollegiate contest. The 6 April contest at the Lexington Opera House, which Grehan won, was heralded in the
Lexington Morning Transcript's front-page coverage as "the most exciting and
successful that has yet been held." The *Transcript* noted approvingly that
fifty members of the faculties of the colleges represented were seated on the
stage in support of the event, and it called the orations "intellectual treats."
The *Transcript*'s account, though overwhelmingly laudatory, gently chided
the students for drowning out the music of Saxton's Band with their cheers
and college yells. The Cecropians' victory was tempered two months later,
in June 1894, by the loss of their expensive and genteel furnishings when a
small tornado damaged the roof of Morrison College above the Cecropian
hall, "drenching the new Brussels carpets . . . and warping the bottoms of
new opera chairs." However, this setback would quickly be assuaged by their
good fortune at the upcoming Chautauqua Assembly.[17]

On 3 July 1894, a week after the Cecropians' encounter with the tornado, the eighth Chautauqua Assembly opened in Woodland Park. The park
was described by the *Kentucky Leader* as a retreat from the "heat and glare of
the city," a cool oasis of "grand forest trees casting their deep shadows over
the smoothly shaven green turf." The *Leader* provided a detailed list of the
social elite who were camping in the Chautauqua tents or staying in Park
House, the hotel that housed "not only the social life of Chautauqua, but

of Lexington." The women's clubs of Lexington mingled in collaboration in the tent of the Fortnightly Club, their exertions perhaps presaging the Progressive Era activities of Lexington women after the turn of the century. Nevertheless, the Victorian era was still represented at Chautauqua in 1894: in Mrs. L. V. Dodge's lecture on "Social Purity," she instructed mothers in their "duty" to be ever vigilant, to "know what her child [was] doing at each and every hour, and shield it from the slightest [moral] pollution." On 12 July the *Leader* headline declared that "Oratory Has Full Sway at Lexington Chautauqua Today" and noted that "ever since oratorical contests were inaugurated at Chautauqua they have proven wonderfully successful as a drawing card." Again, as at the intercollegiate contest that April, a Cecropian orator representing Kentucky University won the contest. This time it was twenty-four-year-old Charles A. Thomas, a student from Australia, for his oration "The Universal Republic." Upon the announcement of his victory, he "was hoisted on the shoulders of his jubilant college mates and borne around the grounds, high above the heads of the shrieking, yelling crowd who followed." Such enthusiasm and public acclaim would literally and figuratively carry the college orators aloft through the remainder of the decade.[18]

In 1895 the *(Lexington) Press-Transcript* provided its readers with extensive coverage of the annual intercollegiate oratorical contest at the opera house on 5 April and, in what became something of a press tradition, printed the entire text of the winning oration. The *Press-Transcript* had also reported on the primary and preliminary contests at State College and Kentucky University to select each school's representative to the intercollegiate event. By now, the importance of the intercollegiate contest was affecting on-campus society activities. For instance, by 1895, the Patterson birthday celebration, originally a noncompetitive entertainment (open session) in honor of the State College president, had been turned into a primary contest to select the orator to represent the Patterson Society in the intersociety contest—which, for the only time, would choose a Normal Society (male) orator as the State College representative in 1895. Across town at Kentucky University, the Cecropians were once again victorious. However, at the intercollegiate competition that year, the day belonged to Georgetown College and its representative, J. M. Shelburne. The *Press-Transcript*'s coverage of the 1895 intercollegiate contest suggests how thoroughly the region's college students, the competing orators and their female admirers, and other followers of this entertainment commandeered many of the public spaces of Lexington. According to the *Press-Transcript* accounts, the crowds gathered for the intercollegiate contest filled and "took over" not only the opera house but also the streets, the railway station, and the hotels of the city.[19]

Later that year these same public scenes were replayed on "College Day" (now capitalized in the press) at Chautauqua. According to the *Kentucky Leader*, trains brought large crowds from the outlying towns, "the hotel lobbies were filled with the gossiping college enthusiasts," and the hotel parlors hosted "large numbers of pretty girls who had come along to help cheer the respective representatives to victory." The 1895 Chautauqua began on 1 July, and on the Fourth the *Leader* reported that huge crowds celebrated the day at Woodland Park, which in the 1890s became the major (white) venue for this patriotic holiday. According to the *Leader*, babies, children, and lovers all enjoyed "the shady delights of Woodland" that day; "the sturdy mechanic, whose play days are too few, [was there] with his wife and little ones out for a glad holiday." The featured speaker, ex–Confederate general John B. Gordon, once again recounted the glories of the Lost Cause to those assembled. The collegiate oratorical contest at Chautauqua was held on 11 July. The previous day, however, belonged to twenty-three-year-old Madeline McDowell (Breckinridge), who had stood before the Chautauqua convocation of women's clubs to read "an excellent paper upon 'Socialism in Fiction' which was the occasion of much congratulation to the young writer." The following day, the *Leader's* front-page headline declared, "Oratory Reigns Supreme at Chautauqua Today . . . The Annual Oratorical Contest Is On." The *Leader* reported that "the largest crowd since the Fourth" was on hand for "College Day"; later, the *K. U. Enroll* would claim that 5,000 people had witnessed Periclean Society member Wood Ballard's victory for his oration entitled "Great Men of the Future."[20]

Just as 1894 had been Kentucky University's year at these public oratorical contests, 1896 seemed to belong to State College. Patterson Society member John T. Geary won the gold medal in the intercollegiate contest— the first victory for State College in this competition. Later that year, Union Society member William Sugg took second place at the Chautauqua College Day contest—the first time State College had a prize winner at Woodland Park. The *Lexington Daily Leader* gave extensive front-page coverage to the intercollegiate contest in April, printing the official yell of each participating college, a history of the previous contests, a detailed description of the gold medal fashioned for the occasion, and the full text of the winning oration. It cannot go unnoticed by the careful reader, however, that the press also contained harbingers of the changing times: the students attended an intercollegiate baseball game the afternoon of the contest, and the faculty at Kentucky University had just rejected a petition to organize two Greek-letter fraternities, Kappa Alpha and Kappa Sigma, on campus. Nevertheless, on the night of this ninth annual intercollegiate contest, oratory still held sway over athletics and social fraternities in the students' minds as they and members of the public listened to six orations and the music of Saxton's Orchestra and then cheered wildly as they paraded through the streets carrying aloft the winning orator. At Chautauqua that July, where, according to the *Leader,* a rendition of "Dixie" always met with "applause from [this] Southern audience," College Day 1896 was described as "by long odds the gala day of Chautauqua, the Glorious Fourth not excepted," and it was noted that "a spirit of good humor and general hilarity prevailed."[21]

And so it went for the remainder of the decade and through the turn of the century—or rather, so it *seemed* to go. Although these two off-campus public entertainments controlled by college literary society members continued to be highly popular and invariably received extensive coverage in the Lexington press, there were also signs of problems and signs of change. At State College in 1898 the faculty challenged the idea that the oratorical contests were the exclusive domain of the literary societies. Whereas in 1894 the faculty minutes reflect that the professors understood and accepted the idea that they were considering whether to allow "the *Societies* [emphasis added] to enter again the Oratorical contests of the Kentucky Colleges," by May 1898 the faculty passed a motion "that any student of the college who is not a member of a Literary Society shall be allowed to participate in primary oratorical contests." In addition to faculty threats to literary society exclusivity, there was internal strife in the Inter-Collegiate Oratorical Association brought about, at least in part, by the Lexington schools' success in the contests. At the intercollegiate contests during this period, the Lexington schools frequently claimed the winning orator and seemed to be moving toward almost total domination of the event by century's end: Periclean Society member R. E. Moss won for Kentucky University in 1899, and State College Union Society member Leonidas Ragan won the gold medal in 1900. Even earlier, in February 1897, the executive committee of the Inter-Collegiate Oratorical Association had met at the Phoenix Hotel in Lexington to discuss moving the contest to Louisville because, in part, some members felt that holding the contests in Lexington created "some prejudice on the part of judges in favor of Lexington contestants." The discussion was contentious, and the subsequent vote in favor of moving the contest, opposed by the Lexington schools' committeemen, was never acted on. Nevertheless, the incident suggests the tension and strain within the student organization overseeing the intercollegiate event.[22]

In addition to faculty threats and internal discord, there were other warning signs of challenge and change. Although the oratorical competition at the opera house was perhaps still "the contest long treasured in thought and dream by the college boy," college athletics were increasingly vying for the collegians' and the public's attention in the late 1890s. For instance, an 1898 article in the *Lexington Morning Herald* carried the headline "K. U. News: Base Ball and Other Topics of Interest"; one of those "other topics" was the preliminary contest at Morrison Chapel to choose the school's intercollegiate orator. In addition to rising competition from other student events, there was the emerging problem of negative press coverage. Although the intercollegiate contest was still generally lauded in the press, there was now an occasional negative note struck as well. An 1898 *Herald* account complained of the noise and atmosphere: "It savors of tin horns and flying streamers, of outlandish yells and unearthly hubbub, of racket and noise and racket still." In earlier years there had occasionally been mention of the tremendous noise created by the cheering, but it had generally been encouraging, or at least good-natured, in tone. However, despite challenge, discord, and complaint, the intercollegiate contest was still front-page news in the *Herald* as the new century began. In 1900, two years after the outbreak of the Spanish-American War, the *Herald* put State College Union Society member Leonidas Ragan's picture on the front page, along with the full text of his winning oration "The Open Door," a speech arguing in favor of American imperialistic expansionism.[23]

Meanwhile, there were signs in the Lexington press that the Kentucky Chautauqua Assembly was simultaneously in the midst of success, struggle, and change around the turn of the century. In 1900 the *Lexington Morn-*

ing Herald continued to tout the Chautauqua in glowing terms as a great success, arguing that, for the past thirteen years, Woodland Park had "been the tenting ground for the intellectually inclined and the pleasure loving of the State. . . . [They] come for a season of study and relaxation, [and] for intellectual pursuits among entrancing sylvan scenes. . . . They are drawn together in the mutual pursuit of enjoyment and education." Despite such tributes in the press, problems had begun to surface. In 1897 the *Lexington Daily Leader* reported that, while "everybody [was] sorry to see the park gates close" at the end of the session, there had been an "unpleasant surprise," in that the event was $27,000 in debt and would have "an inadequate fund for meeting the expenses" unless additional donations were forthcoming. Accompanying these warning signs of financial difficulties were signals of cultural change that did not augur well for the traditional Chautauqua. Whereas southern evangelist Sam Jones had been enthusiastically praised in the Lexington press when he addressed the first Chautauqua in 1887, when he returned eleven years later the *Leader* was quite critical, finding him too harsh and coarse for his "refined" Lexington audience, many of whom were "supremely disgusted" by his remarks. The *Leader* was especially unhappy about Jones's criticism of the state capital: "He mentioned the idea of placing lever[s] under places to lift them to higher and better things. [Then] he said: 'But I don't believe there is room enough between Frankfort and hell to get a lever.'" To make matters worse, Jones expressed the opinion that many of the men in the audience were drunkards and that the women were unjustifiably vain. Though the *Leader* took pains to acknowledge Jones's renowned piety and benevolent works, it expressed "the wish . . . that he would lay aside coarse language and needless jest, . . . and be of the opinion that morality and refinement go hand in hand." The *Leader*'s appeal was on behalf of readers now considered too urbane, sophisticated, and refined for such traditional and outdated fare left over from an earlier decade.[24]

The fare offered at the Lexington Chautauqua was indeed changing. For one thing, motion pictures had arrived and had been offered at the Chautauqua as early as 1897. Those shown by the American Vitagraph Company in 1899 were highly successful, in part because the audience could watch these thrilling motion pictures at Chautauqua "under the auspices of cultural uplift." At any rate, the *Lexington Daily Leader* on 6 July 1899 noted that the motion pictures were a "hit with the audiences at Chautauqua [and]

... their popularity has called for repetition." In addition to new entertainments, new collegiate extracurricular agencies were making their appearance at Chautauqua. The Kappa Alpha Fraternity (Southern) held its Twentieth Biennial Convention in Lexington during the 1899 Chautauqua Assembly. According to the *Leader's* coverage of the event, a chapter of Kappa Alpha had been secretly organized at Kentucky University in 1891 and had finally been recognized and approved by the institution in 1896; another chapter had been organized at State College in 1893. Fraternity delegates from eleven southern states attended the Lexington convention, and the *Leader* made much of their meeting, their banquet at the Phoenix Hotel, and their attendance "in a body" at the Chautauqua.[25]

In the meantime, the College Day oratorical contest continued to occupy a prominent place on the Chautauqua agenda. In 1897 the *Lexington Daily Leader* reported that "the college boys took the town [on College Day]. . . . And, the [Chautauqua] auditorium was packed with friends and admirers." In 1898 the *Leader* noted that the Chautauqua grounds were "literally a mass of gay [college] ribbons" on College Day and, in a stark contrast to the paper's criticism of Jones's address only days earlier, expressed only the highest praise for the student orators: "The seven speakers were all fine looking Kentucky sons and all bore themselves with the dignity and gravity befitting the important and responsible position thrust upon them as representatives of their respective colleges." The following year the *Leader*, in a nod to the contest's acknowledged success, noted that "College Day is always a big one with the Chautauqua management [and] . . . the contest [for 1899] promises to be full of interest." Yet, for College Day, as for the entire Chautauqua, there were the telltale signs of challenge, discord, and change.[26]

Reflecting the rising extracurricular competition for student interest and loyalty, in 1897 the *Lexington Daily Leader* identified the first- and second-place winners of the Chautauqua oratorical contest—Kentucky University Cecropian Society member James N. Elliott and State College Patterson Society member John T. Geary—as also being members of the Kappa Alpha Fraternity chapters at their respective schools. By 1900 Kappa Alpha was even sporting its own tent at Woodland Park. Added to the appearance of new collegiate affiliations on the Chautauqua scene were signs of controversy and discord within the College Day contest itself. In 1896 the *Leader* had noted that the Chautauqua contest victor, J. M. Shelburne of Georgetown College, was not only a student but also an experienced minister, which "of course gave him advantage over the others." In 1898 the Chautauqua victor representing Kentucky University, Howard Cree, was not a student but an alumnus of the College of the Bible, having graduated in 1897. The following year the *Leader* reported that Kentucky University had been disqualified from the 1899 Chautauqua contest under a new Inter-Collegiate Oratorical Association rule that barred those "in active practice in the pulpit" from the competition, as they "held a superior advantage" over all others—a rule that made it clear that "only students, not preachers should participate." The appearance of such controversy and discord in the press suggests that the contest was at times buffeted by internal tensions and stresses. In addition to external challenges and internal discord, there were ominous signs of change, especially at the end of this period. For instance, by 1900, even though the *Leader* continued to praise the Chautauqua contest, a perfunctory, slightly bored tone had crept into its coverage; it wrote of "the usual enthusiasm" and the "old familiar yells," and it stated rather indifferently that, "as usual there was the atmosphere of music and flowers on the platform." Such apathetic rhetoric in the local press may have reflected a lessening of the public's ardor for these contests.[27]

Regardless of the challenge, criticism, discord, and forces of change that touched these off-campus, literary society–controlled public entertainments during the 1890s, the annual intercollegiate oratorical contest at the Lexington Opera House and the annual College Day oratorical contest at the Lexington Chautauqua in Woodland Park were remarkably popular and successful events. Raucous yet genteel, imbued with the pleasures of competitive sport while acknowledging the intellectual aspirations and pretensions of both participants and audience, these oratorical contests were a singular fixture of the city's Gilded Age cultural life. Yet, only five years into the twentieth century, the Chautauqua contest had ended, and the intercollegiate contest had retreated to the campus chapel.

1901–1905: Loss and Retreat

On 12 April 1901 nineteen-year-old State College Patterson Society and Kappa Alpha Fraternity member Clarke Tandy won the fourteenth annual intercollegiate oratorical contest at the Lexington Opera House with his oration "The Reign of Law"; this was the same oration he had given to win the Patterson Society primary contest in March on Patterson's birthday. The day after the intercollegiate contest the *Lexington Leader* printed the complete financial statement of the Inter-Collegiate Oratorical Association, seemingly indicating that its financial health was becoming increasing important. The *Leader* noted that the association managed to clear $40 on the intercollegiate contest, but the expense statement did not include "the item of lemons, many dozen of which [were] annually used" by the students to ease their throats and vocal cords due to the loud cheering and yelling they engaged in between the orations. This expense was borne by the individual students themselves. Despite the small profit reported, the article left the impression that the contest might be having financial problems. On a happier, if inaccurate, note, the *Leader* reported that the 1901 victory made State College "the first college of the association to win this unique honor two successive years"; actually, Centre College had won the contest in 1892 and again in 1893.[28]

The *Lexington Leader* reported correctly, however, that Kentucky University students had "boycotted" the 1901 contest, owing to a disagreement over the oratorical association's ruling that those studying for or in the ministry could not enter the contests at the opera house and Chautauqua. This argument can be followed in the Kentucky University *Transylvanian* beginning in May 1900, when the magazine reported that the literary societies were incensed by a change in the association's constitution that barred entry to aspiring and practicing ministers. The societies believed that this rule change was aimed directly at some of their orators, and they deeply resented it. The following spring, in March 1901, the *Transylvanian* reported that the Kentucky University students had withdrawn from the oratorical association, and it vigorously defended that decision. Two months later the magazine reported that the Periclean and Cecropian societies had decided to accept an invitation to join the Southern Interstate Oratorical Association and had participated in and won that association's contest held in Austin, Texas, on 15 May. Nevertheless, by April 1902 the *Transylvanian* announced that the dispute between Kentucky University and the other members of the Inter-Collegiate Oratorical Association had been resolved. The magazine advanced the partisan argument that it had become clear to the other schools that the association could not survive without Kentucky

University. The agreement included the following points: (1) only literary society members of the association's member schools could participate in the contests, (2) seniors in and graduates of the "theological department" would continue to be barred, and (3) the intercollegiate contest would be held outside Lexington for the first time in a decade. The last compromise was considered necessary because the Southern Oratorical Association was holding its contest in Lexington that spring, and it was believed that the "state contest" would be more successful if it were held elsewhere. Without dwelling on the concession made by Kentucky University students with regard to ministry students, the *Transylvanian* was obviously pleased "that our differences have been settled, and that K. U. is again a member of the association."[29]

At the same time that the Inter-Collegiate Oratorical Association and its contest were bedeviled by internal strife, controversy, and potential financial problems, the Lexington Chautauqua and its associated oratorical contest were reportedly declining in attendance and interest. The *Lexington Leader,* reporting the falling and disappointing attendance at the 1901 Chautauqua, warned that "the attendance . . . must pick up." The same article suggested that the city buy Woodland Park and convert it to a city park, reserving eleven days per year for the exclusive use of Chautauqua and thereby relieving the Chautauqua Assembly of its bonded indebtedness for the land. When the 1901 session closed, the *Leader* felt the need to reassure the public by quoting the president of the assembly, who stated, "the Chautauqua would be continued and there was no intention whatever of giving up the enterprise." The decline in the Lexington Chautauqua was also reflected in the *Leader*'s coverage of the Fourth of July holiday in 1901. Whereas in former years the Chautauqua's activities essentially *were* the celebration, at least for the city's whites, it was now competing with several other events, including a "St. Joseph picnic at the fairgrounds." As usual, the *Leader* touted the College Day oratorical contest with a front-page headline reading, in part, "College Youth and His Rosy Cheeked Sweetheart Own the City Today." The following day, however, the contest results were only briefly reported on page four, and the paper acknowledged disappointment that "enthusiasm at the grounds was not as high as it has been in years past; neither was there so large an attendance from the student body." Such press accounts clearly suggest that the Chautauqua Assembly and its college oratorical contest were declining in tandem as the new century began.[30]

The 1902 intercollegiate contest was staged at the Danville Opera House on 18 April. Both Lexington schools were represented, as Kentucky University had returned to the contest after settling its dispute with the association. The *Lexington Morning Herald* gave the contest only brief, if front-page, attention, perhaps in part because the contest was staged outside the city and in part because the Lexington schools failed to win a prize. However, the article's headline clearly suggests that college sports were attaining greater importance, sharing press coverage with the oratorical contest: "Georgetown Won [Oratorical] Contest: K. U. . . . Base Ball Team Defeated Central Nine 4 to 3." Apparently, Kentucky University's baseball players were more conspicuous that year than its orators. Kentucky University was not represented at the College Day Chautauqua contest in late June; however, for the second year in a row, State College's Patterson Society member Clarke Tandy won second place in the event. For the first time, first place went to an orator representing Kentucky Wesleyan College, at that time located in Winchester. On the afternoon before the College Day event, the *Lexington Leader* headline announced as a "Hopeful Sign" that box-office receipts were up over the previous year, and it attributed this to "popular lecturer" Leon Vincent's address on "Burns, the Poet of the People." The *Leader* also listed the schools that would be represented at the College Day contest, their orators, and the titles of the orations. The following day the paper gave the event brief front-page coverage. Absent, however, from both the pre- and postevent accounts were the detailed and lively descriptions of the students and their impact on the city and the assembly—descriptions that had been an integral part of the coverage in former years.[31]

The following year, 1903, would prove to be a singular one in the history of these off-campus oratorical entertainments, for at least two reasons. First, this was the last year that the intercollegiate contest would be held at an off-campus Lexington venue. Press coverage of the intercollegiate event also noted several new features that year. For instance, Kentucky Wesleyan College joined the contest for the first time and won the gold medal, to the surprise of many in the audience. Also for the first time, a second-place winner of the contest was announced from the stage. Such changes were intended, no doubt, to garner more interest in the contest. However, the change in tone of the coverage itself was more significant than a new contestant, a change in procedure, or an unexpected result. The *Lexington Morn-*

ing Herald's account seemed to emphasize, without actually saying so, that this was strictly a college affair for college students; gone was any mention of public interest or attendance that had punctuated press reports in earlier years. In addition, the *Herald* printed an advertisement for a college baseball game in the same column—and a larger typeface—directly above its contest coverage, perhaps reflecting, consciously or unconsciously, what the paper considered of *most* interest to its readers. The *Lexington Leader*'s coverage complimented the orators but vehemently complained about the noisy cheering between the orations, sarcastically commenting, "the orchestra [Saxton's], of course, was not supposed to be heard." In fact, the *Leader* seemed less complimentary of the contest itself than of the bejeweled gold medal created for the event by local jeweler Victor Bogaert, deeming it as "handsomer the closer it is viewed. It is a rare bit of the engraver's art." At the same time, the *Leader* made much of the Kappa Alpha Fraternity banquet given the same night and to which the contest orators had been invited as honored guests.[32]

In short, by 1903 local press accounts were virtually styling the intercollegiate oratorical contest as a rowdy student activity accompanied by a fraternity party. This was a far cry from the Gilded Age depictions of the entertainment as a community event—an "intellectual feast"—frequented by "Lexington people in general." These contests had always been, in part, raucous, competitive student rituals; new was the published perception that they were primarily so—a perception that eroded their status as a genteel fixture of community cultural life beyond the college campus. This erosion was heightened by, and perhaps reflected in, the *Herald*'s announcement after the 1903 event that the intercollegiate contest would once again leave the city to be held at the Georgetown Opera House in 1904, under the auspices of Georgetown College. This was part of a plan to hold the contest in the locale of the school sponsoring the event each year, as had been the case in the early years of the competition. In fact, this announcement foretold the end of the contest's reign on the community, off-campus stage. The State College chapel was the venue for the intercollegiate contest in 1905, and it would never again be held off campus. The *Herald* noted that "the chapel held the crowd of 500 comfortably." This remark reflected the fact that attendance had fallen to less than half its rate during the Gilded Age years, when the 1,250-seat Lexington Opera House had been filled to overflowing with students and members of the public from the city and the surrounding region. Even the music was intramural for the 1905 event, being provided by the State College Orchestra rather than a commercial orchestra. John M. Thacker of Central University of Danville (Centre) won for his oration entitled, appropriately, "The New Kentucky." And so, in these changed conditions, the contest managed to survive as an on-campus event through the Progressive Era. For instance, in 1910 the intercollegiate contest would again be staged in the chapel of the State University of Kentucky (the name change occurred in 1908), and in 1916 the event would be held in the chapel of Centre College in Danville.[33]

The second reason for considering 1903 a turning point in the history of the off-campus contests was that Clarke Tandy's persistence and talent finally won him first place in the Chautauqua contest, having finished second the previous two years. These feats, along with his win at the intercollegiate contest in 1901, made him, arguably, the most successful orator in the history of these off-campus events. At the opening of Chautauqua in 1903, the *Lexington Leader* depicted the assembly grounds at Woodland Park as a sylvan idyll "clothed in all the beauty of a primitive forest in summer. The virgin soil under the giant oaks and elms was never greener and the shade never more inviting." Yet this publicized image of a wooded Arcadia of peace and simplicity was deceptive, for under these monarchs of the forest, the complex cultural conflicts of the New South were quite evident. For instance, the Chautauqua Ministers' Institute devoted an entire afternoon's debate to "The Duty of the Church to the Negro." Indeed, one of the learned ministers taking part in this debate, Dr. M. M. Parkhurst, also served as one of the judges for the College Day oratorical contest—a small matter, perhaps, but one suggesting that the milieu in which these student contests took place was not divorced from the social currents of the times. At the Lexington Chautauqua, collegiate extracurricular life was inseparably commingled with community culture.[34]

A tone of sentimental longing for the past suffused the *Lexington Leader*'s coverage of the 1903 Chautauqua oratorical contest: "Today was College Day . . . [and] there was a revival of the old-time interest [as] in the days when College Day was the greatest of the year." Despite this assertion of "revival," the *Lexington Herald* reported that the crowd had not been as large or as enthusiastic as in former times. Nevertheless, both newspapers showed an interest in the contest's winner. Twenty-one-year-old Clarke Tandy had just graduated from State College the month before, and the *Herald* described him as a "handsome, manly appearing young man, easy and graceful [with] a full, resonant voice," adding that "it was freely predicted that he would win this intellectual contest." The *Leader* went even further, touting him as one of the "ablest young men in the State," and it declared his winning oration, "The Hero as Orator," to be "one of the best college orations ever heard at Chautauqua." Tandy's celebrated performance, in retrospect, was climactic, for the following year's contest proved to be a fading companion to an expiring Chautauqua.[35]

Announcing the opening of the eighteenth annual Kentucky Chautauqua Assembly on 28 June 1904, the *Lexington Leader* bravely asserted that "the present session is to be one of the most successful in the Assembly's history." This was wishful thinking, for after the close of the session, the *Lexington Herald* reported that the assembly had incurred a "considerable" deficit of almost $2,000. This financial disaster was blamed on poor attendance caused by bad weather. But something more serious than summer thunderstorms was amiss, as reflected in the perfunctory and limited press coverage given the once celebrated College Day oratorical contest. The *Leader* printed no detailed precontest promotional accounts and advertised the oratorical contest (along with several other entertainments in its Chautauqua program listing for 1 July) only as "Flying banners and college yells. Music by Lexington Military (Saxton's) Band." The *Leader,* in its brief coverage of the contest, rather nostalgically and curtly referred to it as "something of a review of the famous contests of the past when college yells resounded throughout the day," and it summed up the entire event in a single perfunctory sentence: "All of the speakers were roundly applauded and their orations gave evidence of much study and careful thought." Absent were the embellishments that had characterized the enthusiastic press accounts of earlier years, including the detailed descriptions of the contest, the audience's reactions, and the victory celebrations.[36]

In October 1904 a *Lexington Herald* headline announced, "No Renewal of Chautauqua." The accompanying article quoted a member of the assembly's executive board as saying that it would be "impossible to hold another Chautauqua in Lexington." Falling attendance, mounting financial deficits, and the poor condition of the auditorium and other buildings were cited as reasons. The following spring many of the ancient trees were cut down and the buildings razed in an effort to "improve" the city's Woodland Park. The Lexington Chautauqua and much of its sylvan setting had vanished. Gone also was the off-campus venue for public oratorical performance and the opportunity for collegiate literary societies to participate in and contribute to community intellectual life. An unsuccessful "revival" of the Kentucky Chautauqua was mounted in 1907 and again in 1908 in Woodland Park, where a new auditorium had been constructed. These sessions were both popular and financial failures, even though the management in 1907 "deemed it wise to eliminate the study and class features . . . and to make it a series of pleasant and profitable entertainments." Despite such efforts to match what it thought were the public's changing tastes, the management found it necessary to reduce ticket prices to boost attendance in 1907 and admitted the following year, after the session had closed, that attendance had been "disappointing." No further revival of the Chautauqua Assembly was attempted. Collegiate oratorical contests were not on the program of the 1907–1908 sessions, and they were not part of the fare when the Redpath Tent Chautauqua first included Lexington on its circuit in 1916, as the country edged toward its leap into the First World War.[37]

The Sad Fate of Clarke Tandy

And so, by the end of 1904, Lexington's male collegiate literary societies had been deprived of one of their two community venues for public performance and had retreated from the other back to the college chapel, effectively ending their off-campus presence in the city's intellectual life. This occurred simultaneously with a decline in the organizational power, vitality, and influence the societies had exhibited on campus just a decade earlier. Moreover, this decline would gather steam in the years immediately ahead. Perhaps nothing better symbolized the high aspirations, ephemeral fame, and ultimate fate of these societies than the life of Clarke Howell Tandy—a life preserved in the Lexington press and campus publications of his time.

Tandy was born in Hopkinsville, Kentucky, on 11 June 1882. His mother died shortly thereafter and his father, William Tandy, a bank cashier, essentially turned his infant son over to his wife's brother and sister, Dr. F. H. Clarke and Miss Kate Clarke, to raise. Dr. Clarke, accompanied by his

sister and infant nephew, soon moved to Lexington to become superintendent of the Eastern Kentucky Insane Asylum, and Clarke Tandy, carrying
his mother's maiden name as his first, grew up in the Bluegrass city under
the care of his aunt and uncle, although he reportedly spent the summers
with his father in Hopkinsville. He attended Sayre School in Lexington
and then, at age seventeen, entered the academy attached to State College,
matriculating into the college in 1900 at age eighteen.[38]

Tandy excelled at State College, where he exhibited a special talent for
Greek and Latin, and he quickly became a favorite of both President Patterson and Vice President John Henry Neville, who taught many of the classes
Tandy attended. When Tandy applied successfully to become Kentucky's
first Rhodes scholar in 1904, Neville wrote a letter of reference to the authorities at Oxford University in which he mentioned Tandy's oratorical
powers and his valedictory standing in his class at State College; he went
on to say of Tandy that, "in 'manhood, truthfulness, courage, devotion to
duty, sympathy for and protection of the weak, in kindness, unselfishness
and fellowship,' he would, in the estimation of all who know him best, as-
suredly be rated high." Neville also mentioned Tandy's popularity among
his classmates, noting that they had unanimously endorsed him as their
representative in the Rhodes competition. Tandy's campus popularity was
also reflected in the student publication the *Idea,* which published Neville's
letter at the time of Tandy's death and went on to say of him that, "while at
the University he was a leader among his class-mates and was beloved by all
who knew him. His career as an under-graduate . . . was one of honor and
success."[39]

While excelling in the classroom at State College, Tandy also excelled
in extracurricular activities. He was an active member of the Kappa Alpha
Fraternity, one of at least eight male Greek-letter fraternities that had been
established at State College by the time of Tandy's graduation in 1903, and
he was a charter member of the socially exclusive Lamp and Cross Society, described by the *Idea* in 1910 as an honorary senior fraternity whose
members annually chose, or "tapped," ten male students from the junior
class as new pledges. However, it was as an orator and representative of his
literary society, the Patterson, that Tandy achieved his extracurricular fame.
First winning the Patterson Society's gold medal in March 1901, the nineteen-
year-old Tandy went on to win the fourteenth annual intercollegiate oratori-

cal contest at the Lexington Opera House that April for his oration "The Reign of Law." The *Lexington Leader* announced (inaccurately) that he was "the youngest student who ever won this honor in Kentucky." Perhaps reflecting his local notoriety, the following April the *Leader,* calling Tandy a "popular and polished student-writer of State College," published his long, humorous parody of Judge James H. Mulligan's poem "In Kentucky." Written to amuse the female Philosophian Society, Tandy's parody included such lines as: "In all our social scenes / at State College / The Philosophians are queens / At State College."[40]

Although, according to the *Lexington Leader,* Tandy was heavily favored to win the Chautauqua oratorical contest in 1901, he took the second-place prize that year, and again in 1902. He graduated from State College in June 1903 at age twenty-one, valedictorian of a class of forty-seven members. Then, less than a month after graduation, he won first prize at the Chautauqua College Day contest for his oration "The Hero as Orator." Although the popularity of both the Chautauqua Assembly and its College Day oratorical contest were in decline by 1903, Tandy's reportedly stunning performance seemed, momentarily at least, to rejuvenate the contest. The *Leader,* asserting that this contest had been "one of the best in the history of Chautauqua," extolled the virtues of Tandy and his oration: "His effort was one of the best college orations ever heard at Chautauqua. It was thoughtful, clothed with an almost faultless diction and delivered in a manner that proclaimed the characteristics of the orator. [Tandy's] voice is resonant and musical and his appearance pleasing." Tandy seemed to be the ideal literary society–trained orator; he epitomized the eloquent, handsome collegiate gentleman and seemed to portray the protagonist of his own winning oration. Here was a youthful "hero" for both campus and community intellectual culture. Yet, ironically, the heroic image he embodied and promoted was now fading from the cultural spotlight, and Tandy's life would soon add a tragic note to the ironic.[41]

In the fall of 1903 Tandy was employed as an instructor at Smith Preparatory in Cynthiana, Kentucky, while pursuing the Rhodes scholarship. He entered Oxford University in October 1905, reportedly with the intention of obtaining a law degree, but he later changed course and sought a degree in history, hoping to become a college professor. Tandy apparently did well academically at Oxford and graduated in June 1908. After spending the summer touring Europe with his aunt and uncle, he returned to Lexington in August. Shortly thereafter, according to the *Lexington Herald*'s account, he accepted a position in New Jersey as instructor in Latin and English at the Lawrenceville Preparatory School, "an institution having enrolled about 400 male students and being a feeder to Princeton University." Things seemed to be going well, and the headmaster at Lawrenceville, who had "taken a special pride in the ability of his protégé," later stated that Tandy was "hard working and studious during almost all his spare time." On the night of 9 January 1909 Tandy attended a party in one of the school's dormitories and reportedly was his usual witty, bright, happy self. Upon leaving the party sometime later, he returned to his room and committed suicide, shooting himself in the right temple with a pistol. He was twenty-six years old.[42]

Shock and dismay were widely expressed in Lexington as the news of Tandy's death spread. The *Lexington Herald* carried an extensive report on the front page beneath a large photograph of Tandy. The *Lexington Leader* reported that Tandy's death had caused "deep sorrow among the hundreds of friends of the brilliant young man here." Communications from the school in New Jersey indicated that the authorities investigating his death assigned no cause for Tandy's suicide (the word *suicide* was never used in the press accounts), but a reason was quickly asserted by the *Leader:* "It is believed that his act was due to *overstudy* [emphasis added], causing his mind to become temporarily deranged. He had worked long and hard for his degrees, and was always known as one of the most studious young men ever in school here." In another account the paper reported that the announcement of Tandy's death had "cast a pall of gloom over the State University," his having been a "warm friend" of President Patterson and many others on the faculty, and his name still being known to almost every student. Vice President Neville did not live to share in the grief over his "beloved" pupil; he had died suddenly the previous September, in the words of his eulogizer, "full harnessed, mid in the furrow, in the confident expectation of resuming his work on the morrow." Patterson delivered Tandy's eulogy to the assembled students at chapel services on Monday, 11 January 1909, stating, according to the *Leader,* that "Mr. Tandy was one of the most brilliant students that he had ever known" and specifically mentioning Tandy's victory in the intercollegiate oratorical contest in 1901 and his having been the first Rhodes scholar from Kentucky. Patterson ended the eulogy by saying that "the best citizens of the State would bewail the death of her illustrious son." Tandy's body was returned to Lexington by train; his funeral was held on Tuesday, 12 January, at the First Presbyterian Church in Lexington, and he was buried in the Lexington Cemetery. Classes were canceled at the State University, and many students and faculty reportedly attended the funeral. Shortly afterward, a "tribute" to Tandy was printed in the *Idea* in which he was described as "stainless," a "Knight" above reproach, and "brilliant and scholarly . . . an orator who seemed destined to restore his native State to the proud eminence which she once held in the days gone by."[43]

The rhetoric in the public and campus press elevated Clarke Tandy's life and death to the realm of mythical symbol. He was styled as the youthful, eloquent, heroic scholar-orator struck down by "overstudy"—a martyr to the pursuit of the intellectual life. Such a view was no doubt more comforting than the sad and unpleasant reality of a life wasted. And although it seems legitimate and useful and has a certain "poetic" appeal to style Tandy as a symbol for the passing of nineteenth-century oratorical culture and the student literary societies that flourished within it, any analogy between the Lexington societies and their hero Clarke Tandy must not be too finely drawn, for these societies' lapse into irrelevancy would not be so rapid as Tandy's supposed lapse into madness, nor would their eventual demise be as flamboyant as his sudden, melodramatic death. Still, Tandy's life and death symbolized changing times, for the glories of his collegiate oratorical feats marked the end of the Gilded Age, and his sad passing occurred well into the Progressive Era. Five years had passed since literary society–inspired collegiate oratory had been regularly heard in Lexington outside the confines of its campuses. From the late nineteenth century through the first few years of the twentieth, Lexington's collegiate literary societies, through their sponsoring of and competing in public oratorical entertainments staged in municipal venues, had established and maintained an off-campus, community presence in the city's cultural landscape. By the time of Clarke Tandy's suicide in 1909, this was no longer the case, raising the question of what extracurricular agency, if any, had stepped forward to assume this role. The answer lay just beyond Tandy's death in the 1910s, and it would render prophetic a remark made in the State College publication the *Kentuckian* in 1901, in an essay celebrating Tandy's victory in the intercollegiate oratorical contest that spring. The remark buttressed the essayist's argument in support and praise of public speaking in all its forms: "the stage grows more in importance and demand in every successful dramatized life scene." The comment was prescient, for it would be the student agency of the "dramatized life scene," the dramatic club, that would establish the most notable off-campus collegiate presence within "progressive" Lexington's intellectual life during the years preceding America's march into the Great War.[44]

CHAPTER FIVE

"THIS CITY'S NEVER DULL"

Public Culture in Progressive Era Lexington

There still remains a part essential to a proper description of the South
which it is difficult to describe. . . . It is, in fine, the atmosphere of
the land, the thought and feeling, the thousand and one little actions
which go to make up life. In any community . . . it is these little things
which are most elusive to the grasp and yet most essential to any clear
conception of the group life.

—W. E. B. DuBois, *The Souls of Black Folk*, 1903

"Where does the dust come from, and who raises it?" is one of the
questions which the street cleaning committee of the Clean City Club is
beginning to take up actively, and [it] will make a study of . . . efficient
street cleaning methods.

—"Civic Club Will Fight Dust and Dirt in Lexington,"
Lexington Leader, 29 April 1915

Lexington's collegiate literary societies retreated from the community's cultural stage and from the campus spotlight during a period when the Bluegrass city was rapidly evolving from a Victorian to a "progressive" city. Yet
all the while, it remained firmly rooted in the New South—a vibrant, ambitious, optimistic, reformist, fervidly intellectual and yet virulently racist and
often quite violent cultural climate.

On the night of 10 January 1917, forty-nine-year-old Governor A. O.
(Augustus Owsley) Stanley and three friends left Louisville hurriedly aboard
a chartered train to travel overnight toward Murray in far western Kentucky.
A successful, "progressive" politician and a widely respected orator, Stanley
had put his literary society days at State College and Centre College far
behind him. He had served twelve years as a Democrat in the U.S. House

of Representatives before being elected Kentucky's thirty-eighth governor in 1915. However, during that long night aboard the speeding train, one can only wonder whether his mind drifted back to the youthful pleasures and glories attending those halcyon days as a student orator as he prepared himself for one of the most difficult and pivotal public addresses he would ever make. Governor Stanley, impelled by oath, inclination, and circumstance to uphold and defend centralized, bureaucratic, governmental, and judicial authority against any threat posed by civilian enforcement of community will, was traveling to Murray to face and rebuke an angry mob. Enraged by the murder of a white policeman, this mob was seemingly bent on lynching not only the black alleged murderer but also the white judge and prosecutor attempting to shield the accused.[1]

Stanley arrived in Murray on the morning of 11 January 1917. He bravely faced the angry crowds on the streets, gave an impassioned speech in a packed courtroom that dispersed the mob, took the judge and prosecutor aboard his train to ensure their safety, and ordered the continued safekeeping of the accused murderer at another location until he could be duly tried in court. The Lexington press followed the incident in western Kentucky closely and tended to emphasize Stanley's bravery (he had gone to Murray with no guards or security forces), his determination to uphold the rule of law, and his powerful oratorical abilities, which "turned armed men from thoughts of vengeance and sent them away from the court house in tears." In addition, the Lexington papers noted or reprinted other press accounts of the national acclaim Stanley won from black leaders, who praised his defense of the black man's rights, and from those who saw his actions as setting "a splendid example to those States where lawlessness too often is permitted to have its way." Other, more recent accounts of the incident have highlighted (1) the irony attending the praise by blacks, for Stanley was no racial egalitarian; (2) the governor's dogged and sincere determination to uphold his oath of office; and (3) the political ambitions that may have motivated his dramatic behavior (Stanley aspired to be a U.S. senator). Stanley's courtroom speech was published in full by the *Lexington Leader* on 12 January 1917, and it is worth examining because embedded in it are images highly suggestive of the cultural climate in Kentucky at that time.[2]

Stanley's address to the mob at Murray was praised in the *Boston Transcript,* and that article was reprinted in the *Lexington Leader.* The Boston article noted that although "oratory of the good old picturesque flowery kind" had gone out of fashion in the North, "it hasn't become obsolete in Dixie, where people are tremendously moved" by dramatic rhetoric. Stanley began his "Dixiesque" oration with an appeal to civilized behavior, which he grounded in respect for courthouses, judges, and "law and order"; thus, his appeal reflected the growing insistence of the political and economic elite on bureaucratized legal authority and social control. Yet he couched this appeal in the rhetoric of Victorian cultural, and New South racial, superiority:

> Court houses, reverence for law and order, and the willingness of every citizen to look to the law for the vindication of his wrongs and the protection of his property is the essence of civilization, . . . [the] one difference between . . . a [civilized] community and the jungle where a savage chief stands with a knotted club above the body of his dusky spouse to protect her and his simple holdings by the strength of his right arm. . . . When you defy courts and defy judges you lapse into barbarism, you relinquish all claim to civilization.

Stanley continued to try to shame his auditors through an appeal to Victorian parlor images, invoking the home as a sacred place and mothers and wives as its moral authorities:

> Holier than this temple of justice you would desecrate, more sacred than any cathedral lifting its slender spire toward the stars is the fireside. . . . I appeal from the wild and cruel passions of this hour to the sacred priestess of that altar. . . . Go back to your homes, go back to her who bore you in love and travail and who reared you in the fear of God. Go back and look into the gentle eyes of her who wears your name and whose children consecrate her fidelity and devotion, . . . and if they condemn me or this judge, come back and wreak your vengeance upon us both if you can.

In short, this persuasive speech, designed by and for the cultural milieu in which it was given, was interwoven with Victorian images of purity and morality, New South attitudes of white racial superiority, and an intensifying early-twentieth-century insistence on obedience to governmental and judicial authority at every level. Stanley, as a shrewd politician and a capable orator, effectively played on the various sentiments of his audience to win their agreement. That is, he was able to speak to, and within, the culture of his auditors to persuade them to accede to the region's "progressive" notion of justice in that era—a notion of justice that, for the accused black man, Lube Martin, translated into a quick trial and a death sentence carried out the following month. Such instances of "legal lynching" were symptomatic of the fact that governmental authority had not quite gained control of the "mob" in early-twentieth-century Kentucky but rather had reached a compromise with it. This was an accommodation the *Lexington Herald*—frequently more strident in racial matters than the Republican *Lexington Leader*—clearly understood and endorsed in its headlined declaration following Martin's trial: "Crowds Clamoring for Life of Black Are Appeased."[3]

Stanley's intervention at Murray took place near the end of the Progressive Era, a period marked by sweeping political and social reform movements growing out of changes wrought, in the South as elsewhere, by industrialization, immigration, and urbanization and by a rising business- and profession-based middle class whose social values included "order, morality, humanitarianism, efficiency and [economic] development." These times brought great prosperity for some, and the surging technological revolution led to, among other things, the automobile, the telephone, the phonograph, and the motion picture. However, there was also a growing sense of worsening social problems: extreme poverty, horrifying working conditions and escalating labor unrest, dreadful environmental damage, municipal political corruption, widespread addiction and vice, and discrimination against blacks and women, to name a few. The progressive reformers of the era were struggling to control these sweeping changes and solve their attendant problems in order to "create a cleaner, fairer society." The era of progressive reform is usually considered to encompass, roughly, the period from the 1890s to the United States' entry into World War I. However, historian Dewey Grantham has argued that southern progressivism did not lose its "vitality" until after the armistice. He claims that the war itself provided the South with a dynamic milieu for invigorating both the southern progressivist philosophy, which included a "compulsion to preserve cultural values" alongside an urge to expand the role of government in social planning and a

belief in "the value of efficiency and social control" for achieving modernization and social justice, and specific progressivist reform movements such as
expanded social welfare services, prohibition and other morality campaigns,
and female suffrage. The subtitle of Grantham's book on southern progressivism, "the reconciliation of progress and tradition," delineates his central
argument that a balanced tension, an "equilibrium," existed between "the
forces of modernization and . . . cultural tradition" in the South before and
during World War I and that this equilibrium degenerated into an increasingly acrimonious cultural conflict in the years afterward. In equilibrium or
otherwise, Lexington's cultural milieu in the prewar era was a swirling blend
of social forces, resulting in a public clamor of New South, progressive, and,
as war approached, increasingly nationalistic voices.[4]

A SOUTHERN CITY

In the years after 1900, two powerful and countervailing sociopolitical
forces seemed to be in contention in the American South. On the one hand,
at the end of the nineteenth century an imperialist impulse, overriding all anti-
imperialist objections, had resulted in the Spanish-American and Filipino-
American wars and in a nationalistic fervor that blurred and weakened
sectional differences. This fervor induced the imperialist apologist Albert
Beveridge to assert, "We are at last one people." On the other hand, even
though the South had changed profoundly in many ways since the end of
the Civil War, many southern whites refused to forget the war—that most
important symbol of sectionalism; they refused to reconcile themselves to
its outcome and aftermath or, most notably, to accept any change in matters
of race. Thus, "by later standards, virtually every white Southerner was racist." Moreover, even the most reform-minded southern progressives of the
era shared the conviction of the vast majority of southern whites that blacks'
racial inferiority and increasing "degeneracy" required disfranchisement and
strict segregation to maintain social control and order. Reacting with horror
to the bloody Wilmington race riot of 1898, African American attorney and
novelist Charles W. Chesnutt appealed for interracial harmony and understanding and for political and social equality for blacks in his 1901 novel
The Marrow of Tradition. The novel ends with a hopeful yet ominous plea:
"There's time enough, but none to spare."[5]

Chesnutt's book sold poorly and was mostly ignored by whites while Thomas Dixon's 1902 novel, *The Leopard's Spots,* the first part of a trilogy set in the Reconstruction South, sold more than a million copies and received great notoriety in both South and North. Dixon, whose personality and career have been described as "brilliant, complex, and colorful," was born in 1864 and grew up in western North Carolina during Reconstruction. He graduated from Wake Forest University in 1883 and attended Johns Hopkins, where he met lifelong friend Woodrow Wilson. After obtaining a law degree in North Carolina in 1885, Dixon started down a highly successful multiple-career path that would include law, the Baptist ministry, public lecturing, writing, acting, and the production of motion pictures. Dixon has now been almost forgotten, or when he is remembered, he is vehemently disparaged for his works fomenting white hatred and fear of blacks and unequivocally advocating strict racial separation. However, in the Progressive Era, many white Americans, southerners and otherwise, saw him as a vibrant intellectual figure of national stature and seemed to identify with, and endorse, his racial convictions as expressed in *The Leopard's Spots:* "Amalgamation simply mean[s] Africanization. . . . The rule that ha[s] no exception [is] that one drop of Negro blood makes a Negro. . . . *You cannot build in a Democracy a nation inside a nation of two antagonistic races. The future American must be an Anglo-Saxon or a Mulatto.*"[6]

If early-twentieth-century southern novels obsessively dwelled on the more dramatic markers of post–Civil War white southern culture, so too did Lexington (white-controlled) press accounts in this period. These markers included reverence for the Lost Cause, attitudes of racial superiority and the accompanying disparagement of blacks, and a preoccupation with black crime, lynching, and "legal lynching." Such accounts sketch the southern texture of the city's life before the First World War.

The Lost Cause

On the night of 2 April 1917 President Woodrow Wilson, seeking a declaration of war against Germany, told the assembled Congress that Germany was engaged in "warfare against mankind" and that America, by entering the war, would be "keeping the world safe for democracy." A different view was expressed by progressive Republican George W. Norris of Nebraska as the Senate debated the president's request on 4 April. Arguing, in opposition to the declaration of war, that the nation's wealthy had created the war craze and were pushing the country into the conflict to further enrich themselves, Senator Norris remarked, "I feel that we are about to put the dollar sign upon the American flag." Wilson himself had misgivings, and after his speech to Congress he said tearfully to his private secretary: "Think what it was they were applauding. My message today was a message of death for our young men. How strange it seems to applaud that." Regardless of the opposition, ambivalence, and misgivings, pro-war sentiment prevailed in Congress, and Wilson signed the declaration of war against Germany on 6 April 1917.[7]

Neither ambivalence nor misgivings were apparent two months later in the remarks of the Reverend W. O. Sadler of Paris, Kentucky, when he addressed an audience of 1,500 in the Lexington Cemetery at the Confederate Memorial Day exercises on 3 June. Sadler, according to the *Lexington Herald*, compared the European conflict to the Civil War, arguing that the earlier struggle had been based on a "misunderstanding," whereas the current war was based on a clear understanding of the situation and "must be prosecuted to victory" by a united country. His appeal for a united country notwithstanding, Sadler, in keeping with the occasion, praised Jefferson Davis as "the idol of the Southern people," argued that Lincoln had been a southerner at heart, and paid tribute to "the heroic deeds of the wearers of the gray." The event, complete with an elaborate musical program, was sponsored by the Lexington chapter of the United Daughters of the Confederacy (UDC), whose members capped the ceremony by strewing flowers on the graves of Confederate soldiers. This ceremonial tribute to the Lost Cause in the opening days of the United States' military involvement in World War I is representative of the strength of sectional feelings and southern sympathies that still existed in the region, even as the nation entered a new and larger war. These sympathies were expressed primarily in two organizations, the UDC and the Confederate Veterans Association, and in two annual events, Robert E. Lee's birthday in January and Confederate Memorial Day in June.[8]

First organized in the South in 1895, the UDC had at least three chapters in Lexington by the 1910s: the Lexington Chapter, the Major Otis S. Tenney Chapter, and the Bryan Station Chapter. These chapters sometimes met and worked separately and sometimes acted in concert as one organization. The membership of the UDC comprised Lexington's white social and economic elite, and the group met both in various members' homes and in its own "Confederate Room" in the Fayette County courthouse. The UDC's activities were regularly reported in both the news and society columns of the Lexington press. Embedded in two press accounts from 1916 are suggestions of the relative wealth and influence of the membership. The *Lexington Herald* noted in May that, for a regular UDC meeting at a private home on the Versailles Pike, "arrangements have been made to have the interurban cars stop directly in front of the residence." Moreover, at a time when the *Lexington Leader* reported only 1,500 automobiles in use in Fayette County, the members of the UDC were affluent enough not to have to depend on their influence over the interurban line. The *Herald* noted in June that a meeting at a home on the Bowman's Mill Pike had been attended by forty members, "nearly all of whom made the trip by automobile." Likewise suggestive of the members' affluence and influence, the UDC throughout the South "became involved in benevolent, educational, and social work," in addition to its commemorative events. In Lexington, these women engaged in various civic projects designed to raise money for benevolent causes, including an annual spelling match held in the circuit courtroom, with both adults and children participating. Although "everybody in Lexington interested in good spelling or in the philanthropic work of the Daughters of the Confederacy" was invited to the match, the "Social and Personal" column of the *Leader* made it clear that "many of the society people [would] attend and try their powers at spelling."[9]

Lexington was also the home of the John C. Breckinridge Chapter of the United Confederate Veterans Association of Kentucky. Organized across the South in the Gilded Age, the UCV held annual reunions in various southern cities during the 1910s. The local chapter in Lexington regularly sent representatives, and the Lexington press, particularly the Democratic *Lexington Herald,* paid tribute to these yearly gatherings. For instance, in a 1910 editorial in praise of the reunion being held that year in Mobile, Alabama, the *Herald,* though lamenting that the aging veterans were rapidly dying, saw hope in the assertion that "the children of those who believed in the Lost Cause have inherited their parent's love for it." In May 1916 the *Herald* gave extensive coverage to the Confederate veterans' reunion in Birmingham, Alabama. That reunion, attended by several southern governors, was a combined meeting of the UCV, the Sons of Confederate Veterans, and the Confederate Southern Memorial Association, and its program included many prominent speakers as well as various banquets, balls, and receptions. In addition to the usual rhetoric of reminiscence and reverence, two portentous reports came out of the 1916 reunion. First, presaging the country's entry into the European war, the Sons pledged their unconditional support to the government and President Wilson, "should it become necessary for the defense of the nation." Second, although the press reported that there were still 900 veterans' "camps" located throughout the South, it also noted that death was now taking 14 percent of the members each year. This toll spawned the rumor that this might be the last southern-wide reunion. This inexorable trend was also being felt at the local level. When the Breckinridge Chapter of the UCV met in Lexington in April 1915 to elect Major Philip Preston (P. P.) Johnston president of the chapter (due to the death of his predecessor), only sixteen members could be assembled, and most of the meeting was taken up with resolutions of tribute to recently deceased comrades. Indeed, Lexington press accounts suggest that the funerals of Confederate veterans were themselves elaborate public expressions of reverence for the Lost Cause. For instance, when New Hampshire native and Confederate major Otis S. Tenney (for whom a local chapter of the UDC was named) died in April 1916, his death and subsequent funeral at the First Presbyterian Church and interment in the Lexington Cemetery were given extensive front-page coverage in the *Herald*. The paper's eulogy of Tenney revealed the editor's own sentiments:

> Not born among us; inheriting traditions foreign to all things peculiar to Kentucky, he yet became in his . . . convictions [and] sentiments as truly a Kentuckian as any son she ever bore. Reared in an atmosphere intensely . . . anti-Southern, [yet] Morgan had no more gallant follower. . . . Nor did the years . . . weaken [Tenney's] convictions of the righteousness of the cause for which he fought.[10]

Major P. P. Johnston, first elected president of the local UCV in 1915 and reelected the following year, was a wealthy Thoroughbred and trotting horse breeder. He also served as president of the National Trotting Association from 1889 to 1917. In fact, Johnston can be seen as an exemplar of the social prominence of the UCV membership in Lexington. Born in Virginia in 1840, he joined the Confederacy in 1861 and served under General "Jeb" Stuart. After the war he moved to Lexington and studied law in the office of Colonel W. C. P. Breckinridge and at Kentucky University, graduating in 1869. During his career as an attorney he served in both houses of the Kentucky legislature; he was at one time chairman of the Democratic State Central and Executive Committee and was appointed in 1908 as adjutant general of the state by Governor Augustus Willson. Johnston spent a lot of time on his yacht in Florida in the early 1900s, where he occasionally hobnobbed with Andrew Carnegie. Johnston's son, Dr. Marius Early Johnston, had been retained by the Carnegie family in 1907 as one of their private physicians and would marry Carnegie's niece, Nancy Carnegie. Another of Johnston's sons, Philip Preston Johnston Jr., an engineer by training, managed his father's Lexington farms on the Bryan Station Pike after 1901 and married a member of Lexington's socially prominent Preston family, Margaret Wickliffe Preston, on 8 November 1917. Certainly the elder Johnston, through his background, wealth, and social and family connections, contributed to the air of gentility, prominence, and respectability surrounding the Lexington UCV and its activities during the Progressive Era.[11]

The ceremonial activities of the United Daughters of the Confederacy and the United Confederate Veterans in Lexington centered around two annual events commemorating the Lost Cause. The first, sponsored primarily by the UDC on 19 January each year, was the celebration of Robert E. Lee's birthday. In January 1910 the *Lexington Herald* carried an Associated Press article on a controversy that had erupted in Washington, D.C., over ceremonies honoring the Confederate general. However, there was not the slightest suggestion of any public contention in Lexington over the celebration of Lee's birthday at the Fayette County courthouse. Both the *Lexington Leader* and the *Herald* gave the event extensive coverage, with the *Herald's* front-page report appearing under the headline "Lexington Joins South in Honor of General Lee: Circuit Court Room Is Overcrowded by Lovers of Great Leader." This rather genteel program featured an address on Lee's life by attorney and historian Samuel M. Wilson, guitar solos by Henry Saxton, and choral selections by the State University Glee Club. Six years later, in 1916, the event featured an address by Colonel E. Polk Johnson of

Louisville and music by the Lexington High School Orchestra; following the program, there was a reception for Colonel Johnson in the Confederate Room in the courthouse. Less public celebrations of Lee's birthday were also held in the homes of the "ladies of the Confederacy" and were reported in the society columns of the *Herald*.[12]

Confederate Memorial Day was the second public ceremony observed each year in honor of the Lost Cause. The service conducted in 1916 was typical, and the rhetoric of the occasion is instructive. The national Memorial Day had been celebrated in the Lexington Cemetery on 30 May 1916, on which occasion flowers were placed on the graves of both Union and Confederate soldiers. The public rhetoric of that day's featured speaker, President R. H. Crossfield of Transylvania University, was conciliatory and unifying: "The war is over, and we now have One flag, one land, one heart, one hand, one nation evermore." Nonetheless, Confederate Memorial Day was celebrated in the same cemetery under the auspices of the UDC four days later on 3 June, Jefferson Davis's birthday. In fact, these ceremonies were invariably an opportunity to pay tribute to the president of the Confederacy, and the 1916 event was no exception. Former Kentucky governor James McCreary was on hand to introduce the two featured speakers. One was General John B. Castleman of Louisville, a veteran who was passionate in his tribute to Davis: "So long as one Confederate soldier lives upon this earth the name of Jefferson Davis will be enshrined within that heart as the illustrious leader of a sacred cause. O, lofty spirit of earth! The soul of Jefferson Davis! The embodiment of Southern chivalry! Surpassing in dignity and worth and glory all the great ones who toiled for . . . honor, . . . [he] stands unique among the names of men." The other, the Reverend W. E. Ellis of Paris, Kentucky, was equally adamant about the virtue of the South itself: "The South has nothing to take back, nothing to be ashamed of and nothing for which to apologize. Her chivalrous grace and splendor has been unequaled by nations past or present. [Her] character stands without reproach." Following these declarations of fealty to the Lost Cause and its leader, the Daughters scattered flowers on the graves of the Confederate dead, read aloud the name of every Confederate veteran buried in the Lexington Cemetery, and sang a number of southern-oriented songs, most notably "Dixie." The version of "Dixie" sung that day was printed in full in the *Lexington Herald*, and the following lines leave little doubt as to the sectional loyalties and racial sentiments of those who assembled to sing it:

> Look away, look away to Dixie,
> The land where rules the Anglo-Saxon
> The land of Davis, Lee and Jackson,
> Look away to Dixie's land.[13]

Racial Disparagement and the Humor of Humiliation

One of the era's most notable, and notorious, public expressions of the volatile combination of war, Reconstruction, and race was *The Birth of a Nation,* D. W. Griffith's film version of Thomas Dixon's novel *The Clansman.* In February 1915 Dixon, faced with the possibility that the movie might be suppressed due to its controversial nature, turned to his friend Woodrow Wilson, who agreed to view the film at the White House. The southern-born, Democratic president, moved and impressed by the movie, exclaimed afterward, "It is like writing history with lightning. And my only regret is that it is all so terribly true." The audacious Dixon then approached Douglas White, chief justice of the Supreme Court, and requested that he and the other justices view the film. White refused at first but then, upon learning that the film portrayed the original Ku Klux Klan, related to Dixon that he himself had been a member and agreed to view the movie. That same night *Birth of a Nation* was shown to the justices of the Supreme Court and several members of the House and Senate as well. Once such powerful patrons had viewed the film, Dixon was able to overcome all objections, and *Birth of a Nation* opened in New York on 3 March 1915 to immediate acclaim, notoriety, and controversy. Race riots and opposition by local boards of censorship accompanied the film's distribution across the nation. There is no question that the film glorified the Lost Cause and the Ku Klux Klan, condemned Reconstruction, and demonized and disparaged blacks at every turn. Dixon's biographer, Raymond Cook, put the matter plainly: "the Negro is depicted as obnoxious and as but little removed from barbarism. . . . Biased as the film is it is no wonder that it created such bitter controversy."[14]

Lexington escaped neither the film nor the controversy it engendered.

It was shown at the opera house for the first time between 20 and 26 March 1916. Gregory Waller, in his book about popular amusements in Lexington during this era, devotes nine pages to an analysis of local press accounts surrounding the prescreening controversy and postscreening reaction to the film and concludes that they reflected race relations in the city at the time. Indeed, despite protests and calls for censorship from the community's black intelligentsia and some influential segments of the white community as well, the film was shown to reportedly enthusiastic "overflow" crowds. Waller's extensive reading of local newspaper accounts of the city's experience with *Birth of a Nation* offers compelling evidence that Progressive Era Lexington was a place of New South racial attitudes and relations. Waller details the mixed, sometimes ambivalent, but seemingly always paternalistically racist reactions to *Birth of a Nation* by several of Lexington's white elites. One citizen worth mentioning that Waller cites in a related context is the "widely respected superintendent of schools, M. A. Cassidy." In his discussion of local attempts at film censorship, Waller quotes Cassidy as taking a strong stand against any "immoral . . . trashy, vulgar improbable motion picture"; the superintendent took an equally strong stand in favor of cultivating students' "taste for pure, pleasing and instructive motion pictures." Perhaps Cassidy had already been to the Louisville showing of *Birth of a Nation* when the *Lexington Herald* reported in early March 1916 that, "in discussing the film, 'The Birth of a Nation,' which is billed to show in Lexington the latter part of this month, M. A. Cassidy, superintendent of schools, said yesterday that he believed the picture contained unusual educational qualities, and endorsed its presentation in Lexington."[15]

In addition to the film's endorsement in the name of education by this locally esteemed educator, the *Herald* recounted endorsements of the film's historical "accuracy" by ordinary citizens recalling their own firsthand experiences. According to the *Herald*, after residents of the Kentucky Confederate Home viewed the film in Louisville, the veterans drafted a letter stating that they saw themselves "in those stirring scenes—for many of us were in the scenes depicted . . . when we were boys doing our duty and taking part in the fray. The scenes were wonderfully reproduced." Based on these Confederate veterans' remarks and those of the school superintendent, it is clear that the racial attitudes depicted in *Birth of a Nation* were not abhorrent to a wide spectrum of the white population. Racial attitudes were manifested in the white Lexington press in many other contexts as well, and one particular item clearly implies that the local (white) culture could tolerate—and perhaps even enjoy—trivializing, commercializing, and just plain "poking fun" at this otherwise serious, even volatile, topic. In April 1916 the *Herald,* in what was obviously meant to be a humorous play on words, ran a local hardware company's advertisement for screen doors and windows in which, above a large drawing of an insect, were the words: "Coming Again: 'The Birth of a Nation of Flies.'"[16]

Humor attending race—or rather the disparagement of blacks *as* humor—appeared in various forms in the local press during this era. First, there was the comic strip. For instance, in "Scoop the Cub Reporter," a strip appearing in the *Lexington Herald* in 1916, the jocularity was frequently based on the belittlement of blacks. In one episode a black janitor is depicted as a mentally incompetent fool, misunderstanding the simplest of instructions; in another, a jealous wife blackens her lecherous husband's face with burnt cork to make him so repugnant that "no skinny blonde thing will want to smile attchuh." The disparagement of blacks in the guise of humor found its way into the rhetoric of news columns as well. Reporting on the stabbing of one black woman by another in January 1916, the *Herald* suggested that the crime was the "result of a fight, sponsored by the God of free love and caused by the alienation of the affections of 'Lawrence.'" In 1916 the *Herald* ran a front-page story under the headline "Gold Fish Stolen; Negro Is Arrested." According to the article, "John Johnson is a negro, but he likes the sight of gold." Johnson, who "had money on the mind . . . but was shy on the coin," was standing in a Negro saloon on Water Street talking to his "dusky" girlfriend on the telephone when he "walled" his eyes and "spied" something gold in a bowl on the bar. Thinking it to be real gold, he grabbed a goldfish out of the bowl and ran down the street. The article reported that the fish was not in Johnson's possession when he was arrested, and police officers said, "he must have eaten it." The reporter obviously fabricated the motives behind the alleged behavior of the black man to make him appear laughably ignorant, foolish, and incompetent, as well as criminal and repulsive. Whatever the man's motives, his punishment meted out in court the following day was no joke—he received twenty days in jail and costs. No fabrication was necessary to amuse and entertain white readers in another 1916 *Herald* article under the headline "Negro Dances His Way to Freedom." It reported that a black man, Ollie Brown, who had been arrested for "using insulting language" toward a white performer in a minstrel show, had been freed only after he obeyed the judge's order to dance for the spectators in the courtroom.[17]

The hapless Ollie Brown had been arrested at a performance that was almost by definition a form of humor based on race. African American historian Kevin Gaines, in *Uplifting the Race,* emphasizes the racist, demeaning aspects of minstrelsy and argues that the genre was designed to depict blacks as immoral and subordinate. He states, "the most insidious aspect of minstrelsy, well into the twentieth century, was its mockery of African Americans' aspirations to equal status." Nevertheless, there is some evidence that minstrelsy, for whatever reason, was popular with blacks as well as whites. Minstrelsy provided entertainment that was apparently considered hilarious by whites and blacks alike throughout the New South, and professional minstrel shows were regularly booked at the Lexington Opera House in the early 1900s to entice both races to fill the theater seats. In addition to professional performances, amateur minstrel shows put on by local whites were a feature of Lexington life in the 1910s, and even high school students were enlisted in perpetuating the minstrel stereotypes that Gaines refers to as the "cultural dimension of white supremacy." In the spring of 1916 the *Lexington Herald* both promoted and reported on the fourth annual minstrel show performed at the opera house by students from Lexington's white Morton High School—an event designed to raise money for the school's athletic association. The paper referred to the student performers as "laugh producers [who] will appear as knights of the burnt cork."[18]

Although the white Lexington press promoted and participated in white Lexingtonians' amusement at the expense of their fellow black citizens, it also printed evidence of a harsh and sometimes hysterical wish by whites to disassociate themselves from blacks and the black community. Three examples illustrate this trend. In March 1916 the *Lexington Herald* reported that a white man, Jolly Duncan, was suing the paper for $31,000 because two years earlier it had wrongly referred to him as a Negro when it reported his conviction for forgery. Duncan alleged that because of that story, he had "almost" been placed in a cell with Negroes, his former friends and associates had shunned or ridiculed him, and "as a result of the mental and physical anguish caused him by the statement, he is now confined to his bed unable to move his body or feed himself." Perhaps less hysterical, but no less adamant, was the statement of Captain F. Van Der Ven of Lexington's Salvation Army. In February 1916 he wrote a letter to the *Herald* to clear up several misconceptions that might affect the organization's image and fund-raising efforts, including his emphatic reassurance that "there is no colored branch of the army in town." Harsh rhetoric toward blacks was not confined to the Democratic *Herald* but appeared in the Republican *Lexington Leader* as well. For instance, in January 1910 the *Leader* printed a large advertisement for *Pearson's* magazine with the headline "What Miscegenation Is Doing to Southern White Folks." The text began: "The crossing of black and white blood is becoming a distinct menace to the white race of the South—the purest Anglo-Saxon in this country."[19]

In George C. Wright's *A History of Blacks in Kentucky,* he notes that Desha Breckinridge, editor of the *Lexington Herald* in the years after 1900, opposed racial hatred and unequal treatment of blacks and condemned Dixon's *The Clansman,* yet he simultaneously championed white supremacy, strict segregation, and black disfranchisement—a position that we would now label both contradictory and paternalistic. In January 1916 Breckinridge's *Herald* printed an article that was the epitome of racial paternalism. The article sentimentally reminisced about the days of slavery in Savannah, Georgia, and described how elderly former slaves received Christmas gifts of sweaters and caps in 1915 from the benevolent son of a former slave owner. The article clearly implied that these ex-slaves had been better off under the slavery system, stating that the elderly blacks "were loquacious in their thanks. They curtsied and scraped their feet, and the air was full of 'god bless you, Masser,' and 'Tank you, Masser.' These expressions came from the ancient men and women of ebony hue who had passed from an environment where they were well cared for, well housed and fed into one which too often spelled hunger and want. Mr. Heyward had a good and kind word for each of the old negroes, who look upon him as a sort of twentieth-century Santa Claus." The *Herald* at times portrayed blacks in a positive, even heroic, light—as long as it could clearly situate the black person in a subordinate position. In January 1916 a white engineer was injured and in danger of drowning after a rock bridge abutment he was working on near Lexington collapsed. The *Herald's* headline—"Negro Assistant Rescues Engineer after He Falls in Cedar Creek"—and the accompanying text lauded and gave full credit to the black man who had rescued his employer at the risk of his own life.[20]

RACE AND CRIME

Unfortunately, Lexington press accounts featuring a positive image of blacks (however paternalistic) were often overshadowed if not rendered "invisible" by the many sensationalized accounts of black criminals and black crimes. Moreover, if the language of such accounts in the Gilded Age had been dehumanizing and brutal, the rhetoric surrounding black crime in the new century was scarcely less so. This rhetoric rendered *Negro* synonymous with *criminal,* and it perpetuated the menacing black stereotypes that fueled white anxiety and hatred. A sampling of Lexington headlines reveals the impact:

Reward Offered for Two Escaped Negroes
Desperate Negro in Death Cell at Paris
Negro Is Held on a Charge of Murder
Old Soldier Says Negro Took Money
Negro Is Held for Mistreating a Girl
Negro Charged with Malicious Shooting
Cynthiana Negro Admits Charge of Incendiarism
Negress Runs Amuck
Negro with Pistol Threatens Traveler

Although these examples appeared in the Democratic *Lexington Herald,* the Republican *Lexington Leader* was not above the use of inflammatory racial rhetoric either. For example, a May 1916 headline announced, "Wild Negro Cuts Up Three People."[21]

Writing in 1903, W. E. B. DuBois understood black crime as being largely the result of a racist southern social order: "In well-nigh the whole rural South the black farmers are peons, bound by law and custom to an economic slavery, from which the only escape is death or the penitentiary. In the . . . cities of the South the Negroes are a segregated servile caste, with restricted rights and privileges. . . . Taxation without representation is the rule of their political life. And the result of all this is . . . lawlessness and crime." DuBois rebuked those who associated crime primarily with blacks, arguing, "when you fasten crime upon this race as its peculiar trait, [blacks] answer that slavery was the arch-crime, and lynching and lawlessness its twin abortion." Across the "color line," the predominant view in the New South era among whites, according to Edward Ayers, was that black crime, committed by "bad niggers" who hated and disdained white authority, was out of control. This viewpoint led many white southerners to engage in, justify, or tolerate barbaric lynching and convict leasing systems. Ayers asserts that after the turn of the twentieth century, race relations in the South were often characterized by a situation in which "whites did not like the new generation of black people, . . . blacks longed for revenge, . . . [and] it seemed that the two races grew further apart each year." In 1906, the year of the Atlanta race riot, white fear and anger were fueled by that city's newspapers, where "accounts of black rape, murder, degeneration, and insolence filled [the] columns." Likewise, Lexington press accounts of crimes allegedly committed by blacks reflected and shaped white attitudes.[22]

Although the Gilded Age rhetoric of outright approval of lynching was essentially gone from the Lexington press by 1910, the *Herald* in particular continued to print numerous lynching stories in a rather matter-of-fact tone, with no explicit or implied outrage or even disapproval. In contrast, the *Lexington Leader*'s coverage expressed some notes of disapproval, however subtle, in its lynching stories. In some *Leader* articles the rhetoric at least indirectly disapproved of lynching, threatened lynching, and mob violence, characterizing these acts as something to be dreaded or to at least be apprehensive about. Headlines included phrases such as "lynching is feared" and "mob violence feared." By 1917 the *Leader* was openly editorializing against lynching as "hideous." Though the press attitude toward lynching and mob violence varied from unspoken acquiesce to explicit disapproval, the legal execution of blacks convicted of crimes against whites—"legal lynching," as it has been called—was reported with unanimous approval and satisfaction. For example, the *Herald* announced in a January 1910 headline that the gallows at Williamstown, Kentucky, had sent a Negro "into eternity" for his "brutal" assault on a white woman two months earlier. The following month the *Leader* reported on the simultaneous hanging of two blacks in the county jail at Kansas City, Missouri, two months after their arrest; the headline read: "Negroes Pay Penalty for Assault upon White Woman." Such executions, which quickly followed perfunctory trials before all-white juries, clearly suggest that although "claiming to be opposed to lynching, many white Kentuckians were perfectly content to see blacks legally executed."[23]

In addition to the nearly instantaneous executions of blacks for capital crimes, press accounts during the 1910s recorded the harsh sentences meted out to African Americans caught up in the judicial system for the crime of theft, petty and otherwise. According to the *Lexington Herald,* in Paris, Kentucky, in February 1910 a black man was sentenced to ninety days' hard labor for stealing brass and copper waste materials from a railroad yard, and another got thirty days for taking a tarpaulin. However, these punishments probably seemed lenient to the black man sentenced in January 1910 to five years in prison for taking a dollar from a white woman's apartment and to the black woman sentenced to three years for stealing a few articles of clothing. These were not isolated cases. On 6 January 1916 the *Lexington Leader* reported that a black man in Lexington had been sentenced to one year in prison for stealing $5, and on the previous day the *Herald* reported that a black man had been sentenced to six months for stealing a single pair of shoes from a Lexington shoe store. More "serious" thefts garnered even stiffer penalties. On 6 January 1910 the *Herald* reported that a local black man had been sentenced to five years in the penitentiary for stealing a steer, and on 3 February 1916 it reported the sentencing of another black man to two years and one day for stealing chickens from some backyard coops in Lexington. Sometimes the punishment was incredibly severe even when the theft was "petty." In April 1915 a Lexington judge sentenced a black man to ten years in the penitentiary for snatching a white woman's purse. Two incidents reported in the *Lexington Herald* in 1910 reveal how differently whites and blacks were treated in the local courts. Two black boys, ages nine and thirteen, who took a white man's buggy and drove it through the streets on a "joy ride" in February were sent away to reform school. In contrast, a few months later, when two State University students forcibly robbed a young black deliveryman at gunpoint outside their dormitory as a "joke," they were simply fined $100 plus court costs.[24]

If the treatment of blacks in Lexington's Progressive Era courtrooms can be described as harsh, an even stronger term is needed to characterize the authorities' reaction to black alleged criminals who attempted to elude or resist capture. The sensationalized press accounts of two such incidents became, briefly, serialized narratives of crime and race—archetypal "case histories" of white racial attitudes in the city.

In March 1916 the Lexington police considered Robert Rice, a thirty-year-old black man who went by the nickname "Buckeye," to be "one of the most desperate criminals [they had] ever had to cope with." The trouble began on the night of 24 February 1916 when a black man allegedly attacked two young white women walking on Rose Street between High Street and the railroad tracks. The two women screamed and fought their assailant, who ran away. The police immediately searched the downtown area and arrested Rice, who was identified by the two women as their attacker after some initial confusion and hesitation on their part. Rice—or "Buckeye," as the press usually referred to him—was charged with detaining a woman against her will and was lodged in the county jail. Approximately two weeks later, on 7 March, Rice (whom the *Lexington Herald* referred to as a "degenerate" in the next day's headline) and two other black prisoners overpowered their guards and escaped from the Fayette County Jail. Two days later the *Herald* reported that the escapees were still at large, despite the usual offer of a $25 reward for each of them. On 24 March the deputy jailer, acting on a tip that a "strange negro" had been spotted in the basement of St. Joseph's Hospital in the "colored ward," confronted Rice and exchanged gunfire with him in the midst of the patients. Neither man was wounded, but Rice escaped in the confusion. At this point, the *Herald* and the *Lexington Leader* reported that the police suspected "Buckeye" of several burglaries that had occurred since his escape, and Rice's prior prison terms had come to light, which, according to the *Leader*, "stamp[ed] him as a dangerous criminal." The *Herald* reported on 27 March that "Robert Rice, better known as 'Buckeye,' a negro desperado" had been captured the day before in a house on Thomas Street without violence. He had apparently hidden his revolver (later found) as the police approached and given up peacefully; he was placed in leg irons at the jail. On 19 April 1916, just over three weeks after his recapture, Rice was transferred to the State Reformatory in Frankfort to begin serving the term of twenty-four years meted out by the circuit court for his various offenses. Thus, justice was swift and, because he was not killed by the police or anyone else, "progressive."[25]

Perhaps not so progressive was the fate, two months later, of a black man the *Lexington Leader* described in its 3 June headline as the "Unknown

Negro." This label, repeatedly used by the Lexington press for unidentified blacks suspected of crimes, was doubtless related to what W. Fitzhugh Brundage has called the "growing fear of black criminality" among southern whites in the late nineteenth and early twentieth centuries—a fear that certain "classes" of blacks were getting out of control, especially the "black vagabonds." These "black vagabonds" were young black males, made migratory by economic and social disruption, who moved restlessly from place to place, strangers wherever they went. Hence, these migrants were often "unknown" to, and therefore feared by, the residents and authorities of any particular locale.[26]

Under its "Unknown Negro" headline, the *Lexington Leader* announced that a "strange black man" and four white residents of the city had been wounded by gunfire in a melee inside a house at 210 Ormsby Avenue. According to the account, a black man had been retained by Mrs. A. A. Robertson, a white woman, to mow her yard. Upon finishing the job, he entered the house and, without saying a word, pulled a pistol and shot at Mrs. Robertson, wounding her slightly. The sound of the pistol shot and the woman's screams brought a police detective and several other men running—men described by the paper as a "citizen's posse." When he was discovered hiding in an upstairs closet, the "frenzied" black man opened fire, wounding two of the "posse" members slightly. The detective was more severely wounded as he returned fire, seriously wounding the suspect. All the wounded parties were subsequently transported to St. Joseph's Hospital. Placed in the segregated "colored" ward, the suspect initially refused to give his name or address, but the police continued to interrogate him, despite his life-threatening wounds. Two days later he admitted that his name was Will Pearl and that he had come to Lexington from Chicago. He steadfastly refused to say why he had shot Mrs. Robertson. The police were not allowed to interview Mrs. Robertson because of her "extreme nervous condition," but the investigation revealed that Pearl had reportedly been sleeping outside near the railroad tracks for several weeks and that he had allegedly shot at and slightly wounded a black woman the week before when she refused to give him money. Though it provided no information about the condition of the black woman reportedly injured by Pearl, the *Lexington Herald* offered a detailed account of the suffering of each of the white persons wounded in the Ormsby Avenue shoot-out, all of whom quickly recovered. The account ended with the claim that "the negro's viciousness again asserted itself at the hospital yesterday when he attempted to bite one of the Sisters when she was giving him medicine." Believing that he was only "shamming," the police continued to question Pearl even though he complained of feeling extremely ill, but they learned only that he was originally from Mississippi. Although Pearl had originally been expected to recover, his condition worsened, and on 15 June a brief notice in the *Herald* announced that the "negro desperado" was dead.[27]

When Will Pearl died the matter was dropped, and the press never clarified exactly what happened at 210 Ormsby Avenue that June day. What was clear, however, was white Lexingtonians' fear of and fascination with black criminality. This attitude often fueled a readiness to accept the word of a white person directed against a black person and to publicly label a black suspect, especially a "stranger," as a vicious, frenzied desperado before a single allegation had been heard in court. In sum, those conditions that had characterized the city in the Gilded Age—racial segregation, distrust, disparagement, and injustice, along with a zealous enshrinement of the Lost Cause—were obviously still present in the 1910s, suggesting a rather static social climate. However, forces of change and reform were at work even within this context. During that same season in 1916 when "Buckeye" was taken to Frankfort in chains and Will Pearl died of his wounds in the "colored" ward, the city was preparing to open, on 4 July, a new "colored" park, Douglass Park, on the Georgetown Road for the "amusement and recreation . . . of the colored people of Lexington." The city budget for 1916 contained an appropriation of $4,000 for this purpose. New or improved municipal recreational facilities, even segregated facilities for blacks, were indicative of an impulse toward reform and modernization that swept through the South, and through the entire nation, during the Progressive Era.[28]

A PROGRESSIVE CITY

Grantham, in *Southern Progressivism*, has noted that "the South's perennial concern with the 'race question' no doubt gave a special color to its social reform; but it is apparent, nevertheless, that the South shared in the national reform ethos, . . . developing its own brand of progressivism." Grantham argues that progressivism in the early twentieth century, in the South as elsewhere, was a movement to reform society grounded in three major themes: social control and governmental regulation, social justice and the relief of human suffering, and social efficiency. In fact, however unjust it now appears, the racial climate in Lexington in the 1910s, characterized in part by strict segregation and harsh treatment of blacks by the legal authorities, accorded with many southern progressive reformers' arguments in favor of social control and regulation. These reformers, according to Grantham, believed that such practices and policies would "bring order and tranquillity to race relations, enable black people to develop their own institutions, and demonstrate to the whole nation that the South's social arrangements were workable." Race relations, of course, was only one aspect of the era's crowded reform agenda, which also included female suffrage, prohibition, control and regulation of business, restriction of child labor, the "scientific charity" movement, public health, and municipal reform. Wherever the reform impulse was directed, the progressive agenda was largely based on the idea that social improvement required greater efficiency in both business and governmental activities and that such efficiency would be achieved via scientific knowledge created or applied by professional experts. As it happened, the solutions these experts would create, advocate, and manage were increasingly manifested as governmental rather than private services, reflecting the fact that in the South, as elsewhere, progressivism was "a movement for positive government."[29]

A Parade of Experts

By 1916 *efficiency* had become something of a watchword in the Lexington press, where the concept was applied to a wide spectrum of issues. For example, one Dr. John Huber linked rest and diet with efficient workers and stated that workplace efficiency "decreases as fatigue begins." Likewise, the overall theme at the Kentucky Educational Association meeting held in April 1916 was "efficiency and economy in public education." The assembled educators reportedly asserted that most progressive boards of education in the state had come to recognize that merely attending the annual meeting of the KEA "increase[d] the teacher's efficiency at once." Apparently, they had concluded that just rubbing shoulders with and listening to one's colleagues made one a more efficient educator.[30]

The belief that expertise led to efficiency resulted in the influx of many "expert" consultants into the city and to a call for proficiency and special-ization in the provision of local services. In January 1916 the *Lexington Leader* announced that "progressive optimism" had infused the Board of Commerce meeting on 12 January, where the members expressed their dis-pleasure with the municipal government's position that the city parks were essentially "finished" and its related proposal to abolish the position of park superintendent. The board chose a committee to meet with city officials to plead that the position be continued and that "the work of enlarging the park system be prosecuted industriously and extensively." Apparently, the board's optimism was warranted and its influence felt, for in May 1916 the city procured the services of "park and landscape expert", John C. Olmsted, the son of Frederick Law Olmsted, a name synonymous with the development of the urban park in Victorian America. According to the *Lexington Herald,* John Olmsted had been in Lexington in 1905 to advise the city on landscaping Woodland Park and was now back in the city again, retained at a fee of $250 by the Park Commission, to make a "tour of inspection" of the city's parks and playground system and "pass on" plans for improvements drawn up by city officials. As if to reinforce Olmsted's credibility, in the headlines of the *Herald* he was invariably identi-fied as an "expert."[31]

Olmsted was not the only outside expert brought to Lexington in 1916 to advise and inform the city. Beneath the headline "Road Expert to Be Sent into Fayette," the *Lexington Herald* reported in May 1916 that Judge Frank A. Bullock's request for a "road expert" to advise on "specifications and materials" for the construction of county roads had been granted by the Bureau of Public Roads of the U.S. Department of Agriculture. And in March 1917 a *Herald* headline, "$165,000 Wasted on Pauper Idiots," summed up the opinion of Dr. Thomas Haines, director of the Kentucky Survey for the Commission on Provision for the Feeble-Minded, an arm of the National Committee for Mental Hygiene. He had addressed a meeting of Lexington's Associated Charities, the city's own organizational manifes-tation of the Progressive Era's scientific charity movement. Reflecting the progressive impulse toward institutionalization, Dr. Haines advised the assembled that Kentucky was wasting money by caring for the mentally challenged in its communities and that what these people needed, for their own protection and society's, "was the safekeeping an institution would give them." A similar opinion had been voiced the year before in a *Herald* article reprinted from the *Louisville Times* in which "institutional care for idiots and imbeciles" was advocated for reasons of efficiency, economy, and public protection and to prevent procreation among the "feeble-minded." These were the views and recommendations of Alexander Johnson, the field agent of the National Association for the Prevention of Feeble-Mindedness, and they appeared under the headline "Kentucky Custom of Dealing with Idiots Censured by Expert." This move toward seeking consultation from specialists or experts was also reflected in the provision of community services. For example, the *Herald* printed a long article in June 1916 touting the effectiveness of the local board of education's three new full-time truant officers under the headline "Truants in Lexington Schools Are Fewer Than Ever Before Due to Efficient System." Similarly, another *Herald* article in May 1916 detailed the demand of a citizens' committee headed by Mrs. Desha Breckinridge that the city jail employ a full-time female matron to work exclusively with the female prisoners.[32]

The Progressive Era impulse toward efficiency and specialized expertise that permeated Lexington's civic life was also felt on the city's campuses. For instance, when the students at State College appealed to the administration in 1910 for better dormitories, they argued that "the efficiency of the student in the classroom . . . is controlled to a large extent by his home [dormitory] life." In another example, in 1912 the student editors of the *Idea* encouraged Kentucky high school graduates to join them at State University by arguing, "The large modern-day problems are . . . being broken down into a multitude of special problems, each of which must undergo investigation by a specialist. . . . In other words, the professions are becoming more and more specialized, [and] the college man is able to meet these conditions of this new age." And, in tandem with the "expert" remarks of Haines and Johnson on the "feeble-minded," two student members of the genetics class at State University wrote a letter to the *Lexington Leader* in which they argued that much of the charity work being done was misdirected, in that it was encouraging the "reproduction of hereditary mental and physical unsoundness" by maintaining "defectives" outside of institutions and thereby allowing the "indiscriminate multiplication of imperfect humans."[33]

Municipal Reform

The impetus toward efficiency through expertise in the Progressive Era was joined with a call for structural change in municipal government so that it might better "apply business methods to public service" and thus improve and expand urban services. It was thought that such methods, along with improved services, would attract business investment and lead to economic growth. In addition, these structural reforms were aimed at reducing corruption in city governance in an era of political "bossism." Prominent among such reformist schemes was the city commission form of municipal government, which was replacing the mayor-council system in many cities throughout the South. Unlike under the city council system, in which each member was elected from a specific area, or ward, of the city, all commission members were elected from the city at large, and "each commissioner was responsible for a city department and functioned as both legislator and administrator." This progressive call for municipal reform had reached Lexington by 1910, when the *Lexington Leader* reprinted an article in support of the effort under the headline "Dead Cities Brought to Life: How the Commission Plan of Government Has Revived American Municipalities." Lexington voters adopted the commission plan in November 1911, and there is evidence in the Lexington press that this municipal reform was accompanied by a shift toward public rather than private responsibility for urban services. For instance, in the realm of public health and sanitation, what was initially a privately inspired and organized reform effort was subsequently appropriated by the city commissioners, who then carried out this responsibility in ways that the civic reformers never dreamed of.[34]

In the early twentieth century much of the South experienced recurring epidemics of infectious diseases, and a public health reform movement began "based on the diffused efforts of social reformers and pressure groups." In January 1910 the *Lexington Herald* published two separate reports announcing death and disease figures, by race and sex, for 1909. The leading cause of death in the city was the "white plague," or tuberculosis, which reportedly took eighty-eight lives during 1909, followed by pneumonia, which reportedly killed fifty-eight. Among the many other infectious or communicable diseases reported in the city during 1909 were smallpox, diphtheria, and typhoid fever. In this environment, where health had become linked with sanitation, the problem was confronted in both the public and private spheres. Aimed at the latter, the local press printed editorials, such as one in the *Lexington Leader* in April 1915 exhorting women to "increase the efficiency" of the "administration of household affairs" by adopting the "science of housekeeping." Articles were also directed at women—under such titles as "Living Scientifically," "Physical Culture and Scrubbing," and "Housework and Beauty"—linking housework and cleaning with science and efficiency and with hygiene, health, and physical beauty.[35]

The public sphere included the streets, alleys, and yards in front of and behind these (hopefully) efficiently and scientifically cleaned homes, and a concerted effort to clean up Lexington's public spaces began in the 1910s as a private reform effort. During this period, "clean-up and local improvement campaigns . . . [were] among the most prevalent reform endeavors in Southern towns and cities." Spearheaded by a local civic- and public health–minded private organization, the Clean City Club, "Clean-up Days" were organized in Lexington in 1915. Over a six-day period in April public school children, supervised by their teachers, raked and cleaned yards and carried refuse from basements, attics, yards, and alleys to the curbside. The use of pupils and teachers was aided, no doubt, by the fact that M. A. Cassidy, superintendent of schools, was chairman of the club's Clean-up Committee. The city government cooperated with and aided the effort by contracting with a private company to haul the rubbish generated by the campaign to the city's dumps. By all accounts, the effort was a great success. The *Lexington Leader* quipped after the first day: "The dumps are fat and germ hosts are in retreat. Clean-up forces have raised a thousand pyramids in a day. The spring dirt carnival is on." In a more serious vein, the same report quoted health officer Dr. Nathan Simmons as saying, "The work done within these six days will be reflected in the actual health of the city." At the end of the campaign the *Leader* printed Cassidy's open letter thanking all involved and asserting, "the work that has been done not only means a cleaner and healthier city, but more in the fine practical lesson in home and civic cleanliness which has been impressed upon the youth of the city." Although the yards, vacant lots, and back alleys may have been improved, there was still the matter of the public streets, and the *Lexington Herald* weighed in with an editorial unfavorably comparing Lexington with Charlotte, North Carolina. The editor had recently visited that city and noted that in Charlotte, never "did we see a heap of trash, a dirty gutter or wandering sheet of paper or fruit peeling, such as one meets in the busiest section of Lexington, and continually in the residence sections." A few days later the *Leader* reported that the Clean City Club had formed a Clean Streets Committee that would study the problem in Lexington before approaching city officials with "recommendations for cost and methods for efficient cleaning" of the streets.[36]

The 1915 Clean-up Days campaign was a privately inspired, benevolent, nonbureaucratic, community-wide endeavor that used the labor of schoolchildren while simultaneously teaching them a lesson in civic virtue. The effort was characterized by civic goodwill and cooperation between private reformers and city officials, who courteously provided assistance. The campaign's format and apparent success were emulated the following year in smaller surrounding towns, including Paris and Winchester. However, in Lexington in 1916, the endeavor quickly evolved and took on the characteristics of an autocratic, bureaucratically driven, government-controlled "service." The Clean City Club and Cassidy, with the endorsement of the local Civic League, once again approached Mayor James Rogers and the Board of Commissioners to provide appropriations for hauling the trash gathered during the Clean-up Days, and the *Lexington Herald* backed the effort with an editorial approving of the entire scheme, including the use of the city's schoolchildren: "Train them to look with disapproving eye upon dirty streets and alleys and gutters. Make it certain that when they come to have the authority . . . the town will be clean from center to circumference—clean physically, clean morally, clean educationally. Surely there can be no doubt that the city authorities will perpetuate the custom of a Clean Up Day." Nevertheless, despite favorable rhetoric and "custom," the mayor and the commissioners refused to appropriate funds. Moreover, they took the position that the "cleaning up of premises should be taken care of entirely at the expense of the owners and occupants of the property" and stated that the city's health officer would be going "thoroughly over the city, giving notice to clean up where required, and if not complied with, . . . to be followed by prosecution in police court." Although the *Herald* declared a few days later that "'Clean-Up-Day' Is Now Assured for Lexington" and noted that the Clean City Club endorsed the plan, in truth, the city had assumed complete control of this public health issue. The effort's "educational" and civic-benevolent aspects had been stripped away; its provisions were legally

prescribed and enforced, and the project was being overseen by a city bureaucrat rather than a private club of volunteers. Even though the commissioners characterized the actual cleanup of premises and the subsequent
removal of refuse as a private, individual responsibility rather than a public
service, this responsibility would be regulated, evaluated, and enforced by
the city bureaucracy. And so, in one year's time, Clean-up Day in Lexington
had evolved from a privately organized, benevolent, civic reform effort into
a "progressive," public, bureaucratized, governmental function under the
city's "reformed" municipal system. In sum, then, Lexington press accounts
suggest that in the 1910s—an era marked by the catchwords *efficiency* and
expertise, municipal reform, and increasing governmental control and regulation—the city was indeed awash in progressive influences.[37]

A City of Culture

Popular Culture

Popular culture in Lexington during the 1910s was perhaps most obviously
exemplified by the motion picture. The decade witnessed the opening of
several new movie theaters in Lexington, including the Ada Meade, the Ben
Ali, and the Strand. Arguably, motion pictures came to dominate the commercial entertainment market in the city. Nevertheless, popular entertainment did not reside in the movie theaters alone. Two other venues for public
amusement offer a glimpse into the nature of popular culture in Lexington
immediately prior to national mobilization for war: the Ransom Avenue
carnivals and the combined automobile and fashion show.[38]

On 17 April 1916 the *Lexington Herald* announced that the arrival of
the Con T. Kennedy Shows, a carnival traveling to the city from Knoxville,
Tennessee, for a one-week engagement, would be delayed due to the need to
remove the wheels from all the wagons aboard the show's thirty-car train so
they could pass through the numerous tunnels between the two cities. Despite this delay, the carnival, brought to Lexington under the auspices of the
local Shriners' Oleika Arab Patrol, arrived the following day and began to
set up its midway on the vacant land on Ransom Avenue between Main and
High streets. The show's proprietor, in a display of public relations savvy, invited all the employees of the city's two newspapers to attend the carnival free

of charge, and about sixty-five *Lexington Leader* employees and "more than a score" from the *Herald* took him up on the offer. They were in the company of "thousands of amusement seekers . . . treated to a wonderful exhibition of cleverness, beauty, and hair-raising performance." The *Herald*'s report of opening night made a point of suggesting that the attractions were "exhibitions that for clean, wholesome amusement are seldom seen." These attractions included "The Miracle," a tableau in which an apparently "charming" young woman assumed a number of guises, including the Statue of Liberty; "The Motordrome," a slanted wooden oval on which a daredevil performed motorcycle stunts "that would be credited only to one who is crazy"; four French midgets described by the *Herald* as "cute and charming . . . [and] jolly and winning as can be"; six-year-old Siamese twins joined at the hip, who provided "some of the best amusement at the show with their banters and jokes"; the "Garden of Allah," featuring an "oriental" dancer who impressed the *Herald*'s correspondent with her "gracefulness and ability"; and a "Wonders" show that featured "many interesting people."[39]

Mayor James Rogers and the Board of Commissioners agreed to close Ransom Avenue to motor traffic during the Kennedy Shows' presence for reasons of safety. In recognition of the potential public disorder these carnivals generated, Chief of Police J. J. Reagan placed two officers at the carnival during the day and five at night "to see that good order is maintained." Despite the police presence and the event's praise in the local press, several residents of East Main Street complained of gambling and other disorders at the Kennedy carnival and asked the city to "permit no more exhibitions of the kind" within its limits. Nevertheless, the Smith Greater Shows, billed as "the show that raised the standard," with "no immoral shows—no gambling" and featuring "Miss May Collier, the lady high diver," was advertised as coming to Lexington for the week of 29 May under the auspices of the Blue Grass Federation of Labor. Angered that their recent complaint and request had apparently been ignored, a committee of "East Main Street women" appeared at the mayor's office on the day the Smith carnival was scheduled to open at the Ransom Avenue location to protest its presence. In response, the mayor immediately met with the other commissioners, and they consulted the city's attorney as to their options. The attorney informed them that the Smith carnival had obtained a proper license to exhibit at the Ransom Avenue site, and nothing could be done to stop it. Mayor Rogers, who would not release the names of the protesting women to the press, took the public position that he was "very much put out" that the Federation of Labor had "put one over" on the city government, obtaining the license before the commissioners "got wise" to the fact that the labor-sponsored carnival would be held at the same spot where the Shriners' Kennedy carnival had engendered such vehement protest from nearby residents. Furthermore, he announced, an ordinance would soon be drafted to prohibit all carnivals within the city limits. It can be assumed from the mayor's swift and solicitous response that the protesters were of the respectable middle class. It can also be assumed that their objection was, in part, a censure of taste and class, in that the aforementioned ordinance referred to these carnivals as "annoying" and suggested that, among other detrimental effects, they brought "undesirable persons into the city."[40]

Despite such genteel complaints, the "Labor Carnival," as the *Lexington Leader* began to refer to it, opened with a street parade led by the carnival's band, and "all the labor unions of the city" marched in it. The proceeds of this carnival were to be devoted to the purchase of textbooks and the renovation of a hall in support of a series of six "university extension" lectures. This lecture series "on popular educational themes calculated to interest working men" had been developed in March 1916 after Henry Stites Barker, president of the University of Kentucky, met with and spoke before the local Federation of Labor. The first lecture was delivered at Labor Hall on 7 April by the dean of the graduate school, A. S. McKenzie, on "European and American Workingmen," and the second was presented by President Barker himself on 13 April on "Labor Laws." Joseph Kett has written about the complexities of the American university extension movement: its Chautauqua roots, the professoriat's attempts before 1900 to bring university culture into contact with the working class and thus bring its "influence to bear upon the Social Question (the gap between the social classes)," the loss of faith by the end of the nineteenth century in the ability of "culture" to bridge this gap, and the movement's subsequent revival—in part as a public relations ploy to enhance the image of the university—whereby vocationally oriented, "practical" courses were tailored by academic experts to the specific educational interests of various "diverse subpopulations" of a complex and segmented society. Reflecting this university extension "revival," the 1916 lectures were touted in the Lexington press as being of "practical

. . . value to the busy worker desirous of increasing his knowledge of useful information." In any case, this attempt to raise money via a carnival to further the practical education of local laboring men through university extension backfired, failing to show a profit and serving only to highlight local class animosities. Although attendance at the carnival had been good on opening night, subsequent bad weather contributed to the venture's poor financial return, prompting the Federation of Labor to request a refund of its $75 license fee for the event, since it had been sponsored for charitable and educational purposes. City officials angrily refused and later passed an ordinance prohibiting all future carnivals in the city. Despite the thousands of local citizens who had attended the two carnivals that spring, the mayor was quoted as saying that "street carnivals have had their day in Lexington, and are no longer a drawing card for the better element of our people."[41]

No such complaints of annoyance or fears of attracting the "undesirable" were publicly voiced when, at the end of March 1916, commercialism, civic pride, and ambition and "cheap amusement" merged in a singular event at the Shelburne Tobacco Warehouse on the southwest corner of Pine Street and South Broadway in Lexington. In January the *Lexington Herald* announced that plans were being drawn up to repeat the automobile show that had been held by the local Automobile Dealers Association for the first time the previous year in a tent downtown on Cheapside, next to the courthouse. Through February and early March various locations were explored before the Shelburne facility was selected as the site for the exhibit. Meanwhile, the secretary of the Chamber of Commerce, H. L. Burch, had brokered an arrangement between the "automobile men" and local retail clothing merchants to hold a combination automobile exhibit and spring fashion show. Several dates for this combined exhibition of cars and clothing were prematurely announced in the press, but after several scheduling delays, a four-day event running from 29 March through 1 April was finally settled on. By mid-March several committees had been formed by the auto and clothing retailers' associations, and the arrangements were being closely followed in the local press. The event would exhibit approximately ninety new automobiles provided by dealers not only from Lexington but also from Louisville, Cincinnati, and other cities, as well as a variety of automobile-related products ranging from oil to fire extinguishers. Moreover, in the words of the *Herald,* "as an instance of how complete the Automobile section really is, there is a booth advertising the merits of auto insurance."[42]

In addition to the automobile-related exhibits, there would be a "style" show for three successive evenings, featuring spring fashions provided by Lexington clothing merchants and modeled by eight female and six male students from the city's colleges. Interspersed with the fashion modeling, local amateur dancers would perform cakewalks, polkas, fox-trots, and other dance numbers, and music for the entire program would be provided by Miss Hogarty's Orchestra. The warehouse itself was elaborately decorated and equipped by a crew of twenty men. White wooden latticework was erected to conceal the ceiling and partition the individual exhibition booths, and hanging floral baskets filled with greenery (smilax) were strung from the ceiling and around the walls. Restrooms for both men and women were installed, and the women's restroom was furnished with maids and attendants throughout the event. In addition, the *Lexington Herald* observed that a "patriotic note prevails throughout—American flags . . . [and] the Confederate banner appear everywhere." Lighting was provided by hundreds of colored electric lightbulbs, and telephones were installed throughout the building "for the convenience of the patrons of the show." A stage was erected for the fashion show and dance performances, and it was decorated to be "a representation of a drawing room done in the latest black and white [wall]paper." Perhaps somewhat ironic in this rigidly segregated city, the combining of black and white in home decorating was apparently extremely fashionable and was promoted in the "Social and Personal" column of the *Herald:* "Black and white table china, black and white wall paper, black and white rugs and furniture and curtains and upholstery and hangings. . . . The fad . . . is one that persists. But the black and white dinner is rather new. . . . Of course, it is impossible to have all the food black and white, but the ingenious woman can think of many black and white combinations."[43]

Along with the twenty-nine automobile, tire, and parts and equipment exhibitors, other "subscribers" to the event included thirty-three local clothing stores, other merchants, banks, and the two local newspapers. Both papers printed glowing, promotional editorials touting the upcoming automobile and style show and asserting that it demonstrated Lexington's enterprising spirit and importance as a regional retail center. They argued that the event would contribute to the city's economic well-being and growth and suggested that, in the *Lexington Leader*'s words, the show "should have the cooperation of everyone interested in the prosperity of Lexington." The *Lexington Herald* went even further, attributing an educational component to the event: "Central Kentucky will get a liberal education in clothes and motor cars this week." The economic and educational themes were repeated in the mayor's proclamation for the attraction, printed in the *Lexington Leader* on opening day, 29 March 1916, in which he stated that the show's organizers had designed the event "for the better prosperity of this city, and the instruction of those who come . . . that they . . . may be edified and enlightened." The exhibit opened that afternoon with much fanfare, including speeches by the mayor and other notables and orchestral music. The crowd was large and reportedly enthusiastic, and many of the attendees arrived on the sixteen extra streetcars the Kentucky Traction and Terminal Company made available on its East Main–South Broadway line. Twenty-five thousand free tickets had been distributed by the participating businesses beforehand, and attendance on the first afternoon and evening exceeded all expectations, according to the *Lexington Herald:* "That crowd was the thing—it overshadowed the fashions and automobiles last night; more people than have ever been attracted to a similar event in the history of [this] center of Culture and Agriculture." With an estimated 5,000 people in the building at any one time, several cars on display were damaged by spectators climbing on them to see the fashion show on stage, and several women reportedly fainted in the stifling heat. Nevertheless, the first day was declared a great success, and the *Herald*'s headline was exuberant: "Thousands Learn of Mechanical Marvels of Machine Construction and Stop Test of Motors Only to Watch Dancing of Beautiful Blue Grass Girls Who Wear Fashion's Best with Natural Charm." Unfortunately, the *Herald* was unable to provide visual evidence of the crowds inside the warehouse because "the scarcity of chemicals due to the European war" allowed no flash photography, and the "time exposure" photograph printed on the front page captured only the cars, as "none of the visitors remain[ed] in front of the camera long enough to affect the film."[44]

During the entire four-day run of the automobile and style show, the press reported large crowds that were delighted by the decorations, the automobile exhibits, the fashion modeling, and the dancing and musical entertainment. The city seemed quite pleased with the event as a commercial and promotional venture. Certainly, the businesses involved declared it a great success; more than forty new automobiles were sold during the exhibit, and the "stimulated" clothing merchants announced plans to conduct a fall fashion show "on an even more elaborate plan." Sounding the only negative note, the *Lexington Leader* suggested that the Shelburne facility was unsuitable in "design and interior arrangement" for such a show. This was the beginning of the paper's campaign to promote the construction of a combination city hall, auto and style show building, and auditorium—a "municipal building" that would enable Lexington to compete with Louisville and other cities for the convention and exhibition trade. After all, the *Leader* argued, "these [shows] cannot be held on the streets nor can they be properly conducted in a tobacco warehouse." Beyond its economic importance, the show was a cultural event that offered free amusement to those crowds "representative of Lexington and the surrounding country," including "hundreds of country folk" who turned the event into "market-amusement, auto and style knowledge day[s]." There was no obvious attempt in the press to tie the exhibit to Lexington "society" or the city's "best people." Although the entertainment was respectable, and the event was touted as one of "edification and enlightenment" (with regard to motor cars and clothing styles, at least), there were no pretensions in the press rhetoric to gentility or "culture." The Automobile and Style Show of 1916 served the city's desire for commercial boosterism while offering the masses "cheap" (in this case, free) and popular amusement that was apparently more respectable and acceptable than street carnivals and certainly far less controversial than the film *Birth of a Nation*, which 15,000 people had reportedly seen at the Lexington Opera House the previous week.[45]

High Culture

If street carnivals and automobile and fashion shows, along with motion pictures, are suggestive of popular culture in Lexington during the 1910s, the activities of the Woman's Club of Central Kentucky (WCCK) are evocative of the city's genteel high culture and intellectual life during this same period. Thomas D. Clark, in his introduction to Loretta Brock's history of the WCCK, highlights this club as an important institutional example of Lexington's cultural heritage, citing it as a "dynamic force in the cultural advancement . . . of the community." Likewise, Nancy K. Forderhase, in a separate introduction to the same volume, suggests that the club contributed to the city's cultural life in the years before World War I through "the various Departments . . . [that] sponsored frequent musical and literary offerings, invited prominent speakers to give public lectures, and supported cultural and artistic programs for children." Such events would have been in keeping with the era's ideal of wedding intellectual pursuits with efficient public service. This ideal was pursued by many of these clubs and was perhaps best expressed by Mrs. Josiah E. Cowles, president of the General Federation of Women's Clubs, who argued in 1917, in true progressive form, that the club movement had evolved from small groups meeting for self-improvement to "great organizations . . . whose chief aim is public service, and who use study and culture as a means of increasing efficiency." From a much more recent perspective, it has been argued that these clubs, by "appropriating the ideology of selfless womanhood," used their public service projects to avoid charges of selfishness and thereby created "political cover for their self-improvement projects." Regardless of their motivation, these clubs provided their members with opportunities for both public service and intellectual self-improvement. Turning to the latter, the members of the WCCK sought to improve themselves through, among other things, the study of the dramatic arts.[46]

Through the 1910s the list of organized departments, functioning committees, and "study classes" of the Lexington-based Woman's Club of Central Kentucky read like a catalog of intellectual endeavors. For instance, the club's January 1910 calendar of activities, published in the *Lexington Herald,* included meetings of the Departments of Social Science, Literature, Fine Arts, and Current Events, along with meetings of the Shakespeare and Faust study classes. By February 1916 a Department of Drama Study had been added to the list. Brock has emphasized the WCCK's "fascination with drama," noting that drama had been nurtured in the Department of Literature before the formation of a separate drama department, and by 1914 a "Playgiving Committee" (also referred to in the *Herald* in 1916 as the "Play Producing Committee") had been created to stage plays for the club. In May 1916, for example, the *Herald* reported that the committee had arranged the club's "dramatic event of the year"—for an audience described as "one of the largest at the Club this season"—consisting of "two very charming plays": *How He Lied to Her Husband* by George Bernard Shaw, and *Chasing Butterflies: A Dramatic Trifle* by Elizabeth Cary Williamson. Williamson was described by the *Herald* as "one of Lexington's brightest and most attractive girls." Later that month the Drama Study Department presented its last program of the season, "one of entertainment rather than study," consisting of an "interpretation" of two one-act plays performed by, among others, Margaret Wickliffe Preston, who was also chairperson of the club's Department of Literature that year.[47]

The appeal of dramatic performance to the WCCK members fit well with the club movement's twofold impulse toward refinement and reform. First, the stage had long been associated with genteel culture and the intellectual life. For instance, an 1884 article in the *Atlantic Monthly* had argued that the role of the press should be similar to that of the stage, since "the stage's purpose was to entertain, cultivate, refine, and elevate." Second, along with pretensions to refinement, theatrical performances were seen in the early 1900s as having great educational potential by many progressive reformers, including Jane Addams, who "started to stress the potential of drama to inject force into moral truths that sounded hollow and platitudinous from the lectern" and instituted amateur theatrical performances at Hull House. Whether driven by genteel pretensions, intellectual interests, the progressive spirit, the pleasures attached to entertainment, or perhaps all these things, Margaret Preston and her fellow club members were certainly not alone in their fascination with drama and the staging of amateur plays. Nor were such interests and aspirations a new phenomenon in the city. Amateur theatrical performances had furnished entertainment in Lexington even before professional troupes first arrived in 1810. Nevertheless, the years preceding the United States' entry into World War I were particularly fertile for such endeavors. In May 1916 the *Lexington Herald* ran a full-page advertisement soliciting newspaper subscriptions that began with the Shakespearean quote "the play's the thing." It touted the city's many amusements, especially its wide variety of theatrical offerings, and bragged that "this city's never dull, for she gets the best things going in things theatrical." The claim of quality aside, Lexington certainly had "things going" in terms of the quantity of amateur offerings available. Press reports from 1916 suggest that the city was saturated with amateur theatrical performances staged by churches, schools, and civic organizations.[48]

Lexington's churches, both white and black, seemingly shared the WCCK's infatuation with dramatics. On 16 January 1916 the *Lexington Herald* announced that the members of St. Paul's Catholic Church had organized a dramatic club that would be giving several "amateur theatrical performances" during the course of the year. On the same day the *Lexington Leader* reported in its "Colored Notes" feature that the "drama known as 'The Deacon's Tribulations'" was to be given at the St. Paul African Methodist Episcopal Church and that admission for the performance would be ten cents. Fund-raising seems to have been an integral aspect of these performances. On 22 March the *Herald* reported that the Ida Harrison Mission Circle of the Central Christian Church had performed *Her First Assignment*—a "delightful little one-act play" that was "in every way . . . a brilliant success"—to raise money "for the good work the members are doing." The latter part of May 1916 was a particularly active time for church theatricals. For instance, organizations in the black First Baptist Church staged two plays during the month—*Cinderella* and *Men Not Wanted*. And at the Episcopal Christ Church Cathedral a play in two acts, *The Mission of Letty*, was staged by the church's Girls' Friendly Society.[49]

Along with church groups, grammar school and high school students frequently staged theatrical productions. In February 1916 the *Lexington Herald* reported that the annual play produced by the senior class of Morton High School that year, *Higbee of Harvard*, had filled the auditorium to capacity. That April the "entire student body" of the Chandler Normal School—a private high school for blacks founded in 1889 by the American Missionary Association of the Congregational Church on land adjoining the Georgetown and Newtown pikes—presented the operetta *Princess Chrysanthemum* at the Lexington Opera House. Tickets for the production, priced from fifteen to fifty cents, were sold at Ballard's Drugstore, and the *Lexington Leader* reported that "a good sized and appreciative audience" saw "unquestionably one of the most attractive performances of the season." In May the superintendent of the city's "colored" schools, William Fouse, announced in the *Leader*'s "Colored Notes" that Russell School would celebrate May Day with a performance of *The Minstrel, Basket Ball, Crowning the Queen of May, The Flying Machine*, and other "features," the profits to be used for "scholarship and school supplies." And at their June commencements, both the (white) city grammar schools and the (white) Fayette County grade schools and high schools gave performances consisting of singing, dancing, and the re-creation of historical scenes and tableaux.[50]

Lexington's civic organizations also embraced dramatics to raise money, promote their cause, or showcase their members' thespian talents. The Lexington Association for Infant Welfare, reporting on its activities and progress before the city's Board of Commissioners in January 1916, suggested that fund-raising was essential to its work and that "amateur theatricals" were effective "in keeping these lines of work in progress." Whereas fund-raising seemed to be the primary motivation of the Association for Infant Welfare, promotion of the organizational "cause" seemed to be the primary concern of the Fayette County Equal Rights Association, a women's rights organization founded in 1888, when it staged a one-act comedy, *How the Vote Was Won*, at the Phoenix Hotel in May 1915. Fund-raising, promotion, and artistic and social pretensions were combined when the members of the Daughters of the American Revolution (DAR) produced a program of three one-act plays interspersed with dance numbers on 4 March 1916 at the Ada Meade Theater. Promoting the event in its society column, the *Herald* suggested that it would be "of interest in society" and noted that "many box parties and theater parties will be given. There will be a crowded house for this delightful entertainment." DAR members and other "well known Lexington people" wrote, produced, and performed in this production, which was styled as a "Matinee Comique." In an incident perhaps symbolic of the complex social and economic tensions of the time, the performance was delayed for more than an hour when the theater's stage manager refused to raise the curtain after discovering that some of the members of the black orchestra hired for the event were nonunion. The orchestra leader possessed a union card, but some of his musicians did not. Finally, it was decided to pay the entire orchestra, ask the musicians to leave the building, and then use music "furnished by a Victrola" for the dance numbers.[51]

Perhaps the most ambitious amateur theatrical production taking place in Lexington in 1916, and certainly the one employing the largest number of residents in the cast, was the "Kirmess" staged at the Lexington Opera House on 15 and 16 February under the auspices of the Baby Milk Supply Society for the benefit of its Baby Milk Fund. The *Kirmess*, as the *Lexington Leader* explained to its readers, had originated in Europe, where it was a fair associated with a religious observance, but in this country it had come to mean an indoor entertainment, usually connected with charity fund-raising. Initially conceived as a relatively modest undertaking, the idea stimulated the imagination of several of the city's social elites, and soon plans were under way for a major theatrical and social affair. The *Lexington Herald* began touting the event as the largest amateur show ever held on a local stage. According to the plans, which were closely followed by the press, the Kirmess itself was to be a musical and dance extravaganza complete with a large orchestra, elaborate costumes and scenery, and several separate acts, or "scenes," carrying titles such as "The Bohemians," "The Midsummer Night's Dream," and "The Cabaret Scene." The production would employ an all-volunteer cast of 350 young "society" men, women, and children. In addition, a king and queen of the Kirmess would be crowned on opening night, and it was soon announced that the king for the first night would be Governor A. O. Stanley. Lieutenant Governor James Black would serve as king on the second night, with a young debutante, Miss Cary Gratz Johnstone, "one of the most beautiful and most charming young ladies in the whole State of Kentucky," serving as the queen.[52]

Along with the performance at the opera house, the organizers planned a massive street parade to be held in conjunction with the event. Designed to include four brass bands, including one from the state university; fire department and mounted police contingents; and more than seventy-five "gaily decorated automobiles" carrying all the Kirmess singers and dancers in full costume, as well as the Board of Commissioners and other city officials, the Kirmess Parade was scheduled for Saturday, the twelfth. It would begin and end in front of the Phoenix Hotel, where Mayor Rogers would present Governor Stanley with the keys to the city. A full dress rehearsal of the Kirmess performance would take place at the hotel immediately after the parade. Also planned was the Kirmess Ball, to be held at the Phoenix Hotel following the last performance on the night of the sixteenth. The ball was clearly a "society" affair, and among those on the reception committee were such notables as Governor Stanley, Mayor Rogers, Desha Breckinridge, and Henry Stites Barker and their respective spouses.[53]

Not everything went as planned. First, Saturday's street parade had to be canceled due to rain. It was rescheduled for Monday night, only to be canceled again due to snow and extreme cold (the temperature dropped to two degrees Fahrenheit that evening). Second, a controversy arose over one of the Kirmess scenes to be enacted. The *Lexington Herald* reported rumors that the cabaret scene would be "positively naughty," with those "young society men and women" taking part smoking cigarettes and drinking "real" wine "in full view of the audience." This immediately created an uproar among the families of the participants, and the Kirmess organizers had to ask the *Lexington Leader* to announce that the "ladies connected with the Kirmess performances indignantly deny that anything ugly will be permitted." Finally, Governor Stanley and Lieutenant Governor Black backed out at the last minute and did not attend. Despite these setbacks, the Kirmess was performed, $1,200 was raised for the Baby Milk Fund, and the "grand" ball after the final night's performance was described as a "charming and brilliant gathering." Reviewing the Kirmess, the *Herald* exuberantly declared that "perhaps never in the history of amateur theatricals in this community did so many prominent and talented young Lexingtonians participate in a similar enterprise." The Kirmess had been an opportunity not only for the popular exercise of amateur theatrics and charitable endeavor but also for a public display of the cultural pretensions of Lexington's "prominent" class.[54]

Members of Lexington's gentry class also approached the dramatic arts in ways more reflective and certainly less exhibitionistic and grandiose than the Kirmess. One such approach was the intellectual study of drama as artistic and literary expression. Beginning on 17 January 1916 Elizabeth Shelby Kincaid offered a series of ten lectures on modern art and ethics as reflected in contemporary drama. Following each lecture, held on consecutive Monday afternoons at Kincaid's home at 423 West Second Street in Lexington, there was the "usual charming social hour," complete with tea, cakes, and conversation. Kincaid, one of the first three female students to be admitted to State College in the early 1880s, was both the daughter and the sister of prominent members of the State College Board of Trustees. She had been hired by the school in 1903, though not formally as a member of the faculty, to lecture on English literature and literary criticism. Her freelance lecture series, however, was not under the auspices of the university; nor was it a program of the WCCK, even though there were many eminent club members among the fifty-odd attendees. Participants included Mrs. Wickliffe Preston, former president of the WCCK from 1906 to 1908 and 1910 to 1912; her daughter, Margaret Preston, chair of the club's Department of

Literature; Laura Kincaid, chair of the club's Department of Social Service; and Mrs. Charles Berryman, leader of the club's 1915 project to open the first public art museum in Lexington in Gratz Park. Also present was Cary Gratz Johnstone, the queen of that February's Kirmess.[55]

Elizabeth Kincaid's remarks to her genteel, intellectually aspiring followers were acknowledged each week by the local press, particularly by the *Lexington Leader,* which published detailed descriptions of and long excerpts from her lectures in its society column. Her first lecture was an introductory one in which she outlined the basic theme of the series. This theme was grounded in an epistemological and axiological certitude holding, in her words, that artistic beauty, truth, and ethics "have fixed qualities and are really subject to no changes in time or interpretation." From this basic assumption she argued (1) that society had gone astray because it had reached such a high level of materialism, doubt, and skepticism that humanity had been "set up in place of God and Creed"; (2) that the dominant idea in the arts had become one of revolt against accepted beliefs and institutions; and (3) that modern drama often "attempts . . . to overthrow established ideas of right, charity towards all sin now being the ruling thought." She perceived this trend in the contemporary arts as a "shallow and lulling" sentimentality, and she "protested against the best people giving support to trashy plays and witless musical comedies."[56]

Each of the nine weekly lectures that followed was devoted to a synopsis of a contemporary drama, often one currently or recently playing on the stage in New York or elsewhere, and a critique of the play and its author based on the thesis set forth in the introductory lecture—a thesis that held, in short, that modernity had led to error: "The chief tenet of the modern thinker is charity but charity to the wrongdoer, their hardness towards intolerance is far greater than the opposition to evil." Kincaid emphasized this viewpoint throughout the course of lectures. For instance, on 14 February she reviewed and critiqued a drama currently being performed on the New York stage. The play, *Searchlights,* had been written in 1915 by the British playwright and author Horace Annesley Vachell, whose only son had been killed in the European war that same year. Even though Kincaid gave a brief nod of approval to Vachell's use of the war as a symbolic searchlight illuminating the "finer impulses of sacrifice," her remarks were largely an attack on the author's motives, style, and theme. Arguing that "no man can work both well and hastily," she suggested that *Searchlights* had been rapidly and carelessly turned out to satisfy "the commercial spirit of the age," and she labeled it a piece of literature "loose and flimsy in style, cheap in word and phrase, and lacking . . . the principles of truth." Nevertheless, she explained, she had chosen the play for the lecture series because it was "in accord with the idea of a modern drama," in that it depicted and represented "a protest [which] is distinctly modern, never against the error but against the creed and custom which consider it wrong, the emphasis constantly placed where it does not belong. . . . This modern sentimental interpretation manifests a gentleness towards sin and a relentlessness towards anything which protests against the wrongdoer." In contrast, in her lecture of 6 March she praised *The Faithful,* a play by John Edward Masefield (who would become poet laureate of England in 1930), as a drama Shakespearean in nature in terms of its true depiction of the inevitable results of sin. And she described Masefield as "tower[ing] above his fellows . . . [and] out of harmony with the writers of the present time who are destructive and revolutionary."[57]

The theme and tone running through Kincaid's series of lectures, and their reportedly enthusiastic reception by her auditors, suggest that a segment of Lexingtonians who partook of the pleasures of "high culture" were seeking a bulwark against the forces of change and a reassuring reaffirmation of tradition, stability, and the status quo. This impulse was perhaps understandable at a time when events in the world beyond Lexington offered no such assurance of stability, as the inhabitants of the city prepared for the coming of war.

A PREPARED CITY

By 1916 news coverage and editorial opinion in the local press were preparing Lexingtonians for the fortitude, discipline, and sacrifice that would be required by the nation's participation in the First World War. At the beginning of the European war in 1914, there was no unanimity of opinion in Kentucky regarding the belligerents, and most Kentuckians generally favored isolation and neutrality. However, by May 1915 German submarines (U-boats) had sunk the *Lusitania* and thereby killed 114 Americans. The attacks on Allied shipping continued for the remainder of the year and were still being perpetrated up until May 1916, when threats from the Wilson administration led the Germans to temporarily suspend U-boat operations. The *Lexington Herald*'s 21 April 1916 editorial made it quite clear where the paper stood. The editorial cited the Germans' "inhuman and barbaric warfare against non-combatants" and their "submarine brutality," and it staunchly backed President Wilson's March 1916 ultimatum to the German government. The following spring, as submarine attacks resumed and formal hostilities with Germany approached, the *Lexington Leader* was likewise in full cry with an extensive series of editorials—all printed prior to Wilson's formal appeal to Congress for a declaration of war on 2 April—suggesting that (1) the pacifists were wrong in opposing military preparedness, (2) universal military training (conscription) was a good idea and would be helpful to the nation's youth, (3) war with Germany was inevitable if the United States was to avoid humiliation, and (4) "the voice of the American press is for war." Meanwhile, in May 1916 the *Herald* had printed a large drawing by George Willard Bonte of a skeletal apparition of death wading in the ocean and guiding a German submarine with its hands. Superimposed on the drawing was a poem, also by Bonte, entitled *The Iron Shark*. The poem is repeated here, in part, to suggest the press's power to play on and shape the attitudes and emotions of the city's inhabitants:

> A demon hand guides the Stygian craft—
> A demon crew of the imps of hell
> Await the signal, fore and aft,
> To vomit a brimstone shell. . . .
> Stealthily creeping within close range,
> A ship's gray hull will burst,
> ·And feed to the deep-sea monster strange
> The women and children first.
> For the Iron Shark's work is to kill the breed
> That for years to come will fight
> To free mankind from Attila's Greed.[58]

Pancho Villa

The tensions produced by German submarine warfare were heightened in the spring of 1916 by a threat to American interests along the Mexican border. Unstable governments in Mexico had repeatedly been toppled by revolutionary forces, and the Wilson administration chose to get involved in Mexican affairs both diplomatically and militarily. In 1915 Washington gave preliminary recognition to a Mexican government led by the successful revolutionist Venustiano Carranza, after having briefly flirted with Carranza's former lieutenant and now rival, Pancho Villa. Villa felt betrayed by the U.S. government, which had once looked on him favorably as a force for democracy. In an apparent act of revenge, his soldiers killed American citizens in Mexico in January 1916 and then across the border in New Mexico in March 1916. In response, Wilson, with the consent of the Carranza government, sent American troops under the command of General John J. Pershing across the border in pursuit of Villa and his "bandits." Over the next year, the American troops failed to effectively engage Villa's forces or to capture him, succeeding only in clashing with the Mexican army and provoking a military and diplomatic confrontation with the Carranza government. By March 1917 Wilson was largely preoccupied by the war in Europe, so he withdrew American forces and formally recognized the Carranza government, having, by one account, "spent four years of effort and [having] gained nothing but a lasting Mexican hostility toward the United States."[59]

Kentuckians experienced the campaign against Villa in at least three ways: firsthand, indirectly, and vicariously through the press. For an example suggesting all three, the *Lexington Leader* in January 1917 explained to its readers that Governor A. O. Stanley had been forced to confront the Murray lynch mob with no security forces because "almost every available member of the Kentucky National Guard [is] mobilized on the Mexican border." As the Villa episode began to unfold in the spring of 1916, it was dramatized by the *Lexington Herald* in the racially charged language of the time, and the reports vilified the Mexicans in every way. On 10 March the *Herald* reported Villa's attack on Columbus, New Mexico, in which sixteen Americans were killed; the initial American military response was likewise reported, including one front-page headline that announced, "One Hundred of Greasers Killed." Characterizing Villa as an "outlawed Mexican Bandit," the lead article emphasized the chase given by the troopers of the Thirteenth U.S. Cavalry following the surprise raid on Columbus and suggested that the Mexicans had been bested in a fight five miles south of the border. A companion article on the same page quoted an American woman who claimed that while being held captive by Villa for nine days she heard him say that he intended to seek aid from Germany and Japan to "help me kill Americans." Further arousal of jingoistic sentiment followed. On 27 March, under the headline "Lexington Boy on Border Anxious to Pursue Villa," the *Herald* printed a letter to the editor from Twelfth Infantry private Orville Bradly. Bradly, who thought that "a letter from the front might be interesting" to the public, wrote that his unit was "doing border duty, protecting the border peoples from any further raids by these blood-thirsty Greaser outlaws." However, he wrote, they were all anxious to "get into Mexico after Villa and his band. . . . It can't come too quick for us boys."[60]

The provocative rhetoric continued in the *Lexington Herald* in the weeks ahead. On 14 April 1916 the *Herald* editorialized, under the title "Villa the Mexican Submarine," that there was no difference between Villa and the German naval officer who had sunk the *Lusitania;* both had "murdered peaceful American citizens." The editorial supported the effort to pursue Villa across the border into Mexico and insisted that this be done, even though the job would be harder than "the capture of Geronimo, the Apache chief, [which] was difficult enough." On 16 April the *Herald* expressed its unhappiness with the Mexican government's request that U.S. forces withdraw and allow it to deal with Villa, arguing that President Carranza "would not hesitate to betray the whole American force." The paper insisted that President Wilson fully support the American troops in Mexico until Villa had been dealt with. The editorial also suggested that even though the United States possessed many advantages, including being the richest nation on earth, having limitless resources, and having "the largest homogeneous population to be found among the Caucasian races," the leaders in Washington had not utilized these advantages to prepare for the inevitable problems with Mexico. This, the editor argued, had led to the current inability to bring Villa to heel and to deal forcefully with the Mexican government. In subsequent editorials the *Herald* stridently maintained that American prestige was on the line in the Mexican situation; it opposed negotiations with Carranza as humiliating to the United States and suggested that the situation had become a "comic opera" due to Washington's inability to capture Villa. In addition, with fear of Germany hovering in the background, the paper was adamant in linking the Mexican issue to the larger concern over national preparedness: "Just how criminally negligent our Nation has been in the matter of national defense could not have been better illustrated than it has been by this serio-comic chase of the one-time patriot Villa. . . . Between preparedness and calamity we must make [a] choice, and make it now. . . . The *Herald* has besought our representatives in Congress to take immediate action in favor of adequate defenses."[61]

The Preparedness Parade

The *Lexington Herald*'s editorials stressing the urgent need for national military preparedness were reinforcing and exposing the paper's readers to sentiments widely held across the nation. It has been argued that the incidents on the Mexican border in 1916 were a "dress rehearsal" for U.S. military involvement in Europe and that the Villa affair gave impetus to an already established, organized movement in the United States agitating for industrial and military preparedness for national defense. This movement manifested itself, in part, through street parades and demonstrations in many cities in support of preparedness. There were even summer training camps for civilians that offered "military" training to those college students, young professionals, and businessmen willing to pay for the experience. Even prior to the start of war in Europe in 1914, a small but vocal and influential minority had expressed its unhappiness with the state of the country's military forces and openly called for a national program to prepare the United States to defend itself and prosecute its military interests. After 1914 this preparedness lobby, led by such public figures as Theodore Roosevelt, grew in power and influence despite the opposition of women's organizations, pacifists, labor groups, and powerful individuals, including Henry Ford.[62]

Editorials and news reports kept the concept of preparedness before the Lexington public in 1916. The *Lexington Herald* editorialized that "Preparedness Brings Peace" and reported on huge preparedness parades held in larger cities, such as the 13 May parade in New York in which 150,000 people marched in "the greatest civil parade in the history of the country," and the 3 June Chicago parade that boasted more than a million spectators and took "eleven and one-half hours in passing." Shortly after the Chicago demonstration, Lexingtonians, caught up in the national fervor, began preparations for their own preparedness parade. On 9 June 1916 the *Lexington Herald* reported on a meeting of the Sons of the American Revolution at the

Fayette National Bank during which the organization's president, General Roger D. Williams, suggested that Lexington have a "mammoth Preparedness Parade" on Flag Day the following Wednesday. The event emulated the spirit of "similar events held in many other cities in the past few days," and it was asserted that such a demonstration would be "truly indicative of the sentiment of Lexingtonians and the people of Central Kentucky on the subject of preparedness."[63]

A committee was immediately formed to promote and organize the event, and much like the Kirmess in February, the preparedness parade almost instantly became a major community undertaking. Both Lexington papers gave the event support and prominent coverage from the outset, and with only six days to organize the parade, the role of the local press was crucial. This was explicitly asserted by the *Herald,* whose publisher, Desha Breckinridge, was a member of the Sons and had been at the 8 June meeting: "Details of the demonstration will be published daily in the city newspapers, and those who are to participate are requested to keep informed in that way . . . as it would be virtually impossible to reach all concerned by any other means." On 9 June the *Herald* published in the "Social and Personal" column an "urgent invitation" to the women of Lexington and central Kentucky to participate in the parade, stating, "these patriotic demonstrations have been given in many of the large cities and all the women feel it a duty and privilege to be among the 'paraders.'" On the same day the *Lexington Leader* published a long list of organizations and individuals being invited to participate and announced, "it is the purpose of the committee . . . to interest every man, woman and child in Central Kentucky to march in the big parade." The *Herald* weighed in with editorials decrying the grave threats facing the country—threats that demanded national preparedness—and strongly implied that every patriotic citizen would be at the parade. Thus, the *Herald* could suggest by Sunday, 11 June, that the parade would be "the biggest in the city's history" and announced that more than forty businesses had agreed to decorate their storefronts with American flags and bunting in the national colors and to give their employees time off to attend the parade and the speeches to follow.[64]

By Monday, 12 June, the *Lexington Leader* reported that the call had gone out to, and been accepted by, many local organizations to participate in the upcoming parade, including several fraternal and labor groups. In addition, Unionist members of the local post of the Grand Army of the Republic had agreed to march, and Major P. P. Johnston, president of the Breckinridge Chapter of the United Confederate Veterans, had accepted the invitation on behalf of that organization. The *Leader* also reported that a meeting of the Fayette Equal Rights Association (FERA) had been held on the parlor floor of the Phoenix Hotel and that the suffrage organization had agreed to participate as a body in the march, placing arrangements in the hands of three prominent members. One of the three was Margaret Preston, the FERA's recording secretary at the time. She recalled in her diary attending this meeting with her mother and being invited to play the role of Columbia, the Goddess of Liberty, at the upcoming parade. Such roles for women in public ceremonies were common after the Civil War and have been described as "feminine allegories [of civic virtue]; . . . civic symbolism conveyed by living women." Columbia often represented Liberty and the United States in the World War I era, and the image of the "stern goddess" was frequently used in American war propaganda, sometimes appearing as "a formidable-looking woman clad in a long, nightgown-like garment with a steel helmet on her head . . . [and] holding an American flag."[65]

It was not surprising that Margaret Preston was chosen for this role of honor in the parade: she was a member of a locally prominent family, was vice president of the WCCK, and had many influential friends in the city, including her future father-in-law, Major P. P. Johnston, who was serving as grand marshal of the preparedness parade. The *Lexington Herald* referred to Preston as both a "young girl" (she was thirty-one at the time) and a "popular woman" who would be representing Columbia and "guarding Old Glory on the platform." On the reviewing stand she would be flanked by Colonel Richard C. Morgan (the eighty-year-old brother of General John Hunt Morgan) of the United Confederate Veterans in a gray uniform and Captain Jack Sheehan of the Grand Army of the Republic in a blue uniform "as guards of honor . . . [to] symbolize Kentucky's motto: 'In Union There is Strength.'" Other participants in the "guard of honor" on the platform would be dressed in the uniforms of the army and navy to represent the need for current military preparedness.[66]

The parade would form up at Third Street and Broadway, turn left at Main Street, and pass the reviewing stand at the Fayette County courthouse; from there it would proceed out to the auditorium at Woodland Park, where patriotic speeches would be given, including a keynote address by Dr. W. A. Ganfield, president of nearby Centre College. On the morning of the parade the *Lexington Herald* announced that "Everything is in Readiness for the Big Celebration" and published a list of more than fifty organizations, groups of government officials, professional associations, and others participating in the march. The *Herald* also noted that arrangements had been made to include "the colored people," at their request, but with "the time being too short," the blacks could not organize "their marchers [so] they decided to have a preparedness parade of their own on July 4. . . . For this reason there will be no colored people in the parade today." (As it turned out, black citizens of the city held a parade on 4 July, but it was part of the dedication ceremony for the opening of Frederick Douglass Park, "the first public park for colored people ever opened in Lexington," and there was no mention of "preparedness" in the press in connection with the event.) That afternoon, following the parade and ceremonies, the *Lexington Leader,* under the headline "The Bluegrass Raises Its Voice for Preparedness," asserted that 20,000 people had watched from the sidewalks and buildings as 10,000 people had marched in the two-mile-long procession that took an hour to pass the reviewing stand. The following day the *Herald* put the number of marchers, almost all of whom were carrying American flags, at 5,000, but it agreed in every other respect with the *Leader* that "the patriotic sentiment of National preparedness [was] impressively emphasized by the citizens of Lexington and Central Kentucky today."[67]

The *Lexington Herald*'s coverage of the Flag Day ceremonies gave extensive space to Centre College president Ganfield's speech at the auditorium in Woodland Park. In that speech he depicted Civilization as an allegorical female character and offered his suggestion for a fitting tribute to the women of America, saying, "upon the great monument, erected to and inscribed with the names of the Nation's famous, should be left a single block, snow white, and dedicated to American women." Perhaps in the spirit of such rhetoric, both newspapers paid tribute to Margaret Preston's depiction of Columbia, the *Lexington Leader* referring to her as "queenly," and the *Herald* publishing a large front-page picture of her and the "guards of honor," noting proudly that she was the granddaughter of General William Preston "of Mexican war fame." Recalling the day in her diary, Preston wrote that she had worn a white dress with a large American flag draped over it and "a very pretty . . . gold paper crown with a five-pointed star" sent to her for the occasion by a friend. She noted that "Colonel Dick Morgan," in his Confederate uniform, called for her at her family's apartment on Hampton Court in his automobile and drove her downtown to the reviewing stand. She thought the parade a "great success" and added, "there were thousands in line, men, women, and children. I knew hundreds of the men and women in line, and it was really very inspiring."[68]

Margaret Preston—reform-minded worker in her suffrage association, leader in the cultural and intellectual pursuits of her women's club, and scion of a prominent Lexington family whose sympathies lay emphatically with the Lost Cause—represented more than Columbia, Goddess of Liberty, on Flag Day 1916. She had been chosen to play a key role in an ardent public demonstration by the city's elite as one of their own; she had been escorted to the event by a former Confederate colonel in full dress uniform to stand, inspired, in review of a massive, whites-only parade in support of national military preparedness less than a year before the United States entered the European conflict. As she stood there on the reviewing stand in June 1916, she represented not only a female allegory of civic virtue but also a significant segment of Lexington cultural life in the Progressive Era.

CHAPTER SIX

"In Her Most Charming, Characteristic Way"

Lexington's Margaret Preston in the Progressive Era

Years ago, in 1900, when my father attained his fiftieth birthday, I
remember his saying over and over again, "Half a century, Lord, Lord,
half a century." And now, I recall incidents beginning fifty years ago [in
1890]. The world has seen tremendous changes in that period of time,
and the life I describe has really ceased.

—Margaret Preston Johnston, handwritten
autobiographical essay, circa early 1940s

As thirty-year-old Margaret Wickliffe Preston stood on the reviewing stand
representing Columbia at Lexington's preparedness parade on 14 June 1916,
her thoughts might have turned for a moment to her absent father, Robert Wickliffe ("Wick") Preston, who had died, at age sixty-three, two years
earlier, on 13 June 1914. Having initially survived a paralyzing stroke, he
had been confined for some time to Lexington's St. Joseph's Hospital before
suffering a fatal heart attack. Margaret had been at a luncheon bridge party
when she received word, by telephone, of her father's death, and in her diary
she expressed regret that she had not gone to see "Papa" the day before, as she
had intended. In his memoirs, Lexington attorney Joseph Tanner remembered Margaret's father as "fine looking" and a "real feller" before the turn of
the century, and he suggested that Wick Preston could have been described
as a "high (not holy) roller." Tanner did not elaborate on this description,
but certainly Preston enjoyed, and subsequently lost, a good deal of money.
The scion of an eminent Bluegrass family, Robert Wickliffe Preston was the
only son of General William Preston, a onetime U.S. minister to Spain and
a Yale- and Harvard-educated soldier who had distinguished himself first in

the Mexican War and then as a Confederate general in the Civil War. General Preston's great-grandfather, John Preston, had immigrated from Ireland to Virginia in 1740; his grandfather, Colonel William Preston of Smithfield, Virginia, had been a "decided, active, and efficient" Whig during the Revolutionary War; and his father, Captain William Preston, had served under General Anthony Wayne during the Revolution before settling in Louisville, Kentucky. In 1840 General Preston married Margaret Wickliffe, his second cousin, and they had five daughters in addition to their one son. General Preston, who was among John Hunt Morgan's pallbearers at the Confederate idol's Lexington funeral and reburial in the city's cemetery in April 1868, spent the years after the Civil War managing the large estate on the Bryan Station Pike that he had inherited from his father-in-law, prominent attorney and state legislator Robert Wickliffe, who had once been Kentucky's largest slaveholder.[1]

Indeed, Robert Wickliffe Preston had been named to honor his mother's father, and according to his grandson, Robert Wickliffe Preston Johnston, he had been "adored . . . spoiled and indulged" as a child. Johnston may have heard this description of his grandfather from his mother, Margaret, for in a handwritten, autobiographical essay penned in the early 1940s, she referred to her father as having been "petted and indulged from his birth." She illustrated her observation with an anecdote: upon learning that a batch of new bedroom wallpaper might contain arsenic, her grandmother had exclaimed, "Oh me, that is Wick's room. I must give it to one of the girls." At any rate, the family certainly indulged Wick Preston in terms of the educational opportunities provided, first at Washington and Lee University in Lexington, Virginia, and then at the University of Virginia in Charlottesville. Indeed, Wick Preston apparently enjoyed the fruits of these educational opportunities throughout his adulthood; his front-page obituary in 1914 stated that "much of his life . . . was spent reading the classics of the English Language . . . [and he] was especially well read in the English novelists." Like his father before him, Wick Preston received a law degree from Harvard and practiced for a short time in New York City before returning to Fayette County to farm.[2]

On 1 February 1883 Wick Preston married his third cousin, Sarah (Sallie) Brant McDowell. Sarah McDowell was born in Abingdon, Virginia, and early in her life her father, Dr. James McDowell, was appointed consul to Constantinople. Sarah's earliest memory of that city, as retold later by her daughter, Margaret, was "of a dark-skinned man walking before her and

her sister and exclaiming to all in hearing distance, 'make way for the prin-
cesses.'" Afterward the McDowell family lived for several years in France,
specifically, "for the sake of the children, . . . in Tours, where the best French
was to be heard," and later in Paris. Eventually the McDowells returned to
America, where Sarah lived with her grandmother, Sarah Brant, in St. Louis
until her marriage to Wick Preston. Sarah Preston "had an exceptional education for a woman at the turn of the century"; she had studied literature
and wrote poetry, could speak several languages, and in later years would
become, in the words of the *Lexington Leader,* "a leader in the cultural life
of Lexington." She was generally considered quite cultured, refined, and
charming, and Margaret recalled that General Preston had remarked that
"the crowning glory of my life is Wick's wife." Wick, who "loved horses,"
and his bride rented a 200-acre farm about six or seven miles from Lexington between the Bryan Station and Maysville (Paris) pikes, "a place well
adapted to the rearing of race horses." They called the farm Muir, and it is
now part of the property known as Payson Stud.[3]

The Early Years

Wick and Sarah Preston's first child, Margaret Wickliffe, was born on 1
September 1885 and was named for her paternal grandmother; their second (and last) child, William, was born on 28 August 1887. The family
lived on their rented farm in what Margaret remembered as an "old . . .
large, square brick house with four tall white columns in front." She also
recalled a smaller brick building in the yard that housed her father's office
and billiard room, as well as stables and several other outbuildings. The family, which Margaret called "a family in the old-fashioned sense of the word
. . . a household," also included Sarah Preston's grandmother from St. Louis,
Sarah Brant, whom the children called Mam, and Mam's sister "Mrs. Warren," whom they called Aunt Mamie. Margaret remembered that "these
. . . two old ladies in the family" were widows and invariably wore black.
Also "important in the family" were Elsie (Lucille Figibel), the "extremely
dignified [Alsatian] housekeeper" who had been Sarah Preston's nurse, lady's
maid, and companion in France, and Elsie's niece Cecile, known in the
family as "our beloved 'Keckie.'" Keckie would be Margaret's "inseparable
companion" in her youth and young adulthood. Margaret's son, Robert

Wickliffe Preston Johnston, recalled that Keckie, who often looked after him as a child, "came as a scullery maid . . . [but] she was a dear, dear friend. She started out as a servant and worked her way up, and became more and more important. And, my mother loved her—I loved her. She was a dear person." In concluding her description of the household, Margaret, in her own manner, included some of the black residents of the farm in this "old-fashioned" family: "There were various colored people about the place. I remember the cook, Celia, who was always good to me. And, I played with her daughters, Lila and Tavinia. Then, I remember Will, who helped us on our ponies. Such was the family."[4]

During the early years of Margaret's life, things seemed to be going well for all the Prestons. In May 1890 Margaret's aunt, Susan Preston, married General William Draper of Hopedale, Massachusetts. General Draper was a former Union officer and a member of a very wealthy and influential cloth manufacturing family that had operated fabric mills in New England since before the Revolutionary War. Six months later another of her aunts, Jessie Preston, married George A. Draper of Boston, the brother of William, further cementing the alliance between these two notable American families—one a fabulously rich, northern manufacturing power, and the other a prominent bastion of the upper South's planter class. Jessie's wedding took place in the drawing room of General Preston's Lexington mansion, and the *Kentucky (Lexington) Leader* described the occasion in minute detail: the profusion of flowers throughout the house, the table decorations in the banquet rooms so high "they reached half way to the ceiling," the four "mammoth" wedding cakes, the gold table service at the bridal table, the china bearing the Preston family crest, and the elaborate gowns and jewelry worn by the bride and her many female guests. Jessie's young niece and nephew were present at her lavish wedding, and the *Leader* noted that "tiny Miss Margaret and Master William Preston were figures just stepped out from an old painting in white silk, lined with pale blue satin. They are the handsome babies of Mr. and Mrs. Wickliffe Preston."[5]

And so, as the 1890s began, young Margaret Preston's extended family was one of wealth and prominence. Her father was a gentleman farmer and member of the prestigious Lexington Gun Club, and her mother was an admired and cultured young wife. Times seemed good at Muir, and Margaret recalled that her father "apparently was on the verge of a happy and successful life." She went to the wheat fields with him one evening as the full moon rose and remembered his happy reference to the crop as "dollar wheat." And although she had no recollection of their growing tobacco, she had fond memories of "the hemp, the beautiful grass, and the horses." Each Sunday the family went into Lexington to attend the Episcopal Christ Church Cathedral, sitting in a front pew with Margaret's grandmother and namesake, Margaret Wickliffe Preston. Though success seemed assured for Margaret's father, he apparently managed his finances unwisely, was caught unprepared for the depression of the 1890s, and was financially ruined during the panic of 1893. Writing of this depression's effect on agrarian Kentucky, Hambleton Tapp and James Klotter have observed that "most of the distress in the state centered in western Kentucky." Wick Preston's experience suggests that there were harsh effects in the Bluegrass as well. Margaret recalled 1893 as "that black year." She wrote, "I recall hearing of Coxey's army, and poor, dirty men came by tramping, asking for food. And the year wore on. And, one day Keckie showed me in my old nursery an advertisement in the paper announcing the sale of Papa's horses." That announcement appeared on the front page of the *Kentucky (Lexington) Leader* on 7 January 1894 and lamented, "the many friends of Mr. R. Wickliffe Preston will hear with regret that he has made an assignment. . . . Mr. Preston is a gentleman who is endeared to a large circle of friends . . . who extend to him their hearty good wishes in a time when, like a multitude of others, he must yield to the inevitable hard pressure of the times." On 24 January 1894 Wick Preston's Thoroughbred horses, Jersey cows, and other farm and personal property were sold at auction. The *Leader's* account sketched an almost festive scene in which a "wholesome burgoo" was served to the large crowd, and candidates for city offices circulated among the throng, seeking votes. However, Margaret remembered only the sadness: "Papa's fine horses went under the hammer. They sold for almost nothing. From that day, my father's life was ruined. He was only forty-three, and this financial failure seemed to be a frustration of all his hopes."[6]

School Days

After the auction, it appears that the Wickliffe Preston family lived primarily on "family" money. General Preston had died in 1887, and when his son went bankrupt in 1894 he immediately moved his family in with his widowed mother. Margaret, who was nine years old when the family retreated to town, recalled that "Grandma [Margaret Wickliffe] Preston" lived in "a very large old house that she had inherited from her step-mother, Mrs. Robert [Mary Owen Todd Russell] Wickliffe. Mrs. Wickliffe's father was Col. [John] Todd who was killed at the battle of Blue Licks in 1782." This house, originally known as Glendower, was located on West Second Street in Lexington and later became a private hotel, Preston Inn; even later, in the 1930s, it was used as quarters for St. Joseph Hospital nurses before being demolished in 1942. In one wing of the house lived Grandma Preston with her maid, and in another wing lived young Margaret and her father, mother, and brother, William; Mam and Aunt Mamie; and Keckie. Keckie's aunt Elsie had returned to France "to spend her last days." In 1898, four years after Margaret's family moved into the Preston home, both her great-grandmother, Sarah Brant, and her grandmother, Margaret Wickliffe Preston, died. Wick Preston managed to maintain the residence at Glendower for five more years until the house was "sold out of the family" in 1903.[7]

Margaret's recollection of the years on Second Street was that they were a time of religious, political, and literary instruction at home as well as at school. Although Margaret and William were taken to church each Sunday, their mother did not allow them to go to Sunday school, preferring to teach them herself by having them read aloud from Psalms and from John Bunyan's *Pilgrim's Progress*. In addition, Margaret read the Bible aloud to her great-grandmother and learned backgammon from her grandmother. Grandma Preston also read James Boswell's *Life of Samuel Johnson* to Margaret and William, taught them spelling "from a blue-back speller," and made Margaret "copy selections from Shakespeare and learn them by heart." The children also attended Miss Ella Williams's private, coeducational preparatory school, located at 177 North Upper Street, in the former parsonage of the McChord (Second) Presbyterian Church, between 1895 and 1900 and then at 355 North Broadway until the founder's death in 1915, when the school closed. In Ella Williams's front-page obituary in March 1915, the *Lexington Herald* stated, "Miss Williams had a marvelous influence over the lives of young people. She was attractive to both boys and girls and they were anxious to please her." Margaret, writing in the 1940s, recalled her as "a strict Presbyterian, and a good Republican, and, so at school, I heard a different point of view from home where we were Episcopalians and Democrats." The differences in perspective at school and at home were pronounced, and these contrasts served to stimulate thought at the time and memories later: "Miss Ella taught us to salute the flag, and when the Spanish war came on in 1898, we all recited 'Remember the Maine' . . . with gusto. Dewey sailed into Manila Bay and we were much excited." Yet at home, "father was an anti-imperialist." And there were other contrasts: "At school, Miss Ella was for a high tariff; at home, Papa was for free trade."[8]

By 1902, the year Margaret turned seventeen, her diary reveals that she was immersed in educational endeavors and in social and cultural pursuits and entertainments. From January through June of that year, Margaret recorded faithfully in her diary a weekday routine of school (Miss Williams's) in the mornings; reading for pleasure at the city library in the afternoons, or sometimes taking long walks, shopping, or attending plays; and studying (French, Latin, history), practicing the piano, and, again, reading for pleasure in the evenings. Her reading material was quite eclectic and included such works as *Gondola Days* by Hopkinson Smith, *A Lady of the Regency* by Stephney Rawson, "a book of quotations compiled by Emerson," and the *House Party,* "a collection of twelve unsigned stories by famous authors." Frequently Keckie accompanied Margaret on her walks or went shopping with her; she also fitted and altered Margaret's clothing and washed her hair. In the afternoons and on Saturdays, clothed and coiffed by Keckie, Margaret would frequently attend adult social gatherings with her mother or those of her own age group. On 2 January 1902 she dressed up in her "white wool dress, blue sash, and garnets" and hosted a euchre party at her home for eight girls, including Gretchen Miller, who would become her brother William's wife in 1911. That spring, Margaret and her mother attended a series of lectures on the dramatic arts given by Elizabeth Shelby Kincaid—occasions both social and explicitly educational in nature. Kincaid's general theme for this particular lecture course was "The Development of Personality," and among the specific topics discussed were "Lancelot and Guinevere"; "'Elizabeth Bennet,' the heroine of 'Pride and Prejudice'"; and "'Ulysses,' the new play by Stephen Phillips." Margaret and her mother also attended lectures and meetings of the Woman's Club of Central Kentucky and the United Daughters of the Confederacy. Sarah Preston was an active and prominent member of both organizations; for instance, she helped organize the annual UDC spelling matches at the courthouse, and she would be elected president of the WCCK in 1906. On Sunday mornings Margaret invariably attended services at Christ Church Cathedral, and Sunday afternoons and evenings were often spent taking walks, going for rides in the family's carriage, reading, practicing the piano, and studying her school lessons.[9]

In 1902 the teenaged Margaret made an appearance at a variety of public events and entertainments. For instance, on the night of 4 January she and her mother attended a concert to hear "Madame Nevada." On 21 May she "went with Mrs. Headley to the Oratorical Contest. It was quite amusing." And on 28 June she recorded that she and "about a dozen of my friends" rented "Tent No. 12" at the Lexington Chautauqua and "gave a large tea. . . . There were about eighty guests, boys and girls. . . . I wore my blue lawn dress and white hat." However, consonant with her enjoyment of Elizabeth Kincaid's lectures on drama, Margaret's diary suggests that stage plays, both professional and amateur, made up the bulk of her public entertainment fare, and she frequented both matinee and evening performances. On the afternoon of 4 January she attended, with a friend and the friend's mother, a matinee performance at the Lexington Opera House of the play *Human Hearts,* which Margaret deemed "a pathetic drama which was shriekingly funny." On 8 January she attended, with Keckie, a matinee performance of *Way Down East* and noted in her diary that "several of the actors were very good." On 4 February she met Keckie at the opera house after school for a matinee performance of *Lover's Lane,* which she thought was "acted by a second rate company and wasn't much account." On the night of 3 April she sat with the Headley family in the parquet at the opera house to watch a play she did not name, starring actress Julia Marlowe; she noted that "it cost $2.50 which was excessive. I enjoyed it extremely." On the night of 10 April she went with her mother to the opera house to see *Quality Street* starring Maude Adams and was elated: "the play was charming, . . . and I have never seen anything prettier or better acted." On the afternoon of 24 May she "went to an amateur play which was very good." And again on the night of 27 May she and Keckie "went to an amateur play . . . at the Opera House." She mentions others in her diary, but these are sufficient to suggest that stage plays—far more so than the odd oratorical entertainment or occasional musical concert—were the staple of Margaret's public entertainment fare as a teenager in Lexington in the early 1900s. Indeed, she felt familiar enough with the genre to record her own critique of the literary, artistic, and entertainment merits of each performance she attended.[10]

MEADOW WOOD

Before the First World War, Victorian Americans allowed themselves to play and to travel for pleasure if they could convince themselves that it was beneficial for their health, character, or intellect. By the early twentieth century, summer vacations had become common among the middle class, although this often meant camping at the local Chautauqua or a brief trip to a nearby health spa, because most could not afford long vacations at distant locations. The wealthier classes recommended longer holidays for their peers. President William Howard Taft, for instance, suggested that men of affairs should take two to three months off each year, and Supreme Court Justice Henry Bishoff suggested "two months for professional men, one month for businessmen, and two weeks for clerks." Although her parents were no longer well off, Margaret Preston was blessed with wide and wealthy family connections that made it possible for her to enjoy many of the pleasures of the "better" classes, including lengthy summer respites out of town. In her diary entry for 11 July 1902 Margaret wrote: "We left home for the summer. . . . I was very sorry to leave Papa and Keck." That morning had been spent packing, and then family and friends had seen Margaret and her mother off at the train station as they began their annual sojourn—lasting two months or longer—to Virginia.[11]

Beginning in 1900, Margaret, her mother, and often her brother spent the summer at Meadow Wood, a country estate near the small town of Chalk Level, Virginia. Her father seldom accompanied them and usually remained in Lexington, sometimes living in rooms at the Lexington Club during their absence. Margaret described Meadow Wood as "an old country place in southern Virginia . . . about forty miles from Lynchburg and about the same distance from Danville." Located on a parcel of land that had once been part of a 700-acre plantation, Meadow Wood was "a simple two-story white frame house built in 1855." The property had belonged to Aunt Mamie Warren, and on her death it had passed to her adopted daughter, Alice (Mrs. Robert) Wooding. A bewildering array of "cousins" and "aunts" from

Margaret's extended family, "literally scores of people to whom we had some kind of affinity," also visited Meadow Wood each summer and fall, and Margaret loved to tell strangers about this complex of relatives "in order to confuse them." In this atmosphere, Margaret remarked, "the world was not a lonesome place. The difficult thing was to find time apart from the social group of relatives and friends."[12]

Margaret apparently kept no diary during the summer of 1902, making only a short entry covering 12 July through 3 September to indicate her whereabouts during that period. However, her daily diary entries from mid-August to mid-September 1907 offer a glimpse into her lifestyle at this Virginia estate. Her time there was clearly one of leisure and recreation, and her daily schedule was that of someone on a holiday. In the mornings she typically "rested" or "sat around," read, played bridge or tennis, rode her horse (named Blanche), walked to the "ice-pond" with her mother, went for carriage rides, and frequently embroidered. This last activity she apparently did not continue into later adulthood, for her son remembered his mother as being "not the least bit domestic." (In fact, he recalled that although Margaret belonged in later years to a "ladies' sewing circle," the members never really sewed but only met at one another's homes to eat and talk. On one occasion one of the women tore the hem of her dress and asked Margaret for a needle and thread to repair it. Margaret turned to her husband and asked, "Preston, where *is* our needle?") Evenings were occupied with masquerade, birthday, euchre, or bridge parties; picnics; moonlight rides to visit neighbors; and reading. It is generally acknowledged that reading, both for enjoyment and as a means of self-improvement, was of great importance in the Victorian home, and "reading filled the leisure hours of many Victorian women." Historian Thomas Schlereth has argued that the Victorian era extended to the First World War, and when Margaret visited Meadow Wood in the early twentieth century, reading was certainly an important part of daily life. At times, various female members of the household read aloud to the others, but more frequently they read silently for their individual pleasure. One of several books Margaret read during her stay in 1907 was the novel *Hopes and Fears* by Charlotte M. Yonge. As was her custom, Margaret noted in her diary her own critical analysis, calling the book "a very good picture of mid-Victorian, middle-class life." To a great extent, that description also applied to the life Margaret lived while on holiday in the Virginia countryside.[13]

Margaret cherished her visits to Meadow Wood and returned yearly by train during the prewar years. In 1910, for instance, she and her mother stopped in West Virginia at White Sulphur Springs, a fashionable health resort made popular by the hydropathy cure then in vogue. However, Margaret confided to her diary that she found the people rather "dull" and the resort disagreeable. She was impatient to get to Meadow Wood (which the family also referred to as Chalk Level, the nearest small town): "The place [White Sulphur Springs] is beautifully situated, the hotel is attractive and comfortable, but I do not like watering place[s]. There are so many people to speak to, and it is all quite aimless. I will be glad to get to Chalk Level." Margaret's brother shared her fondness for the Virginia estate. On 1 August 1910 William wrote to her from Calgary, Canada, where he had gone to homestead and farm, and expressed his regret that she had "found it so dull at the White Sulphur" compared with Meadow Wood. He then went on to express his own feelings for the Virginia farm: "Chalk Level is a dear old place and I often think of the many happy hours I spent there. . . . I think those were the happiest moments of my boyhood days."[14]

BROTHER WILLIAM

All the surviving letters from William Preston to his older sister, Margaret, suggest that he was quite fond of her. He addressed her as "My Dear Sister" and closed his letters by asking her to always think of him as her "true" or "loving" brother. Apparently quite devoted to his family, William kept both his parents and his sister informed of his activities when he was away from them, and these letters sketch an outline of his life in the Progressive Era. In the fall of 1904 he was attending State College in Lexington as a freshman. He had joined the Kappa Alpha Fraternity and was attending parties with his future wife, Gretchen Miller. He wrote to Margaret, then in her first year at Bryn Mawr College in Pennsylvania, of his academic travails: "I think I am going to fail when examinations come." William remained at State College until after his sophomore year, transferring to the University of Virginia in the fall of 1906. His father's wealthy sister, Jessie Preston Draper, who resided with her husband in Hopedale, Massachusetts, paid his expenses at the Charlottesville school so that he could continue the Preston family tradition; both his grandfather and his father had attended the university.

When William first arrived in Charlottesville in September 1906 he stayed at least one evening at the Clermont Hotel and wrote to his mother on hotel stationery to advise her that he had arrived safely. This letter written by nineteen-year-old William contains a rare expression of this upper-class Lexington family's views of the "color line": "You know, I saw something that certainly did surprise me in Virginia. While I was eating supper [in the hotel dining room] I looked across the room and saw a black nigger eating with two white men. What do you think of that? I think it is awful. It would not be so bad in the North, but what do you think the South is coming to[?]"[15]

William failed his courses that first semester and decided that the University of Virginia was "far different from State [College]." As he explained to his mother in a letter written in January 1907, he had mistakenly thought that he could do just "enough work to keep up in my classes without killing myself, so to speak." He promised to redouble his efforts, but it was to no avail. Near the end of May 1907 he wrote to his mother that the dean had graciously advised, but not compelled, him to withdraw due to his poor grades and had suggested that he study law if he returned someday. However, what William really wanted to be was a gentleman farmer, like his father before him. He sent his mother a postcard in April 1907 featuring a drawing of a country "squire" and wrote above it, "This is what I would like to be." Thus, he did not return to Virginia but remained in Lexington and began taking classes in agriculture at State College in the fall of 1907. He wrote to his mother at Meadow Wood that Aunt Jessie Draper had offered him $1,000 for his college expenses and added, "She certainly has been good to me and[,] in fact[,] to all of us." But his father, Wickliffe, writing to William from the Hotel Havlin in Cincinnati, where he had gone to seek medical help for a "rupture," clearly thought his son should pursue an avenue to success other than higher education: "one year and a thousand gone and no practical results. I do hope she may offer the same to advance you in other ways."[16]

William eventually took his father's advice, and in the spring of 1909 he was writing letters home from Canada, where he had gone to purchase a homestead to farm. On stationery from the Arlington Temperance Hotel in Calgary, he reassured his mother that the soil was rich, the weather fine, and the town, though it looked like "it was built in a night," prosperous and growing; the locals were surely correct, he wrote, in calling it "the Chicago of the West." A month later he wrote an equally optimistic letter to Margaret, although he did complain that the rainy season had begun and that "the weather has not been what it might since I have been here." Nevertheless, William persisted and was still farming near Calgary a year later. However, his 1 August 1910 letter to Margaret at Meadow Wood contained a strong note of doubt, and he advised her against investing family assets in land in Alberta because "the seasons here are uncertain." (Margaret apparently ignored his advice, for among her papers is a tax bill for $5 for two lots in Calgary, payable 30 June 1912.) Despite his misgivings, William seemed determined to stay in Canada, and he wrote to Margaret in September 1910 of his engagement to Gretchen Miller, whom he had loved since he was thirteen, when Margaret had first introduced them. He wrote that they planned to live on his farm in Canada after their marriage in Lexington the following February, and he called Gretchen "a brave girl to be willing to come up here to the far Northwest." William and Gretchen were married on 28 February 1911, and they both wrote cheerful letters to Margaret that spring and summer. William assured her that "everything is O.K. and the crops are all doing well," and Gretchen informed her that "we are as happy as we can be up here to-gether, and I feel positive that I am not going to mind the life at all." Despite Gretchen's brave assertions, Margaret noted in her diary on 13 December 1911 that "Wm & Gretchen reached home this morning"—and they were home to stay. In February 1912 William wrote to Margaret, who was visiting New York City at the time, that he and Gretchen had just purchased a farm, located on the Georgetown Road, for $150 per acre. Gretchen likewise wrote to Margaret of her plans for the new house and that their furniture had finally arrived from Canada. Margaret noted in her diary on 15 March 1912 that "Gretchen & William spent last night at their new home, so we may say that they are settled."[17]

Margaret at College

Margaret herself had seemed anything *but* settled a few years earlier in 1904, for she had just been admitted, at age nineteen, to Bryn Mawr College in Pennsylvania. Things had begun well enough. Margaret had longed to go to college, and she received both inspiration and private tutoring from her cousins Linda and Mary Neville, the daughters of State College professor John H. Neville. The Neville sisters, who had themselves gone to Bryn Mawr, were teaching privately in Lexington at the time. With their encouragement and help, Margaret passed her entrance exams in the spring of 1904 and soon received congratulatory letters from Aunt Jessie Draper indicating that she would be delighted to pay Margaret's college and personal expenses. This was no small gift, for the tuition, room, and board came to almost $700 for the year, and she sent Margaret another $300 for clothing, living, and traveling expenses. Armed with a private preparatory education and her aunt's wealth, Margaret moved into Bryn Mawr's brandnew Rockefeller Hall, "the gift of Mr. John D. Rockefeller," an impressive edifice of gray stone and many amenities: "Students are expected to provide their own rugs and towels, but in every other respect the rooms are completely furnished. . . . There are open fire-places in all the studies and in many single rooms, but the rooms are sufficiently heated by currents of air passing over steam-heated pipes; the air is changed every ten minutes and the temperature is regulated by a thermostat in each room. Electric light is introduced into every room." Barbara Miller Solomon, in her history of women's higher education in America, notes that although "going to college became an accepted part of growing up for women in certain social groups" in the pre–World War I era, the expense involved and the lack of public financial aid assured that college was "a privilege for the fortunate." Margaret's attendance at Bryn Mawr reflected her good fortune in having a wealthy aunt, but her situation was hardly unique. As Solomon also notes, "occasionally assistance from an interested relative . . . enabled young people to obtain a college education. An aunt subsidized the daughter of Elizabeth Cady and Henry Stanton at Vassar."[18]

From the moment she arrived on the Bryn Mawr campus, Margaret was extremely homesick. Although accustomed to traveling, she was now living far from home and the support of her large extended family. She wrote many years later, "I nearly died of homesickness. I can yet remember how homesick I was." The mail, however, was her link to home. In one of her first letters to her mother from Bryn Mawr in October 1904, she wrote that she had cried for a long time on the train; she stated that she "hated this spot" and wished she would not have to return after Christmas. Wistfully, she added, "Perhaps I will get sick and then I can go home." Margaret soon learned that Bryn Mawr, an institution originally focused on moral discipline, had changed its emphasis to "academic rigor." In her first semester she was taking courses in French literature, French composition, English composition, English literature, elocution, history of Christian doctrine, and physical culture. She wrote to her brother, "My lessons are very hard," and added, "People talk through their hat when they say that you don't have to study at college. There is an awful lot to do." Likewise, she complained to her mother, "I never felt so rushed in all my life, even at Miss Linda's [Neville]." Nor was Margaret initially happy with the social life at Bryn Mawr: "These formal college teas are simply fearful entertainments. You meet upperclassmen, who think it as impossible to talk to a freshman as a duchess would to a butcher's wife. If you want to feel your own insignificance go to college as a freshman. . . . The blood is on Miss Linda's [Neville] head for having brought me to this spot. It really is just like a prison. The life is so narrow and restricted and the talk is all shop, there being absolutely no broadening element."[19]

Throughout that first fall at Bryn Mawr, Margaret continued to write to her mother of her dislike of the school and her course work, especially German, and her exhaustion from the long hours of study, her fear of failure, and her bouts of anxiety: "I have studied all afternoon and some this evening, but the more I studied, the more nervous and restless I became. . . . Oh, when will this year be over. I feel so nervous and curious tonight." This tone of distress was common in her correspondence, and in another letter she likened herself to a convict: "I feel as if I were in prison and could never get away." These letters alarmed Margaret's family at home. In addition to her mother's frequent letters of reassurance, her father, who did not write often, did so in late November 1904: "My dear Margaret, I have intended writing, but posted Mama's letters instead. . . . I hope you are over your homesickness. I know it is a dreadful ordeal. If at Christmas you are not reconciled, I'd not wish you to feel compelled to continue a second term if it is too irksome. I really do not think much of schools or mobs of any kind which always are more or less vulgar." In early December 1904 Mary Neville also wrote a long letter of encouragement and advice to Margaret, telling her not to put too much emphasis on what her German teacher thought of her and begging her not to worry about her course work: "I certainly expect that I wasted too much strength and time in worrying while I was at Bryn

Mawr. If I had not been so foolish I should have slept better and done better work and . . . been much happier." Even Keckie's husband (though married, she continued to "supervise" the Preston household on a daily basis), E. P. Harrison, wrote a kind letter of encouragement to Margaret, reassuring her that his "dear Cecile" would soon be returning from France, where she was visiting her Aunt Elsie. Harrison, circulation manager for the *Lexington Leader,* also forwarded the local newspapers to Margaret, perhaps attempting to lessen her homesickness, and assured her that he was "very glad of the opportunity to send them."[20]

Despite all this hubbub, and perhaps in spite of herself, Margaret began to acclimate to Bryn Mawr through her extracurricular life, for she was soon included in a peer group that offered friendship, emotional support, and distraction from the rigors of the curriculum. She shared a table in the dining room with eight other girls, and a clique quickly formed. Margaret wrote to her mother about this new group of friends, who had chosen the name "Aryans" for themselves because, as Margaret put it, "we studied them so much in English and because we have primitive table manners." In November one of the girls invited the others to her rooms for an "Aryan" party, where they ate "hunks of bread, butter, and sausages"; the plates, knives, and forks were fashioned of rough pieces of wood, and several of the girls wore "marvelous savage costumes." Margaret could not help but admit, "We really had a very amusing time, for it was such a funny idea. . . . We did stunts, which is a phase of my education that has been sadly neglected." Margaret, who loved chocolate passionately, often invited the Aryans to her room to talk and indulge. This camaraderie helped Margaret survive, and she actually began to flourish at college. Some of these relationships were quite long lasting; she corresponded with several of these college friends for many years afterward.[21]

Despite her father's assurances that she could remain at home, Margaret returned to Bryn Mawr in January 1905 after the Christmas break. Although she continued to struggle with German and French, she had begun to do well in some of her other classes, happily telling her mother soon after her return to school that she had received the comment "decidedly good" from her teacher on an English quiz and that, with one exception, "all the Aryans passed." Even so, Margaret remained a rather nervous student: "I get so frightened when I read in class . . . that my hands get icy cold and tremble. I know it is foolish, but I can't help it." Nonetheless, her life was by no means confined solely to academic struggle and stress. In addition to the comforts and distractions provided by her fellow Aryans, Margaret continued to enjoy stage plays, both on campus and off. Plays were frequently given by the students, and Margaret wrote one scene for the freshman play in February 1905. In addition, she often visited nearby Philadelphia over the weekends, where she went shopping and attended the theater with her "Aunt Tallie," a relative on her mother's side who was apparently quite fond of Margaret and provided her with a home-away-from-home during her time at Bryn Mawr. To cite only two examples of their frequent theatergoing, in January 1905 she went with Aunt Tallie to see *Romeo and Juliet,* and in February they saw John Drew at the Broad Street Theater in *The Duke of Killiecrankie;* she wrote to her mother that the latter play was "charming, so funny in every line." Margaret also attended the professional theater with her college friends; for instance, she went into Philadelphia with fellow student Elizabeth Wright to see Lionel Barrymore in *The Other Girl,* a play she described in a letter to her brother as "a ridiculous farce which amused us very much."[22]

Margaret's social life at college was not confined to "aunts" and female friends. In March 1905 she was introduced to Charles Horner, a Princeton student from Louisville and one of several young men who showed an interest in Margaret while she was at Bryn Mawr. Apparently, Princeton students called on Bryn Mawr women so frequently that Princeton was called the "Bryn Mawr Annex." At any rate, Horner began to call on Margaret regularly, taking her for chauffeured automobile rides and to the theater. At first she seemed enamored of him, describing him to her mother as "extremely nice, tall, good-looking, and rather reserved, very gentlemanly." However, although Horner continued to pursue Margaret throughout her two years at Bryn Mawr, he apparently turned out to be *too* reserved, and her ardor for him cooled. Disillusioned, she complained to her mother in November 1905, "Charles Horner is positively a clam. It is dreadful trying to talk to him. I think even you would give up." Nevertheless, she continued to see him, somewhat reluctantly, and in March 1906, ever the stage play enthusiast, wrote to her mother that she had accompanied him to "a real melodrama, one of those that William is so fond of." This outing occasioned the following observation—at once astute and sophomoric—of popular entertainment and social class by this twenty-year-old college coed:

> I hadn't been to a play like that since I was 13 and I was struck by the old stock plot of forged wills, etc. . . . The acting was naturally absurd. The audience was interesting too. I had a good view for we were in a box. The people were the real working-classes, perfectly respectable and American or Irish. Many of the women had brought children, even babies. They were much more ready to laugh than to applaud, [and] even the villain was laughed at instead of hissed. Of course, every old thread-bare moral maxim was vigorously clapped.

Indeed, Margaret's letters during her college days were filled with her own unique observations of class and manners. Having just attended a play with college friends at the Garrick Theater in Philadelphia—one with "a delicious amateur detective, a burlesque of Sherlock Holmes"—they walked up Chestnut Street, "which is always a gay sight on Saturday Afternoons . . . all the second-rate smart people crowd the sidewalks and you see many fashionable costumes." If not always kind, Margaret's observations often displayed a lively wit. After visiting relatives in Princeton, New Jersey, Margaret wrote to her mother describing two visitors who had come calling one evening: "After supper one of cousin Margaret's protégés—a little Jap—called and showed us his Japanese water-colors. Then a young professor, Mr. Lallou, called. He is very interesting, really he talks quite epigrammatically and is unusual altogether. The Millers have no use for him because he is an atheist and proud of the fact (as if it mattered at all what a man of twenty-five believes, but Presbyterian Princeton is all stirred up and intends to fire him)."[23]

In addition to the distractions provided by suitors, friends, relatives, and, of course, the theater, Margaret showed an interest in benevolent activities while at Bryn Mawr—a proclivity she retained in the years ahead. Beginning in the 1880s, the collegiate experience often included the college settlement movement, which attempted to provide students with a self-enriching experience and an opportunity to "serve and improve society" by living with the poor. Though Margaret did not join a settlement herself, she was interested in the movement. She attended a lecture on college settlements by "a New York woman" in November 1905 and the following February visited a settlement house on Stanton Street in New York City, where her cousin, Mary Preston, was living and working at the time. Margaret accepted her cousin's invitation to see the settlement house "with joy" and described it in a letter to her mother: "[It] is a church settlement and in the one building is a church, a kindergarten-room, a cooking school-room, a billiard-room for men, an office, a kitchen, a dining-room, and the bed-rooms and sitting-room of the workers." Margaret not only showed an interest in benevolent programs while in college but also contributed to them. In October 1904 and again in May 1905 she made cash donations to St. John's Collegiate Institute and Industrial School in Corbin, Kentucky, and received letters of thanks from Emma Morrell, a teacher at the school. Under the auspices of the Episcopal Church in the diocese of Lexington, St. John's was an educational and religious missionary outreach program to "the boys and girls residing in the Mountains of Eastern Kentucky." Margaret remained quite active in the various endeavors of the Episcopal Church in the years ahead, but her benevolence toward educational efforts ranged beyond those of the diocese. For instance, shortly after Berea College lost its legal battle over the Day Law, she received a letter in August 1909 from William Frost, president of the college, thanking her for her "kind gift for the 'Adjustment Fund,' which is to provide the Lincoln Institute for the colored people of Kentucky."[24]

Margaret did well enough academically during the spring term of her freshman year that her mother wrote to congratulate her: "Dearest, I am bursting with pride . . . you see, I am still early Victorian. I look to men to be intellectual[,] women fascinating . . . you are both." Thus flattered and encouraged, and after a summer's respite at Meadow Wood, Margaret returned for a second year at Bryn Mawr in the fall of 1905. However, still struggling with the discipline required for long hours of study, the pressures of exams, and her nervous reaction to classroom performance, Margaret apparently experienced severe symptoms of anxiety and required a physician's aid and medication. A consulting physician from Philadelphia diagnosed Margaret in October 1905 as being "in a very overwrought, nervous condition, suffering in fact from Neurasthenia," and recommended that she be withdrawn from school. A fashionable, faddish "disease" among the Victorians, *neurasthenia* was coined in 1881 by neurologist Dr. George Miller Beard, who recognized it as being primarily a malady of "the comfortable classes." In addition, with its many and varied psychosomatic symptoms, "neurasthenia provided a respectable covering term for many distressing, but not life-threatening, complaints." To Aunt Jessie Draper, however, the matter was deadly serious, and she wrote to Margaret's mother, "If Margaret were my child, and had an acute attack of nerves, I *would not keep her at college.*" Aunt Jessie also wrote to Margaret the same day, enclosed a check for $500 for Margaret's doctor bills and dormitory room, and made it clear that even if she did not remain at college, she could keep the money. Furthermore, she stated, "as I promised you another year at Bryn Mawr [I] will give you what your board and tuition will cost for you to get clothes for your debut, or as you prefer spending it."[25]

Despite professional advice and inducements from Aunt Jessie, Margaret remained at college, with her mother's support. She wrote to her mother on 2 November 1905 that her doctor thought her improved and had reduced her medication: "He told me I looked well, and to have the tonic renewed, tho not to take so much at a time." She was so improved by the end of November that her father wrote, "I did not write when you were ill at beginning of session. Mamma kept me informed and I did not wish to influence your joint decision. I am so glad that you have recovered." Indeed, Margaret did recover and successfully completed her second year at Bryn Mawr in June 1906. Nevertheless, throughout the spring of 1906, while her parents were leasing and moving into the large and elegant Bodley House at 200 Market Street in Lexington and her mother was being elected president of the Woman's Club of Central Kentucky, Margaret agonized over whether to return to school for a third year. In February 1906 she wrote to her mother of her uncertainty: "I don't suppose . . . I would come back, and I certainly don't want to except that I should like to have a degree from Bryn Mawr." Again in March she wrote, "Of course, I would like the honor of a degree, but I am so tired of working and I want to be at home so much." In the end, "home" won out, for she did not return to Bryn Mawr in the fall of 1906. For the next eleven years Margaret lived in Lexington with her family, first in Bodley House on Market Street until October 1912, and then in the Waverly Apartments on nearby Hampton Court. For Margaret, these would be years of social pleasure, benevolent service, progressive effort, and intellectual endeavor, but they would also include a long and devoted courtship with the man who would become her husband in November 1917, Philip Preston Johnston Jr.[26]

PHILIP PRESTON JOHNSTON JR.

After leaving Bryn Mawr, Margaret spent much of the summer of 1906 at Meadow Wood and was a Bluegrass debutante the following fall and winter season—her expensive gowns compliments of Aunt Jessie. A schedule defined by travel, leisure, and social pleasure continued into the spring of 1907. Her diary makes it clear that after returning home in April from a trip to visit friends and relatives in the Northeast, she resumed a routine filled with parties, dances, dinners, picnics, and carriage and automobile rides, along with, as was her custom, reading at home or at the library, going to plays, and attending various club and civic meetings with her mother. Margaret was free to pursue this lifestyle in large part because she had no need for paid employment. Though not rich, her parents provided her with a comfortable home, and her aunt continued to furnish her with a supplementary income. In addition to periodic large gifts of cash, Margaret regularly received $100 per month from Aunt Jessie until Jessie's death in 1917, whereupon Margaret was given a final bequest of $2,000.[27]

The spring of 1907 found Margaret with a very active social calendar, and she was being escorted to a variety of events by an assortment of young men. On Friday, 12 April 1907, she noted in her diary that she had attended a "cotillion . . . with Preston Johnston." This was the first reference in her diary to Philip Preston Johnston Jr., and like his own family, Margaret omitted his first name and would always refer to him as "Preston." At this time, she included his last name in her diary entries, suggesting no particular feeling of closeness or familiarity. It was almost a month (3 May) before she mentioned him again in her diary, having sat beside him at a supper party in Versailles, Kentucky, and danced with him afterward. A few days later, on 9 May, he called on her at home in the evening, after which he began to call once or twice a week and occasionally took her to dinner parties and other social gatherings. By late June, reflecting a growing familiarity, Margaret was referring to him simply as Preston, and from time to time he would come for supper and spend the entire evening with her and her family. Shortly after Margaret left for Meadow Wood in July 1907, Preston wrote her a straightforward, polite, newsy letter, which would be typical of his correspondence to her through the years. His missives were always solicitous for her well-being, sympathetic toward her slightest discomfort or frustration, and filled with stories of farming, farm life, and the politics, gossip, and social life of Lexington. Margaret responded to Preston's letter in warm but polite tones, describing the trip on the train and her daily life at Meadow Wood. They continued to correspond through the summer of 1907, learning more about each other and revealing aspects of their personal preferences and personalities. For instance, Preston, who was thirty years old at the time, wrote to Margaret expressing his feeling of ambivalence upon seeing men and women drinking highballs and beer during the intermission at a dance in Lexington: "It didn't look very nice to me at a public dance, but of course anybody that wanted to had a perfect right." Margaret, typical of her brand of wit, wrote to Preston that her fellow house guests wanted to play bridge so much that it left her no time to read anything other than magazines such as the *Ladies' Home Journal,* which, she quipped, "tends to soften the brain." On 28 September, knowing that Margaret would be returning soon, Preston was characteristically straightforward: "The Bluegrass German Club has been reorganized and will give the first german [dance] Oct. 18th. Will you go with me to it?" She wrote back that she accepted "with pleasure" but could not resist adding, "I wonder how they chose that name for a german club, it sounds so common someway, as if it were the name of a brand of whiskey." And so, a long and affectionate courtship had begun.[28]

Preston, eight years older than Margaret, was born on 13 May 1877, one of five sons of Sallie Chiles Johnston, a member of a "prominent pioneer family," and Confederate Civil War veteran Major P. P. Johnston. Major Johnston, a native of Shiloh, Virginia, graduated from the Kentucky University College of Law in 1868; he became president of the National Trotting Association in 1889 and president of the Breckinridge (Lexington) Chapter of the United Confederate Veterans in 1915. In his role as leader of the Lexington UCV, Major Johnston represented what has been referred to as the "Inner Lost Cause," those former rebels who justified secession, rationalized defeat, and idolized the Confederacy, organizing to celebrate it and keep its memory alive. The major and his family resided on his wife's ancestral farm on the Bryan Station Pike, where he bred Thoroughbred and trotting horses; of his five sons, it was his namesake, Preston, who perhaps most loved and would devote himself to this farm. Preston left home in his late teens to enter Louisiana State University, where he joined the Sigma Nu Fraternity. However, never happy being away from the family farm for long, he returned to Lexington to complete his college education and at age twenty-two was one of six students awarded a degree in mechanical engineering by State College in 1899. Seeking professional employment after graduation, Preston moved to Chattanooga, Tennessee, where he worked briefly as a draftsman for the Cincinnati, New Orleans & Texas Pacific Railway. However, homesick and dissatisfied, he complained about the hard work and low pay and longed to return home to manage the family farm. His father wrote to him in November 1899 supporting his desire to return to the farm; indeed, his father offered to give notice to their current farm manager and to place Preston in the position at $25 a week. But shortly thereafter his father had second thoughts, having run into State College president James K. Patterson on the street in Lexington and asking his advice on the matter. Patterson strongly recommended that young Preston remain employed as an engineer. Major Johnston, who had previously served on the State College Board of Trustees, admired Patterson for being "a long headed old fellow," and he cautioned Preston in a letter that "[Patterson] may be right. The farmer is a hewer of wood and a drawer of water for the corporations and the trusts. They allow him a haphazard chance to make a living but no opportunity to accumulate a fortune. It may be better to get in with the class that squeezes the life out of the farmer than to be one of the farmers." Despite Major Johnston's ambivalence, he eventually acquiesced to his son's desire, and Preston returned home shortly after the turn of the century to manage the Johnston farm; he would continue to do so throughout the Progressive Era and beyond. Preston and Margaret were very much alike, in that both were the privileged offspring of prominent Bluegrass families, and both found the challenges of the world beyond their homes to be a painful struggle requiring a sacrifice they were not willing to make.[29]

Both Preston and Margaret also came from very loving and supportive families. The Johnston family members were close and concerned about one another's welfare, and they corresponded in times of separation. Their surviving letters offer snapshots of their sentiments, their lives, and their lifestyles. Preston's mother, Sallie Chiles Johnston (who would die suddenly of a heart attack in 1904), wrote to him in August 1900, not only displaying her obvious affection for him but also revealing their family lifestyle as a blend of the cosmopolitan and the agrarian. In this letter she expressed her ardent desire for him to come home to Lexington so that she could see him, described in detail the recent renovations and improvements to the family yacht in Florida, and ended her letter with a postscript, explaining that a neighbor's horse had kicked one of their horses through the fence and had broken its leg, forcing Preston's brother, Marius, to shoot the injured animal.[30]

Two of Preston's younger brothers, John Pelham Johnston and Marius Early Johnston, followed Preston to State College, both receiving their degrees in 1900. Pelham, like Preston, majored in mechanical engineering; he would later become a prominent Lexington attorney. Pelham wrote to Preston in January 1900, describing his struggles with his senior year course work and relaying the local news. Pelham's letter portrayed 1900 Lexington as a violent place, rife with murders and shootings, including an incident involving Pelham. Three strange men had attempted to stop him as he rode home from college one evening and had fired several shots at him when he spurred on his horse. Marius, who received his medical degree from Columbia University in New York, wrote to Preston in October 1907 (signing the letter, as usual, "your loving brother") with the news that he had become the personal physician to Mrs. Lucy Coleman Carnegie, the widow of Andrew Carnegie's brother, Thomas. Marius traveled with Mrs. Carnegie and her large family and stayed with them for extended periods at their private retreat, Cumberland Island, located off the coast of Georgia near Fernandina, Florida. According to Marius's nephew, Robert Wickliffe Preston Johnston, Lucy Carnegie reigned "like Queen Victoria" at the Cumberland Island estate. Marius apparently made a favorable impression on the queen and her subjects, and he later cemented his relationship with the Carnegie family by marrying Lucy Carnegie's once-divorced daughter, Nancy, on 17 April 1912. Marius's letters to Preston in 1907–1908, when he first went to work for the Carnegies, were filled with anecdotes related to the lifestyle of this famous American family. In May 1908 Marius wrote that a nine-foot alligator had been killed in the fish pond in the Carnegies' yard, and they had had it skinned for the hide. That afternoon, he noted, he must "go and see if Mrs. C. [Lucy] wants to go snake hunting. This is one of our favorite amusements." The adventurous Marius would also go on African hunting safaris and Arctic expeditions before marrying and establishing a residence back home in Lexington. Even then, he and his wife, Nancy, "a very rich woman," traveled a great deal. He practiced medicine only sporadically, which, according to his nephew, "was too bad, for he was a surgeon, and a very good one. . . . He was a charming and lovely man, a fine man. . . . It was a great waste that he did not continue his profession."[31]

Unlike Marius, Preston was quite content to remain at home in the Bluegrass after his brief sojourn to Tennessee. Throughout the Progressive Era he managed his father's Fayette County farm and involved himself in local civic affairs. First and foremost a farmer, Preston sought to make his farming progressive and to carry his farming interests into the public, political sphere. In Kentucky, as throughout the South, there was a movement in the Progressive Era to support efficiency in agriculture through "scientific farming" and agricultural education through the agricultural colleges' extension services. Preston, in a prime example of his faith in science and his attempt to be a progressive, scientific farmer, wrote to Margaret in October 1911 that a cholera outbreak had killed some of his hogs and he had sought the help of the State University Agricultural Experiment Station to have the remainder of the hogs immunized with a cholera serum: "It is rather expensive, but it absolutely immunizes those that are not sick and sometimes saves sick ones." Margaret, in an October 1914 letter, explicitly referred to Preston as being a "scientific farmer," and he was a publicly active one as well. The American Tobacco Company's "Tobacco Trust" aggressively suppressed tobacco prices in the early years of the twentieth century, leading to revolt in some areas of western Kentucky and to the violent excesses of the night riders. There was also a nonviolent response to the trust in both central and western Kentucky, consisting of a movement to establish cooperatives to pool and store tobacco and thus force the trust to offer higher prices. Preston was quite active in this effort and wrote to Margaret in October 1909 that he was trying to convince farmers in the area to join the pool: "I am glad it [the campaign to pool tobacco] is near[ly] over because it has taken a lot of my time, but I am going to try and get as much more pooled as I can."[32]

Preston did not limit his civic involvement to issues associated with farming. He also served on the Fayette County Board of Education, and Margaret wrote from Meadow Wood to congratulate him when he was made chairman in August 1910. Preston exhibited a special interest in school architecture and construction and in teachers' salary schedules, and his letters to Margaret on these matters reveal that his racial attitudes were consonant with those of many white southerners at the time. He wrote to Margaret in 1911 that he was creating a salary schedule for the district's teachers to ensure that black teachers would not be paid more than white teachers, regardless of the number of students they taught. He was also personally designing two new county school buildings to be constructed, one for whites and one for blacks, and he felt strongly that they should not look identical: "The negro school plan I am working on is practically the same inside and the windows [are] the same as for the whites, but I have changed the door and porch so that it will look different on the outside and be a little less expensive. I want to give the negroes a good building well lighted, but not [one] to look like the white schools." In her reply, Margaret expressed her support of the idea "to make the colored schools look different from the white schools." Neither Preston nor Margaret ever engaged in written racial rhetoric as explicit as that of her brother, William, when he complained of the black diner at the Charlottesville hotel. Nevertheless, their letters exhibited their racial views and attitudes. Margaret, for instance, sometimes referred to blacks as "darkies" and northerners, pejoratively, as "d— Yankees." It must be kept in mind that Preston's father and Margaret's grandfather had both been Confederate officers, and their sentiments reflected their upbringing. Preston, for instance, insisted on attending the unveiling of the General John Hunt Morgan statue in Lexington on 18 October 1911, even though he was quite ill with an infection at the time. Margaret was a member of both the Children of the Confederacy and the Daughters of the Confederacy. Therefore, although Preston's service on the school board displayed a commendable sense of public responsibility for education, his efforts were not "color blind." Although he remained interested in educational matters, the venue for Preston's public service shifted in 1914, when he was nominated to serve on the Board of Trustees at the State University in Lexington. Margaret was sure he would be elected and stated, "I feel so proud, for it is a great honour to be chosen from among so many alumnae [sic]." Margaret's optimism was well founded, and Preston received a letter in December 1914 from W. T. Lafferty, secretary of the board and dean of the College of Law, confirming his election to the Board of Trustees and inviting him to begin attending board meetings immediately.[33]

Margaret felt free to express her pride in Preston's appointment because she had confessed her love for him and had promised to marry him three years earlier in 1911; by 1914 their letters were openly and ardently affectionate. In February 1914 she wrote to him while visiting in Massachusetts: "My dearest, I love you and I think of you so much . . . and I am so thankful that I have such a good, honest, true man to love and to love me." Their courtship had already lasted seven years by 1914, and their formal engagement and marriage had been delayed by her reluctance to leave home during her father's extended illness. Still, it appeared that they would certainly marry in 1914. Margaret hoped to marry that October and wrote to Preston that she already felt as if they were "spiritually husband and wife." Meanwhile, Preston was actively scrutinizing building magazines for the ideal house, which he planned to construct for them on the Johnston family farm. However, the death of Margaret's father in June 1914 heightened her concern for her mother's welfare and accentuated her hesitance to marry and leave her mother alone, since Sarah Preston was reluctant to live with her daughter once she married. By September 1916 the ever-faithful Preston was gently and affectionately nudging Margaret forward and offering ample reassurances:

> I am so glad that you have talked to your mother and that our plans are getting settled into something definite. It hardly seems real after the long time that we have waited and talked about it [marriage]. I love you so much and you are so good and sweet. . . . I hope that your mother won't make up her mind so irrevocably that she can't come to live with us at some future date. . . . In the meantime you will be close to her and your responsibilities not so great that you can't see a lot of her. I know that her comfort and happiness mean so much to you and I hope that it will be all for the best. I want to help you in every way I can and I want you to be happy.

Finally, more than a year later, on 8 November 1917, Margaret and Preston were married. Shortly thereafter, Margaret received an affectionate, congratulatory letter from her distant cousin and owner of the *Lexington Herald,* Desha Breckinridge, in which he playfully addressed her as "the Sweetest Young Married Woman in the Whole State" and expressed his hope that she and Preston had enjoyed their honeymoon in New York. Margaret and Preston lived that winter at Hampton Court with her mother and then took up residence on the Johnston farm, where they would raise two sons— Philip Preston Johnston (III), born in 1918, and Robert Wickliffe Preston Johnston, born in 1920. Several years after Preston's death in 1937, at age fifty-nine, Margaret would, with sorrow, pay written tribute to him as "a Christian, a gentleman, a devoted husband and father." In retrospect, Margaret had taken on the responsibilities, joys, and sorrows of marriage just as the prewar Progressive Era ended, an era in which she had lived a relatively carefree and leisured life that was benevolent, progressive, and cultured.[34]

MARGARET AND THE CIVIC LIFE

With the stressful, if exhilarating, Bryn Mawr experience behind her, and with the emotional support of a devoted suitor and a loving, generous, and socially prominent family, Margaret was able to lead a happy, privileged, and civically active life between 1906 and her marriage in late 1917. She has been portrayed elsewhere as a full-fledged member of Lexington's leisure class, engaging in a seemingly endless round of activities composed of "'motor-car' rides, . . . parties, . . . attend[ing] political rallies and football games, and lunch[ing] frequently at the country club." Unquestionably, she was a member of Lexington's social elite; her name appeared frequently on the "society" pages of the local press throughout this era. Moreover, Margaret lamented that "the sheltered, protected lady" was a disappearing role, and "soon there won't be any more ladies in that sense of the word, except among the plutocratic classes." In a passage typical of her wit, she expressed to Preston her reaction to a book entitled *Woman and Labour* by Olive Schreiner, which she labeled "a very remarkable book. But, it makes me feel like a drone on the face of the earth. She [Schreiner] thinks there is no hope for the race unless women work like the dickens, that is, raise large families and be doctors, lawyers, and business people besides. It makes you kind of breathless to read it." However, it is also clear from her diaries and correspondence, and from local press accounts, that she was much more than a social butterfly.

When Margaret died in April 1964, both Lexington papers and the *Louisville Courier-Journal* printed obituary articles, and all three referred to her as a "civic leader." Margaret began to assume the role of civic leader in the Progressive Era, and in these early years of the new century, her civic life was one of active benevolent concern and progressive reform effort.[35]

The Industrial School

For Victorian Americans, both "religious fervor and educational earnestness" shaped a moral imperative to strive for both personal and social improvement. Moreover, in the early twentieth century, many young women found in voluntarism an outlet for their need to strive, be useful, and expand and further their own interests and personal development. These impulses led them to join clubs and organizations involved in religious, charitable, and educational endeavors. For Margaret, voluntarism and religious fervor combined in her active and faithful participation in the decorating activities of the Altar Guild (serving as vice president in 1916) and in the various functions of the Women's Auxiliary at Lexington's Christ Church Cathedral, where she eventually became a vestryman. Moreover, as previously mentioned, she financially supported church-sponsored charitable and educational institutions such as St. John's Collegiate Institute and Industrial School. Looking back on all her activities during the years before the First World War, Margaret clearly considered her work for the church most important: "life was very full, with all kinds of civic, social, and charitable activities. Above these, was always Church and duties connected therewith."[36]

In the secular realm, Margaret combined "educational earnestness," benevolence, and voluntarism in her work at the Industrial School in Lexington. This charitable, privately operated, manual arts training school had been established in 1876 as the Saturday Industrial School, and the *Lexington Morning Transcript* referred to it in 1885 as a "true charity" for the poor, sometimes hungry, but nevertheless "bright faced children . . . from the homes of our mechanics." These were children who, the *Transcript* made clear, needed to be controlled as well as helped: "If any scholars of the school are caught begging in the streets, they are liable to dismissal. It is pathetic to see how many of them gather in, in inclement weather. . . . On such days it is almost impossible to get near the stoves for the crowds of little forms, many of them far too thinly clad." During the Progressive Era the Industrial School was located at the northeast corner of Fourth and Upper streets in Lexington, in the building that would later house the Phillis Wheatley YWCA. Since its inception the school had been operated on Saturday mornings by volunteer teachers——mostly women——and offered a range of subjects to both boys and girls, including, by 1910, "Sewing . . . Cooking, Chair-caning and Woodcarving and Carpentry." By 1913 embroidery and basketry had been added, and night classes in millinery and dressmaking were offered for older students. The thriving institution reported an overall enrollment of 352 pupils during the 1912–1913 school year.[37]

Margaret Preston was one of six volunteer assistants supervised by Margaret Hunt in her classroom at the Industrial School on Saturday morning, 9 November 1907. She noted in her diary that "the children are all tiny in that room, just learning the stitches on samples. . . . It is a fine work and I think I shall enjoy it." Apparently, she did enjoy it, for her diaries reflect that whenever she was not traveling, she worked at the school on Saturday mornings from October through May each year until she married in the fall of 1917. Margaret understood her role at the school as one of *serving* these working-class children, referring to the last regular Saturday of the school year before the annual closing ceremonies in May as the "last serving Saturday." Margaret served the Industrial School and its students in a variety of ways. By the summer of 1913 she was listed among the officers of the school, serving as auditor as well as teacher. When the school held an exhibition and sale in May 1915 to raise funds for the night classes, she was in charge of the "Candy Table." At the closing exercises each May, prizes were awarded and a program of music and recitations was performed for the audience. After this ceremony in 1916, Margaret noted in her diary, "I gave each of my ten little girls . . . a small coin purse." For the most part, however, what Margaret and the other volunteers gave was their time and effort. Each year the school provided a Christmas dinner for the children. On 1 January 1916 the *Lexington Leader* reported that 200 children had been fed at the event: "The officers and teachers were in charge and attended to all of the details of the menu and serving with their own fair hands." If such rhetoric placed Margaret amid a scene of Victorian benevolence, she could also be found laboring as a member of the Lexington Civic League, an agency quite suggestive of the progressive reform impulse.[38]

The Civic League

While in college, Margaret had dabbled in activities associated with progressive reform, having on one occasion traveled to Philadelphia to tell stories to children at the Front Street Settlement House. However, she had been somewhat disillusioned by that experience when one or more of the children stole money from her purse. "That shows how little an effect all this work really has on them," she wrote. "Excuse me from ever living in the slums if I can help it." Despite this early, rancorous reaction to the travails of social service, Margaret's circle of friends and relatives was replete with women caught up in the social welfare reform efforts characteristic of the Progressive Era—intimates who, by their example, had a definite influence on Margaret. In 1907, not long after Margaret left Bryn Mawr, her college friend "Phoenix" wrote with obvious pleasure about "hearing a Russia lecture at Hull House, and meeting Jane Addams in a chummy manner." Another friend from Bryn Mawr, "Peggy," described to Margaret, with humor rather than rancor, her own struggles in the field of "social work" in 1910: "I mustn't forget my last, despairing attempt to do some Social Work. I'm quite proud of it—it has resulted in my teaching various women how to cut out 'garments' for themselves or their children. Theoretically, that is, I teach them. Actually, I do the cutting while they nurse the last baby, and give me advice!" Mary Neville, Margaret's cousin, wrote of her sister Linda's persistent benevolent efforts in Lexington: "Linda is still working at the typewriter and the telephone, and rushing to the Charity Building or the hospital." And, of course, Margaret's mother was active in progressive reform endeavors, becoming in 1906 a charter member of the "Anti Child Slavery League of America," whose certificate of membership stated its creed and charge: "Believing that child labor injures the children, and is therefore a serious danger to the nation; desiring to prevent it by all lawful means; promising aid that wrongful employment of children may be prevented, and that children shall attain their rightful growth, morally, mentally, and physically; pledging personal efforts to secure, if possible, the rescue from bondage and the sending to school of at least one child."[39]

Seemingly even more influential than her mother's activism and idealism was the inspiration Margaret received from one of her distant cousins, Madeline ("Madge") McDowell Breckinridge. Margaret was somewhat in awe of her older cousin, and when Breckinridge and another civic activist spoke at the opera house in May 1909, Margaret noted in her diary that "both spoke well, but Madge was truly eloquent." Years later Margaret referred to Madge as "one of the most brilliant women I have ever known." By the time Margaret left Bryn Mawr, Madge (Mrs. Desha) Breckinridge was already active and prominent in the field of progressive reform, having received inspiration and guidance from her sister-in-law and pioneering professional social worker Sophonisba Breckinridge. Madge had been among the founders in 1900 of both the Associated Charities, which attacked the problems of the poor in Lexington with the casework methods identified with "scientific" charity, and the Lexington Civic League, which sought to improve the civic climate of the city by establishing a variety of progressive programs. These programs included community playgrounds and parks and, after a four-year campaign, the Lincoln School, built in 1912 in the Lexington slum known as Irish Town to offer a progressive blend of educational and social services to the poor.[40]

Margaret had become active in the Civic League at least by the spring of 1909, when her diary reveals that she was on the music committee for a league-sponsored public lecture. She would serve on other, more important, committees in the years to come. On 8 November 1912 a typed letter from the membership committee soliciting dues was mailed to 200 Civic League members, and this letter succinctly spelled out the progressive efforts and accomplishments of the league to that time: "Several movements that have since become institutions in this town originated in the League, [and] among the most important of these are: The successful effort to introduce manual training in our city schools[;] The movement for the establishment of playgrounds in various parts of the city[;] The idea of the necessity for a Juvenile Court; Yard improvement work; Raising funds for the building of the Model [Lincoln] School in the West End." The letter was written and signed by Margaret and the two other women on the league's membership committee. Her husband-to-be, Preston Johnston, had helped stamp and seal the letters at the Preston family's new apartment on Hampton Court the night before. Two weeks later, on 30 November 1912, Margaret, who had helped solicit funds to construct the Lincoln School, attended the dedication ceremonies. The program of the event preserved in her diary indicates that the Morton High School Orchestra provided the music, the children of the school performed songs and dances, and Sophonisba Breckinridge, among others, spoke at the ceremony. Margaret wrote in a matter-of-fact manner about the day in her diary: "It was a very interesting occasion. The speeches were good and not too long, and the children did their part well. After the meeting we looked at the school building."[41]

Margaret had been appointed by Madge Breckinridge the previous year to form the new Civic League membership committee made up of, as Madge put it, "young persons like yourself, who are not yet quite worked to death like the rest of us old stagers, and who have more friends and social acquaintances." Madge wrote to Margaret on 15 March 1911 on league stationery to remind her of this appointment and to give other instructions about the various tasks and duties to be carried out. Indeed, Madge depended on Margaret to perform so many chores related to her civic projects that Mary Neville wrote to Margaret at Meadow Wood in 1914 and asked, "How has Madge been able to accomplish anything with you and Linda [Neville] away?" Mary's question was consistent with the many letters Margaret received from Madge, especially after 1910, asking for her help, giving her instructions, and urging her on. Madge was apparently well aware that she called on her young cousin a great deal; in 1918 she closed a letter to Margaret with this fact in mind: "With best love to you and hoping you'll get some rest with . . . me out of town." Margaret served the Civic League (and therefore Madge) in a variety of capacities throughout the Progressive Era. In February 1915 she was elected first vice president of the league while continuing to serve on the membership and dues committees. In 1917 Margaret also served as vice chair of the league's playground committee, and Madge wrote to her that summer discussing playground expenditures, including the need to send Arthur Leland, a former supervisor of Louisville's playgrounds, $25 for drawing up the plans for Lexington's playgrounds. Madge, turning somber sectionalism into lighthearted banter embedded in a compliment, described Leland as a "splendid young Yankee, full of ideas and energy."[42]

Margaret's early experience collecting dues for the Lexington Civic League led to additional work and responsibility. However, Margaret's contact with Madge was not all work, for she also socialized with Madge and her husband, Desha, owner of the *Lexington Herald,* dining and playing bridge with the couple occasionally. Nevertheless, a series of diary entries in 1916 indicate that Margaret and Madge worked many hours a day for two weeks that July in Madge's office in the McClelland Building to develop a comprehensive, indexed card file of the Civic League's financial contributors. By December 1916 Margaret was serving on an auditing committee when it was decided that they would have to consult an "expert accountant . . . to go over the books as they are complicated." Perhaps bolstered by such appeals to, and reliance on, professional expertise, Margaret began serving as the Civic League treasurer in January 1917, responsible for, among other things, paying the bills. Her role as an official of the Civic League brought Margaret into formal contact with community leaders throughout the city. For instance, on 11 January 1917 Margaret and two other league officials met, somewhat unsuccessfully, with Mayor James Rogers to try to persuade him to increase the annual appropriations for playgrounds: "The Mayor promised us $1000 last year, but said that he could not increase that sum to $1500 as we wished." Nor was there instant success later that month when she represented the league in a meeting with the school board: "We requested the board to buy a moving-picture machine for the schools, and we offered to pay half the cost. The board was very polite, but gave no definite reply." Margaret evidently pursued this project, or similar ones, for some time, as there is evidence that she was corresponding two years later with R. E. Gumm, manager of Exhibitors Supply Company, an Indianapolis firm that dealt in "Motion Picture Machines and Supplies."[43]

One further meeting between Margaret, as Civic League treasurer, and the community's leadership illustrates how southern progressives in the early twentieth century often functioned, to quote one historian, "both as agents of modernization and as guardians of Southern tradition." In 1917, as Margaret recorded it in her diary, the league wished to encourage recreational work in the city's black schools and wanted to donate funds to purchase equipment for this purpose; indeed, this was a project in which Margaret "was very much interested." Therefore, on 9 March 1917, Margaret and two other league members, Mrs. Gilmour and Mr. Mummert, went to the Russell School, where they "had a talk with the colored principal." Margaret almost always recorded in her diary the names of those she interacted with, but apparently she did not find it necessary (or perhaps even desirable) to name the "colored principal" she met with that day. Nor did she give any indication that she was aware that she lived only a few blocks from the North Upper Street home of principal William Fouse and his wife, Lizzie, or that the Fouses were outstanding members of the city's black civic and intellectual elite. If, indeed, she was as unaware of the Fouses' accomplishments and contributions as her terse, indifferent diary entry suggests, it was doubtless because the opaque social barrier of segregation and white supremacy erected before, during, and especially after the Civil War—a barrier sanctified as southern tradition by her own time—made it impossible for her to really *see* them. However, if Margaret's attitudes toward race were rooted in the archaic past, her attitudes toward (white) women's civic rights and duties were linked with the modernistic future.[44]

The Equal Rights Associations

Historians of the women's suffrage movement in Kentucky have broadly portrayed it as a white, gentry-class struggle to achieve political parity, a movement fueled by the national, mainstream progressive reform impulse and undergirded by New South attitudes. For the women involved, this movement reinforced a sense of self, group, and regional identity—attributes that defined the movement throughout the South. In light of this blend of elements, it is little wonder that Margaret Preston became a suffragist. Margaret was certainly a progressive in her volunteer endeavors, and she was certainly a southerner by self-identification as well as background, writing to Preston in 1914, *"I am glad my lot is cast in the South."* Moreover, the two women she idealized and most admired, her mother and her cousin and mentor, Madge Breckinridge, were both suffragists. In fact, Breckinridge and Laura Clay were Kentucky's two premier suffrage leaders, Madge succeeding Clay as president of the Kentucky Equal Rights Association (KERA) in 1912 after concluding "that without the vote, she and other women would never have the political power to achieve the other reforms she so much wanted." Of course, as James Klotter has written, Breckinridge and Clay were only "the most visible parts of the [Kentucky suffrage] story, for numerous other women had aided greatly," and among these less celebrated soldiers in the battle for the vote was Margaret Preston.[45]

Claudia Knott, in her work on the Kentucky suffrage movement, has argued that "the story of the school suffrage campaign from 1907 to victory in 1912 is essentially an account of the growing sentiment among clubwomen for woman suffrage." Certainly, by 1910 both Margaret and her mother had become quite active in the local suffrage movement, their interest doubtless intensified through their close association with the Woman's Club of Central Kentucky and its affiliation with the Kentucky Federation of Woman's Clubs. The federation had taken an acute interest in school reform and, consequently, in the school suffrage issue, which involved the right of (literate, and thus largely white) women to the vote on local school matters. Margaret, who was visiting in Richmond, Virginia, wrote to Preston on 14 January 1910 and asked, "Did you go to the grand School Suffrage meeting? Tell me of it." She was referring to a meeting of advocates of school suffrage at the Lexington Opera House on 12 January. In announcing the meeting on 10 January, the *Lexington Leader* noted that Mrs. Wickliffe Preston, Margaret's mother, would preside and that this meeting would be "the best and most largely attended that has ever been held in this city in the interest of that cause." Preston Johnston was sympathetic to women's suffrage, writing to Margaret in 1910 that he viewed it as "the right thing." He answered Margaret's query with due respect, noting, "I went to the mass meeting. . . . There was a very good crowd, . . . [and] Mrs. Preston presided very gracefully." Margaret's mother was very much engaged in the cause of equal rights for women. For instance, she presided over a series of classes and lectures advocating equal suffrage for women beginning on 7 February 1910. Shortly thereafter, in April, she was listed by the *Lexington Herald* as one of "several prominent women of Lexington . . . identified with the Central Kentucky Woman's Club" to telegram the director of the census in Washington to protest "against the wording of census instructions classing house wives as having no occupation."[46]

Margaret returned home in time to join the fray. On 10 February 1910 the *Lexington Leader* reported that a delegation of "representative women from Lexington, Louisville, and other cities," headed by Madge Breckinridge and including Margaret Preston, had called on legislators in Frankfort and "made earnest and eloquent pleas for the right of the mothers of Kentucky to be heard in matters concerning the education of their children." Margaret wrote in her diary that she, Madge, Linda Neville, and several others had caught the "Interurban" train to Frankfort that morning and returned to Lexington that afternoon with some satisfaction: "I left the Capital as soon as we heard the [Senate] committee report favorably on the bill, . . . [and] caught the 4:30 Interurban back home." The school suffrage bill ultimately failed in 1910 but would pass in 1912, largely due to the work of KERA. Margaret and her mother were members of both KERA and the local Fayette Equal Rights Association (FERA), and on 23 January 1913 Margaret was elected secretary of the latter. The organization's minute book for 1917–1918 indicates that she continued to serve as secretary until the end of May 1918, when she stepped down as the birth of her first child approached and Mrs. Whitney Hostetter became secretary pro tem.[47]

In additional to her FERA secretarial duties, Margaret was very active in other aspects of the local suffrage movement between 1913 and 1918. In April 1915, for instance, when Mrs. Pethick-Lawrence, "the noted English Suffragist," spoke at the Ben Ali Theater, Margaret was identified by the *Lexington Leader* as being in charge of the "ushers and distribution of Literature." By 1915 there was growing public acceptance of suffrage in Kentucky, and the movement's increase in popularity inevitably influenced the students on the city's campuses. Reflecting this growing influence, as well as the excitement surrounding the upcoming 1915 National Suffrage Day to be celebrated in Lexington on 1 May, a number of female State University students met in the Philosophian Literary Society room in Patterson Hall on the evening of 5 March to form a campus Equal Rights Association, and "twenty-four of the young ladies joined," according to the *Lexington Herald.* Two months later, in an editorial under the title "National Suffrage Day," the pro-suffrage *Herald* urged all Lexingtonians to attend the suffrage parade beginning at Gratz Park and ending at Duncan Park: "In a thousand cities and in ten thousand villages in the United States, today men and women of every political party, of every religious faith, of every grade of intelligence, education and influence will give public demonstration of their belief that equal rights in political matters should be given to men and women." Margaret was among those in charge of decorating the suffrage parade automobiles with flags, and she was stationed at the Third Street entrance to Gratz Park. "I and a number of other girls were quite busy giving out the flags with which the motor-cars were decorated. Then . . . I rode in the parade in the Breckinridge car with Desha." Continuing her suffrage work, in September 1915 Margaret was involved in soliciting subscribers for the *Woman's Journal and Suffrage News,* receiving a letter of thanks and encouragement from the journal's managing editor, Agnes E. Ryan. Once again in May 1916 she was on the planning committee of the annual suffrage parade and noted the event in her diary entry of 6 May: "The great event of the day was the suffrage parade. The weather was ideal, and the number of people in the procession far exceeded my expectations. I was very proud of the way the whole thing worked out . . . I carried a transparency with the motto 'Suffrage Moves On.'"[48]

Indeed, true to the motto Margaret carried in the 1916 parade, suffrage, along with everything else, was moving on, toward the war years. In June 1916 Margaret represented Columbia in the preparedness parade at the invitation of FERA; sometime late in 1917, in an undated memorandum, Margaret summarized FERA's war-related work, which ranged from recruiting for the Red Cross to knitting woolen garments for the army, and she ended this summary with a rather staunch blend of patriotism and suffragism: "In addition to this direct patriotic work, the FERA has continued its propanda [sic] for woman suffrage, since it believes that the world cannot be made safe for democracy until women as well as men have the ballot." Despite such rhetoric, and despite Margaret's considerable civic efforts, it would be disingenuous to leave the impression that she was an unmitigated zealot, for she repeatedly resisted taking top leadership roles and refused to take it all too seriously.[49]

When Margaret was first elected secretary of FERA in January 1913, she confided to her diary that she wanted to "beg off," and in 1915 she complained in her diary about the work involved. In February 1915 she resisted Madge's attempt to have her elected to the top position at the Civic League: "I was terrified, because she wanted me elected president. By great efforts I got off with being elected 1st Vice Pres. . . . I was surely glad to get home safely." In December 1916 she resisted Madge again: "Madge wants me to be the next president [of the Civic League], but I prefer to be the next treasurer instead, as there is less notoriety." And although Margaret did assist in making the arrangements for the Pethick-Lawrence suffrage lecture in April 1915, she flatly refused to take complete charge of the affair. Moreover, as much as she admired Madge, she sometimes found her zeal a little trying: "Madge came in the motor and took Mamma and me for a ride. Madge talked volubly of suffrage, as usual. After supper I was so tired that I turned out all the lights." Nor did Margaret lack a sense of humor, reacting to opponents of suffrage with amusement rather than anger or outrage. She jovially wrote to Preston in August 1910 from Meadow Wood of her attempt to convince "an unenlightened, . . . extremely prejudiced" male of the merits of equal suffrage: "Of course, he was not convinced, but . . . our whole conversation was very funny, anyway." The same reaction was evident in September 1916 when Margaret participated on the affirmative side in a public debate on suffrage at a Baptist Church near Meadow Wood. She later recorded her amusement in her diary and in a letter to Preston: "I wish you could have heard the arguments on the other side. They were the funniest you have ever heard in all your life." Margaret could also step back from her strong feelings on the issue of equal rights and humorously note her own inconsistencies. For instance, although she quite seriously insisted to Preston in the fall of 1916 that their Episcopal marriage vows should be changed to place men and women on an equal basis, when she wrote to him that same fall of a motoring incident she observed, "We went over the most awful road, and I must say that, suffragette as I am, I prefer having a man to drive me in the dark on a terrible road."[50]

Margaret's ability to detach herself through her sense of humor from the emotionally volatile subjects of women's suffrage and equal rights, her ability to resist (on occasion) her persuasive mentor's demands on her time and energy, and her occasional shunning of top leadership positions might suggest that she was not as dedicated as some of her peers in the reform movement. Or it might simply reflect the fact that Margaret harbored other interests and reserved some of her time and physical, emotional, and intellectual energy to pursue those interests. Though quite committed, she was not willing to place herself unvaryingly among those progressive, reform-minded women whom her cousin Eugene Simpson amusedly referred to in 1914 as being "constantly ready to immolate themselves upon current events."[51]

MARGARET AND THE INTELLECTUAL LIFE

Historian Donald Scott has noted that, by the mid-nineteenth century, "older models of genteel intellectuality in which culture was the pastime of a leisured class" were no longer viable for many. However, that model best describes Margaret Preston's intellectual life in the first two decades of the twentieth century, for her social and financial situation allowed her a "leisured" approach, rather than having to develop what Scott has referred to as a "serious vocational commitment to reflection." Even so, her commitment to intellectual endeavor was, arguably, no less "serious" than the commitment of those who wed their intellectual vitality to a remunerative career. Among the intellectual interests to which Margaret was committed, three stand out in her diaries and letters: private reading, the small-group literary pursuits of her Woman's Club, and the public theater as both art and entertainment.[52]

Reading

Reading "filled the leisure hours" of Victorian middle- and upper-class women prior to the First World War. But reading was more than simply recreation. Victorian Americans approached reading not only as a leisure activity but also as a serious undertaking; indeed, it has been argued that reading was the "central activity of Victorian intellectual life." Among the most common entries in Margaret Preston's diaries throughout the Progressive Era were the notations about reading—in the evenings at home, in the mornings at the city library, and during her visits to Virginia and elsewhere. At the end of February 1911 Margaret listed those works she had read over the previous months, comprising forty titles of mostly fiction and poetry by American and European authors including James Lane Allen, Jane Austen, Honoré de Balzac, George Eliot, Percy Bysshe Shelley, and William Butler Yeats, among others. The fact that she made the list for herself in her private diary suggests that what she read was important to her. Margaret and her family owned many books, and when they moved from the Bodley House to Hampton Court in October 1912, she lamented that most of their books would have to be stored, since they could take "only about 100 books to the flat." Perhaps no one was more aware of the importance Margaret placed on reading than her future husband, Preston Johnston, who apparently read less, both quantitatively and qualitatively, than she did. Early in their relationship Preston willingly acknowledged his shortcomings in this area, but he eventually suffered her admonishments nevertheless. In a 1910 letter written to her at Meadow Wood, he specifically equated reading with intellectual prowess and expressed his feelings of inferiority in this regard. Noting that he had been reading only newspapers and a few magazines while she had been reading the English poets Keats and Shelley, he conceded, "I suppose my intellect will have to remain feeble while you are spending the summer polishing yours up." Despite Preston's strategy of deference and self-effacement, Margaret eventually took him to task for his bad reading habits: "I am sorry you read such trashy books. There are a lot of good ones over at Marius' [his brother]. Why don't you borrow some of his Kiplings to read[?] . . . They are dandy stories—I should love to browse around in Marius' library, for he has so many things that I should love to read."[53]

Among the things Margaret loved to read in the prewar years—and she mentioned a profusion of works in her diaries—were magazines, which she often read at the city library. The literary magazines such as *Atlantic Monthly, Harper's,* and *Century* (formerly *Scribner's Monthly*) were the national arbiters of literary and intellectual matters from the mid-nineteenth to early twentieth centuries, and Margaret read not only these established works of "intellectual journalism" but also the new-century arbiters of style and fashion such as *Vogue,* first published in 1909. Thomas Bender, noted historian of American intellectual life, has reminded us that Edgar Allan Poe defended and justified magazines as a legitimate, necessary form of American letters in modern, hurried times, when "men are forced upon the curt, the condensed, . . . upon journalism in lieu of dissertation." Margaret, however, enjoyed ample time to read, and her fare included many novels. An avid fan of novelists, Margaret seemed quite thrilled when she met and went for an automobile ride with the famous Octave Thanet (Alice French) while visiting Illinois in 1911. One of her favorite authors—one she read repeatedly—was the English historical romance novelist Maurice Hewlett. Hewlett, who championed the cause of women's suffrage, was a very successful and popular author who reached the pinnacle of his literary career in the decade prior to the Great War, having been, by one account, "a historical novelist . . . without equal in his own generation." At any rate, Margaret enjoyed his work: Hewlett's novel *Halfway House* was among the books Margaret included in her February 1911 list; she read his *Mrs. Lancelot* in January 1913, described *The Little Iliad* as a "most delightful book" in August 1916, and found his *Love and Lucy* "entertaining" in January 1917. Margaret also admired H. G. Wells, the English author considered one of the important literary figures exemplifying the transition between the Victorian and modern periods in English literature. On 31 January 1917 Margaret sat up until midnight reading Wells's *The Research Magnificent,* published in 1915. Wellsian scholar Alfred Borrello has suggested that this novel represents Wells's optimistic faith and trust "in the power of a properly conducted education" to save humanity. Two days later she noted in her diary that she was reading Wells's *Mr. Britling Sees It Through,* published in 1916. This is a less optimistic work that New York intellectual and literary essayist Randolph Bourne, writing in the *Dial* in 1916, suggested is an "index of what war is doing to our education."[54]

In addition to magazines and novels, Margaret, an avid theatergoer since adolescence, read plays. In September 1909 she wrote to Preston Johnston from Meadow Wood that she was reading many of the plays of Henrik Ibsen, including *A Doll's House, Ghosts,* and *Hedda Gabler;* in November 1914 she read George Bernard Shaw's *Pygmalion,* which she found "extremely funny," and also several plays she found "delightful," including *Pantaloon, The Twelve Pound Look, Rosalind,* and *The Will* by Scottish author and playwright Sir James Matthew Barrie, most famous for his *Peter Pan;* in January 1915 she called Englishman John Galsworthy's *The Mob* "a wonderful play"; and in July 1915, after reading Oscar Wilde's *Lady Windermere's Fan,* she described it as "a very clever play, which has begun to seem quite old fashioned." Poetry was also prominent on Margaret's reading agenda; indeed, it was partly by sending her volumes of poetry by Shelley, Yeats, and Sir Walter Scott that Preston Johnston had endeared himself to her. In January 1917 Margaret worked for several hours at the city library to develop a program of "Southern war poems" to present to a meeting of the local chapter of the Children of the Confederacy, an organization with which she had long been associated. This endeavor illustrates a confluence of major threads in Margaret's life: her southern roots, her intellectual interests, and her public activities. In fact, poetry was often the vehicle by which Margaret carried her love of private reading into her public life as a prominent member of the Woman's Club of Central Kentucky.[55]

The Department of Literature

Margaret, like her mother, was extremely active in the Woman's Club of Central Kentucky during the Progressive Era. She was first elected recording secretary of the WCCK in March 1908, at the end of her mother's first term as president of the club. Subsequently, Margaret was elected second vice president in 1916 and was reelected in 1917. By 1915 her literary proclivities also led Margaret to chair the club's Department of Literature, succeeding her mother in that position. Margaret would remain chairperson of this department into the 1920s and would remain generally active in the Woman's Club throughout her life. She was still listed as an officer (second auditor) in the 1959–1960 WCCK yearbook, only four years prior to her death.[56]

The Department of Literature met regularly in the prewar years to hear lectures on, discuss, and critique the lives and works of a wide array of literary luminaries. A few weeks after Kentucky artist and poet Robert Burns Wilson died at the end of March 1916, the *Lexington Leader* announced that because his death was "so lamented," he would be honored at the next meeting of the Woman's Club Department of Literature: "Miss Margaret Preston, the chairman, is arranging a Robert Burns Wilson program, and a sketch of his life . . . [and] readings from his poems will be among the features." Margaret subsequently organized and presided over a program consisting of a biographical remembrance of Wilson by Mrs. A. M. Harrison that, according to the *Lexington Herald,* "touched a sympathetic chord in many hearts." This biographical sketch of Wilson was followed by "well chosen selections from his poems [that] were beautifully read" by Sarah Preston, Margaret's mother.[57]

Robert Burns Wilson was not the only poet whose passing would be lamented and whose memory would be honored with a literary program at the Department of Literature in 1916. On 22 April 1915 twenty-seven-year-old English poet Rupert Brooke, a "young man of remarkable beauty and charm," died of blood poisoning aboard a French hospital ship. Brooke's personal attractiveness and charm and his untimely death during the war contributed to his romanticized image, summarized by biographer Timothy Rogers as a combination of "the 'beautiful young poet' myth, and . . . the aura which clings to Brooke as a 'war poet.'" At any rate, Margaret read his poems in January 1916 and was quite taken with them: "During the morning I read the poems of Rupert Brooke. . . . They are perfectly wonderful, and I am so glad that I have read them." This admiration apparently inspired her to arrange a program devoted to Brooke at the Department of Literature's meeting on 5 April 1916. According to the *Lexington Leader,* Margaret presided and "introduced the subject in her most charming, characteristic way," after which a paper on the poet's life was presented by Elizabeth King

Smith and several of his poems were read by Laura Kincaid. To conclude the program, "Miss Preston added a word . . . telling of the college life of the poet and reading a poem by Mrs. F. A. Dangerfield lamenting his loss to Rugby School, Cambridge University, and the world." That night Margaret recorded in her diary that the audience had been small due to bad weather, but she and her mother thought the paper presented had been excellent—so good, in fact, that when Preston visited that evening, Margaret "read him Elizabeth Smith's paper, and several of the Brooke poems."[58]

The program devoted to Rupert Brooke was conducted entirely by Woman's Club members, but outside speakers were often invited to address the meetings as well, and these occasions sometimes represented a coalescence of university and community intellectual endeavors. Such was the case when Margaret asked twenty-five-year-old Reuben Thornton Taylor, an instructor of English at State University of Kentucky, to speak to the Department of Literature on the poetry of Englishman Francis Thompson. Taylor was born into "a prominent [LaGrange] Kentucky family" in 1891 and entered State University in Lexington in 1909, where he majored in English literature; he also joined the staff of the student publications the *Idea* and the *Kentuckian* and became a member of the Kappa Sigma social fraternity and the Canterbury (Literary) Club. While in college, his studiousness earned him the nickname "Book" or "Bookie," by which he was generally known. Upon his graduation from State University in 1914, Bookie Taylor was immediately hired by his alma mater as an instructor in the English Department, and he taught there briefly until he left for Oxford University in the fall of 1916, having been awarded a Cecil Rhodes scholarship. When Taylor vacated his instructor's position, it was filled by Frances Jewell, a Lexingtonian who would go on to serve as dean of women at the University of Kentucky in the 1920s and would become the wife of the university's third president, Frank McVey.[59]

Margaret Preston and Frances Jewell were well acquainted, working and socializing together in the Woman's Club. Margaret first met Bookie Taylor on 22 November 1915 when she accompanied Jewell to a tea party where he was present. Margaret was favorably impressed by Taylor at their first meeting: "Mr. Taylor is a young instructor at the State University who Laura [Kincaid] thinks may speak for my department at the Club. He seemed very nice, and I shall try to get him for February to do Francis Thompson." On 1 December Margaret noted in her diary that she had written to Taylor, inviting him to speak at the club the following February. Taylor accepted the invitation and called on Margaret at home in January 1916: "Mr. Reuben Thornton Taylor, who is to speak for my department at the Club . . . called. I took him for a long walk, and found him very entertaining." On the morning of 2 February 1916 Margaret spent several hours at the library reading material on Francis Thompson in preparation for the biographical remarks she would make that afternoon on the troubled life of the drug-addicted poet, remarks that would serve as prelude and introduction to Taylor's address. Both Lexington papers reported on Taylor's performance at the Woman's Club in glowing terms. The *Lexington Herald* stated that he had given a "valuable and most delightful address," and the *Lexington Leader* called his performance "brilliant. . . . The paper was beautifully expressed and gracefully given. Mr. Taylor is a critic of cleverness and discernment, and with power of interpretation, not omitting the flashes of wit and keen sense of the fitness of things." Margaret's private thoughts, illustrative of her intellectual self-confidence and independence, differed somewhat from the laudatory public rhetoric of the local press: "My meeting came in the afternoon. . . . Bookie . . . was the star of the occasion. . . . I spoke my piece about the life of Frances Thompson, then came Bookie. His paper was very good and well prepared, but his delivery was poor, and he read the poetry badly." Despite this private critique of Taylor's performance, Margaret continued to enjoy her association with him and counted him as a friend She referred to Bookie as being "charming as usual" when he called on her in April 1916 to collect his essay on Thompson, which she had borrowed. She danced with him several times at the country club a month later, and she noted in her diary in December that she had written to him at Oxford. Nevertheless, their relationship was in essence social and cerebral rather than private and amorous, a friendship that both reflected and furthered the cross-pollination of campus and community intellectual life occurring in the city at the time.[60]

The Theater

Margaret's love of reading carried her not only into a public leadership role in the Department of Literature but also undergirded what was seemingly her favorite form of public entertainment: the theater. This is not to say that Margaret did not attend the cinema in the prewar era—a medium that was beginning to "dominate the local commercial entertainment market" in Lexington in the 1910s. In September 1912, in the first reference to moviegoing in her diaries, Margaret stated that she and another woman "walked downtown and saw the moving pictures at the Orpheum," which had opened earlier that year on East Main Street. Throughout the 1910s she continued to occasionally attend and sometimes enjoy motion pictures. For instance, in 1915, at another newly opened Lexington theater, the Ben Ali, she saw John Barrymore in *The Dictator* and considered it a "very good moving picture." She also saw the movie *Joan of Arc* at the Ben Ali in 1917 and found it "really wonderful." Nevertheless, she complained in a 1917 letter to Preston that movies hurt her eyes and noted, "I was bored, as I always am at moving pictures." In contrast, although Margaret often criticized the quality of specific live performances of plays, she never disparaged them en masse and seemed to thoroughly admire and enjoy the genre.[61]

As noted earlier, Margaret frequently attended plays in adolescence and while at Bryn Mawr, and this habit continued into her young adulthood, whether she was at home in Lexington or visiting elsewhere. At times she complained of not going to the theater frequently enough, and in fact, her visits to relatives in the Northeast often seemed in large measure to be planned around playgoing, or what might be called "theater vacations." Between 1910 and 1920 competition from film essentially ended the national system of New York–based touring commercial theatrical companies, the so-called combination companies that brought the professional stage to small cities and towns throughout the nation beginning in the 1870s. Therefore, Margaret traveled to the Northeast in the 1910s in part to see the professional stage performances that were becoming increasingly difficult to see at home in Lexington. A trip she made to Massachusetts and New York in 1914 provides a case in point. She wrote to Preston on 5 February 1914 that in the two weeks since she had left Lexington she had been "very fortunate in going to public amusements," including operas, concerts, and plays, and she named three professional stage plays she had seen: "'The Whip,' a melodrama of English sporting life; 'Where Dreams Come True,' a very pretty musical comedy; and 'Under Cover,' a dramatized detective story." She concluded by noting that she had enjoyed them all, "as I love things of that kind." A few days later she wrote to say that she had seen "Bernard

Shaw's play, 'Caesar and Cleopatra.' It was a splendid performance, and I enjoyed every minute of it." Other letters posted to Preston during this two-month trip indicate that she also saw *Hamlet* and at least two other professionally produced plays before her return to Lexington.[62]

At home in Lexington, Margaret enjoyed not only the locally available professional performances but also those staged in a variety of amateur venues, some of which were interwoven with her religious, political, and civic concerns. For instance, she enjoyed plays with a religious focus given at her church and was quite distressed in February 1916 when the weather prevented her from attending one: "I wanted very much to go to a little play given by the Junior Auxiliary at the Parish House, but rain poured all the afternoon. I started out, but came back as it was so wet, and I was afraid of catching cold." Margaret also enjoyed amateur productions with political themes. Such was the case on the evening of 3 May 1915, when she had supper with Preston and other friends at the Phoenix Hotel and then saw "the little amateur suffrage play, 'How the Vote Was Won,' given in the ballroom." She thought this play in support of female enfranchisement to be "very well given. We enjoyed it very much, and had quite a gay evening." Margaret's civic-benevolent concerns intersected with the amateur stage as well. When the Kirmess was staged at the opera house in February 1916 to raise money for the Baby Milk Fund, Margaret not only attended but also assisted the effort by selling candy. She noted later that "the performance went off very well," and $1,200 had been raised for the milk fund. Margaret's love of amateur theatrics also intersected with her civic reform interests when she and her mother attended a luncheon of the Associated Charities in January 1917 that included a play performed by local college students: "During lunch, a little play was given by Transylvania students showing how a family can be rehabilitated [*sic*] by organized charity methods." Such examples are not intended to suggest that Margaret required amateur performances to support a religious, political, or civic agenda, for she attended them just as readily for their aesthetic and entertainment value. Such was the case when she attended another collegiate extracurricular production in Lexington in June 1916: "Preston and I went to Hamilton College to see the plays of the Marlowe Club. They were excellently given, and I enjoyed every minute. . . . [They] may present 'Blue Roses' again in the autumn with men in the male characters." Margaret ended this private review of the Hamilton

College plays with a short remark quite characteristic of her in the prewar years, when she was an exuberant young woman with an enthusiastic appreciation for all of life, including the life of the mind: "We all enjoyed the plays immensely."[63]

In sum, Margaret Preston, scion of a prominent central Kentucky family and full-fledged member of Lexington's gentry class, led a life during the Progressive Era in which southern tradition and progressive reform intermingled, much as these cultural forces did throughout the city at large. In addition, Margaret was a relatively well-educated and cultured young woman whose intellectual life revolved, in large measure, around private reading, small-group literary efforts, and public entertainment centered around professional and amateur stage plays; indeed, these personal interests and endeavors, taken together, represented one model of intellectuality that the community could produce at that time. Certainly, Margaret's love of the dramatic arts was by no means hers alone, for a great many amateur plays were being staged and patronized throughout the city during the prewar years, suggesting considerable community interest and demand. Moreover, Margaret's attendance at plays performed by college students suggests that the community's interest in, and demand for, amateur dramatics was having an influence on the city's campuses as well.

CHAPTER SEVEN

THE DRAMATIC CLUBS TAKE THE STAGE

An Extracurricular Succession in Prewar Lexington

What's the matter with the literary society? Has it become a back
number? Does it no longer function in our college life?
—Editorial, *Crimson Rambler,* 9 May 1919

The large crowd, composed of students and theatre lovers, was enthusiastic
in its applause and happily caught the spirit from the start. The Strollers
play has now become an anticipated theatrical event of the year.
—*Lexington Leader,* 14 April 1916

When Margaret Preston exercised her taste for the theatrical arts during
the prewar years, she was, on an individual level, expressive of broad cultural trends. These trends would bring change to student life on campus
and beyond. This change, in turn, would ensure that although the collegiate extracurriculum would continue to play a role in the community's
intellectual life, the literary societies would no longer be the major players.
Nineteenth-century oratorical culture, the sine qua non of the Gilded Age
literary societies, which were defined and nurtured by it, had collapsed before the onslaught of the new culture of professionalism characteristic of
the Progressive Era; the societies would not survive this collapse, nor the accompanying changes in public taste for the arts of expression. Symptomatic
of both waning community interest and weakening organizational vitality,
the literary society–sponsored, off-campus public entertainments ceased in
Lexington after 1904, and although their open-to-the-public, on-campus
entertainments continued through the prewar years, these also suffered a
diminution of vitality, popularity, and importance. These developments co-

incided with the erosion of literary society popularity and organizational loyalty among the students at large and, moreover, among society members themselves. At one time essentially the only agency of student life beyond the classroom, before the century's turn the literary societies were already being joined on the city's campuses by a growing field of contending extracurricular attractions, including athletics, Greek-letter fraternities, and a variety of clubs created around specific interests and activities ranging from music to dramatics. Inevitably, divided interest and loyalty followed in the wake of these additional choices. It is perhaps impossible to pinpoint one historical moment when student interest was first seen shifting away from the societies or when divided loyalties became a threat to the societies' preeminence, but four such moments are highly suggestive: (1) in 1890, Kentucky University's student paper the *Focus* began to compartmentalize its coverage of the societies (and other activities such as sports) into discrete columns or regular feature articles, no longer assuming that the societies and their activities essentially *were* the campus news; (2) in the early 1890s, literary society members at both Kentucky University and State College began to hold memberships in other student organizations as well; (3) in 1896, students "attended the base ball game in a body" in the afternoon prior to that night's intercollegiate oratorical contest at the Lexington Opera House; and (4) in 1903, the winners of the intercollegiate oratorical contest gained additional notoriety and prestige by being the guests of honor at a Kappa Alpha Fraternity banquet. At any rate, student interests and tastes evolved and changed along with those of the larger culture, competing extracurricular organizations proliferated, and student loyalties became divided. In the wake of this change and competition, the Lexington collegiate literary societies found themselves in a struggle to remain relevant, and in the ensuing years, the societies attempted to adapt. For example, the Cecropian Literary Society at Kentucky University, apparently reacting to growing student interest in dramatics, reached beyond its traditional activities to form its own dramatic club, which performed *The Mouse Trap* in Morrison Chapel in 1905. Likewise, the Philothean and Phileusebian literary societies of Transylvania's College of the Bible, no doubt reacting to the growing influence of sports on campus, played basketball before "scores of members and sympathizers" for an "intersociety championship" in 1910.[1]

The Decline of the Literary Society
in the Prewar Era

At the beginning of the new century, the student press at Kentucky University reflected the strength and vitality of the literary societies there; yet at the same time, they were the harbingers of the societies' difficulties and decline. On the one hand, the societies and their activities appeared in regular, prominent feature articles in the students' monthly magazine the *Transylvanian,* and each society merited its own titled column in each issue. On the other hand, there were indications of problems within the literary societies and of competition from other extracurricular organizations. In the January 1900 issue the editor lamented the poor attendance at some of the societies' meetings, chastised the members who did not attend regularly, and ended his complaint with a demand: "Either resign from the organization [literary society] or attend its meetings." Moreover, whereas the table of contents for the January 1900 issue of the *Transylvanian* included the customary heading, "The Literary Societies," in April 1900 there was a new heading—"The Societies and the Fraternities"—reflecting the growing strength of competing organizations. By 1905 the *Transylvanian* occasionally omitted the separate section with "societies" in the heading, reporting the activities of the literary societies and a variety of other extracurricular groups, along with numerous miscellaneous items, in the "Locals" section of the magazine. Symbolic of changing student priorities, in the May 1905 issue only one society, the Philothean, was briefly featured, whereas three full pages were devoted to athletics. Moreover, the societies seemed to garner the most attention when they were associated with dramatics—not one of their traditional functions or areas of interest. For instance, the February 1905 *Transylvanian* devoted five pages to the text of a humorous play written by a student, a spoof of Shakespeare depicting the intense rivalry between the Periclean and Cecropian societies, and the April 1905 issue devoted a full page to coverage of the play given in Morrison Hall by the Cecropian Society Dramatic Club.[2]

Five years later, in the spring of 1910, the societies at Transylvania University (Kentucky University had been renamed in 1908) had clearly slipped in status and importance within the pages of the student monthly. "The Societies" no longer appeared *at all* in the table of contents; when reported, news of their activities was almost invariably scattered among similar coverage of the many other extracurricular groups in the unnumbered pages of

246 • Taking the Town

the "Locals" section at the back of the magazine. In the April 1910 issue the oratorical primary held to determine the school's representative at the intercollegiate contest was reported beneath—and occupied no more space than—the regular meeting of the Tennis Club. Society-sponsored oratory could still garner attention, however, particularly if the school's orator was the victor. When Philothean Society member Joseph Thomas Watson won the intercollegiate oratorical contest at Morrison Hall in May 1911, the *Transylvanian* printed his picture and his seven-page oration, "The South— Our Heritage and Opportunity," in full.[3]

The period after 1910 was increasingly difficult for the Transylvania literary societies. By May 1915 the school's new student newspaper, the *Crimson Rambler,* could only both worriedly and hopefully summarize the societies' year as follows: "Notwithstanding the fact that the interest in literary societies at Transylvania has been about at as low ebb this year as at any time in their history, it has been far from total extinction." Although this front-page article in the newspaper's first edition went on to enumerate plans to "inject some of the much-needed 'pep' into this phase of our college work," the language of the piece clearly suggests that the societies were struggling to survive. This theme continued in an editorial printed the following October entitled "Literary Societies and Transylvania Spirit." Here the editor argued—based on the unstated but understood premise that the literary societies were not receiving student support—that the societies represented the entire institution as much as the athletic teams, glee clubs, and dramatic clubs did, and for this reason, students should support the societies to demonstrate their school spirit. Such appeals carried an undertone of desperation, as did the efforts of the societies themselves to retain interest and members. Those societies receiving positive attention in the *Rambler* during the 1915–1916 school year did so not for traditional programs of oratory or debate but rather for their novel attempts to amuse their members and attract new ones with society-sponsored activities unheard of in the Gilded Age. For instance, the *Rambler* gave front-page attention in November 1915 to a Halloween party, complete with "spooky" decorations and ample refreshments, hosted by the Periclean Society in its hall for the other societies and a number of invited guests, male and female. Such events were largely designed to garner some badly needed positive attention and thus serve as a recruitment tool. This intent was made explicit in October 1915 when the

Rambler reported that the Ossolian Society session included a short play acted out by some of the members and that, "after the program was completed, a circle was formed, and the girls played games. Later a committee served ice-cream cones. About forty of the college girls were there, and many expressed their intention of becoming Ossolians at the next meeting."[4]

Despite this effort at recruitment, the *Crimson Rambler* noted the following month that Ossolia was considering an amendment to its constitution that would "admit as associate members women who are only indirectly connected with the college. If this carries, she [Ossolia] will receive much help which would otherwise be denied to her." Clearly, this highly unusual move to recruit members outside the student body was an admission of distress. Despite attractive inducements and unprecedented recruitment schemes, the *Rambler* noted a month later, "little more than a quorum attended the meeting of Ossolia on Friday, the third. It seems that Women's Glee Club interests are taking all the spare time available and hence cutting down somewhat the attendance." Nevertheless, Ossolia was not ready to give up. In February 1916, as enthusiastically reported in the *Rambler,* the society employed both "innocent" gambling and matchmaking to enliven its image and, hopefully, its fortunes when it hosted a Washington's birthday party for "about a dozen couples." At one point in the evening, "all settled down to a game of 'Progressive George,' played with innocent little dice-like cubes. Mr. Lykins, winner of five games, won a red, white and blue George Washington hat. To choose partners for refreshments, each girl threw a ball over a curtain. The boy who got the ball became her partner."[5]

All this suggests that by 1916, the literary societies at Transylvania had strayed far from their traditional roles and purposes in a struggle to survive. Oratory—the quintessential purpose and activity of the literary society—as well as the competitive contests it had spawned and served, had lost the high status and large following enjoyed in the Gilded Age. This was reflected in the pages of the *Crimson Rambler* in 1916. The front page of the 10 March 1916 edition was completely occupied by two articles under the headlines "Exit Basket Ball" and "Enter Base Ball." On 7 April the front page continued to be dominated by baseball news, while the announcement of the preliminary oratorical contest to choose the school's representative in the state contest was buried on page five. And on 12 May, as baseball and track captured the *Rambler's* front page, a small piece on page three noted the upcoming intercollegiate oratorical contest at Danville and suggested that if a party of fifteen students could be gathered to make the trip, lower rates could be secured for transportation and lodging. This was a far cry from the late Gilded Age, when the oratorical contests were front-page news on and off campus, and special trains were chartered to transport the crowds to these events. The societies at Transylvania tried to compensate by mimicking the activities of social clubs, dramatic clubs, and the like, but unfortunately, although they might still amuse their members and attract a few new ones, they could no longer differentiate themselves from these other organizations. Consequently, the societies could no longer offer their members the status and distinction they once had.[6]

The Transylvania societies' decline is also evident in a comparison of the school's yearbooks for 1910 and 1915. In the 1910 *Crimson* six literary societies were featured: three for the College of Arts (Periclea, Cecropia, and Ossolia), and three for the College of the Bible (Phileusebia, Philothea, and Theosebia). The smallest (Ossolia) listed fifteen members, and the largest (Phileusebia) listed forty-five. The average membership for the six societies was thirty. In 1915 only the three Arts College societies were featured in the *Crimson;* all three of the Bible College societies had become defunct in the five-year interval. The largest of the three remaining societies in 1915 (Ossolia) listed twenty-two members, and the smallest (Cecropia) sixteen members. The average membership for the three societies was nineteen. Thus, between 1910 and 1915, the number of literary societies had been halved, and the average membership had dropped by more than a third. Moreover, in the 1910 yearbook the pages featuring the literary societies preceded those devoted to the other student organizations, including Greek-letter fraternities and athletic teams; in the 1915 edition the societies appeared after the fraternities, honorary societies, and several other student organizations, indicative of their decrease in status. Finally, a look at the members of the graduating classes in the two yearbooks reveals society decline from another angle. The 1910 yearbook featured thirty-five graduating seniors (male and female) from the Arts and Bible Colleges; of these, twenty-six, or 74 percent, were literary society members. Although most participated in a variety of extracurricular organizations, for six of the thirty-five graduating seniors, a literary society appeared to be their only extracurricular affiliation. Five years later, of the thirty seniors graduating from the Arts and Bible Colleges, only eleven, or 37 percent, were literary society members. (Although the Bible College literary societies were no longer functioning in 1915, seniors' previous affiliation was listed.) None of the 1915 graduates listed a literary society as their only extracurricular activity, and they all belonged to at least five other student organizations. Therefore, in this five-year interval, literary society membership in the graduating class had declined by approximately one third, and society membership as the sole extracurricular affiliation had vanished. In short, these two yearbooks offer a picture of the decline or demise of literary societies at Transylvania.[7]

Across town at State University, a similar tale of literary society decline was unfolding in the pages of the student weekly the *Idea.* There, as at Transylvania, the literary societies were being forced to share space in the student press with a large number of other extracurricular organizations. Furthermore, in a radical change from the Gilded Age *State College Cadet,* the societies' coverage in the *Idea,* a publication founded in 1908, was sporadic, and they were often displaced by other attractions and relegated to the back pages, even though the paper had a member from each society on its governing board. For instance, in the 28 January 1909 edition, the Patterson Society's annual declamatory contest was given only a few lines at the bottom of the last column of page seven, underneath reports of the activities of two fraternities and the campus YMCA. In the eight-page 11 November 1909 *Idea,* an issue largely devoted to football articles and editorials, there was no mention at all of the societies. Nor were these isolated incidents. A reading of the *Idea* during this period leaves little doubt that sports, along with other extracurricular activities, were eclipsing, interfering with, and even reshaping the rhetoric of literary society activities. Society members did not necessarily perceive these other extracurricular forces as a threat or as abhorrent in any way, for their interests were now multiple and their loyalties divided. For instance, in November 1909 the Neville Literary Society held a Thanksgiving reception and dance in honor of the football team. Indeed, sports metaphors were being used to describe and encourage interest in literary society contests. The *Idea*'s October 1910 issue announced that "the contest will certainly give old Union a good 'kick off' for the literary game of the year." In December 1910 the *Idea* printed the rather suggestive remark that "since the football season is over, much interest is being manifested in the Literary Societies. . . . Those who were unable to become football heros now have the splendid opportunity to win honors in the Literary Societies." Clearly, although there is sympathy for and some optimism about the societies, football and its heroes now took precedence. Moreover, sports were directly interfering with society functions: on 22 February 1912 the annual Union Literary Society oratorical contest—once the premier event on Washington's birthday—was held in the afternoon rather than the evening "so as not to conflict with the Vanderbilt basket-ball game."[8]

While the student press at State University was ignoring or slighting the societies while favoring other student activities, it was also printing accounts lamenting a lessening of student interest in the societies and their activities, exhortations to current society members to more vigorously support their societies, and anxious efforts to recruit new members and encourage campus interest. In January 1909 the *Idea* chastised members of the Union Society: "Many of the old members are missing a great deal by not attending more often. . . . We should all attend our society as often as possible." The following September the paper again complained about "the few members of the Patterson Literary Society . . . present at its weekly meeting Saturday night." Occasionally the paper offered excuses for the poor attendance at society meetings. Reporting on an October 1909 meeting of the Patterson Society, the paper suggested that "on account of the inclemency of the weather, only a very small crowd was present." When the *Idea* was not admonishing society members to be more active or rationalizing their poor attendance, it was decrying the lack of interest in joining the societies and the lack of interest in their activities. For instance, in October 1909 the *Idea* worried openly about declining student interest in society membership: "It is a lamented fact that more students do not belong to them [literary societies]." The previous spring a student writer had already complained about those who did not support the societies' activities: "Of course, there are some of our fellows who take little interest in a literary contest, . . . but we as students owe it to our University to support her in all her intercollegiate contests." By 1910 the *Idea* noted with chagrin that only one-sixth of the student body of 600 belonged to a literary society. (By comparison, the 1894 yearbook indicates that more than half the students were society members.) Moreover, by January 1911 an anxious editorial asked, "Why is there so little interest manifested in the Literary feature of our college life?" It ended by exhorting the students to "give the Literary Societies the necessary attention, participate in the contests and debates, seek to raise higher and higher the literary standard of our school." Such exhortations were common. At the beginning of 1910 the *Idea* pleaded that "all students who have any literary ambition should join one of the societies. Come out and hear these gentlemen." And at the end of 1910 there was this attempt to lure new members: "Literary Societies make the evening of meeting very pleasant. You should join and learn to touch with speech the heart of the hearer."[9]

To these admonishments, laments, and exhortations in the student press was added the open and adamant, but seemingly ineffectual, support of Henry Stites Barker, State University's second president. In March 1911 the *Idea* reported that Barker showed "the proper spirit" by being "interested heart and soul in every student activity which makes for upright conduct." His speech to a combined meeting of the Philosophian, Union, and Patterson societies was reportedly filled with praise: "The central thought of President Barker's talk was the positive value of Literary Society work. He said, that in his opinion, no other feature of college life contributed so much of real culture." Barker did not directly address the weakened condition of the societies, but his remarks clearly reflected his concern and his uncertainty about what he might do to help: "It is of the utmost importance to the University that the Literary Societies be encouraged. I can not say now just what will be done, but there will be some changes, and we mean to stand by your work." Nine months later, in December 1911, Barker again addressed a joint session of the Patterson and Union societies and spoke of "his hopes and desires to see the literary societies equal any other phase of college life," implying, of course, that they no longer did. He also repeated his assurance that something would be done to bring about this change. Barker, a former Union Society member himself, no doubt meant well. But in fact, the administration and faculty of the university were themselves engaged in undermining the literary society, or at least in co-opting a major portion of its traditional curriculum. In January 1911 the *Idea* ran an article informing the students that an oratory class was being conducted by Assistant Professor Edward F. Farquhar (of the College of Arts and Sciences) to "teach the boys how to stand squarely on their feet and to discuss intelligently the most vital questions of the day"—an excellent description of one of the literary society's quintessential services. And so, by March 1912, a note of resignation had crept into the now-familiar editorial disapproval of student disinterest: "They [the students] will not attend the literary societies, and they will not even attend an open literary [society] programme or contest. They are absolutely indifferent to all such work."[10]

By 1912, then, the student body was far less enthralled by oratory and debate than were the cohorts of earlier years, and they were being lured from the literary society by both competing extracurricular attractions and faculty curricular offerings. Literary society membership at State University no longer served, as it had in the 1890s and at the turn of the century, to distinguish or differentiate students in a positive way. Nor was society membership necessary to attain a position of high status among one's fellow students. This is illustrated in the columns of a new feature instituted by the editors of the *Idea* in late March 1912 entitled "Who's Who and Why": "The purpose of this innovation is to acquaint the student body with the records of the men who have done things in our college life." The editors intended these articles to be "sketches" of the collegiate accomplishments of "the most prominent [male] students in the University." In fourteen student sketches published in the spring of 1912 under the title "Who's Who and Why," exactly half of the subjects were identified in the text as being literary society members; half were not so identified, and all boasted multiple extracurricular affiliations. In other words, by the spring of 1912, being a "big man on campus" at State University did not require literary society membership; it had become just one option among a large number of items on the menu of college life. On Lexington's campuses, literary society membership had gone from being an almost universal condition of student life in the nineteenth century to being a marker of high status and a way to differentiate oneself from others in a positive way at the turn of the century to being essentially irrelevant to one's status among fellow students by the 1910s.[11]

If the Lexington collegiate press of the 1910s was chronicling the decline and irrelevancy of the literary societies, this process could be observed in the community press as well. In January 1910 the *Lexington Herald* made a rather explicit plea to the community and the campus for literary society support, urging everyone to attend a Patterson Society declamatory contest at the university chapel and suggesting that those attending would "encourage the literary spirit by their presence." This article echoed pleas in the student press that "all students who may have any literary ambition should join one of the literary societies." In contrast, apparently no such entreaties were necessary to enlist local support for the activities of the Greek-letter fraternities; the city's elite were readily lending a hand. For instance, when the State University chapter of Sigma Alpha Epsilon held its annual "program dance" at Merrick Lodge in April 1910, the *Lexington Herald* reported that it had been a great success, "a brilliant . . . charming event." The *Herald* noted that in addition to the prominent Lexingtonians hosting and chaperoning the affair, Woman's Club president Sarah (Mrs. Wickliffe) Preston and suffragist leader Laura Clay were among the prominent invited guests.[12]

One can also discern the decline of the literary societies by the press coverage of their Washington's birthday celebrations. Indeed, in the Gilded Age and at the turn of the century, Washington's birthday was essentially *the* literary society event at both Kentucky University and State College and for the Lexington community as well. On 22 February 1910 the Washington's birthday celebration at Transylvania University was still "under the auspices of the literary societies." The event was announced in that morning's *Lexington Herald,* which listed the titles of the six orations as well as the names of the six orators, all of whom were identified by the society they represented. All this was as it had been in the 1880s and 1890s, except that the account was quite brief and was buried on page eight. In addition, the societies at Transylvania had to share space in the *Herald* with the Delta Delta Delta Fraternity (sorority), whose tea that afternoon in honor of the chapter's second birthday was announced on page five. Five years later, in 1915, the *Herald* only briefly mentioned the Washington's birthday celebration at Transylvania at the end of a front-page article discussing what businesses would be closed that day. Moreover, the piece made no mention of the literary societies, saying only that "students of Hamilton College and the College of the Bible will join the students of Transylvania in the exercises." The following year, in 1916, the *Lexington Leader* published a short second-page piece covering all the Washington's birthday events throughout the city, including a brief mention of the celebration at Transylvania. There was no mention of the literary societies in this article, which noted only that one student gave a "principal address" and two others "made short talks appropriate to the day." Obviously, the number of speakers had been halved since 1910, and the titles of the addresses were omitted from the press coverage. These examples suggest that the literary societies became "invisible" at their own on-campus event, and the titled orations became merely "principal address[es]," or "short talks." In 1917 the *Leader* seemed to consider the Washington's birthday celebration held at the St. Paul's School auditorium by the Blue-grass Council of the Knights of Columbus to be the best and most important event of 22 February in Lexington, noting in a lengthy piece that the auditorium was overflowing with a huge crowd. The reporter argued that the Knights' celebration "was one of the most entertaining and instructive ever given in Lexington on a similar occasion." The reporter's subjectivity and exuberant rhetoric notwithstanding, the piece clearly, if indirectly, suggest that the community prominence of the Transylvania literary societies' 22 February celebrations had severely declined.[13]

At State University of Kentucky an even more dramatic Washington's birthday scenario was unfolding in the pages of the Lexington press. The Union Literary Society's formal, public celebration of Washington's birthday—an event consisting of orations interspersed with orchestral music that had evolved through the years into an oratorical contest—had been the society's signature entertainment in the Gilded Age; indeed, it had been *the* celebration of 22 February at the school into the new century, even after the other societies began participating in the event in 1895. On 22 February 1910, without even mentioning the Union Society or the traditional celebration, the *Lexington Herald* announced, "On Tuesday afternoon the young ladies' basket ball team of State University will celebrate the birthday of the Father of His Country by a contest with the girls' basket ball team of the Maysville High School in the Buell Armory at 3:30 o'clock. . . . The game will be open to the public, and the State University students will celebrate the day's holiday by attending." For mention of the Union Society, an interested reader would have to turn to the university's student weekly, the *Idea,* to be informed that, "on account of circumstances which could not be avoided [and were left unstated], the annual [oratorical] contest of the Union Literary Society was not held, and the only amusement of any kind was a basket ball game." In its decline, the Union Society had lost even its association with the celebration. The following year, in the view of the *Idea,* the school's "grand celebration on the birthday of George Washington" would be a "hilarious evening in our chapel" planned by Professor Edward Farquhar and consisting of "decorations, band and instrumental music, representatives from the four literary societies, [the] Glee Club, and various other amusements." Clearly, faculty control, in the person of Professor Far-quhar, had arrived. In February 1916 the *Lexington Leader* announced in a matter-of-fact manner that "plans for a big Washington's Birthday Celebration at State University were formulated at the regular faculty meeting yesterday," and the *Herald* later reported that the event had consisted of music and a speech to the assembled by Judge Charles Kerr on "Preparedness." The following year the *Herald* reported that the event at State University would consist of a public address in the chapel by "Dr. Harvey W. Wiley, pure food expert," followed by a faculty luncheon at the Phoenix Hotel. The *Herald* also noted that "all class work will be suspended for the day, leaving the students free to attend the meeting." And so, as war approached, the local press chronicled the fact that the Washington's birthday celebration had ceased to be a literary society event altogether. Now orchestrated by the administration, it had become an affair designed primarily to entertain the faculty, the interested public, and—if they wished to attend—the students, with lectures by invited, expert guests on the broad themes of the time: war and progressivism.[14]

In sum, then, the oratorically grounded Lexington collegiate literary societies, whose off-campus, community performance role had essentially ended in 1904, were also exhibiting serious symptoms of on-campus decline by 1910. Essentially, they had become weak and irrelevant extracurricular agencies well before the United States entered the Great War. However, as the literary society waned, another student agency with intellectual pretensions centered in dramatic performance rather than the oratorical arts not only became popular on the Lexington campuses but also assumed a significant off-campus performance role in the community.

THE DRAMATIC CLUBS TAKE CENTER STAGE

The collegiate dramatic clubs of the early twentieth century can best be understood by positioning them within the context of (1) the important cultural changes in language and rhetorical style impinging on public entertainment at the turn of the century, (2) the challenges and changes facing the professional American theater during this era, and (3) the national amateur theatrical movement emerging, in part, in response to these cultural and theatrical developments. To begin with, cultural historian Lawrence Levine counts the changes in language and rhetorical style among those salient factors affecting public entertainment at the century's turn, arguing that "the oratorical mode, which so dominated the nineteenth century . . . hardly survived into the twentieth." In politics the electorate no longer tolerated the long, florid speeches of an earlier era, and what was true in politics was also true in other arenas. Levine quotes the *New York Times* as proclaiming in 1909, specifically with regard to theatrical entertainment, that "philosophy in action, not in words, represents the ideal of what is best and most desirable." In broad terms, in the emerging cultural environment of the new twentieth century, public taste demanded entertainment that was less "a rostrum for the speaker . . . [and more] a visual arena for acting out human drama." Such cultural changes clearly suggest, at least in part, why the oratorically grounded student literary societies were in decline and a much brighter scenario was unfolding for student groups wedded to amateur dramatics.[15]

Meanwhile, in the realm of the professional stage, theater historian Benjamin McArthur has called the period between 1880 and 1920 the "golden age of the American theatre as a national institution." By "theatre," McArthur means the professional, commercial, or "legitimate" theater devoted to nonmusical stage plays—the theater that was, until the rise of the motion picture, "the standard American entertainment." The legitimate theater included the nontouring, permanent theater stock companies that "formed the normal producing unit through much of the nineteenth century." It also included the national touring system made up of largely New York–based professional companies, the "combination companies" that somewhat dominated the national market after their advent in the 1870s. However, both McArthur and fellow theater historian Gerald Bordman have noted that in the 1910s, and especially after 1914, the competition from film had all but ended the national touring system of combination companies, as well as much of the "once healthy production of original plays for regional audiences" by the nontouring, regional stock companies. In addition, Bordman has observed that although going to the theater was still associated with the "well-bred" and the "good life," there was growing dissatisfaction with what critics considered the superficiality, "crass" commercialism, and archconservatism of the legitimate theater. In this environment the legitimate theater essentially retreated to New York, where it continued to thrive despite the critics, the movies, and the economic difficulties associated with war fear and, subsequently, war fever. Reflecting an optimistic outlook, as well as an attitude linking an affinity for the stage to status and class, one Broadway producer wrote in 1915, "As long as civilization endures, the stage will form one of its chief sources of amusement, but by the same token, the screen will always be the theatre of the many."[16]

It was this environment in the 1910s—a dearth of professional theater for regional audiences who still craved stage plays (what Kenneth Macgowan, writing in the late 1920s, called "the play-starved public"), combined with a growing dissatisfaction with the quality of the professional stage—that helped generate the nationwide flowering of the amateur stage, known as the "Little Theater Movement." This movement, which originated in Europe in the 1880s and had spread to America by the 1910s, was grounded in the production of amateur, noncommercial stage plays in local venues throughout the country—plays that were meant to satisfy the playgoing public's desire for artistically motivated, inexpensive, high-quality productions. Significantly, observers of and advocates for the Little Theater Movement (and amateur theater in general), writing between the 1910s and the late 1930s, consistently included college and university theatrical productions in this movement. Moreover, these campus-generated theatrical productions were originally the province of the extracurriculum, with the primary agencies of this activity being the student dramatic clubs. These clubs are defined here as artistically motivated student organizations engaged in the production of amateur, noncommercial stage plays performed both on campus and off for the benefit of club members, the student body, and the playgoing public—activities that were not a part of, or incorporated into, the formal institutional curriculum. Student dramatic clubs had staged plays on a few campuses even before the American Revolution, and they became more widely popular in the antipuritanical collegiate environment of the 1890s. Moreover, their origination, popularity, and vitality continued in some places through the Progressive Era and beyond. However, in a process that began at Harvard (with the work of Professor George Pierce Baker) in 1908, became widespread by 1918, and was essentially complete everywhere by the late 1920s, the purposes and activities of the extracurricular dramatic clubs—similar to the fate of the literary societies—were co-opted, or absorbed, by a faculty-controlled curricular system of dramatics courses and play production.[17]

On-Campus Players

Student interest in things theatrical did not, of course, spring to life full-blown in the 1910s. In his 1896 novel *Summer in Arcady*, James Lane Allen uses the excitement of the stage as a prelude to the difficulties his young hero will experience at State College in Lexington: "One night he had come from the theatre—after an hour or more about town—and he was feeling ungovernably alive; and when he got into his [dormitory] room and lighted his student's lamp, [he] did not wish to go to bed, and did not wish to get his lessons." Such delights and excitements attending the theatrical arts would motivate students to stage their own performances before the turn of the century, and although they never referred to themselves as "dramatic clubs," the first collegiate extracurricular groups to produce plays on Lexington campuses were the female literary societies. The first to do so was the Philosophian Society at State College. At their first open session on the campus in June 1882, Philosophian members performed a short comedy entitled *All Is Fair in Love,* and by the century's end the Philosophians were producing plays at their open sessions on a regular basis—productions that became, in effect, their signature event. In fact, by the late prewar era, when the societies were generally in decline, the Philosophians were still able to garner some prominence on campus, and some attention in the local press, with their annual dramatic productions. For instance, in February 1914 the *Lexington Leader* reported that "a splendid audience composed of the faculty, alumni members of the Philosophian Literary Society and a large number of the students witnessed an excellent production" of a comedy, *The Higher Education,* performed at the school's Buell Armory by society members. The following year the *Lexington Herald* announced the Philosophians' annual play, *A Kentucky Belle,* and made it clear that society members played every part themselves: "The girls will play the men's parts in the production." In 1916 the Philosophians flirted with the idea of breaking with tradition, announcing that they would perform Shakespeare's *Twelfth Night* on the lawn in front of Patterson Hall. However, they soon changed their minds and performed the play as usual at the Buell Armory, where, the *Herald* noted, "a large audience . . . showered applause and praise for the gifted young artists." And, in their last on-campus production in the prewar era, the Philosophian Society performed *A Southern Cinderella* on 31 March 1917, two days before Woodrow Wilson appealed to Congress for a declaration of war with Germany. The *Herald* called the performance a great success and noted—in what now seems a wistful look backward to another golden age—"the large receipts of last evening will be used to start a new library for the society."[18]

The Philosophians, though apparently the first, were not the only collegiate female literary society to give dramatic performances on a Lexington campus. They were joined in the prewar years by the Ossolian Society at Transylvania, which performed an annual play in Morrison Chapel during commencement week. In 1916, for instance, the *Lexington Leader* suggested that the Ossolian play scheduled for 5 June, *Pre-Digested Politics,* would be, on the whole, "a representative of Transylvania's art." Despite the desperately needed boost in popularity these regular dramatic productions gave the female literary societies, the male societies showed little inclination to emulate them. However, in what can now be seen as an extracurricular transitional moment in time, in 1905 the male Cecropian Literary Society at Kentucky University formed the Cecropian Dramatic Club, enrolled several young women from both Kentucky University and Hamilton College as members, and in March 1905 performed a one-act farce by William Dean Howells, *The Mousetrap,* in Morrison Chapel. The *Leader's* review suggested that the play had been "credibly presented" and noted that "a large crowd was in attendance, every seat in the hall being taken." For reasons unknown, the Cecropian Dramatic Club did not survive for long, but its theatrical efforts would soon be assumed and enlarged by extracurricular dramatic clubs at Transylvania and State universities. These clubs would not be associated with the literary societies or any other preexisting campus organization; rather, they would be independent student organizations whose sole reason for being was the exercise of the dramatic arts.[19]

The Lexington literary societies confined their dramatic presentations to campus venues, as did the Marlowe Club of Hamilton College, the city's first bona fide, independent collegiate dramatic club. Kentucky University had assumed control of the all-female Hamilton College on North Broadway in 1903 and had converted it into the first two-year junior college in the state. By the 1910s the annual on-campus productions of the Marlowe Club were significant and respected cultural events in the city. Founded in 1906, the Marlowe Club had been named in honor of Julia Marlowe, the famous American actress and women's rights activist (and a friend of Susan B. Anthony). Marlowe was widely considered to be "the quintessence of Victorian womanhood," enjoying a virtuous reputation "based upon upright behavior on stage and off." Both the local newspapers acknowledged and praised the annual productions of the Marlowe Club. For instance, in May 1910 the *Lexington Herald* announced that the club would present a two-act comedy, *Two Strings to Her Bow,* in the college chapel; in May 1914 the *Lexington Leader* suggested to readers that the club's productions were "always of a high order"; and in 1916 the *Herald* announced that the Marlowe Club would "give two interesting one-act plays" at its 5 June event, *Weeping Wives* and *Blue Roses,* and that the performance would have "a strong cast chosen from the talented members of the Club." Such on-campus entertainments doubtless had an impact on the cultural life of the city at large. Margaret Preston was in the audience at the club's 5 June performance and noted in her diary that she "enjoyed every minute." However, if student dramatic clubs were to assume a role in community life tantamount to that once enjoyed by the literary societies, they would have to take their dramatic performances out into community venues, and two Lexington collegiate dramatic clubs would do just that during the 1910s.[20]

Off-Campus Players

Transylvania University historian John D. Wright Jr., alluding to the early years of the twentieth century, writes of a "proliferation of extracurricular activities and organizations" at the school; University of Kentucky historian James Hopkins, referring to the same period, notes that "numerous . . . organizations appeared on the campus"; and Helen Deiss Irvin, in her photographic history of the University of Kentucky, says of the 1910s that "interest groups were springing up as clubs all over the campus." Unfortunately, none of these institutional historians specifically mentions the student dramatic clubs among their examples. Nevertheless, these coeducational student groups were significant extracurricular organizations during the period, and like the literary societies, they were motivated in part by intellectual aspirations; through their production of plays, they sought to inspire and enlighten, as well as to entertain. Moreover, in the years between 1910 and U.S. entry into the First World War, both the Transylvania (University) Dramatic Club and the Strollers (Dramatic Club) at the State University of Kentucky succeeded the literary societies in establishing an off-campus presence and role in Lexington's cultural life.[21]

Although the founding of the Transylvania Dramatic Club in the fall of 1909 preceded the founding of the club at State University by a few months, the students at State University were the first to perform in public, staging a show at the Lexington Opera House in February 1910. The Transylvania students may well have been envious of and motivated by the positive public attention received by the as yet unnamed group from State University. Likewise, State University students with an interest in dramatics may have been inspired during the fall of 1909 by a number of reputedly excellent professional theater troupes scheduled to appear in the city's theaters that season. In September the student weekly the *Idea* enthusiastically encouraged students to take advantage of these theatrical offerings: "In looking over the booking list, it is remarkable the number of high-class companies that will be in Lexington this season. . . . This is a rare advantage that all college men may not have soon again." At any rate, subsequent newspaper and student press accounts suggest that two different groups with theatrical aspirations emerged on the State University campus that winter. One of these groups was composed of students in the English Department, and the *Lexington Leader* reported on 6 January 1910 that, with the department's approval and support, a professional actor and former student at the school, James B. Cunningham, had been induced to come to Lexington to "coach a dramatic club" for a performance at the city's opera house in February. Shortly thereafter it was announced that this club would perform *Richelieu*, the historical drama by English author Lord Edward Bulwer-Lytton, an ambitious effort described by the *Lexington Herald* as "the most pretentious offering ever attempted by local talent." The *Leader* quickly chimed in, noting the wide public interest in the play and the intellectual benefits to be had from attending the performance: "A popular topic of discussion now is 'Richelieu' to be presented at the Opera-house by State University students February 4 and 5, and judging from the amount of interest being manifested by the students . . . and the general public at large, 'Richelieu' will be a great local amateur event. . . . The intellectual upliftings to be obtained through witnessing . . . 'Richelieu' are too numerous . . . to undertake a description." On campus, the *Idea* promoted the play as well and ended its exhortation to the students to attend with "nine 'Rahs for 'Richelieu.'" The play was performed at the Lexington Opera House on 4 and 5 February and was declared a great success in both the student and the local press. The *Idea* had high praise for the student performers: "The production of 'Richelieu' did honor to the students who rendered Lord Lytton's powerful drama, and they well deserve the applause which has been accorded to them." The local press printed descriptions reminiscent of those of the literary societies' Gilded Age oratorical performances at the opera house: Governor Augustus Willson attended the first night and personally "came up on stage and congratulated the players heartily"; the boxes were "draped with flags and college pennants," and the audience was described, no doubt predictably, as "brilliant and fashionable."[22]

While the English Department students were rehearsing *Richelieu,* another student group at State University, calling itself the Alpha Dramatic Club, began a brief existence. It was announced in January 1910 in both the *Lexington Leader* and the *Idea* that in April this dramatic club would produce a play, written by a club member, called *What to Expect at College.* The players would be coached, and the play directed, by Julia Connelly, an instructor of elocution at Hamilton College who reportedly had much experience in such matters owing to her association with the Marlowe Club. According to the *Lexington Herald,* editor in chief of the *Idea,* Perry Cassidy, had asked for a leave of absence from the paper to pursue his interests with the Alpha Dramatic Club. Reports in both the *Leader* and the *Idea* took pains to explain that the Alpha Dramatic Club's play was not connected with, nor was it meant to interfere with, the production of *Richelieu.* However, in April 1910 an article in the *Idea* made it clear that the production of *What to Expect at College* had run into financial and "casting" difficulties. There is no evidence that the play was ever performed, and the Alpha Dramatic Club soon ceased to exist. Indeed, it was as if it had never existed when, on 17 February 1910, the *Idea* announced, "at last a Dramatic Club has been organized here," reporting that a group of twenty students had met the previous Saturday to create the club. *Richelieu* cast member Alpha Hubbard was elected temporary chairman. Hubbard, in fact, was an example of students' having multiple extracurricular affiliations, for he was also serving as president of the Patterson Literary Society and would win the Patterson Society oratorical contest the following month. At any rate, the formation of State University's dramatic club can properly be said to have occurred in February 1910, although the name "Strollers"—a word traditionally denoting itinerant actors—would not be adopted until the following school year.[23]

James B. Cunningham, who had been brought to Lexington to coach the State University students in their performance of *Richelieu,* had played the starring role himself. Although he presumably received some remuneration for his services from the English Department and its head, Professor A. S. McKenzie, Cunningham was in no respect a member of the faculty. He left Lexington shortly after the opera house performances to continue his acting career. The day before the first performance of *Richelieu,* however, Cunningham went to Transylvania and spoke to the students in Morrison Chapel on the topics of acting and the stage, and he made it clear that all Transylvania students would be welcome at the *Richelieu* performances: "He told the students that space would be reserved for box parties from the different clubs or fraternities or classes of Transylvania." As it happened, a group of students had just formed a new dramatic club on the Transylvania campus in the fall of 1909, and they were apparently still getting organized when Cunningham spoke in Morrison Chapel. Cunningham's address and the success of *Richelieu* could only have inspired the new Transylvania club to move forward with a production of its own. In any case, the *Lexington Herald* announced in April 1910 that the Transylvania University Dramatic Club would "give a play the latter part of May, 'Sweet Lavender,' by A. W. Pinero." Both the *Herald* and the *Lexington Leader* ran promotional articles for and reviews of this performance, which took place in the Woodland Auditorium on 27 May 1910. The *Herald* noted the large audience present and observed that the performance had been a greater success "than even the most enthusiastic student believed it would be." Meanwhile, the *Leader* exclaimed that the "Transylvania Dramatic Club covers itself in glory in its initial performance. . . . The first attempt . . . to present a play was a big success financially and from an artistic point of view." The exuberant newspaper rhetoric aside, the two new student dramatic clubs, both organized during the 1909–1910 school year, had managed to perform successfully before their fellow students *and* the Lexington public in off-campus, community venues in the first year of their existence.[24]

The prewar dramatic clubs at Transylvania and State universities were extracurricular student organizations. However, it should be made clear that these clubs received varying degrees of guidance, direction, encouragement, and support from faculty members. In addition to being coached by Cunningham, the State University club was "under the personal direction of

Prof. A. S. McKenzie." Likewise, the dramatic club at Transylvania had produced its first play under the direction of Professor Robert Emmett Monroe, who had arrived at Transylvania the year before as an assistant professor of modern languages in the Arts College. Edward Saxon, who directed the Transylvania Dramatic Club for several years in the 1910s, was instructor in expression in the College of the Bible. Certainly, such faculty guidance and patronage of extracurricular organizations was common at both schools: President Loos had presided over many literary society functions at Kentucky University during the Gilded Age; President Patterson had taken an active role and interest in the literary society named for him at State College; and State College professor Ruric Roark had inspired, helped organize, and given guidance to the turn-of-the-century Normal Department societies. Regardless of this faculty presence and influence, however, the prewar dramatic clubs were by no means faculty-controlled organizations, nor were they part of the formal institutional curriculum. This was certainly true at State University, where, after 1911, the direction and production of plays were essentially under the control of the students themselves, although they continued to have faculty patronage; in 1912 both the *Idea* and the *Lexington Herald* noted that Professor McKenzie "had had the privilege of witnessing a recent rehearsal," and the *Idea* made it clear that a student was both stage manager and director of the Strollers' 1912 production. Thus, the prewar dramatic clubs, with their own elected student boards of officers, were clearly recognized as extracurricular, student-controlled organizations. At Transylvania the Dramatic Club always appeared in the yearbook with the other extracurricular organizations and was placed in the "Student Activities" section of the school's catalogs, along with the other student groups. And at State University in 1912 the *Idea* made explicit reference to the Dramatic Club's status there: "'The Strollers' are a regularly constituted student organization."[25]

And so, with faculty encouragement and guidance, the student dramatic clubs at Transylvania and State universities were off to an auspicious beginning in 1910, and they would continue in the prewar years (with two exceptions in the Transylvania club's case) to produce annual off-campus dramas for the students and the public. In the spring of 1911 the Transylvania Dramatic Club joined the State University Strollers in having an opportunity to take the Lexington Opera House stage, performing *One of the Eight,* described by the *Lexington Leader* as "a four-act comedy of college life" on the evening of 6 April 1911, followed by a matinee performance the next day. The *Leader*'s reviewer suggested that "credible performances [had been] given by [the] Transylvania students to highly pleased audiences" and noted that "several beautiful songs" had been sung between the acts by the Transylvania Quartette. Several patterns emerged from these initial efforts. First, both dramatic clubs would usually perform their annual off-campus plays at the opera house in the prewar era; the exceptions were 1914 and 1915, when the performances were held at the new Ben Ali Theater, just prior to its change to an all-movie format in May 1915. Second, the Transylvania Dramatic Club would consistently produce only comedies for its off-campus performances, whereas several of the plays performed by the State University Strollers would be dramas. Third, the productions of both groups, reminiscent of the literary societies' off-campus oratorical entertainments of the Gilded Age, consistently included musical offerings before or at interludes during the performance. True to form on all three counts, the Strollers' April 1911 production of *Brown of Harvard,* a "college" play with dramatic as well as comedic aspirations, was performed at the opera house, and the music was furnished, according to the *Leader,* by "a selected orchestra of the best musicians in the city." The *Leader* also noted that all the scenery had been built by the students and that "handsome souvenir programs" had been prepared, "the frontpiece being a sketch of a boat race, a principal feature of the play." The Strollers had held a student contest to design the cover of the souvenir program for *Brown of Harvard,* with two free tickets as the prize. And the organization had apparently become such a popular campus attraction in its second year that it could state with obvious self-assurance that anyone in the company who missed a rehearsal would be immediately replaced. *Brown of Harvard* played "to a crowded house" at the opera house on 20 April and was dubbed a "high-class performance" by the *Leader.*[26]

In 1912 and 1913 the Transylvania Dramatic Club continued to attract positive press attention with its opera house comedies, while the Strollers did likewise with dramas. Demonstrating the complex nature of campus life during this time, the *Lexington Herald* noted in 1912 that the proceeds from the Transylvania Dramatic Club's productions went to support the Transylvania University Athletic Association. In 1913 the *Leader* suggested the rather complex organizational structure of the Transylvania Dramatic Club itself by publishing a list of its officers, which included a president, vice president, secretary, stage manager, club director, business manager and treasurer, and a properties manager. Meanwhile, the Strollers' 1912 and 1913 dramas were highly acclaimed in the local press. Their 1912 production of *The Virginian,* a western drama adapted by Owen Wister from his novel of the same title, was a particularly successful venture. Upon *The Virginian*'s professional opening at the Manhattan Theater in New York in 1904, drama critic James Metcalfe had given it a rather lukewarm endorsement, referring to the play in *Life* magazine as "far from . . . the worst dramatization of a novel ever made." However, eight years later the Strollers' production of the play was unreservedly praised by the *Herald,* which called *The Virginian* "a remarkably strong drama . . . admirably played" by the Strollers, who had "put on a delightful portrayal." The reviewer went on to call it "the best amateur play ever given in this city"—a remark proudly reprinted on the front page of the *Idea* the following week. As was typical of these productions, the *Herald* listed a large number of prominent Lexington women as "patronesses" of the performance, including Elizabeth Shelby Kincaid, who was considered very well acquainted with the literature of the dramatic arts. The *Herald*'s coverage of *The Virginian* also included a list of the twenty-eight cast members, suggesting the minimum number of club members at the time (all cast members were club members), as well as a list of the organization's officers, including president, vice president, secretary and treasurer, business manager, publicity and program managers, electrician, master of properties, and stage electrician. Like its counterpart at Transylvania, the Strollers was a highly organized club.[27]

In March 1913 the Strollers were again praised in the local press for their performance of *The Lost Paradise,* a French drama translated and adapted by Henry C. DeMille. That year the Strollers began a tradition of taking their annual production to other Kentucky locations after its Lexington debut. On 16 March 1913 the *Lexington Leader* stated that the opera house performance of *The Lost Paradise* had cleared $300, making it "eminently successful from every point of view." It also reported that, after consultation with university president Henry Barker "as to the advisability of presenting the show in another city," a performance of the play had been scheduled for 28 March at the Masonic Theater in Louisville—a performance that was "expected to strengthen [the] prestige of the university." Then in 1914 the club changed both its customary genre and its Lexington venue, staging a comedy, *The College Widow* by George Ade, at the new Ben Ali Theater on Main Street. The press coverage did not reveal the reason for the move, but one can easily speculate that it would have been desirable and prestigious to perform in this elaborate and beautiful facility that had just opened the previous year. The *Lexington Herald*'s headlines for its review of the Strollers' 1914 production were exuberant: "Crack Cast Plays 'The College Widow' . . . State University Thespians Win New Laurels . . . Event of the Season . . . Brilliant Audience Attends."[28]

The Strollers performed at the Ben Ali Theater again in 1915, producing another comedy of college life, *Charley's Aunt,* by Brandon Thomas. This popular English farce, first produced professionally in 1892, was apparently a stunning success for the Strollers on the Lexington stage, and both newspapers published highly enthusiastic review articles. Noting that the music for the production, provided by the State University Orchestra, was excellent, the *Leader* reviewer went on to assert that the Strollers "fairly out did themselves last night in their performance. . . . State's players have presented a creditable production each season, . . . but last night's play was the best in their history." Commenting on the audience at the Ben Ali, the *Herald* reviewer noted that "members of the faculty, sprinkled sedately in among the happy school girls and their gallants, vied with numerous friends of the young Thespians throughout the city in paying homage to the . . . members of the crack Stroller organization." Although such press descriptions are clearly idealized, they confirm that these productions were patronized by many members of the community beyond the campus. Buoyed by the homage and press acclaim, the Strollers again took their show on the road in 1915, scheduling a performance of *Charley's Aunt* at the Georgetown Opera House for 1 February.[29]

Individual cast members were also singled out for praise by the local press, revealing something of the players themselves. For instance, the male lead in the Strollers' 1915 production, Leo Sandman, had acted in two previous plays and had stage-managed a third; he was also a member of the university's Glee Club, where "he earned quite a reputation as a soloist." Sandman had apparently crossed the line between amateur and professional performers, for according to the *Herald,* he had left school the previous year to tour on the Keith vaudeville circuit before returning to his studies at State University.[30]

Another play performed in Lexington in 1915 in which Leo Sandman and several other Strollers participated is worth mentioning here, even though it was not, strictly speaking, a Strollers production. It is worth mentioning because it symbolized the intermingling of extracurricular life with university and community culture in the Progressive Era. A number of Strollers were cast members of *Call of the Blood,* a drama written by State University professor J. T. C. Noe and performed at the Ben Ali Theater on the evening of 14 April 1915 under the auspices of the Social Service Department of the Woman's Club; both the play and its cast received prominent attention and critical acclaim in the local press. The Social Service Department of the Woman's Club was chaired by Frances Jewell, who would assume her position as instructor in the English Department at State University that fall. The proceeds of the play were earmarked for the club's social settlement project, called "Neighboring Settlement House," which was planned to be located on Whitney Avenue. Here, then, were student dramatics in the service of progressive reform at the behest of a coalition of university intellectuals and civic elites. And so, through its main productions and through the acclaim and attention received by individual members taking part in other productions serving diverse purposes, by 1915 the Strollers Dramatic Club of State University had garnered much desirable community attention and prestige for itself and for the university as well.[31]

Meanwhile, in the 1913–1915 period, the Transylvania Dramatic Club produced a successful comedy at the opera house in 1913, failed to produce an off-campus play in 1914, and tried a new off-campus venue in 1915, utilizing, like the Strollers, the Ben Ali Theater. In 1913 the Transylvania players presented the comedy *Esmeralda,* an "extremely popular" play written in 1881 by William Gillette, the successful American actor and dramatist. The day before the performance the *Lexington Leader* announced that the house would be a mixture of Transylvania students and members of Lexington society and that there would be many box parties given by the Transylvania fraternities and by "society" people as well. After the performance the *Leader* praised the production, listed many of those attending, and expressed the hope that many others could have such "an opportunity to see a really good amateur company at work." For reasons that are unclear, the Transylvania

Dramatic Club did not produce an off-campus play in 1914. The local press noted that on 4 February 1914 the club would "give a program at chapel hour at Transylvania this morning." This unnamed performance also appeared in the Transylvania yearbook's calendar of events for 1914, with the entry for 4 February merely stating that "the dramatic club gives us a sample of their talent. Let us say, in the words of our honored president, 'We hope you will come again.'" No other performance was listed in the yearbook's calendar. Perhaps one possible explanation, also recorded in the yearbook calendar, was the fear that spread among students and faculty when smallpox broke out on the campus during March and April, disrupting both classroom and extracurricular efforts. Whatever the cause of the interruption in 1914, the Transylvania Dramatic Club returned to an off-campus venue, the Ben Ali Theater, in February 1915 with a production of *Going Some,* described by the *Lexington Herald* as a "great Western comedy" by Rex Beach and Paul Armstrong. Interestingly, the *Herald*'s review of the play was written by Enoch Grehan, himself rather symbolic of the evolution in cultural taste for the expressive arts. As a Kentucky University Cecropian Literary Society member, Grehan had won the intercollegiate oratorical contest in 1894. By 1915, he was head of State University's Journalism Department and the faculty adviser to the Strollers Dramatic Club. At any rate, praising the production of *Going Some* by the Transylvania students, Grehan suggested—perhaps not altogether objectively, as he was an alumnus—that it had been performed "in a manner that would have excited the envy of professionals." The *Leader*'s reviewer was likewise enthusiastic about these student actors: "There is a lot of first-class theatrical talent at Transylvania University, and the best of it was brought to the fore at the Ben Ali Theatre last night." To be sure, local press reviews of collegiate theatrical performances in this period were almost invariably effusively complimentary and cannot be taken as an objective evaluation of artistic quality. Nevertheless, the publicity and prestige that such public recognition (and flattery) gave the students and their organizations must have been a significant factor in firmly establishing their role in the community and in the cultural life of the city by 1915. Thus established, the next two years would be significant for these student dramatic clubs, each year for a different reason.[32]

Leaving 1916 aside momentarily and jumping ahead to the spring of 1917, declaration of war with Germany and its allies greatly preoccupied and disrupted life in Lexington and on its campuses as well. Nevertheless, the University of Kentucky Strollers, by far the larger and seemingly stronger of the two student dramatic clubs, managed to produce a "comedy-drama" at the opera house, *The Lion and the Mouse* by Charles Klein, a month before the actual declaration of war, and it was apparently enthusiastically received. Over at Transylvania, however, by March 1917 students were organizing and marching in volunteer military companies on campus in anticipation of war. Perhaps in part due to these circumstances, the only 1917 production by the Transylvania club would occur in December in Morrison Chapel, and it was simply a repeat of the December 1916 on-campus performance of "the old English drama" *David Garrick*. By the end of 1917 the club had adopted the name "Stagecrafters," and the Transylvania Stagecrafters would survive the difficult war years and go on to produce plays in the brighter postwar years, as would the Strollers at the University of Kentucky. In fact, the latter's student weekly, the *Kentucky Kernel*, could have been speaking of the early development and subsequent growth and prestige of both organizations when it wrote in 1920 about the Strollers: "From a small unrecognized band of enthusiasts in dramatic art, forced to meet in hallways and private rooms for want of friendlier shelter, depending on turn of circumstance for financial succor, they have grown, because of the real appeal of their work, to be what they are at present, an organization of large membership, to whose ranks it is an honor to be admitted and one much sought after." However, returning to the prewar years, 1916 appears to have been the high point for both organizations.[33]

With the Ben Ali Theater's conversion to an all-movie theater in May 1915, both the Strollers and the Transylvania Dramatic Club returned to the opera house in 1916. In January the *Lexington Leader* printed a small piece providing insight into the mechanism by which students became members of these clubs. Noting that the "annual tryout for membership" in the Transylvania Dramatic Club had just been held, the article stated that six students had given readings, "displaying their dramatic ability before the club members," and all had been accepted as new members. Obviously, prospective applicants were screened, however rigorously, for acting ability by the membership prior to their inclusion in the club. Shortly after the Transylvania club's membership tryout, the *Lexington Herald* announced that the comedy *The Fortune Hunter*, by Winchell Smith, had been selected as the club's production that year. A later account in the *Herald* informed readers that *The Fortune Hunter* was "a high class play . . . a great play by a well known author [that] has had an enormous run on the professional stage." Nevertheless, the article continued, the Transylvania club was capable of rendering the play in an excellent manner, as "every year the audiences, and enthusiasm, and praise increase for this club." After the initial announcement of the play's selection in February, there were at least nine additional accounts in the Lexington newspapers related to the club's production of *The Fortune Hunter* before and after the 25 and 26 April performances at the opera house. Once again, Enoch Grehan heaped compliments on the Transylvania club in his review for the *Herald,* referring to it as, among other things, an "excellent organization of amateur players." Grehan could not resist mentioning, however, that the sets for the Transylvania play had been designed by Eugene Gribbin, a member of the Strollers. Even before the performances, the male and female leads were featured and praised in the local press. Obviously, whereas the collegiate civic hero in turn-of-the-century Lexington had been an orator, by 1916 this hero had become a thespian.[34]

While the Transylvania Dramatic Club was screening and admitting its six new members in January 1916, the Strollers at State University (the Lexington press still referred to the school by this name in the spring of 1916) was entertaining its twenty-seven new members with a tea held in "the Strollers room in the main building of the university." The *Lexington Herald* referred to this room as the "Strollers' studio" and reported that it had been newly and beautifully furnished. Occupying a room in the "main building" was symbolic of this student organization's high status on campus—a status once enjoyed only by the literary societies, which had now been consigned to rooms elsewhere. In 1916 the local press seemed to follow every move the Strollers made, with the *Leader* announcing in early January that the group was in the process of "trying to find a suitable play for presentation, but has nothing definite under consideration so far." When the Strollers returned to playwright George Ade (author of their 1914 production *The College Widow*) for another comedy, *Father and the Boys,* the *Herald* praised the selection in a detailed article in which it called the Strollers' productions "an important event in social and university circles." The *Herald* also made special mention of the on-campus popularity of the club: "The fact that all the students are interested in the effort of the Strollers to present a play each year in the name of the school was shown by how they crowded into the chapel for the Amateur Night performance last fall." Both local newspapers subsequently printed a number of articles covering the club's cast tryouts, the cast chosen, and the rehearsals. In one article highlighting the cast, the *Leader* reminded its readers that "this club[,] which is composed entirely of students at the university[,] has each year since its organization presented in this city a successful amateur performance and has built up for itself an enviable reputation." Moreover, in an article concerning rehearsals, the *Herald* noted that plans were already being completed "for a tour of the neighboring towns of the Blue Grass by the Strollers after the Lexington Performance . . . since the influence of the club was strengthened materially by last year's trips."[35]

As the Strollers' 1916 performance at the opera house neared, the press printed many promotional articles related to the club, its cast members, and the upcoming production, revealing that these things were inextricably interwoven with the culture of the community. Two such accounts also suggest the local racial climate. Referring to a female cast member, the *Herald* observed that she "has made her reputation at the university as a star in negro dialect parts, and will [now] have an opportunity to show her ability as a 'white lady of class.'" Moreover, the *Herald* noted in mid-March that the Strollers had been unsuccessful in booking the opera house for "the middle of this month" and would have to delay the performance until later. This was no doubt the case because the film *Birth of a Nation* was playing to large crowds at the opera house between 20 and 26 March. The interrelatedness of the dramatic clubs and the community was evident in less troubled waters as well. Strollers member Eugene Gribbin had not only designed the sets for both the Strollers and the Transylvania Dramatic Club in 1916 but also designed the poster advertising the automobile and style show held at the Shelburne Tobacco Warehouse that year. In addition, the *Herald* noted that two of the cast members for *Father and the Boys* had also performed in the Kirmess held in February 1916 for the benefit of a local social service effort. Moreover, the lists of patrons and patronesses of the Strollers' 1916 play published by both newspapers included State University president Henry Barker and a number of professors, as well as many prominent community residents, including Desha Breckinridge and his wife, Madeline McDowell Breckinridge, owners of the *Herald*. On 13 April 1916, the date of the Strollers' performance, the *Leader* printed its "social calendar"—a textual snapshot of the city's cultural life—for that afternoon and evening, in which the student dramatic club was clearly visible: "On the calendar for today are: the meeting of the Lexington Chapter U. D. C. [United Daughters of the Confederacy] at the home of Mrs. Ernest Cassidy; Professor Farquhar's lecture for the Woman's College Club; Dr. MacCartney's lecture at the Lexington Public Library; the performance of 'Father and the Boys' by the Strollers at the Lexington Opera House; the Parcel Post Sale this evening at 7:30 . . . given by the Christian Endeavor Societies of Central Christian Church."[36]

Father and the Boys was heavily promoted in the press before the performance, and afterward the rhetoric of the reviews was predictably exuberant and highly complimentary. However, what is striking about this rhetoric is its similarity to that used to describe the literary society–sponsored oratorical events of twenty years earlier. The *Lexington Herald* referred to the evening of the Strollers' performance as "college night" at the opera house, reminiscent of the Lexington Chautauqua's "college day" featuring its collegiate oratorical contest. Other circumstances seemed strangely similar as well. On the afternoon of the performance of *Father and the Boys,* State University's cadet battalion paraded through the streets of downtown Lexington in honor of the Strollers, just as students had paraded in honor of the literary society orators competing at the opera house in the 1890s. That evening, orchestral music accompanied the Strollers' performance, just as it had at the oratorical contests held at the opera house years earlier. Moreover, the *Herald* reported that, in response to the Strollers' performance, "the historic building rang from pit to gallery with the enthusiasm of youth in which State University collegians showed pardonable pride and unlimited loyalty"—just as the building had resounded with cheers and college yells accompanying the oratorical performances in earlier years. And finally, at the Strollers' annual banquet held at the Phoenix Hotel a few weeks after the 1916 performance, the cast members were ceremoniously awarded "pins," much as the literary society orators had been awarded medals for their achievements at the intercollegiate and Chautauqua events. Clearly, in the role of participant in the community's cultural life by a Lexington college student, the actor had stepped into the orator's shoes.[37]

And so it was that in the four decades preceding the United States' entry into World War I, two collegiate extracurricular agencies with intellectual pretensions and aspirations—the literary societies and the dramatic clubs—were, in their turn, prominent organizations on Lexington's campuses. Both of these agencies offered their student members not only the fruits of group socialization and camaraderie but also the opportunity to achieve peer and public admiration and applause through expressive performances designed to inspire, enlighten, and entertain—designed, that is, to appeal to the life of the mind. Moreover, nurtured by and subject to changing tastes for the arts of expression, first the literary societies and then the dramatic clubs carried their activities beyond the campus to establish a distinctive role in the intellectual life of the Bluegrass city.

POSTWAR LEXINGTON—
SO LONG, GILDED AGE

But blessed are they that mourn, for verily there is more joy in the death
of one literary society than in the existence of ninety and nine who are
about to die.
> —*Crimson Rambler* 6, no. 4 (17 October 1919)

"What do you men want here?" asked Governor Morrow. "We came to
see if you would not give us that nigger," they replied.
> —*Lexington Leader,* 5 February 1920

ON THE CAMPUS: THE LITERARY SOCIETIES
"KILLED AND BURIED"

Lexington's collegiate literary societies, like those everywhere, ultimately lost
the struggle to retain relevance and student loyalty, and in so doing, their
fate was sealed. In the years immediately following World War I the literary
societies in Lexington had declined to the point that—if not already defunct—they were small, obscure clubs lost in a sea of campus organizations.
This situation was not without its mourners, however. At Transylvania University, near the end of the spring semester in 1919, the student weekly
newspaper the *Crimson Rambler,* lamenting the serious lack of student interest in and patronage of the campus literary societies, published a melan-
choly editorial entitled "What's the Matter with the Literary Society?" in
which the writer pleaded for renewed student support. Five months later, in
October 1919, the few remaining, discouraged members of Transylvania's
once-prominent Cecropian Literary Society announced that, "in view of the
changed situation in college life," the society was being "killed and buried."
They held an "appropriate service" for the organization in Morrison Chapel
a few days later, thereby publicly and formally disbanding and mourning
the fifty-four-year-old organization that had, according to one student cor-

respondent, "outlived its usefulness." At the ceremony held in Morrison Chapel, the minister eulogizing Cecropia seemed to comment on the general state of literary societies at that time: "But blessed are they that mourn, for verily there is more joy in the death of one literary society than in the existence of ninety and nine who are about to die." The following month, Transylvania's male Periclean and female Ossolian societies merged to form a coed Periclean Society in the hope that "a keener interest will be aroused in the meetings." Thus, at Transylvania, where there had been six active literary societies in 1900, by 1920 there was only one small, struggling literary society among twenty-eight extracurricular organizations (not including athletic teams) featured in the school's yearbook. Moreover, this process of demise seemed to be occurring at educational institutions throughout the region. In February 1920, under the headline "Another School Kills Literary Societies," the *Crimson Rambler* noted that "the days of the old literary societies are gone at the Kentucky Military Institute. . . . In place of the literary societies they have put up . . . new, up-to-date clubs. . . . [For instance,] the Dramatic Club will try to develop theatrical talent."[1]

Across town at the University of Kentucky (the name adopted by statute in 1916), four of the traditional literary societies, the Patterson, Union, Philosophian, and Horace Mann (as well as a society in the law school, the Henry Clay Law Society), were still functioning during the 1919–1920 school year, but here too, the student press reveals a tale of severe decline. In its second issue of the new school year, the student newspaper the *Kentucky Kernel,* offering no special status to the societies, simply lumped them in with other student "clubs" in an article urging freshmen to join in the extracurriculum. Thus, at the University of Kentucky the literary society, far from being the predominant, high-status student organization it had been in the 1890s and at the century's turn, was by 1919 just one more club in a crowded field of extracurricular attractions. And worse, it was no longer even a popular attraction. When the *Kernel* announced that both the Kentucky intercollegiate oratorical contest and the first annual Southern Interstate Oratorical League contest would be held in the university's chapel in March, it also printed an editorial acknowledging the lack of interest on campus in oratory and oratorical contests. The editorial complained that the students gave their support and admiration to the athlete but not to the orator, even though both trained hard for their respective events, and it concluded with a question for the student body: "So is it fair to give hearty support to one and ignore the efforts of the other?" Nevertheless, a month later the student paper buried its brief coverage of the Patterson Society's annual on-campus oratorical contest on page eight while devoting most of the front page to the university's premier dramatic club, the Strollers. Moreover, although Patterson Society member Clifford Smith had just won both the Kentucky intercollegiate and southern interstate contests, the *Kernel* published a long letter from a student who attacked the societies for being "agencies designed, quite badly, to encourage effective public speaking" and bluntly declared them all to be in an "anemic state." This student suggested that there should be only one literary society at the university at most and noted that there was general campus apathy toward debates and the intersociety and intercollegiate oratorical contests, which were "not popular events." The correspondent praised only the female Philosophian Society—for "its charming annual dramatic productions." A week later the *Kernel* published another long student letter in response. This student made no attempt to defend the societies, agreeing that they were no longer very popular, and focused his argument on a defense of public speaking contests, which, though not well attended, were a necessary part of the university's commitment to "intellectual development . . . fostered by competition along intellectual lines."[2]

Yet another clear indication that the literary societies' day was past concerned the basic intellectual services the societies performed for their members—their public speaking curriculum of debate and oratory. The curriculum in the societies' halls has been characterized elsewhere as complementary to (as opposed to being in revolt against) the formal, institutional curriculum, and the warm mutual regard and support between the societies and presidents Patterson at State College and Loos at Kentucky University strongly suggests that this had been the case through the Gilded Age and beyond. However, the societies' curriculum at the University of Kentucky appears to have been largely co-opted by, or absorbed into, the institutional curriculum by 1920. When the *Kentucky Kernel* announced that Clifford Smith had won the "championship of the South" in the Southern Interstate Oratorical League contest, it did not mention his affiliation with the Patterson Society and essentially gave credit for the victory to the faculty and the formal curriculum: "Much of the good work accomplished in these oratorical contests has been due to the diligence and interest exhibited by Professor [E. C.] Mabie, who is in charge of the work in oratory in the University." The same was true of debate. The university fielded an intercollegiate debate team during the 1919–1920 academic year, but it had no observable ties to the literary societies that had once been virtually synonymous with the activity on campus. Rather, the debate team was chosen by Professor Mabie from the members of his "advanced debate class," which was a course offering in the Department of English.[3]

At the same time Mabie was organizing his debate team in the fall of 1919, the female Philosophian Society, one of the most stable and active societies since its inception in 1882, was planning to put on an "old-time circus with side shows and [a] menagerie," as well as free food, in the recreation room of Patterson Hall, the female dormitory. The *Kernel* explained, "The main purpose of the entertainment is to arouse interest in the Philosophian Literary Society and to encourage a greater number of the new girls [to apply] for entrance into the society." Unfortunately, this attempt to arouse interest represented a rather apt metaphor for the situation, for by 1919–1920 the literary societies at the University of Kentucky had become, at best, a "side show." In the 1920 yearbook the *Kentuckian,* the four functioning literary societies were featured, along with a crowded field of twenty-four other student organizations and clubs; five years later, only one society, the Philosophian, was still featured. Such was the fate of the Lexington collegiate literary societies in the postwar years.[4]

ON THE STREET: ANGRY MEN AND THE RULE OF LAW

Postwar Lexington experienced the forces of change beyond its campuses, and on the city's streets these forces shaped matters of life and death. Ten-year-old Geneva Hardman was known to her neighbors, teacher, and classmates as an intelligent, studious, and cheerful child, a leader in her class at school. She was the daughter of Emma Hardman, a widow with eight children. One of Emma Hardman's adult sons, Tupper Hardman, was a well-known Fayette County landowner, farming land along the Tates Creek Pike. Geneva, three of her brothers, and one sister resided with their mother in a house on the Harrodsburg Pike near the small South Elkhorn settlement, a few miles from Lexington. Geneva left home at about 7:30 on the morning of 4 February 1920, carrying her books and umbrella (there was a cold drizzle), to walk the 300 yards to school. She never arrived. About fifteen minutes later a passerby, Speed Collins, found her book satchel and coat hood in the road next to a large cornfield adjoining the Hardman home. Thinking the child had accidentally dropped these items, Collins took them to the school, only to learn that Geneva was not there. The teacher, fearing Geneva had become ill and returned home, sent several children to the Hardman house to inquire about her. Mrs. Hardman was alarmed to learn that Geneva had not reached school and began frantically searching for her daughter, as did several men from a nearby store who had been alerted by the schoolchildren that a child was missing.

A search of the muddy cornfield next to the Hardman home revealed Geneva's body. She had been dragged behind a shock of corn, and her skull and face had been battered beyond recognition with a large rock, which lay nearby. Even though a recent ice storm had felled the telephone lines, word of the gruesome discovery spread rapidly, and soon an armed posse, estimated at several hundred men, was searching for a likely suspect: a stranger to the neighborhood—a black man in an army uniform—who had been seen walking in the vicinity just before Geneva's disappearance. Later that day three men, including a local doctor and a Versailles, Kentucky, police officer, captured the suspect, who identified himself as Will Lockett. When apprehended, Lockett, a World War I veteran, was still wearing his army uniform and was also wearing or carrying (reports varied) muddy, bloodstained overalls. Rushed by automobile to Lexington, Lockett reportedly confessed during the trip that he had committed the murder, and he reiterated this confession later that day at the Lexington police station. According to the *Lexington Leader*, Lockett was lucky to have survived his capture, which it attributed to the fact that he had been apprehended by only three men, one of them a policeman, and then hurriedly taken to jail. As the *Lexington Herald* put it, "had any considerable party of the searchers found the man, it is believed that he would have been lynched without delay."[5]

William Lockett, by self-report age thirty-three at the time of his arrest, was a man whose life had been cloaked in secrets and lies, some of them terrible. Shortly before his death, he would at least partially reveal some of those secrets in his confession to R. F. Chilton, warden of the state prison at Eddyville, Kentucky. His real name was not William Lockett but Petrie

Kimbrough, and he had been born and raised not in Henderson, Kentucky, as he first reported, but in the small farming community of Pembroke in western Kentucky, not far from the Tennessee line. (Ironically, Lockett's father, Charles Kimbrough, had reportedly once been in the employ of Warden Chilton's father.) Having spent most of his life as a farm laborer, Lockett joined the army in the summer of 1918, served eleven months in the 413th Reserve Labor Battalion at Camp Taylor in Louisville, and was honorably discharged in May 1919. After his discharge he apparently made his way to the Lexington area, which he had first been attracted to several years earlier by the "colored fair." Although Lockett suggested at his trial that he had never been in serious trouble before and had no idea why he killed Geneva Hardman, he later confessed to Chilton that she was by no means his first victim. According to press reports of his death-house confession at Eddyville, he had murdered four women between 1905 and 1919, strangling each of his victims, all of whom were apparently unknown to him.[6]

Upon hearing of Lockett's capture and incarceration, members of the posse and others rushed to the jail at Lexington, where officers attempted to calm the situation. "You didn't see the body, did you?" shouted the crowd, which was quickly developing into an angry lynch mob. Fearing violence, the authorities spirited Lockett out of the jail and took him to the State Reformatory at Frankfort. Selected members of the crowd in Lexington were then allowed to inspect the inside of the jail, and when they failed to find the suspect there, a large number of men departed by automobile and train for Frankfort. They would be met there by Governor Edwin Morrow and local law enforcement officers. Morrow, a progressive Republican and strong foe of the Ku Klux Klan, supervised the arrangements to protect the prisoner from the lynch mob, and he met personally with three of the first men to arrive from Lexington to discuss their concerns and demands. This discussion was recorded by the *Lexington Leader:* "'What do you men want here?' asked Governor Morrow. 'We came to see if you would not give us that nigger,' they replied. . . . 'Tell the mother of this poor child,' said Governor Morrow, 'that the law will be enforced in this case. There will be no miscarriage of justice here. Tell this poor woman that the man who killed her little child will be punished to the full extent of the law.'" Morrow's personal courage and assertiveness, a strong show of armed force prepared to resist the mob from Lexington, and promises of swift justice defused the situation and turned away the would-be lynchers, leaving Lockett safe, for the moment, behind the walls of the reformatory. Lockett himself expressed a clear understanding of his situation: "I know that I haven't long to live, that I'll have to die, but I don't want to be killed by a mob."[7]

This seeming detente between governmental authorities and a contingent of outraged white citizens on the night of 4 February proved illusory, and a combination of official miscalculation and public emotion resulted in violence and death at the Lexington courthouse five days later. Despite rumors that Lockett would be lynched if he were returned to Fayette County, circuit court judge Charles Kerr and Fayette County judge Frank Bullock, in consultation with other local officials, decided to hold the trial in Fayette County and asked Governor Morrow to send state militia troops to guard the courthouse. Judge Kerr and his associates apparently hoped that a display of state authority would avert a civil disturbance, and they believed that a swift trial held in Lexington would make the city a "showcase for other Kentucky towns in sustaining proper judicial procedures with appropriate security against the threat of anarchical mob action." Both Lexington papers ran editorials in support of allowing a "swift and certain" judicial process to proceed unhindered, although the *Lexington Herald* expressed some lingering ambivalence, stating on 6 February, "if ever a crime in Fayette County offered the occasion for lynch law it was the murder of little Geneva Hardman." However, the editorial went on to denounce mob violence as a crime and to conclude that "it is certainly much more impressive as a deterrent . . . to have the majesty of the law upheld and adequate punishment inflicted by the authority of the State rather than by the irresponsible act of a few individuals." The city's Negro Civic League issued a statement deploring the murder while supporting law and order, and it called for an orderly trial. Geneva Hardman's brother, Tupper, issued a statement supporting the judicial process and decrying mob violence. And the *Lexington Leader*'s banner headline of the day before the trial gave clear warning to those contemplating disorder: "Troops with Machine Guns and Automatic Rifles, Special Deputy Sheriffs, City and County Officers to Protect Lockett." Although the *Herald* noted that Judge Kerr was confident that "there would be no disorder," he would soon be proved wrong.[8]

Lockett's trial began in the Fayette County courthouse at 9:00 on the morning of 9 February 1920. Thirty-five minutes later, he had publicly confessed to the murder, and Judge Kerr had sentenced him to die in the electric chair at the penitentiary at Eddyville one month later, on 11 March. However, the trial was immediately overshadowed by events occurring outside the building. A large and angry crowd had gathered, and soon shouts of "lynch the brute" were heard; men rushed forward, one reportedly with a rope in hand. The state militia troops and the police guarding the entrance fired on them, resulting in six men dead or dying, along with many others wounded. Among the dead were several local farmers and a Lexington Prudential life insurance salesman. Some in the crowd returned fire, and at least one police officer was wounded. The crowd scattered, but many were now even more enraged and began looting nearby shops, including Joe Rosenberg's Pawnshop on South Limestone Street, for their guns and ammunition. Others returned to the street in front of the courthouse to hurl eggs, insults, and threats at the troops. Anger, fear, and dismay spread throughout the city. On the University of Kentucky campus that afternoon, president Frank McVey addressed the faculty senate, asking faculty members to do everything they could to keep the students from going downtown, lest their presence be interpreted as approval of the mob spirit. His progressive viewpoint was in full display as he urged the faculty to "do all in their power toward building up a healthy sentiment in the minds of the youth for absolute regnancy of law." Meanwhile, fearing further mob violence after dark, Governor Morrow requested federal troops from Louisville's Camp Zachary Taylor. The army troops arrived by train in the late afternoon and marched through the streets with bayonets fixed to restore order. The city was placed under martial law and would remain so until 22 February, when the soldiers were finally withdrawn.[9]

In the days that followed, two separate special grand juries were impaneled to investigate the incident. Margaret Preston Johnston's brother, William, was a member of the first grand jury, which was dismissed owing to technical issues involving how the jurors had been selected. In his charge to the second special grand jury on 21 February 1920, Judge Kerr urged the members to uphold and enforce the law in words that revealed his personal viewpoint and mind-set: "In our reverence for the law I trust we are not divided as people or a community. Passion may blind, but it cannot break that devotion to established order which is the birthright of the Anglo-Saxon." Despite Kerr's urging that those who broke the law be held accountable, the jury decided that it would be in the best interest of the community not to indict anyone for their role in the mob action. Although the *Lexington Herald* defended the grand jury's decision as, "under the circumstances[,] the wiser course," the *Lexington Leader* was disappointed with the decision and published an editorial entitled "Justice Miscarries." Both papers printed stories on both sides of the issue—sympathizing with the families of the men killed, and defending the officials and their need to uphold the rule of law. Local pulpits took up the cause of law and order as well, at the governor's urging: "Lexington ministers on Sunday complied with the request of Governor Edwin P. Morrow that at least a part of their sermons be devoted to urging law observance as opposed to mob violence."[10]

Despite all the furor, controversy, and turmoil surrounding the Lockett trial and the violent confrontation it sparked, in many ways, life in Lexington continued as normal, seemingly undaunted and undisturbed. On Monday, 16 February 1920, while the city remained under martial law, the Marlowe Club at Hamilton College presented a short play, "A Funny Word," in the college chapel, followed by a reception. On Wednesday, 18 February, the Reading Circle of the Woman's Club held its monthly meeting, where a "general discussion of the latest books" took place. And on Saturday, 21 February, the day before martial law ended and army troops were withdrawn from Lexington, University of Kentucky professor George Whiting spoke on "Tendencies in Modern Poetry" at a meeting of the Woman's Club Department of Literature, presided over by its chair, Margaret Preston Johnston. On 11 March Petrie Kimbrough, aka Will Lockett, was electrocuted at Eddyville as two of Geneva Hardman's brothers and seventeen other Lexingtonians looked on.[11]

And so, just as it had in the Gilded Age, Lexington in the years after the First World War showed itself to be a place of refinement and gentility on the one hand, and a place of violence and racism on the other. Just as Chautauqua sessions and college literary societies existed in the same social space with the public humiliation, disparagement, and harsh treatment of blacks and the public approval of lynching during the Gilded Age, the Woman's Club and the college dramatic clubs shared the public space with the murder of Geneva Hardman and its ugly aftermath in 1920. Simply put, in both periods the charming and genteel coexisted with the alarming and brutish. Having said this, it is nevertheless true that the courthouse machine gun emplacement and the soldiers' fusillade heralded a cultural gulf separating 1920 from the Gilded Age. The use of deadly, officially sanctioned force against white citizens intent on avenging the murder of a white child at the hands of a black man would have been most unlikely in the 1880s and 1890s, when the local press (and presumably a substantial number of its readers) openly approved and applauded the lynching of criminal suspects, especially those who were black. This mind-set would be challenged and eroded by the progressive impulse of the early twentieth century, with its insistence on centralized, bureaucratized governmental control. And of course, the argument between these opposing points of view has long since been settled. John D. Wright Jr. aptly titled his 1986 essay on the Lockett incident, published in the *Register of the Kentucky Historical Society,* "Lexington's Suppression of the 1920 Will Lockett Lynch Mob." The title suggests the central theme of the essay: that the incident symbolizes the triumph of good over evil, of government-sanctioned legal authority over the threat to this authority by extralegal, nongovernmental forces, that is, by mob rule. Wright emphasizes this point clearly when he quotes a February 1920 magazine article on the Lockett incident: "The evils of lynch law are not confined to the wrong done to the person lynched; they strike at the root of all government." During the early twentieth century the impulse to regulate social life by legal, bureaucratic, centralized authority was also bolstered by the southern progressive economic philosophy, which held that, simply put, lynching was bad national public relations and therefore bad for business. Arguably, Lexington remained as racist in 1920 as it had been in 1890, and the line between the lynch mob and "legal lynching" in the Lockett incident was a fine one. Nevertheless, the forces of change visible on Lexington's courthouse steps in February 1920 were harbingers of the national progress toward civil rights and equal justice that would be won during the course of the twentieth century. The lynch mob mentality of the Gilded Age had become an obsolete, dysfunctional liability in postwar, progressive Lexington, and no rational person could argue that this was not a good thing. Yet it can be argued that the end of any era is a mixed blessing, rendering obsolete the charming, inspiring, and civilizing aspects of a community's cultural life, as well as the most alarming of its uncivil earmarks. When the Bluegrass city said so long to the Gilded Age, it said good-bye to the literary society on its campuses as well as the lynch mob on its streets.[12]

APPENDIXES

A. LEXINGTON COLLEGIATE LITERARY SOCIETIES

Transylvania/Kentucky University

Antebellum Male Societies
Transylvania Philosophical Society: 1805–1806 (?)
Union Philosophical Society: 1818–1840 (?)
Transylvania Whig Society: 1823–1842
Adelphi Society: 1837–1857
Franklin Society: 1861–1865
Philothean Society: 1861–1865 (attached to the Bible College with the inception of Kentucky University at the end of the Civil War; see below)

Postbellum Societies
Arts College
Cecropian Society (male): 1865–1919
Periclean Society (male): 1865–1919 (merged with Ossolia to become coed, 1919–1925 [?])
Ossolian Society (female): 1890–1895 (reorganized in 1896 as Cornelia), 1914–1919
Cornelia Society (female): 1896–1913 (?) (merged with Alethea into a new Ossolia in 1914)
Alethea Society (female): 1900–1913 (?) (merged with Cornelia into a new Ossolia in 1914)

Bible College
Philothean Society (male): 1861–1914 (?); defunct by 1915
Christomeathean Society (male): 1870–1878
Phileusebian Society (male): 1886–1914 (?); defunct by 1915
Theosebian Society (female): 1906–1910 (?); defunct by 1915

A&M College (of Kentucky University)
Union Society (male): 1869–1878 (continued at State College when A&M separated from Kentucky University; see below)

State College/State University (of Kentucky)
Union Society (male): 1869–early 1920s
Philosophian Society (female): 1882–late 1920s (?)
Patterson Society (male): 1886–1920s; sporadically through 1957 (?)
Neville Society (female): 1904–early 1920s

Normal Department/College of Education
Normal Society (coed): 1890–1907
Horace Mann Society (coed): 1901 (?)–early 1920s
Roark Society (coed): 1905 (survived only a few months)

B. Postbellum Lexington Collegiate Literary Society Paraphernalia

Transylvania/Kentucky University

Arts College

Alatheian (1900)/Alethean (1905) (female)
 Motto: *Esse quam videri* (To be rather than to seem)
 Colors: Royal purple and old gold (1905)
 Flower: Pansy (1905)
 Paper: *The Truth*

Cecropian (male)
 Motto: *Sic itur ad astra* (Such is the way to immortal fame)
 Colors: Red and white (1897); maroon and white (1905)
 Yell: Rah, rah, rah! / Boom-ti-a! / We are the boys / of Ce-cro-pia! (1905)
 Paper: *The Shield*

Cornelian (female)
 Motto: *Nulla Vestigia Retrorsum* (No going backward)
 Colors: Green and white (1897)
 Yell: Green and white! / Colori! Yi! Hi! / Cornelia! K.U. / Literi! Si! Ty! (1897)
 Flower: White carnation (1905)
 Paper: *The Jewel*

Ossolian (female)
 Motto: *Pas pour l'ecole mais pour la vie nous apprenons* (We learn not for school but for life)
 Paper: *The Echo*

Periclean (male)
 Motto: *Per ardua ad alta* (Through difficulties to the heights of wisdom)
 Colors: Navy blue and pure white (1897); old gold and navy blue (1905)
 Yell: Wah! Huh! Wah! / Wah; Huh! We-a! / We are the boys / Of Periclea (1897); Wah, Hoo, Wah! / Wah, Hoo, We-a! / We are the boys / Of Per-i-clea! (1905)
 Paper: *The Owl*

Bible College

Phileusebian (male)
 Motto: *Epi ten teleioteta pheroreoa* (Let us press on to perfection)
 Colors: Scarlet and sky blue (1905)
 Yell: Hoo, gah, hah! / Hoo, gah, hah! / Phileuse! Phileuse! / Phileusebi-ah! (1905)
 Paper: *The Anchor*

Philothean (male)
 Motto: *Agrupneite kai proseuchesthe* (Watch and pray)
 Colors: Light shades of pink and green (1905)

Yell: E-ah! E-ah! / Phi-lo-the-a! / We are thum, / And thum are we-ah! (1905)
    Paper: *The Clavis*
Theosebian (female)
    Motto: *Semper Paratae* (Always ready)
    Colors: Light blue and gold
    Flower: Lily of the valley

State College/State University (of Kentucky)

Neville (female)
    Motto: *Tout bien ou rien* (Everything well, or nothing)
    Colors: Green and gold (1910)
    Flower: Sunflower (1910)
Normal (coed)
    Motto: Forward to excellence
    Paper: *Roark Enterprise*
Patterson (male)
    Motto: *Post proelia praemia* (After battles come rewards)
    Colors: Purple and old gold (1910)
    Paper: *The Spectator*
Philosophian (female)
    Motto: *Nulla Vestigia Retrorsum* (No going backward)
    Colors: Red and black (1894)
    Paper: *The Star*
Union (male)
    Motto: *Jamais Arriere* (Never backward)
    Colors: Pink and white (1910)
    Paper: *The Student*

C. Kentucky State Intercollegiate Oratorical Contests, 1888–1905

Date	Location	Representation	Winner	Oration Title	Source
21 April 1888	Central University chapel, Richmond	Central University, Centre College, Georgetown College, Kentucky University, State College	Centre College: Lucien D. Noel	"Progressive Thought"	*Lexington Morning Transcript*, 22 April 1888, 4
5 April 1889	Lexington Opera House	Central University, Centre College, Kentucky University, State College	Kentucky University: Henry T. Duncan (Periclean Society)	"The New South"	*K. U. Crimson* 1897, 96; *Lexington Morning Transcript*, 6 April 1889, 1; *Kentucky (Lexington) Leader*, 7 April 1889, 4
4 April 1890	Second Presbyterian Church, Danville	Central University, Centre College, Georgetown College, Kentucky University, State College	Centre College: Henry L. Godsey	"Shall the Minority Be Heard?"	*Lexington Morning Transcript*, 5 April 1890, 1

(continued)

C. Kentucky State Intercollegiate Oratorical Contests, 1888–1905 *(continued)*					
Date	Location	Representation	Winner	Oration Title	Source
10 April 1891	Lexington Opera House	Central University, Centre College, Georgetown College, Kentucky University, State College	Georgetown College: John M. Stevenson	"Conservatism and Reform in Government"	*Lexington Morning Transcript*, 11 April 1891, 1
1 April 1892	Scott County courthouse, Georgetown	Central University, Centre College, Georgetown College	Centre College: Martin D. Hardin	"What Next? The Advancement of Science"	*Lexington Morning Transcript*, 2 April 1892, 1
7 April 1893	Lexington Opera House	Central University, Centre College, Georgetown College, Kentucky University	Centre College: J. H. Swango	"The Plutocrat"	*Lexington Morning Transcript*, 8 April 1893, 1
6 April 1894	Lexington Opera House	Central University, Centre College, Georgetown College, Kentucky University, State College	Kentucky University: Enoch Grehan (Cecropian Society)	"By Their Fruits Ye Shall Know Them: Great Characters of History"	*K. U. Crimson* 1897, 96; *Lexington Morning Transcript*, 7 April 1894, 1

(continued)

C. KENTUCKY STATE INTERCOLLEGIATE ORATORICAL CONTESTS, 1888–1905 (continued)					
Date	Location	Representation	Winner	Oration Title	Source
5 April 1895	Lexington Opera House	Central University, Centre College, Georgetown College, Kentucky University, State College	Georgetown College: J. M. Shelburne	"When Thou Saidist, Seek Ye My Face, Thy Face Will I Seek"	*(Lexington) Press-Transcript*, 6 April 1895, 1
3 April 1896	Lexington Opera House	Central University, Centre College, Georgetown College, Kentucky University, State College	State College: John T. Geary (Patterson Society)	"Evolution of the Republic"	*Lexington Daily Leader*, 28 March 1896, 3; 3 April 1896, 1; 4 April 1896, 1
2 April 1897	Lexington Opera House	Central University, Centre College, Georgetown College, Kentucky University, State College	Georgetown College: William Poe Stuart	"Silent Voices"	*Lexington Morning Herald*, 3 April 1897, 1

(continued)

C. KENTUCKY STATE INTERCOLLEGIATE ORATORICAL CONTESTS, 1888–1905 *(continued)*					
Date	Location	Representation	Winner	Oration Title	Source
1 April 1898	Lexington Opera House	Central University, Centre College, Georgetown College, Kentucky University, State College	Central University: Garniss W. Hunter	"Religion and Its Relation to Reform"	*Lexington Morning Herald*, 2 April 1898, 5
7 April 1899	Lexington Opera House	Central University, Centre College, Georgetown College, Kentucky University, State College	Kentucky University: R. E. Moss (Periclean Society)	"Men Will Rise on Stepping Stones of Their Dead Selves to Higher Things"	*K. U. Crimson 1897*, 96; *Lexington Morning Herald*, 8 April 1899, 1, 4, 5
13 April 1900	Lexington Opera House	Central University, Centre College, Georgetown College, Kentucky University, State College	State College: Leonidas Ragan (Union Society)	"At the Open Door"	*Lexington Morning Herald*, 30 March 1900, 6; 14 April 1900, 1, 4

(continued)

	C. KENTUCKY STATE INTERCOLLEGIATE ORATORICAL CONTESTS, 1888–1905 *(continued)*				
Date	Location	Representation	Winner	Oration Title	Source
12 April 1901	Lexington Opera House	Central University, Centre College, Georgetown College, State College	State College: Clarke Tandy (Patterson Society)	"The Reign of Law"	*Lexington Leader*, 27 March 1901, 2; 13 April 1901, 4
18 April 1902	Danville Opera House	Central University (Danville), Georgetown College, Kentucky University, State College	Georgetown College: A. K. Wright	"On the Heights There Is Liberty"	*Lexington Morning Herald*, 19 April 1902, 1
10 April 1903	Lexington Opera House (last time)	Central University, Georgetown College, Kentucky University, Kentucky Wesleyan College (Winchester), State College	Kentucky Wesleyan College: Joseph B. Harris	"The Bulwark of the Anglo-Saxons"	*Lexington Morning Herald*, 11 April 1903, 1; *Lexington Leader*, 11 April 1903, 5

(continued)

C. Kentucky State Intercollegiate Oratorical Contests, 1888–1905 (continued)					
Date	Location	Representation	Winner	Oration Title	Source
8 April 1904	Georgetown Opera House	Central University, Georgetown College, Kentucky University, Kentucky Wesleyan College (Winchester), State College	Kentucky University: Homer W. Carpenter (Cecropian Society)	"The Higher Ministry of Beauty"	*K. U. Crimson* 1905, 79; *Lexington Morning Herald*, 7 April 1904, 8; 9 April 1904, 1
28 April 1905	State College chapel	Central University, Georgetown College, Kentucky University, Kentucky Wesleyan College (Winchester), State College	Central University: John M. P. Thacker	"The New Kentucky"	*Lexington Herald*, 28 April 1905, 2; 29 April 1905, 1

	D. Lexington Chautauqua "College Day" Oratorical Contests at Woodland Park, 1889–1904			
Date	Representation	First Place/Oration Title	Second Place/Oration Title	Source
29 June 1889	Central University (Richmond), Centre College, Georgetown College, Kentucky Wesleyan College (Millersburg)	Central University: John Van Lear "The Triumph of Truth"	Centre College: A. O. Stanley "The Inner Struggle"	*Lexington Morning Transcript*, 30 June 1889, 1; *Kentucky (Lexington) Leader*, 30 June 1889, 2
7 July 1890	Central University (Richmond), Centre College, Georgetown College, Kentucky University	Centre College: S. M. Wilson "A Vindication of Napoleon"	Georgetown College: J. C. Cantrill "A Political Evil and Its Remedy"	*Kentucky (Lexington) Leader*, 6 July 1890, 7; 7 July 1890, 5
6 July 1891	Central University (Richmond), Centre College, Georgetown College, Kentucky University, Kentucky Wesleyan College (Millersburg)	Central University: J. T. Jackson "Freedom Our Heritage, Its Consummation Our Trust"	Centre College: Martin T. Hardin "Our South"	*Kentucky (Lexington) Leader*, 6 July 1891, 4; 7 July 1891, 5
8 July 1892	Central University (Richmond), Centre College, Georgetown College, Kentucky University	Centre College: Henry L. Godsey "Shall We Distrust?"	Central University: J. Lyle Irvine "International Commerce"	*Kentucky (Lexington) Leader*, 8 July 1892, 1
6 July 1893	Berea College, Central University (Richmond), Centre College, Georgetown College, Kentucky University	Centre College: James L. McWilliams "Human Possibilities"	Kentucky University: Phillip W. Breitenbucher (Cecropian Society) "Modern Chivalry"	*K. U. Crimson* 1897, 96; *Kentucky (Lexington) Leader*, 6 July 1893, 1

(continued)

D. Lexington Chautauqua "College Day" Oratorical Contests at Woodland Park, 1889–1904 *(continued)*				
Date	Representation	First Place/Oration Title	Second Place/Oration Title	Source
12 July 1894	Asbury College (Wilmore), Central University (Richmond), Centre College, Georgetown College, Kentucky University, Kentucky Wesleyan (Winchester), State College	Kentucky University: Charles A. Thomas (Cecropian Society) "The Universal Republic"	Centre College: Bert Goodloe "The Golden Era of Humanity"	*K. U. Crimson, 1897,* 96; *Kentucky (Lexington) Leader,* 12 July 1894, 6; 13 July 1894, 6
11 July 1895	Central University (Richmond), Centre College, Georgetown College, Kentucky University, Kentucky Wesleyan (Winchester), State College	Kentucky University: Wood Ballard (Periclean Society) "Great Men of the Future"	Georgetown College: John S. Norris "Napoleon Bonaparte"	*K. U. Crimson 1897,* 96; *Lexington Daily Leader,* 11 July 1895, 1; 12 July 1895, 5; *K. U. Enroll* 1, no. 1 (12 September 1895): 1
9 July 1896	Central University (Richmond), Centre College, Georgetown College, Kentucky University, Kentucky Wesleyan (Winchester), State College	Georgetown College: J. M. Shelburne "When Thou Saidst Seek Ye My Face, Lord, My Heart Said, Thy Face Will I Seek"	State College: William Herbert Sugg (Union Society) "The Dangers of Centralization"	*Lexington Daily Leader,* 23 February 1896, 5; 9 July 1896, 3; 10 July 1896, 3

(continued)

D. Lexington Chautauqua "College Day" Oratorical Contests at Woodland Park, 1889–1904 *(continued)*				
Date	Representation	First Place/Oration Title	Second Place/Oration Title	Source
8 July 1897	Central University (Richmond), Centre College, Georgetown College, Kentucky University, Kentucky Wesleyan (Winchester), State College	Kentucky University: James N. Elliott (Cecropian Society) "Devotion to Duty the Measure of Happiness"	State College: John T. Geary (Patterson Society) "Evolution of the Republic"	*K. U. Crimson 1897,* 80; *Lexington Daily Leader,* 28 March 1896, 3; 8 July 1897, 8; 9 July 1897, 8
8 July 1898	Asbury College (Wilmore), Central University (Richmond), Centre College, Georgetown College, Kentucky University, Kentucky Wesleyan (Winchester), State College	Kentucky University: Howard Cree (? Society, alumnus, College of Bible class of 1897)[1] "The Real Man"	Central University: R. G. Gordon "The Nation and the State"	*Lexington Daily Leader,* 8 July 1898, 8; 9 July 1898, 2; 5 July 1899, 1
6 July 1899	Central University (Richmond), Centre College, Georgetown College, Kentucky Wesleyan College (Winchester), State College	Central University: B. H. Conner "Blot on the Scrutcheon"	State College: Robert M. Allen (Union Society) "At the Threshold"	*Lexington Morning Herald,* 29 March 1899, 4; *Lexington Daily Leader,* 5 July 1899, 1; 7 July 1899, 8

(continued)

Date	Representation	First Place/Oration Title	Second Place/Oration Title	Source
29 June 1900	Central University (Richmond), Centre College, Georgetown College, Kentucky University, Kentucky Wesleyan (Winchester), State College	State College: Robert M. Allen (Union Society) "New Conditions and New Duties"	Centre College: Allen W. Gullion "The Man on Horseback and the Man Afoot"	*Lexington Daily Leader,* 29 June 1900, 1; *Lexington Morning Herald,* 30 June 1900, 4
28 June 1901	Central University (Richmond), Centre College, Georgetown College, Kentucky Wesleyan (Winchester), State College[2]	Georgetown College: A. K. Wright "On the Heights There Is Liberty"	State College: Clarke Tandy (Patterson Society) "The Reign of Law"	*Lexington Leader,* 27 March 1901, 2; 28 June 1901, 1; 29 June 1901, 4
27 June 1902	Central University (Danville), Georgetown College, Kentucky Wesleyan (Winchester), State College	Kentucky Wesleyan: Joseph B. Harris "Napoleon's Personality"	State College: Clarke Tandy (Patterson Society) "The New Theology"	*Lexington Leader,* 26 June 1902, 8; 27 June 1902, 1

(continued)

D. Lexington Chautauqua "College Day" Oratorical Contests at Woodland Park, 1889–1904 *(continued)*

Date	Representation	First Place/Oration Title	Second Place/Oration Title	Source
9 July 1903	Central University (Danville), Georgetown College, Kentucky University, Kentucky Wesleyan (Winchester), State College [3]	State College: Clarke Tandy (Patterson Society) "The Hero as Orator"	Kentucky University: John Shishmanian (? Society) "The Spirit of Washington beyond the Seas"	*Lexington Leader*, 9 July 1903, 1; 10 July 1903, 3; *Lexington Morning Herald*, 10 July 1903, 1
1 July 1904 [4]	Central University (Danville), Georgetown College, Kentucky University, Kentucky Wesleyan (Winchester), State College	Georgetown College: James Hugh Snyder "Life and Song"	Central University: Paul B. Collins "Radiant Energy"	*Lexington Leader*, 1 July 1904, 1

1. As a result of Cree's participation, Kentucky University was disqualified from the contest in 1899.

2. Kentucky University had dropped out of the Kentucky Oratorical Association.

3. Kentucky University returned to the contest.

4. The Lexington Chautauqua disbanded in 1904. When it reappeared in altered form in 1907, the "College Day" oratorical contests were not part of the program.

E. PRINCIPAL OFF-CAMPUS STUDENT DRAMATIC CLUB PERFORMANCES, 1910–1917

Date	Lexington Stage	Drama Club	Play Performed	Source[1]
4–5 February 1910	Opera House	State University (unnamed)	*Richelieu*	*Lexington Leader*, 5 February 1910, 8
27 May 1910	Woodland Auditorium	Transylvania Dramatic Club	*Sweet Lavender*	*Lexington Herald*, 28 May 1910, 2
20 April 1911	Opera House	State University Strollers	*Brown of Harvard*	*Lexington Leader*, 21 April 1911, 7
6–7 April 1911	Opera House	Transylvania Dramatic Club	*One of the Eight*	*Lexington Leader*, 7 April 1911, 2
2 May 1912	Opera House	State University Strollers	*The Virginian*	*Lexington Herald*, 3 May 1912, 6
9 May 1912	Opera House	Transylvania Dramatic Club	*The Private Secretary*	*Lexington Herald*, 10 May 1912, 8
14 March 1913	Opera House	State University Strollers	*The Lost Paradise*	*Lexington Leader*, 15 March 1913, 5
26 May 1913	Opera House	Transylvania Dramatic Club	*Esmeralda*	*Lexington Leader*, 27 May 1913, 11
3 March 1914[2]	Ben Ali Theater	State University Strollers	*The College Widow*	*Lexington Herald*, 4 March 1914, 8
5 January 1915	Ben Ali Theater	State University Strollers	*Charley's Aunt*	*Lexington Leader*, 16 January 1915, 2

(continued)

E. Principal Off-Campus Student Dramatic Club Performances, 1910–1917 (*continued*)

Date	Lexington Stage	Drama Club	Play Performed	Source[1]
26 February 1915	Ben Ali Theater	Transylvania Dramatic Club	*Going Some*	*Lexington Leader*, 27 February 1915, 2
13 April 1916	Opera House	State University Strollers	*Father and the Boys*	*Lexington Leader*, 14 April 1916, 16
25–26 April 1916	Opera House	Transylvania Dramatic Club	*The Fortune Hunter*	*Lexington Herald*, 26 April 1916, 2
10 March 1917[3]	Opera House	State University Strollers	*The Lion and the Mouse*	*Lexington Leader*, 11 March 1917, 6

1. These sources are only representative. Both newspapers carried multiple stories related to these performances.
2. There is no evidence in either the local newspapers or the Transylvania yearbook *The Crimson* that the Transylvania Dramatic Club performed an off-campus play in 1914, although it presented a dramatic program at Morrison Chapel on 4 February.
3. Although the Transylvania Dramatic Club apparently intended to perform a play at the opera house in March 1917, this did not happen. Instead, the club performed *David Garrick* at Morrison Chapel (as it had the previous year) on 6 December 1917. See *Lexington Herald*, 16 December 1916, 6; 6 December 1917, 8. Also see *The Crimson, 1917*, 149; *The Crimson, 1918*, 129.

NOTES

PROLOGUE

1. For arguments about the importance and former neglect of southern intellectual history, see Michael O'Brien, ed., *All Clever Men, Who Make Their Way: Critical Discourse in the Old South*, Brown Thrasher ed. (Athens: University of Georgia Press, 1992), ix–xv, 1–25. For the need to study the history of specific locales, see Thomas Bender, "The Cultures of Intellectual Life: The City and the Professions," in *New Directions in American Intellectual History*, ed. John Higham and Paul K. Conkin (Baltimore: Johns Hopkins University Press, 1979), 182. Also see Timothy J. Gilfoyle, "America's Heart" [review of *Gotham: A History of New York City to 1892*, by Edwin G. Burrows and Mike Wallace], *Atlantic Monthly*, February 1999, 96–97; the quote is from ibid. For the argument between those who eschew attempts at generalization, causal explanation, or synthesis, preferring to view the mission of writing local history as a search for localized meaning through "thick description" of individual situations, and those who insist that works of local history contribute to a larger synthesis, see Aletta Biersack, "Local Knowledge, Local History: Geertz and Beyond," in *The New Cultural History*, ed. Lynn Hunt (Los Angeles: University of California Press, 1989), 72–96. For the interactive nature of higher education and public culture at the turn of the twentieth century, see Thomas Bender, *New York Intellect: A History of Intellectual Life in New York City, from 1750 to the Beginning of Our Own Time* (Baltimore: Johns Hopkins University Press, 1987), 274, chap. 7. The last quote is from Thomas Bender, *Intellect and Public Life: Essays on the Social History of Academic Intellectuals in the United States* (Baltimore: Johns Hopkins University Press, 1993), 33. Finally, note that the terms *cultural history* and *intellectual history* are now virtually interchangeable. For instance, Michael Roth, in "Performing History: Modernist Contextualism in Carl Schorske's *Fin-de-Siècle Vienna*," *American Historical Review* 99 (June 1994): 729, observed that intellectual history has now been "refitted" as cultural history. As another case in point, see Hunt, *The New Cultural History*, 1–22, for a discussion of the "new" cultural history as an amalgamation of economic, social, and intellectual history under the rubric of cultural history.

2. For the characterization of popular culture as "cheap amusement," see Gregory A. Waller, *Main Street Amusements: Movies and Commercial Entertainment in a Southern City, 1896–1930* (Washington, D.C.: Smithsonian Institution Press, 1995), 28. For the concept of intellectual life being based in "localities" as opposed to professions or academic disciplines, see Bender, "Cultures of Intellectual Life," 183.

3. For the shift from nineteenth-century oratorical culture to a "culture of professionalism" in the early twentieth century, see Gregory Clark and S. Michael Halloran, eds., *Oratorical Culture in Nineteenth-Century America: Transformations in the Theory and Practice of Rhetoric* (Carbondale: Southern Illinois University Press, 1993), 1–26. For another perspective on this transformation, see Bruce E. Kimball, *Orators and Philosophers: A History of the Idea of Liberal Education* (New York: Teachers College Press, 1986), chaps. 5, 6. For the concomitant shift in public preference away from the orator's rostrum and toward the dramatic action of the stage and screen in the early twentieth century, see Lawrence W. Levine, *Highbrow/Lowbrow: The Emergence of Cultural Hierarchy in America* (Cambridge, Mass.: Harvard University Press, 1988), 46–49.

4. For this view of the evolution of the historiography of American higher education, see Laurence R. Veysey, "The History of Education," *Reviews in American History* (December 1982): 281–91. For a discussion of the necessity of studying the historical college student and the extracurriculum and viewing students and their activities as the agents of change and reform on campus, see Frederick Rudolph, "Neglect of Students as a Historical Tradition," in *The College and the Student*, ed. Lawrence E. Dennis and Joseph F. Kauffman (Washington, D.C.: American Council on Education, 1966), 47–58. For the argument that the study of nineteenth-century student life and extracurricular activities will lead to additional insights into higher education and the larger American culture, see James McLachlan, "The American College in the Nineteenth Century: Toward a Reappraisal," *Teachers College Record* 80 (September 1978): 298–99. Also see James McLachlan, "The *Choice of Hercules*: American Student Societies in the Early 19th Century," in *The University in Society*, vol. 2, *Europe, Scotland, and the United States from the 16th to the 20th Century*, ed. Lawrence Stone (Princeton, N.J.: Princeton University Press, 1974), 485. For the argument that understanding the literary societies is necessary to an understanding of the historical American college student and of American academic history, see McLachlan, "*Choice of Hercules*," 472. McLachlan insists that an essential component of the history of higher education, the historical college student, "must be sought in the study of student societies."

5. Frederick Rudolph, in *The American College and University: A History* (1962; reprint, Athens: University of Georgia Press, 1990), chap. 7, describes the extracurriculum developing as a counterpoint to the curriculum and becoming one of the successful forces contending to redefine colleges. Rudolph traces the origins of the literary societies to a student revolt against the austere, formal curriculum and institutional climate of the colonial and antebellum campus. For views consonant with Rudolph's about the on-campus social and intellectual origins of the literary societies, see Helen Lefkowitz Horowitz, *Campus Life: Undergraduate Cultures from the End of the Eighteenth Century to the Present* (Chicago: University of Chicago Press, 1987), 28, chap. 2; Arthur T. Hamlin, *The University Library in the United States: Its Origins and Development* (Philadelphia: University of Pennsylvania Press, 1981),

38; Thomas S. Harding, "College Literary Societies: Their Contribution to the Development of Academic Libraries, 1815–76. I. The Golden Age of College Society Libraries, 1815–40," *Library Quarterly* 29, no. 1 (January 1959): 1; and David Potter, "The Literary Society," in *History of Speech Education in America: Background Studies,* ed. Karl R. Wallace (New York: Appleton-Century-Crofts, 1954), 238–39. For a portrayal of the societies' curriculum as complementary to the formal curriculum, see Louise L. Stevenson, "Preparing for Public Life: The Collegiate Students at New York University, 1832–1881," in *The University and the City: From Medieval Origins to the Present,* ed. Thomas Bender (New York: Oxford University Press, 1988), 150–177. For the reference to "intellectual traditions" represented by persuasion and reason, see Kimball's *Orators and Philosophers.* In this regard, note that Rudolph ties the literary societies to Enlightenment "reason" in *The American College and University,* 137–38. In contrast, McLachlan grounds the American Whig Society at Princeton in the Renaissance and therefore in the oratorical tradition of rhetoric as "persuasion" in *"Choice of Hercules,"* 488, 493. For a fuller discussion of the nineteenth-century oratorical culture and its rhetoric, see Clark and Halloran, *Oratorical Culture,* 1–26. For a discussion of student culture, specifically the literary societies, as a training ground for Victorian middle-class and professional life, see Stevenson, "Preparing for Public Life," 150–77. For a discussion of how literary societies functioned to prepare youth for the competitive, male, adult world of work, see Anthony E. Rotundo, *American Manhood: Transformations in Masculinity from the Revolution to the Modern Era* (New York: Basic Books, 1993), 68–71.

6. Both Horowitz, *Campus Life,* 28–31, and McLachlan, "The American College in the Nineteenth Century," 294–96, argue that the societies were originally "inclusive" of all economic and social classes represented on campus; however, unlike Horowitz, McLachlan claims that they remained so throughout their history. For the view that American higher education was largely the domain of the American Anglo-Saxon middle class, see Colin B. Burke, *American Collegiate Populations: A Test of the Traditional View* (New York: New York University Press, 1982), chaps. 3, 5; The term "working elite" is from ibid., 7. Stevenson, in "Preparing for Public Life," 155–57, also notes the primarily middle-class backgrounds and aspirations of New York University students in the nineteenth century. Burton J. Bledstein, in *The Culture of Professionalism: The Middle Class and the Development of Higher Education in America* (New York: W. W. Norton, 1978), 248–51, chap. 5, argues in the same vein that, even a generation before the Civil War, extracurricular programs reflected the attitudes and aspirations of an arising middle class. For James Lane Allen's depiction of the relative differences in affluence among Kentucky University students after the Civil War, see *The Reign of Law: A Tale of the Kentucky Hemp Fields* (New York: Macmillan, 1900), 45–46, 48, 69, 73–75. For discussion of female collegiate literary societies, see Barbara M. Solomon, *In the Company of Educated Women: A History of Women and Higher Education in America* (New Haven, Conn.: Yale University Press, 1985), 105; and Thomas S. Harding, *College Literary Societies:*

Their Contribution to Higher Education in the United States, 1815–1876 (New York: Pageant Press International, 1971), 315. For a brief mention of the female literary societies at Kentucky University in Lexington, see John D. Wright Jr. *Transylvania: Tutor to the West* (Lexington: University Press of Kentucky, 1980), 294; for a discussion of female and coeducational literary societies at the University of Kentucky, see James F. Hopkins, *The University of Kentucky: Origins and Early Years* (Lexington: University of Kentucky Press, 1951), 175–76.

7. For the societies' contributions to academic rhetorical practice, specifically academic debate, see Potter's discussion of changing debate styles, and the societies' role in these changes, in "The Literary Society," 238–57, and in David Potter, *Debating in the Colonial Chartered Colleges: An Historical Survey, 1642 to 1900,* Contributions to Education No. 899 (New York: Bureau of Publications, Teachers College, Columbia University, 1944), chap. 3; the quote is from p. 122. Also see George V. Bohman, "Rhetorical Practice in Colonial America," in *History of Speech Education in America: Background Studies,* ed. Karl R. Wallace (New York: Appleton-Century-Crofts, 1954), 60–79; Wilbur Samuel Howell, "English Backgrounds of Rhetoric," ibid., 1–47; and Warren Guthrie, "Rhetorical Theory in Colonial America," ibid., 48–59. For the role of debate in the societies, see Rotundo, *American Manhood,* 69–70; Stevenson, "Preparing for Public Life," 164–67; Rudolph, *The American College and University,* 138; Horowitz, *Campus Life,* 26–27, 29; Hamlin, *The University Library,* 38; and McLachlan, *"Choice of Hercules,"* 483–85. For discussions of the organization of society libraries and their contribution to modern academic libraries, see Hamlin, *The University Library,* 38–41; and Harding, "The Golden Age of College Society Libraries." For McLachlan's discussion of the American Whig Society library and its contributions to collegiate intellectual life, see *"Choice of Hercules,"* 477–80. For Harding's argument regarding the societies' contribution to academic freedom, see *College Literary Societies,* 319. For those factors generally associated with the decline and demise of the literary societies, see Rudolph, *The American College and University,* 145–46; Horowitz, *Campus Life,* 29, 37; and Bledstein, *Culture of Professionalism,* 248–54. For a discussion of nineteenth-century cultural shifts that boded ill for these societies, see Stevenson, "Preparing for Public Life," 167–69. In a similar vein, see Louise L. Stevenson, *Scholarly Means to Evangelical Ends: The New Haven Scholars and the Transformation of Higher Learning in America, 1830–1890* (Baltimore: Johns Hopkins University Press, 1986).

8. The first quote is from Richard L. Bushman, *The Refinement of America: Persons, Houses, Cities* (1992; reprint, New York: Vintage Books, 1993), 441. For a description of the audience at a society-sponsored entertainment, see *Lexington Transcript,* 23 February 1894, 8. For excellent, detailed descriptions of elaborately staged society-sponsored entertainments inside the Lexington Opera House and of the parades by students through the streets of Lexington, see *Kentucky (Lexington) Leader,* 7 April 1889, 4; and *Lexington Morning Herald,* 14 April 1900, 1, 4. The

second quote is from *Lexington Daily Leader,* 8 July 1897, 8; the last quote is from *Lexington Morning Herald,* 7 April 1899, 2.

9. For use of the term "high amusement," see Joseph F. Kett, *The Pursuit of Knowledge under Difficulties: From Self-Improvement to Adult Education in America, 1750–1990* (Stanford, Calif.: Stanford University Press, 1994), 147. With regard to "quests" for self-improvement that marked the Gilded Age middle and upper classes, see ibid., chap. 5. For "refinement" and "genteel" respectability, see Bushman, *The Refinement of America,* 273, 389, chap. 12. For the concept of intellectual cultural authority, see Levine, *Highbrow/Lowbrow,* 236, chap. 3; and Willard B. Gatewood, *Aristocrats of Color: The Black Elite, 1880–1920* (Bloomington: Indiana University Press, 1990; First Midland Book ed., 1993), chap. 7; Gatewood also uses the term "genteel performance." The quote is from *Lexington Herald,* 1 March 1916, 8.

10. For a discussion of the cultural changes in language and rhetorical style affecting public entertainment at the turn of the twentieth century, see Levine, *Highbrow/Lowbrow,* 46–49.

11. The conception of collegiate dramatic clubs as originally being extracurricular bodies producing amateur, artistically motivated, noncommercial plays was developed from Percy MacKaye, *The Civic Theatre in Relation to the Redemption of Leisure: A Book of Suggestions* (New York: Mitchell Kennerley, 1912), 219–23; Constance D'Arcy Mackay, *The Little Theater in the United States* (New York: Henry Holt, 1917), 181–204; William Lyon Phelps, *The Twentieth Century Theatre: Observations on the Contemporary English and American Stage* (New York: Macmillan, 1918), 84–85, chap. 3; Kenneth Macgowan, *Footlights across America: Towards a National Theater* (New York: Harcourt, Brace, 1929), 112–13; and Solomon, *In the Company of Educated Women,* 104–6. For the pre-Revolutionary origins of dramatic clubs, see Macgowan, *Footlights across America,* 107–8, 112. For their widespread popularity in the 1890s, see Solomon, *In the Company of Educated Women,* 105; and Horowitz, *Campus Life,* 55. For dramatic clubs as an expression of revolt against puritanical mores, see Macgowan, *Footlights across America,* 112; and Solomon, *In the Company of Educated Women,* 105. For origins and definitions of the Little Theater Movement, see Mackay, *The Little Theater in the United States,* chap. 1; Phelps, *The Twentieth Century Theatre,* 77–80; Macgowan, *Footlights across America,* chap. 1; and Clarence Arthur Perry, *The Work of the Little Theatres: The Groups They Include, the Plays They Produce, Their Tournaments, and the Handbooks They Use* (New York: Russell Sage Foundation, 1933), 9–27. Both Macgowan (9) and Perry (15) directly link collegiate theatrical efforts or student dramatic clubs with the Little Theater Movement. For the argument that the professional, commercial theater retreated to New York in the face of competition from movies in the 1910s, and that this retreat led to the Little Theater Movement and to the general growth of amateur theatrics nationwide, see Macgowan, *Footlights across America,* 3; and Gerald Bordman, *American Theatre: A Chronicle of Comedy and Drama 1914–1930* (New York: Oxford University Press, 1995), preface, 3, 27–28. For the link between

the Little Theater Movement and the inclusion of dramatics courses in the formal curriculum (always applauded in this literature), see Mackay, *The Little Theater in the United States*, 181–82; Macgowan, *Footlights across America*. 112–31; Perry, *The Work of the Little Theatres*, 15; and Jean Carter and Jess Ogden, *Everyman's Drama: A Study of the Noncommercial Theatre in the United States* (New York: American Association for Adult Education, 1938), 28–29. The first quote is from Timothy Dwight, quoted without citation in Macgowan, *Footlights across America*, 107; the second quote is from Hazel Dicken-Garcia, *Journalistic Standards in Nineteenth-Century America* (Madison: University of Wisconsin Press, 1989), 164; the third quote is from Phelps, *The Twentieth Century Theatre*, 78; the fourth quote is from Macgowan, *Footlights across America*, 108; and the last quote is from the title of Bledstein's *The Culture of Professionalism*.

12. Pre- and post-1900 University of Kentucky graduation data from Richard Angelo, letter to author, 8 October 2006; and Richard Angelo, e-mail to author, 19 January 2007. Dr. Angelo developed this information from Ezra Gillis, *The University of Kentucky: Its History and Development: A Series of Charts Depicting the More Important Data, 1862–1955* (Lexington: University of Kentucky, 1956).

CHAPTER ONE: LEXINGTON IN THE GILDED AGE

1. For the text of his address, see George W. Ranck, *Historical Address at the Centennial Celebration of the Settlement of Lexington, Kentucky: April 2, 1879* (Lexington: Transylvania Printing and Publishing Co., 1879), copy available in Special Collections and Archives, Margaret I. King Library, University of Kentucky, Lexington. For discussions of George W. Ranck, see John D. Wright Jr., *Lexington: Heart of the Bluegrass* (Lexington: Lexington–Fayette County Historic Commission, 1982), 113; *The Kentucky Encyclopedia*, 1992 ed., s.v. "Ranck, George W."; and Lowell H. Harrison, *The Civil War in Kentucky* (Lexington: University Press of Kentucky, 1975), 96. The quote is from Hambleton Tapp and James C. Klotter, *Kentucky: Decades of Discord, 1865–1900* (Frankfort, Ky.: Kentucky Historical Society, 1977), 1.

2. The first quote is from Harrison, *Civil War in Kentucky*, 102; the second quote is from James Lane Allen, *The Reign of Law: A Tale of the Kentucky Hemp Fields* (New York: Macmillan, 1900), 85. Bettie L. Kerr and John D. Wright Jr., *Lexington: A Century in Photographs* (Lexington: Lexington–Fayette County Historic Commission, 1984), 30, note Kentucky's rejection of the Thirteenth, Fourteenth, and Fifteenth Amendments. The last quote is from Samuel M. Wilson, *History of Kentucky*, vol. 2, *From 1803 to 1928* (Louisville, Ky.: S. J. Clarke Publishing Company, 1928), 280, copy available in Special Collections and Archives, Margaret I. King Library, University of Kentucky, Lexington. For a discussion of the tense race relations in the New South, see Edward L. Ayers, *The Promise of the New South: Life after Reconstruction,* (New York: Oxford University Press, 1992), 136,

156–57. Kentucky lynching statistics are from George C. Wright, *Racial Violence in Kentucky, 1865–1940: Lynchings, Mob Rule, and "Legal Lynchings"* (Baton Rouge: Louisiana State University Press, 1990), 97, 313.

3. For the political situation in Kentucky after the Civil War and the first quote, see Dewey W. Grantham, *Southern Progressivism: The Reconciliation of Progress and Tradition* (Knoxville: University of Tennessee Press, 1983), 82–83. Also see Ayers, *Promise of the New South*, 8; and Tapp and Klotter, *Decades of Discord*, chap. 1. The second quote is from Tapp and Klotter, *Decades of Discord*, 28.

4. The quotes are from Ranck, *Historical Address*, 3, 6. For the origin of the term *Gilded Age* and the related quote, see Charles W. Calhoun, ed., *The Gilded Age: Essays on the Origins of Modern America* (Wilmington, Del.: Scholarly Resources, 1996), xi. For the last quote, see Grant C. Knight, *James Lane Allen and the Genteel Tradition* (Chapel Hill: University of North Carolina Press, 1935), 117–18.

5. The quote is from Hazel Dicken-Garcia, *Journalistic Standards in Nineteenth-Century America* (Madison: University of Wisconsin Press, 1989), 15. For her thoughts on the term *Victorian,* see Louise L. Stevenson, *The Victorian Homefront: American Thought and Culture, 1860–1880* (New York: Twayne Publishers, 1991), xx.

6. For a discussion of Victorian views of civilization and moral purpose, see Stevenson, *Victorian Homefront*, xx–xxii; the first quote is from p. xxi. For the quotes from his address, see Ranck, *Historical Address*, 6. For Mary P. Ryan's discussion of "female allegories," see *Women in Public: Between Banners and Ballots, 1825–1880* (Baltimore: Johns Hopkins University Press, 1990; Johns Hopkins Paperbacks ed., 1992), 24–30. For a discussion of the cult of "True Womanhood," see Barbara M. Solomon, *In the Company of Educated Women: A History of Women and Higher Education in America* (New Haven, Conn.: Yale University Press, 1985), 25–27, 36–37; the last quote is from p. 25. Stacy A. Cordery, in "Women in Industrializing America," in *The Gilded Age: Essays on the Origins of Modern America*, ed. Charles W. Calhoun (Wilmington, Del.: Scholarly Resources, 1996), 132, notes that writer Barbara Welter first used the phrase "the cult of true womanhood" in 1966 as a label for the Victorian conception of the ideal woman as "pious, pure, domestic, submissive, and leisured."

7. For this view of the influence of the nineteenth-century press, see Dicken-Garcia, *Journalistic Standards*, 30, 46–47, 158–59. The first quote is from O. B. Frothingham, "Voices of Power," *Atlantic Monthly* 53 (February 1884): 176–82, quoted in Dicken-Garcia, *Journalistic Standards*, 159. For the phrase, "historical exhibits," see Richard H. Brodhead, *Cultures of Letters: Scenes of Reading and Writing in Nineteenth-Century America* (Chicago: University of Chicago Press, 1993), 173. Additional quotes are from, respectively, *Lexington Daily Press*, 4 June 1885, 4; 5 June 1885, 2.

8. For the "cartography" of gender and public versus private with regard to the "map" of social space, see Ryan, *Women in Public*, 68–76. For the perspective

on "republican motherhood" taken here, see Stevenson, *Victorian Homefront*, xxvi–xxvii. The quotes are from, respectively, *Lexington Morning Transcript*, 21 August 1885, 3; *Kentucky (Lexington) Leader*, 18 November 1892, 5.

9. The quotes by Ranck are from *Historical Address*, 4, 11. For this description of the Victorian ideal of civilization and the last quote, see Stevenson, *Victorian Homefront*, xxi.

10. For the Victorians' fascination with other cultures, see Thomas J. Schlereth, *Victorian America: Transformations in Everyday Life, 1876–1915* (New York: Harper-Collins, 1991; HarperPerennial, 1992), 196. Quoted headlines are from, respectively, *Lexington Morning Transcript*, 9 September 1885, 2; 15 October 1885, 3; and 14 November 1885, 3; *Lexington Daily Press*, 12 November 1885, 2; and *Lexington Morning Transcript*, 26 November 1885, 3. The last quote is from the *Transcript*, 26 November 1885, 3.

11. The first quote is from *Lexington Daily Press*, 22 January 1885, 3; the second quote is from Ranck, *Historical Address*, 10. For Hamilton College, see Wright, *Heart of the Bluegrass*, 122; and John D. Wright Jr., *Transylvania: Tutor to the West* (Lexington: University Press of Kentucky, 1980), 275–76. For the Eastern Lunatic Asylum, the Lunatic Ball, and this annual dance's place in Lexington society at the turn of the twentieth century, see Wright, *Heart of the Bluegrass*, 59–60, 135. The last quote is from *Lexington Daily Press*, 9 December 1885, 1.

12. *Lexington Morning Transcript*, 8 January 1885, 2; 4 December 1885, 2.

13. *Lexington Daily Press*, 4 January 1885, 6; 2 May 1885, 3; 6 May 1885, 2.

14. For the articles quoted, see *Lexington Morning Transcript*, 12 February 1885, 2; 29 January 1885, 3; 12 February 1885, 4.

15. For this description of nineteenth-century benevolent organizations and the related quotes, see Cordery, "Women in Industrializing America," 113–15. For Mary Ryan's more "calloused" perspective and the related quotes, see *Women in Public*, 54–56. The last quote is from Upton Sinclair, *The Jungle* (New York: Jungle Publishing Company, 1906; Bantam Classic ed., 1981), 204.

16. For the articles quoted, see *Lexington Morning Transcript*, 1 January 1885, 2; *Lexington Morning Transcript*, 22 August 1885, 2; *Lexington Daily Press*, 26 July 1877, 4.

17. The quotes are from Ranck, *Historical Address*, 11. For a discussion of "civic folk mercantilism," see Samuel Haber, *The Quest for Authority and Honor in the American Professions, 1750–1900* (Chicago: University of Chicago Press, 1991), 121.

18. The first quote is from Grantham, *Southern Progressivism*, 16; the second quote is from Henry W. Grady, "The New South," in *Century Readings in American Literature*, 4th ed., ed. Fred Lewis Pattee (New York: Century, 1932), 783–84; the third quote is from Ayers, *Promise of the New South*, 20. For the 1883 promotional guide to Lexington, see George Washington Ranck, *Guide to Lexington, Kentucky: With Notices Historical and Descriptive of Places and Objects of Interest, and a Summary of the Advantages and Resources of the City and Vicinity* (Lexington: Transylva-

nia Printing and Publishing Company, 1883), copy available in Special Collections and Archives, Margaret I. King Library, University of Kentucky, Lexington.

19. See George W. Ranck, *History of Lexington, Kentucky: Its Early Annals and Recent Progress, Including Biographical Sketches and Personal Reminiscences of the Pioneer Settlers, Notices of Prominent Citizens, etc., etc.* (Cincinnati: R. Clarke, 1872), copy available in Special Collections and Archives, Margaret I. King Library, University of Kentucky, Lexington. See also *The Kentucky Encyclopedia*, s.v. "Ranck, George W."; Wright, *Heart of the Bluegrass*, 113. The articles quoted are from *Lexington Daily Press*, 4 January 1885, 4; *Lexington Morning Transcript*, 10 November 1885, 2.

20. The quotes are from Ranck, *Guide to Lexington*, 5–6, 14, 18, 22, 26.

21. Ibid., 31–36; the quotes are from pp. 6, 18.

22. *Lexington, the Central City: A Review of Lexington, Kentucky, as She Is Her Wealth and Industry, Her Wonderful Growth and Admirable Enterprise, Her Great Business Concerns, Her Manufacturing Advances, and Commercial Resources* (New York: John Lethem [1887]), copy available in Special Collections and Archives, Margaret I. King Library, University of Kentucky, Lexington (hereafter, *Review of Lexington*); the quote is from p. 1.

23. For Allen J. Share's discussion of "urban imperialism" and nineteenth-century urban competition between Lexington and other cities of the region, see *Cities in the Commonwealth: Two Centuries of Urban Life in Kentucky* (Lexington: University Press of Kentucky, 1982), 25–27. The quote is from Federal Writers' Project of the WPA for the State of Kentucky, *Lexington and the Bluegrass Country* (Lexington: E. M. Glass, 1938), 12, copy available in Special Collections and Archives, Margaret I. King Library, University of Kentucky, Lexington. For the population figures, see *Review of Lexington*, 22, 26; the quote is from pp. 26–27. Census figures are from Department of the Interior, Census Office, *Statistics of the Population of the United States at the Tenth Census (June 1, 1880)*, vol. 1 (Washington, D.C.: Department of the Interior, Census Office, 1883), 418; *Report on Population of the United States at the Eleventh Census: 1890*, vol. 1 (Washington, D.C.: Department of the Interior, Census Office, 1893), 159, 459; *Twelfth Census of the United States, Taken in the Year 1900*, vol. 1, *Population* (Washington, D.C.: Department of the Interior, Census Office, 1902), 178, 656.

24. The first and second quotes are from *Review of Lexington*, 7, 12–13. For the "model of perfect ladyhood," see Richard L. Bushman, *The Refinement of America: Persons, Houses, Cities* (1992; reprint, New York: Vintage Books, 1993), 333. The last quote is from *Review of Lexington*, 13.

25. The first quote is from Ranck, *Guide to Lexington*, 37–38. For a discussion of Ladies Memorial Associations and the quoted phrases, see Ryan, *Women in Public*, 49. The last quote is from *Review of Lexington*, 29–30. Based on this passage, it is clear that the *Review* was assembled and published late in 1887, for the first Chautauqua Assembly was held at Lexington from 28 June through 8 July of that

year, and on 9 July 1887 the *Lexington Morning Transcript* reported plans to purchase Woodland Park for the Assembly.

26. For the cultural significance of the Chautauqua Assemblies, see Stevenson, *Victorian Homefront*, 157–61. For the quotes related to Gregory A. Waller's view of Chautauqua, see his "Entertainment in the Model Municipality: Chautauqua at the Turn-of-the-Century, 1994 [?]," typescript (photocopy), 9, copy in my possession. For Thomas J. Schlereth's view of Chautauqua and the related quotes, see *Cultural History and Material Culture: Everyday Life, Landscapes, Museums* (Charlottesville: University Press of Virginia, 1990; First Paperback ed., 1992), 221–23. For the account of Sam Jones's address to the Lexington Chautauqua, see *Lexington Morning Transcript*, 9 July 1887, 4. For a discussion of Sam Jones and his prominence and influence, see Ayers, *Promise of the New South*, 173–78.

27. For the "New South creed," see Grantham, *Southern Progressivism*, 16, 25–26. For the press's promotion of Lexington in the early twentieth century, see Gregory A. Waller, *Main Street Amusements: Movies and Commercial Entertainment in a Southern City, 1896–1930* (Washington, D.C.: Smithsonian Institution Press, 1995), 18. The first quote is from *Lexington Morning Transcript*, 29 January 1885, 2; the second, third, and fourth quotes are from *Lexington Daily Press*, 20 March 1885, 2. For Ayers's discussion of the growth and importance of southern railroads, see *Promise of the New South*, 9–13. The fifth quote is from *Lexington Morning Transcript*, 13 March 1885, 2; the last quote is from *Lexington Daily Press*, 4 April 1885, 2, and 19 April 1885, 8. For additional editorials and articles from 1885 reflecting city boosterism, see *Lexington Morning Transcript*, 14 January 1885, 1; 30 January 1885, 2; 26 August 1885, 3; and 13 October 1885, 2; and *Lexington Daily Press*, 18 January 1885, 2; and 12 September 1885, 4.

28. *Lexington Daily Press*, 22 January 1885, 3.

29. *Lexington Morning Transcript*, 11 December 1885, 2.

30. For a discussion of high and low culture in the nineteenth century, see Lawrence W. Levine, *Highbrow/Lowbrow: The Emergence of Cultural Hierarchy in America* (Cambridge, Mass.: Harvard University Press, 1988), chap. 3. For "genteel culture," see Bushman, *The Refinement of America*, xv. For "genteel high culture," see Waller, *Main Street Amusements*, 43. For an extensive discussion of the "genteel performance," see Willard B. Gatewood, *Aristocrats of Color: The Black Elite, 1880–1920* (Bloomington: Indiana University Press, 1990; First Midland Book ed., 1993), chap. 7. The first quote is from Bushman, *The Refinement of America*, 349; for the connection between genteel culture and intellectual life, see ibid., 327. The second quote is from Joseph F. Kett, *The Pursuit of Knowledge under Difficulties: From Self-Improvement to Adult Education in America, 1750–1990* (Stanford, Calif.: Stanford University Press, 1994), 24. The third quote is from Bushman, *The Refinement of America*, 292. For Levine's discussion of nineteenth-century highbrow culture and cultural authority, see *Highbrow/Lowbrow*, 211, 221–22. The fourth quote is from *Lexington Morning Transcript*, 9 October 1885, 2.

31. The quotes are from *Lexington Morning Transcript*, 31 July 1885, 1; 15 August 1885, 2. For the statue "Woman Triumphant," see Wright, *Heart of the Bluegrass*, 37, 103.

32. *Lexington Daily Press*, 27 September 1885, 1.

33. For the strong association among reading and self-improvement, refinement, and the development of intellectual culture in the nineteenth century, see Bushman, *The Refinement of America*, 285–87. For the argument that libraries were viewed as a key instrument for the diffusion of knowledge, the development of literary culture, and the spread of refinement during the Gilded Age, see Kett, *The Pursuit of Knowledge*, 42–43, 205–20. For the motives surrounding the funding of libraries, see Thomas Bender, *New York Intellect: A History of Intellectual Life in New York City, from 1750 to the Beginning of Our Own Time* (Baltimore: Johns Hopkins University Press, 1987), 170, chap. 5. The first quote is from Kett, *The Pursuit of Knowledge*, 208; the second and third quotes are from *Lexington Morning Transcript*, 2 August 1885, 4.

34. For "serious reading," see Stevenson, *Victorian Homefront*, chap. 2. For the importance of the lecture in Victorian America and the first quote, see ibid., 56–57. For the listed markers or symbols of refinement in nineteenth-century America, see Bushman, *The Refinement of America*, 376. For the mention of Henry Ward Beecher, see Stevenson, *Victorian Homefront*, 56. The second quote is from *Lexington Morning Transcript*, 29 March 1885, 2.

35. The quotes are from *Lexington Daily Press*, 1 November 1885, 4; 3 December 1885, 1.

36. For biographical information on Belva Lockwood, see *World Book Encyclopedia*, 1982 ed., s.v. "Lockwood, Belva Ann Bennett." Also see Terry Dunnahoo, *Before the Supreme Court: The Story of Belva Ann Lockwood* (Boston: Houghton Mifflin, 1974). The cited advertisement and quotes are from *Lexington Daily Press*, 17 February 1885, 1; 18 February 1885, 2; 19 February 1885, 2; 21 February 1885, 1.

37. For "cheap amusement," see Waller, *Main Street Amusements*, 28. For the popularity of serialized fiction in the weekly magazines of the 1860s, see Stevenson, *Victorian Homefront*, 42. For late-nineteenth-century newspapers using drama in news stories and serialized fiction to lure readers, see Dicken-Garcia, *Journalistic Standards*, 89–92. Newspaper headlines are from *Lexington Daily Press*, 18 January 1885, 7; *Lexington Morning Transcript*, 17 November 1885, 2.

38. For another view of the integration, and segregation, of high and popular pursuits—of "edification" and "amusement"—in Lexington, see Waller, *Main Street Amusements*, 8–9. The first three quotes are from Wright, *Heart of the Bluegrass*, 104, 105, 106. For the quotes related to the "Cheapside Nuisance," see *Lexington Morning Transcript*, 9 December 1885, 3. For a discussion of Victorian middle-class attitudes regarding the uses of urban space, see George Chauncey, *Gay New York: Gender, Urban Culture, and the Making of the Gay Male World, 1890–1940* (New York: Basic Books, 1994), 3–36. For the argument regarding the "geography of re-

finement," "cultural regions," and "cultural and social polarity," see Bushman, *The Refinement of America,* 353. For the letter from "Justice" and the related quotes, see *Lexington Morning Transcript,* 12 December 1885, 1.

39. For accounts of the 1885 white and "colored" A&M fairs in Lexington, see *Lexington Morning Transcript,* 6 August 1885, 1; 13 August 1885, 2; 26 August 1885, 1; and *Lexington Daily Press,* 30 August 1885, 2; 24 September 1885, 4.

40. For the skating fad during the nickelodeon era, see Waller, *Main Street Amusements,* 72–74; the first quote is from p. 72. For the evolving use of the title "professor" in the nineteenth century, see Bruce E. Kimball, *The "True Professional Ideal" in America: A History* (Cambridge, Mass.: Blackwell Publishers, 1992), 303. For the account of Professor Lank's new skating rink, see *Lexington Morning Transcript,* 4 January 1885, 2. The second quote is from *Lexington Daily Press,* 8 January 1885, 1.

41. The first quote is from *Lexington Daily Press,* 30 August 1885, 7. The second quote is from *Lexington Leader,* 30 April 1896, 3, quoted in Waller, *Main Street Amusements,* 12.

42. For the opera house fire and the new facility, see Wright, *Heart of the Bluegrass,* 102. For the quoted opera house billings, see *Lexington Morning Transcript,* 1 November 1885, 6; 7 November 1885, 4; 12 November 1885, 4; and *Lexington Daily Press,* 14 November 1885, 2.

43. *Lexington Morning Transcript,* 28 November 1885, 1. For the "sacralization of culture" in the nineteenth century, see Levine, *Highbrow/Lowbrow,* 184, chaps. 2 and 3.

44. For descriptions of Gilded Age Woodland Park, see J. Winston Coleman Jr., *The Squire's Sketches of Lexington* (Lexington: Henry Clay Press, 1972), 62; and Wright, *Heart of the Bluegrass,* 100. The quote is from *Lexington Daily Press,* 9 May 1885, 4.

45. For this characterization and a discussion of Victorian parks and the "pleasure garden," see Schlereth, *Victorian America,* 234, 236; the first quote is from p. 236. For the park as a reflection of middle-class values and respectable and safe urban space, see Stevenson, *Victorian Homefront,* 49–52. For the park as space on the "map of Gentility," see Bushman, *The Refinement of America,* 356–59; the second quote is from p. 359. The remaining quotes are from *Lexington Daily Press,* 24 April 1885, 2; 24 June 1885, 4; 9 May 1885, 4; and *Lexington Morning Transcript,* 31 January 1885, 2.

46. The newspaper information and quotes are from *Lexington Daily Press,* 4 September 1885, 2; 31 May 1885, 1; 24 June 1885, 4; 16 July 1885, 2.

47. For a discussion of segregation after Reconstruction, see Wright, *Heart of the Bluegrass,* 154–56; the first quote is from p. 155. For the comments on segregation in the post-Reconstruction era, see Tapp and Klotter, *Decades of Discord,* 90–91; the second quote is from p. 90. Also see George C. Wright, *A History of Blacks in Kentucky,* vol. 2, *In Pursuit of Equality, 1890–1980* (Frankfort: Kentucky Historical

Society, 1992), 54; the third quote is from p. 43. For the development of segregated housing patterns in Lexington following the Civil War, see John Kellogg, "The Formation of Black Residential Areas in Lexington, Kentucky, 1865–1887," *Journal of Southern History* 48, no. 1 (February 1982): 21–52. For the 1883 advertisement for Woodland Park and the related quotes, see *Lexington Daily Transcript,* 1 June 1883, 1.

48. For a detailed discussion of railway segregation in the South, see Ayers, *Promise of the New South,* 137–46; the first and second quotes are from p. 137. For an extensive discussion of the anti–Separate Coach Law movement in Kentucky, see Wright, *History of Blacks in Kentucky,* 69–79; the third quote is from p. 69.

49. Newspaper quotes are from *Lexington Daily Transcript,* 13 September 1881, 4; and *Kentucky (Lexington) Leader,* 4 April 1892, 1; 6 April 1892, 2. For perspectives on the civic motivations of the late-nineteenth-century black "elite" and the related quotes, see Gatewood, *Aristocrats of Color,* 22–23. For the apparent lack of surviving black newspapers, see Waller, *Main Street Amusements,* xix.

50. For local accounts related to the passage of the Separate Coach Law and attempts by blacks to overturn it, see *Kentucky (Lexington) Leader,* 24 May, 1892, 1; 2 October 1893, 2; 4 June 1894, 8; 7 October 1898, 1. For segregation of interurban cars in and around Lexington, see *Lexington Morning Herald,* 26 November 1903, 1.

51. Grady, "The New South," 782–83. I borrowed the term "race question" from Grantham, *Southern Progressivism,* xv. For discussions of the hallmark attributes of New South race relations, see Ayers, *Promise of the New South,* chap. 6; Edward L. Ayers, *Southern Crossing: A History of the American South, 1877–1906* (New York: Oxford University Press, 1995), chap. 5; W. Fitzhugh Brundage, *Lynching in the New South: Georgia and Virginia, 1880–1930* (Urbana: University of Illinois Press, 1993), introduction, chaps. 1–3; Gatewood, *Aristocrats of Color,* chap. 1; Grantham, *Southern Progressivism,* chap. 3; Tapp and Klotter, *Decades of Discord,* 90–93, 378–85; Wright, *History of Blacks in Kentucky,* chap. 2; and Wright, *Racial Violence in Kentucky,* chaps. 2–5.

52. *Lexington Daily Press,* 24 March 1877, 2; *Lexington Daily Transcript,* 26 January 1880, 4; 21 October 1883, 2; and *Lexington Morning Transcript,* 3 April 1894, 3. For a discussion of the "back to Africa" movement and the related quote, see Ayers, *Promise of the New South,* 428–29.

53. *Lexington Morning Transcript,* 9 October 1885, 4; 22 February 1885, 4; 13 August 1885, 2; and *Lexington Daily Press,* 21 January 1885, 3; 29 March 1885, 2; 4 September 1885, 3; 12 April 1885, 8; 23 June 1885, 2.

54. *Lexington Morning Transcript,* 25 December 1885, 1; 9 June 1886, 6; 10 September 1885, 2.

55. For the causes of crime and violence in the New South, see Ayers, *Promise of the New South,* 153–59; the first quote is from p. 155. For views on post–Civil War violence in Kentucky, see Tapp and Klotter, *Decades of Discord,* chap. 17; the second quote is from p. 377. The third quote (regarding Octave Thanet) is from

Ayers, *Promise of the New South*, 477. The last quote is from Octave Thanet, *The Man of the Hour* (Indianapolis: Bobbs-Merrill, 1905), 228–29. For a biography of Alice French, who wrote under the pseudonym Octave Thanet, see George L. McMichael, *Journey to Obscurity: The Life of Octave Thanet* (Lincoln: University of Nebraska Press, 1965).

56. For a discussion of the southern chivalric code, see Brundage, *Lynching in the New South*, 50–52. The first quote is from Clement Eaton, *The Waning of the Old South Civilization, 1860–1880s* (Athens: University of Georgia Press, 1968), 45; the second and third quotes are from *Lexington Daily Press*, 18 August 1885, 4; the last quote is from *Lexington Morning Transcript*, 10 January 1888, 1.

57. The first quote is from Wright, *Racial Violence in Kentucky*, 13. For Brundage's view of lynching and the related quotes, see *Lynching in the New South*, 18. For a thorough definition of lynching, see ibid., 17. For "legal lynching," see ibid., 255–57; and Wright, *Racial Violence in Kentucky*, 12–13. For Brundage's discussion of the different types of lynch mobs, see *Lynching in the New South*, introduction, chap. 1. For the quotes related to defending the established order and preserving the social and racial foundations of southern society, see ibid., 48.

58. For the growing fear among whites of black crime in the New South, see Brundage, *Lynching in the New South*, 52–53; Ayers, *Promise of the New South*, 154–55. For press sensationalism, see Dicken-Garcia, *Journalistic Standards*, 64. The quote is from Charles W. Chesnutt, *The Marrow of Tradition* (1901; reprint, Ann Arbor: University of Michigan Press, Ann Arbor Paperbacks, 1969), 114.

59. Newspaper quotes are from *Lexington Daily Press*, 13 March 1885, 3; *Lexington Morning Transcript*, 15 August 1885, 1; 27 September 1885, 1; 4 December 1885, 1; 18 December 1885, 3; 21 February 1892, 1; and *Lexington Herald*, 23 May 1900, 1. For the relationship between rape and lynching in the New South, see Brundage, *Lynching in the New South*, 52; the last quote is from p. 58.

60. For the causes of extralegal violence in the New South, see Ayers, *Promise of the New South*, 157–58. For a similar perspective, see Brundage, *Lynching in the New South*, 20–21, 99–100; the quote is from p. 99. For the term "folk justice," see ibid., 20. Newspaper quotes are from *Lexington Daily Press*, 19 August 1885, 2; and *Lexington Morning Transcript*, 25 March 1894, 5.

61. For "terrorist" mobs, see Brundage, *Lynching in the New South*, 20–21. For the activities of the Ku Klux Klan in Kentucky after the Civil War, see Wright, *Racial Violence in Kentucky*, 24–36. Quotes are from *Lexington Morning Transcript*, 13 March 1885, 3; 2 September 1885, 1.

62. For the laudatory attitude of the white southern press toward mob violence and lynching in the Gilded Age, see Brundage, *Lynching in the New South*, 35, 67, 89, 164. Newspaper quotes are from *Lexington Morning Transcript*, 12 September 1885, 1; 27 September 1885, 1; 21 October 1885, 2; 18 December 1885, 3. The last quote is from Chesnutt, *Marrow of Tradition*, 233.

63. *Lexington Morning Transcript*, 21 February 1892, 1; 27 March 1894, 1.

64. For the lynching of whites, see Brundage, *Lynching in the New South*, chap. 3; the first two quotes are from p. 92. For the Union City, Tennessee, hanging incident, see *Lexington Daily Press*, 15 April 1885, 2. The quoted headline is from *Lexington Morning Transcript*, 29 September 1885, 1. For a discussion of (white) forces opposed to lynching in the New South, see Brundage, *Lynching in the New South*, 156; the last quote is from p. 3.

65. For the "Cult of the Confederacy," also known as the Lost Cause, see Ayers, *Promise of the New South*, 334. For the Lost Cause in the Bluegrass region, see Tapp and Klotter, *Decades of Discord*, 33–35; the first quote is from p. 35. For cultural continuity between the Old and New South, see Eaton, *Waning of the Old South Civilization*, chap. 6; the last quote is from p. 166.

66. For the location of Confederate monuments, see Ayers, *Southern Crossing*, 261. Newspaper quotes are from *Lexington Daily Press*, 24 July 1885, 2; 5 August 1885, 2; 16 August 1885, 1.

67. Newspaper quotes are from *Lexington Morning Transcript*, 30 October 1885, 2; 9 August 1885, 2; 26 September 1885, 1. For Ayers's sociological and economic perspective on the Lost Cause and the related quotes, see *Southern Crossing*, 261.

CHAPTER TWO: "PUT ME IN CLASS WITH THE WIDOW WHO GAVE THE MITE"

The quote in the chapter title is from a 1919 letter from Joseph Tanner to Joseph Guernsey, published in Joseph C. Guernsey, *50th Reunion Class of 1870, Princeton* (Bryn Mawr, Pa.: Class of 1870, Princeton University, 1921), 53–54, copy available in Wilson Library, Special Collections and Archives, Margaret I. King Library, University of Kentucky, Lexington.

1. Biographical information from Joseph M. Tanner, "Fifty Years' Recollections of Lexington and Vicinity, Its People and Institutions, 1926 (?)," typescript, 5–8, in Special Collections and Archives, Margaret I. King Library, University of Kentucky, Lexington (hereafter, "Recollections"); Alumni Survey Form (n.d.), Alumni Records, in Department of Rare Books and Special Collections, Firestone Library, Princeton University, Princeton, N.J. Many of the pages of Tanner's "Recollections" have more than one page number or no page number at all, and the pages have often been cut and pasted together, with little or no continuity; the page numbers cited are therefore as accurate as possible, under the circumstances. For Tanner as a candidate for city treasurer in 1884, see *Lexington Weekly Press*, 16 February 1884, 1; *Lexington Daily Press*, 17 February 1884, 5. For Tanner's business partner, business address, and home address in 1884, see *Lexington Directory for 1883–1884* (Lexington: Townsend and Co., 1884), 171, 210 (all city directories cited are available in Kentucky Room, Central Branch, Lexington Public Library).

2. For Tanner as city treasurer in 1881, see *Lexington Morning Transcript*, 19 November 1881, 3; *Lexington City Directory for 1881–82* (Lexington: Williams and

Co., 1881), 2. For a discussion of politics and politicians in this period, see James Bolin, "Bossism and Reform: Politics in Lexington, Kentucky, 1880–1940" (PhD diss., University of Kentucky, 1988), 24–37. The first quote is from Tanner, "Recollections," 51. For Claud Johnson's election victory in 1884, see *Lexington Daily Press,* 2 March 1884, 1. Also see Bolin, "Bossism and Reform," 25. For Tanner's beginning law practice and his friendship with James Mulligan, see "Recollections," 50; the last quote is from p. 19.

3. For Tanner's loss in the 1884 election, see *Lexington Daily Press,* 2 March 1884, 1. For a discussion of the reestablishment and rising prestige of the professions, including law, in the late nineteenth century, see Samuel Haber, *The Quest for Authority and Honor in the American Professions, 1750–1900* (Chicago: University of Chicago Press, 1991), chap. 6. For the progression of Tanner's career, see Alumni Survey Form (1906), Alumni Records, in Department of Rare Books and Special Collections, Firestone Library, Princeton University, Princeton, N.J.; Tanner, "Recollections," 2, 7–8. For Tanner's apology to his deceased wife, see ibid., 8.

4. Richard H. Brodhead, *Cultures of Letters: Scenes of Reading and Writing in Nineteenth-Century America* (Chicago: University of Chicago Press, 1993), 173.

5. See Tanner, "Recollections," passim. For the autobiographical sketch, see ibid., 5–8; for examples of Tanner's literary interests, see ibid., 6, 93, 118. The term "oratorical culture" has been borrowed from and is discussed at length in Gregory Clark and S. Michael Halloran, eds., *Oratorical Culture in Nineteenth-Century America: Transformations in the Theory and Practice of Rhetoric* (Carbondale: Southern Illinois University Press, 1993), 1–26. The quote is from Tanner, "Recollections," 118.

6. For Tanner's date of birth, see Alumni Survey Form (n.d.). For Tanner's birthplace, his father, and his memories of the Breckinridge farm and the Breckinridge boys, see "Recollections," 5, 68; the quote is from p. 5. For brief biographical sketches of Robert and W. C. P. Breckinridge, see *The Kentucky Encyclopedia,* 1992 ed., s.v. "Breckinridge, Robert Jefferson" and "Breckinridge, William Campbell Preston."

7. For the dispute between Tanner's father and Breckinridge, see Tanner, "Recollections," 68; for the family's move to Jessamine County, see ibid., 5; the quotes are from ibid., 38, 121. For the ex-Confederate domination of Kentucky's Gilded Age politics, see Hambleton Tapp and James C. Klotter, *Kentucky: Decades of Discord, 1865–1900* (Frankfort: Kentucky Historical Society, 1977), chap. 2; for their use of the term "Confederate Dynasty," see ibid., 228.

8. See Tanner, "Recollections," 5–7; the quote is from p. 7. For a discussion of rural Kentucky schools in the Gilded Age, see Tapp and Klotter, *Decades of Discord,* chap. 9. For a succinct discussion of rural southern schools in general during this period, see Edward L. Ayers, *The Promise of the New South: Life after Reconstruction* (New York: Oxford University Press, 1992), 211, 417–18.

9. For Patterson's role at Transylvania during the Civil War years and Bowman's merger of the two older schools into Kentucky University at the close of the war,

see John D. Wright Jr., *Transylvania: Tutor to the West* (Lexington: University Press of Kentucky, 1980),185, 190–201. The first quote is from James Lane Allen, *The Reign of Law: A Tale of Kentucky Hemp Fields* (New York: Macmillan, 1909), 41; the last quote is from Tanner, "Recollections," 80.

10. For a brief discussion of the College of Arts curriculum and faculty immediately following the Civil War, see Wright, *Tutor to the West*, 201–2. For a more detailed view of the faculty and of the curriculum's classical and rhetorical emphasis, see *Catalogue of the Officers and Students of Kentucky University, for the Session of 1867–68* (Louisville, Ky.: John P. Morton and Company, 1868), 39–43, copy available in Special Collections and Archives, J. Douglas Gay Jr. Library, Transylvania University, Lexington (hereafter, *KU Catalogue, 1867–68*). For Tanner's grades, see "Report, Kentucky University, College of Arts, English School, Session 1867–8 & 1868–9," Class Roles and Faculty Grade Reports, 1862–1893, in Special Collections and Archives, J. Douglas Gay Jr. Library. Course descriptions are from *KU Catalogue, 1867–68*, 39. The quote is from Tanner, "Recollections," 80.

11. Tanner, "Recollections," 81.

12. For Tanner's grades, see "Report of Classes in Greek and German, June, 1869," Class Roles and Faculty Grade Reports, 1862–1893; and "Report, School of Latin and Mental Science, June 26, 1868," Class Roles and Faculty Grade Reports, 1862–1893, in Special Collections and Archives, J. Douglas Gay Jr. Library, Transylvania University, Lexington. For the course descriptions, see *KU Catalogue, 1867–68*, 40–41. For the information on John Henry Neville, see James F. Hopkins, *The University of Kentucky: Origins and Early Years* (Lexington: University of Kentucky Press, 1951), 128, 232. The quotes are from Tanner, "Recollections," 81–82.

13. For Tanner as a Kentucky University Periclean, see the program for the *Fourth Annual Exhibition of the Periclean Society of Kentucky University*, Morrison Chapel, Kentucky University, 9 June 1869, copy in Special Collections and Archives, J. Douglas Gay Jr. Library, Transylvania University, Lexington. For Tanner's transfer to Princeton, see Tanner, "Recollections," 7. For Tanner as a Princeton Whig, see *Catalogue of the American Whig Society, Instituted in the College of New Jersey, 1769* (Princeton, N.J.: American Whig Society, 1914), 32, copy available in Department of Rare Books and Special Collections, Firestone Library, Princeton University, Princeton, N.J. For discussion of students from Kentucky attending schools in the Northeast, see Tapp and Klotter, *Decades of Discord*, 198. For Robert and Desha Breckinridge as Princeton students, see *The Kentucky Encyclopedia*, 1992 ed., s.v. "Breckinridge, Robert Jefferson" and "Breckinridge, Desha." For the information on John Todd Shelby, see Guernsey, *50th Reunion Class of 1870*, 78–80. For the correspondence between the Transylvania and Princeton Whigs, see Jacob Beam, *The American Whig Society of Princeton University* (Princeton, N.J.: American Whig Society, 1933), 147; the last quote is from p. 165.

14. For Tanner's graduation from Princeton, see "Recollections," 7; Alumni Survey Form (1906). For these remarks on the master's degree, see Frederick Rudolph,

The American College and University: A History (1962; reprint, Athens: University of Georgia Press, 1990), 336; and Burton J. Bledstein, *The Culture of Professionalism: The Middle Class and the Development of Higher Education in America* (New York: W. W. Norton, 1978), 275. For Tanner's work in Philadelphia, see Alumni Survey Form (n.d.). For a brief historical description of Girard College, see *The World Book Encyclopedia,* 1982 ed., s.v. "Girard, Stephen." For Tanner's mention of beginning law school in Philadelphia and his return to Kentucky University to complete his education in law, see "Recollections," 7. The first quote is from "Our Boys," *Collegian of Kentucky University* 1 (November 1872): 90, in Special Collections and Archives, J. Douglas Gay Jr. Library, Transylvania University, Lexington. For the College of Law at Kentucky University, see Wright, *Tutor to the West,* 143, 200, 249; the last quote is from p. 143.

15. For M. A. Cassidy's evolving career, see *Lexington Daily Press,* 11 October 1885, 4. For multiple careers in the nineteenth century, see Louise L. Stevenson, "Preparing for Public Life: The Collegiate Students at New York University 1832–1881," in *The University and the City: From Medieval Origins to the Present,* ed. Thomas Bender (New York: Oxford University Press, 1988), 153; Bledstein, *Culture of Professionalism,* 20. For law as the preeminent profession in the mid to late nineteenth century, see Haber, *Quest for Authority and Honor,* 87; Bruce E. Kimball, *The "True Professional Ideal" in America: A History* (Cambridge, Mass.: Blackwell Publishers, 1992), 103, chap. 3. The quote is from Harold Frederic, *The Damnation of Theron Ware* (1896; reprint, Greenwich, Conn.: Fawcett Publications, 1962), 26.

16. The first quote is from Tapp and Klotter, *Decades of Discord,* 269. For the revolt against the classical curriculum after the Civil War, see Rudolph, *The American College and University,* chap. 12; the second quote is from p. 263. The last quote is from *Lexington Daily Press,* 14 June 1872, 4.

17. The first quote is from "Annual Commencement of the Law College," *Collegian of Kentucky University* 1 (February 1873): 139; the second and third quotes are from *Lexington Daily Press,* 22 January 1873, 4. For remarks on the travails of the professions from 1830 to 1880 and the phrase "withering attack," see Haber, *Quest for Authority and Honor,* xii. For career indecision in the nineteenth century, see Bledstein, *Culture of Professionalism,* chap. 5.

18. Stevenson, "Preparing for Public Life," 150–77; the quote is from p. 151.

19. The first quote is from *Lexington Daily Press,* 13 June 1873, 4. For Tanner's account of entering practice with General Huston and the remaining quotes, see "Recollections," 31, 50.

20. Tanner, "Recollections," 31–32, 68, 118.

21. For this view of the evolution of rhetoric during the nineteenth century, see Clark and Halloran, *Oratorical Culture in Nineteenth-Century America,* 1–26. The first quote is from Daniel Calhoun, *The Intelligence of a People* (Princeton, N.J.: Princeton University Press, 1973), 82–83. For a discussion of rhetoric in the nineteenth-century college curriculum and the view that late-nineteenth-century rhetoric was

in decline, see James A. Berlin, *Writing Instruction in Nineteenth-Century American Colleges*, Studies in Writing and Rhetoric Series (Carbondale: Southern Illinois University Press, 1984), chap. 6. Also see Nan Johnson, *Nineteenth-Century Rhetoric in North America* (Carbondale: Southern Illinois University Press, 1991), 15–16, chaps. 1–3. For the announcement of James Mulligan's street-corner addresses and the last quote, see *Lexington Daily Press*, 29 April 1885, 4; 2 May 1885, 4.

22. For the location of Huston's law office and Tanner's home address in 1873, see *Sheppard's Lexington City Directory for 1873 and 1874* (Cincinnati: J. S. Sheppard and Co., 1873), 194, 225. For a short biography of John Breckinridge, see *The Kentucky Encyclopedia*, 1992 ed., s.v. "Breckinridge, John Cabell." Quotations related to the Breckinridge funeral are from *Lexington Daily Press*, 20 May 1875, 1, 2. For Tanner's comments on his tribute to Breckinridge before the Bar Association and the last quote, see "Recollections," 37.

23. For Tanner's marriage, see *Kentucky (Lexington) Gazette*, 29 October 1876, 3. For Tanner's discussion of his wife's family, see "Recollections," 8; the quote is from ibid. For Lizzie Butler Tanner's obituary, see *Lexington Leader*, 28 April 1919, 3. For Tanner's address and his law partner in 1877–1878, see *Lexington City Directory* (Lexington: R. C. Hellrigle and Co., 1877), 63, 102.

24. For Tanner's services on the school board, see Tanner, "Recollections," 43. For Tanner's appointment as acting commonwealth attorney, see Alumni Survey Form (1906). For Tanner's home and business addresses, see *Lexington City Directory for 1881–82*, 182; *Lexington Directory for 1883–1884*, 171, 210.

25. The first quote is from Tanner, "Recollections," 2. For Tanner's real estate dealings and related quotes, see *Lexington Morning Transcript*, 13 December 1885, 3; 15 December 1885, 2. The last two quotes are from Tanner, "Recollections," 55, 132.

26. For Tanner's addresses and business partners for the years given and the related quotes, see *City Directory of Lexington Kentucky, 1887* (Chattanooga, Tenn.: Norwood, Connelly and Co., 1887), 241; *City Directory of Lexington, Ky. 1888* (Lexington: Prather and Snyder, 1888), 218, 253, 267; *City Directory of Lexington, Ky. 1890* (Lexington: J. "Hub" Prather, 1890), 359, 419, 441; *Prather's Directory of the City of Lexington, Kentucky* (Lexington: J. "Hub" Prather, 1895), 252; *The "Blue Grass" Directory of the City of Lexington, Kentucky* (Lexington: "Blue Grass" Directory Company, 1902), 703, 909; *Lexington City Directory 1906–1907* (Lexington: R. L. Polk and Co., 1906), 485; *Lexington City Directory 1908* (Lexington: R. L. Polk and Co., 1908), 580; *Lexington City Directory 1911* (Lexington: R. L. Polk and Co., 1911), 38, 541; *Lexington City Guide 1912–13* (Lexington: R. L. Polk and Co., 1912), 503; *Polk's Lexington City Directory 1914–1915* (Lexington: R. L. Polk and Co., 1914), 527. For the birth dates of Tanner's children, see Alumni Survey Form (n.d.). The last quote is from Tanner's 1915 letter to Guernsey, in Joseph C. Guernsey, *45th Reunion Class of 1870, Princeton* (Philadelphia: Class of 1870, Princeton University, 1916), 45–46, copy available in Wilson Library, Special Collections and Archives, Margaret I. King Library, University of Kentucky, Lexington.

27. For Tanner's delinquent property taxes, see *Lexington Morning Herald,* 27 March 1898, 11; 29 March 1898, 3; 7 March 1899, 3; 28 March 1900, 3. For the 1915 IRS employees' meeting, see *Lexington Leader,* 2 January 1916, sec. 3, p. 8.

28. The first quote is from Tanner, "Recollections," 7 (emphasis added); the second quote is from ibid., 8; the third quote is from 1915 letter from Tanner to Guernsey; the last quote is from 1919 letter from Tanner to Guernsey. For Tanner's loss of the city treasurer seat, see *Lexington Daily Press,* 2 March 1884, 1. For his regrets on not being a Confederate veteran, see Tanner, "Recollections," 38.

29. For this view of the 1895 gubernatorial election in Kentucky, see Tapp and Klotter, *Decades of Discord,* chap. 16. The first quote is from Louis W. Koenig, *Bryan: A Political Biography of William Jennings Bryan* (New York: Capricorn Books, 1975), 10; the second quote is from John D. Wright Jr., *Lexington: Heart of the Bluegrass* (Lexington: Lexington–Fayette County Historic Commission, 1982), 157; the third quote is from Tapp and Klotter, *Decades of Discord,* 366; the last quote is from Edward L. Ayers, *Southern Crossing: A History of the American South, 1877–1906* (New York: Oxford University Press, 1995), 174.

30. The first three quotes are from *Lexington Leader,* 23 February 1897, 2, 4. For the anti-Bryan, anti-silver sentiments of the *Lexington Herald* under the management of the Breckinridges, see Tapp and Klotter, *Decades of Discord,* 279. The last two quotes are from *Lexington Morning Herald,* 21 February 1897, 4.

31. *Lexington Morning Herald,* 27 February 1897, 5; 1 March 1897, 1; 7 March 1897, 4; 9 March 1897, 4; 12 March 1897, 5.

32. Tanner, "Recollections," 69. For a discussion of the depression of the 1890s, see Joseph A. Fry, "Phases of Empire: Late Nineteenth-Century U.S. Foreign Relations," in *The Gilded Age: Essays on the Origins of Modern America,* ed. Charles W. Calhoun (Wilmington, Del.: Scholarly Resources, 1996), 272–73.

33. The year of Tanner's retirement from the IRS is inferred from the fact that he was present at the January 1916 meeting of Seventh District employees, as reported in *Lexington Leader,* 2 January 1916, sec. 3, p. 8, but was not on the list of district employees published in *Lexington Leader,* 11 February 1917, 6. For Tanner's obituary articles and the related quote, see *Lexington Herald,* 20 October 1932, 12; *Lexington Leader,* 20 October 1932, 11. For the letter informing Princeton of his death, see Mrs. W. S. Hutchinson to Office of the Graduate Council, Princeton, 5 December 1932, Alumni Records, in Department of Rare Books and Special Collections, Firestone Library, Princeton University, Princeton, N.J.

34. See Tanner, "Recollections," 12, 18, 64–67; the quote is from p. 113.

35. For the argument that middle-class values and attitudes were synonymous with "Victorian America," see Louise L. Stevenson, *The Victorian Homefront: American Thought and Culture, 1860–1880* (New York: Twayne Publishers, 1991), xx. For Tanner's comments about his wife, see "Recollections," 8.

36. The first quote from Stevenson, "Preparing for Public Life," 163; the second quote is from Henry James, *The American* (1877; reprint, New York: Dell Publish-

ing, 1964), 43. For the term "nineteenth-century oratorical culture," see Clark and Halloran, *Oratorical Culture in Nineteenth-Century America,* 1.

37. The first three quotes are from Tanner, "Recollections," 37, 71; the fourth quote is from 1919 letter from Tanner to Guernsey; the last quote is from Ayers, *Promise of the New South,* 132.

38. For a discussion of nineteenth-century middle-class ambition and the growth and evolving status of the professions that fed this ambition, see Bledstein, *Culture of Professionalism,* chaps. 1–3; Haber, *Quest for Authority and Honor,* 193–205, chap. 6; Kimball, *The "True Professional Ideal,"* chaps. 3, 5. For the linkage between the legal profession and middle-class career and social mobility in the late nineteenth century, see Kimball, *The "True Professional Ideal,"* 180. The quote is from Charles Dickens, *Hard Times* (1854; reprint, New York: New American Library, 1961), 15. For the growth of governmental power and bureaucratic organization during the nineteenth century and the Progressive Era, see Dewey W. Grantham, *Southern Progressivism: The Reconciliation of Progress and Tradition* (Knoxville: University of Tennessee Press, 1983), xix–xx, chaps. 9, 11; Thomas J. Schlereth, *Victorian America: Transformations in Everyday Life, 1876–1915* (New York: HarperCollins, 1992), 75–76.

39. The first quote is from Nan Johnson, "The Popularization of Nineteenth-Century Rhetoric: Elocution and the Private Learner," in Clark and Halloran, *Oratorical Culture in Nineteenth-Century America,* 139; the last quote is from Tanner, "Recollections," 68.

CHAPTER THREE: CAMPUS PROMINENCE

1. For the crowds, student parades, and college yells in Lexington on the morning of the oratorical contest in 1896, see *Lexington Daily Leader,* 3 April 1896, 1. For the description of the winner's medal and of the parade to the Phoenix Hotel following the contest, see *Lexington Daily Leader,* 4 April 1896, 1.

2. For a discussion of the sociology of nineteenth-century parades, see Mary Ryan, "The American Parade: Representations of the Nineteenth-Century Social Order," in *The New Cultural History,* ed. Lynn Hunt (Los Angeles: University of California Press, 1989), 131–53; the quotes are from p. 132. For descriptions of the 1825 parade in honor of Lafayette, see Robert Peter, *History of Fayette County, Kentucky, with an Outline Sketch of the Bluegrass Region* (Chicago: O. L. Baskin and Co., 1882), 405; and George W. Ranck, *History of Lexington, Kentucky: Its Early Annals and Recent Progress, Including Biographical Sketches and Personal Reminiscences of the Pioneer Settlers, Notices of Prominent Citizens, etc., etc.* (Cincinnati: R. Clarke, 1872), 305–7, copies of both available in Special Collections and Archives, Margaret I. King Library, University of Kentucky, Lexington. For a description of the 1826 funeral procession in honor of Jefferson, Adams, and Shelby, see Ranck, *History of Lexington,* 313–14.

324 ◆ Notes to Pages 73-75

3. For the dates of origination of the Union and Whig societies, see "Union Philosophical Society Minutes: 1829–1839," 18, in Special Collections and Archives, J. Douglas Gay Jr. Library, Transylvania University, Lexington. Note, however, that John D. Wright Jr., in *Transylvania: Tutor to the West* (Lexington: University Press of Kentucky, 1980), 96, lists the founding dates as 1821 for the Whig Society and 1829 for the Union Society. There is also evidence of the existence of the Transylvania Philosophical Society as early as 1802 in the *Kentucky (Lexington) Gazette,* 26 March 1802, 2, 3; 30 April 1802, 2; 13 August 1802, 3; 25 January 1803, 4. However, no institutional archival records or documents of this society remain, and it is unclear from the newspaper sources whether this was, strictly speaking, a student society. For the dispute over precedence in processions, see "Union Philosophical Society Minutes: 1829–1839," 12–24. Also see "Transylvania Whig Society, Roster and Minutes: 1829–1834," 12–16, in Special Collections and Archives, J. Douglas Gay Jr. Library.

4. For the cited correspondence, see "Union Philosophical Society Minutes: 1829–1839," 21–22. For William Lewis Breckinridge, see *The Biographical Encyclopaedia of Kentucky of the Dead and Living Men of the Nineteenth Century* (1878; reprint, Easley, S.C.: Southern Historical Press, 1980), 24, copy available in Kentucky Room, Central Branch, Lexington Public Library. Also see James C. Klotter, *The Breckinridges of Kentucky, 1760–1981* (Lexington: University Press of Kentucky, 1986), 33, 40. For Cassius Marcellus Clay, see *The Biographical Encyclopaedia of Kentucky,* 353–54; *The Kentucky Encyclopedia,* 1992 ed., s.v. "Clay, Cassius Marcellus."

5. Both James McLachlan, in "The *Choice of Hercules:* American Student Societies in the Early 19th Century," in *The University in Society,* vol. 2, *Europe, Scotland, and the United States from the 16th to the 20th Century,* ed. Lawrence Stone (Princeton, N.J.: Princeton University Press, 1974), 473, 485, and Jacob Beam, in *The American Whig Society of Princeton University* (Princeton, N.J.: American Whig Society, 1933), 15, note that the American Whig and Cliosophic societies at Princeton grew out of the Well Meaning and Plain Dealing clubs, which dated from 1765. The information regarding Caleb Wallace is from John T. Faris, *The Romance of Forgotten Men* (New York: Harper and Brothers, 1928), chap. 4. For Caleb Wallace and his contributions to the founding of Transylvania University, also see Walter Wilson Jennings, *Transylvania: Pioneer University of the West* (New York: Pageant Press, 1955), 3–35.

6. The first quote is from "Transylvania Whig Society, Roster and Minutes: 1829–1834," 1. For Beam's remarks on societies on other campuses affiliated with the Whig and Cliosophic societies at Princeton, see *The American Whig Society,* 147–48. The last quote is from "Union Philosophical Society Minutes: 1829–1839," 2.

7. The first quote is from Frederick Rudolph, *Mark Hopkins and the Log: Williams College, 1836–1872* (New Haven, Conn.: Yale University Press, 1956), 74.

For the founding and legislative chartering of the Adelphi Society, see "Adelphi Society Minute Book: 1837–1842," 10, 56, in Special Collections and Archives, J. Douglas Gay Jr. Library, Transylvania University, Lexington. For John Hunt Morgan and the Adelphi Society, see James A Ramage, *Rebel Raider: The Life of General John Hunt Morgan* (Lexington: University Press of Kentucky, 1986), 18–20; the second quote is from p. 20. For the Adelphi Society conventions, see "Adelphi Society Minute Book: 1837–1842," 51–55, 129. For descriptions of the Adelphi Society badges and diplomas, see ibid., 12, 133. For the merger of the Transylvania Whigs with Adelphi, see "Adelphi Society Minute Book: 1836–1857," 108–9, in Special Collections and Archives, J. Douglas Gay Jr. Library (note that this book contained Transylvania Whig Society minutes until the merger in 1842, when it began to be used for recording Adelphi Society minutes). For the 1829 fire, see "Union Philosophical Society Minutes: 1829–1839," 1; also see "Transylvania Whig Society, Roster and Minutes: 1829–1834," 1. For the article discussing the Whig Society library holdings, see "Society Libraries," *Transylvanian* 23 (June 1915): 293–95, in Special Collections and Archives, J. Douglas Gay Jr. Library. For the total number of volumes in the library holdings of the Adelphi Society, see "Library Book of the A. A. [Adelphi Alpha] Society," 81, in Special Collections and Archives, J. Douglas Gay Jr. Library. For the first use of the name "Adelphoi" in July 1843, see "Adelphi Society Minute Book: 1836–1857," 164. Note that "Adelphi Society Minute Book: 1836–1857" ends abruptly, containing no entries after 16 January 1857. The last quote is from Wright, *Tutor to the West*, 172; on p. 96, Wright briefly discusses the Whig, Union, and Adelphi societies.

8. For examples of the Adelphi Society meeting at the city library, see "Adelphi Society Minute Book: 1837–1842," 14, 42. The society met there several times during 1837–1838. For mention of the fire, see "Union Philosophical Society Minutes: 1829–1839," 1; also see Wright, *Tutor to the West*, 125.

9. For information on the Union Society's 1830 Washington's birthday celebration and the first quote, see "Union Philosophical Society Minutes: 1829–1839," 43. Also see Robert Wickliffe Jr., Esq., *An Oration, Delivered on the 22nd of February, 1830 at the Request of the Union Philosophical Society of Transylvania* (Lexington: Union Philosophical Society, 1830), in Special Collections and Archives, J. Douglas Gay Jr. Library, Transylvania University, Lexington. For this account of Robert Wickliffe Jr., see Wright, *Tutor to the West*, 152–53. For the Adelphi Society public exhibitions and cited oration titles, see *Adelphoi A. Society Celebration*, Chapel of Morrison College, Transylvania University, 18 August 1845; and *Annual Exhibition of the Adelphoi A. Society*, Chapel of Morrison College, Transylvania University, 18 August 1846, copies of both printed programs in Special Collections and Archives, J. Douglas Gay Jr. Library.

10. This account of the Transylvania societies during the Civil War years was developed from Wright, *Tutor to the West*, 185–87; "Literary Societies," *Kentucky University Tablet* 2 (June 1888): 204; and "Minutes of the Franklin Society, 1864–65,"

2, 6, 13; the last two in Special Collections and Archives, J. Douglas Gay Jr. Library, Transylvania University, Lexington.

11. John Fox Jr., *The Little Shepherd of Kingdom Come* (1903; reprint, New York: Grosset and Dunlap, 1931), 178. Note that here, unfashionably perhaps, Fox is quoted as if he were honestly expressing the nature of antebellum civility and gentility at its best, as he understood it. Viewing things from a different angle, James Klotter, in *Kentucky: Portrait in Paradox, 1900–1950* (Frankfort: Kentucky Historical Society, 1996), 48, employs the same quotation to accuse Fox of promulgating a "skewed remembrance . . . of a world that never really was."

12. For the reopening of Kentucky University under Bowman in 1865, see Wright, *Tutor to the West*, 190–201. The first quote is from James Lane Allen, *The Reign of Law: A Tale of Kentucky Hemp Fields* (New York: Macmillan, 1909), 41. For the history of the Philothean Society, see *Kentucky University Crimson, 1897* (Lexington: Senior Classes of Kentucky University, 1897), 95, in Special Collections and Archives, J. Douglas Gay Jr. Library, Transylvania University, Lexington; the second quote is from ibid. For the Philothean motto in English, see ibid., 92. For the Philothean motto in Greek, the society colors (light shades of pink and green), and the society yell, see appendix B and *Crimson, 1905* (Lexington: Senior Classes of Kentucky University, 1905) [60], in Special Collections and Archives, J. Douglas Gay Jr. Library. For the *Clavis* as the Philothean paper read at exhibitions, see "Commencement Exercises," *Transylvanian* 1 (June 1892): 271. For the chartering of the College of the Bible as an independent institution, see Wright, *Tutor to the West*, 230; the third quote is from p. 293. For the Christomathean Society, see ibid., 294. For a history of the Phileusebian Society and the related quotes, see *Kentucky University Crimson, 1897,* 91. For the Phileusebian motto in English, see ibid., 88. For the Phileusebian motto in Greek, the society colors (scarlet and sky blue), and the society yell, see appendix B and *Crimson, 1905* [58]. For the *Anchor* as the Phileusebian paper read at exhibitions, see "Commencement Exercises," *Transylvanian* 1 (June 1892): 271. For the anchor as a symbol of Christ, note the following quotation from *In Memoriam: Stained Glass Windows of Presbyterian Church* (Lexington: First Presbyterian Church, 1997) [17]: "The anchor . . . is symbolic of Jesus Christ, our sure anchor."

13. For a brief history of the Cecropian and the Periclean societies, see "Literary Societies," *Kentucky University Tablet* 2 (June 1888): 204–5. The first quote is from "Constitution and By-Laws of the Cecropian Society of Kentucky University," in Special Collections and Archives, J. Douglas Gay Jr. Library, Transylvania University, Lexington. For the Cecropian motto and colors (red and white), see ibid., 80. For the poem by George Ranck, see "The Cecropian Colors," *Transylvanian* 11 (February 1901): 116. For the 1905 Cecropian colors (maroon and white) and the society yell, see appendix B and *Crimson, 1905* [56]. For a history of the Cecropian Society, see *Kentucky University Crimson, 1897,* 83; "The Cecropian Name and Shield," *Collegian of Kentucky University* 1 (September 1872): 1, and *Organization*

of Kentucky University [Session 1892–93], n.d., printed poster, single sheet, folded, both in Special Collections and Archives, J. Douglas Gay Jr. Library; Wright, *Tutor to the West,* 293; and "Cecropian Annals," *Collegian of Kentucky University* 2 (August 1873): 234; the second quote is from ibid. Latin translations, unless otherwise noted, are from Jon R. Stone, *Latin for the Illiterati* (New York: Routledge, 1996); and D. P. Simpson, *Cassell's Latin and English Dictionary* (New York: Macmillan, 1987). For the *Shield* as the Cecropian paper read at exhibitions, see "Commencement Exercises," *Transylvanian* 1 (June 1892): 271. For an excellent synopsis of the main student publications (not including the individual society papers, almost none of which have survived, to my knowledge) at Kentucky University up to 1897, including the publication history of each, see *Kentucky University Crimson, 1897,* 97. For a discussion of the American Whig Society's emblematic device, see McLachlan, *"Choice of Hercules."*

14. For a history of the Periclean Society, see *Kentucky University Crimson, 1897,* 87. For the Periclean motto, 1897 colors (navy blue and pure white), and yell, see ibid., 84, and appendix B. For the 1905 Periclean colors (old gold and navy blue) and yell, see appendix B and *Crimson, 1905* [54]. For additional history of the Periclean Society, see *Organization of Kentucky University [Session 1892–93];* Wright, *Tutor to the West,* 293. The quote is from "The Constitution of the Periclean Society of Kentucky University," in Special Collections and Archives, J. Douglas Gay Jr. Library, Transylvania University, Lexington. For the Periclean's legislative charter, see "Local and Personal," *Atlantis: A Monthly Magazine* 1 (February 1886): 62, in Special Collections and Archives, J. Douglas Gay Jr. Library. For the *Owl* as the Periclean paper read at exhibitions, see "Commencement Exercises," *Transylvanian* 1 (June 1892): 271. The suggestion that Allen and Fox may have contributed to the *Owl* is only a pleasant conjecture, as no copies of the paper have survived.

15. For the opening of Kentucky University to women, see Wright, *Tutor to the West,* 250–51. Also see Paul E. Fuller, *Laura Clay and the Woman's Rights Movement* (1975; reprint, Lexington: University Press of Kentucky, 1992), 48–49; the first quote is from p. 49. The second quote is from "Editorial," *Kentucky University Tablet* 3 (May 1889): 181. For the organizational date of the Ossolian Society, see *Organization of Kentucky University [Session 1892–93]; Catalogue of Kentucky University and of the College of the Bible, 1891* (Lexington: Transylvania Printing Company, 1891), 28, copy available in Special Collections and Archives, J. Douglas Gay Jr. Library, Transylvania University, Lexington. The third quote is from "The New Society!!" *Focus* 2 (October 1890): 24, in Special Collections and Archives, J. Douglas Gay Jr. Library. For the poem in honor of the Ossolian Society, see J. M. Mc'Vey, "Marchioness Ossola," *Focus* 2 (November 1890): 62–63. For Margaret Fuller (Ossoli), see *The Oxford Companion to English Literature,* 1985 ed., s.v. "Fuller, (Sarah) Margaret."

16. For the 1892 Ossolian celebration of Washington's and Longfellow's birthdays, see "Ossolian Society," *Transylvanian* 1 (March 1892): 190. For the Ossolian

paper the *Echo*, the Ossolian motto, and the exercises and entertainment of 2 June 1892, see *Second Annual Open Session of the Ossolian Society of Kentucky University,* Morrison Chapel, 2 June 1892, copy of the printed program in Special Collections and Archives, J. Douglas Gay Jr. Library, Transylvania University, Lexington. Also see "Commencement Exercises," *Transylvanian* 1 (June 1892): 271 for the Ossolians' June 1892 commencement week performance. The English translation of the Ossolian motto in French is by Patrick Brooks.

17. For the remarks and quotes about Margaret Fuller, see Thomas Bender, *New York Intellect: A History of Intellectual Life in New York City, from 1750 to the Beginning of Our Own Time* (Baltimore: Johns Hopkins University Press, 1987), 159–60. For the Kentucky University Washington's birthday celebration and related quotes, see *Kentucky (Lexington) Leader,* 22 February 1894, 2. For the 1895 celebration and related quotes, see *(Lexington) Press-Transcript,* 23 February 1895, 4.

18. The first quote is from "Ossolian Society," *Transylvanian* 1 (October 1891): 34. For the second and third quotes and additional history pertaining to the Ossolian and Cornelian societies, see *Kentucky University Crimson, 1897,* 79. For the Cornelian motto in Latin, colors (green and white), and yell, see ibid., 76, and appendix B. For the Cornelians' English translation of their motto, see "Cornelia," *Transylvanian* 10 (September 1901): 18. For the Cornelian flower (white carnation), see *Crimson, 1905* [50]. For reference to the Cornelian Society's publication, the *Jewel,* and the Roman matron Cornelia as the society's namesake, see Wright, *Tutor to the West,* 294. For the Cornelian open session and participation in the Washington's birthday celebration, see *Lexington Morning Herald,* 4 June 1898, 2; 23 February 1899, 3.

19. The first and second quotes are from "The Societies," *Transylvanian* 7 (January 1900): 148; the third and fourth quotes and the Aletheian motto in Latin are from "The Societies," *Transylvanian* 7 (February 1900): 179. For the spelling "Alethean," as well as the society motto, colors (royal purple and old gold), and flower (pansy), see *Crimson, 1905* [52]. For the theme of the Aletheians' first public entertainment and the fifth quote, see "The Societies," *Transylvanian* 7 (May 1900): 307. For local press coverage of this initial Aletheian public entertainment, see *Lexington Morning Herald,* 7 June 1900, 6.

20. Quote from Wright, *Tutor to the West,* 238.

21. See "Librarian's Report, Periclean Society, December 23, 1898," in Special Collections and Archives, J. Douglas Gay Jr. Library, Transylvania University, Lexington. For the cited session of the Bible College Philotheans and the quotes, see "Philothean Society Roster and Minutes, 1887–1903," 108, in Special Collections and Archives, J. Douglas Gay Jr. Library.

22. Quote from "Philosophian Society," *State College Cadet* 3, no. 7 (15 March 1893): 5, in Special Collections and Archives, Margaret I. King Library, University of Kentucky, Lexington. For a brief discussion of Henry A. Saxton and Herman Trost and their orchestral bands, see John D. Wright Jr., *Lexington: Heart of*

the Bluegrass (Lexington: Lexington–Fayette County Historic Commission, 1982), 100. Note that Wright refers to Saxton as "Henry Saxton, Jr.," but the *Lexington City Directory, 1914–15* (Lexington: R. L. Polk and Co., 1915), 480, lists him as "Henry A. Saxton." For Trost as University of Kentucky band director and the performance on his wedding anniversary, see *Lexington Leader,* 27 April 1916, 8.

23. This account of the business relationships among musicians Wolf, Trost, and Saxton was developed from the following sources: James F. Hopkins, *The University of Kentucky: Origins and Early Years* (Lexington: University of Kentucky Press, 1951), 132; *Lexington Directory for 1883–1884* (Lexington: Townsend and Co., 1884), 189; *City Directory of Lexington, Ky. 1890* (Lexington: J. "Hub" Prather, 1890), 323, 410; *Lexington City Directory, 1914–15* (Lexington: R. L. Polk and Co., 1915), 480, 544; *Open Session of the Cecropian Literary Society of Kentucky University,* 12 January 1883; *Periclean Open Session,* 4 February 1887; *Open Session of the Cecrop[i]an Literary Society,* 3 February 1888; *Cecropian Society [Program],* 12 June 1889; *Cecropian Society [Program],* 10 June 1890; *Annual Oratorical Contest of Kentucky University,* 20 May 1892; and *K. U. Enroll* 1, no. 4 (24 October 1895): 4. Note that all city directories cited are available in the Kentucky Room, Central Branch, Lexington Public Library; all the printed programs cited here are available in Special Collections and Archives, J. Douglas Gay Jr. Library, Transylvania University, Lexington.

24. For accounts of Philothean celebrations of Garfield's birthday (19 November) in the 1880s following his assassination in 1881, see *Lexington Morning Transcript,* 19 November 1881, 4; 21 November 1882, 1; 19 November 1885, 2; 20 November 1886, 4; 19 November 1887, 1. The following printed programs are available in Special Collections and Archives, J. Douglas Gay Jr. Library, Transylvania University, Lexington: *Open Session of the Cecrop[i]an Literary Society,* 3 February 1888; *Open Session of the Cecropian Literary Society of Kentucky University,* 12 January 1883; *Annual Entertainment of the Cecropian Society of Kentucky University,* 10 June 1885; *Periclean Open Session,* 13 June 1888; *Second Annual Open Session of the Ossolian Society of Kentucky University,* 2 June 1892. For a brief discussion of James H. Mulligan, see *The Kentucky Encyclopedia,* 1992 ed., s.v., "Mulligan, James Hillary."

25. This account of Garfield's and Washington's birthday celebrations was developed from the following printed programs, all of which are available in Special Collections and Archives, J. Douglas Gay Jr. Library, Transylvania University, Lexington: *Celebration of Garfield's Birthday by the Philothean Society,* 18 November 1884; *Celebration of Garfield's Birthday by the Philothean Society,* 19 November 1885; *Celebration of Garfield's Birthday by the Philothean Society,* 19 November 1886; *Celebration of Garfield's Birthday by the Philothean Society,* 19 November 1887; *Celebration of Washington's Birthday by the Literary Societies of Kentucky University,* 22 February 1889; *Washington Birthday Celebration,* 22 February 1897. For a description of the extracurriculum, including the literary societies, as a counter-

point to the curriculum and as one of the successful forces contending to redefine the colleges, see Frederick Rudolph, *The American College and University: A History* (1962; reprint, Athens: University of Georgia Press, 1990), 136–37, chap. 7; the term "unseen revolution" is from p. 136. Rudolph traces the societies' origins to a student revolt against the austere, formal curriculum and institutional climate of the colonial and antebellum campus. For consonant views on the on-campus social and intellectual origins of the societies, see Helen Lefkowitz Horowitz, *Campus Life: Undergraduate Cultures from the End of the Eighteenth Century to the Present* (Chicago: University of Chicago Press, 1987), 28, chap. 2; Arthur T. Hamlin, *The University Library in the United States: Its Origins and Development* (Philadelphia: University of Pennsylvania Press, 1981), 38; Thomas S. Harding, "College Literary Societies: Their Contribution to the Development of Academic Libraries, 1815–76. I. The Golden Age of College Society Libraries, 1815–40," *Library Quarterly* 29, no. 1 (January 1959): 1; David Potter, "The Literary Society," in *History of Speech Education in America: Background Studies,* ed. Karl R. Wallace (New York: Appleton-Century-Crofts, 1954), 238–39. For a portrayal of the societies' curriculum as complementary to the formal curriculum, see Louise L. Stevenson, "Preparing for Public Life: The Collegiate Students at New York University, 1832–1881," in *The University and the City: From Medieval Origins to the Present,* ed. Thomas Bender (New York: Oxford University Press, 1988), 150–177.

26. For the formation of the Inter-Collegiate Oratorical Association of Kentucky, see *Lexington Morning Transcript,* 27 March 1887, 1. For the first local contest held at Kentucky University and related quotes, see *Lexington Morning Transcript,* 7 April 1888, 4. Also see *Local Oratorical Contest, 1888,* 6 April 1888, printed program in Special Collections and Archives, J. Douglas Gay Jr. Library, Transylvania University, Lexington.

27. For typical reports in the local press of the primary and preliminary oratorical contests at Kentucky University, see *Kentucky (Lexington) Leader,* 25 March 1894, 3; 31 March 1894, 8; *Lexington Press-Transcript,* 27 March 1895, 4; the quote is from ibid. For evidence of Philothean and Phileusebian society representation in the preliminary oratorical contests, see *Lexington Morning Herald,* 11 March 1898, 7; 29 March 1900, 2. Note that the local press often confused the primary (intrasociety) and preliminary (intersociety) contests or used the terms interchangeably. For example, in the *Kentucky (Lexington) Leader,* 1 April 1894, 8, both terms are used to refer to the same contest. To confuse matters further, preliminary contests could also be referred to as local contests.

28. For a brief history of the founding of the Union Literary Society, including the year of its organization and Henry Barker's remark on the name, see Hopkins, *University of Kentucky,* 171. For mention of the Union Society "re-union" meeting in the fall of 1872, see "University News," *Collegian of Kentucky University* 1 (October 1872): 77. The first quote is from "University News," *Collegian of Kentucky University* 1 (November 1872): 92; the second quote is from "University News,"

Collegian of Kentucky University 1 (January 1873): 122. It should be noted that "Minutes of the [Faculty] Senate," 25 November 1870 (Special Collections and Archives, Margaret I. King Library, University of Kentucky), mention an "Adelphian Society" at the A&M College; however, no other specific mention of this society was located. It is quite possible that a society named after the antebellum Adelphi Society at Transylvania functioned for a time at the A&M College after the war. "Minutes of the [Faculty] Senate," 22 October 1875, mentions the Union Society requesting, and being granted, permission to use a certain storage room as its hall.

29. The first quote is from "University News," *Collegian of Kentucky University* 1 (February 1873): 138. For comments on the Union orator at the Washington's birthday celebration of 1873, see "University News," *Collegian of Kentucky University* 1 (March 1873): 157; *Memoria XCIV* (Lexington: Transylvania Printing Company, 1894), 62, in Special Collections and Archives, Margaret I. King Library, University of Kentucky, Lexington. The second quote, in reference to the Union Society paper the *Student*, is from "University News," *Collegian of Kentucky University* 1 (June 1873): 197. For the Union Society motto and colors (pink and white), also see *The [1910] Kentuckian: Yearbook of the State University of Kentucky*, vol. 5 (Lexington: Class of Nineteen Ten, 1910), 196, in Special Collections and Archives, Margaret I. King Library. For extensive discussion of the separation of the A&M College from Kentucky University and its subsequent move to its new campus, see Hopkins, *University of Kentucky*, chap. 6; Wright, *Tutor to the West*, 234–38.

30. The quotes are from *Lexington Morning Transcript*, 23 February 1889, 4; 22 February 1890, 3; 23 February 1894, 8; 23 February 1893, 4. For local newspaper accounts of the dedication of the Washington Monument in 1885, see *Lexington Morning Transcript*, 22 February 1885, 1; *Lexington Daily Press*, 22 February 1885, 1. For local newspaper accounts of the Union Society Washington's birthday celebration at State College between 1885 and 1895 (when it ceased to be a strictly Union event), see *Lexington Daily Press*, 20 February 1885, 4; 22 February 1885, 8; 24 February 1885, 2; 24 February 1888, 4; *Lexington Morning Transcript*, 24 February 1885, 1; 23 February 1886, 1; 23 February 1887, 1; 22 February 1889, 3; 22 February 1890, 3; 21 February 1892, 1; 23 February 1892, 1; 23 February 1893, 4; 23 February 1894, 8; *(Lexington) Press-Transcript*, 23 February 1895, 4; and *Kentucky (Lexington) Leader*, 21 February 1890, 3. No press account of the 1891 celebration was located because the 23 February 1891 *Transcript*—the paper that most consistently reported on this event—was missing from the microfilm collection utilized. Also see "The Student: Union Literary Society, April 25, 1884," typescript dated 28 February 1940, in Special Collections and Archives, Margaret I. King Library, University of Kentucky, Lexington. It is unclear whether the society actually "published" a printed issue of this paper.

31. For the Patterson Society motto and colors (purple and old gold), as well as the assertion that the society's name was suggested by Governor Knott, see *The [1910] Kentuckian: Yearbook of the State University of Kentucky*, 192. For a history of

the Patterson Society, see *Memoria XCIV,* 67–69; the quote is from p. 68. Also see Hopkins, *University of Kentucky,* 171–173; "Minutes [1886–1902] of the Patterson Literary Society," 6 December 1886–30 September 1887, in Special Collections and Archives, Margaret I. King Library, University of Kentucky, Lexington; "Minutes of the [Faculty] Senate," 22 December 1886.

32. For the account of the Patterson Society's first annual open session, see *Lexington Morning Transcript,* 1 June 1887, 1. For Floyd J. Crum and the Crum Medal, see "Minutes [1886–1902] of the Patterson Literary Society," 20 September 1888; *Memoria XCIV,* 68. For Mulligan presenting the medals at the Patterson birthday celebration, see *Kentucky (Lexington) Leader,* 27 March 1894, 7.

33. For local newspaper accounts of the first ten Patterson birthday celebrations held between 1889 and 1898, see *Lexington Morning Transcript,* 27 March 1889, 4; 26 March 1890, 4; 3 April 1893, 4 (the celebration was not held until 2 April in 1893); *Kentucky (Lexington) Leader,* 27 March 1889, 3; 27 March 1890, 4; 27 March 1891, 3; 27 March 1894, 7; *Lexington Daily Press,* 26 March 1892, 4; *(Lexington) Press-Transcript,* 26 March 1895, 1; 27 March 1895, 8; *Lexington Daily Leader,* 28 March 1896, 3; *Lexington Morning Herald,* 27 March 1897, 4; 27 March 1898, 5.

34. For the establishment of the Normal School, also called the Normal Department, and the admission of women to the A&M College, see Terry L. Birdwhistell, "An Educated Difference: Women at the University of Kentucky through the Second World War" (PhD diss., University of Kentucky, 1994), 14–24; Hopkins, *University of Kentucky,* 129–31. For the founding of the Philosophian Society and its connection with the Normal School, see *Memoria XCIV,* 64–66; "The Philosophian Society," *State College Cadet* 6 (June 1896): 115–16; Hopkins, *University of Kentucky,* 175. According to the "Minutes of the [Faculty] Senate," President Patterson and the faculty first met in their new building on Limestone Street on 20 February 1882.

35. For the 1885 Philosophian open session, see *Lexington Morning Transcript,* 18 December 1885, 4; *Lexington Daily Press,* 18 December 1885, 2. For Belle Gunn, see Hopkins, *University of Kentucky,* 197–98. For the Philosophian motto and colors (red and black) and a list of the charter members, see *Memoria XCIV,* 64; the first quote is from p. 65. Also see "Philosophian Society," *State College Cadet* 3, no. 7 (15 March 1893): 5; "The Philosophian Society," *State College Cadet* 6 (June 1896): 116.

36. The first quote is from "The Philosophian Society," *State College Cadet* 6 (June 1896): 116. For the reading of the Philosophian paper the *Star* at the men's oratorical contest, see *Kentucky (Lexington) Leader,* 1 April 1894, 8; *Lexington Morning Transcript,* 1 April 1894, 1. For Breckinridge's speech at the Philosophian exhibition and the excerpts therefrom, see *Lexington Daily Transcript,* 3 June 1882, 1. For the "new woman," see Barbara M. Solomon, *In the Company of Educated Women: A History of Women and Higher Education in America* (New Haven, Conn.: Yale University Press, 1985), 95.

37. For the Philosophian plays cited and the related quotes, see *Lexington Daily Transcript,* 3 June 1882, 2; *Lexington Daily Leader,* 26 February 1899, 2; *Lexington Leader,* 8 December 1900, 4.

38. For the Normal Society motto, see "Constitution, By-Laws and Minutes of the Normal Literary Society," typescript, 33, in Special Collections and Archives, Margaret I. King Library, University of Kentucky, Lexington. For minutes of the first meeting, see ibid., 37. For the congratulatory Union Society letter, see ibid., 42. For mention of the Normal Society paper *Roark Enterprise,* see ibid. The quote is from "The Normal Department," *State College Cadet* 6 (June 1896): 118. For evidence that the Normal Society was divided into sections that met separately as well as jointly, see "Normal Literary Society," *State College Cadet* 3, no. 3 (11 November 1892): 6. For evidence that Normal Society members belonged to other literary societies as well, see "N. L. S.," *State College Cadet* 3, no. 9 (20 May 1893): 5.

39. For the Normal Society's representative at the intercollegiate oratorical contest, see *Lexington Press-Transcript,* 27 March 1895, 8; 6 April 1895, 1. For the election of Ruric Roark as its "Chairman Protem," see "Constitution, By-Laws and Minutes of the Normal Literary Society," 37. For Roark's clash with Patterson and the Board of Trustees, see Hopkins, *University of Kentucky,* 213–14. For evidence of the Roark Literary Society, see "Minutes of the Roark Literary Society, Feb. 1905–May 1905," typescript, in Special Collections and Archives, Margaret I. King Library, University of Kentucky, Lexington. For the Horace Mann Society, see "Constitution, By-Laws, and Rules of Order of the Horace Mann Literary Society," typescript, in Special Collections and Archives, Margaret I. King Library. For evidence of the presence of the Horace Mann Society in the 1920s, see *The Kentuckian 1920: Yearbook of the University of Kentucky,* vol. 21 (Lexington: Class of Nineteen Hundred Twenty, 1920), 221, and *The 1925 Kentuckian: Yearbook of the University of Kentucky,* vol. 26 (Lexington: Class of Nineteen Hundred Twenty-five, 1925), 30, both in Special Collections and Archives, Margaret I. King Library. Also note that Hopkins, *University of Kentucky,* 176, gives Roark credit for organizing "clubs *similar to* [emphasis added] the literary societies" after 1901. I believe that Hopkins was referring to the Roark and Horace Mann societies, but he did not specify; nor did he explain why he felt that these "clubs" were not literary societies by his definition.

40. The quote is from *Lexington Press-Transcript,* 26 February 1896, 8. For the Neville Society motto, colors (green and gold), and flower (sunflower), see *The [1910] Kentuckian: Yearbook of the State University of Kentucky,* 195. For the information on John Henry Neville, see Hopkins, *University of Kentucky,* 232, 259. For the 1907 Neville declamatory contest, see *Lexington Leader,* 31 January 1907, 8.

41. For the suggestion that the societies had a "monopoly," see Wright, *Tutor to the West,* 300. The quote is from Hopkins, *University of Kentucky,* 173.

42. For the prospectus, see *Collegian of Kentucky University* 1 (September 1872): [65]. For a brief history of the *Collegian* and the other student publications produced until 1897, see *Kentucky University Crimson, 1897,* 97, 101.

43. For evidence that the *Collegian* floundered due to unpaid subscriptions, see "Our Paper," *Collegian of Kentucky University* 1 (October 1872): 71; "To Our Subscribers," *Collegian of Kentucky University* 2 (September 1873): 242. The first quote is from *Kentucky University Crimson, 1897*, 97; the second quote is from "College Cliques," *Atlantis* 1 (May 1886): 170.

44. For the oration "Impending Perils," see *Kentucky University Tablet* 1 (March 1887): 28–35. The first and second quotes are from "Literary Societies," *Kentucky University Tablet* 2 (June 1888): 205; the third quote is from "Clippings," *Kentucky University Tablet* 3 (March 1889): 144.

45. The first quote is from "College Athletics," *Kentucky University Tablet* 1 (February 1887): 3. For a discussion of sports at Kentucky University in the late nineteenth century, see Wright, *Tutor to the West*, 301–11; Gregory Kent Stanley, *Before Big Blue: Sports at the University of Kentucky, 1880–1940* (Lexington: University Press of Kentucky, 1996), chap. 1. For the formation of the YMCA at Kentucky University, see *Kentucky University Tablet* 1 (March 1887): [17]. For the founding and early history of the YMCA movement, see Sherwood Eddy, *A Century with Youth: A History of the Y.M.C.A. from 1844 to 1944* (New York: Association Press, 1944), 1–27; the second quote is from p. 5. Also see Paul Edgar Williams, *The Y.M.C.A. College* (St. Louis: Educational Council of the Young Men's Christian Association, 1938), 8. The last quote is from Charles Howard Hopkins, *History of the Y.M.C.A. in North America* (New York: Association Press, 1951), 288.

46. See *Kentucky University Crimson, 1897*, 97; "The New Society!!" *Focus* 2 (October 1890): 24; J. M. Mc'Vey, "Marchioness Ossola," *Focus* 2 (November 1890): 62–63; "Sports," *Focus* 2 (October 1890): 28–29. For an excellent example of how each society was compartmentalized into its own discrete article or column, see *Focus* 2 (November 1890): 72–74.

47. For the first issue and J. M. Mc'Vey as associate editor, see *Transylvanian* 1 (October 1891): 18. For R. H. Crossfield's "The Hero of the Future," see *Transylvanian* 1 (February 1892): 137–42. For the Washington's birthday orations and photographs of the orators, see *Transylvanian* 7 (March 1900): 199–219. The quote is from "Cecropia," *Transylvanian* 7 (January 1900): 147. For a discussion of football's "golden era" at Kentucky University, see Wright, *Tutor to the West*, 306–7. For the bitter football rivalry between Kentucky University and State College in 1901 to 1906, see Stanley, *Before Big Blue*, chap. 2. For the origins and early history of the fraternities at Kentucky University in the late nineteenth century, see Wright, *Tutor to the West*, 300. For the coverage of literary society, fraternity, and athletic association news in the section formerly reserved for the societies alone, see "The Societies," *Transylvanian* 7 (February 1900): 179–83. For the fraternities featured in the 1900 "Commencement Issue," see *Transylvanian* 7 (June 1900): 332–37.

48. See *Kentucky University Crimson, 1897*, 97. Wright has noted in *Tutor to the West*, 298, that the *Crimson Rambler* was the first student newspaper at Transylvania. The quotes are from the editorial section of *K. U. Enroll* 1, no. 2 (26 September

1895): 2. For equal attention given to literary societies and sports, see "Periclea" and "Football Season," *Cloverleaf* 3, no. 1 (27 September 1897): 1, in Special Collections and Archives, J. Douglas Gay Jr. Library, Transylvania University, Lexington.

49. The first and second quotes are from "Lovers of God," *Daily Transylvanian* 2, no. 10 (6 June 1893): 1, in Special Collections and Archives, J. Douglas Gay Jr. Library, Transylvania University, Lexington. For the Cecropian banquet and the quote related to Mc'Vey, see *Daily Transylvanian* 2, no. 12 (8 June 1893): 1. For the last quote, see "The Orange and Blue," *Daily Transylvanian* 2, no. 12 (8 June 1893): 4.

50. See *Kentucky University Crimson 1897*.

51. Ibid.

52. For the *Bayonet* as the first publication at State College and the first quote, see Hopkins, *University of Kentucky,* 180. For a discussion of the literary societies' magazines at Centre College, see Kolan Morelock, "A Preliminary History of the Literary Magazine at Centre College, 1992," typescript, copy in author's possession. The second quote is from *Bayonet* 1 (June 1889): 2, in Special Collections and Archives, Margaret I. King Library, University of Kentucky, Lexington.

53. See *Bayonet* 1 (June 1889). For a brief biography of A. O. Stanley, see *The Kentucky Encyclopedia,* 1992 ed., s.v. "Stanley, Augustus Owsley."

54. For the military system at State College and its implications for student life, see Hopkins, *University of Kentucky,* 168. For a brief discussion of the *State College Cadet,* see ibid., 181. The quote is from *State College Cadet* 2, no. 6 (29 February 1892): 4. Also see *State College Cadet* 3, no. 7 (15 March 1893): 4; "Patterson and Union," *State College Cadet* 2, no. 7 (29 March 1892): [supplement]; "Declamation Contest," *State College Cadet* 3, no. 6 (15 February 1893): 3.

55. For a brief history and description of the YMCA at State College, see *Memoria XCIV,* 70–72; Hopkins, *University of Kentucky,* 177. Note that Hopkins dates the YMCA's founding at State College in 1890 and the YWCA's establishment in 1894, whereas the student publications cited here suggest 1889 and 1896, respectively. For the assertion that 25 percent of male students were Y members and State College YMCA's participation in the state convention, see "Y.M.C.A.," *State College Cadet* 3, no. 7 (15 March 1893): 2. The first quote is from "The Young Women's Christian Association," *State College Cadet* 6 (June 1896): 109–10; the second quote is from "The College Girls," *State College Cadet* 6 (June 1896): 127.

56. For Patterson's opposition to sports, see Stanley, *Before Big Blue,* 16; the first quote is from p. 18. For the beginnings of baseball at State College in 1892, see Hopkins, *University of Kentucky,* 181. For the coverage of sports in the State College student press of the 1890s and the related quotes, see "Base Ball," *State College Cadet* 3, no. 8 (12 April 1893): 4; "Control of Athletics," *State College Cadet* 4, no. 2 (October 1893): 5; "The Track Team," *State College Cadet* 6 (June 1896): 127–28; "Base Ball," *State College Cadet* 6 (June 1896): 127.

57. For Hopkins's discussion of the early annuals, see *University of Kentucky,* 181. For his discussion of fraternities, see ibid., 178. The two fraternities, Kappa

Alpha and Sigma Chi, along with their membership rolls, are featured in *Memoria XCIV,* 51–60. State College enrollment figures for the 1893–1894 academic year are taken from Ezra Gillis, *The University of Kentucky: Its History and Development: A Series of Charts Depicting the More Important Data, 1862–1955* (Lexington: University of Kentucky, 1956), 20, quoted in Birdwhistell, "An Educated Difference," 18. For the 1893–1894 membership of the Philosophian Society, see *Memoria XCIV,* 65. For the 1893–1894 membership lists of the Patterson Society, see "Minutes [1886–1902] of the Patterson Literary Society," 21–23. For mention of student E. J. Hobdy, see *Memoria XCIV,* 69, 71.

58. See "Literary Societies," *State College Cadet* 3, no. 1 (15 September 1892): 3. For the term "expressive life," see Michael O'Brien, ed., *All Clever Men, Who Make Their Way: Critical Discourse in the Old South,* Brown Thrasher ed. (Athens: University of Georgia Press, 1992), xi.

Chapter Four: Community Presence

1. The first three quotes and the last quote are from *Kentucky (Lexington) Leader,* 7 April 1889, 4; the fourth quote is from *Lexington Morning Transcript,* 6 April 1889, 1. For a complete list of dignitaries present, see ibid.

2. The quotes are from *Kentucky (Lexington) Leader,* 7 April 1889, 4. For excellent descriptions of the chartered trains bringing contestants and their friends into Lexington, as well as the enthusiastic throngs and paraders before and after the 1889 contest at the opera house, see *Lexington Morning Herald,* 8 April 1899, 1, 4, 5; 14 April 1900, 1, 4. For the 1889 founding of the United Confederate Veterans, see Edward L. Ayers, *Promise of the New South: Life after Reconstruction* (New York: Oxford University Press, 1992), 334.

3. *Kentucky (Lexington) Leader,* 7 April 1889, 4.

4. For a brief discussion of the formation and function of the Inter-Collegiate Oratorical Association, see James F. Hopkins, *The University of Kentucky: Origins and Early Years* (Lexington: University of Kentucky Press, 1951), 173. For the committee structure and the association's original full name, see *Second Annual Contest of the Inter-Collegiate State Oratorical Association,* Lexington Opera House, 5 April 1889, copy of the printed program in Special Collections and Archives, J. Douglas Gay Jr. Library, Transylvania University, Lexington. For evidence of literary society control of the Inter-Collegiate Oratorical Association, see "K. U. Withdraws," *Transylvanian* 8 (March 1901): 198–99. For press accounts of the literary society events designed to select the orator to represent Kentucky University at the intercollegiate contest, see *Kentucky (Lexington) Leader,* 25 March 1894, 3; 31 March 1894, 8; *Lexington Press-Transcript,* 27 March 1895, 4. For the same process at State College, see, for instance, *Kentucky (Lexington) Leader,* 27 March 1894, 7; *Lexington Press-Transcript,* 27 March 1895, 8; *Lexington Daily Leader,* 23 February 1896, 5.

5. For the account of the first intercollegiate contest at Richmond and the first

quote, see *Lexington Morning Transcript*, 22 April 1888, 4. For Leonard Cox as a member of the Periclean Society, see *Kentucky University Tablet* 2 (March 1888): 132. For A. O. Stanley as a Union Society member, see *Bayonet* 1 (June 1889): 20. For detailed accounts of the 1889 contest, see *Kentucky (Lexington) Leader*, 7 April 1889, 4; *Lexington Morning Transcript*, 6 April 1889, 1; related quotes are from ibid. For evidence that Henry T. Duncan Jr. was a Periclean Society member, see *Kentucky University Crimson, 1897*, 96.

6. The first quote is from *Lexington Morning Transcript*, 6 April 1889, 1. For the 1890 intercollegiate contest and the second and third quotes, see *Kentucky (Lexington) Leader*, 6 April 1890, 4. The last quote is from *Lexington Morning Transcript*, 5 April 1890, 1. For the historians of rhetoric alluded to here who examine the severing of reason from persuasion in rhetorical theory, see James A. Berlin, *Writing Instruction in Nineteenth-Century American Colleges* (Carbondale: Southern Illinois University Press, 1984), chaps. 3, 6; Bruce E. Kimball, *Orators and Philosophers: A History of Liberal Education* (New York: Teachers College Press, 1986); Walter J. Ong, *Ramus, Method, and the Decay of Dialogue: From the Art of Discourse to the Art of Reason* (Cambridge, Mass.: Harvard University Press, 1958; paperback ed., 1983), 49, chap. 12; Walter J. Ong, *Orality and Literacy: The Technologizing of the Word* (1982; reprint, London: Routledge, 1991). For a discussion of Ciceronian rhetoric, see Wilbur Samuel Howell, "English Backgrounds of Rhetoric," in *History of Speech Education in America: Background Studies*, ed. Karl R. Wallace (New York: Appleton-Century-Crofts, 1954), 5–16.

7. For the account of the 1891 intercollegiate contest and related quotes, see *Lexington Morning Transcript*, 11 April 1891, 1. For the life and career of Basil Duke, see Gary Robert Matthews, *Basil Wilson Duke, CSA: The Right Man in the Right Place* (Lexington: University Press of Kentucky, 2005). Also see *The Kentucky Encyclopedia*, 1992 ed., s.v. "Duke, Basil W."; Lowell H. Harrison, *The Civil War in Kentucky* (Lexington: University Press of Kentucky, 1975), 35–36, 57, 60, 62, 65, 68, 79; Hambleton Tapp and James C. Klotter, *Kentucky: Decades of Discord, 1865–1900* (Frankfort: Kentucky Historical Society, 1977), 55, 122, 153, 414, 433. For a brief discussion of the life and career of Samuel M. Wilson, see *The Kentucky Encyclopedia*, 1992 ed., s.v. "Wilson, Samuel MacKay."

8. The first quote is from *Lexington Morning Transcript*, 11 April 1891, 1. For details of the 1892 intercollegiate contest at Georgetown, see *Lexington Morning Transcript*, 2 April 1892, 1. For faculty objections to the intercollegiate contests, see Hopkins, *University of Kentucky*, 174. For the students' rebuttal, see "Some Things Necessary to College Pride," *Transylvanian* 1 (April 1892): 214–15. For the Kentucky University students' boycott of the Washington's birthday celebration in 1893, see *Lexington Morning Transcript*, 22 February 1893, 1; 23 February 1893, 4. The second quote is from "Oratorical Contest," *State College Cadet* 2, no. 7 (29 March 1892): [supplement]. For the meeting between the State College societies and the faculty on the issue of participating in the intercollegiate contests, see *State*

College Cadet 3, no. 7 (15 March 1893): 4. The last quote is from *State College Cadet* 4, no. 2 (October 1893): 4. Also see "Minutes of the [Faculty] Senate," 2 February 1894; 6 February 1894.

9. The first, third, and fourth quotes are from Karl Detzer and Harry P. Harrison, *Culture under Canvas: The Story of Tent Chautauqua* (New York: Hastings House Publishers, 1958), 43, 44, xvi. For observations about the Lexington Chautauqua audiences and the second quote, see Gregory A. Waller, *Main Street Amusements: Movies and Commercial Entertainment in a Southern City, 1896–1930* (Washington, D.C.: Smithsonian Institution Press, 1995), 58. For the argument that the Chautauqua ideals were corrupted by professionalized show-business practices, especially after 1904 on the Redpath Chautauqua circuit, see Frederick J. Antczak and Edith Seimers, "The Divergence of Purpose and Practice on the Chautauqua: Keith Vawter's Self-Defense," in *Oratorical Culture in Nineteenth-Century America: Transformations in the Theory and Practice of Rhetoric,* ed. Gregory Clark and S. Michael Halloran (Carbondale: Southern Illinois University Press, 1993), 208–25; the last quote is from p. 212.

10. The first and second quotes are from *Lexington Morning Transcript,* 22 February 1887, 4; the third quote is from *Lexington Morning Transcript,* 10 March 1887, 4. For a description of the Chautauqua grounds and facilities and the letter from "Rusticus," see *Lexington Morning Transcript,* 26 June 1887, 5. For an account of the opening-day ceremonies, Trost's Band, Patterson's speech, and the planned activities of the session, see *Lexington Morning Transcript,* 29 June 1887, 2. For a description of Sam Jones's closing-day address and related quotes, see *Lexington Morning Transcript,* 9 July 1887, 4. For plans to purchase Woodland Park for the Kentucky Chautauqua Assembly and a detailed list of contributors, see *Lexington Morning Transcript,* 9 July 1887, 2.

11. For the description of the 1888 Chautauqua Assembly, its opening ceremonies, and the related quotes, see the *Kentucky (Lexington) Leader,* 27 June 1888, 1. For the program of the Kentucky College Association meeting and related quotes, see *Kentucky (Lexington) Leader,* 28 June 1888, 1.

12. The first and second quotes are from *Kentucky (Lexington) Leader,* 25 June 1889, 1. For an account of the 1889 Chautauqua educational departments, the new facilities, and the last quote, see *Kentucky (Lexington) Leader,* 28 June 1889, 8. For direct evidence that the Inter-Collegiate Oratorical Association set and enforced the rules governing the Chautauqua contest, see *Lexington Daily Leader,* 5 July 1899, 1.

13. For the *Kentucky (Lexington) Leader*'s account of the 1889 Chautauqua contest and the first quote, see 30 June 1889, 2; for the *Lexington Morning Transcript*'s account of the same contest and the related quotes, see 30 June 1889, 1. For the selection process for Chautauqua contest orators and the related quote, see "Dropping the Curtain," *State College Cadet* 6 (June 1896): 136–37. For the fear that the Chautauqua contest might detract from the intercollegiate contest, see "Editorial," *Kentucky University Tablet* 3 (May 1889): 190.

14. The quotes are from *Kentucky (Lexington) Leader,* 29 June 1890, 8; 6 July 1890, 7; 7 July 1890, 5. For evidence that the faculty and some of the students at State College were opposed to the off-campus contests in the early 1890s, see "Oratorical Contest," *State College Cadet* 2, no. 7 (29 March 1892): [supplement]; *State College Cadet* 3, no. 7 (15 March 1893): 4.

15. For opening night at the Kentucky Chautauqua in 1891, see *Kentucky (Lexington) Leader,* 1 July 1891, 4. For the account of the "colored" picnic on 4 July 1891, see *Kentucky (Lexington) Leader,* 5 July 1891, 2. For the description of the "college boys," see *Kentucky (Lexington) Leader,* 6 July 1891, 4. For the account of the 1891 oratorical contest at Chautauqua, see *Kentucky (Lexington) Leader,* 7 July 1891, 5. For the opening of the 1892 Chautauqua and the schedule of events, see *Kentucky (Lexington) Leader,* 28 June 1892, 1. For the quote describing Bob Taylor, see Detzer and Harrison, *Culture under Canvas,* 134. For the accounts of the closing day of Chautauqua in 1892 and the oratorical contest, see *Kentucky (Lexington) Leader,* 7 July 1892, 5; 8 July 1892, 1.

16. For an example of the advertisements publicizing the upcoming 1893 Chautauqua, see *Kentucky (Lexington) Leader,* 11 June 1893, 10. For Charles Scott as manager of the Lexington Opera House, see Waller, *Main Street Amusements,* 5. For the press account of the 1893 Chautauqua describing its hotel and other facilities, the organizations occupying tents, the sixteen-piece band, and so forth, see *Kentucky (Lexington) Leader,* 27 June 1893, 4. For coverage of the 1893 oratorical contest, including the reference to "college day" and the selection of judges, and the related quotes, see *Kentucky (Lexington) Leader,* 6 July 1893, 1. For Phillip W. Breitenbucher as a Cecropian Society member, see *Kentucky University Crimson 1897,* 96.

17. For the State College societies' 1894 plan for choosing orators for the intercollegiate and Chautauqua contests, see "Minutes of the [Faculty] Senate," 9 March 1894. For the 1894 preliminary contests at Kentucky University and State College, respectively, see *Kentucky (Lexington) Leader,* 31 March 1894, 8; 1 April 1894, 8. For the account of the 1894 intercollegiate oratorical contest and the related quotes, see *Lexington Morning Transcript,* 7 April 1894, 1. For the account of the tornado striking Morrison College and the last quote, see *Kentucky (Lexington) Leader,* 27 June 1894, 6. For a discussion of furnishings such as fine carpets and expensive chairs as markers of gentility and refinement, see Richard L. Bushman, *The Refinement of America: Persons, Houses, Cities* (1992; reprint, New York: Vintage Books, 1993), 256–72.

18. The first three quotes are from *Kentucky (Lexington) Leader,* 28 June 1894, 5. For the description of the women's clubs activities at Chautauqua, the lecture on "Social Purity," and the fourth quote, see *Kentucky (Lexington) Leader,* 6 July 1894, 6. The fifth and sixth quotes are from *Kentucky (Lexington) Leader,* 12 July 1894, 6. For the results of the 1894 Chautauqua oratorical contest and the last quote, see *Kentucky (Lexington) Leader,* 13 July 1894, 6. For Charles A. Thomas as a Cecropian Society member, see *Kentucky University Crimson 1897,* 96.

19. For accounts of the 1895 intercollegiate oratorical contest, see *(Lexington)*
Press-Transcript, 5 April 1895, 2; 6 April 1895, 1. For accounts of the 1895 primary
oratorical contests at Kentucky University and State College, respectively, see *(Lexington) Press-Transcript,* 27 March 1895, 4; 27 March 1895, 8.

20. The first and second quotes are from *Kentucky (Lexington) Leader,* 11 July
1895, 1. For the account of the Fourth of July celebration at Chautauqua in 1895
and the third and fourth quotes, see *Kentucky (Lexington) Leader,* 4 July 1895, 1. For
the account of Madeline McDowell's presentation and the fifth and sixth quotes,
see *Kentucky (Lexington) Leader,* 11 July 1895, 1, 8. For the 1895 Chautauqua
contest and its winner, see *Kentucky (Lexington) Leader,* 12 July 1895, 5. Also see
K. U. Enroll 1, no. 1 (12 September 1895): 1. For Wood Ballard as a Periclean Society member, also see *Kentucky University Crimson 1897,* 96.

21. For the 1896 intercollegiate oratorical contest, see *Lexington Daily Leader,* 2
April 1896, 5; 3 April 1896, 1; 4 April 1896, 1. For Kentucky University's rejection
of the petition to organize social fraternities, see *Lexington Daily Leader,* 3 April
1896, 1. For John T. Geary as a Patterson Society member, see *Lexington Daily
Leader,* 28 March 1896, 3. For William Sugg as a Union Society member, see *Lexington Daily Leader,* 23 February 1896, 5. The first quote is from *Lexington Daily
Leader,* 9 July 1896, 3. For the 1896 Chautauqua contest and the second and third
quotes, see *Lexington Daily Leader,* 10 July 1896, 3.

22. The first two quotes are from "Minutes of the [Faculty] Senate," 2 February
1894; 26 May 1898. For accounts of the intercollegiate oratorical contest between
1897 and 1900, see *Lexington Morning Herald,* 3 April 1897, 1; 2 April 1898, 5; 7
April 1899, 2; 8 April 1899, 1, 4; 14 April 1900, 1. For R. E. Moss as a Periclean
Society member, see *Kentucky University Crimson 1897,* 96. For Leonidas Ragan as
a Union Society member, see *Lexington Morning Herald,* 30 March 1900, 6. For the
Inter-Collegiate Oratorical Association meeting at the Phoenix Hotel and the third
quote, see *Lexington Daily Leader,* 21 February 1897, 5.

23. The quotes are from *Lexington Morning Herald,* 3 April 1897, 1; 11 March
1898, 7; 2 April 1898, 5. For coverage of the intercollegiate contest in 1900, see
Lexington Morning Herald, 14 April 1900, 1, 4.

24. The first quote is from *Lexington Morning Herald,* 27 June 1900, 1. For
Chautauqua's financial problems in 1897 and related quotes, see *Lexington Daily
Leader,* 9 July 1897, 8. For Sam Jones at the 1898 Chautauqua and related quotes,
see *Lexington Daily Leader,* 5 July 1898, 7.

25. For this discussion of motion pictures at the Lexington Chautauqua, see
Waller, *Main Street Amusements,* 58–59; the first quote is from p. 59. The second
quote is from *Lexington Daily Leader,* 6 July 1899, 5. For coverage of the Kappa Alpha convention in Lexington in 1899 and related information, see *Lexington Daily
Leader,* 3 July 1899, 5; 4 July 1899, 6.

26. For accounts of the Chautauqua College Day oratorical contest between
1897 and 1900, see *Lexington Daily Leader,* 8 July 1897, 5; 9 July 1897, 8; 8 July

1898, 8; 9 July 1898, 2; 5 July 1899, 1; 7 July 1899, 8; 29 June 1900, 1, 8; 30 June 1900, 4. Also see *Lexington Morning Herald*, 30 June 1900, 4. The quotes are from *Lexington Daily Leader*, 8 July 1897, 8; 8 July 1898, 8; 5 July 1899, 1.

27. For the 1897 Chautauqua contest winners and their membership in Kappa Alpha, see *Lexington Daily Leader*, 9 July 1897, 8. For James N. Elliott as a Cecropian Society member, see *Kentucky University Crimson 1897*, 80. For John T. Geary as a Patterson Society member, see *Lexington Daily Leader*, 28 March 1896, 3. For Kappa Alpha's Chautauqua tent at Woodland Park, see *Lexington Morning Herald*, 28 June 1900, 4. For J. M. Shelburne as the 1896 Chautauqua contest winner and the first quote, see *Lexington Daily Leader*, 10 July 1896, 3. For Howard Cree as the 1898 Chautauqua victor, see *Lexington Daily Leader*, 9 July 1898, 2. For Cree as an 1897 graduate of the College of the Bible, see *Kentucky University Crimson 1897*, 38. For coverage of Kentucky University's disqualification from the 1899 Chautauqua contest and related quotes, see *Lexington Daily Leader*, 5 July 1899, 1. For the Chautauqua contest in 1900 and related quotes, see *Lexington Daily Leader*, 29 June 1900, 1, 8.

28. For Tandy's victory, see *Lexington Leader*, 27 March 1901, 2. For the Inter-Collegiate Oratorical Association's financial statement and the first quote, see *Lexington Leader*, 13 April 1901, 8. For coverage of the 1901 intercollegiate contest and the second quote, see *Lexington Leader*, 13 April 1901, 4.

29. For the argument pertaining to the exclusion of ministry students and ministers from the intercollegiate contests, see "The Oratorical Contest," *Transylvanian* 7 (May 1900): 303–4; "K. U. Withdraws," *Transylvanian* 8 (March 1901): 198–99; "Editorial," *Transylvanian* 8 (May 1901): 237; "Editorial," *Transylvanian* 9 (April 1902): 197–98; the quote is from ibid., 198.

30. For the suggestion that the city buy Woodland Park and the first quote, see *Lexington Leader*, 30 June 1901, 3. The second quote is from *Lexington Leader*, 6 July 1901, 4. For coverage of the 4 July 1901 celebrations and the third quote, see *Lexington Leader*, 4 July 1901, 1, 4. The fourth quote is from *Lexington Leader*, 28 June 1901, 1. For an account of the 1901 Chautauqua contest and the last quote, see *Lexington Leader*, 29 June 1901, 4.

31. For the 1902 intercollegiate contest and the quoted headline, see *Lexington Leader*, 19 April 1902, 1. For the 1902 Chautauqua receipts, Leon Vincent's lecture and related quotes, and the 1902 College Day contest, see *Lexington Leader*, 26 June 1902, 8. Also see *Lexington Leader*, 27 June 1902, 1.

32. For coverage of the 1903 intercollegiate contest, see *Lexington Morning Herald*, 10 April 1903, 6; 11 April 1903, 1, 6. For the Kappa Alpha banquet and the first quote, see *Lexington Leader*, 11 April 1903, 5. For a detailed description of the gold medal and the second quote, see *Lexington Leader*, 3 April 1903, 4.

33. For the announcement of the location of the 1904 intercollegiate contest at the Georgetown Opera House, see *Lexington Morning Herald*, 11 April 1903, 6. For accounts of the 1904 intercollegiate contest, see *Lexington Morning Herald*, 7

April 1904, 8; 9 April 1904, 1. For coverage of the 1905 intercollegiate contest at the State College chapel and the related quote, see *Lexington Herald,* 29 April 1905, 1. For the seating capacity of the Lexington Opera House, see Waller, *Main Street Amusements,* 4. For an account of the 1910 intercollegiate contest at the chapel of State University, see *Lexington Herald,* 23 April 1910, 1. For the 1916 intercollegiate contest, see *Lexington Herald,* 14 May 1916, 1. For the university's various name changes and the dates of these changes, see *The Kentucky Encyclopedia,* 1992 ed., s.v. "University of Kentucky."

34. The first quote is from *Lexington Leader,* 28 June 1903, 6. For the account of the Chautauqua Ministers' Institute, the quoted title, and the participation of Dr. Parkhurst, see *Lexington Morning Herald,* 8 July 1903, 5. For Parkhurst as one of the judges at the oratorical contest, see *Lexington Leader,* 9 July 1903, 1.

35. For the *Lexington Leader's* precontest coverage of the 1903 Chautauqua College Day oratorical contest and the first quote, see 9 July 1903, 1. For the *Lexington Morning Herald's* account and the second and third quotes, see 10 July 1903, 1. For the fourth and fifth quotes, see *Lexington Leader,* 10 July 1903, 3.

36. The first quote is from *Lexington Leader,* 28 June 1904, 1. For the 1904 Chautauqua deficit, see *Lexington Herald,* 20 July 1904, 5. The second quote is from *Lexington Leader,* 30 June 1904, 3. For the 1904 College Day contest and the third and fourth quotes, see *Lexington Leader,* 1 July 1904, 1.

37. The first two quotes are from *Lexington Herald,* 26 October 1904, 1. For Woodland Park "improvements" in the spring of 1905, see *Lexington Herald,* 17 March 1905, 5; 11 April 1905, 5. For the plan to "revive" the Chautauqua Assembly, see *Lexington Herald,* 19 February 1907, 1. For the opening of Chautauqua in 1907 and the third quote, see *Lexington Herald,* 26 June 1907, 1. For the attempt to boost attendance by lowering ticket prices, see *Lexington Herald,* 1 July 1907, 4. For accounts of the 1908 Chautauqua, see *Lexington Herald,* 24 June 1908, 1; 28 June 1908, 1; July 1908, 9. For accounts of the Redpath Chautauqua in Lexington in 1916, see *Lexington Herald,* 1 July 1916, 6; 2 July 1916, 5; 9 July 1916, 4; 9 July 1916, sec. 3, p. 7. Also see Waller, *Main Street Amusements,* 221–24, for the Redpath Chautauqua in Lexington.

38. Biographical information on Clarke Tandy was developed from *Lexington Leader,* 13 April 1901, 4; 10 July 1903, 3; 11 January 1909, 8; *Lexington Herald,* 11 January 1909, 1, 8; Marguerite McLaughlin, O. M. Shedd, and R. C. Stoll, "Clarke Howell Tandy," *Mechanical Engineering & Electrical Engineering Record* 2 (January 1909): 47, copy available in Special Collections and Archives, Margaret I. King Library, University of Kentucky, Lexington.

39. For Tandy as Kentucky's first Rhodes scholar, see *Lexington Leader,* 11 January 1909, 8; Hopkins, *University of Kentucky,* 172; Carl B. Cone, *The University of Kentucky: A Pictorial History* (Lexington: University Press of Kentucky, 1990), 26. The quotes are from "Clark Howell Tandy," *Idea* 1, no. 17 (21 January 1909): 1, in Special Collections and Archives, Margaret I. King Library, University of Kentucky, Lexington.

40. For the Greek-letter fraternities on the State College campus by 1903, see *Blue and White '03* (Lexington: Kentucky State A&M College, 1903), in Special Collections and Archives, Margaret I. King Library, University of Kentucky, Lexington. For the Lamp and Cross Society, see "Lamp and Cross," *Idea* 2, no. 35 (28 April 1910): 7; also see Hopkins, *University of Kentucky,* 178–79. For Tandy's victory at the 1901 intercollegiate contest and the first quote, see *Lexington Leader,* 13 April 1901, 4. Note that the *Leader*'s assertion that nineteen-year-old Tandy was the youngest orator to win the intercollegiate contest was probably inaccurate. According to the *Lexington Morning Transcript,* 11 April, 1891, 1, John M. Stevenson was eighteen when he won the fourth annual intercollegiate contest in 1891. For the text of Tandy's poem "At State College" and the second and third quotes, see *Lexington Leader,* 1 April 1902, 4. For James H. Mulligan and his poem "In Kentucky," see *The Kentucky Encyclopedia,* 1992 ed., s.v. "Mulligan, James Hillary"; James C. Klotter, *Kentucky: Portrait in Paradox, 1900–1950* (Frankfort: Kentucky Historical Society, 1996), 189.

41. For the 1901 Chautauqua contest, see *Lexington Leader,* 28 June 1901, 1; 29 June 1901, 4. For the Chautauqua contest in 1902, see *Lexington Leader,* 26 June 1902, 8; 27 June 1902, 1. For the 1903 Chautauqua contest and the quotes, see *Lexington Leader,* 10 July 1903, 3. Also see *Lexington Morning Herald,* 10 July 1903, 1.

42. For this account of Tandy's life between his graduation from State College and his death, and the quotes, see *Lexington Herald,* 11 January 1909, 1, 8. Also see *Lexington Leader,* 11 January 1909, 8.

43. For the *Lexington Herald*'s announcement of Tandy's death and the first two quotes, see 11 January 1909, 1, 8. For the *Lexington Leader*'s account of the reaction to Tandy's death, Patterson's eulogy, and the related quotes, see 11 January 1909, 1. For the memorial tribute to Neville and the related quote, see William Benjamin Smith, "In Memoriam: John Henry Neville," *Mechanical Engineering & Electrical Engineering Record* 2 (October 1908): 11. For the *Lexington Herald*'s account of Tandy's funeral, see 13 January 1909, 1. For the memorial tribute to Tandy and the related quotes, see *Idea* 1, no. 16 (14 January 1909): 5.

44. The quote is from "The Intercollegiate Oratorical Contest," *Kentuckian: A Monthly Magazine,* Alumni Number (September 1901): [6], copy available in Special Collections and Archives, Margaret I. King Library, University of Kentucky, Lexington.

CHAPTER FIVE: "THIS CITY'S NEVER DULL"

The quote in the chapter title is from *Lexington Herald,* 28 May 1916, sec. 4, p. 9.

1. This account of Governor Stanley and the January 1917 incident at Murray was developed from James C. Klotter, *Kentucky: Portrait in Paradox, 1900–1950* (Frankfort: Kentucky Historical Society, 1996), 68–69, 226; *The Kentucky Encyclo-*

pedia, 1992 ed., s.v. "Stanley, Augustus Owsley"; George C. Wright, *Racial Violence in Kentucky: 1865–1940: Lynchings, Mob Rule, and "Legal Lynchings"* (Baton Rouge: Louisiana State University Press, 1990), 192–94; Dewey W. Grantham, *Southern Progressivism: The Reconciliation of Progress and Tradition* (Knoxville: University of Tennessee Press, 1983), 373–74. Grantham counts Stanley among the progressive, reform-minded southern governors of the Wilson era. Lexington press accounts of the Murray incident include *Lexington Leader,* 11 January 1917, 1; 12 January 1917, 1; 15 January 1917, 4; 19 February 1917, 1; 23 February 1917, sec. 2, p. 8; *Lexington Herald,* 11 January 1917, 1; 12 January 1917, 1; 23 February 1917, 3. For the idea that a hallmark of the Progressive Era, particularly in the South, was the call for centralized governmental and bureaucratic control to achieve social order, see Grantham, *Southern Progressivism,* chaps. 5, 9, 11; W. Fitzhugh Brundage, *Lynching in the New South: Georgia and Virginia, 1880–1930* (Urbana: University of Illinois Press, 1993), chap. 8.

2. The first two quotes are from *Lexington Leader,* 12 January 1917, 1; 15 January 1917, 4. For praise of Stanley by national black leaders, see *Lexington Leader,* 3 March 1917, 7. Also see Klotter, *Portrait in Paradox,* 68–69; Wright, *Racial Violence in Kentucky,* 192–94.

3. The first four quotes are from *Lexington Leader,* 15 January 1917, 4; 12 January 1917, 1. For accounts of Martin's trial and death sentence, see *Lexington Leader,* 23 February 1917, 8; *Lexington Herald,* 23 February 1917, 3; the last quote is from ibid. For a discussion of legal lynching, or what Wright terms "color-coded justice: racial violence under the law," see his *Racial Violence in Kentucky,* chap. 8.

4. This interpretation of the southern progressivist philosophy and reform effort was largely drawn from Grantham, *Southern Progressivism,* especially the introduction and chap. 13; the first quote is from p. xviii. For a broad, national view of social changes, attendant problems, and reform efforts during this era, I also drew from Meirion Harries and Susie Harries, *The Last Days of Innocence: America at War, 1917–1918* (New York: Random House, 1997), chap. 1; the second quote is from p. 21. Also see Sean Dennis Cashman, *America in the Age of the Titans: The Progressive Era and World War I* (New York: New York University Press, 1988), chaps. 8–10; Neil A. Wynn, *From Progressivism to Prosperity: World War I and American Society* (New York: Holmes and Meier, 1986), chaps. 1–4. The last three quotes are from Grantham, *Southern Progressivism,* 390, 411, 415. For a complementary perspective on progressivism and the progressivist agenda prior to World War I, see Richard Lowitt, *George W. Norris: The Persistence of a Progressive, 1913–1933* (Urbana: University of Illinois Press, 1971), preface, chaps. 1–3. Note that when Lowitt published this book he was a professor of history and associate dean of the College of Arts and Sciences at the University of Kentucky.

5. For the contending imperialist and anti-imperialist forces in the United States at the time of the Spanish-American War, see Barbara Tuchman, *The Proud*

Tower, a Portrait of the World before the War: 1890–1914 (New York: Macmillan, 1966; Bantam Books, 1967), chap. 3; the first quote is from p. 178. For white southerners' intransigence after the Civil War, see Edward L. Ayers, *Promise of the New South: Life after Reconstruction* (New York: Oxford University Press, 1992), 370, 409; the second quote is from p. 432. For the racial stance of southern progressives, see Grantham, *Southern Progressivism,* 126–27. The third quote is from Charles W. Chesnutt, *The Marrow of Tradition* (1901; reprint, Ann Arbor: University of Michigan Press, Ann Arbor Paperbacks, 1969), 329. For the Wilmington riot as Chesnutt's motivation, see Robert M. Farnsworth's introduction, ibid., viii. For a discussion of Chesnutt's life and literary works, also see Ayers, *Promise of the New South,* 366–71.

6. Biographical information on Thomas Dixon is from Raymond A. Cook, *Thomas Dixon* (New York: Twayne Publishers, 1974); the first quote is from p. 8. The second quote is from Thomas Dixon Jr., *The Leopard's Spots: A Romance of the White Man's Burden—1865–1900* (New York: Grosset and Dunlap, 1902), 386–87; emphasis in original.

7. For an account of Wilson's declaration of war speech to Congress and the quotes attributed to him, see Harries and Harries, *Last Days of Innocence,* 71–73. For Senator Norris's opposition to U.S. entry into the war and his speech to the Senate, see Lowitt, *George W. Norris,* 72–76; the quote is from p. 74.

8. *Lexington Herald,* 4 June 1917, 2.

9. For the names of the various local UDC chapters, see, for instance, *Lexington Leader,* 3 January 1916, 8; 12 January 1916, 8. For reference to the UDC meetings in the "Confederate Room," see *Lexington Leader,* 3 January 1916, 8. The first two quotes are from *Lexington Herald,* 11 May 1916, 1; 9 June 1916, 8. For the number of automobiles in Fayette County, see *Lexington Leader,* 26 March 1916, Automobile section, 14. The third quote is from Grantham, *Southern Progressivism,* 203; the fourth quote is from *Lexington Herald,* 16 March 1916, 9; the last quote is from *Lexington Leader,* 16 March 1916, 8.

10. For the organization of the UCV throughout the South, see Ayers, *Promise of the New South,* 334. The first quote is from *Lexington Herald,* 20 April 1910, 4. For coverage of the Birmingham reunion in 1916, see *Lexington Herald,* 14 May 1916, sec.1, p. 2; 17 May 1916, 1; the second quote is from ibid. For Johnston's election as president of the Breckinridge Chapter of the UCV, see *Lexington Leader,* 1 April 1915, 1; *Lexington Herald,* 2 April 1915, 3. For press accounts of Tenney's death and funeral, see *Lexington Herald,* 1 April 1916, 1, 3; 3 April 1916, 1, 3; *Lexington Leader,* 3 April 1916, 7. The last quote is from *Lexington Herald,* 3 April 1916, 4. For additional examples of press coverage of Confederate veterans' funerals in 1916 and use of the rhetoric of the Lost Cause, see *Lexington Herald,* 22 February 1916, 4; 30 April 1916, 1, 3; 25 May 1916, 6; 26 May 1916, 1; 2 June 1916, 1.

11. For Johnston's reelection as president of the Breckinridge UCV, see *Lexington Herald,* 23 April 1916, 2. For Johnston as head of the National Trotting Associa-

tion, see, for instance, *Lexington Leader,* 10 February 1910, 2. Other biographical information on P. P. Johnston is from his obituary in *Lexington Herald,* 11 February 1925, 1. For Johnston's social connections with Andrew Carnegie through his son, Marius, see Marius Johnston to Philip Preston Johnston Jr., 23 October 1907, and 13 March 1912, Philip Preston Johnston Jr. Correspondence File, Philip Preston Johnston Jr. Papers, in Preston-Johnston Papers, Special Collections and Archives, Margaret I. King Library, University of Kentucky, Lexington, Kentucky (hereafter, PPJ Correspondence File). Information on Marius Johnston's marriage to Nancy Carnegie is from Robert Wickliffe Preston Johnston, interview with Kolan Morelock, 5 October 1998, tape on file with author; for the date (17 April 1912) of their marriage, see printed wedding announcement, single sheet, in PPJ Correspondence File. For the wedding date of Philip Preston Johnston Jr. and Margaret Wickliffe Preston, see printed wedding invitation, single sheet, in PPJ Correspondence File; *Lexington Herald,* 9 November 1917, 6; *Lexington Leader,* 9 November 1917, sec. 2, p. 2.

12. For the controversy surrounding the Robert E. Lee birthday ceremonies in Washington, D.C., see *Lexington Herald,* 20 January 1910, 1. For coverage of the celebration of Lee's birthday in Lexington in 1910, see *Lexington Leader,* 20 January 1910, 4; *Lexington Herald,* 20 January 1910, 1, 4. For the celebration of Lee's birthday in 1916, see *Lexington Herald,* 14 January 1916, 4; 16 January 1916, 1; 19 January 1916, 1. For examples of Lee's birthday celebrations in private homes, see *Lexington Herald,* 19 January 1916, 7; 20 January 1916, 7.

13. For an account of the 30 May 1916 Memorial Day services and the first quote, see *Lexington Herald,* 31 May 1916, 1, 6. For the 3 June 1916 Confederate Memorial Day services and the second quote, see *Lexington Herald,* 4 June 1916, 1, 3. For the *Lexington Leader's* coverage of the same event and the third quote, see 4 June 1916, 3. For the last quote, see *Lexington Herald,* 3 June 1916, 1.

14. For the involvement of Woodrow Wilson and other officials in the effort to market *The Birth of a Nation* and the controversy surrounding its distribution and screening, see Cook, *Thomas Dixon,* 114–17; the quotes are from pp. 113, 115.

15. For the screening of *The Birth of a Nation* in Lexington, see Gregory A. Waller, *Main Street Amusements: Movies and Commercial Entertainment in a Southern City 1896–1930* (Washington, D.C.: Smithsonian Institution Press, 1995), 151–60; the first three quotes are from pp. 91, 146. The last quote is from *Lexington Herald,* 9 March 1916, 9.

16. The quotes are from *Lexington Herald,* 27 February 1916, 5; 2 April 1916, 7.

17. For the "Scoop the Cub Reporter" comic strips, see *Lexington Herald,* 1 February 1916, 9; 5 January 1916, 9. For the stabbing incident, see *Lexington Herald,* 16 January 1916, sec. 2, p. 3. For the stolen goldfish incident, see *Lexington Herald,* 18 April 1916, 1; 19 April 1916, 13. For the black man being ordered to dance in the courtroom, see *Lexington Herald,* 23 April 1916, 3.

18. The first two quotes are from Kevin K. Gaines, *Uplifting the Race: Black*

Leadership, Politics, and Culture in the Twentieth Century (Chapel Hill: University of North Carolina Press, 1996), 67. For the comedic appeal of minstrelsy to blacks as well as whites, see Ayers, *Promise of the New South,* 376. For Lexington Opera House bookings of professional minstrel shows to attract both races, see Waller, *Main Street Amusements,* 45. For accounts of the Morton High School minstrel show, see *Lexington Herald,* 15 April 1916, 6; 23 April 1916, 8; 6 May 1916, 2. The last quote is from *Lexington Herald,* 23 April 1916, 8.

19. The quotes are from *Lexington Herald,* 8 March 1916, 8; 19 February 1916, 10; *Lexington Leader,* 6 January 1910, 12.

20. See George C. Wright, *A History of Blacks in Kentucky,* vol. 2, *In Pursuit of Equality, 1890–1980* (Frankfort: Kentucky Historical Society, 1992), 50–52. For the Savannah Christmas account and the related quote, see *Lexington Herald,* 31 January 1916, 12. For the account of the rescue of the engineer, *Lexington Herald,* 10 January 1916, 16.

21. The quoted headlines are from *Lexington Herald,* 6 January 1910, 5; 8 January 1910, 2; 20 January 1910, 2; 28 January 1910, 3; 7 April 1915, 6; 30 April 1915, 8; 22 January 1916, 3; 15 April 1916, 6; 1 May 1916, 1; *Lexington Leader,* 27 May 1916, 8. For additional headlines in the *Lexington Herald* identifying criminal suspects by race (i.e., "Negro" or "Negress") and thereby linking blacks with crime, see 4 January 1910, 1; 6 January 1910, 1; 25 January 1910, 7; 26 January 1910, 10; 30 January 1910, 3; 31 March 1910, 2; 8 April 1910, 1; 9 April 1910, 5; 14 April 1910, 2, 4; 24 May 1910, 2; 4 April 1915, 3; 11 April 1915, 4, 8; 13 April 1915, 8; 20 April 1915, 11; 28 April 1915, 6; 30 April 1915, 8; 1 January 1916, 7; 8 January 1916, 8; 30 January 1916, 6; 31 January 1916, 1, 8; 4 February 1916, 8; 6 February 1916, 3; 10 February 1916, 6; 3 March 1916, 3; 12 March 1916, 2; 18 March 1916, 6; 22 March 1916, 2; 1 April 1916, 10; 7 April 1916, sec. 3, p. 5; 8 April 1916, 6; 9 April 1916, 3; 12 April 1916, 10; 22 April 1916, 12; 13 May 1916, 5; 28 May 1916, 8; 14 June 1916, 10.

22. W. E. B. DuBois, *The Souls of Black Folk* (1903; reprint, New York: Vintage Books, 1990), 34, 80. For a discussion of race relations and white perceptions of black crime in the New South era, see Ayers, *Promise of the New South,* 154–55, 427–37; the quotes are from pp. 427–28, 436.

23. For examples of accounts of lynching and other mob violence in the *Lexington Herald* during this era, see 2 March 1910, 1; 25 April 1910, 5, 6; 1 January 1916, 5; 22 January 1916, 1; 13 February 1916, sec. 2, p. 6; 18 February 1916, 2; 2 April 1916, 6; 16 May 1916, 3. The quoted headlines are from *Lexington Leader,* 21 January 1910, 10; 16 April 1915, 2. For the *Lexington Leader's* antilynching editorial, see 29 January 1917, 4. Also see *Lexington Leader,* 1 January 1917, sec. 2, p. 2. For the *Lexington Herald's* report of the execution at Williamstown, see 8 January 1910, 1. For the *Lexington Leader's* report of the execution at Kansas City, see 8 February 1910, 10. For a discussion of "legal lynching" and "color-coded justice," see Wright, *Racial Violence in Kentucky,* chaps. 7, 8 passim; the last quote is from p. 222.

24. See *Lexington Herald,* 19 February 1910, 2; 30 January 1910, 5; *Lexington Leader,* 6 January 1916, 6; *Lexington Herald,* 15 January 1916, 10; 6 January 1910, 5; 3 February 1916, 2; 15 April 1915, 2; 10 February 1910, 4; 9 May 1910, 6; 13 May 1910, 5. Perhaps justice was served "informally" when the *Lexington Herald* reported on 15 May 1910 that a student committee had "forced" these two young men to leave the university for the "good name" of the school. For the campus perspective on this incident, see "Students Forced to Leave," *Idea* 2, no. 35 (19 May 1910): 8, in Special Collections and Archives, Margaret I. King Library, University of Kentucky, Lexington.

25. The quotes are from *Lexington Herald,* 26 March 1916, 1; *Lexington Leader,* 26 March 1916, sec. 2, p. 1; *Lexington Herald,* 27 March 1916, 1. Also see *Lexington Leader,* 25 February 1916, sec. 2, p. 1; 30 March 1916, 5; *Lexington Herald,* 25 February 1916, 6; 8 March 1916, 1, 3; 9 March 1916, 5; 29 March 1916, 12; 5 April 1916, 8; 19 April 1916, 2; 20 April 1916, 5.

26. The headline is from *Lexington Leader,* 3 June 1916, 1. For two other examples of the term "unknown Negro" in headlines, see *Lexington Herald,* 3 May 1910, 1; *Lexington Leader,* 28 March 1917, sec. 2, p. 1. For Brundage's discussion of the white fear of black criminality, especially the "black vagabonds," see *Lynching in the New South,* 53, 81, chap. 2.

27. For this account of Will Pearl, see *Lexington Leader,* 3 June 1916, 1; 4 June 1916, 1; 5 June 1916, 3; *Lexington Herald,* 5 June 1916, 1, 7; 6 June 1916, 1; 15 June 1916, 1. The quote regarding Pearl's "viciousness" is from *Lexington Herald,* 5 June 1916, 7.

28. *Lexington Leader,* 25 January 1916, 1. For the preparation and planned opening of Douglass Park, see *Lexington Herald,* 31 March 1916, sec. 2, p. 8; *Lexington Leader,* 9 May 1916, 8. For Lexington's 1916 city budget figures, see *Lexington Leader,* 7 February 1916, 1, 12.

29. For the view that improved public services and facilities were connected with progressive reform efforts concerned with both social justice and social efficiency, see Grantham, *Southern Progressivism,* chaps. 7, 9 passim; the first quote is from p. xv. For Grantham's discussion of the major themes of progressive reform, see ibid., xix–xxii, chaps. 5, 7, 9; the second quote is from p. 125. The last quote from George Brown Tindall, *The Emergence of the New South, 1913–1945* (Baton Rouge: Louisiana State University Press, 1967), 32; quoted in Grantham, *Southern Progressivism,* xix. For a detailed study of the emergence of the scientific charity movement in Lexington and its struggle with the Salvation Army to become the dominant social welfare "reform style" during the Progressive Era, see Karen Tice, "Battle for Benevolence: Scientific Disciplinary Control vs. Indiscriminate Relief: Lexington Associated Charities and the Salvation Army, 1900–1918," *Journal of Sociology and Social Welfare* 19 (June 1992): 59–77.

30. *Lexington Herald,* 21 April 1916, sec. 2, p. 3; *Lexington Herald,* 20 April 1916, 3.

31. For the Board of Commerce meeting and the related quote, see *Lexington Leader,* 12 January 1916, 1. For accounts of Olmsted's visit to Lexington, see *Lexington Herald,* 3 May 1916, 4; 4 May 1916, 1; 5 May 1916, 1, 3.

32. For the account of the "road expert," see *Lexington Herald,* 4 May 1916, 3. For Haines's address to the Associated Charities and the related quote, see *Lexington Leader,* 22 March 1917, 2. For attempts to develop institutions for the handicapped in the South during the Progressive Era, see Grantham, *Southern Progressivism,* 218. For the *Louisville Times* article and the related quote, see *Lexington Herald,* 15 April 1916, 7. For the new truant officers, see *Lexington Herald,* 11 June 1916, sec. 3, p. 1. For the request for a female police matron, see *Lexington Herald,* 2 May 1916, 1.

33. "Dormitory Influence," *Idea* 2, no. 36 (26 May 1910): 4; untitled editorial, *Idea* 4, no. 33 (9 May 1912): 6; *Lexington Leader,* 25 January 1916, 3. For a discussion of the movement in higher education toward social change through expertise, see Douglas Sloan, "The Teaching of Ethics in the American Undergraduate Curriculum, 1876–1976," in *Ethics Teaching in Higher Education,* ed. Daniel Callahan and Sissela Bok (New York: Plenum Press, 1980), 1–57.

34. For a discussion of progressive efforts to expand and improve urban services—and thereby foster economic development—through municipal reform plans, including the commission form of city government, see Grantham, *Southern Progressivism,* 275–90; the first two quotes are from p. 283. The quoted headline is from *Lexington Leader,* 12 February 1910, 3. For a detailed discussion of the campaign for, and adoption of, the commission plan in Lexington and its relationship with political "bossism," see James Bolin, "Bossism and Reform: Politics in Lexington, Kentucky, 1880–1940" (PhD diss., University of Kentucky, 1988), 94–100. Bolin (103) also cites the commission government in Lexington as an instance of "progressive reform" but argues that it did not result in the demise of political "bossism"; he notes that the continued power of the political bosses kept Lexington in a "conservative mold" before the First World War.

35. For a discussion of the epidemics that swept the South and the public health movement that arose in response, see Grantham, *Southern Progressivism,* 310–18; the first quote is from p. 311. For 1909 disease and death statistics, see *Lexington Leader,* 10 January 1910, 9; 30 January 1910, 3. For the "Science of Housekeeping" editorial and the related quotes, see *Lexington Leader,* 12 April 1915, 4. For the articles linking housework and hygiene with efficiency and beauty, see *Lexington Leader,* 13 April 1916, 5; 16 April 1916, sec. 2, p. 4; 20 April 1916, 10.

36. The first quote is from Grantham, *Southern Progressivism,* 288; the second, third, and fourth quotes are from *Lexington Leader,* 12 April 1915, 1, 6; the fifth quote is from *Lexington Leader,* 18 April 1915, 3; the sixth quote is from *Lexington Herald,* 17 April 1915, 4; the last quote is from *Lexington Leader,* 29 April 1915, 1.

37. For the "Clean-up Days" in Paris and Winchester, see *Lexington Herald,* 7 April 1916, 2; 12 April 1916, 2. The first quote is from *Lexington Herald,* 23 March 1916, 4. For Cassidy's appeal to the city commissioners and the Civic League's en-

dorsement, see *Lexington Herald*, 25 March 1916, 1, 3. For the mayor's and other commissioners' opposition to the Clean City Club plan and the second quote, see *Lexington Herald*, 28 March 1916, 8; the quoted headline is from *Lexington Herald*, 31 March 1916, 8. For a related account of this incident, see *Lexington Herald*, 2 April 1916, 8.

38. For the convincing argument that motion pictures dominated the commercial entertainment market in Lexington in the 1910s, see Waller, *Main Street Amusements*, 96–97, chap. 5.

39. This account of the Con T. Kennedy Shows was developed from *Lexington Herald*, 17 April 1916, 6; 18 April 1916, 16; 19 April 1916, 6; *Lexington Leader*, 19 April 1916, sec. 2, pp. 1, 6; 21 April 1916, 8. The quotes are from *Lexington Herald*, 19 April 1916, 6.

40. The first quote is from *Lexington Leader*, 19 April 1916, sec. 2, p. 6. For the Smith Greater Shows advertisement and the related quotes, see *Lexington Leader*, 28 May 1916, sec. 4, p. 4. For the protest over the Smith Shows, the reaction of the mayor and commissioners, and the related quotes, see *Lexington Leader*, 29 May 1916, 1; *Lexington Herald*, 30 May 1916, 11. For the wording of the anticarnival ordinance and the last quote, see *Lexington Leader*, 9 June 1916, 16.

41. For the "Labor Carnival" and related quotes, see *Lexington Leader*, 30 May 1916, 3. For Barker's speech to and subsequent meeting with the Federation of Labor, see *Lexington Leader*, 20 March 1916, 6; 23 March 1916, 13. For the decision to offer a series of six lectures and the related quote, see *Lexington Leader*, 24 March 1916, 8. For McKenzie's lecture, see *Lexington Leader*, 7 April 1916, 9. For Barker's lecture, see *Lexington Leader*, 13 April 1916, 1. For a discussion of the university extension movement, see Joseph F. Kett, *The Pursuit of Knowledge under Difficulties: From Self-Improvement to Adult Education in America, 1750–1990* (Stanford, Calif.: Stanford University Press, 1994), 182–204, 299–307; related quotes are from pp. 190, 222. For the quote regarding the intended audience for the extension lectures, see *Lexington Leader*, 2 April 1916, sec. 4, p. 8. For the Federation of Labor's request for a refund of the license fee and the ordinance prohibiting street carnivals, see *Lexington Leader*, 9 June 1916, 16; *Lexington Herald*, 10 June 1916, 6. The last quote is from *Lexington Leader*, 5 June 1916, 1.

42. This account of the auto and style show was developed from *Lexington Leader*, 29 March 1916, 1, 8; *Lexington Herald*, 30 January 1916, sec. 2, p. 4; 17 February 1916, 8; 25 March 1916, 1, 3; 26 March 1916, Automobile section, 1; 28 March 1916, 7; 30 March 1916, 1, 8. The quote is from *Lexington Herald*, 30 March 1916, 8.

43. This account was developed from *Lexington Herald*, 25 March 1916, 1, 3; 26 March 1916, 1; 26 March 1916, Automobile section, 1; 28 March 1916, 7; 30 March 1916, 1, 8. The quotes are from *Lexington Herald*, 30 March 1916, 8; 25 March 1916, 3; 30 March 1916, 1; 1 April 1916, 9.

44. The quotes are from *Lexington Leader*, 26 March 1916, 4; *Lexington Her-*

ald, 26 March 1916, 4; *Lexington Leader,* 29 March 1916, 1; *Lexington Herald,* 30 March 1916, 1. Also see *Lexington Herald,* 28 March 1916, 1; *Lexington Leader,* 29 March 1916, 1, 8; 30 March 1916, 1, 8.

45. For press reports on the large crowds, see *Lexington Leader,* 30 March 1916, 1, 8; 1 April 1916, 1, 8; *Lexington Herald,* 31 March 1916, 1, 6; 1 April 1916, 1, 3. For the number of automobiles sold, see *Lexington Leader,* 2 April 1916, sec. 2, p. 4. For the announcement of a follow-up fall fashion show and the first quote, see *Lexington Leader,* 1 April 1916, 1. For the editorial promoting an all-purpose municipal building and the second quote, see *Lexington Leader,* 30 March 1916, 1. The third quote is from *Lexington Leader,* 10 May 1916, 4. For additional *Lexington Leader* articles on the campaign for an all-purpose municipal building, see 31 March 1916, 1, 4; 2 April 1916, 1, 4; 3 April 1916, 6. For the quotes characterizing the crowds at the auto-style show and its educational nature, see *Lexington Herald,* 31 March 1916, 1, 6. For attendance at *Birth of a Nation,* see *Lexington Leader,* 26 March 1916, 1.

46. The first quote is from Thomas D. Clark's introduction to Loretta Gilliam Brock, *A History of the Woman's Club of Central Kentucky, 1894–1994* (Lexington: Woman's Club of Central Kentucky, 1996), ix. The second quote is from Nancy K. Forderhase's introduction to ibid., xiii. The third quote is from *Lexington Leader,* 25 March 1917, sec. 4, p. 5. For the argument that the clubs' public service projects were self-serving and the last two quotes, see Anne Ruggles Gere, *Intimate Practices: Literacy and Cultural Work in U.S. Women's Clubs, 1880–1920* (Urbana: University of Illinois Press, 1997), 12.

47. For the monthly activity calendars of the WCCK, see *Lexington Herald,* 2 January 1910, 4; 30 January 1916, sec. 3, p. 3. For the WCCK's prewar interest in dramatics and the related quotes, see Brock, *A History of the Woman's Club,* 75. For the term "Play Producing Committee," see, for instance, *Lexington Herald,* 30 April 1916, sec. 3, p. 4. For the account of the plays and the related quotes, see *Lexington Herald,* 7 May 1916, sec. 3, p. 5; also see *Lexington Leader,* 7 May 1916, sec. 3, p. 5. For the Drama Study Department's "entertainment," see *Lexington Herald,* 7 May 1916, sec. 3, pp. 1, 4; 13 May 1916, 7. For Margaret Preston as chair of the Department of Literature, see, for instance, *Lexington Herald,* 30 January 1916, sec. 3, p. 3.

48. The first quote from the *Atlantic Monthly* is cited in Hazel Dicken-Garcia, *Journalistic Standards in Nineteenth-Century America* (Madison: University of Wisconsin Press, 1989), 164. For the progressives' impulse to educate the public and their view of the theater as an educative force, see Kett, *Pursuit of Knowledge,* 321–22, chap. 9; the second quote is from p. 297. For a discussion of amateur theatrical productions in early Lexington, see Beryl Meek, "A Record of the Theater in Lexington, Kentucky from 1799–1850" (master's thesis, State University of Iowa, 1930), chap. 2, copy available in Kentucky Room, Central Branch, Lexington Public Library. The last quote is from *Lexington Herald,* 28 May 1916, sec. 4, p. 9.

49. For church dramatic clubs and the related quotes, see *Lexington Herald,* 16 January 1916, sec. 2, p. 6; *Lexington Leader,* 16 January 1916, sec. 4, p. 6; *Lexington Herald,* 22 March 1916, sec. 2, p. 2; *Lexington Leader,* 16 May 1916, 6; 22 May 1916, 9; *Lexington Herald,* 28 May 1916, sec. 3, p. 3.

50. For the Morton High School senior class play, see *Lexington Herald,* 5 February 1916, 3. For the Chandler Normal School, see Wright, *A History of Blacks in Kentucky,* 118–19; John D. Wright Jr., *Lexington: Heart of the Bluegrass* (Lexington: Lexington–Fayette County Historic Commission, 1982), 119–20. For the Chandler Normal School production at the opera house and related quotes, see *Lexington Leader,* 23 April 1916, sec. 4, p. 6; 25 April 1916, 12; 28 April 1916, 5. For the Russell School's May Day performance, see *Lexington Leader,* 17 May 1916, 3. For the city and county school commencement programs, see *Lexington Leader,* 5 June 1916, 7; 6 June 1916, 5; *Lexington Herald,* 4 June 1916, 10.

51. For the account of the Association of Infant Welfare and related quotes, see *Lexington Herald,* 16 January 1916, sec. 4, p. 8. For the suffrage play at the Phoenix Hotel, see *Lexington Herald,* 4 May 1915, 1. For the Fayette County Equal Rights Association, see Wright, *Heart of the Bluegrass,* 151. For the DAR production at the Ada Meade Theater and related quotes, see *Lexington Herald,* 4 March 1916, 7; 5 March 1916, 1; also see *Lexington Herald,* 22 February 1916, 7; 27 February 1916, sec. 3, p. 3; 3 March 1916, sec. 2, p. 1; 5 March 1916, sec. 3, p. 2.

52. This account of the Kirmess was developed from *Lexington Herald,* 5 February 1916, 5; 6 February 1916, sec. 3, p. 1; 8 February 1916, 7; 13 February 1916, sec. 3, pp. 1, 2; *Lexington Leader,* 16 February 1916, 6. The quote is from *Lexington Herald,* 6 February 1916, sec. 3, p. 1.

53. For a detailed description of the planned street parade and the related quote, see *Lexington Herald,* 12 February 1916, 12. For the complete list of members of the Kirmess Ball Reception Committee, see *Lexington Herald,* 13 February 1916, sec. 3, p. 2.

54. For the cancellation of the parade and related weather reports, see *Lexington Herald,* 13 February 1916, 3, 4, sec. 3, p. 1; 15 February 1916, 4; *Lexington Leader,* 14 February 1916, 1. For the controversy over the cabaret scene and related quotes, see *Lexington Herald,* 14 February 1916, 6; *Lexington Leader,* 14 February 1916, 1. For the money raised for the Baby Milk Fund, see *Lexington Herald,* 17 February 1916, 6. For a detailed description of the Kirmess Ball and the related quote, see *Lexington Herald,* 17 February 1916, 7. For the last-minute cancellation by the governor and lieutenant governor and the last quote, see *Lexington Herald,* 16 February 1916, 1, 2.

55. For the announcement of Kincaid's course of lectures and a schedule of them, see *Lexington Herald,* 16 January 1916, sec. 3, p. 1. For a description of the "social hour," see *Lexington Leader,* 15 February 1916, 7. For the personal information about Kincaid, see Terry L. Birdwhistell, "An Educated Difference: Women at the University of Kentucky through the Second World War" (PhD diss., University

of Kentucky, 1994), 15–17, 52–53; James F. Hopkins, *University of Kentucky: Origins and Early Years* (Lexington: University of Kentucky Press, 1951), 234–35. For a complete list of those attending Kincaid's course of lectures, see *Lexington Leader,* 18 January 1916, 7. For Mrs. Wickliffe Preston's tenure as WCCK president, see Brock, *A History of the Woman's Club,* 139. For Margaret Preston as chair of the Literature Department and Laura Kincaid as chair of the Social Service Department, see, for instance, *Lexington Herald,* 30 January 1916, sec. 3, p. 3. For Mrs. Charles Berryman's leadership role in establishing Lexington's first public art museum, see Brock, *A History of the Woman's Club,* 165. For an extended discussion of nineteenth-century, middle-class women's study clubs, see Theodora Penny Martin, *The Sound of Our Own Voices: Women's Study Clubs 1860–1910* (Boston: Beacon Press, 1987). Martin argues that these clubs, which met in members' homes, linked intellectual and moral improvement so that "piety was linked to learning, and education to formation of moral character" (34).

56. *Lexington Leader,* 18 January 1916, 7.

57. For the *Lexington Leader*'s coverage of all ten Kincaid lectures, see 18 January 1916, 7; 25 January 1916, 8; 1 February 1916, 7; 8 February 1916, 8; 15 February 1916, 7; 22 February 1916, 8; 29 February 1916, 10; 7 March 1916, 8; 14 March 1916, 8; 21 March 1916, 6. For supplementary articles in the *Lexington Herald,* see 16 January 1916, sec. 3, p. 1; 25 January 1916, 5; 12 March 1916, sec. 3, p. 1; 21 March 1916, 16. The first quote is from *Lexington Leader,* 25 January 1916, 8. For Kincaid's lecture on Vachell's play and the related quotes, see *Lexington Leader,* 15 February 1916, 7. For Horace Annesley Vachell, see Stanley J. Kunitz and Howard Haycraft, eds., *Twentieth Century Authors: A Biographical Dictionary of Modern Literature* (New York: H. W. Wilson, 1942), 1436–37; Hal May, ed., *Contemporary Authors: A Bio-Bibliographical Guide to Current Writers in Fiction, General Nonfiction, Poetry, Journalism, Drama, Motion Pictures, Television, and Other Fields,* vol. 120 (Detroit: Gale Research, 1987), 392. For Kincaid's lecture on Masefield's play and the related quote, see *Lexington Leader,* 7 March 1916, 8. For John Edward Masefield, see *The Oxford Companion to English Literature,* 1985 ed., s.v., "Masefield, John Edward."

58. For Kentuckians' opinions about the European war, see Klotter, *Portrait in Paradox,* 235. For the sinking of the *Lusitania* and other Allied shipping incidents and Wilson's request for a war declaration, see Harries and Harries, *The Last Days of Innocence.* 37–40, 61–73. For the cited editorials and related quotes, see *Lexington Herald,* 21 April 1916, 4; *Lexington Leader,* 14 February 1917, 4; 15 February 1917, 4; 16 February 1917, 4; 19 February 1917, 4; 9 March 1917, 4; 11 March 1917, 4; 19 March 1917, 4; 22 March 1917, 4. The quote related to the war sentiments of the American press is from *Lexington Leader,* 22 March 1917, 4. For "The Iron Shark," see *Lexington Herald,* 19 May 1916, 9.

59. This account of Villa, Carranza, and the Mexican incident is largely drawn from Allen Brinkley, Richard N. Current, Frank Freidel, and T. Harry Williams,

American History, a Survey, vol. 2, *Since 1865,* 8th ed. (New York: McGraw-Hill, 1991), 662–64; the quote is from pp. 663–64.

60. The quotes are from *Lexington Leader,* 11 January 1917, 1; *Lexington Herald,* 12 March 1916, 1; 27 March 1916, 4.

61. The quotes are from *Lexington Herald,* 14 April 1916, 4; 16 April 1916, 4; 27 April 1916, 4. For other *Lexington Herald* editorials dealing with Villa or preparedness, see 9 May 1916, 4; 11 May 1916, 4.

62. For the Villa affair as a "dress rehearsal" for U.S. military involvement in Europe, see Edward M. Coffman, *The War to End All Wars: The American Military Experience in World War I* (1968; reprint, Lexington: University Press of Kentucky, 1998), 13–15. For the preparedness lobby, see Harries and Harries, *The Last Days of Innocence,* 37–40.

63. The editorial title is from *Lexington Herald,* 27 May 1916, 4. For the New York parade and the related quote, see *Lexington Herald,* 14 May 1916, 1, sec. 2, p. 3. For the Chicago parade and the related quote, see *Lexington Herald,* 4 June 1916, 12. For the Sons of the American Revolution meeting and related quotes, see *Lexington Herald,* 9 June 1916, 1, 8.

64. The first three quotes are from *Lexington Herald,* 10 June 1916, 5; 9 June 1916, 10; *Lexington Leader,* 9 June 1916, 12. For *Lexington Herald* editorials related to the preparedness parade, see 10 June 1916, 4; 11 June 1916, 4; 12 June 1916, 4. The last quote is from *Lexington Herald,* 11 June 1916, 1.

65. For the *Lexington Leader's* coverage of the organizational meetings prior to the preparedness parade, see 12 June 1916, 1, 5. For Margaret Preston as FERA recording secretary, see Margaret Preston Diary, 23 January 1913, Margaret Preston Johnston Papers, in Preston-Johnston Papers, Special Collections and Archives, Margaret I. King Library, University of Kentucky, Lexington (hereafter, MP Diary); also see *Fayette Equal Rights Association Minute Book,* 6 October 1917–4 June 1918, in Fayette Equal Rights Association Records, 1917–1920, in Special Collections and Archives, Margaret I. King Library. For Preston's comments on the FERA meeting prior to the preparedness parade, see MP Diary, 12 June 1916. The first quote is from Mary Ryan, *Women in Public: Between Banners and Ballots, 1825–1880* (Baltimore: Johns Hopkins University Press, 1990; paperback ed., 1992), 44–45. For a discussion of Columbia as a "stern goddess" in American prewar propaganda, see Ronald Schaffer, *America in the Great War: The Rise of the War Welfare State* (New York: Oxford University Press, 1991; paperback ed., 1994), 6–12; the last quote is from p. 7.

66. For Margaret Preston as the vice president of the WCCK, see MP Diary, 9 May 1916. The first three quotes are from *Lexington Herald,* 12 June 1916, 1; the last quote is from *Lexington Leader,* 13 June 1916, 7.

67. For the parade route, see *Lexington Herald,* 13 June 1916, 1, 3. For the first quote, the list of participating groups, and the "colored people" quotes, see *Lexington Herald,* 14 June 1916, 1, 6. For the parade connected with the dedication of

Douglass Park, see *Lexington Leader,* 5 July 1916, 5. The last two quotes are from *Lexington Leader,* 14 June 1916, 1. Also see *Lexington Herald,* 15 June 1916, 1, 6.

68. *Lexington Herald,* 15 June 1916, 1, 6; *Lexington Leader,* 14 June 1916, 1; MP Diary, 14 June 1916.

CHAPTER SIX: "IN HER MOST CHARMING, CHARACTERISTIC WAY"

The quote in the chapter title is from *Lexington Leader,* 6 April 1916, 8.

1. For Wickliffe Preston's front-page obituary with biographical details, see *Lexington Herald,* 14 June 1914, 1. Margaret Preston Diary, 12 June 1914, 13 June 1914, Margaret Preston Johnston Papers, in Preston-Johnston Papers, Special Collections and Archives, Margaret I. King Library, University of Kentucky, Lexington (hereafter, MP Diary). The quotes describing Wickliffe Preston are from Joseph M. Tanner, "Fifty Years' Recollections of Lexington and Vicinity, Its People and Institutions, 1926 (?)," typescript, 19, in Special Collections and Archives, Margaret I. King Library. General William Preston's lineage is from Orlando Brown, *Memoranda of the Preston Family* (Frankfort, Ky.: Hodges, Todd and Pruett, 1842), 1–10, reprinted copy in Special Collections and Archives, Margaret I. King Library; the quote related to Colonel William Preston is from p. 6. For General William Preston, also see *The Kentucky Encyclopedia,* 1992 ed., s.v. "Preston, William"; for Robert Wickliffe, see ibid., s.v. "Wickliffe, Robert." For General Preston as Morgan's pallbearer, see James A. Ramage, *Rebel Raider: The Life of General John Hunt Morgan* (Lexington: University Press of Kentucky, 1986), 249.

2. The first quote is from Robert Wickliffe Preston Johnston, interview with Kolan Morelock, 5 October 1998, tape on file with the author (hereafter, RWPJ interview). The second and third quotes are from Margaret Preston Johnston [Autobiographical Essay], circa early 1940s, 7, Margaret Preston Johnston Papers, in Preston-Johnston Papers, Special Collections and Archives, Margaret I. King Library, University of Kentucky, Lexington (hereafter, MPJ Autobiographical Essay; the essay is not paginated, so the page numbers provided are as accurate as possible under the circumstances). For Wickliffe Preston's educational background and the last quote, see *Lexington Herald,* 14 June 1914, 1.

3. For the front-page marriage announcement of Wickliffe Preston and Sarah Brant McDowell, see *Daily Lexington Transcript,* 1 February 1883, 1. Biographical information related to Sarah Brant McDowell is from *Lexington Herald,* 28 February 1923, 1; *Lexington Leader,* 28 February 1923, 8; MPJ Autobiographical Essay. The first two quotes are from MPJ Autobiographical Essay, 5–6. The third quote is from Loretta Gilliam Brock, *A History of the Woman's Club of Central Kentucky, 1894–1994* (Lexington: Woman's Club of Central Kentucky, 1996), 139. The fourth quote is from *Lexington Leader,* 28 February 1923, 8. The fifth quote is from MPJ Autobiographical Essay, 8. For the location and size of the Preston farm and the last quote, see ibid., 2. For the name "Muir," see ibid., 5. The current name

of the farm and the comment that Wick Preston "loved horses" are from RWPJ interview.

4. For the announcement of Margaret Preston's birth, see *Lexington Morning Transcript,* 3 September 1885, 2. For the exact date of Margaret's birth, I relied on her tombstone in the Johnston Family Cemetery, Johnston Farm, Johnston Road, Fayette County, Kentucky. I took the date of her brother William's birth from his tombstone in section 28, Lexington Cemetery. Quotes are from MPJ Autobiographical Essay, 10, 2, 1, 5, 8; RWPJ interview; MPJ Autobiographical Essay, 9.

5. For biographical information on General William Draper, including his marriage to Susan Preston, see *Lexington Leader,* 29 January 1910, 6; 31 January 1910, 8. For the marriage of Jessie Preston to George A. Draper and the related quotes, see *Kentucky (Lexington) Leader,* 7 November 1890, 4.

6. For Wick Preston as a member of the Lexington Gun Club, see *Lexington Daily Press,* 1 August 1885, 4. The first three quotes are from MPJ Autobiographical Essay, 8, 10; for the family's church attendance, see ibid., 9. For the underlying causes of the depression in the early 1890s and Coxey's "army," see Worth Robert Miller, "Farmers and Third-Party Politics," in *The Gilded Age: Essays on the Origins of Modern America,* ed. Charles W. Calhoun (Wilmington, Del.: Scholarly Resources, 1996), 251–52. For the effects of the depression in the South, see Edward L. Ayers, *Promise of the New South: Life after Reconstruction* (New York: Oxford University Press, 1992), 98, 112, 119, 252–54, 283–84. For the depression in Kentucky, see Hambleton Tapp and James C. Klotter, *Kentucky: Decades of Discord, 1865–1900* (Frankfort: Kentucky Historical Society, 1977), 297–98; the fourth quote is from p. 297. The fifth and sixth quotes are from MPJ Autobiographical Essay, 10. The seventh quote is from *Kentucky (Lexington) Leader,* 7 January 1894, 1. Also see *Kentucky (Lexington) Leader,* 24 January 1894, 1. The last quote is from MPJ Autobiographical Essay, 11.

7. The first three quotes are from MPJ Autobiographical Essay, 11, 12. For the deaths of Margaret's grandmother and great-grandmother in 1898, see ibid., 15. For information about the house, Glendower, and the last quote, see Bettie L. Kerr and John D. Wright Jr., *Lexington: A Century in Photographs* (Lexington: Lexington–Fayette County Historic Commission, 1984), 77.

8. For Margaret and William's instruction at home and the first two quotes, see MPJ Autobiographical Essay, 13. For Miss Williams's school, see Kerr and Wright, *Lexington: A Century in Photographs,* 63, 163. For Ella Williams's front-page obituary and the third quote, see *Lexington Herald,* 7 March 1915, 1. For the remaining quotes, see MPJ Autobiographical Essay, 14.

9. This account of Margaret Preston's life during 1902 was developed from MP Diary, 1 January–11 July 1902. The quotes are from ibid., 12 January 1902, 15 January 1902, 3 January 1902, 6 January 1902, 3 February 1902, 17 March 1902. For Margaret's description of her brother William's wedding, see ibid., 11 February 1911. For Sarah Preston organizing a UDC spelling match, see ibid., 18 November

1913. For Sarah Preston as president of the WCCK in 1906, see Brock, *A History of the Woman's Club*, 139.

10. The quotes are from MP Diary, 4 January 1902, 21 May 1902, 28 June 1902, 4 January 1902, 8 January 1902, 4 February 1902, 3 April 1902, 10 April 1902, 24 May 1902, 27 May 1902.

11. For Victorian Americans at play and the middle-class vacation in the early twentieth century, see Thomas J. Schlereth, *Victorian America: Transformations in Everyday Life, 1876–1915* (New York: HarperCollins, 1991; HarperPerennial, 1992), 209–17; the first quote is from p. 214. The second quote is from MP Diary, 11 July 1902.

12. For Wick Preston residing at the Lexington Club, see Wickliffe Preston to Margaret Preston, 22 July 1907, 1 September 1907, Margaret Preston Johnston Correspondence File, Margaret Preston Johnston Papers, in Preston-Johnston Papers, Special Collections and Archives, Margaret I. King Library, University of Kentucky, Lexington (hereafter, MPJ Correspondence File). The quotes are from MPJ Autobiographical Essay, 15–17.

13. This account of Margaret Preston's daily life at Meadow Wood was developed from MP Diary, 17 July–14 October 1907. The first and second quotes are from RWPJ interview. For the importance of reading in Victorian America, see Louise L. Stevenson, *The Victorian Homefront: American Thought and Culture, 1860–1880* (New York: Twayne Publishers, 1991), chap. 2. For the view that the Victorian era extended to World War I, see Schlereth, *Victorian America*, xii; the third quote is from p. 210. The last quote is from MP Diary, 23 September 1907.

14. For the White Sulphur Springs resort, see Schlereth, *Victorian America*, 214. For Margaret Preston's assessment of the people she met at White Sulphur Springs, see MP Diary, 26 July 1910; the first quote is from ibid., 24 July 1910. The last two quotes are from William Preston to Margaret Preston, 1 August 1910, MPJ Correspondence File.

15. For typical wording of letters to his sister, see William Preston to Margaret Preston, 4 December 1904, 11 February 1906, MPJ Correspondence File. For William at State College in 1904 and the first quote, see William Preston to Margaret Preston, 4 December 1904, MPJ Correspondence File. For his attention to Gretchen Miller in the fall of 1904, see William Preston to Margaret Preston, 20 October 1904, MPJ Correspondence File. For evidence that Aunt Jessie Draper was financing William's attendance at the University of Virginia, see William Preston to Sarah (Mrs. Wickliffe) Preston, 4 February 1907, Sarah McDowell Preston Correspondence File, Sarah McDowell Preston Papers, in Preston-Johnston Papers, Special Collections and Archives, Margaret I. King Library, University of Kentucky, Lexington (hereafter, SMP Correspondence File). The last quote is from William Preston to Sarah Preston, 11 September 1906, SMP Correspondence File.

16. The first and second quotes are from William Preston to Sarah Preston, 31 January 1907, SMP Correspondence File. For William's explanations of his

withdrawal from the University of Virginia, see William Preston to Sarah Preston, [?] May 1907, 26 May 1907, SMP Correspondence File. The third quote is from William Preston to Sarah Preston [postcard], 15 April 1907; the fourth quote is from William Preston to Sarah Preston, [?] September 1907; the fifth quote is from Wickliffe Preston to William Preston, 4 September 1907, all in SMP Correspondence File. For William's course of study in the agricultural school, see William Preston to Sarah Preston, 14 September 1907, SMP Correspondence File. (Note that correspondence to William Preston during the early twentieth century is located in his mother's correspondence file.)

17. The first and second quotes are from William Preston to Sarah Preston, 17 April 1909, SMP Correspondence File; the third quote is from William Preston to Margaret Preston, 11 May 1909, MPJ Correspondence File; the fourth quote is from William Preston to Margaret Preston, 1 August 1910, MPJ Correspondence File. For evidence of Margaret's investments in Canada, see *City of Calgary: Demand for Taxes 1912*, 30 June 1912, Margaret Preston Johnston Papers, in Preston-Johnston Papers, Special Collections and Archives, Margaret I. King Library, University of Kentucky, Lexington. The fifth quote is from William Preston to Margaret Preston, 27 September 1910, MPJ Correspondence File. For William Preston and Gretchen Miller's wedding date, see MP Diary, 28 February 1911. The sixth quote is from William Preston to Margaret Preston, 12 June 1911, MPJ Correspondence File; the seventh quote is from Gretchen Miller Preston to Margaret Preston, 11 March 1911, MPJ Correspondence File; the eighth quote is from MP Diary, 13 December 1911. For discussion of the 1912 purchase of William and Gretchen Preston's farm on the Georgetown Road, see Gretchen Miller Preston to Margaret Preston, 8 February 1912, and William Preston to Margaret Preston, 11 February 1912, MPJ Correspondence File. The last quote is from MP Diary 15 March 1912.

18. For the Neville sisters tutoring Margaret, see MPJ Autobiographical Essay, 18. For Linda Neville, see *The Kentucky Encyclopedia*, 1992 ed., s.v. "Neville, Linda"; for Linda Neville's obituary and eulogy, see *Lexington Herald*, 3 June 1961, 1, 10. Less celebrated than her sister, Mary Neville died many years earlier; for her brief obituary article, see *Lexington Herald*, 13 October 1931, 1. For Aunt Jessie's congratulatory letters, see Jessie Preston Draper to Margaret Preston, 22 June 1904, 18 July 1904, MPJ Correspondence File. For expenses at Bryn Mawr for the 1904–1905 academic year, see itemized receipt dated 17 October 1904, MPJ Correspondence File. The first and second quotes are from *Rockefeller Hall*, a four-page printed description of the facility, including floor plans, attached to Jessie Preston Draper to Margaret Preston, 18 July 1904, MPJ Correspondence File. The last three quotes are from Barbara M. Solomon, *In the Company of Educated Women: A History of Women and Higher Education in America* (New Haven, Conn.: Yale University Press, 1985), 66, 71, 78.

19. The first quote is from MPJ Autobiographical Essay, 18; the second and third quotes are from Margaret Preston to Sarah Preston, 10 October 1904, SMP

Correspondence File. For the emphasis on "academic rigor" at Bryn Mawr, see Solomon, *In the Company of Educated Women,* 49. The remaining quotes are from Margaret Preston to William Preston, 17 October 1904, 19 November 1904; Margaret Preston to Sarah Preston, 31 October 1904, [?] November 1904, SMP Correspondence File.

20. For Margaret's continuing struggle to adjust to college life, see Margaret Preston to Sarah Preston 5 November 1904, 8 November 1904, 10 November 1904, 12 November 1904, 15 November 1904, 17 November 1904, 30 November 1904, SMP Correspondence File. The quotes are from Margaret Preston to Sarah Preston 13 November 1904, SMP Correspondence File; Margaret Preston to Sarah Preston, 8 November 1904, SMP Correspondence File; Wickliffe Preston to Margaret Preston, 20 November 1904, MPJ Correspondence File; Mary Neville to Margaret Preston, 4 December 1904, MPJ Correspondence File; E. P. Harrison to Margaret Preston, 19 December 1904, MPJ Correspondence File. For E. P. Harrison as circulation manager, see *Lexington Leader,* 2 January 1910, 4.

21. The quotes are from Margaret Preston to Sarah Preston, 18 November 1904, SMP Correspondence File. For Margaret's chocolate parties for the "Aryans," see Margaret Preston to Sarah Preston, 6 February 1905, SMP Correspondence File. Margaret corresponded with several of her college friends long after she left Bryn Mawr. For example, see "Phoenix" to Margaret Preston, 25 June 1907; Ethel Phillips Vick to Margaret Preston, 4 April 1909; Marjorie Young to Margaret Preston, 14 February 1910; Anne Jackson to Margaret Preston, 26 November 1911, MPJ Correspondence File. In the many letters from "Phoenix," the writer referred to both herself and Margaret only by this nickname, which they had apparently called each other at college.

22. The first two quotes are from Margaret Preston to Sarah Preston, 6 January 1905; the third quote is from Margaret Preston to Sarah Preston, 9 January 1905. Margaret mentions writing the scene for the freshman play in Margaret Preston to Sarah Preston, 15 February 1905. For mention of *Romeo and Juliet,* see Margaret Preston to Sarah Preston, 13 January 1905, The fourth quote is from Margaret Preston to Sarah Preston, 11 February 1905; the last quote is from Margaret Preston to William Preston, 19 February 1905. All the cited letters are in SMP Correspondence File.

23. For Margaret's introduction to Charles Horner, see Margaret Preston to Sarah Preston, 7 March 1905, SMP Correspondence File. The quotes are from Margaret Preston to Sarah Preston, 12 March 1905, 12 November 1905, 23 March 1906, 26 November 1905, 26 April 1905, all in SMP Correspondence File.

24. For the college settlement movement, see Solomon, *In the Company of Educated Women,* 109–10; the first quote is from p. 110. The second quote is from Margaret Preston to Sarah Preston, 26 November 1905, SMP Correspondence File; the third and fourth quotes are from Margaret Preston to Sarah Preston, 11 February 1906, SMP Correspondence File. See Emma Morrell to Margaret Preston, 30 October 1904, 4 May 1905, MPJ Correspondence File. The fifth quote is from *St.*

John's Collegiate Institute and Industrial School, n.d., four-page brochure, in Kentucky Education Collection, Special Collections and Archives, Margaret I. King Library, University of Kentucky, Lexington. For information about St. John's, also see *Lexington Leader,* 18 May 1908, 2. For a succinct discussion of the Day Law, see *The Kentucky Encyclopedia,* 1992 ed., s.v. "Day Law." The last quote is from William Frost to Margaret Preston, 3 August 1909, MPJ Correspondence File.

25. The first quote is from Sarah Preston to Margaret Preston, [?] May 1905, MPJ Correspondence File; the second quote is from Dr. J. A. Bayard Kane to Mrs. Wickliffe (Sarah) Preston, 4 October 1905, SMP Correspondence File. For this description of neurasthenia and the third and fourth quotes, see Schlereth, *Victorian America,* 289–90. The fifth quote is from Jessie Preston Draper to Sallie (Sarah) Preston, 15 October 1905, SMP Correspondence File; the last quote is from Jessie Preston Draper to Margaret Preston, 15 October 1905, MPJ Correspondence File.

26. The first quote is from Margaret Preston to Sarah Preston, 2 November 1905, SMP Correspondence File; the second quote is from Wickliffe Preston to Margaret Preston, 26 November, 1905, MPJ Correspondence File. Copy of the original lease for 200 Market Street, dated 1 April 1906, is in SMP Correspondence File. For Mrs. Wickliffe (Sarah) Preston's election as president of the WCCK, see *Lexington Leader,* 4 March 1906, sec. 2, p. 2. The third and fourth quotes are from Margaret Preston to Sarah Preston, 16 February 1906, 18 March 1906, SMP Correspondence File. For the move to the Waverly Apartments on Hampton Court, see MP Diary, 29 October 1912. To my knowledge, Margaret never mentioned the Waverly Apartments by name in writing, referring simply to the apartment or the "flat," but several pieces of correspondence to her at Hampton Court do contain the name of the apartments, including a letter on Civic League stationery from Madge Breckinridge; see Mrs. Desha Breckinridge to Margaret Preston, 2 August 1917, MPJ Correspondence File. For local press coverage of Margaret Preston's marriage to Philip Preston Johnston Jr. on Thursday, 8 November 1917, see *Lexington Herald,* 9 November 1917, 6; *Lexington Leader,* 9 November 1917, sec. 2, p. 2.

27. For Aunt Jessie Draper's providing the money for Margaret's debutante gowns, see Jessie Draper to Margaret Preston, 2 November 1906, MPJ Correspondence File. For Margaret's trip to the Northeast in the early spring of 1906 and her daily activities upon her return to Lexington, see MP Diary, 15 February–15 July 1906. For Margaret's monthly allowance from Aunt Jessie, see Jessie Draper to Margaret Preston, 28 April 1915, MPJ Correspondence File. For Jessie (Mrs. George A.) Draper's obituary and eulogy in the Lexington press, which indicates that she died at her Boston home only hours after her daughter, Helen Draper, married the nephew of former President William Howard Taft on 10 February 1917, see *Lexington Leader,* 12 February 1917, 6. In May 1917 George Draper, Jessie's widower, wrote to Margaret to say that the monthly allowance was ending and that Jessie had bequeathed Margaret a final sum of $2,000; see George A. Draper to Margaret Preston, 31 May 1917, MPJ Correspondence File.

28. The first quote is from MP Diary, 12 April 1907. For mention of Philip Preston Johnston Jr. (hereafter, Preston Johnston) in Margaret's diary in the spring and summer of 1907, see MP Diary, 3 May 1907, 9 May 1907, 16 May 1907, 24 May 1907, 26 May 1907, 2 June 1907, 3 June 1907, 9 June 1907, 13 June 1907, 18 June 1907, 26 June 1907, 4 July 1907, 6 July 1907, 13 July 1907, 14 July 1907, 15 July 1907. For the first located letter from Preston to Margaret when she was in Virginia during the summer and fall of 1907, see 22 July 1907, MPJ Correspondence File. For Margaret's letter in response, see Margaret Preston to Preston Johnston, 25 July 1907, Philip Preston Johnston Jr. Correspondence File, Philip Preston Johnston Jr. Papers, in Preston-Johnston Papers, Special Collections and Archives, Margaret I. King Library, University of Kentucky, Lexington (hereafter, PPJ Correspondence File). The second quote is from Preston Johnston to Margaret Preston, 26 August 1907, MPJ Correspondence File; the third quote is from Margaret Preston to Preston Johnston, 5 August 1907, PPJ Correspondence File; the fourth quote is from Preston Johnston to Margaret Preston, 22 September 1907, MPJ Correspondence File; the last quote is from Margaret Preston to Preston Johnston, 28 September 1907, PPJ Correspondence File.

29. For Preston Johnston's date of birth, his attendance at LSU, and the first quote, see *Lexington Herald*, 18 January 1937, 1. Preston's date of birth is also on his tombstone in the Johnston Family Cemetery, Johnston Farm, Johnston Road, Fayette County, Kentucky. For Major P. P. Johnston's 1868 graduation from law school, see *Catalogue of Kentucky University, 1899–1900* (Lexington: Transylvania Printing Company, 1900), 92, copy available in Special Collections and Archives, J. Douglas Gay Jr. Library, Transylvania University, Lexington. Note that this issue of the Kentucky University catalog contains the majors and graduation dates of all graduates of the institution between 1841 and 1900. For Major P. P. Johnston as head of the National Trotting Association, see *Lexington Leader*, 10 February 1910, 2; for his election as head of the Breckinridge UCV, see *Lexington Herald*, 2 April 1915, 3. For the term "Inner Lost Cause," see Ramage, *Rebel Raider*, 251. Evidence that Preston Johnston was a member of Sigma Nu at LSU is from A. K. Read to Preston Johnston, 29 July 1901, PPJ Correspondence File; and RWPJ interview. For Preston's employment in Chattanooga, Tennessee, see (signature illegible), Cincinnati, New Orleans & Texas Pacific Railway, to Preston Johnston, 25 September 1899, PPJ Correspondence File; *Kentuckian: A Monthly Magazine* (September 1901): 12, copy available in Special Collections and Archives, Margaret I. King Library, University of Kentucky, Lexington. For Major Johnston's support of his son's desire to manage the family farm, see P. P. Johnston to Preston Johnston, 11 November 1899, PPJ Correspondence File. For Major P. P. Johnston as a member of the State College Board of Trustees, see *Lexington Leader*, 5 June 1890, 8. The last two quotes are from P. P. Johnston to Preston Johnston, 26 November 1899, PPJ Correspondence File.

30. For biographical information on Sallie Chiles Johnston, see her obituary

article in *Lexington Morning Herald,* 20 February 1904, 6. For her letter to Preston in Tennessee, see Sallie Chiles Johnston to Preston Johnston, 13 August 1900, PPJ Correspondence File.

31. For the graduation of Pelham and Marius from State College in 1900, see *Kentucky State College Commencement* (pamphlet), 7 June 1900, PPJ Correspondence File; *Kentuckian: A Monthly Magazine* (September 1901): 3, copy available in Special Collections and Archives, Margaret I. King Library, University of Kentucky, Lexington. For biographical information on John Pelham Johnston, see his obituary article in *Lexington Herald,* 6 September 1935, 1, 3. For the violence of Lexington life, see Pelham Johnston to Preston Johnston, 27 January 1900, PPJ Correspondence File. Biographical information on Marius Johnston from RWPJ interview; obituary article, *Lexington Herald,* 6 March 1960, 1. For Marius's relationship to the Carnegie family, see *Lexington Leader,* 17 January 1916, 3; 29 March 1916, 1. For Marius's employment by the Carnegie family and the first quote, see Marius Johnston to Preston Johnston, 23 October 1907, PPJ Correspondence File. The second, fourth, and last quotes are from RWPJ interview; the third quote is from Marius Johnston to Preston Johnston, 23 May 1908, PPJ Correspondence File. For a detailed description of Marius hunting big game in Africa, see Preston Johnston to Margaret Preston, 26 August 1911, MPJ Correspondence File. The date of the marriage of Marius Johnston and Nancy Carnegie is from a printed wedding announcement, single sheet, in PPJ Correspondence File.

32. For the Progressive Era agricultural education movement and scientific farming methods, see Dewey W. Grantham, *Southern Progressivism: The Reconciliation of Progress and Tradition* (Knoxville: University of Tennessee Press, 1983), 332–33; James C. Klotter, *Kentucky: Portrait in Paradox, 1900–1950* (Frankfort: Kentucky Historical Society, 1996), 125–26. The first quote is from Preston Johnston to Margaret Preston, 25 October 1911, MPJ Correspondence File; the second quote is from Margaret Preston to Preston Johnston, 11 October 1914, PPJ Correspondence File. For the "Tobacco Trust" and efforts to break it, see Grantham, *Southern Progressivism,* 324–26; Klotter, *Portrait in Paradox,* 57–65. The last quote is from Preston Johnston to Margaret Preston, 1 October 1909, MPJ Correspondence File.

33. For Preston as school board chairman, see Margaret Preston to Preston Johnston, 20 August 1910, PPJ Correspondence File. For Preston's discussion of teacher salary schedules, see Preston Johnston to Margaret Preston, 1 August 1911, MPJ Correspondence File. For Preston's discussion of school building plans and the first quote, see Preston Johnston to Margaret Preston, 24 July 1911, MPJ Correspondence File. The second quote is from Margaret Preston to Preston Johnston, 28 July 1911, PPJ Correspondence File. For Margaret's use of the terms "darkies" and "d— Yankees," see Margaret Preston to Preston Johnston, 29 September 1911, 20 July 1911, PPJ Correspondence File. For Preston at the unveiling ceremony for the Morgan statue, see Preston Johnston to Margaret Preston, 19 October 1911,

MPJ Correspondence File. For Margaret's membership in the Children of the Confederacy, see *Lexington Herald*, 24 April 1910, sec. 3, p. 2; for her membership in the Daughters of the Confederacy, see *Lexington Herald*, 3 December 1939, 1. For Preston's nomination as a State University trustee, see Preston Johnston to Margaret Preston, 19 September 1914, MPJ Correspondence File. The last quote is from Margaret Preston to Preston Johnston, 22 September 1914, PPJ Correspondence File. For Preston's confirmation to the Board of Trustees, see W. T. Lafferty to Preston Johnston, 3 December 1914, PPJ Correspondence File.

34. For evidence of Margaret's promise to marry Preston in 1911, see Preston Johnston to Margaret Preston, 2 March 1912, MPJ Correspondence File. The first quote is from Margaret Preston to Preston Johnston, 10 February 1914, PPJ Correspondence File. For Margaret's desire to marry in October 1914, see Margaret Preston to Preston Johnston, 11 February 1914, PPJ Correspondence File. The second quote is from Margaret Preston to Preston Johnston, 20 February 1914, PPJ Correspondence File. For other examples of Margaret's ardent love letters to Preston during this period, see Margaret Preston to Preston Johnston, 25 January 1914, 5 February 1914, 8 February 1914, PPJ Correspondence File. For Preston's home-building plans, see Preston Johnston to Margaret Preston, 5 February 1914, MPJ Correspondence File. The third quote is from Preston Johnston to Margaret Preston, 11 September 1916, MPJ Correspondence File. For local press coverage of Margaret and Preston's marriage, see *Lexington Herald*, 9 November 1917, 6; *Lexington Leader*, 9 November 1917, sec. 2, p. 2. The fourth quote is from Desha Breckinridge to Margaret Preston Johnston, 27 November 1917, MPJ Correspondence File. For the date of Preston's death (17 January 1937), see *Lexington Herald*, 18 January 1937, 1. The dates of birth and death of Philip Preston Johnston [III] (28 August 1918–10 November 1964) and the date of birth of Robert Wickliffe Preston Johnston (30 May 1920) are from their respective tombstones in the Johnston Family Cemetery, Fayette County, Kentucky. The last quote is from MPJ Autobiographical Essay, 23.

35. For Margaret Preston as an upper-class social butterfly and the first quote, see Klotter, *Portrait in Paradox*, 93. For a sampling of the "society" columns in which Margaret Preston's name appeared, see *Lexington Herald*, 2 January 1910, 2; 4 January 1910, 5; 5 January 1910, 8; 7 January 1910, 8; 13 February 1910, sec. 3, p. 3; 9 April 1910, 6; 2 January 1916, sec. 3, p. 1; 11 February 1916, 9; 30 April 1916, sec. 3, p. 1; 2 May 1916, 9; 3 May 1916, 9; 5 May 1916, 9; 1 June 1916, 9; 3 January 1917, 5; 8 May 1917, 5; *Lexington Leader*, 2 January 1916, sec. 3, p. 4; 9 January 1916, sec. 3, p. 3; 23 January 1916, sec. 3, p. 2; 23 April 1916, sec. 3, p. 3; 4 May 1916, 8; 9 May 1916, 6; 28 January 1917, sec. 2, p. 4; 21 March 1917, sec. 2, p. 2; 25 March 1917, sec. 3, p. 8. The second and third quotes are from Margaret Preston to Preston Johnston, 18 September 1914, PPJ Correspondence File; the last quote is from Margaret Preston to Preston Johnston, 20 March 1914, PPJ Correspondence File. For Margaret's obituary and eulogy, see *Lexington Herald*, 1

May 1964, 1, 10; *Lexington Leader,* 30 April 1964, 1, 12; *Louisville Courier-Journal,* 1 May 1964, 12.

36. For the moral imperative of Victorian Americans and the first quote, see Schlereth, *Victorian America,* 243. For voluntarism among college-educated women, see Solomon, *In the Company of Educated Women,* 122–23. Margaret apparently joined the Women's Auxiliary of Christ Church Cathedral in 1908, as suggested by a letter from the Reverend William Capers to Margaret Preston, 20 March 1908, MPJ Correspondence File. For Margaret as a vestryman, see *Lexington (Sunday) Herald Leader,* 3 December 1939, 1. Margaret's diaries are replete with references to her work with the Altar Guild; for example, see MP Diary, 24 December 1907, 5 April 1908, 22 December 1910, 21 December 1912, 16 March 1913, 22 November 1914, 27 March 1915, 22 December 1915, 22 December 1916. For Margaret as vice president of the Altar Guild, see MP Diary, 30 October 1916. The last quote is from MPJ Autobiographical Essay, 21.

37. For the founding of the Saturday Industrial School in 1876, see Melba Porter Hay, "Madeline McDowell Breckinridge: Kentucky Suffragist and Progressive Reformer" (PhD diss., University of Kentucky, 1980), 44. The first three quotes are from *Lexington Morning Transcript,* 22 October 1885, 2; the last quote is from *Lexington Herald,* 22 May 1910, 3. Also see *Lexington Herald,* 1 June 1913, 6. For the location of the Industrial School in 1909, see the street map in *Transylvania University Catalogue Number 1910–1911* (Lexington: Transylvania University, 1911), back page, copy available in Special Collections and Archives, J. Douglas Gay Jr. Library, Transylvania University, Lexington.

38. The first quote is from MP Diary, 9 November 1907. Evidence of Margaret's work at the Industrial School can be found throughout her diaries from 1907 through 1917. The second quote is from MP Diary, 14 May 1910. For Margaret as Industrial School auditor, see *Lexington Herald,* 1 June 1913, 6. For Margaret in charge of the "Candy Table," see *Lexington Herald,* 20 May 1915, 11; *Lexington Leader,* 23 May 1915, 2. The third quote is from MP Diary, 13 May 1916; the last quote is from *Lexington Leader,* 1 January 1916, 8.

39. For a succinct history and description of the Settlement House movement before and during the Progressive Era, see Schlereth, *Victorian America,* 257–60. The first quote is from Margaret Preston to Sarah Preston, 11 February 1906, SMP Correspondence File; the second quote is from "Phoenix" to Margaret Preston, 25 June 1907, MPJ Correspondence File; the third quote is from "Peggy" to Margaret Preston, 27 December 1910, MPJ Correspondence File; the fourth quote is from Mary Neville to Margaret Preston, 14 August 1910, MPJ Correspondence File; the last quote is from *Certificate of Membership: Anti Child Slavery League of America,* 10 October 1906, single sheet, in SMP Correspondence File. For a detailed discussion of child labor reform in the South during the Progressive Era, see Grantham, *Southern Progressivism,* 178–99.

40. The first two quotes are from MP Diary, 25 May 1909, 3 January 1917.

For Madeline McDowell Breckinridge, the Associated Charities, the Lexington Civic League, and the Lincoln School, see Hay, "Madeline McDowell Breckinridge," chaps. 3, 5; *The Kentucky Encyclopedia,* 1992 ed., s.v. "Breckinridge, Madeline McDowell"; John D. Wright Jr., *Lexington: Heart of the Bluegrass* (Lexington: Lexington–Fayette County Historic Commission, 1982), 138–39; Kerr and Wright, *Lexington: A Century in Photographs,* 145. For Madeline McDowell Breckinridge and her struggles on behalf of "scientific charity," see Karen Tice, "Battle for Benevolence: Scientific Disciplinary Control vs. Indiscriminate Relief: Lexington Associated Charities and the Salvation Army, 1900–1918," *Journal of Sociology and Social Welfare* 19 (June 1992): 59–77. For a concise biographical sketch of Sophonisba Breckinridge, see *The Kentucky Encyclopedia,* 1992 ed., s.v. "Breckinridge, Sophonisba Preston"; Wright, *Heart of the Bluegrass,* 152.

41. For Margaret on the Civic League music committee, see MP Diary, 17 May 1909. The first quote is from Civic League Membership Committee to Messrs. Speyer & Son, 8 November 1912, MPJ Correspondence File. For Preston Johnston helping with the letters, see MP Diary, 7 November 1912. The last quote is from MP Diary, 30 November 1912. Also see *Dedication Exercises of Lincoln School,* 30 November 1912, printed program, single sheet, in or attached to MP Diary, 30 November 1912.

42. The first quote is from Madeline (Madge) Breckinridge to Margaret Preston, 15 March 1911, MPJ Correspondence File; the second quote is from Mary Neville to Margaret Preston, 22 October 1914, MPJ Correspondence File; the third quote is from Madeline (Madge) Breckinridge to Margaret Preston, [?] August 1918, MPJ Correspondence File. For examples of Madge's correspondence to Margaret on Civic League matters, see Madeline (Madge) Breckinridge to Margaret Preston, 31 July 1911, 20 August 1911, 12 April 1917, 18 April 1917, 2 August 1917; Madeline (Madge) Breckinridge to Margaret Preston Johnston, 20 August 1918, 21 September 1918, 16 October 1918, MPJ Correspondence File. For Margaret's election as vice president of the Civic League, see MP Diary, 22 February 1915; also see *Lexington Herald,* 23 February 1915, 1. For Margaret as vice chair of the playground committee, see *Lexington Leader,* 21 April 1916, 4. The last quote is from Madeline (Madge) Breckinridge to Margaret Preston, 2 August 1917, MPJ Correspondence File.

43. For Margaret's socializing with the Breckinridges, see MP Diary, 1 February 1917. For Margaret working with Madge on the Civic League's card files, see MP Diary, 7 July–22 July 1916. For the location of Madge's office, see MP Diary, 1 February 1917. For a photograph and description of the McClelland Building, Lexington's first "high-rise" building, which is still standing on the northeast corner of Short and Upper streets, see Kerr and Wright, *Lexington: A Century in Photographs,* 160. The first quote is from MP Diary, 20 December 1916. For Margaret as treasurer of the Civic League, see MP Diary, 2 December 1916, 21 December 1916, 20 January 1917, 22 January 1917. The second and third quotes are from

MP Diary, 11 January 1917, 24 January 1917. The last quote is from R. E. Gumm to Margaret Preston Johnston, 18 June 1919, MPJ Correspondence File.

44. The first quote is from Grantham, *Southern Progressivism,* 419. For Margaret's meeting with the "colored principal" and the remaining quotes, see MP Diary, 9 March 1917. The statement that William and Lizzie Fouse were members of Lexington's black elite is based on evidence from the following sources: Wright, *Heart of the Bluegrass,* 172, 182; Kerr and Wright, *Lexington: A Century in Photographs,* 235; George C. Wright, *A History of Blacks in Kentucky,* vol. 2, *In Pursuit of Equality, 1890–1980* (Frankfort: Kentucky Historical Society, 1992), 29, 173. For William Fouse's obituary article, listing many of his activities and accomplishments, see *Lexington Herald,* 2 June 1944, 24. Also see Harvey C. Russell, *The Negro Education Association: 1877–1946* (Norfolk, Va.: Guide Quality Press, 1946), 34, copy available in Special Collections and Archives, Paul G. Blazer Library, Kentucky State University, Frankfort; "Educator in Retirement after 45 Years Service," undated newspaper article summarizing the career of William Fouse, in Whitney M. Young Sr. Collection, Special Collections and Archives, Paul G. Blazer Library; John B. Caulder and Henry H. Hill to Whitney M. Young [Sr.], 18 March 1938 (a letter listing Fouse's accomplishments and nominating him for the Lincoln Institute's Lincoln Award), in Whitney M. Young Sr. Collection. William Fouse completed his master's degree in education at the University of Cincinnati in 1937, and a copy of his thesis, "Educational History of the Negroes of Lexington Kentucky," is located in Special Collections and Archives, Margaret I. King Library, University of Kentucky, Lexington. For a brief biography of Lizzie B. Fouse, see her obituary article in *Lexington Herald,* 23 October 1952, 30. Also, the Fouse Family Papers, in Special Collections and Archives, Margaret I. King Library, reflects their many activities and interests. Finally, for a sampling of newspaper articles reflecting the local prominence of William and Lizzie Fouse and their religious, educational, civic, and intellectual activities and accomplishments during the Progressive Era, see *Lexington Herald,* 27 March 1915, 12; 3 January 1916, 4; 9 January 1916, 5; 12 March 1916, 8; *Lexington Leader,* 14 June 1914, sec. 4, p. 5; 4 October 1914, sec. 2, p. 6; 5 April 1915, 5; 10 April 1915, 5; 18 April 1915, 7; 21 April 1915, 9; 28 April 1915, 5; 15 November 1915, 4; 3 January 1916, 11; 26 January 1916, 5; 26 January 1916, sec. 4, p. 6; 30 January 1916, sec. 4, p. 3; 5 February 1916, 3; 13 February 1916, sec. 4, p. 3; 24 February 1916, 6; 8 March 1916, sec. 4, p. 6; 12 March 1916, sec. 4, p. 6; 21 March 1916, 2; 23 March 1916, 8; 7 April 1916, 3; 9 April 1916, sec. 4, p. 6; 12 April 1916, 13; 16 April 1916, sec. 4, p. 6; 27 April 1916, 1, 6; 28 April 1916, 7; 1 May 1916, 3; 21 May 1916, sec. 4, p. 6; 23 May 1916, 12; 28 May 1916, sec. 4, p. 5; 29 May 1916, 2; 4 June 1916, sec. 4, p. 6; 6 June 1916, 6; 8 June 1916, 2; 10 June 1916, 5; 1 January 1917, 5; 9 January 1917, 3; 14 January 1917, 7; 4 February 1917, sec. 2, p. 11; 8 February 1917, 2; 24 February 1917, 8; 4 March 1917, sec. 3, p. 5; 11 March 1917, sec. 4, p. 7; 14 March 1917, 3; 18 March 1917, sec. 2, p. 11.

45. Note that Margaret Preston belonged to both the Kentucky Equal Rights

Association and the Fayette Equal Rights Association, and sometimes in her diary she referred to the latter simply as "the Equal Rights Association." This brief description of the Kentucky suffrage movement was developed from Paul E. Fuller, *Laura Clay and the Woman's Rights Movement* (1975; reprint, Lexington: University Press of Kentucky, 1992), 87; Claudia Knott, "The Woman Suffrage Movement in Kentucky" (PhD diss., University of Kentucky, 1980), 1–4. Also see Grantham, *Southern Progressivism*, 212. For a brief history of KERA, see *The Kentucky Encyclopedia*, 1992 ed., s.v. "Kentucky Equal Rights Association (KERA)." The first quote is from Margaret Preston to Preston Johnston, 10 February 1914, PPJ Correspondence File; the second quote is from Hay, "Madeline McDowell Breckinridge," 139; the last quote is from Klotter, *Portrait in Paradox*, 111.

46. The first quote is from Knott, "The Woman Suffrage Movement in Kentucky," 246. For a concise discussion of school suffrage in Kentucky, see *The Kentucky Encyclopedia*, 1992 ed., s.v. "Women's Suffrage." The second quote is from Margaret Preston to Preston Johnston, 14 January 1910, PPJ Correspondence File; the third quote is from *Lexington Leader*, 10 January 1910, 2; the fourth quote is from Preston Johnston to Margaret Preston, 25 August 1910, MPJ Correspondence File; the fifth quote is from Preston Johnston to Margaret Preston, 16 January 1910, MPJ Correspondence File. For the first of a series of suffrage classes presided over by Sarah Preston, see *Lexington Herald*, 8 February 1910, 10; *Lexington Leader*, 8 February 1910, 8. The last two quotes are from *Lexington Herald*, 12 April 1910, 5.

47. The first and second quotes are from *Lexington Leader*, 11 February 1910, 4; the last quote is from MP Diary, 10 February 1910. For Margaret's election as secretary of FERA, see MP Diary, 23 January 1913. Also see *Fayette Equal Rights Association Minute Book*, 6 October 1917–4 June 1918, in Fayette Equal Rights Association Records, 1917–1920, Special Collections and Archives, Margaret I. King Library, University of Kentucky, Lexington.

48. The first and second quotes are from *Lexington Leader*, 5 April 1915, 7. For the growing public acceptance of the suffrage cause during 1913 and 1914, see Knott, "The Woman Suffrage Movement in Kentucky," 253. The third quote is from *Lexington Herald*, 7 March 1915, 1; the fourth quote is from ibid., 1 May 1915, 4. For other accounts of the 1915 Suffrage Day parade, see *Lexington Herald*, 1 May 1915, 1; *Lexington Leader*, 25 April 1915, sec. 3, p. 8; 30 April 1915, 11. The fifth quote is from MP Diary, 1 May 1915. For Margaret's involvement with the *Woman's Journal and Suffrage News*, see Agnes E. Ryan to Margaret Preston 25 September 1915, MPJ Correspondence File. For an article on the 1916 suffrage parade in Lexington, see *Lexington Leader*, 25 April 1916, 1. The last quote is from MP Diary, 6 May 1916.

49. For the FERA meeting at which Margaret was invited to represent Columbia, see MP Diary, 12 June 1916. The quote is from *FERA Minute Book*.

50. For Margaret's hesitation to become FERA secretary, see MP Diary, 23 January 1913. For her complaint about the workload, see MP Diary, 26 October 1915.

The first two quotes are from MP Diary, 22 February 1915, 2 December 1916. For Margaret's refusal to organize the Pethick-Lawrence lecture, see MP Diary, 16 March 1915. The third quote is from MP Diary, 16 August 1915; the fourth and fifth quotes are from Margaret Preston to Preston Johnston, 20 August 1910, PPJ Correspondence File; the sixth quote is from Margaret Preston to Preston Johnston, 18 September 1916, PPJ Correspondence File. For the suffrage debate at the Baptist Church in Virginia, see MP Diary, 15 September 1916. For Margaret's views on the Episcopal wedding vows, see Margaret Preston to Preston Johnston, 26 September 1916, PPJ Correspondence File. The last quote is from Margaret Preston to Preston Johnston, 4 August 1916, PPJ Correspondence File.

51. Eugene Simpson to Margaret Preston, 24 March 1914, MPJ Correspondence File.

52. Donald Scott, "The Profession that Vanished: Public Lecturing in Mid-Nineteenth-Century America," in *Professions and Professional Ideologies in America*, ed. Gerald L. Geison (Chapel Hill: University of North Carolina Press, 1983), 17.

53. The first quote is from Schlereth, *Victorian America*, 210; the second quote is from Stevenson, *The Victorian Homefront*, 30. For the complete list of books recorded in Margaret Preston's diary at the end of February 1911, see MP Diary, "February 14, 1910–February 28, 1911," back page and flyleaf. The third quote is from MP Diary, 7 October 1912; the fourth quote is from Preston Johnston to Margaret Preston, 10 August 1910, MPJ Correspondence File; the last quote is from Margaret Preston to Preston Johnston, 20 August 1916, PPJ Correspondence File.

54. For a discussion of literary magazines and their importance in intellectual matters, see Thomas Bender, *New York Intellect: A History of Intellectual Life in New York City, from 1750 to the Beginning of Our Own Time* (Baltimore: Johns Hopkins University Press, 1987), 164, 168, 177, 207–8, 214; Richard H. Brodhead, *Cultures of Letters: Scenes of Reading and Writing in Nineteenth-Century America* (Chicago: University of Chicago Press, 1993), 122, 126–31; Joseph F. Kett, *The Pursuit of Knowledge under Difficulties: From Self-Improvement to Adult Education in America, 1750–1990* (Stanford, Calif.: Stanford University Press, 1994), 176–77; Stevenson, *Victorian Homefront*, 156. The term "intellectual journalism," is from Bender, *New York Intellect*, 168. For the founding of *Vogue*, see William Packer, *The Art of Vogue Covers 1909–1940* (London: Peerage Books, 1987), 5–27. For Margaret's reading of magazines, see MP Diary, 3 December 1914, 28 June 1915, 26 November 1915, 31 January 1917. The first quote is from Edgar Allan Poe, "Marginal Notes . . . No. II. A Sequel to the 'Marginalia' of the *Democratic Review*," *Godey's Lady's Book*, September 1845, in *Complete Works of Edgar Allen Poe*, ed. James A. Harrison (New York: AMS Press, 1965), XVI, 82, quoted in Bender, *New York Intellect*, 157. For Margaret's encounter with Octave Thanet, see Margaret Preston to Preston Johnston, 22 July 1911, PPJ Correspondence File. For a biography of Octave Thanet (Alice French), see George L. McMichael, *Journey to Obscurity: The Life of Octave Thanet* (Lincoln: University of Nebraska Press, 1965). For a detailed account of the

life and work of Maurice Hewlett, see Arthur Bruce Sutherland, "Maurice Hewlett: Historical Romancer" (PhD diss., University of Pennsylvania, 1938), copy available in Margaret I. King Library, University of Kentucky, Lexington. For Hewlett as a champion of women's suffrage, see ibid., 176; the second quote is from ibid., 173. For Margaret's reading of Hewlett's works and her comments on them, see MP Diary, "February 14, 1910–February 28, 1911," back page and flyleaf, 31 January 1913; Margaret Preston to Preston Johnston, 25 August 1916, PPJ Correspondence File; MP Diary, 10 January 1917. For H. G. Wells as an important transitional author, see Frank M. Tierney, introduction to *Scientific Romances of H. G. Wells : A Critical Study,* by Stephen Gill (Ontario: Vesta Publications, 1975), 6–7. The third quote is from Alfred Borrello, *H. G. Wells: Author in Agony* (Carbondale: Southern Illinois University Press, 1972), 41; the last quote is from Randolph Bourne, "Randolph Bourne, article in *Dial,* 28 December 1916," in *H. G. Wells: The Critical Heritage,* ed. Patrick Parrinder (London: Rutledge and Kegan Paul, 1972), 241. For Randolph Bourne, see Bender, *New York Intellect,* 232–37; for the *Dial,* see ibid., 158, 249–50.

55. For the Ibsen plays Margaret was reading in 1909, see Margaret Preston to Preston Johnston, 22 September 1909, PPJ Correspondence File. For Margaret's reading of Shaw's *Pygmalion* and her reaction, see MP Diary, 7 November 1914. For Margaret's reading of Barrie's plays and her reaction to them, see MP Diary, 21 November 1914. For a brief biography of Barrie, see *The Oxford Companion to English Literature,* 1985 ed., s.v. "Barrie, Sir J(ames) M(atthew)." For the plays listed, see J. M. Barrie, *The Plays of J. M. Barrie, in One Volume* (New York: Charles Scribner's Sons, 1929). For Galsworthy's play *The Mob* and Margaret's reaction, see MP Diary, 1 January 1915. For a brief biography of Galsworthy, see *The Oxford Companion to English Literature,* 1985 ed., s.v. "Galsworthy, John." For Wilde's *Lady Windermere's Fan* and the related quote, see MP Diary, 19 July 1915. For the poetry he sent to Margaret at Meadow Wood, see Preston Johnston to Margaret Preston, 10 August 1910, 28 August 1910, MPJ Correspondence File. The last quote is from MP Diary, 8 January 1917.

56. For Margaret's election as WCCK recording secretary, see MP Diary, 7 March 1908. For her election as vice president, see MP Diary, 4 March 1916; *Lexington Leader,* 5 March 1916, sec. 3, p. 4. For her reelection as vice president, see MP Diary, 3 March 1917; *Lexington Leader,* 4 March 1917, sec 2., p. 3. Margaret apparently succeeded her mother as chair of the WCCK Department of Literature in late 1914 or early 1915. Brock, in *A History of the Woman's Club,* 165, notes that Sarah Preston was the chair in October 1914. Margaret clearly indicates that she had assumed this position early in January 1915, calling a meeting of the department "my meeting" (see MP Diary, 6 January 1915). An article in the *Lexington Leader,* 4 April 1915, sec. 3, p. 3 explicitly refers to Margaret as the chair. For Margaret as Department of Literature chair in 1922, see *April 1922 Calendar Woman's Club of Central Kentucky,* single sheet, MPJ Correspondence File. For Margaret as

second auditor of the WCCK, see *Woman's Club of Central Kentucky Yearbook for 1959–1960* (Lexington: WCCK, 1960), 4–5.

57. For Robert Burns Wilson, see Tapp and Klotter, *Decades of Discord,* 274–75, 289; *The Kentucky Encyclopedia,* 1992 ed., s.v. "Wilson, Robert Burns." The first two quotes are from *Lexington Leader,* 16 April 1916, sec. 3, p. 3; the third and fourth quotes are from *Lexington Herald,* 4 May 1916, 7.

58. The first quote is from *The Oxford Companion to English Literature,* 1985 ed., s.v. "Brooke, Rupert Chawner." For a biography of Brooke, including details of his death, see Timothy Rogers, *Rupert Brooke: A Reappraisal and Selection from His Writing, Some Hitherto Unpublished* (New York: Barnes and Noble, 1971), chap. 2; the second quote is from p. 7. The third quote is from MP Diary, 5 January 1916; the fourth and fifth quotes are from *Lexington Leader,* 6 April 1916, 8; the last quote is from MP Diary, 5 April 1916.

59. Biographical information on Reuben Thornton ("Bookie") Taylor was developed from *The [1914] Kentuckian: Yearbook of the State University of Kentucky,* vol. 10 (Lexington: Class of Nineteen Fourteen, 1914), 39, in Special Collections and Archives, Margaret I. King Library, University of Kentucky, Lexington; Reuben Thornton Taylor Alumni Survey Form (1938), Alumni Records, Special Collections and Archives, Margaret I. King Library; *Louisville Herald Post,* 1 February 1936, 4; the first quote is from ibid. For Frances Jewell, see Terry L. Birdwhistell, "An Educated Difference: Women at the University of Kentucky through the Second World War" (PhD diss., University of Kentucky, 1994), chap. 2; *The Kentucky Encyclopedia,* 1992 ed., s.v. "McVey, Mary Frances (Jewell)." For Frances Jewell succeeding Bookie Taylor as English instructor at State University, see *Lexington Herald,* 17 May 1916, 1.

60. The first quote is from MP Diary, 22 November 1915. Also see MP Diary, 1 December 1915. The second quote is from MP Diary, 23 January 1916. For a brief description of the troubled life of poet Francis Thompson, see *The Oxford Companion to English Literature,* 1985 ed., s.v. "Thompson, Francis." The third quote is from *Lexington Herald,* 3 February 1916, 7; the fourth quote is from *Lexington Leader,* 3 February 1916, 7; the last two quotes are from MP Diary, 2 February 1916, 6 April 1916. Also see MP Diary, 10 May 1916, 8 December 1916.

61. For the argument that cinema was beginning to dominate the Lexington entertainment market in the 1910s and the first quote, see Gregory A. Waller, *Main Street Amusements: Movies and Commercial Entertainment in a Southern City, 1896–1930* (Washington, D.C.: Smithsonian Institution Press, 1995), 96. For the Orpheum Theater, see ibid., 66, 92–98. The second and third quotes are from MP Diary, 21 September 1912, 2 September 1915. For Margaret's attendance at *Joan of Arc* and her comments, see MP Diary, 4 September 1917. For the Ben Ali Theater, see Waller, *Main Street Amusements,* 97, 101–10. The last quote is from Margaret Preston to Preston Johnston, 30 January 1917, PPJ Correspondence File.

62. For the professional touring combination companies and their decimation by competition from film in the 1910s, see Benjamin McArthur, *Actors and Ameri-*

can Culture, 1880–1920 (Philadelphia: Temple University Press, 1984), preface, chap. 1. For Margaret's lament that she could not attend more plays, see MP Diary, 25 September 1915, 4 January 1917. The first and second quotes are from Margaret Preston to Preston Johnston, 5 February 1914, PPJ Correspondence File; the third quote is from Margaret Preston to Preston Johnston, 10 February 1914, PPJ Correspondence File. Also see Margaret Preston to Preston Johnston, 15 February 1914, 22 February 1914, 4 March 1914, PPJ Correspondence File.

63. For Margaret attending professionally produced plays in Lexington, see MP Diary, 6 December 1913, 16 April 1914, 25 September 1915, 7 March 1916, 4 January 1917. The first three quotes are from MP Diary, 12 February 1916, 3 May 1915. For Margaret at the Kirmess and the fourth quote, see MP Diary, 15 February 1916. The last three quotes are from MP Diary, 29 January 1917, 5 June 1916.

CHAPTER SEVEN: THE DRAMATIC CLUBS TAKE THE STAGE

1. For each literary society compartmentalized into discrete article or column, see *Focus* 2 (November 1890): 72–74. For evidence of multiple and combined student extracurricular affiliations in the 1890s, see *Memoria XCIV* (Lexington: Transylvania Printing Company, 1894), in Special Collections and Archives, Margaret I. King Library, University of Kentucky, Lexington; *Kentucky University Crimson, 1897* (Lexington: Senior Classes of Kentucky University, 1897), in Special Collections and Archives, J. Douglas Gay Jr. Library, Transylvania University, Lexington. The first quote is from *Lexington Daily Leader,* 3 April 1896, 1. For an account of the Kappa Alpha banquet, see *Lexington Leader,* 11 April 1903, 5. For the Cecropian Dramatic Club play, see *Transylvanian* 12 (April 1905): 165. For the Bible College literary society basketball game and related quotes, see *Lexington Herald,* 18 February 1910, 10; 19 February 1910, 3.

2. The first is quote from *Transylvanian* 7 (January 1900): 146. For the quoted table of contents headings, see *Transylvanian* 7 (January 1900): 121; *Transylvanian* 7 (April 1900): 251. For the greater attention to sports, see *Transylvanian* 12 (May 1905): 191–93, 202. For the play spoofing society rivalry, see *Transylvanian* 12 (February 1905): 118–22. For the Cecropian Dramatic Club play, see *Transylvanian* 12 (April 1905): 165.

3. For the report of the Tennis Club meeting and the oratorical primary, see *Transylvanian* 18 (April 1910) "Locals" section, unpaginated. Also see "Locals" sections in the January, February, March, and May issues of the 1910 *Transylvanian* for coverage, or the lack thereof, of literary society news. For "The South—Our Heritage and Opportunity," see *Transylvanian* 19 (June 1911): 301–7. For Joseph T. Watson as a Philothean member, see "The Philothean Literary Society," in *The Crimson, 1910,* vol. 12 (Lexington: Senior Classes of Transylvania University, College of the Bible, and Hamilton College, 1910), in Special Collections and Archives, J. Douglas Gay Jr. Library, Transylvania University, Lexington.

4. The first two quotes are from *Crimson Rambler* 1, no. 1 (21 May 1915): 1. For the editorial "Literary Societies and Transylvania Spirit," see *Crimson Rambler* 2, no. 6 (15 October 1915): 4. For the Periclean Halloween party, see *Crimson Rambler* 2, no. 9 (5 November 1915): 1. The last quote is from *Crimson Rambler* 2, no. 7 (22 October 1915): 2.

5. *Crimson Rambler* 2, no. 10 (12 November 1915): 2; 2, no. 14 (10 December 1915): 8; 2, no. 23 (25 February 1916): 2.

6. For the quoted headlines, see *Crimson Rambler* 2, no. 25 (10 March 1916): 1. For the front-page baseball story and page-five preliminary oratorical contest, see *Crimson Rambler* 2, no. 28 (7 April 1916): 1, 5. For the front-page baseball and track stories and the page-three intercollegiate oratorical contest, see *Crimson Rambler* 2, no. 33 (12 May 1916): 1, 3.

7. See *The Crimson, 1910; The Crimson, 1915*, vol. 17 (Lexington: Senior Classes of Transylvania, College of the Bible, and Hamilton College, 1915), in Special Collections and Archives, J. Douglas Gay Jr. Library, Transylvania University, Lexington.

8. For literary society representation on its Board of Directors, see *Idea* 2, no. 34 (12 May 1910): 1, 7. For the societies' shrinking presence, see *Idea* 1, no. 18 (28 January 1909): 7; 2, no. 10 (11 November 1909). For an example of no mention of literary societies, see *Idea* 4, no. 1 (14 September 1911). For the Neville Society dance honoring the football team, see *Idea* 2, no. 11 (18 November 1909): 6. The quotes are from *Idea* 3, no. 7 (20 October 1910): 2; 3, no. 14 (8 December 1910): 1; 4, no. 21 (15 February 1912): 2.

9. The quotes are from *Idea* 1, no. 16 (14 January 1909): 7; 2, no. 4 (30 September 1909): 5; 2, no. 8 (28 October 1909): 8; 2, no. 7 (21 October 1909): 4; 1, no. 30 (22 April 1909): 1; 3, no. 19 (19 January 1911): 4; 2, no. 18 (20 January 1910): 6; 3, no. 15 (15 December 1910): 1. For the statistics on literary society membership in 1910, see *Idea* 3, no. 4 (29 September 1910): 4. Percentages of literary society membership in the mid-1890s derived from *Memoria XCIV* (see chapter 3).

10. The quotes are from *Idea* 3, no. 28 (23 March 1911): 8; 4, no. 13 (7 December 1911): 1; 3, no. 17 (12 January 1911): 7; 4, no. 27 (28 March 1912): 4. For Edward F. Farquhar, see James F. Hopkins, *The University of Kentucky: Origins and Early Years* (Lexington: University of Kentucky Press, 1951), 285.

11. The quotes are from *Idea* 4, no. 26 (21 March 1912): 4. For student biographical sketches under "Who's Who and Why," see *Idea* 4, no. 26 (21 March 1912): 5; 4, no. 28 (4 April 1912): 5; 4, no. 29 (11 April 1912): 5; 4, no. 30 (18 April 1912): 5; 4, no. 31 (25 April 1912): 5; 4, no. 32 (2 May 1912): 5.

12. The first two quotes are from *Lexington Herald*, 23 January 1910, sec. 3, p. 2. For the Sigma Alpha Epsilon "program dance" and the last quote, see *Lexington Herald*, 17 April 1910, sec. 3, p. 1.

13. The first quote is from *Lexington Herald*, 22 February 1910, 8. For the an-

nouncement of the Delta Delta Delta tea, see ibid., 5. The remaining quotes are from *Lexington Herald,* 22 February 1915, 1; *Lexington Leader,* 22 February 1916, 2; 23 February 1917, sec. 2, p. 1.

14. The first quote is from *Lexington Herald,* 22 February 1910, 3; the second quote is from *Idea* 2, no. 23 (24 February 1910): 1; the third, fourth, and fifth quotes are from *Idea* 3, no. 23 (16 February 1911): 1; the sixth quote is from *Lexington Leader,* 15 February 1916, 7. For coverage of the 1916 Washington's birthday celebration, see *Lexington Herald,* 23 February 1916, 5. The last two quotes are from *Lexington Herald,* 22 February 1917, 6, 7.

15. For a discussion of the cultural changes in language and rhetorical style affecting public entertainment at the turn of the twentieth century, see Lawrence W. Levine, *Highbrow/Lowbrow: The Emergence of Cultural Hierarchy in America* (Cambridge, Mass.: Harvard University Press, 1988), 46–49; the first and third quotes are from p. 46. The quote from the *New York Times,* 14 March 1909, is quoted in ibid., 46.

16. For American theater in general between 1880 and 1920, see Benjamin McArthur, *Actors and American Culture, 1880–1920* (Philadelphia: Temple University Press, 1984), preface, chap. 1; the first three quotes are from pp. x, xi, 5. For a discussion of the criticisms of the legitimate theater and its tenure on Broadway between 1914 and 1918, see Gerald Bordman, *American Theatre: A Chronicle of Comedy and Drama, 1914–1930* (New York: Oxford University Press, 1995), preface, 3–82; the fourth quote is from the preface; the last quote is from Daniel Frohman, quoted without citation, ibid., 28.

17. For the argument that aesthetic dissatisfaction with the legitimate theater contributed to the growth of the amateur Little Theater Movement, see Bordman, *American Theatre,* 3. For the argument that the legitimate theater's retreat to New York contributed to the Little Theater Movement, see McArthur, *Actors and American Culture,* preface; Kenneth Macgowan, *Footlights across America: Towards a National Theater* (New York: Harcourt, Brace, 1929), chap. 1; the quote is from p. 3. For origins and definitions of the Little Theater Movement, see Constance D'Arcy Mackay, *The Little Theater in the United States* (New York: Henry Holt, 1917), chap. 1; William Lyon Phelps, *The Twentieth Century Theatre: Observations on the Contemporary English and American Stage* (New York: Macmillan, 1918), 77–80; Macgowan, *Footlights across America,* chap. 1; Clarence Arthur Perry, *The Work of the Little Theatres: The Groups They Include, the Plays They Produce, Their Tournaments, and the Handbooks They Use* (New York: Russell Sage Foundation, 1933), 9–27. Both Macgowan (9) and Perry (15) directly link college theatrical efforts or the student dramatic clubs with the Little Theater Movement. The conception of the collegiate dramatic clubs offered here as originally being extracurricular bodies producing amateur, artistically motivated, noncommercial plays was developed from Percy MacKaye, *The Civic Theatre in Relation to the Redemption of Leisure: A Book of Suggestions* (New York: Mitchell Kennerley, 1912), 219–23; Mackay, *The*

Little Theater in the United States, 181–204; Phelps, *The Twentieth Century The-atre,* 84–85, chap. 3; Macgowan, *Footlights across America,* 112–13; and Barbara M. Solomon, *In the Company of Educated Women: A History of Women and Higher Education in America* (New Haven, Conn.: Yale University Press, 1985), 104–6. For the pre-Revolutionary origins of the dramatic clubs, see Macgowan, *Footlights across America,* 107–8, 112. For their widespread popularity in the 1890s, see Solomon, *In the Company of Educated Women,* 105; Helen Lefkowitz Horowitz, *Campus Life: Undergraduate Cultures from the End of the Eighteenth Century to the Present* (Chi-cago: University of Chicago Press, 1987), 55. For the dramatic clubs as an expres-sion of revolt against puritanical mores, see Macgowan, *Footlights across America,* 112; Solomon, *In the Company of Educated Women,* 105. For Baker's pioneering the effort at Harvard to include dramatics in the curriculum, see MacKaye, *The Civic Theatre,* 219–23; Mackay, *The Little Theater in the United States,* 183; Phelps, *The Twentieth Century Theatre,* 83–84; Macgowan, *Footlights across America,* 112–17. For the link between the Little Theater Movement and the inclusion of dramat-ics courses in the formal curriculum, see Mackay, *The Little Theater in the United States,* 181–82; Macgowan, *Footlights across America,* 112–31; Perry, *The Work of the Little Theatres,* 15; Jean Carter and Jess Ogden, *Everyman's Drama: A Study of the Noncommercial Theatre in the United States* (New York: American Association for Adult Education, 1938), 28–29. Note that Phelps (*The Twentieth Century Theatre,* 84) writing in 1918, stated, "courses on contemporary drama are now a regular part of the curriculum in most American universities." And by 1929 Macgowan (*Footlights across America,* 108) saw the process of absorbing drama study and play production into the curriculum as an accomplished fact.

18. The first quote is from James Lane Allen, *Summer in Arcady* (1896; reprint, New York: Macmillan, 1909), 81. For the Philosophian play performed in 1882, see *Lexington Daily Transcript,* 3 June 1882, 2. For turn-of-the-century productions by the Philosophians, see *Lexington Daily Leader,* 26 February 1899, 2; *Lexington Leader,* 8 December 1900, 4. The second quote is from *Lexington Leader,* 27 Febru-ary 1914, 9; the third quote is from *Lexington Herald,* 3 March 1915, 5. For the Philosophians changing the location of their play, see *Lexington Leader,* 27 April 1916, 1; 3 May 1916, 4. The last two quotes are from *Lexington Herald,* 7 May 1916, sec. 3, p. 3; 1 April 1917, sec. 2, p. 3.

19. The first quote is from *Lexington Leader,* 15 May 1916, 9. For the Osso-lian performance of *Pre-Digested Politics,* also see *Crimson Rambler* 2, no. 33 (12 May 1916): 7. The second and third quotes are from *Lexington Leader,* 1 April 1905, 8. The *Leader* article on *The Mouse Trap* was reprinted in *Transylvanian* 12 (April 1905): 165. For the Cecropian Dramatic Club, also see *The Crimson, 1905,* 107.

20. For a brief history of Hamilton College, see *The Kentucky Encyclopedia,* 1992 ed., s.v. "Hamilton College"; also see John D. Wright Jr., *Transylvania: Tu-tor to the West* (Lexington: University Press of Kentucky, 1980), 275–76. For the

founding of the Marlowe Club and its naming in honor of Julia Marlowe, see *The Crimson, 1908,* vol. 10 (Lexington: Senior Classes of Kentucky University and the College of the Bible, 1908), 238, in Special Collections and Archives, J. Douglas Gay Jr. Library, Transylvania University, Lexington. For the remarks regarding Julia Marlowe, see McArthur, *Actors and American Culture,* 155, 158; the first two quotes are from p. 158. For the local press announcements of the Marlowe Club's performance and the related quotes, see *Lexington Herald,* 22 May 1910, sec. 3, p. 3; *Lexington Leader,* 24 May 1914, sec. 2, p. 2; *Lexington Herald,* 21 May 1916, sec. 3, p. 4. The last quote is from Margaret Preston Diary, 5 June 1916, Margaret Preston Johnston Papers, in Preston-Johnston Papers, Special Collections and Archives, Margaret I. King Library, University of Kentucky, Lexington.

21. Wright, *Tutor to the West,* 301; Hopkins, *The University of Kentucky,* 176; Helen Deiss Irvin, *Hail Kentucky! A Pictorial History of the University of Kentucky* (Lexington: University of Kentucky Press, 1965), 47.

22. The first quote is from *Idea* 2, no. 2 (16 September 1909): 1; the second quote is from *Lexington Leader,* 6 January 1910, 6; the third quote is from *Lexington Herald,* 23 January 1910, 5. For Edward Bulwer-Lytton, see *The Oxford Companion to English Literature,* 1985 ed., s.v. "Bulwer-Lytton, Edward George Earle." For a synopsis of Lytton's play *Richelieu,* see James M. Salem, *Drury's Guide to Best Plays,* 3d ed. (Metuchen, N.J.: Scarecrow Press, 1978), 196–97. The fourth quote is from *Lexington Leader,* 23 January 1910, 3; the fifth quote is from *Idea* 2, no. 20 (3 February 1910): 1; the sixth quote is from *Idea* 2, no. 21 (10 February 1910): 1; the seventh and eighth quotes are from *Lexington Leader,* 5 February 1910, 8; the last quote is from *Lexington Herald,* 5 February 1910, 5. For additional press reports on the production of *Richelieu,* see *Lexington Leader,* 28 January 1910, 8; 1 February 1910, 2; *Lexington Herald,* 2 February 1910, 4; 4 February 1910, 2; 5 February 1910, 4.

23. This account of the Alpha Dramatic Club and *What to Expect at College* was developed from *Idea* 2, no. 19 (27 January 1910): 7; 2, no. 30 (14 April 1910): 1; *Lexington Leader,* 16 January 1910, 7; *Lexington Herald,* 18 January 1910, 4; 23 January 1910, 6. The quote is from *Idea* 2, no. 22 (17 February 1910): 1. For Hubbard as a member of the cast of *Richelieu,* see *Lexington Herald,* 23 January 1910, 5. For Hubbard as president of the Patterson Society, see *The [1910] Kentuckian: Yearbook of the State University of Kentucky,* 192. For Hubbard winning the Patterson Society contest, see *Idea* 2, no. 28 (31 March 1910): 1. For the first located mention of "Strollers" as the name of the State University's student dramatic club, see *Idea* 3, no. 29 (30 March 1911): 2.

24. Cunningham's exit from Lexington shortly after the performances of *Richelieu* has been inferred from remarks in *Idea* 2, no. 2 (10 February 1910): 1, that he would be welcome at the university whenever he returned and wishing him "abundant success" in his "chosen" career. For the founding of the Transylvania Dramatic Club in the fall of 1909, see *The Crimson, 1911,* vol. 13 (Lexington:

Senior Classes of Transylvania University, College of the Bible, and Hamilton College, 1911), 118, in Special Collections and Archives, J. Douglas Gay Jr. Library, Transylvania University, Lexington. For Cunningham's address to the Transylvania students and the first quote, see *Lexington Herald,* 3 February 1910, 4. The second quote is from *Lexington Herald,* 16 April 1910, 10. For playwright A. W. Pinero, see *The Oxford Companion to English Literature,* 1985 ed., s.v. "Pinero, Sir Arthur Wing." For a synopsis of Pinero's play *Sweet Lavender,* see Salem, *Drury's Guide to Best Plays,* 244. The third quote is from *Lexington Herald,* 28 May 1910, 2; the last quote is from *Lexington Leader,* 28 May 1910, 2. For articles promoting the performance of *Sweet Lavender,* see *Lexington Herald,* 15 May 1910, 8; *Lexington Leader,* 22 May 1910, 24.

25. The first quote is from *Idea* 3, no. 5 (6 October 1910): 6. For Professor R. E. Monroe directing the work of the Transylvania Dramatic Club, see *Lexington Leader,* 22 May 1910, 24; also see *Transylvania University Catalogue Number 1909–1910* (Lexington: Transylvania University, 1910), 6, copy available in Special Collections and Archives, J. Douglas Gay Jr. Library, Transylvania University, Lexington. For Edward Saxon as director of the Transylvania Dramatic Club, see *Lexington Leader,* 24 February 1915, 11; *Lexington Herald,* 26 April 1916, 2. For Saxon as instructor of expression in the College of the Bible, see *The Crimson, 1917,* vol. 19 (Lexington: Senior Classes of Transylvania College, College of the Bible, and Hamilton College, 1917), 54, in Special Collections and Archives, J. Douglas Gay Jr. Library. The second quote is from *Idea* 4, no. 32 (2 May 1912): 1; *Lexington Herald,* 1 May 1912, 9. For the Transylvania Dramatic Club's listing in the school catalog under "Student Activities," see *Transylvania College Bulletin, the Catalogue 1915–1916* (Lexington: Transylvania University, 1916), 55, copy available in Special Collections and Archives, J. Douglas Gay Jr. Library. For the Transylvania Dramatic Club featured among other extracurricular organizations in the student yearbook, see *The Crimson, 1911,* 118. The last quote is from *Idea* 4, no. 32 (2 May 1912): 1.

26. The first quote is from *Lexington Leader,* 2 April 1911, 28; the second and third quotes are from *Lexington Leader,* 7 April 1911, 2. For the Ben Ali's conversion to an all-movie theater in May 1915, see Gregory A. Waller, *Main Street Amusements: Movies and Commercial Entertainment in a Southern City, 1896–1930* (Washington, D.C.: Smithsonian Institution Press, 1995), 97, 101. The fourth, fifth, and sixth quotes are from *Lexington Leader,* 20 April 1911, 3. For a critical review of the 1906 New York production of *Brown of Harvard,* see Anthony Slide, ed., *Selected Theatre Criticism,* vol. 1, *1900–1919* (Metuchen, N.J.: Scarecrow Press, 1985), 35–36. For the articles in the *Idea* regarding the program cover design contest and the consequences of missing rehearsal, see 3, no. 29 (30 March 1911): 7, 2. The last two quotes are from *Lexington Leader,* 21 April 1911, 7.

27. For the profits of Transylvania Dramatic Club being used to support the Athletic Association, see *Lexington Herald,* 9 May 1912, 12. For the list of Tran-

sylvania Dramatic Club officers, see *Lexington Leader*, 27 May 1913, 11. For additional press accounts of the Transylvania Dramatic Club plays at the Lexington Opera House in 1912 and 1913, see *Lexington Herald*, 10 May 1912, 8; *Lexington Leader*, 25 May 1913, sec. 3, p. 2. The first quote is from James Metcalfe, review of *The Virginian*, by Owen Wister and Kirke La Shelle (Manhattan Theater, New York), in *Life* (4 February 1904), 118–19, quoted in Slide, *Selected Theatre Criticism*, 302. For the *Lexington Herald*'s coverage of the Strollers' production of *The Virginian* and the related quotes, see 3 May 1912, 6; also see *Lexington Herald*, 1 May 1912, 9; *Idea* 4, no. 33 (9 May 1912): 1.

28. For the announcement of the Strollers' March 1913 performance in Louisville and the first three quotes, see *Lexington Leader*, 16 March 1913, 2. For additional coverage of the Strollers' production of *The Lost Paradise*, see *Lexington Leader*, 13 March 1913, 12; 14 March 1913, 6, 9; 15 March 1913, 5. For a synopsis of *The Lost Paradise*, see Salem, *Drury's Guide to Best Plays*, 110. The last quote is from the headlines of the *Lexington Herald* review article, 4 March 1914, 8. For coverage of *The College Widow*, also see *Lexington Herald*, 3 March 1914, 10. For a critical review of the 1904 New York production of *The College Widow*, see Slide, *Selected Theatre Criticism*, 57–58.

29. For the State University Orchestra's performance of *Charley's Aunt* and the first quote, see *Lexington Leader*, 16 January 1915, 2. The second quote is from *Lexington Herald*, 16 January 1915, 6. For a synopsis of *Charley's Aunt*, see Salem, *Drury's Guide to Best Plays*, 317–18. Also see *The Oxford Companion to English Literature*, 1985 ed., s.v. "Charley's Aunt." For the announcement of the Strollers' performance of *Charley's Aunt* at the Georgetown Opera House, see *Lexington Herald*, 31 January 1915, 2.

30. For Sandman, see *Lexington Herald*, 15 January 1915, 10.

31. For the performance of *Call of the Blood* and the related information, see *Lexington Leader*, 14 April 1915, 8; 15 April 1915, 7.

32. For *Esmeralda*, Gillette, and the first quote, see McArthur, *Actors and American Culture*, 174. For the *Lexington Leader*'s remarks just prior to the performance of *Esmeralda*, see 25 May 1913, sec. 3, p. 2. For the review of *Esmeralda* and the second quote, see *Lexington Leader*, 27 May 1913, 11; also see *Lexington Leader*, 10 May 1913, 10. The third quote is from *Lexington Herald*, 4 February 1914, 8; the fourth quote is from *The Crimson, 1914*, vol. 14 (Lexington: Senior Classes of Transylvania University, College of the Bible, and Hamilton College, 1914), "Calendar 1913–1914," 4 February, in Special Collections and Archives, J. Douglas Gay Jr. Library, Transylvania University, Lexington. For the smallpox outbreak at Transylvania, see *The Crimson, 1914*, "Calendar 1913–1914," March and April. For Grehan's review of *Going Some* and the fifth and sixth quotes, see *Lexington Herald*, 27 February 1915, 4. For Grehan as the 1894 intercollegiate oratorical contest winner, see *Lexington Morning Transcript*, 7 April 1894, 1. For Grehan as head of the State University Journalism Department and faculty adviser to the Strollers, see

Lexington Herald, 13 January 1916, 5. For the *Lexington Leader's* review of *Going Some* and the seventh quote, see 27 February 1915, 2.

33. For war-related disruption on the Transylvania campus, see Wright, *Tutor to the West,* 331–36; for the effects at the University of Kentucky, see Irvin, *Hail Kentucky,* 51. Also see John D. Wright Jr., *Lexington: Heart of the Bluegrass* (Lexington: Lexington–Fayette County Historic Commission, 1982), 161–65. For a critical review of a 1905 professional performance of the "comedy-drama" *The Lion and the Mouse,* see Slide, *Selected Theatre Criticism,* 157. For the Strollers' version of *The Lion and the Mouse,* see *Lexington Leader,* 25 February 1917, sec. 2, p. 5; 9 March 1917, 2; 11 March 1917, 6; 14 March 1917, 11; 18 March 1917, Second Fashion section, 2; *Lexington Herald,* 4 March 1917, sec. 3, p. 3; 10 March 1917, 4; 11 March 1917, 6. For the Transylvania Dramatic Club's first performance of *David Garrick,* see *Lexington Herald,* 16 December 1916, 6. For an account of students drilling for war on the Transylvania campus, see *Lexington Herald,* 20 March 1917, 8. For the second performance of *David Garrick,* see *Lexington Herald,* 6 December 1917, 8. The name "Stagecrafters" first appears in the 6 December 1917 entry in the calendar of activities in *The Crimson, 1918,* vol. 23 (Lexington: Senior Classes of Transylvania College and the College of the Bible, 1918), 129, in Special Collections and Archives, J. Douglas Gay Jr. Library, Transylvania University, Lexington: "David Garrick was presented by the Stagecrafters." Since I found no reference to "Stagecrafters" in the press during the spring of 1917, I inferred that the organization must have adopted the name in the fall of 1917. The last quote is from *Kentucky Kernel* 10, no. 23 (26 March 1920): 4.

34. For the Ben Ali's conversion to an all-movie theater in May 1915, see Waller, *Main Street Amusements,* 97. The first two quotes are from *Lexington Leader,* 14 January 1916, sec. 2, p. 5. For the announcement of the Transylvania Dramatic Club's play, see *Lexington Herald,* 4 February 1916, 9. The third and fourth quotes are from *Lexington Herald,* 23 April 1916, sec. 4, p. 4. For Gribbin as the set designer and the last quote, see *Lexington Herald,* 26 April 1916, 2. For press accounts of the Transylvania club's male and female leads, see *Lexington Leader,* 23 April 1916, sec. 4, p. 5; 25 April 1916, 5. For additional press accounts of the club's production of *The Fortune Hunter,* see *Lexington Leader,* 16 April 1916, sec. 3, p. 1; 25 April 1916, 8; 26 April 1916, 7; *Lexington Herald,* 17 April 1916, Bluegrass Farmers section, 5; 20 April 1916, 12.

35. For the Strollers' new members, see *Lexington Leader,* 7 January 1916, 4. The first quote is from *Lexington Leader,* 16 January 1916, sec. 3, p. 2. For the reference to the "Strollers' studio," see *Lexington Herald,* 21 January 1916, 9. As mentioned, the literary societies no longer had rooms in the "main building"; during this period, the Patterson Society met in the Gymnasium Building (see *Idea* 4, no. 18 [25 January 1912]: 6), the Union Society met in the Alumni Building (see *Idea* 4, no. 3 [28 September 1911]: 5), and the Philosophian Society met in Patterson Hall, the women's dormitory (see *Lexington Herald,* 18 March 1917, sec. 3, p.

2). The second quote is from *Lexington Leader,* 7 January 1916, 4; the third quote is from *Lexington Herald,* 13 January 1916, 5; the fourth quote is from *Lexington Herald,* 27 February 1916, sec. 3, p. 2. For the Strollers' tryouts, cast selection, and rehearsals, see *Lexington Herald,* 2 February 1916, 9; 6 February 1916, 6; 7 February 1916, 6; 13 February 1916, sec. 4, p. 5; 5 March 1916, sec. 3, p. 1; 11 March 1916, 7; 12 March 1916, sec. 3, p. 2; *Lexington Leader,* 4 February 1916, 4; 14 February 1916, 5; 27 February 1916, sec. 3, p. 7. The fifth quote is from *Lexington Leader,* 27 February 1916, sec. 3, p. 7; the last quote is from *Lexington Herald,* 13 February 1916, sec. 4, p. 5.

36. The first quote is from *Lexington Herald,* 5 March 1916, sec. 3, p. 1; the second quote is from *Lexington Herald,* 12 March 1916, sec. 3, p. 3. For Gribbin as set designer and poster creator, see *Lexington Herald,* 7 April 1916, sec. 2, p. 2. For the Strollers participating in the Kirmess, see *Lexington Herald,* 9 April 1916, 5. For the lists of patrons, see *Lexington Herald,* 13 April 1916, 9; *Lexington Leader,* 12 April 1916, 10. The last quote is from *Lexington Leader,* 13 April 1916, 8.

37. For accounts promoting or reviewing the Strollers' production, see *Lexington Herald,* 12 April 1916, 16; 13 April 1916, 16; 14 April 1916, sec. 2, pp. 1, 3; *Lexington Leader,* 7 April 1916, 16; 9 April 1916, sec. 3, p. 3; 14 April 1916, 16. For "college night" at the opera house and the quote regarding student enthusiasm, see *Lexington Herald,* 14 April 1916, sec. 2, p. 3. For the street parade and the orchestral accompaniment, see *Lexington Herald,* 12 April 1916, 16; *Lexington Herald,* 13 April 1916, 16. For the Strollers' banquet and the awarding of pins to the cast members, see *Lexington Herald,* 27 May 1916, 7; 28 May 1916, 3.

Epilogue

1. "What's the Matter with the Literary Society?" *Crimson Rambler* 5, no. 29 (9 May 1919): 2. For the decision to disband the Cecropian Society and the first four quotes, see *Crimson Rambler* 6, no. 3 (10 October 1919): 1. For the Cecropian "funeral ceremony" and the fifth quote, see *Crimson Rambler* 6, no. 4 (17 October 1919): 1, 4. The University of Kentucky student newspaper the *Kentucky Kernel* 10, no. 5 (24 October 1919): 2 (in Special Collections and Archives, Margaret I. King Library, University of Kentucky, Lexington), also took note of the passing of the Transylvania society. For the merger of the Periclean and Ossolian societies and the sixth quote, see *Crimson Rambler* 6, no. 10 (29 November 1919): 1. For the extracurricular organizations in the 1920 yearbook, see *The Crimson, 1920,* vol. 22 (Lexington: Senior Classes of Transylvania College, College of the Bible, and Hamilton College, 1920), 59–109, in Special Collections and Archives, J. Douglas Gay Jr. Library, Transylvania University, Lexington. The last two quotes are from *Crimson Rambler* 6, no. 18 (13 February 1920): 4.

2. For the distinction between "societies" and "clubs," see *Kentucky Kernel* 10, no. 2 (3 October 1919): 1. The first quote is from *Kentucky Kernel* 10, no. 19 (27

February 1920): 4. For the page-eight coverage of the Patterson's birthday contest, Clifford Smith as a Patterson Society member, and the front-page coverage of the Strollers, see *Kentucky Kernel* 10, no. 24 (2 April 1920): 1, 8. For Smith's oratorical victories, see *Kentucky Kernel* 10, no. 20 (5 March 1920): 1, 7; 10, no. 21 (12 March 1920): 1. For the student letter critical of the societies and the related quotes, see *Kentucky Kernel* 10, no. 28 (30 April 1920): 5. For the response to this letter and the related quote, see *Kentucky Kernel* 10, no. 29 (7 May 1920): 4.

3. For the literary society curriculum and the formal, institutional curriculum as complementary, see Louise L. Stevenson, "Preparing for Public Life: The Collegiate Students at New York University, 1832–1881," in *The University and the City: From Medieval Origins to the Present*, ed. Thomas Bender (New York: Oxford University Press, 1988), 150–77. For a contrasting description of the societies as a counterpoint to or a revolt against the formal curriculum, see Frederick Rudolph, *The American College and University: A History* (1962; reprint, Athens: University of Georgia Press, 1990), 136–37, chap. 7. For the Southern Interstate Oratorical League contest and the first two quotes, see *Kentucky Kernel* 10, no. 21 (12 March 1920): 1. For the debating team and the related quote, see *Kentucky Kernel* 10, no. 3 (10 October 1919): 1.

4. For the announcement of the Philosophian circus and the related quotes, see *Kentucky Kernel* 10, no. 5 (24 October 1919): 1. For the four literary societies featured (and pictured) in the 1920 yearbook, see *The Kentuckian 1920: Yearbook of the University of Kentucky*, vol. 21 (Lexington: Class of Nineteen Hundred Twenty, 1920), 214, 221, 228, 229, in Special Collections and Archives, Margaret I. King Library, University of Kentucky, Lexington. For the Philosophian as the sole society featured (and pictured) in the 1925 yearbook, see *The 1925 Kentuckian: Yearbook of the University of Kentucky*, vol. 26 (Lexington: Class of Nineteen Hundred Twenty-five, 1925), 228, in Special Collections and Archives, Margaret I. King Library.

5. For this account of Geneva Hardman, her family, and the circumstances of her disappearance, see *Lexington Leader*, 4 February 1920, 1, 2; *Lexington Herald*, 5 February 1920, 1, 2. For descriptions of the crime scene, the posse, and the capture of Will Lockett, see *Lexington Leader*, 4 February 1920, 1, 2; 5 February 1920, 1, 3; *Lexington Herald*, 5 February 1920, 1, 2; the quote is from ibid., 2. For an alternative account of the Hardman-Lockett incident, see John D. Wright Jr., "Lexington's Suppression of the 1920 Will Lockett Lynch Mob," *Register of the Kentucky Historical Society* 84 (Summer 1986): 263–79. Also see Don Edwards, "Attempted Lynching Is Also Part of History," *Lexington Herald-Leader*, 13 May 1997, B1.

6. This biographical sketch of William Lockett (Petrie Kimbrough) is from *Lexington Herald*, 10 February 1920, 2; 9 March 1920, 1; *Lexington Leader*, 8 March 1920, 1.

7. For events at the Lexington jail, see *Lexington Herald*, 5 February 1920,

1, 2; the first quote is from ibid., 1. Also see *Lexington Leader,* 5 February 1920, 1, 2. For the events in Frankfort, see *Lexington Leader,* 5 February 1920, 2. For Governor Edwin Morrow, see *The Kentucky Encyclopedia,* 1992 ed., s.v. "Morrow, Edwin Porch." The last two quotes are from *Lexington Leader,* 5 February 1920, 2; 6 February 1920, 1.

8. For the decision to hold the trial in Fayette County and petition the governor for troops, see *Lexington Herald,* 6 February 1920, 1, 6; 7 February 1920, 1. Also see Wright, "Lexington's Suppression of the 1920 Will Lockett Lynch Mob," 267–68; the first quote is from p. 268. For editorials supportive of judicial authority and due process, see *Lexington Herald,* 6 February 1920, 4; 8 February 1920, sec. 2, p. 1; *Lexington Leader,* 5 February 1920, 4; 8 February 1920, 4. The second quote is from *Lexington Leader,* 5 February 1920, 4; the third and fourth quotes are from *Lexington Herald,* 6 February 1920, 4. For the Negro Civic League's press release, see *Lexington Leader,* 6 February 1920, 9. For the statement by Tupper Hardman, see *Lexington Leader,* 7 February 1920, 1. The quoted headline is from *Lexington Leader,* 8 February 1920, 1; the last quote is from *Lexington Herald,* 8 February 1920, 3.

9. For accounts of the Lockett trial and the mob violence outside the courthouse, see *Lexington Leader,* 9, February 1920, 1, 2; *Lexington Herald,* 10 February 1920, 1, 2. The first quote is from *Lexington Leader,* 9, February 1920, 1. For those killed or wounded by the authorities, see *Lexington Leader,* 9 February 1920, 1, 2; 10 February 1920, 1; 11 February 1920, 1; *Lexington Herald,* 10 February 1920, 1, 2; 11 February 1920, 1, 9; 12 February 1920, 1. For looting, see *Lexington Leader,* 9 February 1920, 2. For McVey's address and the second quote, see *Lexington Herald,* 10 February 1920, 8. For federal troops and martial law in Lexington, see *Lexington Herald,* 10 February 1920, 1, 2; 13 February 1920, 1, 2; 17 February 1920, 1; 22 February 1920, 1, 8; *Lexington Leader,* 9 February 1920, 1, 2; 10 February 1920, 1; 17 February 1920, 1; 22 February 1920, 1.

10. For the special grand juries, see *Lexington Herald,* 13 February 1920, 1, 2; 14 February 1920, 1, 3; 15 February 1920, 1, 3; 20 February 1920, 1; 27 February 1920, 1, 5; 28 February 1920, 4; *Lexington Leader,* 12 February 1920, 1; 13 February 1920, 4; 14 February 1920, 1; 15 February 1920, 1; 21 February 1920, 1; 27 February 1920, 1; 29 February 1920, 4. For William Preston as grand juror, see *Lexington Herald,* 15 February 1920, 1; *Lexington Leader,* 14 February 1920, 1. The first quote is from *Lexington Leader,* 21 February 1920, 1; the second quote is from *Lexington Herald,* 28 February 1920, 4. For "Justice Miscarries," see *Lexington Leader,* 29 February 1920, 4. For accounts sympathetic to the families of the men killed and in defense of the officials, see *Lexington Leader,* 10 February 1920, 4; 12 February 1920, 1; 16 February 1920, 1, 2; 21 February 1920, 1; *Lexington Herald,* 10 February 1920, 1, 2, 4; 11 February 1920, 1, 9; 11 February 1920, 4; 12 February 1920, 1; 15 February 1920, sec. 2, p. 1. For the churches' defense of law and order and the last quote, see *Lexington Leader,* 16 February 1920, 5.

11. For the Marlowe Club play and the Department of Literature meeting, see *Lexington Leader,* 22 February 1920, sec. 2, p. 4. For the Reading Circle meeting, see *Lexington Leader,* 15 February 1920, sec. 2, p. 1.

12. Quote from "Vindicating the Law," *Outlook,* 18 February 1920, 268, in Wright, "Lexington's Suppression of the 1920 Will Lockett Lynch Mob."

BIBLIOGRAPHY

BOOKS AND ARTICLES

Allen, James Lane. *The Reign of Law: A Tale of the Kentucky Hemp Fields.* New York: Macmillan, 1900.
———. *Summer in Arcady.* New York: Macmillan Company, 1896; reprint, New York: Macmillan, 1909.
Antczak, Frederick J., and Edith Seimers. "The Divergence of Purpose and Practice on the Chautauqua: Keith Vawter's Self-Defense." In *Oratorical Culture in Nineteenth-Century America: Transformations in the Theory and Practice of Rhetoric,* ed. Gregory Clark and S. Michael Halloran, 208–25. Carbondale: Southern Illinois University Press, 1993.
Axell, James. *The European and the Indian: Essays in the Ethnohistory of Colonial North America.* New York: Oxford University Press, 1981.
Ayers, Edward L. *The Promise of the New South: Life after Reconstruction.* New York: Oxford University Press, 1992.
———. *Southern Crossing: A History of the American South, 1877–1906.* New York: Oxford University Press, 1995.
Barrie, J. M. *The Plays of J. M. Barrie, in One Volume.* New York: Charles Scribner's Sons, 1929.
Beam, Jacob. *The American Whig Society of Princeton University.* Princeton, N.J.: American Whig Society, 1933.
Bender, Thomas. "The Cultures of Intellectual Life: The City and the Professions." In *New Directions in American Intellectual History,* ed. John Higham and Paul K. Conkin, 181–95. Baltimore: Johns Hopkins University Press, 1979.
———. *Intellect and Public Life: Essays on the Social History of Academic Intellectuals in the United States.* Baltimore: Johns Hopkins University Press, 1993.
———. *New York Intellect: A History of Intellectual Life in New York City, from 1750 to the Beginning of Our Own Time.* Baltimore: Johns Hopkins University Press, 1987.
Berlin, James A. *Writing Instruction in Nineteenth-Century American Colleges.* Studies in Writing and Rhetoric Series. Carbondale: Southern Illinois University Press, 1984.
Biersack, Aletta. "Local Knowledge, Local History: Geertz and Beyond." In *The New Cultural History,* ed. Lynn Hunt, 72–96. Los Angeles: University of California Press, 1989.
The Biographical Encyclopaedia of Kentucky of the Dead and Living Men of the Nineteenth Century. Cincinnati: J. M. Armstrong, 1878; reprint, Easley, S.C.: Southern Historical Press, 1980.

Bledstein, Burton J. *The Culture of Professionalism: The Middle Class and the Development of Higher Education in America.* New York: W. W. Norton, 1978.

The "Blue Grass" Directory of the City of Lexington, Kentucky. Lexington: "Blue Grass" Directory Company, 1902.

Bohman, George V. "Rhetorical Practice in Colonial America." In *History of Speech Education in America: Background Studies,* ed. Karl R. Wallace, 60–79. New York: Appleton-Century-Crofts, 1954.

Bordman, Gerald. *American Theatre: A Chronicle of Comedy and Drama, 1914–1930.* New York: Oxford University Press, 1995.

Borrello, Alfred. *H. G. Wells: Author in Agony.* Carbondale: Southern Illinois University Press, 1972.

Bourne, Randolph. "Randolph Bourne, Article in *Dial,* 28 December 1916." In *H. G. Wells: The Critical Heritage,* ed. Patrick Parrinder, 239–43. London: Rutledge and Kegan Paul, 1972.

Briggs, Irene, and Raymond F. DaBoll. *Recollections of the Lyceum and Chautauqua Circuits.* Freeport, Me.: Bond Wheelwright Company, 1969.

Brinkley, Allen, Richard N. Current, Frank Freidel, and T. Harry Williams. *American History, a Survey,* 8th ed. Vol. 2, *Since 1865.* New York: McGraw-Hill, 1991.

Brock, Loretta Gilliam. *A History of the Woman's Club of Central Kentucky, 1894–1994.* Lexington: Woman's Club of Central Kentucky, 1996.

Brodhead, Richard H. *Cultures of Letters: Scenes of Reading and Writing in Nineteenth-Century America.* Chicago: University of Chicago Press, 1993.

Brown, Orlando. *Memoranda of the Preston Family.* Frankfort, Ky.: Hodges, Todd and Pruett, 1842.

Brundage, W. Fitzhugh. *Lynching in the New South: Georgia and Virginia, 1880–1930.* Urbana: University of Illinois Press, 1993.

Burke, Colin B. *American Collegiate Populations: A Test of the Traditional View.* New York: New York University Press, 1982.

Bushman, Richard L. *The Refinement of America: Persons, Houses, Cities.* New York: Knopf, 1992; New York: Vintage Books, 1993.

Calhoun, Charles W., ed. *The Gilded Age: Essays on the Origins of Modern America.* Wilmington, Del.: Scholarly Resources, 1996.

Calhoun, Daniel: *The Intelligence of a People.* Princeton, N.J.: Princeton University Press, 1973.

Carter, Jean, and Jess Ogden. *Everyman's Drama: A Study of the Noncommercial Theatre in the United States.* New York: American Association for Adult Education, 1938.

Cashman, Sean Dennis. *America in the Age of the Titans: The Progressive Era and World War I.* New York: New York University Press, 1988.

Catalogue of the American Whig Society, Instituted in the College of New Jersey, 1769. Princeton, N.J.: American Whig Society, 1914.

Catalogue of Kentucky University and of the College of the Bible, 1891. Lexington: Transylvania Printing Company, 1891.

Catalogue of Kentucky University, 1899–1900. Lexington: Transylvania Printing Company, 1900.

Catalogue of the Officers and Students of Kentucky University, for the Session of 1867–68. Louisville: John P. Morton and Company, 1868.

Chauncey, George. *Gay New York: Gender, Urban Culture, and the Making of the Gay Male World, 1890–1940.* New York: Basic Books, 1994.

Chesnutt, Charles W. *The Marrow of Tradition.* With an introduction by Robert M. Farnsworth. New York: Houghton, Mifflin, 1901; reprint, Ann Arbor: University of Michigan Press, Ann Arbor Paperbacks, 1969.

City Directory of Lexington Kentucky, 1887. Chattanooga, Tenn.: Norwood, Connelly and Co., 1887.

City Directory of Lexington, Ky. 1888. Lexington: Prather and Snyder, 1888.

City Directory of Lexington, Ky. 1890. Lexington: "Hub" Prather, 1890.

Clark, Gregory, and S. Michael Halloran, eds. *Oratorical Culture in Nineteenth-Century America: Transformations in the Theory and Practice of Rhetoric.* Carbondale: Southern Illinois University Press, 1993.

Coffman, Edward M. *The War to End All Wars: The American Military Experience in World War I.* New York: Oxford University Press, 1968; reprint, Lexington: University Press of Kentucky, 1998.

Coleman, J. Winston, Jr. *The Squire's Sketches of Lexington.* Lexington: Henry Clay Press, 1972.

Cone, Carl B. *The University of Kentucky: A Pictorial History.* Lexington: University Press of Kentucky, 1990.

Cook, Raymond A. *Thomas Dixon.* New York: Twayne Publishers, 1974.

Cordery, Stacy A. "Women in Industrializing America." In *The Gilded Age: Essays on the Origins of Modern America,* ed. Charles W. Calhoun, 111–35. Wilmington, Del.: Scholarly Resources, 1996.

Detzer, Karl, and Harry P. Harrison. *Culture under Canvas: The Story of Tent Chautauqua.* New York: Hastings House, 1958.

Dicken-Garcia, Hazel. *Journalistic Standards in Nineteenth-Century America.* Madison: University of Wisconsin Press, 1989.

Dickens, Charles. *Hard Times.* London: Bradbury and Evans, 1854; reprint, New York: New American Library, 1961.

Dickerson, Donna Lee. *The Course of Tolerance: Freedom of the Press in Nineteenth-Century America.* Westport, Conn.: Greenwood Press, 1990.

Dixon, Thomas, Jr. *The Clansman: An Historical Romance of the Ku Klux Klan.* New York: Grosset and Dunlap, c. 1905.

———. *The Leopard's Spots: A Romance of the White Man's Burden—1865–1900.* New York: Grosset and Dunlap, c. 1902.

DuBois, W. E. B. *The Souls of Black Folk.* Chicago: A. C. McClurg, 1903; reprint, New York: Vintage Books, 1990.

Dunnahoo, Terry. *Before the Supreme Court: The Story of Belva Ann Lockwood.* Boston: Houghton Mifflin, 1974.

Dzuback, Mary Ann. "Retrospective: Professionalism, Higher Education, and American Culture: Burton J. Bledstein's *The Culture of Professionalism.*" *History of Education Quarterly* 33 (Fall 1993): 375–85.

Eaton, Clement. *The Waning of the Old South Civilization, 1860–1880s.* Athens: University of Georgia Press, 1968.

Eddy, Sherwood. *A Century with Youth: A History of the Y.M.C.A. from 1844 to 1944.* New York: Association Press, 1944.

Faris, John T. *The Romance of Forgotten Men.* New York: Harper and Brothers, 1928.

Federal Writers' Project of the WPA for the State of Kentucky. *Lexington and the Bluegrass Country.* Lexington: E. M. Glass, 1938.

Fox, John, Jr. *The Little Shepherd of Kingdom Come.* New York: Charles Scribner's Sons, 1903; reprint, New York: Grosset and Dunlap, 1931.

Frederic, Harold. *The Damnation of Theron Ware.* New York: Stone and Kimball, 1896; reprint, Greenwich, Conn.: Fawcett Publications, 1962.

Frothingham, O. B. "Voices of Power." *Atlantic Monthly* 53 (February 1884): 176–82.

Fry, Joseph A. "Phases of Empire: Late Nineteenth-Century U.S. Foreign Relations." In *The Gilded Age: Essays on the Origins of Modern America,* ed. Charles W. Calhoun, 261–88. Wilmington, Del.: Scholarly Resources, 1996.

Fuller, Paul E. *Laura Clay and the Woman's Rights Movement.* With a foreword by A. Elizabeth Taylor. Lexington: University Press of Kentucky, 1975, 1992.

Gaines, Kevin K. *Uplifting the Race: Black Leadership, Politics, and Culture in the Twentieth Century.* Chapel Hill: University of North Carolina Press, 1996.

Gatewood, Willard B. *Aristocrats of Color: The Black Elite, 1880–1920.* Bloomington: Indiana University Press, 1990; First Midland Book ed., 1993.

Gere, Anne Ruggles. *Intimate Practices: Literacy and Cultural Work in U.S. Women's Clubs, 1880–1920.* Urbana: University of Illinois Press, 1997.

Gilfoyle, Timothy J. "America's Heart." Review of *Gotham: A History of New York City to 1892,* by Edwin G. Burrows and Mike Wallace. *Atlantic Monthly,* February 1999, 95–98.

Gill, Stephen. *Scientific Romances of H. G. Wells : A Critical Study.* Ontario, Canada: Vesta Publications, 1975.

Gillis, Ezra L. *The University of Kentucky: Its History and Development: A Series of Charts Depicting the More Important Data, 1862–1955.* Lexington: University of Kentucky, 1956.

Grady, Henry W. "The New South." In *Century Readings in American Literature,* 4th ed., ed. Fred Lewis Pattee, 780–84. New York: Century, 1932.

Grantham, Dewey W. *Southern Progressivism: The Reconciliation of Progress and Tradition.* Knoxville: University of Tennessee Press, 1983.

Guernsey, Joseph C. *45th Reunion Class of 1870, Princeton.* Philadelphia: Class of 1870, Princeton University, 1916.

————. *50th Reunion Class of 1870, Princeton.* Bryn Mawr, Pa.: Class of 1870, Princeton University, 1921.

Guthrie, Warren. "Rhetorical Theory in Colonial America." In *History of Speech Education in America: Background Studies,* ed. Karl R. Wallace, 48–59. New York: Appleton-Century-Crofts, 1954.

Haber, Samuel. *The Quest for Authority and Honor in the American Professions, 1750–1900.* Chicago: University of Chicago Press, 1991.

Hamlin, Arthur T. *The University Library in the United States: Its Origins and Development.* Philadelphia: University of Pennsylvania Press, 1981.

Harding, Thomas S. "College Literary Societies: Their Contribution to the Development of Academic Libraries, 1815–76. I. The Golden Age of College Society Libraries, 1815–40." *Library Quarterly* 29, no. 1 (January 1959): 1–26.

————. "College Literary Societies: Their Contribution to the Development of Academic Libraries, 1815–76. II. The Decline of College Society Libraries, 1841–76." *Library Quarterly* 29, no. 2 (April 1959): 94–112.

————. *College Literary Societies: Their Contribution to Higher Education in the United States 1815–1876.* New York: Pageant Press International, 1971.

Harries, Meirion, and Susie Harries. *The Last Days of Innocence: America at War, 1917–1918.* New York: Random House, 1997.

Harrison, Lowell H. *The Civil War in Kentucky.* Lexington: University Press of Kentucky, 1975.

Hopkins, Charles Howard. *History of the Y.M.C.A. in North America.* New York: Association Press, 1951.

Hopkins, James F. *The University of Kentucky: Origins and Early Years.* Lexington: University of Kentucky Press, 1951.

Horowitz, Helen Lefkowitz. *Campus Life: Undergraduate Cultures from the End of the Eighteenth Century to the Present.* Chicago: University of Chicago Press, 1987.

Howell, Wilbur Samuel. "English Backgrounds of Rhetoric." In *History of Speech Education in America: Background Studies,* ed. Karl R. Wallace, 1–47. New York: Appleton-Century-Crofts, 1954.

Hunt, Lynn. "Introduction: History, Culture, and Text." In *The New Cultural History,* ed. Lynn Hunt, 1–22. Los Angeles: University of California Press, 1989.

In Memoriam: Stained Glass Windows of First Presbyterian Church. Lexington: First Presbyterian Church, 1997.

Irvin, Helen Deiss. *Hail Kentucky! A Pictorial History of the University of Kentucky.* With an introduction by Holman Hamilton. Lexington: University of Kentucky Press, 1965.

James, Henry. *The American.* Boston: Houghton, Mifflin, 1877; reprint, New York: Dell, 1964.

Jennings, Walter Wilson. *Transylvania: Pioneer University of the West.* New York: Pageant Press, 1955.

Johnson, Nan. *Nineteenth-Century Rhetoric in North America*. Carbondale: Southern Illinois University Press, 1991.

———. "The Popularization of Nineteenth-Century Rhetoric: Elocution and the Private Learner." In *Oratorical Culture in Nineteenth-Century America: Transformations in the Theory and Practice of Rhetoric*, ed. Gregory Clark and S. Michael Halloran, 139–57. Carbondale: Southern Illinois University Press, 1993.

Kellogg, John. "The Formation of Black Residential Areas in Lexington, Kentucky, 1865–1887." *Journal of Southern History* 48, no. 1 (February 1982): 21–52.

The Kentucky Encyclopedia. Lexington: University Press of Kentucky, 1992.

Kerr, Bettie L., and John D. Wright Jr. *Lexington: A Century in Photographs*. Lexington: Lexington–Fayette County Historic Commission, 1984.

Kett, Joseph F. *The Pursuit of Knowledge under Difficulties: From Self-Improvement to Adult Education in America, 1750–1990*. Stanford, Calif.: Stanford University Press, 1994.

Kimball, Bruce E. *Orators and Philosophers: A History of Liberal Education*. With a foreword by Joseph L. Featherstone. New York: Teachers College Press, 1986.

———. *The "True Professional Ideal" in America: A History*. Cambridge, Mass.: Blackwell, 1992.

Klotter, James C. *The Breckinridges of Kentucky, 1760–1981*. Lexington: University Press of Kentucky, 1986.

———. *Kentucky: Portrait in Paradox, 1900–1950*. Frankfort: Kentucky Historical Society, 1996.

Knight, Grant C. *James Lane Allen and the Genteel Tradition*. Chapel Hill: University of North Carolina Press, 1935.

Koenig, Louis W. *Bryan: A Political Biography of William Jennings Bryan*. New York: Capricorn Books, 1975.

Kunitz, Stanley J., and Howard Haycraft, eds. *Twentieth Century Authors: A Biographical Dictionary of Modern Literature*. New York: H. W. Wilson Company, 1942.

Levine, Lawrence W. *Highbrow/Lowbrow: The Emergence of Cultural Hierarchy in America*. Cambridge, Mass.: Harvard University Press, 1988.

Lexington City Directory. Lexington: R. C. Hellrigle and Co., 1877.

Lexington City Directory for 1881–82. Lexington: Williams and Co., 1881.

Lexington Directory for 1883–1884. Lexington: Townsend and Co., 1884.

Lexington City Directory 1906–1907. Lexington: R. L. Polk and Co., 1906.

Lexington City Directory 1908. Lexington: R. L. Polk and Co., 1908.

Lexington City Directory 1911. Lexington: R. L. Polk and Co., 1911.

Lexington City Directory 1914–15. Lexington: R. L. Polk and Co., 1915.

Lexington City Guide 1912–13. Lexington: R. L. Polk and Co., 1912.

Lexington, the Central City: A Review of Lexington as She Is Her Wealth and Industry, Her Wonderful Growth and Admirable Enterprise, Her Great Business Concerns, Her Manufacturing Advances, and Commercial Resources. New York: John Lethem [1887].

Lowitt, Richard. *George W. Norris: The Persistence of a Progressive, 1913–1933.* Urbana: University of Illinois Press, 1971.

Macgowan, Kenneth. *Footlights across America: Towards a National Theater.* New York: Harcourt, Brace, 1929.

Mackay, Constance D'Arcy. *The Little Theater in the United States.* New York: Henry Holt, 1917.

MacKaye, Percy. *The Civic Theatre in Relation to the Redemption of Leisure: A Book of Suggestions.* New York: Mitchell Kennerley, 1912.

Martin, Theodora Penny. *The Sound of Our Own Voices: Women's Study Clubs 1860–1910.* Boston: Beacon Press, 1987.

Matthews, Gary Robert. *Basil Wilson Duke, CSA: The Right Man in the Right Place.* Lexington: University Press of Kentucky, 2005.

May, Hal, ed. *Contemporary Authors: A Bio-Bibliographical Guide to Current Writers in Fiction, General Nonfiction, Poetry, Journalism, Drama, Motion Pictures, Television, and Other Fields,* vol. 120. Detroit: Gale Research, 1987.

McArthur, Benjamin. *Actors and American Culture, 1880–1920.* Philadelphia: Temple University Press, 1984.

McLachlan, James. "The American College in the Nineteenth Century: Toward a Reappraisal." *Teachers College Record* 80 (September 1978): 287–306.

———. "The *Choice of Hercules:* American Student Societies in the Early 19th Century." In *The University in Society,* vol. 2, *Europe, Scotland, and the United States from the 16th to the 20th Century,* ed. Lawrence Stone, 449–94. Princeton, N.J.: Princeton University Press, 1974.

McLaughlin, Marguerite, O. M. Shedd, and R. C. Stoll. "Clarke Howell Tandy." *Mechanical Engineering and Electrical Engineering Record* 2 (January 1909): 46–50.

McMichael, George L. *Journey to Obscurity: The Life of Octave Thanet.* Lincoln: University of Nebraska Press, 1965.

Metcalfe, James. Review of *The Virginian,* by Owen Wister and Kirke La Shelle (Manhattan Theater, New York). *Life,* 4 February 1904, 118–19.

Miller, Worth Robert. "Farmers and Third-Party Politics." In *The Gilded Age: Essays on the Origins of Modern America,* ed. Charles W. Calhoun, 235–60. Wilmington, Del.: Scholarly Resources, 1996.

Morelock, Kolan. "A Preliminary History of the Literary Magazine at Centre College." Typescript, 1992.

O'Brien, Michael, ed. *All Clever Men, Who Make Their Way: Critical Discourse in the Old South.* Brown Thrasher ed. Athens: University of Georgia Press, 1992.

Ong, Walter J. *Orality and Literacy: The Technologizing of the Word.* London: Methuen, 1982; reprint, London: Routledge, 1991.

———. *Ramus, Method, and the Decay of Dialogue: From the Art of Discourse to the Art of Reason.* Cambridge, Mass.: Harvard University Press, 1958; reprinted in paperback, 1983.

The Oxford Companion to English Literature. New York: Oxford University Press, 1985.

Packer, William. *The Art of* Vogue *Covers 1909–1940.* London: Peerage Books, 1987.

Perry, Clarence Arthur. *The Work of the Little Theatres: The Groups They Include, the Plays They Produce, Their Tournaments, and the Handbooks They Use.* New York: Russell Sage Foundation, 1933.

Peter, Robert. *History of Fayette County, Kentucky, with an Outline Sketch of the Bluegrass Region.* Chicago: O. L. Baskin, 1882.

Phelps, William Lyon. *The Twentieth Century Theatre: Observations on the Contemporary English and American Stage.* New York: Macmillan, 1918.

Poe, Edgar Allan. "Marginal Notes . . . No. II. A Sequel to the 'Marginalia' of the *Democratic Review.*" In *Complete Works of Edgar Allan Poe,* ed. James A. Harrison. New York: AMS Press, 1965.

Polk's Lexington City Directory 1914–1915. Lexington: R. L. Polk and Co., 1914.

Potter, David. *Debating in the Colonial Chartered Colleges: An Historical Survey, 1642 to 1900.* Contributions to Education No. 899. New York: Bureau of Publications, Teachers College, Columbia University, 1944.

———. "The Literary Society." In *History of Speech Education in America: Background Studies,* ed. Karl R. Wallace, 238–58. New York: Appleton-Century-Crofts, 1954.

Prather's Directory of the City of Lexington, Kentucky. Lexington: J. "Hub" Prather, 1895.

Ramage, James A. *Rebel Raider: The Life of General John Hunt Morgan.* Lexington: University Press of Kentucky, 1986.

Ranck, George W. *Guide to Lexington, Kentucky: With Notices Historical and Descriptive of Places and Objects of Interest, and a Summary of the Advantages and Resources of the City and Vicinity.* Lexington: Transylvania Printing and Publishing Company, 1883.

———. *Historical Address at the Centennial Celebration of the Settlement of Lexington, Kentucky: April 2, 1879.* Lexington: Transylvania Printing and Publishing Company, 1879.

———. *History of Lexington, Kentucky: Its Early Annals and Recent Progress, Including Biographical Sketches and Personal Reminiscences of the Pioneer Settlers, Notices of Prominent Citizens, Etc., Etc.* . Cincinnati: R. Clarke, 1872.

Rogers, Timothy. *Rupert Brooke: A Reappraisal and Selection from His Writing, Some Hitherto Unpublished.* New York: Barnes and Noble, 1971.

Roth, Michael S. "Performing History: Modernist Contextualism in Carl Schorske's *Fin-de-Siècle Vienna.*" *American Historical Review* 99 (June 1994): 729–45.

Rotundo, Anthony E. *American Manhood: Transformations in Masculinity from the Revolution to the Modern Era.* New York: Basic Books, 1993.

Rudolph, Frederick. *The American College and University: A History.* New York: A. Knopf, 1962; reprint, Athens: University of Georgia Press, 1990.

————. *Mark Hopkins and the Log: Williams College, 1836–1872.* New Haven, Conn.: Yale University Press, 1956.

————. "Neglect of Students as a Historical Tradition." In *The College and the Student,* ed. Lawrence E. Dennis and Joseph F. Kauffman, 47–58. Washington, D.C.: American Council on Education, 1966.

Russell, Harvey C. *The Negro Education Association: 1877–1946.* Norfolk, Va.: Guide Quality Press, 1946.

Ryan, Mary. "The American Parade: Representations of the Nineteenth-Century Social Order." In *The New Cultural History,* ed. Lynn Hunt, 131–53. Los Angeles: University of California Press, 1989.

————. *Women in Public: Between Banners and Ballots, 1825–1880.* Baltimore: Johns Hopkins University Press, 1990; paperback ed., 1992.

Salem, James M. *Drury's Guide to Best Plays,* 3d ed. Metuchen, N.J.: Scarecrow Press, 1978.

Schaffer, Ronald. *America in the Great War: The Rise of the War Welfare State.* New York: Oxford University Press, 1991; paperback ed., 1994.

Schlereth, Thomas J. *Cultural History and Material Culture: Everyday Life, Landscapes, Museums.* Charlottesville: University Press of Virginia, 1990; paperback ed., 1992.

————. *Victorian America: Transformations in Everyday Life, 1876–1915.* New York: HarperCollins, 1991; HarperPerennial, 1992.

Scott, Donald. "The Profession that Vanished: Public Lecturing in Mid-Nineteenth-Century America." In *Professions and Professional Ideologies in America,* ed. Gerald L. Geison, 12–28. Chapel Hill: University of North Carolina Press, 1983.

Share, Allen J. *Cities in the Commonwealth: Two Centuries of Urban Life in Kentucky.* Lexington: University Press of Kentucky, 1982.

Sheppard's Lexington City Directory for 1873 and 1874. Cincinnati: J. S. Sheppard and Co., 1873.

Simpson, D. P. *Cassell's Latin and English Dictionary.* New York: Macmillan, 1987.

Sinclair, Upton. *The Jungle.* New York: Jungle Publishing Company, 1906; Bantam Classic ed., 1981.

Slide, Anthony, ed. *Selected Theatre Criticism,* vol. 1, *1900–1919.* Metuchen, N.J.: Scarecrow Press, 1985.

Sloan, Douglas. "The Teaching of Ethics in the American Undergraduate Curriculum, 1876–1976." In *Ethics Teaching in Higher Education,* ed. Daniel Callahan and Sissela Bok, 1–57. New York: Plenum Press, 1980.

Smith, William Benjamin. "In Memoriam: John Henry Neville." *Mechanical Engineering and Electrical Engineering Record* 2 (October 1908): 4–11.

Solomon, Barbara M. *In the Company of Educated Women: A History of Women and Higher Education in America.* New Haven, Conn.: Yale University Press, 1985.

Stanley, Gregory Kent. *Before Big Blue: Sports at the University of Kentucky, 1880–1940.* Lexington: University Press of Kentucky, 1996.

Stevenson, Louise L. "Preparing for Public Life: The Collegiate Students at New York University, 1832–1881." In *The University and the City: From Medieval Origins to the Present,* ed. Thomas Bender, 150–77. New York: Oxford University Press, 1988.

———. *Scholarly Means to Evangelical Ends: The New Haven Scholars and the Transformation of Higher Learning in America, 1830–1890.* Baltimore: Johns Hopkins University Press, 1986.

———. *The Victorian Homefront: American Thought and Culture, 1860–1880.* New York: Twayne Publishers, 1991.

Stone, Jon R. *Latin for the Illiterati.* New York: Routledge, 1996.

Tanner, Joseph M. "Fifty Years' Recollections of Lexington and Vicinity, Its People and Institutions." Typescript, 1926.

Tapp, Hambleton, and James C. Klotter. *Kentucky: Decades of Discord, 1865–1900.* Frankfort: Kentucky Historical Society, 1977.

Thanet, Octave. *The Man of the Hour.* Indianapolis: Bobbs-Merrill, 1905.

Tice, Karen. "Battle for Benevolence: Scientific Disciplinary Control vs. Indiscriminate Relief: Lexington Associated Charities and the Salvation Army, 1900–1918." *Journal of Sociology and Social Welfare* 19 (June 1992): 59–77.

Tindall, George Brown. *The Emergence of the New South, 1913–1945.* Baton Rouge: Louisiana State University Press, 1967.

Transylvania College Bulletin, the Catalogue 1915–1916. Lexington: Transylvania University, 1916.

Transylvania University Catalogue Number 1910–1911. Lexington: Transylvania University, 1911.

Tuchman, Barbara. *The Proud Tower, a Portrait of the World before the War: 1890–1914.* New York: Macmillan, 1966; New York: Bantam Books, 1967.

Veysey, Laurence R. "The History of Education." *Reviews in American History* (December 1982): 281–91.

Waller, Gregory A. "Entertainment in the Model Municipality: Chautauqua at the Turn-of-the-Century." Typescript, 1994.

———. *Main Street Amusements: Movies and Commercial Entertainment in a Southern City, 1896–1930.* Washington, D.C.: Smithsonian Institution Press, 1995.

Wickliffe, Robert, Jr., Esq. *An Oration, Delivered on the 22nd of February, 1830 at the Request of the Union Philosophical Society of Transylvania.* Lexington: Union Philosophical Society, 1830.

Williams, Paul Edgar. *The Y.M.C.A. College.* St. Louis: Educational Council of the Young Men's Christian Association, 1938.

Wilson, Samuel M. *History of Kentucky,* vol. 2, *From 1803 to 1928.* Louisville: S. J. Clarke Publishing Company, 1928.

Woman's Club of Central Kentucky Yearbook for 1959–1960. Lexington: Woman's Club of Central Kentucky, 1960.

The World Book Encyclopedia. Chicago: World Book–Childcraft International, 1982.

Wright, George C. *A History of Blacks in Kentucky,* vol. 2, *In Pursuit of Equality, 1890–1980.* Frankfort: Kentucky Historical Society, 1992.

———. "Oral History and the Search for the Black Past in Kentucky." *Oral History Review* 10 (1982) : 73–91.

———. *Racial Violence in Kentucky, 1865–1940: Lynchings, Mob Rule, and "Legal Lynchings."* Baton Rouge: Louisiana State University Press, 1990.

Wright, John D., Jr. *Lexington: Heart of the Bluegrass.* Lexington: Lexington–Fayette County Historic Commission, 1982.

———. "Lexington's Suppression of the 1920 Will Lockett Lynch Mob." *Register of the Kentucky Historical Society* 84 (Summer 1986): 263–79.

———. *Transylvania: Tutor to the West.* Lexington: University Press of Kentucky, 1980.

Wynn, Neil A. *From Progressivism to Prosperity: World War I and American Society.* New York: Holmes and Meier, 1986.

DISSERTATIONS AND THESES

Birdwhistell, Terry L. "An Educated Difference: Women at the University of Kentucky through the Second World War." PhD diss., University of Kentucky, 1994.

Bolin, James. "Bossism and Reform: Politics in Lexington, Kentucky, 1880–1940." PhD diss., University of Kentucky, 1988.

Fouse, William H. "Educational History of the Negroes of Lexington, Kentucky." Master's thesis, University of Cincinnati, 1937.

Hay, Melba Porter. "Madeline McDowell Breckinridge: Kentucky Suffragist and Progressive Reformer." PhD diss., University of Kentucky, 1980.

Knott, Claudia. "The Woman Suffrage Movement in Kentucky." PhD diss., University of Kentucky, 1989.

Meek, Beryl. "A Record of the Theater in Lexington, Kentucky from 1799–1850." Master's thesis, State University of Iowa, 1930.

Shiflett, Orvin Lee. "The Origins of American Academic Librarianship." PhD diss., Florida State University, 1979. Ann Arbor: University Microfilms International, 1980.

Sutherland, Arthur Bruce. "Maurice Hewlett: Historical Romancer." PhD diss., University of Pennsylvania, 1938.

GOVERNMENT DOCUMENTS

Department of Commerce, Bureau of the Census. *Thirteenth Census of the United States Taken in the Year 1910,* vol. 1, *Population.* Washington, D.C.: Department of Commerce, Bureau of the Census, 1913.

———. *Fourteenth Census of the United States Taken in the Year 1920,* vol. 1, *Population.* Washington, D.C.: Department of Commerce, Bureau of the Census, 1921.

Department of the Interior, Census Office. *Report on Population of the United States at the Eleventh Census: 1890,* vol. 1. Washington, D.C.: Department of the Interior, Census Office, 1893.

———. *Statistics of the Population of the United States at the Tenth Census (June 1, 1880),* vol. 1. Washington, D.C.: Department of the Interior, Census Office, 1883.

———. *Twelfth Census of the United States, Taken in the Year 1900,* vol. 1, *Population.* Washington, D.C.: Department of the Interior, Census Office, 1902.

MANUSCRIPT COLLECTIONS

Department of Rare Books and Special Collections, Firestone Library, Princeton University, Princeton, N.J.

Special Collections and Archives, Paul G. Blazer Library, Kentucky State University, Frankfort, Ky.

Special Collections and Archives, J. Douglas Gay Jr. Library, Transylvania University, Lexington, Ky.

Special Collections and Archives, Margaret I. King Library, University of Kentucky, Lexington, Ky.

Index

academic freedom, 5
Ada Meade Theater (Lexington), 171, 181
Adams, Forepaugh, and Sells Circus, 33
Adams, John, 72
Adams, Maude, 202
Addams, Jane, 179
Ade, George, 267, 271, 272–73
Adelphi Alpha Society (Transylvania), 75, 77, 331n28
Adelphi Beta Society (Danville, Ky.), 75
Agricultural and Mechanical College, 54, 85, 89–90, 92, 285, 331n28
agricultural college extensions, 219
Alatheian (Alathean/Aletheian/Alethean) Literary Society, 82–83, 96
Allen, James Lane
  on Bible College students, 4–5
  as Chautauqua judge, 119
  on Civil War legacy, 13
  on Kentucky University, 53, 78
  as *Owl* contributor, 80
  The Reign of Law, 5
  salutatory speech given by, 56–57
  Summer in Arcady, 258
All Is Fair in Love (comedy), 258
Alpha Dramatic Club, 262
Altar Guild, 223
American, The (James), 67
American Tobacco Company, 219
American Vitagraph Company, 127
American Whig Society (Hampden-Sydney College), 74
American Whig Society (Princeton), 55, 73, 74, 80, 324n5
Anchor (Phileusebian Society paper), 78–79

Antczak, Frederick, 116
Anthony, Susan B., 259
Anti Child Slavery League of America, 225
anti–Separate Coach Law campaign, 10, 37–38
Armstrong, Paul, 269
art museums, 184
Associated Charities, 166, 226, 241
athletics
  dramatic society funding of, 265
  increased local press coverage of, 254
  increased student press coverage of, 99, 104–5, 245, 246, 247–48, 249–50
  as intercollegiate oratorical contest competition, 125, 126, 132
  as literary society competition, 7, 98, 99, 100, 244
  Patterson opposed to, 104
Atlanta (Ga.) race riot (1906), 160
Atlantic Monthly, 235
Atlantis (Kentucky University literary magazine), 80, 97
"Aunt Jessie." *See* Draper, Jessie Preston
Automobile and Fashion Show, 171, 174–77, 272
Automobile Dealers Association, 174
automobiles, 150
Ayers, Edward, 26, 37, 41, 43, 48, 64, 160

Baby Milk Fund, 181–83, 241
Baby Milk Supply Society, 181
Back to Africa movement, 39
Bacon College (Harrodsburg, Ky.), 77
  See also Kentucky University
Baird's Minstrels, 34

Baker, George Pierce, 257
Ballard, Wood, 124
Ballard's Drugstore (Lexington), 180
Barker, Henry Stites, 89, 173, 182,
   251, 266, 272
Barrie, James Matthew, 236
Barrymore, John, 240
Barrymore, Lionel, 211
baseball
   increased student press coverage of,
      247
   as intercollegiate oratorical contest
      competition, 125, 132
   intercollegiate series in, 105
   as literary society competition, 98,
      99, 244
   at State College, 105
   in Woodland Park, 36
basketball, 244, 250, 254
Bayonet (State College student
   monthly), 103
Beach, Rex, 269
Beam, Jacob, 74
Beard, George Miller, 214
Beecher, Henry Ward, 30
Ben Ali Theater (Lexington)
   all-movie format of, 265, 270,
      378n34
   dramatic society performances in,
      265, 267, 268, 269
   opening of, 171
   Preston (Margaret) at, 231, 240
Bender, Thomas, 1, 235
benevolent associations, 20–21, 120
Berea College (Berea, Ky.), 213
Berry, Betty, 102
Berryman, Mrs. Charles, 184
Beveridge, Albert, 147
Birmingham (Ala.), 150–51
Birth of a Nation, The (film; 1915),
   154–55, 177, 272
Bishoff, Henry, 203

Black, James, 182, 183
black crime, 43, 148, 159–64
black culture and intellectual life, 10,
   32–33, 37–38, 228–29
black disenfranchisement, 158
black middle class, 38
Blue Grass Federation of Labor,
   172–73, 174
Blue Roses (drama), 260
Board of Home Mission, 40
Bodley House (Lexington), 214–15
Bogaert, Victor, 91, 133
Bonte, George Willard, 186
boosterism, 177
Bordman, Gerald, 256
Borrello, Alfred, 236
Boston Transcript, 144
Bourbon Democrats, 14, 47, 63
Bourne, Randolph, 236
Bowman, John, 52–53, 78
boycotts, 37–38
Boyton, Paul, 36
Bradley, William O., 63
Bradly, Orville, 188
Brant, Sarah, 197, 200
Breckinridge, Desha
   at Kirmess, 182
   as *Lexington Morning Herald* owner,
      64
   Preparedness Parade and, 190
   Preston (Margaret) and, 222, 227,
      231
   as Princeton graduate, 55
   racial views of, 158
   as Strollers patron, 272
Breckinridge, John C., 60, 67
Breckinridge, Madeleine McDowell
   ("Madge")
   as civic leader, 167
   as orator, 124, 226
   Preston (Margaret) influenced by,
      225–28

as Strollers patron, 272
as suffragist, 229, 230
Breckinridge, Robert J., 51–52, 55
Breckinridge, Sophonisba, 226–27
Breckinridge, W. C. P.
  law office of, 55, 152
  as *Lexington Morning Herald* owner,
    64
  oratorical skills of, 58–59
  as Philosophian Society guest
    speaker, 93–94
  Tanner and, 52, 67
Breckinridge, William Lewis, 73
Bredalbane Farm (Scott County, Ky.),
  51–52
Breitenbucher, Phillip W., 121
Brock, Loretta, 177–78
Brooke, Rupert, 237, 238
Brown, Ollie, 157
Brown of Harvard (drama), 265
Brundage, W. Fitzhugh, 42, 44, 46, 163
Bryan, William Jennings, 59, 63–64
Bryn Mawr College (Bryn Mawr, Pa.),
  207–14
Buckley, Claude, 117
Buckner, Clay, 87
Buell Armory, 258
Bullock, Frank A., 166, 281
Bulwer-Lytton, Edward, 261–63
Burch, H. L., 174
Burr, Aaron, 73
Bushman, Richard, 28
Butler, John, 60
Butler, Lizzie, 60

Caesar and Cleopatra (Shaw), 241
Calgary (Alberta, Canada), 206–7
Calhoun, Charles W., 14–15, 309n6
Call of the Blood (Noe), 268
campus culture, 10–11
Cane Run Presbyterian Church
  (Harrodsburg, Ky.), 74

Canterbury Literary Club (State
  University), 238
Carnegie, Andrew, 152
Carnegie, Lucy Coleman, 218–19
carnivals, 171–74
Carranza, Venustiano, 187, 188
Cassidy, M. A., 56, 155, 169, 170
Cassidy, Mrs. Ernest, 273
Castleman, John B., 153
Cecropian Dramatic Society, 259
Cecropian Literary Society, 83, 96
  declining membership in, 248
  disbanding of, 275–76
  dramatic performances by, 244, 245,
    259
  founding of, at Kentucky University,
    79–80
  Inter-Collegiate Oratorical
    Association and, 112, 130
  in intercollegiate oratorical contests,
    121, 122, 123, 128, 130, 269
  motto of, 79
  in oratorical contests, 88
  orchestras hired by, 85
  as Ossolian Society mentor, 81
  printed programs of, 86, 87
  student press coverage of, 101, 102,
    245
  student publications and, 97
  Washington's Birthday celebrations
    of, 87
censorship, 154, 155
Central Christian Church (Lexington),
  180
Central University (Richmond, Ky.)
  athletics at, 105
  Inter-Collegiate Oratorical
    Association and, 111
  in intercollegiate oratorical contests,
    109–11, 119, 120
  intercollegiate oratorical contests at,
    112

Centre College (Danville, Ky.), 73
  Inter-Collegiate Oratorical
    Association and, 111
  in intercollegiate oratorical contests,
    109–11, 113–14, 119, 120, 130, 134
  student press at, 103
Centre College Courant, 103
Centre College Magazine, 103
Century Magazine, 235
Chalk Level (Va.), 203–5, 215
Chandler Normal School (Lexington),
    180
Chaperone (comedy), 94
charity, public
  Eastern Lunatic Asylum, 18
  Kirmess and, 181–83
  poverty relief programs, 18–21
  Preston (Margaret) and, 223–24
  scientific charity, 165, 166–67, 226,
    348n29
  UDC and, 150
Charley's Aunt (Thomas), 267–68
Charlotte (N.C.), 169–70
Chasing Butterflies (Williamson), 179
Chautauqua (Kentucky Assembly,
    Lexington)
  accommodations at, 120–21, 122–23
  audience at, 116
  controversy at, 128–29
  decline of, 131, 134–35, 138
  establishment of, 26, 116–17
  first assemblies at, 117–18,
    311–12n25
  fraternities at, 128
  ICOA and, 118
  motion pictures at, 127–28
  New South conflicts at, 134
  Preston (Margaret) at, 202
  racial segregation at, 120
  unsuccessful revivals of, 136
  Victorian values exemplified in,
    25–26

  Woodland Park and, 35
  See also College Day Oratorical
    Contest
Chautauqua Minister's Institute, 134
Chautauqua movement, 6, 116, 173
Cheapside (Lexington), 32, 71, 174
Cheek, S. R., 118
Chesnutt, Charles W., 43, 45, 147–48
Chicago (Ill.), 189
Chi Epsilon Chi sorority, 100
Children of the Confederacy, 236
Chinese immigrants, 18, 40
chivalric code of honor, 41–42, 72–73,
    75
Christ Church Cathedral (Lexington),
    180, 199, 202, 223
Christomathean Literary Society, 78
churches, theatrical performances by,
    180
Cincinnati, New Orleans & Texas
    Pacific Railway, 217
Cincinnati Southern Railroad, 37
circuses, 33
city commission government type, 168,
    349n34
city council government type, 168
civic folk mercantilism, 21
Civic League, 170
civic organizations, 181–83
Civil Rights Act (1875), 36
Civil War, 13, 52, 77, 89, 147, 149,
    196
  See also Lost Cause of the
    Confederacy
Clansman, The (Dixon), 154, 158
Clarke, F. H., 136–37
Clarke, Kate, 136–37
Clark, Thomas D., 177–78
Clavis (Philothean Society paper), 78,
    87
Clay, Cassius Marcellus, 73, 80
Clay, Green, 73

Clay, Henry, 73
Clay, Laura, 80, 229, 253
Clay Monument (Lexington), 23
Clean City Club, 143, 169–71
Clean Streets Committee, 170
Clean-up Days, 169–71
Cliosophic Society (Princeton), 55, 73, 74, 324n5
Cloverleaf (Kentucky University student weekly), 100–101, 102
College Day Oratorical Contest (Chautauqua Assembly), 111, 138, 295–99
  1889–1893, 115–21
  1894–1900, 122–23, 124–25, 126–29
  1901–1905, 131, 134–36
College of New Jersey (Princeton), 73, 80
College of the Bible (Lexington)
  alumni of, barred from intercollegiate oratorical contests, 129
  establishment of, as independent entity, 78, 83
  literary societies at, 78–79, 83, 88, 96, 244, 285 (*see also* Christomathean Literary Society; Phileusebian Literary Society; Philothean Literary Society; Theosebian Literary Society)
  literary society decline at, 248–49, 253
college settlement movement, 212–13
College Widow, The (Ade), 267
Collegian of Kentucky University (student monthly), 56, 57, 79, 89, 97
Collins, Speed, 279
Colored Citizens Protective League, 37
Colored Fair, 10, 32–33
commercialism, 47
Commission on Provision for the Feeble-Minded, 166–67

community intellectual life, 1
  dramatic societies and, 141, 272–73
  literary society oratorical performances, 3, 77, 107, 121
Confederate Dynasty, 52
Confederate Memorial Day, 149, 153–54
Confederate Monument (Lexington), 25, 47
Confederate Southern Memorial Association, 151
Connelly, Julia, 262
Con T. Kennedy Shows, 171–72
Cook, Raymond, 154
Cornelian Literary Society, 101
  Alatheian Society as competition of, 83
  motto of, 82, 92
  Ossolian Society becomes, 82, 95–96
  paper published by, 82
  student press coverage of, 102
  in Washington's Birthday celebrations, 87
  See also Ossolian Literary Society
county court days, 32
Cowles, Mrs. Josiah E., 178
Cox, Leonard G., 88, 112
Cozine, Lulu, 82
Cree, Howard, 129
Crimson (Transylvania yearbook), 248–49
Crimson Rambler (Kentucky University student newspaper), 100, 243, 246–48, 275, 334n48
Crossfield, R. H., 99, 153
Crum, Floyd J., 91
Crum, George W., 91
Crum Medal, 91
Cunningham, James B., 261, 263, 375n24

Daily Transylvanian (student newspaper), 101

Damnation of Theron Ware, The
  (Frederic), 56
Dangerfield, Mrs. F. A., 238
Danville Opera House, 132
Darnaby, Catherine, 82
Daughters of the American Revolution
  (DAR), 181
Davis, Jefferson, 149, 153
debate, faculty co-optation of, 278
DeLong, Mrs. E. B., 62
Delta Delta Delta sorority, 253
DeMille, Henry C., 266–67
Democratic Party, 14, 47, 63–64
Detzer, Karl, 116
Dial, 236
Dickens, Charles, 68
Dickerson College (Carlisle, Pa.), 74
Dictator, The (film), 240
diphtheria, 168
disease epidemics, 168
"Dixie," 153–54
Dixon, Thomas, 148, 154, 158
Dodge, Mrs. L. V., 123
Doll's House, A (Ibsen), 236
domesticity, 20
Douglass Park (Lexington), 164, 192
dramatic societies, collegiate, 2–3
  ascendancy of, 7, 257, 276
  community life and, 272–74
  defined, 257
  as extracurricular activity, 8, 263,
    373n17
  faculty coaches, 261, 262, 263,
    375n24
  faculty co-optation of, 8–9, 257,
    263–64, 374n17
  first independent, 259–60
  forerunners of, 94
  high point of, 270
  historical/cultural context of, 255–57
  Little Theater Movement and,
    307n11, 373n17

off-campus players, 141, 260–73
on-campus players, 258–60
See also specific societies
Draper, George A., 198, 360n27
Draper, Helen, 360n27
Draper, Jessie Preston (Margaret's
  aunt), 198, 205, 208, 214, 215,
  360n27
Draper, William, 198
DuBois, W. E. B., 143, 159–60
Duke, Basil, 114
Duncan, Henry, Jr., 110, 112–13
Duncan, Jolly, 157–58
Duncan Park (Lexington), 231
Dwight, Timothy, 8

Eastern Kentucky Insane Asylum, 137
Eastern Lunatic Asylum (Lexington),
  18, 84
Eaton, Clement, 47
Echo (Ossolian Society paper), 81, 86
Eddyville (Ky.), 279–80
education
  classical traditions in, 56–57
  efficiency in, 165
  manual training in, 226
  oratorical culture and, 69
  transitional years, 57–58
  university extension movement, 173–74
efficiency, 165–67, 171, 219
egalitarianism, 80
Elliott, James N., 128
Ellis, W. E., 153
epidemics, 168
Esmeralda (Gillette), 268
ethnocentrism, 17–18, 33, 40–41
Exhibitors Supply Company, 228
experts, 166–67, 171
extracurriculum
  campus-generated theater as, 257
  as counterpoint to curriculum,
    304n5

dramatic societies and, 8
literary societies and, 4
multiple affiliations in, 102, 244,
252, 262
social class and, 305n6
as student creation, 3–4

fairs, 32–33
Faithful, The (Masefield), 185
Farquhar, Edward F., 251, 254–55, 273
Father and the Boys (Ade), 271, 272–73
Fayette Bar Association, 60
Fayette County Board of Education,
220
Fayette County courthouse, 150
Fayette County Equal Rights
Association, 181
Fayette County Jail, 162
Fayette County Schools, 56, 180–81
Fayette Equal Rights Association
(FERA), 80, 191, 231, 232
Fayette National Bank, 190
Federal Writers' Project, 1
feminism, 81
fiction, serialized, 31
"Fifty Years' Recollections of Lexington
and Vicinity" (Tanner), 49, 50–51
Figibel, Lucille ("Elsie"), 197
Filipino-American War, 201
film censorship, 154, 155
"Fire King of the World" (daredevil),
36
First Baptist Church (Lexington), 180
First Presbyterian Church (Lexington),
140, 151
First World War. *See* World War I
Fitzhugh, R. H., 39
Focus (Kentucky University student
magazine), 81, 98–99, 244
See also *Transylvanian*
"folk justice," 44
football, 98, 100, 104, 249–50

Ford, Henry, 189
Forderhase, Nancy K., 178
Fortnightly Club, 123
Fortune Hunter, The (Smith), 270–71
Fouse, Lizzie, 10, 229
Fouse, William, 10, 180, 228–29,
366n44
Fox, John, Jr., 71, 80, 326n11
Franklin Literary Society, 77
fraternities, social
at Chautauqua, 128
as dramatic society audience, 268
increased local support of, 253
increased student press coverage of,
245, 249
as intercollegiate oratorical contest
competition, 125, 133
at Kentucky University, 100
as literary society competition, 7,
100, 106, 244
in Preparedness Parade, 190–91
at State College, 105
See also specific fraternities
Frederic, Harold, 56
Front Street Settlement House
(Philadelphia, Pa.), 225
Frost, William, 213
Fuller, Margaret, 81

Gaines, Kevin, 157
Galsworthy, John, 236
gambling, 172
Ganfield, W. A., 192
Garfield, James A., 86, 87
Garrick Theatre (Philadelphia, Pa.),
212
Geary, John T., 124, 128
gender stereotypes, Victorian-era,
15–17, 28–29, 67, 93–94, 104,
259–60, 309n6
General Federation of Women's Clubs,
178

George's Orchestra, 86
Georgetown College
  Inter-Collegiate Oratorical
    Association and, 111
  in intercollegiate oratorical contests,
    114, 119, 120, 123, 128–29
Georgetown Opera House, 133
Ghosts (Ibsen), 236
Gilded Age, 7
  characteristics of, 14–15, 80
  ex-Confederate domination of
    Kentucky politics during, 52
  Tanner as exemplification of, 50–51,
    66–69
Gillette, William, 268
Girard College (Philadelphia, Pa.),
    55–56
Going Some (Beach and Armstrong), 269
Gordon, John B., 124
governmental regulation, 146–47, 165,
    168, 344n1
Grady, Henry W., 21, 38
Graham, Robert, 53–54
Grand Army of the Republic, 191
Grant, Ulysses S., 47–48
Grantham, Dewey, 146–47, 164–65,
    344n1
Gratz Park (Lexington), 184, 231
Gray, Thomas, 51, 63
Great Depression, 66
Great War. *See* World War I
Grehan, Enoch, 122, 269, 271
Gribbin, Eugene, 271, 272
Griffith, D. W., 154
Guernsey, Joseph, 62, 63
Guide to Lexington, Kentucky (Ranck),
    21–23, 25
Gumm, R. E., 228
Gunn, Belle, 92

Haines, Thomas, 166–67
Halfway House (Hewlett), 235

Hamilton College (Lexington), 18,
    241–42, 253, 259–60, 262
Hamlet (Shakespeare), 241
Hampden-Sydney College (Va.), 73,
    74
Hampton Court (Lexington), 234,
    360n26
Hardman, Emma, 278
Hardman, Geneva, murder of,
    278–83
Hardman, Tupper, 278, 281
Hard Times (Dickens), 68
Harlan, John, 56
Harper's Weekly, 31, 235
Harrison, Cecile ("Keckie"), 197–98,
    200, 201, 202
Harrison, E. P., 210
Harrison, Harry P., 116
Harrison, Mrs. A. M., 237
Hart, Joel, 28
Hayes, Rutherford B., 39
Hedda Gabler (Ibsen), 236
Henry Clay Law Society, 276
Hewlett, Maurice, 235
high culture, 27–31, 177–85
Higher Education, The (comedy),
    258
History of Blacks in Kentucky, A
    (Wright), 158
Hobdy, E. J., 106, 122
Home of the Friendless (Lexington),
    20–21
Hopes and Fears (Yonge), 204
Hopkins, James F., 96, 105, 260,
    333n39, 335n55
Hopson, J. M., 37
Horace Mann Literary Society (State
    College), 95, 276, 333n39
Horner, Charles, 211
Horowitz, Helen Lefkowitz, 305n6
Hostetter, Mrs. Whitney, 231
Howells, William Dean, 259

How He Lied to Her Husband (Shaw), 179
Hubbard, Alpha, 262
Huber, John, 165
Hull House (Chicago, Ill.), 179
humor, racial, 156–57
Huston, John B., 58–59, 60
Hutchinson, Mrs. W. S., 66

Ibsen, Henrik, 236
Idea (State University student publication)
    dramatic society coverage of, 261–62, 264, 375n24
    on efficiency and expertise, 167
    literary society decline chronicled in, 249–52, 254–55
    Tandy eulogized in, 137
    Taylor ("Bookie") on staff of, 238
immigration, 146
industrialization, 47, 146
Industrial School (Lexington), 223–24
"Inner Lost Cause," 216
Inter-Collegiate (Intercollegiate) Oratorical Contests, 289–93
    1889–1893, 111–15, 121
    1894–1900, 122, 123–26
    1901–1905, 129–31, 132–34
    decline of, 276–77
    student press coverage of, 246, 247–48
Inter-Collegiate (Intercollegiate) State Oratorical Association, 88
    Chautauqua contest rules established by, 118, 129
    establishment of, 111
    financial difficulties of, 130
    internal strife within, 125–26, 130–31
    literary society control of, 111–12
Internal Revenue Service (IRS), 50, 62, 68–69, 322n33

Iron Shark, The (Bonte), 186
Irvin, Helen Deiss, 260

James, Henry, 67
Jefferson, Thomas, 72
Jewel (Cornelian Society paper), 82
Jewell, Frances, 238, 268
Joan of Arc (film), 240
Johnson, Alexander, 167
Johnson, Claud M., 49–50
Johnson, E. Polk, 152–53
Johnson, John, 156
Johnson, Nan, 59, 69
Johnston, John Pelham, 218
Johnston, Marius Early, 152, 218–19
Johnston, Philip Preston ("P. P."), 151–52, 191, 216–17
Johnston, Philip Preston, Jr., 152
    birth of, 216
    children of, 222
    as civic leader, 219–21
    courtship with Margaret Wickliffe Preston, 215–17, 221, 226
    death of, 222
    early employment history of, 217
    education of, 217
    family of, 217–19
    marriage to Margaret Wickliffe Preston, 221–22, 233
    racial attitudes of, 220
    reading habits of, 234–35
    as scientific farmer, 219
    suffrage movement as viewed by, 230
Johnston, Philip Preston, III, 222, 363n34
Johnston, Robert Wickliffe Preston, 196, 197–98, 218, 222, 363n34
Johnston, Sallie Chiles, 216, 218
Johnstone, Cary Gratz, 182, 184
Jones, J. L., 60
Jones, Sam, 117, 127
Juvenile Court, 226

Kansas City (Mo.), 160–61
Kappa Alpha fraternity, 102
    intercollegiate oratorical contest
        winners honored by, 244
    at Kentucky University, 100, 125,
        128
    local press coverage of, 133
    Preston (William) as member of, 205
    at State College, 105, 128
    Tandy as member of, 129, 137
    Twentieth Biennial Convention
        (Lexington, 1899), 128
Kappa Sigma fraternity, 100, 125, 238
"Keckie." *See* Harrison, Cecile
Kentuckian, 140–41, 238, 278
Kentucky (Lexington) Gazette, 60
Kentucky (Lexington) Leader
    on anti–Separate Coach campaign,
        37–38
    on Chautauqua, 118
    on female literary society
        performances, 82
    intercollegiate oratorical contest
        coverage of, 109–11, 113, 118,
        119–23, 124
    on Preston family members, 198,
        199
    Victorian gender stereotypes in, 17
Kentucky Agricultural and Mechanical
    (A&M) Association, 32–33
Kentucky Belle, A (drama), 258
Kentucky College Association, 117–18
Kentucky Confederate Home
    (Louisville), 155
Kentucky Education Association, 165
Kentucky Equal Rights Association
    (KERA), 229, 231
Kentucky Federation of Woman's
    Clubs, 230
Kentucky Historical Society, 284
Kentucky Kernel, 270, 276–77, 278
Kentucky legislature, 80

Kentucky Military Institute, 276
Kentucky National Guard, 187
Kentucky Supreme Court, 38, 74
Kentucky Survey for the Commission
    on Provision for the Feeble-
    Minded, 166–67
Kentucky Traction and Terminal
    Company, 176
Kentucky University, 152
    Arts College, 5, 53–55, 79–83, 88,
        102, 285, 286
    athletics at, 98, 99, 100, 132
    Bible College, 5, 78–79, 102, 285,
        286 (*see also* College of the Bible
        [Lexington])
    boosterism for, 22
    Chautauqua contests initially avoided
        by, 119
    College of Law, 49, 56–57, 216
    dramatic performances at, 259–60
    fraternities at, 100, 125, 128
    Inter-Collegiate Oratorical
        Association and, 111
    in intercollegiate oratorical contests,
        109–11, 119–20, 121, 122,
        125–26, 129, 132
    intercollegiate oratorical contests
        boycotted by, 130–31
    Lexington cultural life and, 2–3
    literary societies at, 55, 77, 78–90,
        96, 285, 286
    literary society oratorical
        performances, 5–7
    literary society public lectures, 30
    Preparatory Academy, 102
    Ranck centennial address delivered
        at, 13, 14–15
    renaming of (1908), 245
    student press at, 97–102
    students not allowed to enter
        intercollegiate oratorical contests,
        115

Tanner as student at, 52–55
Transylvania University merged with, 52–53, 78
Woodlands campus, 89
yell of, 71
See also Transylvania University
Kentucky University Athletic Association, 102
Kentucky University Crimson (yearbook), 101–2
Kentucky University Tablet, 77, 79, 80–81, 97–98, 119
See also *Transylvanian*
Kentucky Wesleyan College (Millersburg, Ky.), 119, 132
Kerr, Charles, 51, 255, 281, 282–83
Kett, Joseph, 28, 173
Kimbrough, Petrie (aka "Will Lockett"), 279–83
Kincaid, Elizabeth Shelby, 183–85, 201, 202, 266
Kincaid, Laura, 184, 238
Kirmess, 181–83, 241
Kirmess Ball, 182
Kirmess Parade, 182
Klair, William ("Billy"), 50
Klein, Charles, 270
Klotter, James, 199, 229
Knight, Grant C., 15
Knights of Columbus, 254
Knott, Claudia, 229
Knott, Proctor, 91
Koenig, Louis, 63
K. U. Enroll (student biweekly magazine), 85, 100–101, 124
Ku Klux Klan, 42, 44, 154, 280

labor unions, 172–73, 174, 189, 190–91
Ladies Memorial Associations, 25
Lady Windermere's Fan (Wilde), 236
Lafayette, Marquis de, 72

Lafferty, W. T., 221
Lamp and Cross Society, 137
Langston, Dr., 39
Lank, O. A., 33
Lawrenceville Preparatory School, 139
lectures, public
Kincaid's drama series, 183–85, 201, 202
at Lexington Opera House, 33–34, 225–26
literary societies as sponsors of, 30–31
Preston (Margaret) at, 201, 202
university extension movement and, 173–74
Lee, Robert E., 48, 149, 152–53
legal profession, 50, 56, 68
Leland, Arthur, 227
Lell's Hall (Lexington), 33
Leopard's Spots, The (Dixon), 148
Levine, Lawrence, 28, 255–56
Lewellen, G. A., 86
Lexington (Ky.)
commercial orchestral bands in, 84–85
high culture in, 27–31
popular culture in, 31–36
population of, 24
Lexington, as New South city, 2, 27–31
boosterism, 21–27, 48, 177
Lost Cause of the Confederacy, 46–48, 148–54
lynching, 41–46, 148
race relations, 38–41, 143, 148, 154–59
Lexington, as Progressive Era city
efficiency and expertise, 165–67, 171
municipal reform, 168–71, 349n34
paradox of, 283–84
preparedness, 185–93
scientific charity, 166

Lexington, the Central City, 13, 23–25
Lexington and the Bluegrass Country
(WPA), 1
Lexington Association for Infant
Welfare, 181
Lexington Board of Commerce, 166
Lexington Board of Commissioners,
170, 172, 181, 182
Lexington Board of Education, 167
Lexington Cemetery, 47, 140, 151,
153
Lexington Chamber of Commerce,
174
Lexington Civic League, 226–29
Lexington courthouse, 28–29
Lexington Daily Leader
intercollegiate oratorical contest
coverage of, 71, 124–25, 127,
128–29
on movies at Chautauqua, 127–28
Lexington Daily Press
on black crime, 43
on chivalry and violence, 41–42
on classical traditions in education,
56–57
on "folk justice," 44
on Grant's death, 47–48
on Huston, 58
on Lockwood lecture, 31
on lynching, 46
on Mulligan speeches, 59–60
New South boosterism in, 26–27
poverty as viewed in, 19
on public charity, 18
on race relations, 39, 40
serialized fiction in, 31
on Tanner commencement address,
57
Victorian ethnocentric attitudes of, 33
Victorian gender stereotypes in, 16,
29
on Woodland Park, 35–36

Lexington Daily Transcript, 93–94
Lexington Gun Club, 198
Lexington Herald
Automobile and Style Show
promoted by, 175–76
on *Birth of a Nation,* 155
black crime as portrayed in, 43, 159,
161, 162, 163–64
on Chautauqua decline, 135
on Confederate holidays, 152,
153–54
dramatic society coverage of,
258–59, 260, 264, 266, 267–68,
269, 270–72, 273
editorship of, 52, 55
employees invited to carnival,
171–72
on expert consultants, 165
increased fraternity coverage of, 253
intercollegiate oratorical contest
coverage of, 134–35
literary society decline chronicled in,
252–53
on literary society oratorical
performances, 7
on Lockett trial, 283
lynching as portrayed in, 160, 281
preparedness advocated by, 187–89
Preparedness Parade as covered by,
190, 191, 192
on Preston family members, 230,
237
on public health, 169–71
racial attitudes in, 146, 156–59,
187–89
on Tandy suicide, 139
Tanner obituary in, 66
on theatrical performances, 179, 180,
181, 182, 183
on UCV reunions, 150–51
on UDC, 150
Washington's Birthday coverage, 253

on WCCK, 178–79
on WWI and Civil War, 149
WWI supported by, 186
Lexington High School Orchestra, 153
Lexington Leader
Automobile and Style Show
promoted by, 175–76
on automobile ownership, 150
black crime as portrayed in, 159,
161, 162–63
on Chautauqua decline, 131
on Confederate holidays, 152
dramatic society coverage of, 243,
258, 259, 260, 261, 263, 265–66,
267, 268, 269, 271, 272–73
employees invited to carnival,
171–72
on expert consultants, 165
on female literary society
performances, 94
on Industrial School Christmas
dinner, 224
intercollegiate oratorical contest
coverage of, 95, 130, 134, 135,
138
literary society decline chronicled in,
253–54, 255
on Lockett trial, 283
lynching as portrayed in, 160–61,
275, 280
Preparedness Parade as covered by,
190–91, 192
Preston (Margaret) reads at college,
210
on Preston family members, 197,
231, 237
on public health, 143, 169, 170
on public lectures, 184
racial attitudes in, 146, 158
Stanley's Murray speech reprinted in,
144–45
on suffrage movement, 230

on Tandy suicide, 139–40
on Tanner, 64, 66
on theatrical performances, 180,
181–82, 183
Washington's Birthday coverage of,
253–54
WWI supported by, 186
Lexington Library Association, 29–30
Lexington Military Band, 135
Lexington Morning Herald
on female literary society
performances, 82, 83
fraternity coverage of, 133
intercollegiate oratorical contest
coverage of, 109, 126–27, 132–33
sports coverage of, 133
Tanner's political career and, 64–65
Lexington Morning Transcript
on black crime, 43
businessmen listed in, 61
on Chautauqua, 116–17
on Cheapside, 32
on chivalry and violence, 42
on female literary society
performances, 92–93
on "folk justice," 44
on Grant's death, 48
on Industrial School, 223–24
intercollegiate oratorical contest
coverage of, 110, 112–15, 118–19,
122
KKK as portrayed in, 44
letters to the editor, 27–28
on library construction, 29–30
on literary society oratorical contests,
88
on literary society oratorical
performances, 90–91
on lynching, 44–46
on minstrel shows, 34
New South boosterism in, 26
poverty as viewed in, 18–21

Lexington Morning Transcript, cont.
  on race relations, 39, 40
  Ranck promoted as mayor by, 22
  serialized fiction in, 31
  Victorian ethnocentric attitudes of,
    40–41
  Victorian gender stereotypes in,
    16–17, 28–29
  on Woodland Park, 36
Lexington Negro Civic League, 281
Lexington Opera House
  Birth of a Nation shown at, 177
  dramatic society performances at,
    261–62, 264–65, 270
  fire at, 33–34
  as fixed intercollegiate oratorical
    contest venue, 115, 121
  intercollegiate oratorical contests at,
    6, 71–72, 95, 109–11, 112–13,
    114–15, 123–24, 129–30,
    133–34, 137–38
  minstrel shows at, 157
  public lectures at, 30, 33–34,
    225–26
  theatrical performances at, 180,
    181–83, 201, 241
Lexington Park Commission, 166
Lexington Press-Transcript
  on coeducational literary societies, 95
  on female literary society
    performances, 82
  intercollegiate oratorical contest
    coverage of, 123–24
  on literary society oratorical contests,
    88
Lexington Salvation Army, 158
Lexington Society for Improving the
  Condition of the Poor, 18
libraries
  academic, literary societies and
    development of, 5
  funding of, 29–30

  intellectual significance of, 313n33
  of literary societies, 75, 76, 83–84,
    259
Life magazine, 266
Lincoln, Abraham, 149
Lincoln School (Lexington), 226
Lion and the Mouse, The (Klein), 270
literary societies, collegiate, 2–3, 69
  antebellum, at Transylvania
    University, 72–78, 285
  aspirations of, 104
  chartering of, 80
  coeducational, 5, 94–95
  community significance of, 273–74
  competing student organizations, 244
  curriculum of, 87, 92
  decline of, 3, 5, 7, 9, 140–41, 143,
    243–55, 275–78, 378n35
  dramatic performances by, 94,
    258–59
  as extracurricular activity, 3–4
  faculty/administration support of,
    251
  female, 5, 80–83, 92–94, 100–101,
    258–59
  influence on student publications,
    97–106
  intercollegiate oratorical contestants
    chosen by, 119, 125–26
  libraries of, 75, 76, 83–84, 259
  local press coverage of, 252–53
  membership of, 4–5
  mottoes adopted by, 78
  off-campus presence of, 121, 136
  open session printed programs of,
    86, 87
  oratorical contests held by, 87–88
  oratorical performances offered by,
    5–7, 84–87
  origins of, 304n5
  postbellum, at Kentucky University,
    78–90, 96, 285, 286

Princeton influence on, 73, 74
public lectures sponsored by, 30
social class and, 305n6
at State College, 90–96, 285
status attached to membership in,
    106–7
student press coverage of, 244
student publications and, 96
See also specific societies
literary society publications (State
    College)
The Bayonet, 103
The Spectator, 91, 92
The Star, 93
The Student, 89, 90
See also *State College Cadet, The*
literary society publications
    (Transylvania/Kentucky
    University)
The Anchor, 78–79
The Atlantis, 80, 97
The Clavis, 78, 87
The Collegian of Kentucky University,
    56, 57, 79, 89, 97
The Echo, 81, 86
The Jewel, 82
The Owl, 80, 86
The Shield, 79, 86
The Student, 89, 90
The Truth, 83
Little Iliad, The (Hewlett), 235
Little Shepherd of Kingdom Come, The
    (Fox), 71
Little Theater Movement, 8, 9, 257,
    307–8n11, 373n17
Lockett, Will, 279–83, 284
Lockwood, Belva Anne, 30–31
Logan, F. V., 117–18
Loos, Charles L., 87, 88, 92, 110, 264,
    277
Lost Cause of the Confederacy, 46–48,
    148–54

Confederate monuments, 14, 25, 47
Davis's Birthday celebrations, 149,
    153
"Dixie," 153–54
Grant's death and, 47–48
holidays honoring, 48, 149, 152–54
"Inner Lost Cause," 216
as oratorical topic, 114, 124
political impact of, 14
UCV and, 110
See also lynching; United Confederate
    Veterans; United Daughters of the
    Confederacy
Lost Paradise, The (adapt. DeMille),
    266–67
Louisiana State University, 217
Louisville (Ky.), 126, 266–67
Louisville Courier-Journal, 223
Louisville Times, 167
Love and Lucy (Hewlett), 235
Lunatic Ball, 18
Lusitania, sinking of, 185, 188
lynching, 42–46, 144, 275
defined, 42
in Fayette County (1878), 14
"legal," 42, 146, 148, 160–61, 284
local press coverage of, 43, 44–46,
    148, 160–61, 187, 284
as New South hallmark, 39
rule of law and, 280–83, 284
Lynching in the New South (Brundage),
    42

Mabie, E. C., 278
MacArthur, Benjamin, 256
Macgowan, Kenneth, 8–9, 257,
    307n11, 373n17
Madison, James, 73
Man of the Hour, The (Thanet), 41
Marlowe, Julia, 202, 259–60
Marlowe Club, 241–42, 259–60, 262,
    283

Marrow of Tradition, The (Chesnutt), 43, 147–48
Martin, Lube, 146
Martin, Theodora Penny, 353n55
Masefield, John Edward, 185
Masonic Hall (Lexington), 20–21, 266–67
mass assemblies, 6
Mathis, Julia, 82
McClintock, W. D., 117
McCreary, James, 153
McDowell, James, 196–97
McDowell, Sarah Brant. *See* Preston, Sarah McDowell
McKenzie, A. S., 173, 263, 350n41
McKinley, William, 64
McLachlan, James, 305n6
McVey, Frank, 10, 282
Mc'Vey, J. M., 81, 99, 101
Meadow Wood (Chalk Level, Va.), 203–5, 215
Meiler's Orchestra, 81, 86–87
Memoria (State College yearbook), 89, 105–6
Mexican Revolution, 186–89
Mexican War, 196
middle class, 305n6
military preparedness
    Mexican Revolution and, 186–89
    for WWI, 189–93
Miller, Gretchen, 201, 205
Milton, John, 51
minstrelsy, 34, 157
miscegenation, 158
Miss Ella Williams's School (Lexington), 200
Miss Hogarty's Orchestra, 175
Mob, The (Galsworthy), 236
Mobile (Ala.), 150
mob violence, 10, 39, 42, 46, 144, 160, 187, 280–83
    See also lynching

Monroe, Robert Emmett, 264
Morgan, John Hunt, 75, 196, 220
Morgan, Richard C., 191, 193
Morrell, Emma, 213
Morrison Chapel (Kentucky University)
    Cecropian Society eulogized at, 275–76
    commencement addresses at, 56–57
    Cunningham address at, 263
    dramatic society performances in, 244, 259
    lecture series at, 30
    literary society oratorical contests at, 55, 88, 98, 126
    literary society oratorical performances at, 84, 86
    Ranck centennial address delivered at, 13, 14
    Washington's Birthday celebrations at, 77, 115
    women's literary society performances at, 81
Morrison College (Kentucky University), 79, 122
Morrow, Edwin P., 280–81, 282, 283
Morton High School (Lexington), 157, 226
Moss, R. E., 125
motion pictures, 8, 127–28, 171, 240
Mousetrap, The (Howells), 259
Mr. Britling Sees It Through (Wells), 236
Mrs. Lancelot (Hewlett), 235
Muir (Preston family farm), 197–99
Mulligan, Dennis, 49–50
Mulligan, James H., 50, 59–60, 86, 91, 138
Muncie, Mollie, 94
municipal reform, 168–71, 349n34
Murray (Ky.), 144–47, 187

musical interludes, 77, 81, 84–85, 90, 93, 110, 113, 121
Musselman, Nancy, 87

National Association for the Prevention of Feeble-Mindedness, 167
National Committee for Mental Hygiene, 166
nationalism, 147
National Suffrage Day (1915), 231
National Trotting Association, 151–52, 216
Native Americans, 17, 40–41
Neal, W. L., 61
neurasthenia, 213–14
Neville, John H., 53, 54, 95, 137, 208
Neville, Linda, 208, 209, 225, 227, 230
Neville, Mary, 208, 209, 225, 227
Neville Literary Society (State College), 95, 96, 249
New Departure Democrats, 14
New England Club (New York, N.Y.), 21, 38
Newport (R.I.) Times, 34
New South, 15, 67
  business expansion, 21, 46–47
  chivalric code of honor, 41–42
  lynching, 42–44, 46
  New South Creed, 21
  racial attitudes in, 145
  rural schools of, 52
  See also Lexington, as New South city
Newton Literary Society, 77
New Woman, 94
New York (N.Y.), 189
New York Evening Post, 27–28
New York Times, 256
New York University, 87
"nickelodeon" era, 33
Noe, J. T. C., 268
Noel, Lucien, 112

Normal Literary Society (State College), 94–95, 123, 264
Normal School, 92
Norris, George W., 148–49

Olmsted, Frederick Law, 35
Olmsted, John C., 166
One of the Eight (drama), 264–65
oratorical contests, 71–73
  intercollegiate, 106
  preliminary (intersociety), 88, 119, 122, 123, 126, 247, 330n27
  Preston (Margaret) attends, 202
  primary (intrasociety), 88, 122, 123, 330n27
oratorical culture
  decline of, 51, 59, 140–41, 243, 255–56
  literary societies grounded in, 4, 5
  Tanner and, 51, 53, 58–60, 67, 69
oratorical performances, 77
  off-campus, 107
  on-campus public, 107
orchestral bands, commercial, 84–85
Orpheum Theater (Lexington), 240
Ossoli, Angelo, 81
Ossolian Literary Society, 92
  annual open session of, 86–87
  declining membership in, 100, 248
  dramatic performances by, 247, 259
  founding of, at Kentucky University, 81
  local press coverage of, 81–82
  merged with Periclean Society, 276
  paper published by, 86
  recruitment schemes of, 247
  student press coverage of, 246–47
  See also Cornelian Literary Society
Other Girl, The (drama), 211
Owl (Cecropian Society paper), 80, 86
Oxford University, 137, 138

pacifism, 189
Pantaloon (Barrie), 236
parades
   community life and, 77
   for dramatic societies, 273
   for Kirmess, 182
   of literary societies, 71–73, 77, 109
   preparedness, 189–93, 232
   suffrage, 231–32
   as Victorian-era entertainment, 6
Paris (Ky.), 161, 170
Parkhurst, M. M., 134
parks, public, 35–36, 166
Patterson, James K.
   birthday celebrations for, 92, 123
   as Chautauqua speaker, 117
   as Kentucky University Latin
      professor, 54–55
   literary societies supported by, 10,
      91, 264, 277
   Preston (William) and, 217
   Roark and, 95
   as State College president, 110
   Tandy and, 137, 139–40
   Transylvania University operated as
      high school by, 53, 77
   as University of Kentucky president,
      53
Patterson Literary Society (State
      College), 96
   Barker address to, 251
   decline of, 276, 277, 378n35
   faculty implored to reverse
      intercollegiate contest decision,
      115
   founding of, at State College, 91
   in intercollegiate oratorical contests,
      122, 123, 128, 129–30, 137–38
   local press coverage of, 91–92,
      252–53
   magazine published by, 103
   membership of, 105–6

motto of, 91
   oratorical contests, 91–92, 262
   Patterson's Birthday celebration of,
      92
   student press coverage of, 104, 250,
      277
   Tandy as member of, 137–38
Patterson Medal, 91
Pearl, Will, 163–64
"Peggy" (Margaret Preston's friend),
      225
Pennsylvania Institute for Instruction
      of the Blind, 55
Periclean Literary Society, 71, 96
   declining membership in, 248
   founding of, at Kentucky University,
      79
   Inter-Collegiate Oratorical
      Association and, 112, 130
   in intercollegiate oratorical contests,
      110, 112, 124, 125, 130
   library of, 83–84
   motto of, 80
   open sessions held by, 86, 87
   in oratorical contests, 88
   Ossolian Society merged with, 276
   paper published by, 80, 86
   student press coverage of, 101, 246
   student publications and, 97
   Tanner as member of, 55, 56
Perry, Clarence Arthur, 307n11,
      373n17
Pershing, John J., 187
Peter Pan (Barrie), 236
Pethick-Lawrence, Mrs. (British
      suffragist), 231, 232
Phileusebian Literary Society, 83, 96
   declining membership in, 248
   founding of, at Kentucky University,
      78
   in intersociety basketball games, 244
   motto of, 78–79

paper published by, 78
in preliminary oratorical contests, 88
in Washington's Birthday
celebrations, 87
Phillis Wheatley YWCA (Lexington),
224
Philosophian Literary Society (State
College), 92–94, 96
Barker address to, 251
decline of, 276, 378n35
dramatic performances by, 258–59,
277
Equal Rights Association formed by,
231
founding of, at State College, 92
membership of, 105–6
motto of, 92
student press coverage of, 277
Tandy's parody of, 138
Philothean Literary Society, 83, 96
declining membership in, 248
founding of, at Kentucky University,
78
Garfield's Birthday celebrations of,
86, 87
in intercollegiate oratorical contests,
246
in intersociety basketball games, 244
meetings of, 84
motto of, 78
paper published by, 78
in preliminary oratorical contests, 88
student press coverage of, 101, 245
student publications and, 97
"Phoenix" (Margaret Preston's friend),
225
Phoenix Hotel (Lexington), 255
FERA meeting at, 191
Inter-Collegiate Oratorical
Association meeting at, 126
Kappa Alpha banquet at, 128
Kirmess Ball at, 182

as parade destination, 71, 182
Strollers annual banquet at, 273
suffragist play performed at, 181,
241
Pinero, A. W., 263
Plain Dealing Club (Princeton), 73,
324n5
playgrounds, 226, 227, 228
Plessy v. Ferguson, 36
pneumonia, 168
popular culture, 31–36, 171–77
Populism, 64
Potter, David, 5
poverty, Victorian attitudes toward,
18–21
Pre-Digested Politics (drama), 259
Preparedness Parade, 189–93, 232
press, collegiate, 96
at Kentucky University, 97–102
at State College, 103–6
See also specific publications
press, Lexington. *See specific newspapers*
Preston, Jessie. *See* Draper, Jessie
Preston
Preston, John, 196
Preston, Margaret Wickliffe, 2, 152
as "Aryan" member, 210–11
benevolent interests of, 212–13
birth of, 197
at Bodley House, 214–15
Breckinridge (Madeleine) as mentor
of, 225–28, 229
childhood of, at Muir farm, 197–99
children of, 222, 231
as civic leader, 222–33
as Civic League member/officer,
226–29
college education of, 205, 207–14
college social/intellectual life of,
211–12
as Columbia in Preparedness Parade,
191–93, 232

Preston, Margaret Wickliffe, *cont.*
  courtship with P. P. Johnston Jr.,
    215–17, 221, 226
  death of, 223
  early education of, 200–201
  early social/intellectual life of, 201–3
  at Glendower, 199–200
  at Hampton Court, 234
  as Industrial School teacher, 223–24
  Lexington residences of, 360n26
  love of reading, 200, 204, 234–36
  marriage to P. P. Johnston Jr.,
    221–22, 233
  at Meadow Wood, 203–5
  neurasthenia episode of, 213–14
  as Progressive Era exemplification,
    242
  racial attitudes of, 228–29
  religious life, 200, 202, 223, 241
  social class as viewed by, 212
  as suffragist, 191, 229–33
  suitors of, 211
  Taylor ("Bookie") and, 238–39
  as theatergoer, 202–3, 211–12,
    239–42, 260
  as WCCK Literature chair, 179,
    183–84, 236–39, 283, 369n56
Preston, Margaret Wickliffe (Margaret's
  grandmother), 200
Preston, Mary (Margaret's cousin), 213
Preston, Robert Wickliffe ("Wick";
  Margaret's father), 195–97, 205,
  206, 209, 221
Preston, Sarah McDowell (Margaret's
  mother), 214
  birth/childhood of, in France, 196–97
  as civic leader, 225
  as fraternity guest, 253
  Margaret's marriage and, 221
  marriage to "Wick" Preston, 196
  as suffragist, 229–30, 231
  as UDC member, 201–2

  as WCCK officer, 183, 201–2, 236
Preston, Susan (Margaret's aunt), 198
Preston, William (Margaret's brother)
  birth of, 197
  childhood of, at Muir farm, 198
  as farmer, 205, 206–7
  at Glendower, 200
  as Lockett jury member, 282
  marriage to Gretchen Miller, 201,
    207
  racial attitudes of, 206, 220
  university education of, 205–6
Preston, William (Margaret's
  grandfather), 192, 195–96, 199,
  205
Preston, William (Revolutionary War
  captain), 196
Preston, William (Revolutionary War
  colonel), 196
Princeton University, 49, 55, 66,
  73–74
professionalism, culture of, 3, 57,
  120–21, 243
Progressive Era, 66
  characteristics of, 68, 146–47,
    164–65, 243, 344n1
  New Woman during, 94
  Preston (Margaret) as exemplification
    of, 242
  time span of, 146
  women and voluntarism during, 223,
    225
  See also Lexington, as Progressive Era
    city
Pygmalion (Shaw), 236

race relations
  dramatic societies and, 272
  during Gilded Age, 13–14, 160
  post-WWI, 283–84
  during Progressive Era, 165, 228–29
racial segregation

during Gilded Age, 13–14
impact on black intellectual life, 37–41
at intercollegiate oratorical contests, 120
legislation of, 36–37
in popular fairs, 32–33
Preparedness Parade and, 192
Preston (William) and, 220
during Progressive Era, 165
in public parks, 164, 192
Racial Violence in Kentucky, 1865–1940 (Wright), 42
racism, 159–60
Ragan, Leonidas, 126
railroads, 26–27, 37–38
Ranck, George W.
  centennial address given by, 13, 14–16, 17
  Guide to Lexington, Kentucky, 21–23, 25
  as literary society member, 77, 79
  as New South booster, 21, 48
  real estate business of, 61
  student press coverage of, 101
Ransom Avenue carnivals, 171–74
Ray, S. B., 95
reading, 200
  intellectual culture developed through, 313n33
  as Victorian-era entertainment, 204, 234
Reagan, J. J., 172
Reconstruction, 13, 67
Redpath Tent Chautauqua, 136
reformism, 146, 164–65
  drama and, 179
  mental health, 166–67
  municipal, 168–71
  public health, 168–71
  women and, 225
Register of the Kentucky Historical Society, 284

Reign of Law, The (Allen), 5
republican ideology, 4, 5, 57
republican motherhood, 17
Republican Party, 63–64
Research Magnificent, The (Wells), 235–36
Review of Lexington, 311–12n25
Rice, Robert, 162
Richelieu (Bulwer-Lytton), 261–63
Richmond (Ky.), 88
Roark, Ruric, 95, 264
Roark Enterprise (Normal Society paper), 94
Roark Literary Society (State College), 95, 333n39
Robertson, Mrs. A. A., 163
Rogers, James, 170, 172–73, 182, 228
Rogers, Timothy, 237
roller skating, 33
Roosevelt, Theodore, 189
Rosalind (Barrie), 236
Rudolph, Frederick, 74, 87, 304n5
Russell School (Lexington), 180
Ryan, Agnes E., 231

Sadler, W. O., 149
Salvation Army, 158, 348n29
Sandman, Leo, 267–68
Saturday Industrial School (Lexington), 223–24
Saxon, Edward, 264
Saxton, Henry A., 84, 85, 117, 152
Saxton and Trost Military Band, 85
Saxton and Trost Orchestra, 85, 86
Saxton and Trost's Band, 117
Saxton's Band, 122, 135
Saxton's Orchestra, 85, 125
Sayre Female Institute, 16
Schlereth, Thomas, 25, 204
Schreiner, Olive, 222
scientific charity, 166, 226, 348n29
scientific farming, 219

"Scoop the Cub Reporter" (comic strip), 156
Scott, Charles, 121
Scott, Donald, 233–34
Scott County Courthouse (Georgetown, Ky.), 115
Searchlights (Vachell), 184–85
Second Presbyterian Church (Danville, Ky.), 113–14
Second Presbyterian Church (Lexington), 77, 200
Sells Brothers' "Arabian Circus," 33
Separate Coach Law (1892), 37
serialized fiction, 31
Shakespeare, William, 241, 258
Sharp, Stephen G., 49, 61
Shaw, George Bernard, 179, 236, 240–41
Sheehan, Jack, 191
Shelburne, J. M., 123, 128–29
Shelburne Tobacco Warehouse (Lexington), 174–77
Shelby, Isaac, 72
Shelby, John Todd, 55
Shield, 79, 86
Shriners, 171–73
Siemers, Edith, 116
Sigma Alpha Epsilon fraternity, 253
Sigma Chi fraternity, 105
Sigma Nu fraternity, 217
silver, Democratic controversy over, 63–64
Simpson, Eugene, 233
Sinclair, Upton, 20
skating rinks, 33
slavery, 158, 160
smallpox, 168
Smith, Clifford, 277
Smith, Elizabeth King, 237–38
Smith, Winchell, 270–71
Smith Greater Shows, 172–74
Smith Preparatory School (Cynthiana, Ky.), 138

social justice, 165
Solomon, Barbara Miller, 208
Sons of Confederate Veterans, 151
Sons of the American Revolution, 189–90
Southern Cinderella, A (drama), 258
southern intellectual life, academic portrayals of, 1
Southern Interstate Oratorical Association, 130, 131, 276
Southern Progressivism (Grantham), 164–65
Spanish-American War, 126, 201
Spectator (Patterson Society paper), 91, 92
sports. *See* athletics
Stanley, A. O.
   as intercollegiate oratorical contestant, 103, 112, 119
   Kirmess and, 182, 183
   Murray lynch mob and, 143–47, 187
   as Progressive Era governor, 344n1
   as Union Society member, 103
Stanton, Elizabeth Cady, 208
Stanton, Henry, 208
Star (Philosophian Society paper), 93
State College
   athletics at, 104–5
   boosterism for, 22
   Chautauqua contests initially avoided by, 119, 121
   curricular changes at, 11
   dramatic performances at, 258–59
   efficiency and expertise at, 167
   first female admissions, 92, 183
   fraternities at, 105
   Inter-Collegiate Oratorical Association and, 111
   in intercollegiate oratorical contests, 109–11, 122, 124, 125–26, 130
   Johnston family members attending, 217

Lexington cultural life and, 2–3
literary societies at, 90–96, 285
literary society oratorical
  performances, 5–7
literary society public lectures, 30
name change of, 134
Preston family members attending,
  205
student press at, 103–6
students not allowed to enter
  intercollegiate oratorical contests,
  115
Tandy as orator at, 137–38
YMCA at, 335n55
See also State University
State College Alumni Association, 103
State College Board of Trustees, 95,
  183, 217
State College Cadet, The
  establishment of, 103–4
  intercollegiate oratorical contest
    coverage of, 115, 119
  literary society coverage of, 93, 94,
    106
State College Orchestra, 134
State College YMCA, 106
State University, 238
  crimes committed by students at,
    161
  dramatic societies at, 9, 259, 261–64
  Equal Rights Association formed at,
    231
  literary society decline at, 249–53,
    254–55
  name change of (1916), 276
  State College becomes, 134
  Washington's Birthday celebrations
    at, 254–55
State University Agricultural
  Experiment Station, 219
State University Board of Trustees,
  220–21

State University Glee Club, 152, 267
State University Orchestra, 267
State University Strollers Dramatic
  Club. See Strollers Dramatic Club
Stevenson, John M., 114, 343n40
Stevenson, Louise, 57, 87
St. John's Collegiate Institute and
  Industrial School (Corbin, Ky.),
  213, 223
St. Joseph Hospital (Lexington), 200
St. Paul African Methodist Episcopal
  Church (Lexington), 180
St. Paul's Catholic Church (Lexington),
  180
Strand Theater (Lexington), 171
Strollers Dramatic Club, 243
  annual banquet of, 273
  drama repertoire of, 265
  faculty coaches, 269
  impact of WWI on, 269–70
  joint productions with Transylvania
    Dramatic Club, 264–65
  local press coverage of, 266–68,
    271–73
  name of, 262
  off-campus presence of, 260, 272–73
  on-campus popularity of, 271–72
  student press coverage of, 277
Stuart, J. E. B., 152
Student (Union Society paper), 89, 90
Sugg, William, 124
Summer in Arcady (Allen), 258
Sweet Lavender (Pinero), 263

Taft, William Howard, 203, 360n27
Tandy, Clarke
  birth of, 136
  eulogies for, 139–40
  intercollegiate oratorical contests
    won by, 129–30, 132, 134, 135,
    137–38, 343n40
  as Rhodes scholar, 137, 138–39

Tandy, Clarke, *cont.*
  suicide of, 139
  as symbol of changing times, 140–41
  teaching career of, 138, 139
Tandy, William, 136
Tanner, Joseph Marion, 2
  birth of, 51
  bureaucratic career of, 50, 62, 65–66
  children of, 61–62
  death of, 66
  education of, 49, 52–58, 69
  as Gilded Age exemplification,
      50–51, 66–69
  as literary society member, 55, 69
  marriage of, 60
  memoirs of, 49, 50–51, 59, 66, 67,
      195
  oratorical skills admired by, 58–59,
      69
  political career of, 49–50, 61, 63–65
  on Preston ("Wick"), 195
  professional career of, 50, 55–56, 58,
      60–63, 68–69
  racial attitudes of, 67–68
  reasons for political failure, 63–66
  retirement of, 66, 322n33
Tanner, Lizzie Butler, 60
Tanner, Louise, 62
Tanner, Mary, 62
Tanner, Oliver Hazard Perry, 51
Tanner, Thomas, 62
Tapp, Hambleton, 199
Taylor, Bob, 120
Taylor, Reuben Thornton ("Bookie"),
    10, 238–39
Tenney, Otis S., 151
Thacker, John M., 134
Thanet, Octave, 41, 235
theater, amateur, 255, 257
  See also Little Theater Movement
theater, professional, 255, 256–57
theatrical performances

by church groups, 180
by civic organizations, 181–83
lecture series on, 183–85
Preston (Margaret) at, 202–3,
    211–12, 239–42
by school groups, 180–81
by WCCK, 178–79
See also dramatic societies, collegiate
Theosebian Literary Society, 248
Thomas, Brandon, 267–68
Thomas, Charles A., 123
Thompson, Francis, 238–39
Todd, John, 200
Transylvanian (Kentucky University
    student monthly), 102
  declining literary society coverage of,
      99–100, 245–46
  on Inter-Collegiate Oratorical
      Association, 111–12, 130–31
  on intercollegiate oratorical contest
      rules, 115
  literary society coverage of, 75,
      82–83
Transylvania Philosophical Society,
    324n3
Transylvania Stagecrafters, 270,
    378n33
Transylvania: Tutor to the West (Wright),
    96
Transylvania University
  antebellum literary societies at,
      72–78, 285
  Arts College, 248
  Bible College, 244, 248–49
  Board of Trustees, 72, 73
  dramatic performances at, 259
  dramatic societies at, 9, 259, 260–61,
      263
  foundation of, 73
  Kentucky University merged with,
      52–53, 78
  Library, 86

literary society decline at, 245–49, 253–54, 275–76
Medical Department building, 76
student publications at, 334n48
Washington's Birthday celebrations at, 253–54
WWI military preparations at, 270
See also Kentucky University
Transylvania University Athletic Association, 265
Transylvania University Dramatic Club
comedy repertoire of, 265
foundation of, 261, 375n24
impact of WWI on, 270
joint productions with Strollers, 264–65
local press coverage of, 263, 265–66, 270–71
membership tryouts for, 270
name change of, 270
off-campus presence of, 260, 268–69
organizational structure of, 265–66
Transylvania University Tennis Club, 246
Transylvania Whig Society, 55, 72–74, 75, 76, 80
"Triumph of Chastity, The" (sculpture; Hart), 28–29
Trost, Herman G., 84–85
Trost's Band, 117, 119
Trost's Orchestra, 87, 93
True Womanhood, 16, 24, 67, 93–94, 104, 259–60, 309n6
Truth (Alatheian Society paper), 83
tuberculosis, 168
Twain, Mark, 14
Twelfth Night (Shakespeare), 258
Twelve Pound Look, The (Barrie), 236
Two Strings to Her Bow (comedy), 260
typhoid fever, 168

Union Literary Society (Kentucky University), 88–90, 331n28
Union Literary Society (State College), 96
Barker address to, 251
competing student organizations, 250
decline of, 276, 378n35
declining local press coverage of, 254
faculty implored to reverse intercollegiate contest decision, 115
in intercollegiate oratorical contests, 112, 124, 126
magazine published by, 103
membership of, 105–6
Normal Society and, 94
oratorical contests, 250
public lectures sponsored by, 30–31
student press coverage of, 250
transferred from Kentucky University, 90
Washington's Birthday celebrations of, 90–91, 254
Union Philosophical Society (Dickerson College), 74
Union Philosophical Society (Transylvania), 72–73, 74, 75, 76–77, 89
United Confederate Veterans
annual reunions of, 150–51
Chautauqua tent of, 120
founding of, 47, 110
John C. Breckinridge chapter, 150, 151–52, 191, 216
Lost Cause and, 47, 110, 149
middle-class membership of, 48
in Preparedness Parade, 191
Preston (P. P.) as president of Lexington chapter, 151–52, 191, 216
United Confederate Veterans Association of Kentucky, 150
United Daughters of the Confederacy, 273

United Daughters of the Confederacy,
  cont.
  elite membership of, 150
  founding of, 47
  Lexington chapters, 149–50
  Lost Cause and, 47, 149, 152, 153
  spelling matches held by, 201–2
United States
  federal bureaucracy growth in, 68
  university extension movement in,
    173–74
United States Bureau of Public Roads,
  166
United States Department of
  Agriculture, 166
United States Supreme Court, 36
university extension movement,
  173–74
University of Kentucky
  band, 85
  literary society decline at, 276–77
  See also State College; State
    University
*University of Kentucky: Origins and
  Early Years* (Hopkins), 96
University of Virginia, 206
Uplifting the Race (Gaines), 157
urban imperialism, 23–24
urbanization, 146

Vachell, Horace Annelsey, 184–85
Van Der Ven, F., 158
Van Lear, John, 119
Versailles (Ky.), 66
Victorian Era, 15
  charity during, 18–21
  ethnocentrism during, 17–18, 33,
    40–41
  gender stereotypes during, 15–17,
    24–25, 28–29, 67, 93–94, 104,
    259–60, 309n6
  morality during, 123, 145, 353n55

neurasthenia as fashionable disease
  during, 213–14
  oratorical culture during, 67
  park design during, 35–36
  reading during, 204, 234
  refined entertainment during, 6
  republican motherhood, 17
  summer vacations during, 203
  time span of, 204
  True Womanhood ideal, 16
Villa, Pancho, 186–89
Vincent, Leon, 132
violence, chivalry and, 41–42
Virginian, The (Wister), 266
Vogue magazine, 235

Wallace, Caleb, 73–74
Waller, Gregory, 25, 155
Warner, Charles Dudley, 14
Warner, Hattie, 93
Warren, Mamie, 203
Washington's Birthday celebrations
  declining local press coverage of,
    253–55
  faculty co-optation of, 254–55
  female participation in, 81–82
  literary society decline and, 99, 115,
    247
  literary society involvement in,
    76–77, 81–82, 87, 89, 90
  as on-campus public entertainment,
    5
Watson, Joseph Thomas, 246
Waverly Apartments (Lexington), 214,
  360n26
Weeping Wives (drama), 260
Weller, Jack, 94
Well Meaning Club, 324n5
Wells, H. G., 235–36
Welter, Barbara, 309n6
What to Expect at College (drama), 262
White, Douglas, 154

White, Henry, 54
White Sulphur Springs (W.Va.), 204
white supremacy, 39, 145, 158
Whiting, George, 283
Wickliffe, Margaret, 196
Wickliffe, Mary Owen Todd Russell, 200
Wickliffe, Robert, 196
Wickliffe, Robert, Jr., 76
Widner, G. H., 102
Wilde, Oscar, 236
Wiley, Harvey W., 255
Will, The (Barrie), 236
Williams, Ella, 200–201
Williams, Roger D., 190
Williamsburg Academy, 40
Williamson, Elizabeth Cary, 179
Williamstown (Ky.), 160
Willitis, A. A., 30
Willson, Augustus, 262
Wilmington (N.C.) race riot (1898),
 147
Wilson, Robert Burns, 237
Wilson, Samuel M., 13–14, 114, 152
Wilson, Woodrow
 Birth of a Nation and, 154
 Dixon as friend of, 148, 154
 Villa affair and, 187, 188
 WWI and, 185–86, 258
Winchester (Ky.), 170
Wister, Owen, 266
Wolf, Frank, 85
Wolf and Trost Orchestra, 85
Woman and Labour (Schreiner), 222
Woman's Club, 10, 353n55
Woman's Club of Central Kentucky
 (WCCK)
 high culture and, 177–80
 Preston (Margaret) as Literature
  Dept. chair, 179, 183–84, 236–39,
  283, 369n56
 Preston (Margaret) as president of,
  191

Preston (Sarah) as officer in, 201–2,
 214, 230
 Reading Circle of, 283
 Social Service Department, 268
Woman's Journal and Suffrage News, 231
women
 benevolent associations formed by,
  20–21
 college education of, 208
 lectures given by, 183–84
 literary societies of, 80–83, 92–94,
  100–101
 in public ceremonies, 191
 public lectures given by, 30–31
 Victorian stereotypes of, 15–17,
  24–25
 voluntarism of, 223, 225
Women's Glee Club, 247
women's organizations, 189
women's rights, 30–31, 80, 181,
 229–33
Wooding, Alice, 203
Woodland Auditorium, 263
Woodland Park (Lexington)
 as Chautauqua site, 25, 117, 136,
  312n25
 intercollegiate oratorical contests at,
  111
 landscaping of, 166
 New South boosterism promoting,
  26
 Preparedness Parade speeches
  delivered at, 191–92
 as Victorian park, 35–36
 See also Chautauqua (Kentucky
  Assembly, Lexington)
Woodland Park Association, 35
Works Progress Administration, 1
World War I, 66, 149, 184
 amateur theater preceding, 179
 economic difficulties associated with,
  256–57

World War I, *cont.*
  impact on dramatic societies, 269–70
  impact on professional theater,
    256–57
  preparedness for, 185–86, 189–93
  Progressive Era and, 146, 147
  shortages due to, 176
  U.S. declaration of war in (1917), 7,
    258, 269–70
  Villa affair as dry run for, 189
Wright, Elizabeth, 211
Wright, George C., 37, 42, 158
Wright, John D., Jr., 75, 96, 260, 284,
    334n48

yearbooks, 101–2, 105–6, 248–49,
    264
YMCA, 98, 102, 104, 106, 249,
    335n55
Yonge, Charlotte M., 204
YWCA, 102, 104, 224

Taking the Town